Effective Management

a multimedia approach

6e

Chuck Williams

CENGAGE
Learning·

Australia • Brazil • Japan • Korea • Mexico • Singapore • Spain • United Kingdom • United States

CENGAGE
Learning

Effective Management: a multimedia approach, 6e

Effective Management, 6th Edition
Chuck Williams

© 2014 Cengage Learning. All rights reserved.

Senior Project Development Manager:
 Linda deStefano

Market Development Manager:
 Heather Kramer

Senior Production/Manufacturing Manager:
 Donna M. Brown

Production Editorial Manager:
 Kim Fry

Sr. Rights Acquisition Account Manager:
 Todd Osborne

For product information and technology assistance, contact us at
Cengage Learning Customer & Sales Support, 1-800-354-9706

For permission to use material from this text or product,
submit all requests online at **cengage.com/permissions**
Further permissions questions can be emailed to
permissionrequest@cengage.com

This book contains select works from existing Cengage Learning resources and was produced by Cengage Learning Custom Solutions for collegiate use. As such, those adopting and/or contributing to this work are responsible for editorial content accuracy, continuity and completeness.

Compilation © 2013 Cengage Learning
ISBN-13: 978-1-285-38961-5

ISBN-10: 1-285-38961-1

Cengage Learning
5191 Natorp Boulevard
Mason, Ohio 45040
USA

Cengage Learning is a leading provider of customized learning solutions with office locations around the globe, including Singapore, the United Kingdom, Australia, Mexico, Brazil, and Japan. Locate your local office at:
international.cengage.com/region.
Cengage Learning products are represented in Canada by Nelson Education, Ltd.
For your lifelong learning solutions, visit **www.cengage.com/custom.**
Visit our corporate website at **www.cengage.com.**

Printed in the United States of America

Brief Contents

Contents

Part Two

Part Three

Organizing 247

Preface

Different Minds Learn in Different Ways

Everyone approaches learning differently. Some learn best by listening to lectures, while others learn best by reading and summarizing course material on their own. Others struggle unless concepts and ideas are visually illustrated in charts, models, or graphs, while others need firsthand experience to gain understanding. Of course, many of us learn best when we combine these approaches.

In most introductory courses with most introductory textbooks, however, student learning boils down to one approach: (1) read the textbook; (2) take class notes during the lecture; (3) participate in a bit of class discussion; (4) do a few assignments; and then (5) "cram" the night before each exam. Because nearly all introductory courses and nearly all introductory textbooks use this approach, students who adapt to this approach to learning tend to do well in all of their introductory courses. Yet, a surprisingly large percentage of college students struggle when using this "standard" approach. Consequently, many students work very hard in their introductory courses, but do not do very well. (Ask around. You'll be surprised by the number of students who have much higher grades in upper-level courses.) If the sixth edition of *Effective Management: A Multimedia Approach* is viewed as just another "introductory textbook," with just one approach to learning, think again. Instead of asking students to adapt their learning styles to one way of learning, *Effective Management: A Multimedia Approach* provides a variety of different learning tools to let students create and combine learning methods uniquely suited to the way in which they learn—and not the other way around. By integrating a unique organizing system in each chapter (see the following Chapter Outline and Numbering System, Learning Objectives, and Section Reviews) with an extensive multimedia learning package, we have put together a complete teaching and learning system designed to educate students with all kinds of learning needs in all types of classroom situations. The system is flexible enough to be used in traditional classes, in completely online classes, in combinations of those two, or in independent study. In short, the sixth edition of *Effective Management: A Multimedia Approach* taps into multiple technologies (text, graphics, video, audio, and animation), to teach management to students with all kinds of learning styles.

Using Your Book

With today's busy schedules, very few students have the opportunity to read a chapter from beginning to end in one sitting. Because of their schedules and cognitive styles, today's students take anywhere from two to five study sessions to read a chapter completely. Accordingly, a chapter outline and numbering system, learning objectives, and section reviews are used to break chapters into small, self-contained sections that can be studied separately over multiple study sessions.

Chapter Outline

Each chapter begins with a detailed chapter outline that breaks the chapter into numbered sections and subsections. For example, the outline for the first part of Chapter 4, Planning and Decision Making, looks like this:

Learning Objectives and Numbering System

4-2 How to Make a Plan that Works

Planning is a double-edged sword. If done right, planning brings about tremendous increases in individual and organizational performance. If planning is done wrong, however, it can have just the opposite effect and harm individual and organizational performance.

After reading this section, you should be able to:
4-2 describe how to make a plan that works.

There are several elements involved in making a plan that works.

As depicted in Exhibit 4.1, planning consists of 4-2a setting goals, 4-2b developing commitment to the goals, 4-2c developing effective action plans, 4-2d tracking progress toward goal achievement, and 4-2e maintaining flexibility in planning.

4-2a Setting Goals

The first step in planning is to set goals. To direct behavior and increase effort, goals need to be specific and challenging. For example, deciding to "increase

The numbered information contained in the chapter outline is then repeated in the chapter as learning objectives (at the beginning of major parts of the chapter) and as numbered headings and subheadings (throughout the chapter) to help students remember precisely where they are in terms of the chapter outline.

Section Reviews

Finally, instead of a big summary at the end of the chapter, students will find a detailed review at the end of each section. Together, the chapter outline, numbering system, learning objectives, section headings (which mark the beginning of a section), and section reviews (which mark the end of a section) allow students to break the chapter into small, self-contained sections that can be read in their entirety over multiple study sessions. This format not only makes it easier for busy students to effectively spread their studying across multiple days and times, but it also adapts textbook learning to evolving student-learning styles and preferences.

Finally, all student resources and instructor resources are organized by section and subsection so that students and instructors always know where they are and what they are reviewing.

REVIEW 4-2

How to Make a Plan That Works

There are five steps to making a plan that works: (1) Set SMART goals, or goals that are **S**pecific, **M**easurable, **A**ttainable, **R**ealistic, and **T**imely. (2) Develop commitment to the goals from the people who contribute to goal achievement. Managers can increase workers' goal commitment by encouraging worker participation in goal setting, making goals public, and getting top management to show support for workers' goals. (3) Develop action plans for goal accomplishment. (4) Track progress toward goal achievement by setting both proximal and distal goals and by providing workers with regular performance feedback. (5) Maintain flexibility. Keeping options open through options-based planning and seeking continuous improvement through learning-based planning help organizations maintain flexibility as they plan.

Using the Student Learning Resources That Come with Your Book

To give students access to a wide variety of learning opportunities, this book is supported by an exciting set of multimedia materials on CourseMate (login.cengagebrain.com).

At CourseMate, there are materials to help students learn by reading (text), by seeing (graphics), and by doing (learning modules, self-assessments, and quizzing). There are materials to help learn through audio, video, and combinations of the two. The opening pages of each chapter list the key multimedia learning resources that are available with *Effective Management, 6e*. But that is not all there is. At CourseMate, there are study tools from PowerPoint® to Podcasts.

Visual learners can use CourseMate to watch Management Workplace videos. Each clip takes an in-depth look into daily operations and management issues inside well-known organizations, such as Living Social, Barcelona Restaurant Group, and Theo Chocolate. Discussion questions and comprehension quizzes maximize these resources.

© TETRA IMAGES/CORBIS

Joe Whinney of Theo Chocolate

Most students are interested in finding out about their future potential as managers. Do their skills and perspectives connect with those required to be a successful manager? Each chapter of *Effective Management* gives them the opportunity to find out using a self-assessment related to the content covered in the chapter. Topics range from competitiveness to communication to ethics. Students can find out how their individual attitudes, perspectives, and behaviors affect their ability to manage, as these assessments connect what is being taught in the course with their experiences and skills. The same assessment at the end of the chapters can be found online in CourseMate as well.

Nearly all students quiz themselves over course material when preparing for exams. The quizzes in the Management CourseMate allow them to do this over and over. Short quizzes consisting of true/false and multiple choice questions provide feedback and cover all sections of the chapter. In addition to traditional quizzes, the Management CourseMate includes quizzes related to the videos that go with each chapter.

Text Features

Engaging Style

Chuck's compelling writing style conveys his passion for both management and teaching. The combination of theories and current stories helps students actually relate to how text topics play out in business settings.

What Would You Do?

Chapter-opening *WHAT WOULD YOU DO?* cases create an opportunity for students to confront the real issues that managers face before deciding on a course of action, handling a particular problem, or changing the direction of a company. Students are called upon to put themselves in the situation of the managers at companies like NetFlix, Caterpillar, Disney, AmericanExpress, Waste Management, and SAS.

What Really Works?

Some studies show that two drinks a day increase life expectancy by decreasing the chances of having a heart attack. Other studies show that two drinks a day decrease life expectancy. The results of both sets of studies are presented in very definitive terms, so the conflicting information confuses and frustrates ordinary people who just want to "eat right" and "live right." Managers also have trouble figuring out what works, based on the scientific research published in scholarly business journals. But thankfully, a research tool called meta-analysis, which is a study of studies, is helping management scholars understand how well their research supports management theories. The *What Really Works* features in *Effective Management*, sixth edition, present the results of various meta-analyses using an easy-to-understand statistic called the "probability of success." Concrete study results presented in an accessible format give students the best estimate of what really works in the business world.

Doing the Right Thing

Because managers set the standard for others in the workplace, unethical behavior and practices quickly spread when they do not do the right thing. This sixth edition contains practical, useful advice to help students become more ethical managers or businesspersons by *Doing the Right Thing*. A range of topics is explored throughout the book.

Management Facts and Trends

Management is happening every day in every company. One way to prepare for a career as a manager is by being aware of management trends today. To help students look forward to what might be happening in management tomorrow, there are short boxes titled *Management Fact* and *Management Trend* that give students a short, memorable insight into the direction in which management is headed.

Management Decision

These end-of-chapter assignments are tightly written and focus on a single management situation. Students must decide what to do and then answer several questions to explain their choices.

Management Team Decision

From sports to school to work to civic involvement, working in teams is increasingly part of our experience. *Management Team Decision* exercises have been designed to give students the opportunity to work as management teams to solve various workplace dilemmas.

Practice Being a Manager

These experiential exercises give students the opportunity to role play management scenarios, discuss management dilemmas, and resolve management problems. Most are designed to be started and completed during the class session.

Self-Assessments

Self-assessments give students insights into their attitudes, beliefs, and tendencies that relate to management issues. Each PowerPoint chapter contains a special slide with an embedded spreadsheet to facilitate use of the assessments in the classroom using a simple show of hands. The slide automatically generates a distribution, which students enjoy seeing.

Reel to Real Video

The textual component to the *Management Workplace* videos prepares students for viewing. By directing students' attention to certain chapter topics before they watch the clip or segment, students are better able to connect what they are seeing with the management concepts they have been learning.

Multimedia Resources

CengageNOW

This robust, online course management system gives the instructor more control in less time and delivers better student outcomes—NOW. CengageNOW for *Effective Management 6e* includes teaching and learning resources organized around lecturing, creating assignments, grading, quizzing, and tracking student progress and performance. Flexible assignments, automatic grading, and a gradebook option provide more control while saving valuable time. A Personalized Study diagnostic tool empowers students to master concepts, prepare for exams, and become more involved in class.

CourseMate

Engaging, trackable, and affordable, the new Management CourseMate website offers a dynamic way to bring course concepts to life with interactive learning, study, and exam-preparation tools that support this printed edition of the text. Watch student comprehension soar with all-new flash cards and engaging games, audio summaries, self-assessments, streaming videos, and more in this textbook-specific website. Management CourseMate goes beyond the book to deliver what is needed.

APLIA™

This leading, online assignment solution for management is fully integrated with the text and encourages students to "think like managers." Aplia problem sets provide calculated combinations of both lower order and higher order thinking-skills exercises. Engaging video cases and interactive charts and graphs seamlessly integrate with self-assessments and vivid examples. Instructors can easily hold students accountable for their own engagement. A flexible grading system offers grade analytics and grade book export tools to work with any learning management system. Aplia can be integrated with a variety of Learning Management Systems, such as Blackboard®.

Williams, *Effective Management*, 6th edition on MindTap

MindTap is the first of its kind in an entirely new category: the Personal Learning Experience (PLE). This personalized program of digital products and services uses interactivity and customization to engage students, while offering instructors a wide range of choices in content, platforms, devices, and learning tools. MindTap is device agnostic, meaning that it will work with any platform or Learning Management System and will be accessible anytime, anywhere: on desktops, laptops, tablets, mobile phones, and other Internet-enabled devices. Visit www.cengage.com/mindtap for more information or to see a demo.

Instructor Resources

Instructor Resource CD-ROM

Key instructor ancillaries (Instructor Manual, Test Bank, and PowerPoint®) are provided on an Instructor Resource CD-ROM. The Instructor Manual is organized in such a way as to allow instructors to get going quickly and to minimize the time needed to prepare a superior course. Suggested plans for covering the chapter using lecture, group work, and video are included, along with a brief chapter outline, and teaching tips and solutions for all chapter assignments.

The Test Bank for *Effective Management, 6e* consists of true/false, multiple-choice, scenario, short answer, and essay questions that have been reviewed by management faculty. The Test Bank contains over 2,400 questions, all of which have been tagged using AACSB categories to help collect and manage the data required for accreditation. And to aid with lectures, a comprehensive set of PowerPoint™ slides has been created for each chapter.

Video

The Management Workplace videos are available online and on DVD. CDs containing the video clips can be made on demand using the online digitized files. The Instructor Manual includes detailed teaching notes so that video can be incorporated into the class in a meaningful way.

The Business and Company Resource Center

The Business & Company Resource Center (BCRC) is a premier online business research tool that provides a seamless search of thousands of periodicals, journals, references, financial information, industry reports, company histories, and much more. The BCRC is a powerful and time-saving research tool for students and a wonderful tool instructors can use for building online coursepack and assigning readings and research projects. Visit http://bcrc.swlearning.com to learn more about how this powerful electronic tool integrates a diverse collection of resources to reflect the natural research process and contact the local representative to learn how to include the Business & Company Resource Center with the text.

ExamView

A computerized version of the Test Bank is available on the Instructor Resource CD-ROM and by special request. ExamView allows adding or editing questions, instructions, and answers. It is possible to create, edit, store, print, and otherwise customize all quizzes, tests, and exams. The system is menu-driven, making it quick and easy to use.

Acknowledgements

Let's face it, writing a textbook is a long and lonely process. It's surely the most difficult (and rewarding) project I've ever tackled. And, as I sat in front of my computer with a rough outline on the left side of my desk, a two-foot stack of journal articles on the floor, and a blank screen in front of me, it was easy at times to feel isolated. But, as I found out, a book like this doesn't get done without the help of many other talented people. First, I'd like to thank the world-class team at Cengage for the outstanding support (and patience) they provided while I wrote this book; Scott Person, who heads the Management group at Cengage, was calm, collected, and continuously positive through the major ups and downs of this project; and Tamborah Moore, who managed the production process, was consistently upbeat and positive with me when I deserved otherwise. Authors are prone to complain about their publishers. But that hasn't been my experience at all. Pure and simple, everyone at Cengage has been great to work with throughout the entire project. However, special thanks goes to Jamie Gleich Bryant and her team at B-books, Ltd., who maintained the high quality standards that were set when I began writing. Their enthusiasm, professionalism, commitment, and attention to detail made me a better writer, made this a better book, and made me appreciate my good fortune to work with such an outstanding talent. Thanks, B-books, and here's to many more editions. I'd also like to thank the outstanding set of reviewers whose diligent and thoughtful comments helped shape previous editions and whose rigorous feedback improved the sixth edition.

Ali Abu-Rahma
United States International University

William Acar
Kent State University

David C. Adams
Manhattanville College

Bruce R. Barringer
University of Central Florida

Gayle Baugh
University of West Florida

James Bell
University of Texas, Austin

Greg Blundel
Kent State University, Stark

Katharine A. Bohley
University of Indianapolis

Santanu Borah
University of North Alabama

Angela Boston
University of Texas, Arlington

Michael Boyd
Owensboro Community College

Jon L. Bryan
Bridgewater State College

Victoria Mullennex
Davis & Elkins College

John J. Nader
Grand Valley State University

Charlie Nagelschmidt
Champlain College

Patrick J. Nedry
Monroe County Community College

Stephanie Newport
Austin Peay State University

Don A. Okhomina
Alcorn State University

James S. O'Rourke IV
University of Notre Dame

Rhonda S. Palladi
Georgia State University

Lynne Patten
Clark Atlanta University

Jane Pettinger
Minnesota State University, Moorhead

Clifton Petty
Drury University

John Poirier
Bryant University

David M. Porter Jr.
UCLA

Michael Provitera
Barry University

Abe Qastin
Lakeland College

Robert Raspberry
Southern Methodist University

Kim Rocha
Barton College

Linda Ross
Cleveland Community College

Carol Rowey
Community College of Rhode Island

Amit Shah
Frostburg State University

Penni F. Sikkila
Baker College

Thomas Shaughnessy
Illinois Central College

Michelle Slagle
University of South Alabama

James Smas
Kent State University

James O. Smith
East Carolina University

Charlotte Nix Speegle
Cisco Junior College

Gregory K. Stephens
Texas Christian University

John Striebich
Monroe Community College

Joseph Tagliaferre
Pennsylvania State University

Jennie Carter Thomas
Belmont University

Neal Thomson
Columbus State University

James Thornton
Champlain College

Mary Jo Vaughan
Mercer University

Michael Wakefield
Colorado State University, Pueblo

James Whelan
Manhattan College

Joann White
Jackson State University

Xiang Yi
Western Illinois University

Finally, my family deserves the greatest thanks of all for their love, patience, and support. Writing a textbook is an enormous project with incredible stresses and pressures on authors as well as their loved ones. However, throughout this project, my wife, Jenny, was unwavering in her support of my writing. She listened patiently, encouraged me when I was discouraged, read and commented on most of what I wrote, gave me the time to write, and took wonderful care of me and our children during this long process. My children, Benjamin, Rebecca, and Zack, also deserve special thanks for their patience and for understanding why Dad was locked away at the computer for all of this time. While writing this book has been the most rewarding professional experience of my career, it pleases me to no end that my family is as excited as I am that it's done. So, to Jenny, Benjamin, Rebecca, and Zack: The book is done. Let's play.

About the Author

Chuck Williams is dean of the College of Business at Butler University. He received his BA in psychology from Valparaiso University, and specialized in the areas of organizational behavior, human resources, and strategic management while earning his MBA and PhD in business administration from Michigan State University. Previously, he taught at Michigan State University and was on the faculty of Oklahoma State University and Texas Christian University, where he also served as associate dean of the Neeley School of Business and chair of the Management Department. He was also dean of the Eberhardt School of Business at the University of the Pacific. His research interests include employee recruitment and turnover, performance appraisal, and employee training and goal-setting. Chuck has published research in the *Journal of Applied Psychology*, the *Academy of Management Journal, Human Resource Management Review, Personnel Psychology*, and the *Organizational Research Methods Journal*. He was a member of the *Journal of Management*'s editorial board, and serves as a reviewer for numerous other academic journals. He was also the webmaster for the Research Methods Division of the Academy of Management. Chuck is also a corecipient of the Society for Human Resource Management's Yoder-Heneman Research Award. Chuck has consulted for a number of organizations: General Motors, IBM, JCPenney, Tandy Corporation, Trism Trucking, Central Bank and Trust, StuartBacon, the city of Fort Worth, the American Cancer Society, and others. He has taught in executive development programs at Oklahoma State University, the University of Oklahoma, Texas Christian University, and the University of the Pacific. Chuck teaches a number of different courses, but has been privileged to teach his favorite course, Introduction to Management, for nearly 25 years. His teaching philosophy is based on four principles: (1) courses should be engaging and interesting; (2) there is nothing as practical as a good theory; (3) students learn by doing; and (4) students learn when they are challenged. Chuck has won teaching awards at several universities at the department, business school, and university levels.

Effective Management

Sixth Edition

Chuck Williams

BUTLER UNIVERSITY

PART ONE

Introduction to Management

Chapter One

Management

© JIN LEE/BLOOMBERG/ GETTY IMAGES

Chapter 1 begins by defining management and discussing the functions of management. We look at what managers do, what it takes to be a manager, what companies look for in their managers, the most serious mistakes managers make, and what it is like to make the tough transition from being a worker to being a manager.

Chapter Two

Organizational Environments and Cultures

© SCOTT OLSON/GETTY IMAGES

Chapter 2 examines the internal and external forces that affect business, including how those forces affect the decisions and performance of a company. We cover the general environment that affects all organizations and the specific environment unique to each company.

Chapter Three

Ethics and Social Responsibility

© DANNY MOLOSHOK/ LANDOV

Chapter 3 examines ethical behavior in the workplace and explains how unethical behavior can expose a business to legal penalties. You'll read about the influences on ethical decision making and learn the practical steps that managers can take to improve ethical decision making.

© DIZZO/ISTOCK PHOTO

Management

REEL TO REAL

Management Workplace is at Camp Bow Wow.

© TETRA IMAGES/CORBIS

SELF-ASSESSMENT

Is management for you? Get feedback on the general skills it takes to be a manager by taking the Self-Assessment for this chapter in the book or online.

© ISTOCKPHOTO/ALEXANDER KALINA

ONLINE QUIZZES

Did you get it? Review the main concepts in the chapter by taking the online quizzes on CourseMate!

© ISTOCKPHOTO/PEARLEYE

VIDEO QUIZZES

Get more out of the videos by taking the multimedia video quizzes online.

© ISTOCKPHOTO/DAVID HUGHES

What Would You Do?

Netflix Headquarters, Los Gatos, California.[1]

CEO Reed Hastings started Netflix in 1997 after becoming angry about paying Blockbuster Video $40 for a late return of *Apollo 13*. Hastings and Netflix struck back with flat monthly fees for unlimited DVDs rentals, easy home delivery and returns via prepaid postage envelopes, and no late fees, which let customers keep DVDs as long as they wanted. Blockbuster, which earned up to $800 million annually from late returns, was slow to respond and lost customers in droves.

When Blockbuster, Amazon, and Walmart started their own mail-delivery video rentals, Hastings recognized that Netflix was in competition with "the biggest rental company, the biggest e-commerce company, and the biggest company, period." With investors expecting it to fail, Netflix's stock price dropped precipitously to $2.50 a share. But with an average subscriber cost of just $4 a month compared to an average subscriber fee of $15, Netflix, unlike its competitors, made money from each customer. Three years later, Walmart abandoned the business, asking Netflix to handle DVD rentals on Walmart.com. Amazon, by contrast, entered the DVD rental business in Great Britain, expecting that experience to prepare it to beat Netflix in the United States. But, like Walmart, Amazon quit after four years of losses. Finally, 13 years after Netflix's founding, Blockbuster declared bankruptcy. With DVDs mailed to 17 million monthly subscribers from 50 distribution centers nationwide, Netflix is now the industry leader in DVD rentals.

However, its expertise in shipping and distributing DVDs won't provide a competitive advantage when streaming files over the Internet. Indeed, Netflix's Watch Instantly download service is in competition with Amazon's Video on Demand, Apple's iTunes, HuluPlus at Hulu.com, Time-Warner Cable's TV Everywhere, and DirectTV Cinema, all of which offer movie and TV downloads. Moreover, unlike DVDs, which can be rented without studio approval, U.S. copyright laws require streaming rights to be purchased from TV and movie studios before downloading

content into people's homes. And that creates two new issues. First, does Netflix have deep enough pockets to outbid its rivals for broad access to the studios' TV and movie content? Second, can it convince the studios that it is not a direct competitor? HBO, for instance, won't license any of its original shows, like *The Sopranos*, for Netflix streaming. It also has exclusive rights for up to eight years for content from Twentieth Century Fox and Universal Pictures. HBO co-president Eric Kessler says, "There is value in exclusivity. Consumers are willing to pay a premium for high-quality, exclusive content." If other studio executives think this, Netflix will not acquire the video content it needs to satisfy its customers. Planning involves determining organizational goals and a means for achieving them. So, how can Netflix generate the cash it needs to pay the studios? How can it convince them it's not a competitor so they will agree to license their content?

Netflix must also address the significant organizational challenges accompanying accelerated growth. Hastings experienced the same problem in his first company, Pure Software, where he admitted, "Management was my biggest challenge; every year there were twice as many people and it was trial by fire. I was underprepared for the complexities and personalities." With blazing growth on one hand and the strategic challenge of obtaining studio content on the other, how much time should he and his executive team devote directly to hiring? Deciding where decisions will be made is a key part of the management function of organizing. So, should he and his executive team be directly involved, or is this something that he should delegate? Finally, what can Netflix, which is located near Silicon Valley, home to some of the most attractive employers in the world, Google, eBay, Apple, Hewlett-Packard, and Facebook, provide in the way of pay, perks, and company culture that will attract, inspire, and motivate top talent to achieve organizational goals?

If you were in charge of Netflix, what would you do?

1-1 Management Is...

The management issues facing Netflix are fundamental to any organization: What's our plan? What are top management's key responsibilities? How can we best position the company against key competitors? How can we get things done and put in place controls to make sure plans are followed and goals are met? Good management is basic to starting a business, growing a business, and maintaining a business once it has achieved some measure of success.

We begin this chapter by defining management and discussing the functions of management. Next, we look at what managers do by examining the four kinds of managers and reviewing the various roles that managers play. Then we investigate what it takes to be a manager by reviewing management skills, what companies look for in their managers, the most serious mistakes managers make, and what it is like to make the tough transition from being a worker to being a manager. We finish this chapter by examining the competitive advantage that companies gain from good management. In other words, we learn how to establish a competitive advantage through people.

To understand how important *good* management is, think about mistakes like these: Mistake #1: A new Chinese plant manager at a factory in South Carolina publicly berates his workers when they make errors, creating resentment and alienation among his American workers.[2] Mistake #2: After Motrin failed quality-control tests, managers at McNeil Laboratories, a division of Johnson & Johnson, hired people to buy out all the bottles of Motrin they could find.[3] Is it any wonder that companies pay management consultants nearly $250 billion a year for advice on basic management issues such as how to lead people effectively, organize the company efficiently, and manage large-scale projects and processes?[4] This textbook will help you understand some of the basic issues that management consultants help companies resolve. (And it won't cost you billions of dollars.)

After reading this section, you should be able to:

1-1 describe what management is.

Many of today's managers got their start welding on the factory floor, clearing dishes off tables, helping customers fit a suit, or wiping up a spill in aisle 3. Similarly, lots of you will start at the bottom and work your way up. There's no better way to get to know your competition, your customers, and your business. But whether you begin your career at the entry level or as a supervisor, your job as a manager is not to do the work, but to help others do theirs. **Management** is getting work done through others. Vineet Nayar, CEO of IT services company *HCL Technologies*, doesn't see himself as the guy who has to do everything or have all the answers. Instead, he sees himself as "the guy who is obsessed with enabling employees to create value." Rather than coming up with solutions himself, Nayar creates opportunities for collaboration, peer review, and employee feedback on ideas and work processes. Says Nayar, "My job is to make sure everybody is enabled to do what they do well."[5]

Nayar's description of managerial responsibilities suggests that managers also have to be concerned with efficiency and effectiveness in the work process. **Efficiency** is getting work done with a minimum of effort, expense, or waste. At *FedEx*, efficiency means delivering more packages in less time—but always on time—for less cost. To increase its efficiency, FedEx replaced its primary long-distance cargo plane, the MD-11, with Boeing's 777 jets. Why? Because the 777 carries 14,000 more pounds of cargo and has maximum range that is 2,100 miles more than the MD-11. The 777 can fly also from the United States to Asia without stopping for fuel, so it can make the trip three hours faster than the MD-11. This gives FedEx's Asian customers two extra hours to manufacture products and still get them shipped out for next-day delivery. The company calls the planes a "game changer" in the international package-delivery market.[6]

Efficiency alone, however, is not enough to ensure success. Managers must also strive for **effectiveness**, which is accomplishing tasks that help fulfill organizational objectives such as customer service and satisfaction.

REVIEW 1-1
. . . .
Management Is...
Good management is working through others to accomplish tasks that help fulfill organizational objectives as efficiently as possible.

1-2 Management Functions

Henri Fayol, who was a managing director (CEO) of a large steel company in the early 1900s, was one of the founders of the field of management. Based on his 20 years of experience as a CEO, Fayol argued that "the success of an enterprise generally depends much more on the administrative ability of its leaders than on their technical ability."[7] For example, John Riccitiello, CEO of Electronic Arts (EA), the world's leading computer-game maker, is a serious "gamer." Although it certainly helps that Riccitiello understands EA's products and its hardcore "gamer" customers, EA succeeds not for those reasons, but because of his capabilities as a manager.[8]

After reading this section, you should be able to:
1-2 explain the four functions of management.

According to Fayol, managers need to perform five managerial functions to be successful: planning, organizing, coordinating, commanding, and controlling.[9] Most management textbooks today have updated this list by dropping the coordinating function and referring to Fayol's commanding function as "leading." Fayol's management functions are thus known today

management
getting work done through others

efficiency
getting work done with a minimum of effort, expense, or waste

effectiveness
accomplishing tasks that help fulfill organizational objectives

Exhibit 1.1

© CENGAGE LEARNING

in an updated form as planning, organizing, leading, and controlling. Studies indicate that managers who perform these management functions well are more successful, gaining promotions for themselves and profits for their companies. For example, the more time CEOs spend planning, the more profitable their companies are.[10] A 25-year study at AT&T found that employees with better planning and decision-making skills were more likely to be promoted into management jobs, to be successful as managers, and to be promoted into upper levels of management.[11]

The evidence is clear. Managers serve their companies well when they plan, organize, lead, and control. So we've organized this textbook based on these functions of management, as shown in Exhibit 1.1. The major sections within each chapter of this textbook correspond to learning outcomes and are numbered using a single digit: 1, 2, 3, and so on. The subsections are also consecutively numbered, beginning with the major section number. For example, "1-1" indicates the first learning outcome in Chapter 1, and 1-1-a is the first major section for that learning outcome. This numbering system should help you easily see the relationships among topics and follow the topic sequence. It will also help your instructor refer to specific topics during class discussion.

Now let's take a closer look at each of the management functions: **1-2a planning, 1-2b organizing, 1-2c leading,** and **1-2d controlling.**

1-2a Planning

Planning involves determining organizational goals and a means for achieving them. As you'll learn in Chapter 4, planning is one of the best ways to improve performance. It encourages people to work harder, work hard for extended periods, engage in behaviors directly related to goal accomplishment, and think of better ways to do their jobs. But most importantly, companies that plan have larger profits and faster growth than companies that don't plan.

For example, the question, "What business are we in?" is at the heart of strategic planning. You'll learn about this in Chapter 5. If you can answer the question "What business are you in?" in two sentences or less, chances are you have a very clear plan for your business. But getting a clear plan is not so easy. EBAY paid $2.6 million to acquire Skype, which makes software for free phone and video calls over the Internet. However, eBay eventually sold Skype to a group of investors for $1.9 billion. Why? Because eBay's CEO realized it was a poor fit with its Internet auction site and its PayPal online payment service.[12] You'll learn more about planning in Chapter 4 on planning and decision making, Chapter 5 on organizational strategy, Chapter 6 on innovation and change, and Chapter 7 on global management.

planning
determining organizational goals and a means for achieving them

what *really* works

Meta-Analysis

Some studies show that having two drinks a day increases life expectancy by decreasing the chances of having a heart attack. Yet other studies show that having two drinks a day shortens life expectancy. For years, we've "buttered" our morning toast with margarine instead of butter because margarine was supposed to be better for our health. Now, however, new studies show that the trans-fatty acids in margarine may be just as bad for our arteries as butter. Confusing scientific results like these frustrate ordinary people who want to eat right and live right. They also make many people question just how useful most scientific research really is.

Managers also find themselves questioning the conflicting scientific research published in journals like the *Academy of Management Journal,* the *Academy of Management Review*, the *Strategic Management Journal,* the *Journal of Applied Psychology*, and *Administrative Science Quarterly.* The *Wall Street Journal* may quote a management research article from one of these journals that says that total quality management is the best thing since sliced bread (without butter or margarine). Then, just six months later, the *Wall Street Journal* will quote a different article from the same journal that says that total quality management doesn't work. If management professors and researchers have trouble deciding what works and what doesn't, how can practicing managers know?

Thankfully, a research tool called **meta-analysis** is helping management scholars understand how well their research supports management theories. It is also useful for practicing managers because it shows what works and the conditions under which management techniques may work better or worse in the real world. Meta-analysis involves studying the scientific studies themselves. It is based on this simple idea: If one study shows that a management technique doesn't work and another study shows that it does, an average of those results is probably the best estimate of how well that management practice works (or doesn't work). For example, medical researchers Richard Peto

and Rory Collins averaged all of the different results from several hundred studies investigating the relationship between aspirin and heart attacks. Their analysis, based on more than 120,000 patients from numerous studies, showed that aspirin lowered the incidence of heart attacks by an average of 4 percent. Prior to this study, doctors prescribed aspirin as a preventive measure for only 38 percent of heart-attack victims. Today, because of the meta-analysis results, doctors prescribe aspirin for 72 percent of heart-attack victims.

Fortunately, you don't need a PhD to understand the statistics reported in a meta-analysis. In fact, one primary advantage of meta-analysis over traditional significance tests is that you can convert meta-analysis statistics into intuitive numbers that anyone can easily understand. Each meta-analysis reported in the What Really Works sections of this textbook is accompanied by an easy-to-understand statistic called the "probability of success." As its name suggests, the probability of success shows how often a management technique will work.

For example, meta-analyses suggest that the best predictor of a job applicant's on-the-job performance is a test of general mental ability. In other words, smarter people tend to be better workers. The average correlation (one of those often misunderstood statistics) between scores on general mental-ability tests and job performance is 0.60. However, very few people understand what a correlation of 0.60 means. What most managers want to know is how often they will hire the right person if they choose job applicants based on general mental-ability test scores. Likewise, they want to know how much difference a cognitive-ability test makes when hiring new workers. The probability of success may be high, but if the difference isn't really that large, is it worth a manager's time to have job applicants take a general mental-ability test?

Well, our user-friendly statistics indicate that it's wise to have job applicants take a general mental-ability test. In fact, the probability of success, shown in graphical form here, is 76 percent.

(Continued)

(Continued)

This means that an employee hired on the basis of a good score on a general mental-ability test stands a 76 percent chance of being a better performer than someone picked at random from the pool of all job applicants. So chances are you're going to be right much more often than wrong if you use a general mental-ability test to make hiring decisions.[13]

In summary, each What *Really* Works section in this textbook is based on meta-analysis research, which provides the best scientific evidence that management professors and researchers have about what works and what doesn't work in management. We will use the easy-to-understand index known as the "probability of success" to indicate how well a management idea or strategy is likely to work in the workplace. Of course, no

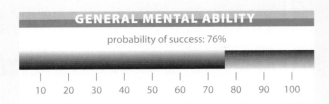

idea or technique works every time and in every circumstance. Nevertheless, the management ideas and strategies discussed in the What Really Works sections can usually make a meaningful difference where you work. In today's competitive, fast-changing, global marketplace, few managers can afford to overlook proven management strategies like the ones discussed in What *Really* Works.

1-2b Organizing

Organizing is deciding where decisions will be made, who will do what jobs and tasks, and who will work for whom in the company. On average, it costs more than $10 billion to bring a new pharmaceutical drug to market. So when PFIZER, the second-largest pharmaceutical firm in the world, acquired Wyeth, the 11th largest, CEO Jeffrey Kindler decided to restructure Pfizer's research and development unit into two parts: one for small molecules or traditional pills, and one for large molecules or drugs made from living cells. Kindler said, "Creating two distinct, but complementary, research organizations, led by the top scientist from each company, will provide sharper focus, less bureaucracy and clearer accountability in drug discovery."[14] In all, the new company will consist of nine businesses, including primary care, vaccines, oncology, consumer and nutritional products, and pharmaceuticals.

You'll learn more about organizing in Chapter 8 on designing organizations, Chapter 9 on managing teams, and Chapter 10 on managing human resources.

meta-analysis
a study of studies, a statistical approach that provides one of the best scientific estimates of how well management theories and practices work

organizing
deciding where decisions will be made, who will do what jobs and tasks, and who will work for whom

leading
inspiring and motivating workers to work hard to achieve organizational goals

1-2c Leading

Our third management function, **leading**, involves inspiring and motivating workers to work hard to achieve organizational goals. For Alan Mulally, CEO of FORD MOTOR COMPANY, a critical part of keeping his employees motivated is to "Communicate, communicate, communicate. Everyone has to know the plan, its status, and areas that need special attention." Accordingly, Mulally distributed a set of cards with Ford's mission on one side and the company's four most important goals on the other. He also hosts a Business Plan Review each week with his top executives to check on company-wide performance, which is tracked via 280 charts, each with the name and picture of the manager responsible. Mulally's leadership brought Ford back from the brink of bankruptcy. In a series of timely maneuvers and shrewd business deals, Mulally secured a $23.6 billion loan and then sold off several noncore brands to raise $23.6 billion prior to the recession, which kept Ford sufficiently capitalized as the world economy slowed. And although General Motors and Chrysler were forced to seek government loans and eventually file for bankruptcy, Ford stayed afloat on its own, posting healthy profits in 2009 and 2010, well ahead of Mulally's promise to make Ford profitable by 2011.[15]

You'll learn more about leading in Chapter 11 on motivation, Chapter 12 on leadership, and Chapter 13 on managing communication.

Doing the Right Thing

Making a Great Workplace

Good managers focus not only on the bottom line, but on the people they manage. One of the most important tasks that a manager has is to make sure that the people whom they are supposed to manage are taken care of. Yvon Chouinard, the founder of the outdoor clothing company, Patagonia, says that the key to her company's success is making sure that employees feel physically and emotionally secure at work, and that they are given the freedom to be creative and solve problems. Patagonia also has an extensive benefits policy that includes child care and flexible scheduling, so that employees don't have to worry about how personal issues might conflict with work. Although some might worry that these expenses hurt the company's bottom line, Chouinard views them as necessary expenses for building a family atmosphere. So, as a manager, do the right thing and make sure to take care of the people you manage.[16]

1-2d Controlling

The last function of management, **controlling**, is monitoring progress toward goal achievement and taking corrective action when progress isn't being made. The basic control process involves setting standards to achieve goals, comparing actual performance to those standards, and then making changes to return performance to those standards. Mike Duke, WALMART's CEO, maintains a red folder for each of the executives who reports to him. Each folder contains a set of goals, problems, and follow-up items related to that manager's responsibilities. Brian Cornell runs Sam's Club, Walmart's discount warehouse chain, and his folder contains recent sales figures, a question regarding real estate purchases for new locations, and a complaint from a Sam's Club member about Member's Mark facial tissue (a private brand sold by Sam's). Regarding the tissue, Duke said, ". . . I keep this in here until Brian tells me it's solved. It's a follow-up mechanism."[17]

You'll learn more about the control function in Chapter 14 on control, Chapter 15 on managing information, and Chapter 16 on managing service and manufacturing operations.

controlling
monitoring progress toward goal achievement and taking corrective action when needed

Management Functions

Henri Fayol's classic management functions are known today as planning, organizing, leading, and controlling. Planning is determining organizational goals and a means for achieving them. Organizing is deciding where decisions will be made, who will do what jobs and tasks, and who will work for whom. Leading is inspiring and motivating workers to work hard to achieve organizational goals. Controlling is monitoring progress toward goal achievement and taking corrective action when needed. Studies show that performing these management functions well leads to better managerial performance.

1-3 Kinds of Managers

Not all managerial jobs are the same. The demands and requirements placed on the CEO of Sony are significantly different from those placed on the manager of your local Wendy's restaurant.

After reading this section, you should be able to:

1-3 describe different kinds of managers.

As not all managerial jobs are the same, not all managers are the same. As shown in Exhibit 1.2 on the next page, there are four kinds of managers, each with different jobs and responsibilities: **1-3a top managers, 1-3b middle managers, 1-3c first-line managers,** and **1-3d team leaders.**

1-3a Top Managers

Top managers hold positions like chief executive officer (CEO), chief operating officer (COO), chief financial officer (CFO), and chief information officer (CIO), and are responsible for the overall direction of the organization. Top managers have the following responsibilities:[18] First, they are responsible for creating a context for change. In fact, the CEOs of AIG, British Petroleum, General Motors, and Massey Energy were all fired precisely because they had not moved fast enough to bring about significant changes in their companies.[19] Thirty-five percent of all CEOs are eventually fired because of their inability to successfully change their companies.[20] Creating a context for change includes forming a long-range vision or mission for the company. As one CEO said, "The CEO has to think about the future more than anyone."[21]

The second responsibility of top managers is to develop employees' commitment to and ownership of the company's performance. That is, top managers are responsible for creating employee buy-in. CAMPBELL SOUP's former CEO, Douglas Conant, says, "To win in the marketplace, we believe you must first win in the workplace. I'm obsessed with keeping employee engagement front and center and keeping up energy around it." Indeed, Conant put that into action in a highly symbolic way when he joined Campbell Soup as the CEO. "When I first got to Camden, N.J., our facility there was surrounded by barbed wire. It looked and felt more like a minimum-security prison than a corporate

top managers
executives responsible for the overall direction of the organization

Exhibit 1.2

Jobs and Responsibilities of Four Kinds of Managers

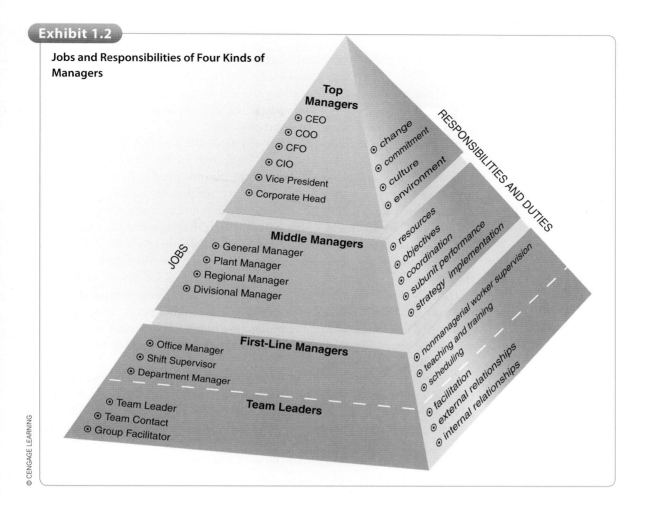

headquarters. I didn't waste any time taking down the fences and replacing them." Said Conant, "Campbell as an organization needed to demonstrate its commitment to its people before they could be expected to demonstrate their own extraordinary commitment to it and its success. This understanding became the basis of what we call the Campbell Promise, which is summed up by the phrase, 'Campbell valuing people, people valuing Campbell.'"[22]

Third, top managers must create a positive organizational culture through language and action. Top managers impart company values, strategies, and lessons through what they do and say to others both inside and outside the company. Kimberly Till, CEO of *Harris Interactive*, a New York–based market research company, emphasizes the importance of frequent communication, saying, "I keep all the employees in the loop through weekly e-mails, town hall meetings and forums, video clips of big decisions, and visits to the offices."[23]

Finally, top managers are responsible for monitoring their business environments. This means that top managers must closely monitor customer needs, competitors' moves, and long-term business, economic, and social trends.

1-3b Middle Managers

Middle managers hold positions like plant manager, regional manager, or divisional manager. They are responsible for setting objectives consistent with top management's goals and for planning and implementing subunit strategies for achieving those objectives.[24] One specific middle-management responsibility is to plan and allocate resources to meet objectives.

A second major responsibility is to coordinate and link groups, departments, and divisions within a company. In February 2008, a tornado destroyed a CATERPILLAR plant in Oxford, Mississippi, the only plant in the company that produced a particular coupling required for many of Caterpillar's machines. The disaster threatened a worldwide production shutdown. Greg Folley, a middle manager in charge of the parts division that included the plant, gave workers two weeks to restore production to pre-tornado levels. He said, "I was betting on people to get it done." He contacted new vendors, sent engineers from other Caterpillar locations to Mississippi to check for quality, and set up distribution operations in another facility. Meanwhile, Kevin Kempa, the plant manager in Oxford, moved some employees to another plant, delivered new training to employees during the production hiatus, and oversaw reconstruction of the plant. The day before the two-week deadline, the Oxford plant was up and running and produced 8,000 parts.[25]

A third responsibility of middle management is to monitor and manage the performance of the subunits and individual managers who report to them. After JOHNSON & JOHNSON's (J&J) McNeil Consumer Healthcare division experienced repeated manufacturing problems that led to a recall of children's Tylenol, Motrin, and Benadryl, J&J's Ajit Shetty, who runs the company's oversight group, was given the responsibility for maintaining quality standards in the company's consumer, medical device, and pharmaceutical segments. The chief quality officers from each business group and the 120 managers of J&J's manufacturing facilities around the world will continue to maintain responsibility for producing safe, high-quality products, but having all of these middle managers work together and report directly to Ajit Shetty should help J&J maintain its high standards in a uniform way.[26]

Finally, middle managers are also responsible for implementing the changes or strategies generated by top managers.

1-3c First-Line Managers

First-line managers hold positions like office manager, shift supervisor, or department manager. The primary responsibility of first-line managers is to manage the performance of entry-level employees who are directly responsible for producing a company's goods and services. Thus, first-line managers are the only managers who don't supervise other managers. The responsibilities of first-line managers include monitoring, teaching, and short-term planning.

First-line managers encourage, monitor, and reward the performance of their workers. When INTUIT bought Paycycle, Jennifer Lepird stayed up all night determining how the salary structure for Paycycle's employees should be integrated with Intuit's. When her acquisition team manager, a first-line

middle managers
managers responsible for setting objectives consistent with top management's goals and for planning and implementing subunit strategies for achieving these objectives

first-line managers
managers who train and supervise the performance of nonmanagerial employees who are directly responsible for producing the company's products or services

manager, thanked her, Jennifer was thrilled; "The fact that somebody took the time to recognize the effort made the long hours just melt away."[27]

First-line managers also teach entry-level employees how to do their jobs. Damian Mogavero's company, *Avero LLC*, helps restaurants analyze sales data for each member of a restaurant's wait staff. Restaurant managers who use these data, says Mogavero, will often take their top-selling server to lunch each week as a reward. The best managers, however, will also take their poorest-selling servers out to lunch to talk about what they can do to improve their performance.[28] Likewise, *Coca-Cola* manager Tom Mattia says, "I try to make every interaction I have with someone on my team a teaching experience. There are always specific work issues that need to get addressed, but then I try to explain my thinking behind an approach so people can get more experience."[29]

First-line managers also make detailed schedules and operating plans based on middle management's intermediate-range plans. By contrast to the long-term plans of top managers (3 to 5 years out) and the intermediate plans of middle managers (6 to 18 months out), first-line managers engage in plans and actions that typically produce results within two weeks.[30]

1-3d Team Leaders

The fourth kind of manager is a team leader. This relatively new kind of management job developed as companies shifted to self-managing teams, which, by definition, have no formal supervisor. In traditional management hierarchies, first-line managers are responsible for the performance of nonmanagerial employees and have the authority to hire and fire workers, make job assignments, and control resources. In this new structure, the teams themselves perform nearly all of the functions performed by first-line managers under traditional hierarchies.[31]

Team leaders have a different set of responsibilities than traditional first-line managers.[32] **Team leaders** are primarily responsible for facilitating team activities toward accomplishing a goal. This doesn't mean team leaders are responsible for team performance. They aren't; the team is. Team leaders help their team members plan and schedule work, learn to solve problems, and work effectively with each other, but the team members own the outcome. The leader is there to bring intellectual, emotional, and spiritual resources to the team. Through his or her actions, the leader should be able to show the others how to think about the work that they're doing in the context of their lives.

Team leaders are responsible for fostering good relationships and addressing problematic ones within their teams. Relationships among team members are crucial to good team performance, and must be well managed. For example, studies show that it's not the surgeon but the interactions between the surgeon and all operating room (OR) team members that determine surgical outcomes. However, at 20 hospitals, 60 percent of the operating room team members—nurses, technicians, and other doctors—agreed with the statement: "In the ORs here, it is difficult to speak up if I perceive a problem with patient care."[33] And when OR team members don't speak up, serious mistakes can occur, no matter how talented the surgeon. Consequently, surgeons are using "safety pauses" to better involve members of their surgical

team leaders
managers responsible for facilitating team activities toward goal accomplishment

teams. The surgeon will pause, ask whether anyone has concerns or comments, and address them if need be. Studies show that safety pauses reduce mistakes, such as operating on the wrong leg or beginning surgery with key surgical instruments missing.[34]

Team leaders are also responsible for managing external relationships. Team leaders act as the bridge or liaison between their teams and other teams, departments, and divisions in a company. For example, if a member of Team A complains about the quality of Team B's work, Team A's leader is responsible for solving the problem by initiating a meeting with Team B's leader. Together, these team leaders are responsible for getting members of both teams to work together to solve the problem. If it's done right, the problem is solved without involving company management or blaming members of the other team.[35]

So the team leader's job involves a different set of skills than traditional management jobs typically do. For example, a Hewlett-Packard ad for a team leader position says, "Job seeker must enjoy coaching, working with people, and bringing about improvement through hands-off guidance and leadership."[36] Team leaders who fail to understand how their roles are different from those of traditional managers often struggle in their jobs. You will learn more about teams in Chapter 9.

REVIEW 1-3

Kinds of Managers

There are four different kinds of managers. Top managers are responsible for creating a context for change, developing attitudes of commitment and ownership, creating a positive organizational culture through words and actions, and monitoring their company's business environments. Middle managers are responsible for planning and allocating resources, coordinating and linking groups and departments, monitoring and managing the performance of subunits and managers, and implementing the changes or strategies generated by top managers. First-line managers are responsible for managing the performance of nonmanagerial employees, teaching entry-level employees how to do their jobs, and making detailed schedules and operating plans based on middle management's intermediate-range plans. Team leaders are responsible for facilitating team performance, managing external relationships, and facilitating internal team relationships.

1-4 Managerial Roles

Although all four types of managers engage in planning, organizing, leading, and controlling, if you were to follow them around during a typical day on the job, you would probably not use these terms to describe what they actually do. Rather, what you'd see are the various roles managers play.

After reading this section, you should be able to:

1-4 explain the major roles and subroles that managers perform in their jobs.

Professor Henry Mintzberg followed five American CEOs, shadowing each for a week and analyzing their mail, their conversations, and their actions. He concluded that managers fulfill three major roles while performing their jobs—interpersonal roles, informational roles, and decisional roles.[37]

In other words, managers talk to people, gather and give information, and make decisions. Furthermore, as shown in Exhibit 1.3, these three major roles can be subdivided into 10 subroles.

Let's examine each major role—**1-4a interpersonal, 1-4b informational,** and **1-4c decisional roles**—and their 10 subroles.

1-4a Interpersonal Roles

More than anything else, management jobs are people intensive. Estimates vary with the level of management, but most managers spend between two-thirds and four-fifths of their time in face-to-face communication with others.[38] If you're a loner, or if you consider dealing with people a pain, then you may not be cut out for management work. In fulfilling the interpersonal role of management, managers perform three subroles: figurehead, leader, and liaison.

In the **figurehead role**, managers perform ceremonial duties like greeting company visitors, speaking at the opening of a new facility, or representing the company at a community luncheon to support local charities. When Wichita-based *Cessna*, the largest manufacturer of general aviation planes in the world, opened a new 101,000-square-foot jet service facility in Mesa, Arizona, CEO Jack Pelton flew in to join Mesa's mayor, Cessna managers, and local workers and their families to celebrate the grand opening.[39]

In the **leader role**, managers motivate and encourage workers to accomplish organizational objectives. In the **liaison role**, managers deal with people outside their units. Studies consistently indicate that managers spend as much time with outsiders as they do with their own subordinates and their own bosses. The New York Jets have an initiative that encourages members of the organization to interact with professionals outside of their fields to learn better management and decision-making processes. General Manager Mike Tannenbaum met J. P. Morgan Chase CEO Jamie Dimon to discuss J. P. Morgan's risk assessment and acquisition processes.[40]

1-4b Informational Roles

Not only do managers spend most of their time in face-to-face contact with others, but they spend much of it obtaining and sharing information. Indeed, Mintzberg found that the managers in his study spent 40 percent of their time

figurehead role
the interpersonal role managers play when they perform ceremonial duties

leader role
the interpersonal role managers play when they motivate and encourage workers to accomplish organizational objectives

liaison role
the interpersonal role managers play when they deal with people outside their units

McDonald's knows the key to growth in China is the quality of its managers, so it opened a training center with the goal of recruiting and retaining top workers. McDonald's invested about $23 million in Hamburger University, which can train about 1,000 people per year for junior and senior management positions. It also teaches franchise owners effective and efficient restaurant operations. McDonald's will build on this foundation by opening 1,000 new stores in China. Hamburger University also enables an entry-level employee to rise to store manager, and with further training, to rise to middle and senior management in the organization.[41]

giving and getting information from others. In this regard, management can be viewed as processing information, gathering information by scanning the business environment and listening to others in face-to-face conversations, processing that information, and then sharing it with people both inside and outside the company. Mintzberg identified three informational subroles: monitor, disseminator, and spokesperson.

In the **monitor role**, managers scan their environment for information, actively contact others for information, and because of their personal contacts, receive a great deal of unsolicited information. Besides receiving firsthand information, managers monitor their environment by reading local newspapers and the *Wall Street Journal* to keep track of customers, competitors, and technological changes that may affect their businesses. Now, managers can also take advantage of electronic monitoring and distribution services that track the news wires (Associated Press, Reuters, etc.) for stories related to their businesses. These services deliver customized electronic newspapers that include only stories on topics the managers specify.

Because of their numerous personal contacts and their access to subordinates, managers are often hubs for the distribution of critical information. In the **disseminator role**, managers share the information they have collected with their subordinates and others in the company. Although there will never be a complete substitution for face-to-face dissemination of information, Serena Software, based in Redwood City, California, uses Facebook to communicate worldwide with its 850 employees. The company relies on Facebook so much for recruiting new employees and marketing that it has become the company's de facto intranet.[42] (You'll read more about intranets in Chapter 15 on communication.)

In contrast to the disseminator role, in which managers distribute information to employees inside the company, managers in the **spokesperson role** share information with people outside their departments and companies.

monitor role
the informational role managers play when they scan their environment for information

disseminator role
the informational role managers play when they share information with others in their departments or companies

spokesperson role
the informational role managers play when they share information with people outside their departments or companies

entrepreneur role
the decisional role managers play when they adapt themselves, their subordinates, and their units to change

1-4c Decisional Roles

Mintzberg found that obtaining and sharing information is not an end in itself. Obtaining and sharing information with people inside and outside the company is useful to managers because it helps them make good decisions. According to Mintzberg, managers engage in four decisional subroles: entrepreneur, disturbance handler, resource allocator, and negotiator.

In the **entrepreneur role**, managers adapt themselves, their subordinates, and their units to change. When *UPS* found nearly 30 percent of its driver candidates were flunking its driver-training program, it abandoned traditional classroom training for high-tech, interactive, training methods. UPS training now includes video-game simulators, and "kinetic learning" modules designed to allow recruits to practice specific scenarios such as walking on ice. It even has an 11,500-square-foot facility with a real driving course that teaches and tests UPS's driving techniques. Thanks to its new, interactive, training methods, only 10 percent of driver trainees fail, leading Allen Hill, UPS's senior vice president of human resources, to conclude that the new training methods have "enhanced the probability of success of these new drivers."[43]

In the **disturbance handler role**, managers respond to pressures and problems so severe that they demand immediate attention and action. When computer hackers replaced wine critic Gary Vaynerchuk's website, CORKD.COM, with pornographic images, Vaynerchuk immediately recorded an apology video, posted it on another website, and then tweeted about the apology video to his 900,000 followers. He also communicated directly with the 65 people who mentioned the incident on their own Twitter accounts. Said Vaynerchuk, "Every person that mentioned Corkd on Twitter got a message from me and a link to the video." Although it took eight hours to restore the Corkd.com website, there was no drop-off in terms of sales or website visits. Furthermore, he received 75 e-mails from customers who appreciated his quick explanation about what had happened.[44]

In the **resource allocator role**, managers decide who will get what resources and how many resources they will get. For instance, as the recession that began in the fall of 2008 deepened, companies slashed production by closing facilities, laying off workers, and cutting pay for surviving workers and managers. But when it came to research and development (R&D) spending, the largest firms spent as much on R&D as they did before, despite revenues falling by nearly 8 percent. Why? Because in prior economic downturns, continued investments in R&D led to the development of successful products such as the iPod and fuel-efficient jet engines. Says Jim Andrew, of the Boston Consulting Group, "Companies by and large realized that large reductions in R&D are suicidal." Therefore, companies such as Intel, which saw a 90 percent drop in its net income, still spent $5.4 billion on R&D. Likewise, 3M, which cut capital spending

disturbance handler role
the decisional role managers play when they respond to severe problems that demand immediate action

resource allocator role
the decisional role managers play when they decide who gets what resources

© MIKE SEGAR/REUTERS/LANDOV

After years of lawsuits, it took Roger Faxon, CEO of EMI Group Ltd., just two days to negotiate the rights to sell Beatles' music on Apple's iTunes stores.

by 30 percent and laid off 4,700 workers, slightly increased its R&D spending so as not to sacrifice future profits from new, innovative products.[45]

In the **negotiator role**, managers negotiate schedules, projects, goals, outcomes, resources, and employee raises. For example, after years of lawsuits, it only took two days for Roger Faxon, the new CEO of *EMI GROUP LTD.*, which owns the rights to sell the Beatles' music, to negotiate a deal to make the legendary band's music available for sale at Apple's iTunes store. Just two months after the agreement was negotiated, 5 million Beatles' songs and 2 million Beatles' albums had been sold and downloaded via iTunes.[46]

REVIEW 1-4

....

Managerial Roles

Managers perform interpersonal, informational, and decisional roles in their jobs. In fulfilling the interpersonal role, managers act as figureheads by performing ceremonial duties, as leaders by motivating and encouraging workers, and as liaisons by dealing with people outside their units. When managers perform their informational role, they act as monitors by scanning their environment for information, as disseminators by sharing information with others in the company, and as spokespeople by sharing information with people outside their departments or companies. In decisional roles, managers act as entrepreneurs by adapting their units to incremental change, as disturbance handlers by responding to larger problems that demand immediate action, as resource allocators by deciding resource recipients and amounts, and as negotiators by bargaining with others about schedules, projects, goals, outcomes, and resources.

1-5 What Companies Look For in Managers

I didn't have the slightest idea what my job was. I walked in giggling and laughing because I had been promoted and had no idea what principles or style to be guided by. After the first day, I felt like I had run into a brick wall (Sales Representative No. 1).

Suddenly, I found myself saying, "Boy, I can't be responsible for getting all that revenue. I don't have the time." Suddenly you've got to go from [taking care of] yourself and say, "Now I'm the manager, and what does a manager do?" It takes awhile thinking about it for it to really hit you . . . a manager gets things done through other people. That's a very, very hard transition to make (Sales Representative No. 2).[47]

The preceding statements were made by two star sales representatives who, on the basis of their superior performance, were promoted to the position of sales manager. As their comments indicate, at first they did not feel confident about their ability to do their jobs as managers. Like most new managers, these sales managers suddenly realized that the performance that led to success early in their careers would not necessarily help them succeed as managers. What then would help them thrive in their new positions? Let's find out.

After reading this section, you should be able to:

1-5 explain what companies look for in managers.

negotiator role
the decisional role managers play when they negotiate schedules, projects, goals, outcomes, resources, and employee raises

When companies look for employees who would be good managers, they look for individuals who have technical skills, human skills, conceptual skills, and the motivation to manage.[48] Exhibit 1.4 shows the relative importance of these four skills to the jobs of team leaders, first-line managers, middle managers, and top managers.

Technical skills are the specialized procedures, techniques, and knowledge required to get the job done. For the sales managers described above, technical skills involve the ability to find new sales prospects, develop accurate sales pitches based on customer needs, and close the sale.

Technical skills are most important for team leaders and lower-level managers because these people supervise the workers who produce products or serve customers. Team leaders and first-line managers need technical knowledge and skills to train new employees and help employees solve problems. Technical knowledge and skills are also needed to troubleshoot problems that employees can't handle. Technical skills become less important as managers rise through the managerial ranks, but they are still important.

Human skills can be summarized as the ability to work well with others. Managers with human skills work effectively within groups, encourage others to express their thoughts and feelings, are sensitive to others' needs and viewpoints, and are good listeners and communicators. Human skills are equally important at all levels of management, from first-line supervisors to CEOs. However, because lower-level managers spend much of their time solving technical problems, upper-level managers may actually spend more time dealing directly with people. On average, first-line managers spend 57 percent of their time with people, but that percentage increases to 63 percent for middle managers and 78 percent for top managers.[49]

Conceptual skills involve the ability to see the organization as a whole, to understand how the different parts of the company affect each other, and to recognize how the company fits into or is affected by its external environment such as the local community, social and economic forces, customers, and the competition. Good managers have to be able to recognize, understand, and reconcile multiple complex problems and perspectives. In other words, managers have to be

technical skills
the ability to apply the specialized procedures, techniques, and knowledge required to get the job done

human skills
the ability to work well with others

conceptual skills
the ability to see the organization as a whole, understand how the different parts affect each other, and recognize how the company fits into or is affected by its external environment

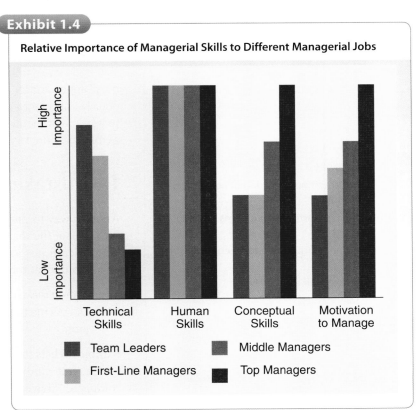

Exhibit 1.4

Relative Importance of Managerial Skills to Different Managerial Jobs

Team Leaders
First-Line Managers
Middle Managers
Top Managers

© CENGAGE LEARNING

smart! In fact, intelligence makes so much difference for managerial performance that managers with above-average intelligence typically outperform managers of average intelligence by approximately 48 percent.[50] Clearly, companies need to be careful to promote smart workers into management. Conceptual skills increase in importance as managers rise through the management hierarchy.

Good management involves much more than intelligence, however. For example, making the department genius a manager can be disastrous if that genius lacks technical skills, human skills, or one other factor known as the motivation to manage. **Motivation to manage** is an assessment of how motivated employees are to interact with superiors, participate in competitive situations, behave assertively toward others, tell others what to do, reward good behavior and punish poor behavior, perform actions that are highly visible to others, and handle and organize administrative tasks. Managers typically have a stronger motivation to manage than their subordinates, and managers at higher levels usually have a stronger motivation to manage than managers at lower levels. Furthermore, managers with a stronger motivation to manage are promoted faster, are rated as better managers by their employees, and earn more money than managers with a weak motivation to manage.[51]

REVIEW 1-5
....

What Companies Look For in Managers

Companies do not want one-dimensional managers. They want managers with a balance of skills. They want managers who know their stuff (technical skills), are equally comfortable working with blue-collar and white-collar employees (human skills), are able to assess the complexities of today's competitive marketplace and position their companies for success (conceptual skills), and want to assume positions of leadership and power (motivation to manage). Technical skills are most important for lower-level managers; human skills are equally important at all levels of management; and conceptual skills and motivation to manage increase in importance as managers rise through the managerial ranks.

motivation to manage
an assessment of how enthusiastic employees are about managing the work of others

Exhibit 1.5

Top 10 Mistakes That Managers Make

1. Insensitive to others: abrasive, intimidating, bullying style
2. Cold, aloof, arrogant
3. Betrayal of trust
4. Overly ambitious: thinking of next job, playing politics
5. Specific performance problems with the business
6. Overmanaging: unable to delegate or build a team
7. Unable to staff effectively
8. Unable to think strategically
9. Unable to adapt to boss with different style
10. Overdependent on advocate or mentor

Source: M. W. McCall Jr., and M. M. Lombardo, "What Makes a Top Executive?" Psychology Today *(February 1983): 26–31.*

1-6 Mistakes Managers Make

Another way to understand what it takes to be a manager is to look at the mistakes managers make. In other words, we can learn just as much from what managers shouldn't do as from what they should do.

After reading this section, you should be able to:

1-6 Discuss the top mistakes that managers make in their jobs.

Exhibit 1.5 lists the top 10 mistakes managers make.

Several studies of U.S. and British managers have compared "arrivers," or managers who made it all the way to the top of their companies, with "derailers," or managers who were successful early in their careers but were knocked off the fast track by the time they reached the middle to upper levels of management.[52] The researchers found that there were only a few differences between arrivers and derailers. For the most part, both groups were talented and both groups had weaknesses. But what distinguished derailers from arrivers was that derailers possessed two or more fatal flaws with respect to the way they managed people. Although arrivers were by no means perfect, they usually had no more than one fatal flaw or had found ways to minimize the effects of their flaws on the people with whom they worked.

The No. 1 mistake made by derailers was that they were insensitive to others by virtue of their abrasive, intimidating, and bullying management style. The authors of one study described a manager who walked into his subordinate's office and interrupted a meeting by saying, "I need to see you." When the subordinate tried to explain that he was not available because he was in the middle of a meeting, the manager barked, "I don't give a damn! I said I wanted to see you now."[53] Not surprisingly, only 25 percent of derailers were rated by others as being good with people, compared to 75 percent of arrivers.

The second mistake was that derailers were often cold, aloof, or arrogant. Although this sounds like insensitivity to others, it has more to do with derailed managers being so smart, so expert in their areas of knowledge, that they treated others with contempt because they weren't experts too.

The third mistake made by derailers involved betraying a trust. Betraying a trust doesn't mean being dishonest. Instead, it means making others look bad by not doing what you said you would do when you said you would do it. That mistake, in itself, is not fatal, because managers and their workers aren't machines. Tasks go undone in every company every single business day. There's always too much to do and not enough time, people, money, or resources to do it. The fatal betrayal of trust is failing to inform others when things will not be done on time. This failure to admit mistakes, quickly inform others of the mistakes, take responsibility for the mistakes, and then fix them without blaming others clearly distinguished the behavior of derailers from arrivers.

The fourth mistake was being overly political and ambitious. Managers who always have their eye on their next job rarely establish more than superficial relationships with peers and coworkers. In their haste to gain credit for successes that would be noticed by upper management, they make the fatal mistake of treating people as though they don't matter.

The fatal mistakes of being unable to delegate, build a team, and staff effectively indicate that many derailed managers were unable to make the most basic transition to managerial work: Quit being hands-on doers and get work done through others. Two things go wrong when managers make these mistakes. First, when managers meddle in decisions that their subordinates should be making—when they can't stop being doers—they alienate the people who work for them. According to Richard Kilburg of Johns Hopkins University, when managers interfere with workers' decisions, "You . . . have a tendency to lose your most creative people. They're able to say, 'Screw this. I'm not staying here.'"[54] Second, because they are trying to do their subordinates' jobs in addition to their own, managers who fail to delegate will not have enough time to do much of anything well.

Mistakes Managers Make

Another way to understand what it takes to be a manager is to look at the top mistakes managers make. Five of the most important mistakes made by managers are being abrasive and intimidating; being cold, aloof, or arrogant; betraying trust; being overly ambitious; and failing to build a team and then delegate to that team.

1-7 The Transition to Management: The First Year

In her book *Becoming a Manager: Mastery of a New Identity*, Harvard Business School professor Linda Hill followed the development of 19 people in their first year as managers. Her study found that becoming a manager produced a profound psychological transition that changed the way these managers viewed themselves and others. As shown in Exhibit 1.6, the evolution of the managers' thoughts, expectations, and realities over the course of their first year in management reveals the magnitude of the changes they experienced.

After reading this section, you should be able to:

1-7 describe the transition that employees go through when they are promoted to management.

Initially, the managers in Hill's study believed that their job was to exercise formal authority and to manage tasks—basically being the boss, telling others what to do, making decisions, and getting things done. One of the managers Hill interviewed said, "Being the manager means running my own office, using my ideas and thoughts." Another said, "[The office is] my baby. It's my job to make sure it works."[55] In fact, most of the new managers were attracted to management positions because they wanted to be in charge. Surprisingly, the new managers did not believe that their job was to manage people. The only aspects of people management mentioned by the new managers were hiring and firing.

Exhibit 1.6

The Transition to Management: Initial Expectations, after Six Months, and after a Year

MANAGERS' INITIAL EXPECTATIONS			AFTER SIX MONTHS AS A MANAGER			AFTER A YEAR AS A MANAGER					
JAN	FEB	MAR	APR	MAY	JUN	JUL	AUG	SEP	OCT	NOV	DEC

MANAGERS' INITIAL EXPECTATIONS	AFTER SIX MONTHS AS A MANAGER	AFTER A YEAR AS A MANAGER
⊙ Be the boss	⊙ Initial expectations were wrong	⊙ No longer "doer"
⊙ Have formal authority	⊙ Fast pace	⊙ Communicating, listening, and giving positive reinforcement
⊙ Manage tasks	⊙ Heavy workload	⊙ Learning to adapt to and control stress
⊙ Job is not managing people	⊙ Job is to be problem-solver and troubleshooter for subordinates	⊙ Job is people development

© CENGAGE LEARNING

After six months, most of the new managers had concluded that their initial expectations about managerial work were wrong. Management wasn't just about being the boss, making decisions, and telling others what to do. The first surprise was the fast pace and heavy workload involved. Said one of Hill's managers, "This job is much harder than you think. It is 40 to 50 percent more work than being a producer! Who would have ever guessed?" The pace of managerial work was startling too. Another manager said, "You have eight or nine people looking for your time . . . coming into and out of your office all day long." A somewhat frustrated manager declared that management was "a job that never ended . . . a job you couldn't get your hands around."[56]

Informal descriptions like this are consistent with studies indicating that the average first-line manager spends no more than two minutes on a task before being interrupted by a request from a subordinate, a phone call, or an e-mail. The pace is somewhat less hurried for top managers, who spend an average of approximately nine minutes on a task before having to switch to another. In practice, this means that supervisors may perform 30 different tasks per hour, whereas top managers perform 7 different tasks per hour, with each task typically different from the one that preceded it. A manager described this frenetic level of activity by saying, "The only time you are in control is when you shut your door; and then I feel I am not doing the job I'm supposed to be doing, which is being with the people."[57]

The other major surprise after six months on the job was that the managers' expectations about what they should do as managers were very different from their subordinates' expectations. Initially, the managers defined their jobs as helping their subordinates perform their jobs well. For the managers, who still defined themselves as doers rather than managers, assisting their subordinates meant going out on sales calls or handling customer complaints. One manager said, "I like going out with the rep, who may need me to lend him my credibility as manager. I like the challenge, the joy in closing. I go out with the reps and we make the call and talk about the customer; it's fun."[58] But when the managers "assisted" in this way, their subordinates were resentful and viewed their help as interference. The subordinates wanted their managers to help them by solving problems that they couldn't solve. Once the managers realized this distinction, they embraced their role as problem solver and troubleshooter. Thus, they could help without interfering with their subordinates' jobs.

After a year on the job, most of the managers thought of themselves as managers and no longer as doers. In making the transition, they finally realized that people management was the most important part of their job. One of Hill's interviewees summarized the lesson that had taken him a year to learn by saying, "As many demands as managers have on their time, I think their primary responsibility is people development. Not production, but people development."[59] Another indication of how much their views had changed was that most of the managers now regretted the rather heavy-handed approach they had used in their early attempts to manage their subordinates. "I wasn't good at managing . . ., so I was bossy like a first-grade teacher." "Now I see that I started out as a drill sergeant. I was inflexible, just a lot of how-to's." By the end of the year, most of the managers had abandoned their authoritarian approach for one based on communication, listening, and positive reinforcement. One manager explained, "Last night at five I handed out an award in the boardroom just to the individual. It was the first time in his career that he had [earned] $100,000, and I gave him a piece of glass [a small award] and said I'd heard a rumor that somebody here just crossed over $100,000 and I said congratulations, shook his hand, and walked away. It was not public in the sense that I gathered everybody around. But I knew and he did too."[60]

Finally, after beginning their year as managers in frustration, the managers came to feel comfortable with their subordinates, with the demands of their jobs, and with their emerging managerial styles. Although being managers had made them acutely aware of their limitations and their need to develop as people, it also provided them with an unexpected reward of coaching and developing the people who worked for them. One manager said, "It gives me the best feeling to see somebody do something well after I have helped them. I get excited." Another stated, "I realize now that when I accepted the position of branch manager that it is truly an exciting vocation. It is truly awesome, even at this level; it can be terribly challenging and terribly exciting."[61]

REVIEW 1-7

The Transition to Management: The First Year

Managers often begin their jobs by using more formal authority and fewer people management skills. However, most find that being a manager has little to do with bossing their subordinates. After six months on the job, the managers were surprised at the fast pace and heavy workload and that "helping" their subordinates was viewed as interference. After a year on the job, most of the managers had come to think of themselves not as doers, but as managers who get things done through others. And because they finally realized that people management was the most important part of their job, most of them had abandoned their authoritarian approach for one based on communication, listening, and positive reinforcement.

1-8 Competitive Advantage through People

Management matters. If you walk down the aisle of the business section in your local bookstore, you'll find hundreds of books that explain precisely what companies need to do to be successful. Unfortunately, the best-selling business books tend to be faddish, changing dramatically every few years. One thing that hasn't changed, though, is the importance of good people and good management: Companies can't succeed for long without them. In his books *Competitive Advantage through People* and *The Human Equation: Building Profits by Putting People First*, Stanford University business professor Jeffrey Pfeffer contends that what separates top-performing companies from their competitors is the way they treat their workforce—in other words, their management style.[62]

After reading this section, you should be able to:

1-8 Explain how and why companies can create competitive advantage through people.

Pfeffer found that managers in top-performing companies used ideas like employment security, selective hiring, self-managed teams and decentralization, high pay contingent on company performance, extensive training, reduced status distinctions (between managers and employees), and extensive sharing of financial information to achieve financial performance that, on average, was 40 percent higher than that of other companies. These ideas, which are explained in detail in Exhibit 1.7, help organizations develop workforces that are smarter, better trained, more motivated, and more committed than their competitors' workforces. And—as indicated by the phenomenal growth and return on investment earned by these companies—smarter, better trained, and more committed workforces provide superior products and service to customers. Such customers keep buying and, by telling others about their positive experiences, bring in new customers.

According to Pfeffer, companies that invest in their people will create long-lasting competitive advantages that are difficult for other companies to duplicate. Indeed, other studies clearly demonstrate that sound management practices can produce substantial advantages in four critical areas of organizational performance: sales revenues, profits, stock market returns, and customer satisfaction.

Exhibit 1.7

Competitive Advantage through People: Management Practices

1. Employment Security—Employment security is the ultimate form of commitment that companies can make to their workers. Employees can innovate and increase company productivity without fearing the loss of their jobs.

2. Selective Hiring—If employees are the basis for a company's competitive advantage, and those employees have employment security, then the company needs to aggressively recruit and selectively screen applicants in order to hire the most talented employees available.

3. Self-Managed Teams and Decentralization—Self-managed teams are responsible for their own hiring, purchasing, job assignments, and production. Self-managed teams can often produce enormous increases in productivity through increased employee commitment and creativity. Decentralization allows employees who are closest to (and most knowledgeable about) problems, production, and customers to make timely decisions. Decentralization increases employee satisfaction and commitment.

4. High Wages Contingent on Organizational Performance—High wages are needed to attract and retain talented workers and to indicate that the organization values its workers. Employees, like company founders, shareholders, and managers, need to share in the financial rewards when the company is successful. Why? Because employees who have a financial stake in their companies are more likely to take a long-run view of the business and think like business owners.

5. Training and Skill Development—Like a high-tech company that spends millions of dollars to upgrade computers or R&D labs, a company whose competitive advantage is based on its people must invest in the training and skill development of its people.

6. Reduction of Status Differences—These are fancy words that indicate that the company treats everyone, no matter what the job, as equal. There are no reserved parking spaces. Everyone eats in the same cafeteria and has similar benefits. The result: much improved communication as employees focus on problems and solutions rather than on how they are less valued than managers.

7. Sharing Information—If employees are to make decisions that are good for the long-run health and success of the company, they need to be given information about costs, finances, productivity, development times, and strategies that was previously known only by company managers.

Source: J. Pfeffer, The Human Equation: Building Profits by Putting People First *(Boston: Harvard Business School Press, 1996).*

In terms of sales revenues and profits, a study of nearly 1,000 U.S. firms found that companies that use *just some* of the ideas shown in Exhibit 1.7 had $27,044 more sales per employee and $3,814 more profit per employee than companies that didn't. For a 100-person company, these differences amount to $2.7 million more in sales and nearly $400,000 more in annual profit! For a 1,000-person company, the difference grows to $27 million more in sales and $4 million more in annual profit![63]

Another study that considers the effect of investing in people on company sales found that poorly performing companies were able to improve their average return on investment from 5.1 percent to 19.7 percent and increase sales by $94,000 per employee. They did this by adopting management techniques as simple as setting performance expectations (establishing goals, results, and schedules), coaching (informal, ongoing discussions between managers and subordinates about what is being done well and what could be done better), reviewing (annual, formal discussion about results), and rewarding employee performance (adjusting salaries and bonuses based on employee performance and results).[64] So, in addition to significantly improving the profitability of healthy companies, sound management practices can turn around failing companies.

To determine how investing in people affects stock market performance, researchers matched companies on *Fortune* magazine's list of "100 Best Companies to Work For in America" with companies that were similar in industry, size, and—this is key—operating performance. Researchers found that people who worked for the "100 Best" companies were consistently much more satisfied with their jobs and employers year after year than were employees in the matched companies. More importantly, those stable differences in employee attitudes were strongly related to differences in stock market performance. From 1998 to 2009, a $100,000 investment in the "100 Best Companies to Work For" would have grown to $266,536 compared to just $134,392 invested in the Standard & Poor's 500, which is a stock index of the 500 largest public companies in the United States.[65] In other words, over those 10 years an investment in the "100 Best" companies doubled investors' money.

Finally, research also indicates that managers have an important effect on customer satisfaction. Many people find this surprising. They don't understand how managers, who are largely responsible for what goes on inside the company, can affect what goes on outside the company. They wonder how managers, who often interact with customers under negative conditions (when customers are angry or dissatisfied), can actually improve customer satisfaction. It turns out that managers influence customer satisfaction through employee satisfaction. When employees are satisfied with their jobs, their bosses, and the companies they work for, they provide much better service to customers.[66] In turn, customers are more satisfied too. Indeed, customers of companies on *Fortune*'s list of "100 Best Companies to Work For," where employees are much more satisfied with their jobs and their companies, have much higher customer satisfaction scores than do customers of comparable companies who are not on *Fortune*'s list. Over an eight-year period, that difference in customer satisfaction also resulted in a 14 percent annual stock market return for the "100 Best" companies compared to a 6 percent return for the overall stock market.[67] You will learn more about the service–profit chain in Chapter 16 on managing service and manufacturing operations.

Competitive Advantage through People

Why does management matter? Well-managed companies are competitive because their workforces are smarter, better trained, more motivated, and more committed. Furthermore, companies that practice good management consistently have greater sales revenues, profits, and stock market performance than companies that don't. Finally, good management matters because it leads to satisfied employees who, in turn, provide better service to customers. Because employees tend to treat customers the same way that their managers treat them, good management can improve customer satisfaction.

 # Management Decision

Making decisions is part of every manager's job. To give you practice at managerial decision making, each chapter contains a Management Decision assignment focused on a particular decision. You'll need to decide what to do in the given situation and then answer several questions to explain your choices.

Should We Try to Make More Money?[68]

To say that the airline industry has experienced some struggles would be a huge understatement. Faced with fears over terrorist attacks and sharp rises in the price of oil, airlines have been losing money at historic rates. In 2009, only four domestic airlines were able to turn a profit, while the five largest carriers lost more than $3 billion combined.

In the midst of these struggles, the industry found an unexpected, but highly lucrative, source of revenue—baggage. For many years, passengers were allowed to travel with up to three pieces of luggage—one item to carry on the plane, and two larger items that could be checked into the storage area. In 2008, American Airlines became the first major airline to charge passengers who wanted to check their baggage. Though widely criticized, other airlines quickly followed suit, charging $15–$35 per bag for each portion of a roundtrip flight.

For airlines, the net effects of baggage fees have been incredible. In 2009, the airlines combined to collect nearly $2 billion in baggage fees alone; Delta Airlines led the entire industry with $550 million. Not surprisingly, baggage fees led passengers to check fewer bags. This has allowed airlines to dedicate more space to cargo, which commands a premium price. What is more, there has been a reduction in the number of mishandled bags, which led to an additional $94 million in savings. Best of all, all of this is essentially "free money"—the airlines did not lower their fares after charging for checked baggage, and they have not had to increase other expenses (such as labor) to collect the fees.

All told, checked-bag fees have been such a success that Spirit Airlines now charges $45 for carry-on baggage that is stored in overhead bins. You are a manager of the lone holdout, Southwest Airlines, which allows passengers to check two bags with no charge. Although Southwest has remained profitable during the industry's struggles, it is difficult to see competitors rake in millions of dollars in additional revenue with virtually no labor. You begin to wonder whether your company shouldn't also charge for bags so that it can maintain a competitive edge. After all, as you well know, the airline industry is unpredictable, and your company could find itself with financial struggles very quickly.

Questions

1. How is this decision emblematic of your job as a manager?

2. What are the advantages and disadvantages of following competitors by charging for checked baggage?

Practice Being a Manager

Finding a Management Job

Management is a wide-ranging and exciting area of work. One way to gain a sense of the possibilities is to study the advertisements for management job openings. Companies advertise their management openings in a variety of ways, including print advertisements in such newspapers as the *Wall Street Journal* (especially its Friday career section) and online ads at job sites like Monster.com and Career-Builder.com.

STEP 1 **Find a job you'd like to have.** Search through the newspaper and online ads and locate several detailed job descriptions for management positions. Select the one that you find most appealing—a job that you could picture yourself interviewing for either in the near future or later in your career. Do not be too concerned about your current qualifications in making your selection, but you should see realistic prospects of meeting the qualifications over time (if a job requires an MBA, e.g., you should see yourself completing this degree sometime in the future). Print your selected detailed job description and bring it to your next class session.

STEP 2 **Share your job description.** In class, your professor will assign you to a pair or group of three. Write your name on your selected management job description, and exchange your job description with your partner(s). Each member of the pair or triad should now have a job description other than their own.

STEP 3 **Think like a hiring manager.** Read the job description you received from your partner. Imagine that you are the manager responsible for hiring someone to fill this position. A human resources specialist in your company has already screened the applicant's résumé and background. Thus, you may assume that your partner has met all the basic qualifications for the job. Your job as a senior manager is to ask questions that might get beyond the résumé to the person—what might you ask to learn whether someone is well suited to thrive in this management job and in your company?

STEP 4 **Take turns interviewing.** Each member of the group should be briefly interviewed (5–10 minutes) for the job he or she selected.

STEP 5 **Debrief.** Discuss your experiences with your partner(s). What was it like to be interviewed for your selected position? What was it like to role-play interviewing someone for a management position? Now imagine the real thing. Brainstorm about how you might prepare yourself over time to be the top candidate for an attractive management position and to be a senior manager responsible for hiring the best-qualified managers for your company.

STEP 6 **Discuss with the class.** Share your interview experiences and brainstorming ideas with the class. Do you hear any similarities across the pairs/triads? What ideas or questions are most significant to you as you consider management job interviews?

Self Assessment

Is Management for You?

Each chapter has a related Self-Assessment to help you consider how your own perspectives influence your management skills. Each assessment tool starts with a short description and ends with basic scoring information. (Your instructor will have interpretations of your scores.) As you advance through the book, take time to review your assessment scores together. Doing so will help you see patterns in your own perceptions and behaviors and give you insights into how those perceptions may affect your performance as a manager.

As you learned in Section 7 of this chapter, many managers begin their careers in management with specific ideas about what it means to be the boss. Although you may want to be a manager because of excitement, status, power, or rewards, knowing how to manage is not automatic; it requires specific skills and competencies, as well as a desire to manage. This assessment is meant to establish your baseline ability in the skills covered in the chapter. It will not tell you whether you should or should not be a manager, or whether you have "what it takes" to be a manager. It will, however, give you feedback on general skills that influence your overall managerial style.[69]

Be candid as you complete the assessment by circling the appropriate responses.

ML = Most like me
SL = Somewhat like me
NS = Not sure
SU = Somewhat unlike me
MU = Most unlike me

1. I can get others to do what I want them to do.
   ML   SL   NS   SU   MU

2. I frequently evaluate my job performance.
   ML   SL   NS   SU   MU

3. I prefer not to get involved in office politics.
   ML   SL   NS   SU   MU

4. I like the freedom that open-ended goals provide me.
   ML   SL   NS   SU   MU

5. I work best when things are orderly and calm.
   ML   SL   NS   SU   MU

6. I enjoy making oral presentations to groups of people.
   ML   SL   NS   SU   MU

7. I am confident in my abilities to accomplish difficult tasks.
   ML   SL   NS   SU   MU

8. I do not like to write.
   ML   SL   NS   SU   MU

9. I like solving difficult puzzles.
   ML   SL   NS   SU   MU

10. I am an organized person.
    ML   SL   NS   SU   MU

11. I have difficulty telling others they made a mistake.
    ML   SL   NS   SU   MU

12. I like to work set hours each day.
    ML   SL   NS   SU   MU

13. I view paperwork as a trivial task.
    ML   SL   NS   SU   MU

14. I like to help others learn new things.
    ML   SL   NS   SU   MU

15. I prefer to work alone.
    ML   SL   NS   SU   MU

16. I believe it is who you know, not what you know, that counts.

     ML   SL   NS   SU   MU

17. I enjoy doing several things at once.

     ML   SL   NS   SU   MU

18. I am good at managing money.

     ML   SL   NS   SU   MU

19. I would rather back down from an argument than let it get out of hand.

     ML   SL   NS   SU   MU

20. I am computer literate.

     ML   SL   NS   SU   MU

SCORING

Start by reversing your scores for items 5, 8, 11, 15, and 16. For example, if you used ML, change it to MU, and vice versa; if you used SL, change it to SU, and vice versa. Now assign each answer a point value.

Number of ML answers _____ times 5 points each = _____

Number of SL answers _____ times 4 points each = _____

Number of NS answers _____ times 3 points each = _____

Number of SU answers _____ times 2 points each = _____

Number of MU answers _____ times 1 point each = _____

TOTAL = _____

You can find the interpretation for your score at www.cengagebrain.com.

Source: From P. Hunsaker, *Management; A Skills Approach*, 2nd ed., pp. 24–25. Copyright © 2005. Used by permission Pearson Education, Inc., Upper Saddle River, NJ.

REEL TO REAL

 MANAGEMENT WORKPLACE

© CENGAGE LEARNING 2013

Camp Bow Wow: Innovative Management for a Changing World

Sue Ryan, a Camp Bow Wow franchisee from Colorado, knows the ins and outs of managing a care center for pets. To help launch her business a few years ago, Ryan recruited experienced pet-care worker Candace Stathis, who came on as a camp counselor. Ryan soon recognized that Stathis was a star performer with a natural ability to work with clients and pets alike, and today serves as the camp's general manager. At Camp Bow Wow, store managers have roles distinct from camp counselors. Whereas counselors typically take care of dogs, answer phones, and book reservations, managers must know how to run all operations and mange people as well. To keep camp running as efficiently as possible, Stathis maintains a strict daily schedule for doggie baths, nail trimmings, feedings, and play time.

What to Watch for and Ask Yourself

1. Identify three skills that companies look for in managers and explain which might be most needed for the Camp Bow Wow leaders highlighted in the video.

2. Which activities at Camp Bow Wow require high efficiency? Which activities require high effectiveness?

3. List two activities that leaders at Camp Bow Wow perform daily, and identify which of the managerial roles discussed in the chapter figure prominently for each.

Endnotes

1. M. Anderson and M. Liedtke (Associated Press), "Hubris—and Late Fees—Doomed Blockbuster," *MSNBC*, September 23, 2010, accessed January 29, 2011, from www.msnbc.msn.com/id/39332696/ns/business-retail/; M. Copeland, "Reed Hastings: Leader of the Pack," *Fortune*, December 6, 2010, 120–130; J. Heilemann, "Showtime for Netflix," *Business 2.0* (March 2005): 36; R. Grover, "Netflix: Premium Cable's Worst Nightmare," *Bloomberg Businessweek*, September 20, 2010, 21–22; and J. Surowiecki, "The Financial Page: The Next Level," *The New Yorker*, October 18, 2010, 28.

2. S. Prasso, "American Made…Chinese Owned," *Fortune*, May 24, 2010, 92.

3. M. Kimes "Why J & J's Headache Won't Go Away," *Fortune*, September 6, 2010, 100–108.

4. "Business Services: Global Industry Guide," *Data Monitor*, January 21, 2010, accessed April 18, 2009, from www.marketresearch.com.

5. V. Nayar, "Corner Office: He's Not Bill Gates, or Fred Astaire," interview by A. Bryant, *New York Times*, February 13, 2010, accessed June 22, 2010, from www.nytimes.com/2010/02/14/business/14cornerweb.html.

6. J. Levitz, "FedEx Looks to 777s to Deliver an Edge," *The Wall Street Journal*, July 14, 2010, B1, B2.

7. D. A. Wren, A. G. Bedeian, and J. D. Breeze, "The Foundations of Henri Fayol's Administrative Theory," *Management Decision* 40 (2002): 906–918.

8. S. Totilo, "The Unexpected Gamer Who Runs EA," *Kotaku*, accessed January 26, 2011, from http://kotaku.com/5568591/the-unexpected-gamer-who-runs-ea.

9. H. Fayol, *General and Industrial Management* (London: Pittman & Sons, 1949).

10. R. Stagner, "Corporate Decision Making," *Journal of Applied Psychology* 53 (1969): 1–13.

11. D. W. Bray, R. J. Campbell, and D. L. Grant, *Formative Years in Business: A Long-Term AT&T Study of Managerial Lives* (New York: Wiley, 1993).

12. G. Fowler, "eBay to Unload Skype in IPO, Citing Poor Fit," *Wall Street Journal*, April 15, 2009, B1; G. Fowler and E. Ramstad, "EBay Looks Abroad for Growth—Online Auctioneer to Buy Korean Site as It Refocuses on E-Commerce, PayPal," *Wall Street Journal*, April 16, 2009, B2; and G. Fowler, "EBay's Earnings Soar with Sale of Skype," *Wall Street Journal*, January 21, 2010, B3.

13. R. J. Grisson, "Probability of the Superior Outcome of One Treatment over Another," *Journal of Applied Psychology* 79 (1994): 314–316; and J. E. Hunter and F. L. Schmidt, *Methods of Meta-Analysis: Correcting Error and Bias in Research Findings* (Beverly Hills, CA: Sage, 1990).

14. A. Johnson, "Pfizer Outlines Post-Wyeth R & D Structure—Company Splits Research on Traditional Drugs from Biologics and Strives to Retain Scientists," *Wall Street Journal*, April 8, 2009, B4.

15. A. Taylor III, "Fixing Up Ford," *Fortune*, May 25, 2009, 44–51 (para 1); N. Bunkley, "Ford Profit Comes as Toyota Hits a Bump," *New York Times*, January 28, 2010, accessed June 23, 2010, from www.nytimes.com/2010/01/29/business/29ford.html; and A. Taylor III, "Fixing Up Ford" (para 2).

16. "A Little Enlightened Self-Interest," Inc.com, June 8, 2010, accessed July 5, 2010, from www.inc.com/top-workplaces/2010/a-little-enlightened-self-interest.html.

17. B. O'Keefe and D. Burke, "Meet the CEO of the Biggest Company on Earth," *Fortune*, September 27, 2010, 80–94.

18. H. S. Jonas III, R. E. Fry, and S. Srivastva, "The Office of the CEO: Understanding the Executive Experience," *Academy of Management Executive* 4 (1990): 36–47.

19. D. Mattioli, "The Year in Review: CEO Changes: Crises Trigger Dramatic Departures—From H-P's Hurd to Pfizer's Kindler, 'Surprise Exits' Stunned Many in 2010, Though Turnover at Top Was Low Overall," *Wall Street Journal*, December 26, 2010, B6.

20. Jonas et al., "The Office of the CEO."

21. Ibid.

22. T. Waghorn, "How Employee Engagement Turned Around Campbell's: An Interview with Douglas Conant, CEO of Campbell Soup Co.," *Forbes*, June 23, 2009, January 17, 2011, from www.forbes.com/2009/06/23/employee-engagement-conant-leadership-managing-turnaround.html.

23. T. Gutner, "Career Journal—90 Days: Plotting a Smooth Course When You Take the Helm," *Wall Street Journal*, March 24, 2009, D5.

24. Q. Huy, "In Praise of Middle Managers," *Harvard Business Review* (September 2001): 72–79.

25. I. Barat, "Rebuilding After a Catastrophe: How Caterpillar Is Responding to Tornado's Lesson," *Wall Street Journal*, May 19, 2008, B1–B2.

26. J. Rockoff, "J & J, Bruised by Recalls, Aims Higher—CEO Weldon Offers Prescription to Regain Consumers' Trust by Revamping Drug Manufacturing, Adding Quality Overseer," *Wall Street Journal*, August 19, 2010, B10.

27. T. Demos, "Motivate without Spending Millions," *Fortune*, April 12, 2010, 37–38.

28. J. Adamy, "A Menu of Options: Restaurants Have a Host of Ways to Motivate Employees to Provide Good Service," *Wall Street Journal*, October 30, 2006, R1, R6.

29. C. Hymowitz, "Today's Bosses Find Mentoring Isn't Worth the Time and Risks," *Wall Street Journal*, March 13, 2006, B1.

30. S. Tully, "What Team Leaders Need to Know," *Fortune*, February 20, 1995, 93.

31. L. Liu and A. McMurray, "Frontline Leaders: The Entry Point for Leadership Development in the Manufacturing Industry," *Journal of European Industrial Training* 28, no. 2–4 (2004): 339–352.

32. "What Makes Teams Work?" *Fast Company*, November 1, 2000, 109.

33. L. Landro, "The Informed Patient: Bringing Surgeons Down to Earth—New Programs Aim to Curb Fear That Prevents

Nurses from Flagging Problems," *Wall Street Journal*, November 16, 2005, D1.

34 Ibid.

35 N. Steckler and N. Fondas, "Building Team Leader Effectiveness: A Diagnostic Tool," *Organizational Dynamics* (Winter 1995): 20–34.

36 Tully, "What Team Leaders Need to Know."

37 H. Mintzberg, *The Nature of Managerial Work* (New York: Harper & Row, 1973).

38 C. P. Hales, "What Do Managers Do? A Critical Review of the Evidence," *Journal of Management Studies* 23, no. 1 (1986): 88–115.

39 "Cessna CEO Joins Mesa Mayor to Open New Jet Center," *Business Wire*, for February 2009, available online at www.Reuters.com.

40 K. Clark and R. Sidel, "Gang Green Meets Wall Street," *Wall Street Journal*, May 5, 2010, accessed June 22, 2010, from http://online.wsj.com/article/SB10001424052748703866704575224480779342098.html?mod=WSJ_hpp_MIDDLENext-toWhatsNewsForth.

41 "Getting into Harvard Easier Than McDonald's University in China," *Bloomberg Businessweek*, January 26, 2011, accessed February 2, 2011, from www.bloomberg.com/news/2011-01-26/getting-into-harvard-easier-than-mcdonald-s-hamburger-university-in-china.html.

42 "100 Best Companies to Work for 2009," *The Sunday Times* (London), March 8, 2009, 20.

43 J. Levitz, "UPS Thinks Out of the Box on Driver Training," *Wall Street Journal*, April 6, 2010, accessed June 22, 2010, from http://online.wsj.com/article/SB10001424052702303912104575164573823418844.html?mod=WSJ_hp_editorsPicks.

44 S. Needleman, "Entrepreneurs 'Tweet' Their Way Through Crises—Twitter Helps Companies Cope with Site Crashes, Weather Delays: 'You Can't Do That with a 1-800 Number,'" *Wall Street Journal*, September 15, 2009, B5.

45 J. Scheck, "R & D Spending Holds Steady in Slump—Big Companies Invest to Grab Sales in Recovery: The iPod Lesson," *Wall Street Journal*, April 6, 2009, A1.

46 L. Greenblatt, "Beatles Sales on iTunes Hit New Milestone," *MusicMix*, January 14, 2011, accessed January 17, 2011, from http://music-mix.ew.com/2011/01/14/beatles-sales-itunes/; and E. Smith, "Day in the Life of Deal—How EMI's New CEO Helped Beatles Clear iTunes Hurdles," *Wall Street Journal*, November 17, 2010, B12.

47 L. A. Hill, *Becoming a Manager: Mastery of a New Identity* (Boston: Harvard Business School Press, 1992).

48 R. L. Katz, "Skills of an Effective Administrator," *Harvard Business Review* (September–October 1974): 90–102.

49 C. A. Bartlett and S. Ghoshal, "Changing the Role of Top Management: Beyond Systems to People," *Harvard Business Review* (May–June 1995): 132–142.

50 F. L. Schmidt and J. E. Hunter, "Development of a Causal Model of Process Determining Job Performance," *Current Directions in Psychological Science* 1 (1992): 89–92.

51 J. B. Miner, "Sentence Completion Measures in Personnel Research: The Development and Validation of the Miner Sentence Completion Scales," in H. J. Bernardin and D. A. Bownas (eds.), *Personality Assessment in Organizations* (New York: Praeger, 1986), 147–146.

52 M. W. McCall Jr., and M. M. Lombardo, "What Makes a Top Executive?" *Psychology Today*, February 1983, 26–31; and E. van Velsor and J. Brittain, "Why Executives Derail: Perspectives across Time and Cultures," *Academy of Management Executive* (November 1995): 62–72.

53 McCall and Lombardo, "What Makes a Top Executive?"

54 J. Sandberg, "Overcontrolling Bosses Aren't Just Annoying: They're Also Inefficient," *Wall Street Journal*, March 30, 2005, B1.

55 Hill, *Becoming a Manager*, p. 17.

56 Ibid., p. 55.

57 Ibid., p. 57.

58 Ibid., p. 64.

59 Ibid., p. 67.

60 Ibid., p. 103.

61 Ibid., p. 161.

62 J. Pfeffer, *The Human Equation: Building Profits by Putting People First* (Boston: Harvard Business School Press, 1996); and *Competitive Advantage through People: Unleashing the Power of the Work Force* (Boston: Harvard Business School Press, 1994).

63 M. A. Huselid, "The Impact of Human Resource Management Practices on Turnover, Productivity, and Corporate Financial Performance," *Academy of Management Journal* 38 (1995): 635–672.

64 D. McDonald and A. Smith, "A Proven Connection: Performance Management and Business Results," *Compensation & Benefits Review* 27, no. 6 (January 1, 1995): 59.

65 "Financial Results," *Great Place to Work*, January 22, 2011, accessed January 22, 2011, from www.greatplacetowork.com/what_we_believe/graphs.php.

66 B. Schneider and D. E. Bowen, "Employee and Customer Perceptions of Service in Banks: Replication and Extension," *Journal of Applied Psychology* 70 (1985): 423–433; and B. Schneider, J. J. Parkington, and V. M. Buxton, "Employee and Customer Perceptions of Service in Banks," *Administrative Science Quarterly* 25 (1980): 252–267.

67 "How Investing in Intangibles—Like Employee Satisfaction—Translates into Financial Returns," Knowledge@Wharton, January 9, 2008, accessed January 24, 2010, from http://knowledge.wharton.upenn.edu/article.cfm?articleid=1873.

68 "Airlines Make a Bundle Through Separate Charges," *Seattle Times*, April 7, 2010, accessed June 30, 2010, from http://seattletimes.nwsource.com/html/travel/2011539200_webtroubleshooter06.html/; H. Martin, "Spirit Airlines Launches $45 Carry-on Fee," *Los Angeles Times*, April 7, 2010, accessed July 1, 2010, from http://articles.latimes.com/2010/apr/07/business/la-fi-spirit7-2010apr07; and C. Negroni, "Less Baggage, Big Savings to Airlines," *New York Times*, April 6, 2010, from www.nytimes.com/2010/04/07/business/07bags.html?src=me.

69 P. L. Hunsaker, *Management: A Skills Approach* (Upper Saddle River, NJ: Pearson Prentice Hall, 2005), 24–25.

Organizational Environments and Culture

REEL TO REAL

© TETRA IMAGES/ CORBIS

Management Workplace is at Camp Bow Wow.

SELF-ASSESSMENT

© ISTOCKPHOTO/ ALEXANDER KALINA

How comfortable are you with ambiguity? Take the Self-Assessment for this chapter in the book or online to find out.

ONLINE QUIZZES

© ISTOCKPHOTO/ PEARLEYE

Did you get it? Review the main concepts in the chapter by taking the online quizzes on CourseMate!

VIDEO QUIZZES

© ISTOCKPHOTO/DAVID HUGHES

Get more out of the videos by taking the multimedia video quizzes online.

What Would You Do?

Waste Management Headquarters, Houston, Texas[1]

Americans generate a quarter billion tons of trash a year, or 4.5 pounds of trash per person per day. Thanks to nearly 9,000 curbside recycling programs, a third of that is recycled. But, that still leaves 3 pounds of trash per person per day to be disposed of. In the past, trash was incinerated, often in local neighborhoods. John Waffenschmidt, vice president for Covanta Energy Corp., remembers that when he delivered newspapers in the 1960s, "I'd go out in the morning and there would be little flakes coming down because there were 4,000 or 5,000 apartment-building incinerators." The rest was incinerated in large power plants, like the one on the east side of the Hudson River that burns 1,900 tons of New York City garbage each day.

© SCOTT OLSON/GETTY IMAGES

With 20 million customers; 273 municipal landfills; 91 recycling facilities; and yes, 17 "waste-to-energy facilities"—that's what large power-generating incinerator plants are called today—WASTE MANAGEMENT, INC., is the largest waste-handling company in the world. It generates 75 percent of its profits from 273 landfills, which can hold 4.8 billion tons of trash. And because it collects only 110 million tons a year, it has plenty of landfill capacity for years to come.

You joined the company a decade ago and, after three and a half short years as deputy general counsel and then chief financial officer, became CEO. That quick promotion prompted you to joke, "I needed to go to a bookstore to see whether I could find a book called *CEO-ING FOR DUMMIES*." Instead, Waste Management sent you to Harvard for an executive program for CEOs, where the most important lesson you learned was to listen, because, as you tell your executive team, "This company and this industry aren't very good at that." And with all of the changes taking place in your industry, Waste Management won't succeed unless it listens. However, corporations, cities, and households are greatly reducing the amount of waste they generate, and thus the amount of trash that they pay Waste Management to haul away

to its landfills. Subaru of America, for instance, has a zero-landfill plant in West Lafayette, Indiana, that hasn't sent any waste to a landfill since 2004. None! And Subaru isn't exceptional in seeking to be a zero-landfill company. Walmart, the largest retailer in the world, has also embraced this goal, stating, "Our vision is to reach a day where there are no dumpsters behind our stores and clubs, and no landfills containing our throwaways." Like those at Subaru and Walmart, corporate leaders worldwide are committed to reducing the waste produced by their companies. Because that represents a direct threat to Waste Management's landfill business, what steps could it take to take advantage of the trend toward zero waste, which might allow it to continue growing company revenues?

Another significant change for Waste Management is that not only are its customers reducing the waste they send to its landfills, they're also wanting what is sent to landfills to be sorted for recycling and reuse. For instance, food waste, yard clippings, and wood—all organic materials—account for roughly one-third of the material sent to landfills. Likewise, there's growing demand for waste companies to manage and recycle discarded TVs,

© DIZZO/ISTOCK PHOTO

computer monitors, and other electronic waste that leaks lead, mercury, and hazardous materials when improperly disposed of. However, the high cost of collecting and sorting recyclable materials means that Waste Management loses money when it recycles them. What can the company do to meet increased customer expectations on one hand, while still finding a way to earn a profit on high-cost recycled materials?

Finally, advocacy groups, such as the Sierra Club, regularly protest Waste Management's landfill practices, deeming them irresponsible and harmful to the environment. From changing social attitudes about waste and recycling, to anti–Waste Management websites, everywhere that Waste Management's top managers look, they see changes and forces outside the company that directly affect how they do business. Should they take on the company's critics and fight back, or should they focus on business and let the results speak for themselves? Should they view environmental advocates as a threat or an opportunity for the company?

If you were in charge of Waste Management, what would you do?

2-1 External Environments and Change

This chapter examines the internal and external forces that affect business. We begin by explaining how the changes in external organizational environments affect the decisions and performance of a company. Next, we examine the two types of external organizational environments: the general environment that affects all organizations, and the specific environment unique to each company. Then, we learn how managers make sense of their changing general and specific environments. The chapter finishes with a discussion of internal organizational environments by focusing on organizational culture.

External environments are the forces and events outside a company that have the potential to influence or affect it. From Walkmans to PlayStation video games and consoles, to its top-of-the-line televisions, Sony's ability to innovate made it one of the world's top electronics companies. However, because of intense competition in its external environment from Apple (iPods, iPhones, and iPads), Microsoft (Xbox 360), Samsung, and Vizio (high-definition TVs), Sony has been forced to cut costs, lay off workers, and try to change its internal culture in order to restore profits (more on that later in the chapter).[2]

Our first task in this chapter is to understand the external environment.

After reading this section, you should be able to:

2-1 discuss how changing environments affect organizations.

What can a manager do to deal with such changing external environments?

Let's begin the discussion by examining the four basic characteristics of changing external environments: **2-1a environmental change; 2-1b environmental complexity; 2-1c resource scarcity; and 2-1d the uncertainty that environmental change, complexity, and resource scarcity can create for organizational managers.**

external environments
all events outside a company that have the potential to influence or affect it

2-1a Environmental Change

Environmental change is the rate at which a company's general and specific environments change. In **stable environments**, the rate of environmental change is slow. Wholesale food distribution changes little from year to year. On the other hand, in **dynamic environments**, the rate of environmental change is fast. The external environment for gaming platforms like *Microsoft*'s Xbox 360 is highly dynamic because competition brings rapid technological changes. When Nintendo's Wii console, which controls games from its wireless controller, sold 74 million units worldwide its first year, Microsoft saw its Xbox 360 game system sales fall far behind and introduced the Kinect motion technology the next year, hoping to catch up.[3]

Although you might think that a company's external environment would be either stable or dynamic, research suggests that companies often experience both. According to **punctuated equilibrium theory**, companies go through long periods of stability (equilibrium) during which incremental changes occur, followed by short, complex periods of dynamic, fundamental change (revolutionary periods), finishing with a return to stability (new equilibrium).[4]

Exhibit 2.1 shows one example of punctuated equilibrium—the U.S. airline industry. Three times in the last 30 years, the U.S. airline industry has experienced revolutionary periods. Airlines had tremendous difficulty operating in the competitive environment created by deregulation and suffered huge losses until they were able to adjust.

environmental change
the rate at which a company's general and specific environments change

stable environment
an environment in which the rate of change is slow

dynamic environment
an environment in which the rate of change is fast

punctuated equilibrium theory
the theory that companies go through long periods of stability (equilibrium) during which incremental changes occur, followed by short, complex periods of dynamic, fundamental change (revolutionary periods), finishing with a return to stability (new equilibrium)

Exhibit 2.1

Punctuated Equilibrium: U.S. Airlines Profits since 1979

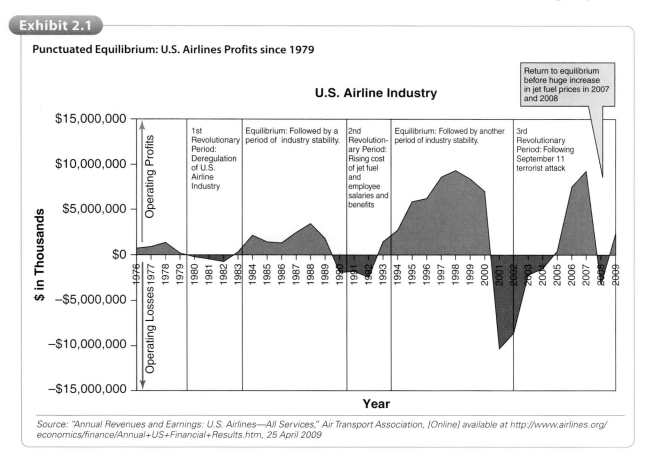

Source: "Annual Revenues and Earnings: U.S. Airlines—All Services," Air Transport Association, [Online] available at http://www.airlines.org/economics/finance/Annual+US+Financial+Results.htm, 25 April 2009

Then, after experiencing record growth and profits, U.S. airlines lost billions of dollars in the early '90s as the industry went through dramatic changes. Key expenses, including jet fuel and employee salaries, which had held steady for years, suddenly increased, and revenues suddenly dropped because of changes in the airlines' customer base. Leisure travelers, who wanted the cheapest flights they could get, replaced business travelers, who typically pay full-priced fares, as the largest customer base.[5] The airlines responded to these changes in their business environment by laying off 5 to 10 percent of their workers, canceling orders for new planes, and eliminating unprofitable routes. These changes helped the airline industry achieve profits far in excess of their historical levels. The industry began to stabilize, if not flourish, just as punctuated equilibrium theory predicts.[6]

The third revolutionary period for the U.S. airline industry began with the terrorist attacks of September 11, 2001, in which planes were used as missiles to bring down the World Trade Center towers and damage the Pentagon. The immediate effect was a 20 percent drop in scheduled flights, a 40 percent drop in passengers, and a $15 billion government bailout to keep the airlines in business. But just as the airlines were heading toward a more stable period of equilibrium in 2006 and 2007, the price of oil jumped dramatically, doubling, if not tripling, the price of jet fuel, which prompted the airlines to charge for luggage and cut flights using older, fuel-inefficient jets.

2-1b Environmental Complexity

Environmental complexity refers to the number and the intensity of external factors in the environment that affect organizations. **Simple environments** have few environmental factors, whereas **complex environments** have many environmental factors. For example, the dairy industry has a relatively simple external environment. Even accounting for decades-old advances in processing and automatic milking machines, milk is produced the same way today as it was 100 years ago. And although food manufacturers introduce dozens of new dairy-based products each year, U.S. milk production has grown a meager 1.25 percent per year over the last decade. In short, producing milk is a highly competitive but simple business that has experienced few changes.[7]

By contrast, consider the environmental changes in the newspaper business. For a century, newspapers made money by selling classified and retail ads. Today, free online versions of newspapers make only 10 percent of the original print-ad revenue from digital ads; sites like Craigslist.org have led to a 29 percent decrease in classified-ad revenue; and customers expect digital editions to be free of charge.[8] The *Wall Street Journal* is one of few papers that has successfully charged for online access because it never allowed free access to its content, so readers are willing to pay to read online.[9]

2-1c Resource Scarcity

The third characteristic of external environments is resource scarcity. **Resource scarcity** is the abundance or shortage of critical organizational resources in an organization's external environment. For example, in many locations throughout the world, water is a scarce resource. This is why a *Dow Chemical* plant in

environmental complexity
the number and the intensity of external factors in the environment that affect organizations

simple environment
an environment with few environmental factors

complex environment
an environment with many environmental factors

resource scarcity
the abundance or shortage of critical organizational resources in an organization's external environment

Texas, faced with water shortages each summer, hired Nalco, a firm that helps companies reduce energy, water, and other natural resource consumption. Nalco's water management systems reduced water consumption at Dow's Texas plant by 1 billion gallons per year.[10]

2-1d Uncertainty

As Exhibit 2.2 shows, environmental change, environmental complexity, and resource scarcity affect environmental **uncertainty**, which is how well managers can understand or predict the external changes and trends affecting their businesses. Starting at the left side of the figure, environmental uncertainty is lowest when environmental change and environmental complexity are at low levels and resource scarcity is small (i.e., resources are plentiful). In these environments, managers feel confident that they can understand, predict, and react to the external forces that affect their businesses. By contrast, the right side of the figure shows that environmental uncertainty is highest when environmental change and complexity are extensive and resource scarcity is a problem. In these environments, managers may not be confident that they can understand, predict, and handle the external forces affecting their businesses.

REVIEW 2-1
. . . .

External Environments and Change

Environmental change, complexity, and resource scarcity are the basic components of external environments. Environmental change is the rate at which conditions or events affecting a business change. Environmental complexity

uncertainty
the extent to which managers can understand or predict which environmental changes and trends will affect their businesses

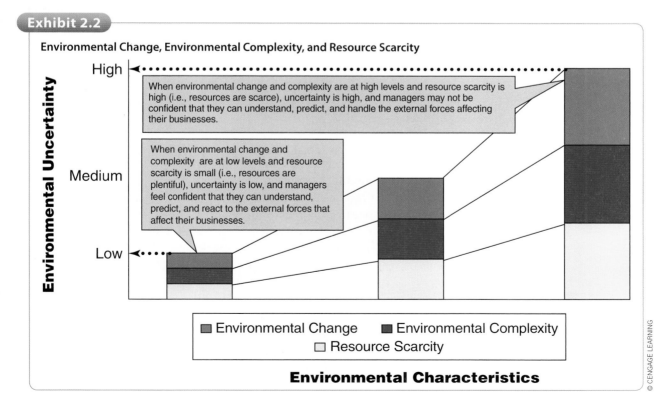

Exhibit 2.2

Environmental Change, Environmental Complexity, and Resource Scarcity

When environmental change and complexity are at high levels and resource scarcity is high (i.e., resources are scarce), uncertainty is high, and managers may not be confident that they can understand, predict, and handle the external forces affecting their businesses.

When environmental change and complexity are at low levels and resource scarcity is small (i.e., resources are plentiful), uncertainty is low, and managers feel confident that they can understand, predict, and react to the external forces that affect their businesses.

Environmental Uncertainty — High, Medium, Low

■ Environmental Change   ■ Environmental Complexity   □ Resource Scarcity

Environmental Characteristics

© CENGAGE LEARNING

is the number and intensity of external factors in an external environment. Resource scarcity is the scarcity or abundance of resources available in the external environment. The greater the degree of environmental change, environmental complexity, and resource scarcity, the less confident managers are that they can understand, predict, and effectively react to the trends affecting their businesses. According to punctuated equilibrium theory, companies experience periods of stability followed by short periods of dynamic, fundamental change, followed by a return to periods of stability.

2-2 General Environment

general environment
the economic, technological, sociocultural, and political trends that indirectly affect all organizations

As Exhibit 2.3 shows, two kinds of external environments influence organizations: the general environment and the specific environment. The **general environment** consists of the economy and the technological, sociocultural, and political/legal trends that indirectly affect *all* organizations. Changes in any

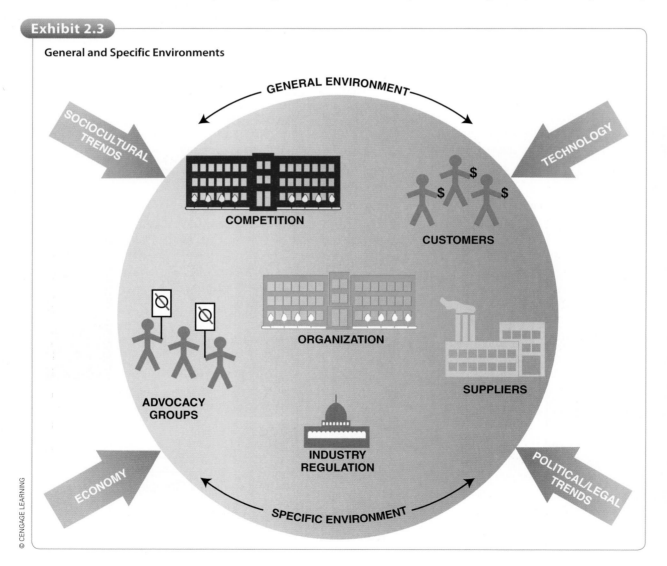

Exhibit 2.3

General and Specific Environments

GENERAL ENVIRONMENT

SOCIOCULTURAL TRENDS

TECHNOLOGY

COMPETITION

CUSTOMERS

ADVOCACY GROUPS

ORGANIZATION

SUPPLIERS

INDUSTRY REGULATION

ECONOMY

POLITICAL/LEGAL TRENDS

SPECIFIC ENVIRONMENT

© CENGAGE LEARNING

sector of the general environment eventually affect most organizations. For example, when the Federal Reserve lowers its prime lending rate, most businesses benefit because banks and credit card companies often lower the interest rates they charge for loans. Consumers, who can then borrow money more cheaply, might borrow more to buy homes, cars, refrigerators, and plasma or LCD flat-screen TVs.

After reading this section, you should be able to:

2-2 describe the four components of the general environment.

By contrast, each organization also has a **specific environment** that is unique to that firm's industry and directly affects the way it conducts day-to-day business. The specific environment, which will be discussed in detail in Section 2-3 of this chapter, includes customers, competitors, suppliers, industry regulation, and advocacy groups.

First, let's take a closer look at the four components of the general environment: **2-2a the economy** and **2-2b the technological, 2-2c sociocultural**, and **2-2d political/legal trends** that indirectly affect all organizations.

2-2a Economy

The current state of a country's economy affects virtually every organization doing business there. In general, in a growing economy, more people are working and wages are growing, and therefore consumers have relatively more money to spend. More products are bought and sold in a growing economy than in a static or shrinking economy. Though an individual firm's sales will not necessarily increase, a growing economy does provide an environment favorable for business growth. In contrast, in a shrinking economy, consumers have less money to spend and relatively fewer products are bought and sold. Thus, a shrinking economy makes growth for businesses more difficult.

Because the economy influences basic business decisions, such as whether to hire more employees, expand production, or take out loans to purchase equipment, managers scan their economic environments for signs of significant change. Unfortunately, the economic statistics that managers rely on when making these decisions are notoriously poor predictors of *future* economic activity. A manager who decides to hire 10 more employees because economic data suggest future growth could very well have to lay off those workers when the economy does not in fact grow. A famous economic study found that at the beginning of a business quarter (a period of only three months), even the best economic forecasters could not accurately predict whether economic activity would grow or shrink *in that same quarter*![11]

Because economic statistics can be poor predictors, some managers try to predict future economic activity by tracking business confidence. **Business confidence indices** show how confident managers are about future business growth. For example, the Conference Board's CEO Confidence Index is a quarterly survey of 100 CEOs of large companies across a variety of different industries that examines attitudes regarding future growth.[12] Another widely cited measure is the Small Business Research Board's Business Confidence Index, which asks 500 small business owners and managers to express their optimism

specific environment
the customers, competitors, suppliers, industry regulations, and advocacy groups that are unique to an industry and directly affect how a company does business

business confidence indices
indices that show managers' level of confidence about future business growth

(or pessimism) about future business sales and prospects.[13] Managers often prefer business confidence indices to economic statistics because they know that other managers make business decisions that are in line with their expectations concerning the economy's future.

2-2b Technological Component

Technology is the knowledge, tools, and techniques used to transform inputs (raw materials, information, etc.) into outputs (products and services). For example, the inputs of authors, editors, and artists (knowledge) and the use of equipment like computers and printing presses (technology) transformed paper, ink, and glue (raw materials) into this book (the finished product).

Changes in technology can help companies provide better products or produce their products more efficiently. For example, advances in surgical techniques and imaging equipment have made open-heart surgery much faster and safer in recent years. Although technological changes can benefit a business, they can also threaten it. For example, PRIME VIEW INTERNATIONAL, based in Taipei, Taiwan, makes the E Ink screens used in popular e-reader devices such as Barnes & Noble's Nook and Amazon's Kindle. Despite the popularity of Prime View's E Ink screens, however, its stronghold on the screen market is being challenged by Qualcomm's mirasol display technology. Like E Ink, mirasol uses low power and can be read in direct sunlight, but unlike E Ink's black-and-white screens, displays in color.[14] In response, Prime View has developed a color version of its E Ink technology. Chapter 6, on organizational change and innovation, provides a more in-depth discussion of how technology affects a company's competitive advantage.

2-2c Sociocultural Component

The sociocultural component of the general environment refers to the demographic characteristics, general behavior, attitudes, and beliefs of people in a particular society. Sociocultural changes and trends influence organizations in two important ways.

First, changes in demographic characteristics, such as the number of people with particular skills or the growth or decline in particular population segments (marital status, age, gender, ethnicity), affect how companies staff their businesses. Married women with children are much more likely to work today than four decades ago. In 1960, only 18.6 percent of women with children under the age of 6 and 39 percent of women with children between the ages of 6 and 17 worked. According to the U.S. Bureau of Labor Statistics, by 2010 those percentages had risen to 57.6 percent and 71.2 percent, respectively.

Second, sociocultural changes in behavior, attitudes, and beliefs also affect the demand for a business's products and services. Today, with more married women with children in the workforce, traffic congestion creating longer commutes, and both parents working longer hours, people are much more likely to value products and services that allow them to recapture free time with their

technology
the knowledge, tools, and techniques used to transform input into output

families. Thus people—especially working mothers—use numerous services to help reduce the amount of time they spend doing chores and household management tasks.

Priscilla La Barbera, a marketing professor at New York University, says, "People are beginning to realize that their time has real value."[15] Brian Wheeler, who runs a concierge service in Washington, DC, that performs personal tasks for busy workers, said, "Many households have two adults working full time, people are working longer hours, and traffic in our region gets worse each year. When you combine these things, there isn't much time for anything outside of work and life maintenance stuff. We give them a hand and magically get things done for them during the day so that when they get home they can actually unwind or spend quality time with their family."[16]

2-2d Political/Legal Component

The political/legal component of the general environment includes the legislation, regulations, and court decisions that govern and regulate business behavior. New laws and regulations continue to impose additional responsibilities on companies. Unfortunately, many managers are unaware of these new responsibilities. For example, under the 1991 Civil Rights Act (www.eeoc.gov/policy/cra91.html), if an employee is sexually harassed by anyone at work (a supervisor, a coworker, or even a customer), the company—not just the harasser—is potentially liable for damages, attorneys' fees, and back pay.[17] Under the Family and Medical Leave Act (www.dol.gov/whd/fmla), employees who have been on the job one year are guaranteed 12 weeks of unpaid leave per year to tend to their own illnesses or to their elderly parents, a newborn baby, or a newly adopted child. Employees are guaranteed the same job, pay, and benefits when they return to work.[18]

Many managers are also unaware of the potential legal risks associated with traditional managerial decisions like recruiting, hiring, and firing employees. Increasingly, businesses and managers are being sued for negligent hiring and supervision, defamation, invasion of privacy, emotional distress, fraud, and misrepresentation during employee recruitment.[19] More than 14,000 suits for wrongful termination (unfairly firing employees) are filed each year.[20] In fact, wrongful termination lawsuits increased by 77 percent during the 1990s.[21] One in four employers will at some point be sued for wrongful termination. It can cost $300,000 to settle such a case once it goes to court, but employers lose 70 percent of court cases, and the former employee is awarded, on average, $1 million or more.[22] On the other hand, employers who settle before going to court typically pay just $10,000 to $100,000 per case.[23]

Not everyone agrees that companies' legal risks are too severe. Indeed, many believe that the government should do more to regulate and restrict business behavior and that it should be easier for average citizens to sue dishonest or negligent corporations. From a managerial perspective, the best medicine against legal risk is prevention. As a manager, it is your responsibility to educate yourself about the laws, regulations, and potential lawsuits that could affect your business. Failure to do so may put you and your company at risk of sizable penalties, fines, or legal charges.

General Environment

The general environment consists of economic, technological, sociocultural, and political and legal events and trends that affect all organizations. Because the economy influences basic business decisions, managers often use economic statistics and business confidence indices to predict future economic activity. Changes in technology that transforms inputs into outputs can be a benefit or a threat to a business. Sociocultural trends, like changing demographic characteristics, affect how companies run their businesses. Similarly, sociocultural changes in behavior, attitudes, and beliefs affect the demand for a business's products and services. Court decisions and new federal and state laws have imposed much greater political and legal responsibilities on companies. The best way to manage legal responsibilities is to educate managers and employees about laws and regulations and potential lawsuits that could affect a business.

2-3 Specific Environment

As you just learned, changes in any sector of the general environment (economic, technological, sociocultural, and political and legal) eventually affect most organizations. Each organization also has a specific environment that is unique to that firm's industry and directly affects the way it conducts day-to-day business.

After reading this section, you should be able to:

2-3 explain the five components of the specific environment.

If your customers decide to use another product; your main competitor cuts prices 10 percent; your best supplier can't deliver raw materials; federal regulators mandate reductions in pollutants in your industry; or environmental groups accuse your company of selling unsafe products, the impact from the specific environment on your business is immediate.

Let's examine how the **2-3a customer, 2-3b competitor, 2-3c supplier, 2-3d industry regulation**, and **2-3e advocacy group components of the specific environment affect businesses.**

2-3a Customer Component

Customers purchase products and services. Companies cannot exist without customer support. Monitoring customers' changing wants and needs is critical to business success. There are two basic strategies for monitoring customers: reactive and proactive.

Reactive customer monitoring involves identifying and addressing customer trends and problems after they occur. One reactive strategy is to listen closely to customer complaints and respond to customer concerns. ACTIVISION-BLIZZARD hosts forums for the Web-based role-playing game World of Warcraft (WOW). In reaction to hateful anonymous posts on the forums, Activision-Blizzard announced forum posters would have to start using their real names, sparking privacy concerns. Three days after creating the policy, because of overwhelming complaints about the new policy, Activision-Blizzard reacted again: users would be allowed to use anonymous names after all.[24]

Companies that respond quickly to customer complaints (i.e., reactive customer monitoring) are viewed much more favorably than companies that are slow to respond or never respond.[25] In particular, studies have shown that when a company's follow-up letter thanks the customer for writing; offers a sincere, specific response to the complaint (not a form letter, but an explanation of how the problem will be handled); and contains a small gift, coupons, or a refund to make up for the problem, customers are much more likely to purchase products or services again from that company.[26]

Proactive monitoring of customers means identifying and addressing customer needs, trends, and issues *before* they occur. HARRAH'S casinos determined that 80 percent of its revenues and 100 percent of its profits come from the 30 percent of its customers who spend only $100 to $500 per visit. To encourage their regular gambling, Harrah's addresses their needs through its electronic "Total Rewards" program cards. The data obtained from those cards helps Harrah's identify what different customers need to keep choosing Harrah's over other casinos. For example, Harrah's offers slot machine players cash rewards, which can be used in the machines.[27] Today, Harrah's gets 43 percent of its customers' gambling business, compared to 36 percent before its Total Rewards program.[28]

2-3b Competitor Component

Competitors are companies in the same industry that sell similar products or services to customers. Ford, Toyota, and Kia all compete for automobile customers. NBC, ABC, CBS, and Fox (along with hundreds of cable channels) compete for TV viewers' attention. McDonald's, Burger King, and Chick-fil-A compete for fast-food customers' dollars. Often the difference between success and failure in business comes down to whether your company is doing a better job of satisfying customer wants and needs than the competition. Consequently, companies need to keep close track of what their competitors are doing. To do this, managers perform **competitive analysis**, which involves identifying your competitors, anticipating their moves, and determining their strengths and weaknesses.

Surprisingly, managers often do a poor job of identifying potential competitors, because they tend to focus on only two or three well-known competitors with similar goals and resources.[29] Coke and Pepsi lost ground to energy drinks, bottled water, and fruit juice because they were so focused on each other.[30] Likewise, Hoover Dirt Devil, and, more recently, Oreck competed fiercely in the market for vacuum cleaners. When Dyson entered the market with its radically different vacuum that maintained significantly more suction power, the company garnered 20 percent market share within its first months on the shelves.[31] Only then did Hoover and Dirt Devil design their own bagless vacuums.

Another mistake managers may make when analyzing the competition is to underestimate potential competitors' capabilities. When this happens, managers don't take the steps they should to continue to improve their products

competitors
companies in the same industry that sell similar products or services to customers

competitive analysis
a process for monitoring the competition that involves identifying competition, anticipating their moves, and determining their strengths and weaknesses

or services. The result can be significant decreases in both market share and profits. For nearly a decade, traditional phone companies ignored the threat to their business from Voice over Internet Protocol (VoIP). Early on, software products like Cool Talk, Internet Phone, and Web Phone made it possible to make inexpensive long-distance phone calls using VoIP. The sound quality was only as good as AM radio, but people who were used to poor-quality sound on their cell phones didn't care because the calls were so much cheaper.[32]

Today, because larger phone companies themselves were slow to adopt VoIP capabilities, they're facing a rash of new, unexpected VoIP competitors, all of which have slashed prices and taken market share using high-speed Internet service. For example, Comcast, a cable-TV provider that also offers high-speed Internet service, gains 10 phone subscribers—at the expense of phone companies like Verizon and AT&T—for every cable-TV subscriber that it loses.[33] VoIP is also threatening the phone companies' wireless services, which now account for most of their profits. Vonage, a VoIP service that typically charges $25 to $35 a month for online phone service, gives Facebook users free VoIP calls to any of their Facebook friends. And if any of those Facebook friends are international, it costs nothing to make an international call.[34]

2-3c Supplier Component

Suppliers are companies that provide material, human, financial, and informational resources to other companies. U.S. Steel buys iron ore from suppliers to make steel products. When IBM sells a mainframe computer, it also provides support staff, engineers, and other technical consultants to the company that bought the computer. If you're shopping for desks, chairs, and office supplies, chances are Office Depot will be glad to help your business open a revolving charge account to pay for your purchases. When a clothing manufacturer has spent $100,000 to purchase new high-pressure "water drills" to cut shirt and pants patterns to precise sizes, the water drill manufacturer, as part of the purchase, will usually train the workers on the machinery.

A key factor influencing the impact and quality of the relationship between companies and their suppliers is how dependent they are on each other.[35] **Supplier dependence** is the degree to which a company relies on a supplier because of the importance of the supplier's product to the company and the difficulty of finding other sources for that product. Chinese mining companies, for example, provide 97 percent of the rare-earth materials, which are used to manufacture TV screens, mobile phones, fiber optics, and electric motors.[36] When China announced it was cutting exports of rare-earth materials, Japanese importers estimated that Japanese companies would face shortages of 10,000 tons a year. "The only real solution to the problem is to buy new mining rights overseas," according to Toru Okabe, an engineering professor at the University of Tokyo. But, he says, "Mines outside of China don't have cost-competitiveness. If China begins to flood the market with cheap supplies again, they wouldn't stand the competition."[37]

Buyer dependence is the degree to which a supplier relies on a buyer because of the importance of that buyer to the supplier's sales and the difficulty of finding other buyers of its products. For example, *AB InBev*, the world's largest

suppliers
companies that provide material, human, financial, and informational resources to other companies

supplier dependence
the degree to which a company relies on a supplier because of the importance of the supplier's product to the company and the difficulty of finding other sources of that product

buyer dependence
the degree to which a supplier relies on a buyer because of the importance of that buyer to the supplier and the difficulty of finding other buyers for its products

brewer, has controlled over 25 percent of global beer sales in recent years, which has given it tremendous bargaining power over suppliers. AB InBev leveraged that bargaining power by paying suppliers, who provide everything from malt to hops to yeast, 120 days after being invoiced. The change from the typical 30-day payment period to 120 days meant that AB InBev's suppliers would have to wait an extra three months to be paid. Delaying payments gives AB InBev an additional $1.2 billion in cash flow per year, but it did so at the expense of its suppliers.[38] There was little, however, that most AB InBev suppliers could do about this change.

As the previous examples show, a high degree of buyer or seller dependence can lead to **opportunistic behavior**, in which one party benefits at the expense of the other. Although opportunistic behavior between buyers and suppliers will never be completely eliminated, many companies believe that both buyers and suppliers can benefit by improving the buyer–supplier relationship.[39] In contrast to opportunistic behavior, **relationship behavior** focuses on establishing a mutually beneficial, long-term relationship between buyers and suppliers.[40]

2-3d Industry Regulation Component

Whereas the political and legal component of the general environment affects all businesses, the **industry regulation** component consists of regulations and rules that govern the practices and procedures of specific industries, businesses, and professions.

Regulatory agencies affect businesses by creating and enforcing rules and regulations to protect consumers, workers, or society as a whole. For

opportunistic behavior a transaction in which one party in the relationship benefits at the expense of the other

relationship behavior the establishment of mutually beneficial, long-term exchanges between buyers and suppliers

industry regulation regulations and rules that govern the business practices and procedures of specific industries, businesses, and professions

Doing the Right Thing

The Language of Bribery

In many foreign countries, bribery is an accepted, and even expected, part of doing business, though there are laws designed to prevent illegal gifts and payments. Because of these laws, bribery has its own jargon or slang that disguises the true nature of the exchange of money. In Italy, for example, a bribe might be called a *spintarella,* "a little push," while it might be called *fakelaki,* "a little purse," in Greece. An offer of a bribe might often be described as something to eat or drink—a *pot-de-vin* ("glass of wine") in France, a *mordida* ("a bite") in Spain, or a *finjaan 'ahwa* ("a cup of coffee") in Syria. How can companies navigate this confusing jumble of foreign slang? James Tillen and Sonia Delman, of the international law firm Miller & Chevalier Chartered, give the following suggestions:

- Incorporate local dialects, slang, and customs into compliance policies and training programs.
- Use role-play exercises with locally relevant language and customs in anticorruption training sessions.
- Instruct employees to clarify any dubious payment requests.
- Include colloquial bribery terms as "red flags" in internal audit modules.[46]

example, the U.S. Department of Agriculture (USDA) and the Food and Drug Administration (FDA) regulate the safety of seafood (as well as meat and poultry) through the science-based Hazard Analysis and Critical Control Points program. Seafood processors are required to identify hazards (toxins, chemicals, pesticides, and decomposition) that could cause the fish they process to be unsafe. They must also establish critical control points to control hazards both inside and outside their fish-processing plants and then establish monitoring, corrective action, and verification procedures to certify that the fish they process is safe to consume.[41]

The nearly 100 federal agencies and regulatory commissions can affect almost any kind of business. For example, the toy industry spent $200 million to increase the safety of its products after 20 million toys produced in China were recalled because of the presence of harmful chemicals. In addition to the voluntary recall by toy retailers and manufacturers, new federal regulations in the Consumer Product Safety Improvement Act of 2008 ban phthalates from children's products and now require products to be tested for them before they are sold.[42]

Overall, the number and cost of federal regulations has nearly tripled in the last 25 years. Today, for every $1 the federal government spends creating regulations, businesses spend $45 to comply with them.[43] In addition to federal regulations, businesses are also subject to state, county, and city regulations. Complying with all of these regulations costs businesses an estimated $1.1 trillion per year, or $5,633 per employee.[44] Surveys indicate that managers rank dealing with government regulation as one of the most demanding and frustrating parts of their jobs.[45]

2-3e Advocacy Groups

advocacy groups
concerned citizens who band together to try to influence the business practices of specific industries, businesses, and professions

Advocacy groups are groups of concerned citizens who band together to try to influence the business practices of specific industries, businesses, and professions. The members of a group generally share the same point of view on a particular issue. For example, environmental advocacy groups might try to get manufacturers to reduce smokestack pollution emissions. Unlike the industry regulation component of the specific environment, advocacy groups cannot force organizations to change their practices. Nevertheless, they can use a number of techniques to try to influence companies, including public communications, media advocacy, Web pages, blogs, and product boycotts.

The **public communications** approach relies on *voluntary* participation by the news media and the advertising industry to send out an advocacy group's message. For example, a public service campaign to encourage people to quit smoking ran the following ads in newspapers and magazines throughout Europe: a photo showing the foot of a young person with a toe tag (indicating the person was dead), with the caption "Smokers die younger"; a picture showing clean lungs next to brown- and black-stained lungs, with the caption "Smoking causes fatal lung cancer"; and a photo of a baby in an intensive care unit hooked up to a respirator, with the caption "Smoking when pregnant harms your baby."[47]

Media advocacy is much more aggressive than the public communications approach. A **media advocacy** approach typically involves framing the group's concerns as a public issue (affecting everyone); exposing questionable, exploitative, or unethical practices; and creating controversy that is likely to receive extensive news coverage. In one of its latest protests, called "McCruelty: I'm Hatin' It," PEOPLE FOR THE ETHICAL TREATMENT OF ANIMALS (PETA) is protesting that McDonald's, which uses 290 million chickens a year, tolerates suppliers using inhumane killing methods—hanging the birds upside down, stunning them in water that carries an electrical current, and then cutting their throats. PETA wants McDonald's suppliers to use gas to kill the birds, which it believes is more humane. Paul Shapiro, who heads the Humane Society's factory farming initiative, said, "It causes less suffering than the conventional method, which is archaic and inhumane." However, Marie Wheatley, president of the American Humane Association, disagrees, saying, "There is not definite proof either is more humane. Both technologies are acceptable in minimizing pain and suffering."[48] A McDonald's spokesperson said the company is committed to "humane treatment of animals by our suppliers in every part of the world where we do business."[49]

A **product boycott** is a tactic in which an advocacy group actively tries to persuade consumers not to purchase a company's product or service. When an explosion on one of BRITISH PETROLEUM'S (BP) oil rigs in April 2010 caused massive amounts of oil to leak into the Gulf of Mexico, many American consumers expressed outrage by boycotting and demonstrating against BP. Tyson Slocum, director of Public Citizen, an advocacy group, said, ". . . This is a fitting response because, after all, BP over the years has spent millions promoting this image of being a green, environmentally friendly company. It was all for show. Boycotting their brand is the best way to counter that kind of charade."[50]

REVIEW 2-3

. . . .

Specific Environment

The specific environment is made up of five components: customers, competitors, suppliers, industry regulation, and advocacy groups. Companies can monitor customers' needs by identifying customer problems after they occur or by anticipating problems before they occur. Because they tend to focus on well-known competitors, managers often underestimate their competition or do a poor job of identifying future competitors. Suppliers and buyers are dependent on each other, and that dependence sometimes leads to opportunistic behavior, in which one benefits at the expense of the other. Regulatory

public communications
an advocacy group tactic that relies on voluntary participation by the news media and the advertising industry to get the advocacy group's message out

media advocacy
an advocacy group tactic that involves framing issues as public issues; exposing questionable, exploitative, or unethical practices; and forcing media coverage by buying media time or creating controversy that is likely to receive extensive news coverage

product boycott
an advocacy group tactic that involves protesting a company's actions by persuading consumers not to purchase its product or service

agencies affect businesses by creating rules and then enforcing them. Overall, the level of industry regulation has nearly tripled in the last 25 years. Advocacy groups cannot regulate organizations' practices. Nevertheless, through public communications, media advocacy, and product boycotts, they try to convince companies to change their practices.

2-4 Making Sense of Changing Environments

In Chapter 1, you learned that managers are responsible for making sense of their business environments. As our discussions of the general and specific environments have indicated, however, making sense of business environments is not an easy task.

After reading this section, you should be able to:

2-4 describe the process that companies use to make sense of their changing environments.

External environments can be dynamic, confusing, and complex.

Let's look at the three-step process managers use to make sense of the changes in their external environments: **2-4a environmental scanning, 2-4b interpreting environmental factors**, and **2-4c acting on threats and opportunities.**

2-4a Environmental Scanning

Environmental scanning involves searching the environment for important events or issues that might affect an organization. Managers scan the environment to stay up-to-date on important factors in their industry. The American Hospital Association, for instance, publishes an "Environmental Scan" annually to help hospital and health system managers understand the trends and market forces that have a "high probability of affecting the health care field."[51] Organizational strategies also affect environmental scanning. In other words, managers pay close attention to trends and events that are directly related to their company's ability to compete in the marketplace.[52]

   Finally, environmental scanning is important because it contributes to organizational performance. Environmental scanning helps managers detect environmental changes and problems before they become organizational crises.[53] Furthermore, companies whose CEOs do more environmental scanning have higher profits.[54] CEOs in better-performing firms scan their firm's environments more frequently and scan more key factors in their environments in more depth and detail than do CEOs in poorer-performing firms.[55]

2-4b Interpreting Environmental Factors

After scanning, managers determine what environmental events and issues mean to the organization. Typically, managers view environmental events and issues as either threats or opportunities. When managers interpret environmental events as threats, they take steps to protect the company from further harm. For example, now that Internet phone service (VoIP) has emerged as

environmental scanning
searching the environment for important events or issues that might affect an organization

a threat, traditional phone companies have responded by spending billions to expand their fiber-optic networks so that they can offer phone (using VoIP), Internet service, and TV packages just like those the cable and satellite companies offer. For example, when this was being written, Comcast was losing 233,000 cable TV subscribers per quarter, while U-Verse, AT&T's digital TV service, and FiOS, Verizon's digital TV service, were adding 264,00 and 303,000 subscribers, respectively, during the same period.[56]

By contrast, when managers interpret environmental events as opportunities, they consider strategic alternatives for taking advantage of those events to improve company performance. To take advantage of the rapid growth of the smartphone market, Apple developed the iPhone. Then CEO Steve Jobs announced the release more than six months in advance to generate hype, stimulate demand, and dampen sales of competitors. Apple then sold 21 million iPhones in its first 18 months on the market, far exceeding its goal of 10 million. Another sign of Apple's success was that the 1-billionth iPhone application was downloaded just nine months after Apple opened its App Store for the iPhone and iPod Touch.[57]

© AP IMAGES/PRNEWSFOTO/APPLE

2-4c Acting on Threats and Opportunities

After scanning for information on environmental events and issues and interpreting them as threats or opportunities, managers have to decide how to respond to these environmental factors. Deciding what to do under conditions of uncertainty is always difficult. Managers can never be completely confident that they have all the information they need or that they correctly understand the information they have. Nonetheless, they must make decisions and take actions that minimize threats and take advantage of opportunities.

In the end, managers must complete all three steps—environmental scanning, interpreting environmental factors, and acting on threats and opportunities— to make sense of changing external environments. Environmental scanning helps managers more accurately interpret their environments and take actions that improve company performance. Through scanning, managers keep tabs on what competitors are doing, identify market trends, and stay alert to current events that affect their company's operations. Armed with the environmental information they have gathered, managers can then minimize the impact of threats and turn opportunities into increased profits.

REVIEW 2-4
. . . .
Making Sense of Changing Environments
Managers use a three-step process to make sense of external environments: environmental scanning, interpreting information, and acting on threats and opportunities. Managers scan their environments based on their organizational

strategies, their need for up-to-date information, and their need to reduce uncertainty. When managers identify environmental events as threats, they take steps to protect the company from harm. When managers identify environmental events as opportunities, they formulate alternatives for taking advantage of them to improve company performance.

2-5 Internal Environments

We have been looking at trends and events outside of companies that have the potential to affect them. By contrast, the **internal environment** consists of trends and events *within* an organization that affect the management, employees, and organizational culture.

After reading this section, you should be able to:

2-5 explain how organizational cultures are created and how they can help companies be successful.

Earlier in the chapter, you learned that innovative new products such as the iPod, iPhone, and Xbox 360, as well as aggressive cost cutting in the booming market for high-definition TVs (i.e., the external environment), hurt Sony's market share and profitability. Sony's problems, however, were directly linked to its hypercompetitive culture, where people in different parts of the company did not communicate with each other and where designing innovative, high-priced products no matter the cost was seen as the most important contribution to the company.

The key component in internal environments is **organizational culture**, or the set of key values, beliefs, and attitudes shared by members of the organization.

Let's take a closer look at **2-5a how organizational cultures are created and maintained, 2-5b the characteristics of successful organizational cultures,** and **2-5c how companies can accomplish the difficult task of changing organizational cultures**.

2-5a Creation and Maintenance of Organizational Cultures

A primary source of organizational culture is the company founder. Founders like Thomas J. Watson Sr. (IBM), Sam Walton (Walmart), and Bill Gates (Microsoft) create organizations in their own images and imprint them with their beliefs, attitudes, and values. Although company founders are instrumental in the creation of organizational cultures, eventually founders retire, die, or choose to leave their companies. When the founders are gone, how are their values, attitudes, and beliefs sustained in the organizational culture? The answer is stories and heroes.

Organizational members tell **organizational stories** to make sense of organizational events and changes and to emphasize culturally consistent assumptions, decisions, and actions.[58] At Walmart, stories abound about founder Sam Walton's thriftiness as he strove to make Walmart the low-cost retailer that it is today.

> In those days, we would go on buying trips with Sam, and we'd all stay, as much as we could, in one room or two. I remember one time in Chicago when we stayed eight of us to a room. And the room wasn't very big to begin with. You might say we were on a pretty restricted budget. (Gary Reinboth, one of Walmart's first store managers)[59]

internal environment
the events and trends inside an organization that affect management, employees, and organizational culture

organizational culture
the values, beliefs, and attitudes shared by organizational members

organizational stories
stories told by organizational members to make sense of organizational events and changes and to emphasize culturally consistent assumptions, decisions, and actions

Sam Walton's thriftiness still permeates Walmart today. Everyone, including top executives and the CEO, flies coach rather than business or first class. When employees travel on business, it's still the norm to share rooms (though two to a room, not eight!) at inexpensive motels like Motel 6 and Super 8. At one of its annual meetings, former CEO Lee Scott reinforced Sam Walton's beliefs by exhorting Walmart employees to bring back and use the free pencils and pens from their travels. Most people in the audience didn't think he was kidding, and he probably wasn't.[60]

A second way in which organizational culture is sustained is by recognizing and celebrating heroes. By definition, organizational heroes are organizational people admired for their qualities and achievements within the organization. AxleTech International in Troy, Michigan, is a global manufacturer and supplier of axles, axle components, brakes, and aftermarket parts for specialty trucks, military vehicles, and off-highway machines used in construction, material handling, forestry, mining, and agriculture. When one of its largest, multimillion-dollar customers phoned on a Thursday night to call in a special order of parts urgently needed by Monday, engineer Richard Clisch took charge. Over the next three days, he contacted suppliers on different continents to make sure critical parts were flown overnight to AxleTech's factory, flew to the customer's plant in New York to double check that additional parts weren't needed, and slept just 30 minutes over a four-day span to heroically deliver the order on time.[61]

2-5b Successful Organizational Cultures

Preliminary research shows that organizational culture is related to organizational success. As shown in Exhibit 2.4, cultures based on adaptability, involvement, a clear mission, and consistency can help companies achieve higher sales growth, return on assets, profits, quality, and employee satisfaction.[62]

Adaptability is the ability to notice and respond to changes in the organization's environment. Cultures need to reinforce important values and behaviors, but a culture becomes dysfunctional if it prevents change. One of the surest ways to do that is to discourage open discussion and disagreement. Zappos.com is an online retailer that is founded on one principle—make customers happy. To help new employees adapt to a culture based on superior customer service, all new employees, whether website designers or box loaders or corporate lawyers, are required to attend the company's four-week training program for customer service representatives. New hires even spend two weeks taking phone calls from customers so that they can have firsthand experience in providing customers with the best possible service.[63] Additionally, cultures that promote higher levels of *employee involvement* in decision making tend to have employees who feel a greater sense of ownership and responsibility.

organizational heroes people celebrated for their qualities and achievements within an organization

Exhibit 2.4

Successful Organizational Cultures

Adaptability

Involvement

Consistency

Clear Vision

Source: D. R. Denison and A. K. Mishra, "Toward a Theory of Organizational Culture and Effectiveness," Organization Science 6 (1995): 204–223.

Company mission is the business's purpose or reason for existing. In organizational cultures with a clear company mission, the organization's strategic purpose and direction are apparent to everyone in the company. When managers are uncertain about their business environments, the mission helps guide the discussions, decisions, and behavior of the people in the company. Novo Nordisk, a pharmaceutical company based in Denmark, has one clear goal: to cure diabetes. Everything it does as an organization—from research and innovation, to marketing, to its social responsibility—is geared toward revolutionizing the way diabetes is treated and prevented. Novo Nordisk's mission is about improving the lives of its customers.[64] Specific mission statements strengthen organizational cultures by letting everyone know why the company is in business, what really matters (i.e., the company's values), and how those values can be used to guide daily actions and behaviors.[65]

Finally, in **consistent organizational cultures**, the company actively defines and teaches organizational values, beliefs, and attitudes. Tony Hsieh, CEO of Zappos.com, developed a list of 10 core values that gave everyone at Zappos shared values and a common corporate language. Then, Hsieh made sure that Zappos's culture played a significant role in hiring decisions. As a result, prospective hires go through two rounds of interviews to make sure they gel with the culture.[66]

Having a consistent or strong organizational culture doesn't guarantee good company performance. When core beliefs are widely shared and strongly held, it is very difficult to bring about needed change. Consequently, companies with strong cultures tend to perform poorly when they need to adapt to dramatic changes in their external environments.[67] Indeed, McDonald's saw its sales and profits decline in the late 1990s as customer eating patterns began to change. To rescue falling performance, the company introduced its Plan to Win, which focused on the five elements that drive its business: people, products, place, price, and promotion.

2-5c Changing Organizational Cultures

As shown in Exhibit 2.5, organizational cultures exist on three levels.[69] On the first, or surface, level are the reflections of an organization's culture that can be seen and observed, such as symbolic artifacts (e.g., dress codes and office layouts) and workers' and managers' behaviors. Next, just below the surface, are the values and beliefs expressed by people in the company. You can't see these values and beliefs, but they become clear if you carefully listen to what people say and observe how decisions are made or explained. Finally, unconsciously held assumptions and beliefs about the company are buried deep below the surface. These are the unwritten views and rules that are so strongly held and so widely shared that they are rarely discussed or even thought about unless someone attempts to change them or unknowingly violates them. Changing such assumptions and beliefs can be very difficult. Instead, managers should focus on the parts of the organizational culture they can control. These include observable surface-level items, such as workers' behaviors and symbolic artifacts,

company mission
a company's purpose or reason for existing

consistent organizational culture
a company culture in which the company actively defines and teaches organizational values, beliefs, and attitudes

Exhibit 2.5

Three Levels of Organizational Culture

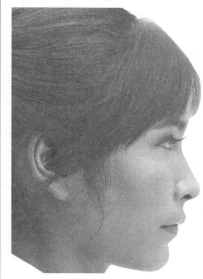

SEEN (Surface level)	• Symbolic artifacts such as dress codes • Workers' and managers' behaviors
HEARD (Expressed values & beliefs)	• What people say • How decisions are made and explained
BELIEVED (Unconscious asumptions & beliefs)	• Widely shared assumptions and beliefs • Buried deep below surface • Rarely discussed or thought about

© VICTOR TONGDEE/SHUTTERSTOCK.COM. © CENGAGE LEARNING 2013

and expressed values and beliefs, which can be influenced through employee selection. Let's see how these can be used to change organizational cultures.

One way of changing a corporate culture is to use behavioral addition or behavioral substitution to establish new patterns of behavior among managers and employees. **Behavioral addition** is the process of having managers and employees perform a new behavior, while **behavioral substitution** is having managers and employees perform a new behavior in place of another behavior. The key in both instances is to choose behaviors that are central to and symbolic of the old culture you're changing and the new culture that you want to create. When Mike Ullman, the former CEO of *JCPenney* took over at the retailer, he thought the company's culture was stuck in the nineteenth century (when the company was started). Employees called each other "Mr." and "Mrs." and casual attire and elaborate office decoration was unacceptable. Ullman quickly determined that the company's stringent code of conduct was, among other things, keeping it from recruiting the talent it needed. Mike Theilmann, the human resources officer, drafted a list of what he called "quick hits," small changes that would have a big impact on the culture. The first of Theilmann's initiatives was a campaign titled "Just Call Me Mike," which he hoped would cure employees of the entrenched practice of calling executives and managers "Mr." and "Mrs."[70]

Another way in which managers can begin to change corporate culture is to change the **visible artifacts** of their old culture, such as the office design and layout, company dress code, and recipients (or nonrecipients) of company benefits and perks like stock options, personal parking spaces, or the private company dining room.

Cultures can also be changed by hiring and selecting people with values and beliefs consistent with the company's desired culture. *Selection* is the process of

behavioral addition
the process of having managers and employees perform new behaviors that are central to and symbolic of the new organizational culture that a company wants to create

behavioral substitution
the process of having managers and employees perform new behaviors central to the "new" organizational culture in place of behaviors that were central to the "old" organizational culture

visible artifacts
visible signs of an organization's culture, such as the office design and layout, company dress code, and company benefits and perks, like stock options, personal parking spaces, or the private company dining room

gathering information about job applicants to decide who should be offered a job. As discussed in Chapter 10 on human resources, most selection instruments measure whether job applicants have the knowledge, skills, and abilities needed to succeed in their jobs. But companies are increasingly testing job applicants to determine how they fit with the company's desired culture (i.e., values and beliefs). Management consultant Ram Charan says, "A poor job match is not only harmful to the individual but also to the company."[71] At PARTNERS + NAPIER, an advertising agency, the three most important values are courage, ingenuity, and family, and these values carry over into the hiring process. According to CEO Sharon Napier, the ideal candidate is curious, willing to try new things, and wants to learn about the products he or she is working on. According to Napier, "If you don't really want to know how something works, if you don't read a lot, then you're not a very curious person. And in our business you really have to be. If I'm going to put you on an account like Kodak, I want you to learn how to make a photo book . . . if you're not interested in digging in, then that'll say a lot about you."[72]

The second step is to ensure that applicants fit with the culture by using selection tests, instruments, and exercises to measure these values and beliefs in job applicants. (See Chapter 10 for a complete review of applicant and managerial selection.) At Southwest Airlines, humor and a good attitude are two of the most important requirements in its new hires. Cofounder and former CEO and board chair Herb Kelleher says, "What's important is that a customer should get off the airplane feeling: 'I didn't just get from A to B. I had one of the most pleasant experiences I ever had and I'll be back for that reason.'"[73]

Corporate cultures are very difficult to change. Consequently, there is no guarantee that any one approach—changing visible cultural artifacts, using behavioral substitution, or hiring people with values consistent with a company's desired culture—will change a company's organizational culture. The best results are obtained by combining these methods. Together, these are some of the best tools managers have for changing culture because they send the clear message to managers and employees that "the accepted way of doing things" has changed.

REVIEW 2-5

Organizational Cultures: Creation, Success, and Change

Organizational culture is the set of key values, beliefs, and attitudes shared by organizational members. Organizational cultures are often created by company founders and then sustained through the telling of organizational stories and the celebration of organizational heroes. Adaptable cultures that promote employee involvement, make clear the organization's strategic purpose and direction, and actively define and teach organizational values and beliefs can help companies achieve higher sales growth, return on assets, profits, quality, and employee satisfaction. Organizational cultures exist on three levels: the surface level, where cultural artifacts and behaviors can be observed; just below the surface, where values and beliefs are expressed; and deep below the surface, where unconsciously held assumptions and beliefs exist. Managers can begin to change company cultures by focusing on the top two levels and using behavioral substitution and behavioral addition, changing visible artifacts, and selecting job applicants with values and beliefs consistent with the desired company culture.

Management Team Decision

Making a New Culture[74]

Home Depot stores used to be known for customer service. A host of friendly employees would help customers navigate a huge inventory, find exactly what they needed, and even provide detailed instruction. Those days seem long gone, though. Under the leadership of the former CEO, the company shifted its focus away from customer service to reducing inventory and cutting costs. Stores that once had an employee in nearly every aisle are now being manned by just a handful, even during the busiest times. Customers who were used to getting helpful, personal attention can no longer find even a cashier, much less someone who can answer their questions on how to use a reciprocating saw.

Marvin Ellison, promoted to CEO in 2008, saw the disastrous results of Home Depot's lack of attention to customers. In the last three months of 2009, the company lost $54 million. To make matters worse, the company's reputation took tremendous hits. For many years, it routinely ranked near the bottom of the University of Michigan's American Customer Satisfaction Index, which measures consumers' evaluations of all major retailers. Even after Home Depot recovered in these rankings slightly, it still lagged far behind competitors like Lowe's and Ace. He had to listen to numerous stories of how consumers would drive an extra 30 minutes, even an hour, to avoid going to Home Depot.

To turn things around, Marvin Ellison has committed to a new company vision, a culture that is dedicated to meeting three goals:

clean warehouses, stocked shelves, and top customer service. He wants employees to set aside a portion of their shift to do nothing else but take care of customers. He wants to revise evaluations so that employees' performance is reviewed primarily on the basis of customer service. He wants to give financial incentives to employees who provide great service. He wants to reduce the number of messages that stores and employees get from headquarters so that they can focus on customers. In short, he wants to restore Home Depot's reputation for providing the very best in customer service.

Ellison has appointed you to a management team in charge of setting up a training and evaluating program that will get the entire company focused on his vision of customer service. You and your team face the difficult task of changing the entire company's culture so that the entire organization is focused on the customer. How will you do it?

For this Management Team Decision, form a group of three or four with other students, to act as the management team, and answer the questions below.

Questions

1. What kind of training and evaluation program would you institute to change Home Depot's culture?

2. Recall from the text that there are three levels of organizational culture. What kind of changes would you make to address each level?

3. How could an analysis of the company's external environment help in establishing a new customer-based culture?

Practice Being a Manager

Navigating Different Organizational Cultures

Effective managers recognize that organizational culture is an important, often critical, element of organizational health and performance.

But recognizing and understanding culture, especially its less visible aspects, is often quite challenging. This exercise will give you some practice in recognizing cultural differences and the challenges and opportunities that managers face as they work with diverse cultures. Suppose that major music-recording company Sony BMG has announced plans to hire several college students to form a team that will invest in the "next big things in music." The selected students will be paid $50,000 per year for working part time. Sony BMG will also allocate up to $10 million for hiring artists, producing records, and so on, based on the team's recommendations.

The new team has been dubbed the Top Wave Team (TWT). If TWT's recommendations are fruitful, the company will sign each member of the team to $150,000 full-time contracts. The company also plans to keep the team together and to give members bonuses and promotions based on their group performance.

Your class has been chosen as the representative college class. The music company is now asking you to form affinity groups by musical preferences in your class (e.g., a Country Music group, an Urban and Hip-Hop group). Each group will nominate one of its members to receive the first $50,000 internship as a TWT team member at Sony BMG. The new TWT group will meet and discuss initial plans and investment recommendations, and then your class will discuss the process and outcomes.

STEP 1 **Choose your musical affinity.** In the class session before this exercise, your professor will ask you to submit a survey form or sheet of paper with your name and your preferred musical genre or identity.

Identify yourself with one of the following musical genres based on (a) preference or affinity ("I prefer this music") and (b) knowledge and understanding ("Of all types of music, I know the most about _____ music/musicians"):

1. Rock
2. Country
3. Religious and Spiritual
4. Urban and Hip-Hop
5. Rap
6. Jazz and R & B
7. Pop and Mainstream
8. Classical
9. Folk and Bluegrass

Your professor will review your submitted preferences and organize affinity groups for the next class session.

STEP 2 **Organize into groups.** Your professor will organize you by musical affinity. If your class is heavily concentrated in one or a few of the musical genres, you may be asked to further divide into smaller groups by subcategories (e.g., Rock—Heavy Metal and Rock—Popular or Hit).

STEP 3 **Prepare your recommendations.** In groups, discuss what is important about your type of music and what investments the TWT team should make. Keep in mind that the investments made by the TWT team could have a big impact on the future of your favorite music. Recommend a dollar amount or percentage of the $10 million that your representative ought to secure for investment in your genre.

Each group should then select one of its members to receive the internship from Sony BMG and represent the group on the TWT team.

STEP 4 **Discuss recommendations before the class.** Nominees from the musical affinity groups should discuss their recommendations before the class. Those not on the TWT should observe the process and take notes on what happens in this meeting.

STEP 5 **Hold the team meeting.** Your professor will allocate a short time for the initial meeting of the TWT. It may occur before or during the class meeting. After the TWT reaches agreement on how it might allocate its investments by genre (or by some alternative approach), reaches impasse, or reaches the time limit, your professor will call an end to the TWT meeting.

STEP 6 **Debrief and discuss.** As a class, discuss the process and outcomes of this exercise. Consider the following questions and/or others posed by your professor:

• Did you sense some cultural affinity with others who shared your musical tastes? Why or why not?

- What expectations might be associated with choosing someone to "represent" a group on a team such as the TWT?

- What tensions and challenges might face each member of the TWT in a real-life setting of serving on a group that represents various cultures?

 ## Self-Assessment

Check Your Tolerance for Ambiguity

Think of the difference between playing chess (where you can see all the pieces and anticipate attacks and plan counterattacks) and playing poker (where no one knows anyone else's hand, and you have to make guesses based on your interpretation of opponents' betting patterns). In chess, there is little ambiguity, whereas in poker there is tremendous ambiguity. Although many people liken business to a game of chess, probably because of the strategic aspects of the game, business is actually more like poker. The business environment is complex and uncertain, and managers never *really* know all the cards the opposition is holding. Managers must learn to adapt to environmental shifts and new developments—sometimes on a daily basis. For some managers, however, this can be a challenging task because everyone has a different comfort level when it comes to ambiguity. For some, not knowing all the details can be a source of significant stress, whereas for others uncertainty can be energizing.

As a manager, you will need to develop an appropriate tolerance for ambiguity. For example, being stressed out every time interest rates change can be counterproductive, but completely ignoring the economic environment can be detrimental to your company's performance.

Complete the following questionnaire to get a sense of your tolerance for ambiguity.[75] Indicate the extent to which you agree with the statements using the following scale:

1. Strongly disagree
2. Moderately disagree
3. Slightly disagree
4. Neutral
5. Slightly agree
6. Moderately agree
7. Strongly agree

1. I don't tolerate ambiguous situations well.

    1   2   3   4   5   6   7

2. I find it difficult to respond when faced with an unexpected event.

    1   2   3   4   5   6   7

3. I don't think new situations are any more threatening than familiar situations.

    1   2   3   4   5   6   7

4. I am drawn to situations that can be interpreted in more than one way.

    1   2   3   4   5   6   7

5. I would rather avoid solving problems that must be viewed from several different perspectives.

    1   2   3   4   5   6   7

6. I try to avoid situations that are ambiguous.

    1   2   3   4   5   6   7

7. I am good at managing unpredictable situations.

    1   2   3   4   5   6   7

8. I prefer familiar situations to new ones.

    1   2   3   4   5   6   7

9. Problems that cannot be considered from just one point of view are a little threatening.

    1   2   3   4   5   6   7

10. I avoid situations that are too complicated for me to easily understand.

    1   2   3   4   5   6   7

11. I am tolerant of ambiguous situations.

    1   2   3   4   5   6   7

12. I enjoy tackling problems that are complex enough to be ambiguous.

    1   2   3   4   5   6   7

13. I try to avoid problems that don't seem to have only one "best" solution.

    1   2   3   4   5   6   7

14. I often find myself looking for something new rather than trying to hold things constant in my life.

    1   2   3   4   5   6   7

15. I generally prefer novelty over familiarity.

    1   2   3   4   5   6   7

16. I dislike ambiguous situations.

    1   2   3   4   5   6   7

17. Some problems are so complex that just trying to understand them is fun.

    1   2   3   4   5   6   7

18. I have little trouble coping with unexpected events.

    1   2   3   4   5   6   7

19. I pursue problem situations that are so complex some people call them "mind-boggling."

    1   2   3   4   5   6   7

20. I find it hard to make a choice when the outcome is uncertain.

    1   2   3   4   5   6   7

21. I enjoy an occasional surprise.

    1   2   3   4   5   6   7

22. I prefer a situation in which there is some ambiguity.

    1   2   3   4   5   6   7

SCORING

Determine your score by entering your response to each survey item below, as follows. In blanks that say *regular score*, simply enter your response for that item. If your response was a 6, place a 6 in the *regular score* blank. In blanks that say *reverse score*, subtract your response from 8 and enter the result. So if your response was a 6, place a 2 (8–6 = 2) in the *reverse score* blank. Add up your total score.

1. regular score _____
2. regular score _____
3. reverse score _____
4. reverse score _____
5. regular score _____
6. regular score _____
7. reverse score _____
8. regular score _____
9. regular score _____
10. regular score _____
11. regular score _____
12. reverse score _____
13. regular score _____
14. reverse score _____
15. reverse score _____
16. regular score _____
17. reverse score _____
18. reverse score _____
19. reverse score _____
20. regular score _____
21. reverse score _____
22. reverse score _____

TOTAL = _____

You can find the interpretation for your score at www.cengagebrain.com.

MANAGEMENT WORKPLACE

Camp Bow Wow: The Environment and Corporate Culture

In 10 years, Camp Bow Wow has grown from a single kennel in Denver, Colorado, to a $40 million business, with more than 150 locations. The transition from a small family business to a national chain, however, required a shift from a family-based culture to a business- and performance-based culture. A key element of Camp Bow Wow's culture is the staff's deep emotional connection with animals. The connection is immediately apparent at corporate headquarters, where offices are bustling with employees and pets alike. According to founder Heidi Ganahal, "What we do is focus on what's important to us, and that's the animals."

What to Watch For and Ask Yourself

1. What aspects of Camp Bow Wow's corporate culture reflect the surface level of the organizational culture? What aspects reflect the values and beliefs? What aspects reflect the unconsciously held assumptions and beliefs?
2. Why did Camp Bow Wow have to change its culture when it became a national franchise?
3. What impact does Heidi Ganahl's personal story have on employees at Camp Bow Wow?

Endnotes

1. J. Ball, "Currents—Power Shift: Climate Change: Garbage Gets Fresh Look as Source of Energy," *Wall Street Journal*, May 15, 2009, A9; J. Fahey, "Waste Not," *Forbes Asia*, July 2010, 46; M. Gunther, "Waste Management's New Direction," *Fortune*, December 6, 2010, 103–108; A. Robinson and D. Schroeder, "Greener and Cheaper: The Conventional Wisdom Is That a Company's Costs Rise as Its Environmental Impact Falls; Think Again," *Wall Street Journal*, March 23, 2009, R4; "2010 Sustainability Report," Waste Management, accessed February 6, 2011, from www.wm.com/sustainability/pdfs/2010_Sustainability_Report.pdf; "Municipal Solid Waste Generation, Recycling, and Disposal in the United States: Facts and Figures for 2008," U.S. Environmental Protection Agency, accessed February 14, 2011, from www.epa.gov/osw/nonhaz/municipal/pubs/msw2008rpt.pdf; and "Zero Waste," Wal-Mart Corporate, accessed February 15, 2011, from http://walmartstores.com/Sustainability/7762.aspx.

2. Y. Kane, "Sony CEO Urges Managers to 'Get Mad'; Conference Told That Company Needs to Be More Innovative, Bold," *Wall Street Journal*, May 23, 2008, B8.

3. B. Fritz, "Once-Hot Nintendo Wii Now Struggling for Sales," *Los Angeles Times,* November 30, 2010; N. Wingfield, "Microsoft Net Slips, but Sales Rise as Kinect Proves Popular," *Wall Street Journal*, January 28, 2011, accessed February 2, 2011, from http://online.wsj.com/article/SB1000142405274870426810457610840219692091 0.html.

4. E. Romanelli and M. L. Tushman, "Organizational Transformation as Punctuated Equilibrium: An Empirical Test," *Academy of Management Journal* 37 (1994): 1141–1166.

5. H. Banks, "A Sixties Industry in a Nineties Economy," *Forbes*, May 9, 1994, 107–112.

6. L. Cowan, "Cheap Fuel Should Carry Many Airlines to More Record Profits for 1st Quarter," *Wall Street Journal*, April 4, 1998, B17A.

7. B. Jones, "The Changing Dairy Industry," Department of Agricultural & Applied Economics & Center for Dairy Profitability, accessed July 25, 2008, from www.aae.wisc.edu/jones/Presentations/Wisc & TotalDairyTrends.pdf.

8. B. Stone, "Revenue at Craigslist Is Said to Top $100 million," *New York Times*, June 9, 2009, accessed August 1, 2010, from www.nytimes.com/2009/06/10/technology/internet/10craig.html?_r=1 & ref=craigslist.

9. J. Falls, "What the Wall Street Journal Has, Few Will Match," *Social Media Explorer*, October 30, 2009, accessed August 1, 2010, from www.socialmediaexplorer.com/2009/10/30/what-the-wall-street-journal-has-few-will-match/.

10. E. Fyrwald, "The King of Water," interview by G. Colvin, *Fortune*, July 5, 2010, 52–59.

11. R. Norton, "Where Is This Economy Really Heading?" *Fortune*, August 7, 1995, 54–56.

12. "CEO Confidence Survey," *The Conference Board*, April 9, 2009, accessed April 27, 2009, from www.conference-board.org.

13. "Despite Recession, U.S. Small Business Confidence Index Increases Six Points; Small Business Research Board Study Finds Increase in Key Indicators," *U.S. Business Confidence*, February 23, 2009, accessed April 27, 2009, from www.ipasbrb.net.

14. T. Tsai and G. Fowler, "Business Technology: Race Heats Up to Supply E-Reader Screens," *Wall Street Journal*, December 29, 2009, B1.

15. J. Fletcher, "Extreme Nesting," *Wall Street Journal*, January 7, 2000, W1.

16. B. Sackett, "A Shopper for All Seasons; The Workplace Concierge Taking Care of Business," *Washington Times*, November 30, 2007, C08.

17. "The Civil Rights Act of 1991," U.S. Equal Employment Opportunity Commission, available online at www.eeoc.gov/policy/cra91.html.

18. "Compliance Assistance—Family and Medical Leave Act (FMLA)," U.S. Department of Labor: Employment Standards Administration Wage and Hour Division, accessed July 25, 2005, from www.dol.gov/compliance/laws/comp-fmla.htm [accessed 25 July 2005].

19. R. J. Bies and T. R. Tyler, "The Litigation Mentality in Organizations: A Test of Alternative Psychological Explanations," *Organization Science* 4 (1993): 352–366.

20. M. Orey, "Fear of Firing," *Businessweek*, April 23, 2007, 52–62.

21. S. Gardner, G. Gomes, and J. Morgan, "Wrongful Termination and the Expanding Public Policy Exception: Implications and Advice," *SAM Advanced Management Journal* 65 (2000): 38.

22. Orey, "Fear of Firing."

23. Ibid.

24. C. Morris, "Activision Battles 'Trolls', Backs Down on Privacy Fears," *CNBC.com*, July 9, 2010, accessed July 10, 2010, from www.cnbc.com/id/38171990/.

25. R. Johnston and S. Mehra, "Best-Practice Complaint Management," *Academy of Management Experience* 16 (November 2002): 145–154.

26. D. Smart and C. Martin, "Manufacturer Responsiveness to Consumer Correspondence: An Empirical Investigation of Consumer Perceptions," *Journal of Consumer Affairs* 26 (1992): 104.

27. C. Binkley, "Lucky Numbers: Casino Chain Mines Data on Its Gamblers, and Strikes Pay Dirt—'Secret Recipe' Lets Harrah's Target Its Low-Rollers at the Individual Level—A Free-Meal 'Intervention,'" *Wall Street Journal*, May 4, 2000; "Harrah's Hits Customer Loyalty Jackpot: SAS Identifies Customers with Highest Potential to Return," *SAS Customer Success*, accessed February 4, 2011, from www.sas.com.

28. T. Mullaney, "Harrah's," *Businessweek* (November 24, 2003): 94.

29. S. A. Zahra and S. S. Chaples, "Blind Spots in Competitive Analysis," *Academy of Management Executive* 7 (1993): 7–28.

30 "The Cola Wars: Over a Century of Cola Slogans, Commercials, Blunders, and Coups," available at www.geocities.com/colacentury/.

31 M. Frazier, "You Suck: Dyson, Hoover and Oreck Trade Accusations in Court, on TV as Brit Upstart Leaves Rivals in Dust," *Advertising Age*, July 25, 2005, 1.

32 J. M. Moran, "Getting Closer Together—Videophones Don't Deliver TV Quality Sound, Visuals, but They're Improving," *Seattle Times*, March 15, 1998.

33 D. Searcey, "Cable's Picture Gets Fuzzier; Market Leader Comcast's Stock Is Hit as Phone Companies Make Gains," *Wall Street Journal*, November 8, 2007, B3.

34 R. Kim, "Vonage Call App Uses Facebook, No Minutes," SFGate.com, August 6, 2010, accessed October 12, 2010, from http://articles.sfgate.com/2010-08-06/business/22205815_1_facebook-call-phone-rings.

35 K. G. Provan, "Embeddedness, Interdependence, and Opportunism in Organizational Supplier-Buyer Networks," *Journal of Management* 19 (1993): 841–856.

36 B. Preuschoff and P. McGroarty, "Rare Earth Shortages Hit Germany," *Wall Street Journal*, October 26, 2010, accessed February 10, 2011, from http://online.wsj.com/article/SB10001424052702303341904575576162454449250.html.

37 Y. Hayashi and J. Areddy, "Japan Scrambles for Rare Earth—Tokyo Seeks to Sidestep Reliance on Uncertain Supplies From China; Issue a Priority Elsewhere, Too," *Wall Street Journal*, October 25, 2010, A10.

38 M. Dalton, "AB InBev Suppliers Feel Squeeze," *Wall Street Journal*, April 17, 2009, B2.

39 D. Birch, "Staying on Good Terms," *Supply Management*, April 12, 2001, 36.

40 S. Parker and C. Axtell, "Seeing Another Viewpoint: Antecedents and Outcomes of Employee Perspective Taking," *Academy of Management Journal* 44 (2001): 1085–1100; and B. K. Pilling, L. A. Crosby, and D. W. Jackson, "Relational Bonds in Industrial Exchange: An Experimental Test of the Transaction Cost Economic Framework," *Journal of Business Research* 30 (1994): 237–251.

41 "Seafood HACCP," U.S. Food and Drug Administration Center for Food Safety & Applied Nutrition, accessed March 12, 2009, www.cfsan.fda.gov/~comm/haccpsea.html.

42 N. Casey and M. Trottman, "Toys Containing Banned Plastics Still on Market; Restrictions on Phthalates Don't Take Effect Until '09; Fears of Reproductive Defects," *Wall Street Journal*, October 23, 2008, D1.

43 S. Dudley, "The Coming Shift in Regulation," *Regulation*, October 1, 2002.

44 S. Dudley, "Regulation and Small Business Competitive," *Federal Document Clearing House*, Congressional Testimony, Prepared Remarks for the House Committee on Small Business Subcommittee on Regulatory Reform and Oversight, May 20, 2004.

45 H. Morley, "Bush Orders Cut in Regulations—Change Will Cut Red Tape for Small Businesses," *Knight-Ridder Tribune*, August 17, 2002.

46 J.G. Tillen and S.M. Delman "A Bribe by Any Other Name," Forbes.com. May 28, 2010, accessed December 10, 2010, from www.forbes.com/2010/05/28/bribery-slang-jargon-leadership-managing-compliance_2.html

47 "EU's Aggressive Anti-Smoking Campaign," *Creative Bits*, http://creativebits.org/eus_agressive_anti-smoking_campaign, January 17, 2005.

48 M. Hughlett, "PETA Targets McDonald's over Slaughter of Chickens," *Chicago Tribune*, February 16, 2009, accessed May 10, 2009, from www.Chicagotribune.com.

49 S. Simon and J. Jargon, "PETA Ads to Target McDonald's," *Wall Street Journal*, May 1, 2009, B7.

50 R. Blake, "Boycotting BP: Who Gets Hurt?" ABCNews.com. June 2, 2010, accessed February 5, 2011, from http://abcnews.go.com/Business/bp-boycotts-spreading-frustration-oil-spill-boils/story?id=10800309.

51 "AHA Environmental Scan 2010," American Hospital Association, accessed February 5, 2010, from www.hhnmag.com/hhnmag_app/gateFold/pages/SEPTEMBER09.jsp.

52 D. F. Jennings and J. R. Lumpkin, "Insights between Environmental Scanning Activities and Porter's Generic Strategies: An Empirical Analysis," *Journal of Management* 4 (1992): 791–803.

53 E. Jackson and J. E. Dutton, "Discerning Threats and Opportunities," *Administrative Science Quarterly* 33 (1988): 370–387.

54 B. Thomas, S. M. Clark, and D. A. Gioia, "Strategic Sensemaking and Organizational Performance: Linkages among Scanning, Interpretation, Action, and Outcomes," *Academy of Management Journal* 36 (1993): 239–270.

55 R. Daft, J. Sormunen, and D. Parks, "Chief Executive Scanning, Environmental Characteristics, and Company Performance: An Empirical Study," *Strategic Management Journal* 9 (1988): 123–139; V. Garg, B. Walters, & R. Priem, "Chief Executive Scanning Emphases, Environmental Dynamism, and Manufacturing Firm Performance," *Strategic Management Journal* 24 (2003): 725–744; and D. Miller and P. H. Friesen, "Strategy-Making and Environment: The Third Link," *Strategic Management Journal* 4 (1983): 221–235.

56 Sharman, "AT&T, Verizon Make Different Calls," *Wall Street Journal*, January 29, 2009, B1; N. Worden and V. Kumar, "Earnings: Comcast Feels the Strain of Economic Slump," *Wall Street Journal*, February 19, 2009, B7.

57 D. Ionescu, "Update: Apple Hits 1 Billion App Store Downloads," *PC World*, April 24, 2009, accessed May 10, 2009, from www.pcworld.com/article/163785/update_apple_hits_1_billion_app_store_downloads.html.

58 D. M. Boje, "The Storytelling Organization: A Study of Story Performance in an Office-Supply Firm," *Administrative Science Quarterly* 36 (1991): 106–126.

59 S. Walton & J. Huey, *Sam Walton: Made in America* (New York: Doubleday, 1992).

60 D. Rushe, "Wal-Martians," *Sunday Times* (London), June 10, 2001, 5.

61 E. Thornton, "Perform or Perish," *Businessweek*, November 5, 2007, 38–45.

62 D. R. Denison & A. K. Mishra, "Toward a Theory of Organizational Culture and Effectiveness," *Organization Science* 6 (1995): 204–223.

63 S. Rosenbaum, "The Happiness Culture: Zappos Isn't a Company—It's a Mission," *Fast Company*, June 6, 2010, accessed August 5, 2010, from www.fastcompany.com/1657030/the-happiness-culture-zappos-isn-t-a-company-it-s-a-mission.

64 "Changing Diabetes," Norvo Nordisk, August 4, 2010, from http://changingdiabetes.novonordisk.com/.

65 S. Yearout, G. Miles, and R. Koonce, "Multi-Level Visioning," *Training & Development*, March 1, 2001, 31.

66 T. Hsieh, "Corner Office: On a Scale of 1 to 10, How Weird Are You?" interview by A. Bryant, *New York Times*, January 9, 2010, accessed June 1, 2010, from www.nytimes.com/2010/01/10/business/10corner.html.

67 A. Zuckerman, "Strong Corporate Cultures and Firm Performance: Are There Trade-offs?" *Academy of Management Executive*, November 2002, 158–160.

68 D. Mattioli, "New Room, New Vantage Point," *The Wall Street Journal*, March 8, 2010, B7.

69 E. Schein, *Organizational Culture and Leadership*, 2nd ed. (San Francisco: Jossey-Bass, 1992).

70 E. Byron, "'Call Me Mike!'—To Attract and Keep Talent, JCPenney CEO Loosens Up Once-Formal Workplace," *Wall Street Journal*, March 27, 2006, B1.

71 C. Daniels, "Does This Man Need a Shrink? Companies Are Using Psychological Testing to Screen Candidates for Top Jobs," *Fortune*, February 5, 2001, 205.

72 A. Bryant, "On Her Team, It's All about Bench Strength," *New York Times*, May 8, 2010, accessed November 11, 2011, from www.nytimes.com/2010/05/09/business/09corner.html.

73 S. Chakravarty, "Hit 'Em Hardest with the Mostest (Southwest Airlines' Management)," *Forbes*, September 16, 1991, 48.

74 The American Customer Satisfaction Index: www.theacsi.org/; and Jena McGregor "Putting Home Depot's House in Order." *Businessweek*, May 18, 2009, 54.

75 D. L. McCain, "The MSTAT-I: A New Measure of an Individual's Tolerance for Ambiguity," *Educational and Psychological Measurement*, 53 (1993): 183–190.

Ethics and Social Responsibility

OUTLINE

REEL TO REAL

© TETRA IMAGES/ CORBIS

Management Workplace is at Theo Chocolate.

SELF-ASSESSMENT

© ISTOCKPHOTO/ ALEXANDER KALINA

What's your ethical baseline? Do the Self-Assessment for this chapter in the book or online to find out.

ONLINE QUIZZES

© ISTOCKPHOTO/ PEARLEYE

Did you get it? Review the main concepts in the chapter by taking the online quizzes on CourseMate!

VIDEO QUIZZES

© ISTOCKPHOTO/DAVID HUGHES

Get more out of the videos by taking the multimedia video quizzes online.

What Would You Do?

American Express Headquarters, New York, New York[1]

With medical costs rising 10 to 15 percent per year, one of the members of your board of directors at American Express mentioned that some companies are now refusing to hire smokers and that the board should discuss this option at the next month's meeting. Nationwide, about 6,000 companies refuse to hire smokers. Weyco, an employee benefits company in Okemos, Michigan, requires all applicants to take a nicotine test. Weyco's CFO says, "We're not saying people can't smoke. We're just saying they can't smoke and work here. As an employee-benefits company, we need to take a leadership role in helping people understand the cost impact of smoking." The Cleveland Clinic, one of the top hospitals in the United States, doesn't hire smokers. Paul Terpeluk, the director of corporate and employee health, says that all applicants are tested for nicotine and that 250 people have lost job opportunities because they smoke. The Massachusetts Hospital Association also refuses to hire smokers. The company's CEO says, "Smoking is a personal choice, and as an employer I have a personal choice within the law about whom we hire and whom we don't."

As indicated by your board member, costs are driving the trend not to hire smokers. According to the U.S. Centers for Disease Control, a smoker costs about $4,000 more a year to employ because of increased health care costs and lost productivity. Breaking that down, a smoker will have 50 percent higher absenteeism, and, when present, will work 39 fewer minutes per day because of smoke breaks, which leads to 162.5 lost hours of annual productivity, roughly one month per year. A smoker will have higher accident rates, cause $1,000 a year in property damage (from cigarette burns and smoke damage), and will cost up to $5,000 more a year for annual insurance premiums. John Banzhaf, executive director of an antismoking group in Washington and a law professor at George

Washington University, says, "Smoking is the biggest factor in controllable health care costs."

Although few would disagree about the costs, others argue it is wrong not to hire smokers. Jay Whitehead, publisher of a magazine for human resources managers, says, "There is discrimination at many companies—and maybe even most companies—against people who smoke." Even if applicants aren't asked whether they smoke, it "doesn't mean that hiring managers turn off their sense of smell." Paul Sherer, a smoker who was fired less than a week after taking a new job, says, "Not hiring smokers affects millions of people and puts them in the same category as women able to bear children, that is, people who contribute to higher health care costs. It's unfair." Law professor Don Garner believes that not hiring smokers is "an overreaction on the part of employers whose interest is cutting costs. If someone has the ability to do the job, he should get it. What you do in your home is your own business.... Not hiring smokers is 'respiratory apartheid.'"

Well, with the meeting just a month away, you've got to prepare for the board of directors' questions. For example, on what basis should the company decide whether to hire smokers? Should the decision be based on what's in the best interest of the firm, what the law allows, or what affirms and respects individual rights? The board is interested in making good decisions for the company, but "doing the right thing" is also one of its core values. Is this an issue of ethics or social responsibility? Is refusing to hire smokers a form of discrimination?

If you were in charge at American Express, what would you do?

3-1 Ethics and the Nature of Management Jobs

The dilemma facing American Express is an example of the tough decisions involving ethics and social responsibility that managers face. Unfortunately, no matter what is decided, someone or some group will be unhappy with the outcome. Managers don't have the luxury of choosing theoretically optimal, win–win solutions that are obviously desirable to everyone involved. In practice, solutions to ethics and social responsibility problems aren't optimal. Often, managers must be satisfied with a solution that just makes do or does the least harm. Rights and wrongs are rarely crystal clear to managers charged with doing the right thing. The business world is much messier than that.

We begin this chapter by examining ethical behavior in the workplace and explaining how unethical behavior can expose a business to penalties under the U.S. Sentencing Commission Guidelines for Organizations. Second, we examine the influences on ethical decision making and review practical steps managers can take to improve ethical decision making. We finish by considering to whom organizations are socially responsible, for what organizations are socially responsible, how organizations can respond to societal expectations for social responsibility, and whether social responsibility hurts or helps an organization's economic performance.

Ethics is the set of moral principles or values that defines right and wrong for a person or group. Unfortunately, numerous studies have consistently produced distressing results about the state of ethics in today's business world. A Society of Human Resources Management Survey found that only 27 percent of employees felt that their organization's leadership was ethical.[2] In a study of 1,324 randomly selected workers, managers, and executives across multiple industries, 48 percent admitted to actually committing an unethical or illegal act such as cheating on an expense account, discriminating against coworkers, forging signatures, paying or accepting kickbacks, and looking the other way when environmental laws were broken.[3]

Not all news is bad, however. When people believe their work environment is ethical, they are six times more likely to stay with that company than if they believe they work in an unethical environment.[4] One study asked 570 white-collar workers which of 28 qualities were important in company leaders. The results? Honesty (24%) and integrity/morals/ethics (16%) ranked by far the highest.[5] (Caring/compassion was third at 7%.) Though much needs to be done to make workplaces more ethical, but—and this is very important—most managers and employees want it to happen.

ethics
the set of moral principles or values that defines right and wrong for a person or group

After reading this section, you should be able to:

3-1 discuss how the nature of management jobs creates the possibility for ethical abuses.

Ethical behavior follows accepted principles of right and wrong. By contrast, unethical management behavior occurs when managers personally violate accepted principles of right and wrong—for example, by lying about company profits or knowingly producing an unsafe product—or encourage others to do so. Because of the nature of their jobs, managers can be tempted to engage in unethical managerial behavior in four areas: authority and power, handling information, influencing the behavior of others, and setting goals.

The *authority and power* inherent in some management positions can tempt managers to engage in unethical practices. Because they often control company resources, there is a risk that some managers will cross the line from legitimate use to personal use of these resources. For example, unless it's in an employee's job description, using an employee to do personal chores, like picking up the manager's dry cleaning, is unethical behavior. Even worse, though, is using one's managerial authority and power for direct personal gain as some managers have done by using corporate funds to pay for extravagant personal parties, lavish home decorating, jewelry, or expensive works of art.

Handling information is another area in which managers must be careful to behave ethically. Information is a key part of management work, because managers collect it, analyze it, act on it, and disseminate it. In doing so, they are expected to be truthful and, when necessary, to keep confidential information confidential. Leaking company secrets to competitors, doctoring the numbers, wrongfully withholding information, and lying are some of the ways managers may misuse information entrusted to them. SATYAM COMPUTER is a leading Indian outsourcing and software company that serves more than a third of the *Fortune* 500 companies and the U.S. government. After years of "doctoring" the books, chairman and cofounder Ramalinga Raju finally admitted that he overstated profits and revenues and created a fake cash balance of $1 billion in hopes of making the company appear more successful than it was so it could attract more business and investment.[6]

Managers must also be careful to behave ethically in the way they *influence the behavior of others*, especially those they supervise. Managerial work gives managers significant power to influence others. If managers tell employees to perform unethical acts (or face punishment), such as faking the numbers to get results, they are abusing their managerial power. This is sometimes called the "move it or lose it" syndrome. "Move it or lose it" managers tell employees, "Do it. You're paid to do it. If you can't do it, we'll find somebody who can."[7]

Although managers can influence their employees' behavior through direct order, they can also do so more indirectly through the *goals they set*. If managers set unrealistic goals, the pressure to perform and achieve those goals can influence employees to engage in unethical business behaviors, especially if they are just short of meeting their goals or a deadline.[8] Hedge fund GALLEON GROUP pushed its stock traders to get illegal inside information about the performance of companies to give them an advantage in buying and selling stocks. Galleon's aggressive investment goals led its senior managers and traders to berate, punish, and fire analysts who couldn't produce inside

ethical behavior
behavior that conforms to a society's accepted principles of right and wrong

information. A former Galleon trader said, "Get an edge or you're gone." So far, 19 of the 26 defendants associated with Galleon's insider trading scandal have pled guilty.[9]

REVIEW 3-1
....

Ethics and the Nature of Management Jobs

Ethics is the set of moral principles or values that define right and wrong. Ethical behavior occurs when managers follow those principles and values. Because they set the standard for others in the workplace, managers can model ethical behavior by using resources for company business and not for personal gain. Furthermore, managers can encourage ethical behavior by handling information in a confidential and honest fashion, not using their authority to influence others to engage in unethical behavior, and setting reasonable rather than unreasonable goals.

3-2 U.S. Sentencing Commission Guidelines for Organizations

A male supervisor is sexually harassing female coworkers. A sales representative offers a $10,000 kickback to persuade an indecisive customer to do business with his company. A company president secretly meets with the CEO of her biggest competitor, and they agree not to compete in markets where the other has already established customers. Each of these behaviors is clearly unethical (and in these cases also illegal).

After reading this section, you should be able to:

3-2 describe the U.S. Sentencing Commission Guidelines for Organizations, and explain how they both encourage ethical behavior and punish unethical behavior by businesses.

Historically, if management was unaware of such activities, the company could not be held responsible for them. Since 1991, however, when the U.S. Sentencing Commission Guidelines for Organizations were established, companies can be prosecuted and punished *even if management didn't know about the unethical behavior.* Penalties can be substantial, with maximum fines approaching a whopping $300 million.[10] An amendment made in 2004 outlines much stricter ethics-training requirements and emphasizes creating a legal and ethical company culture.[11]

Let's examine **3-2a to whom the guidelines apply and what they cover** and **3-2b how, according to the guidelines, an organization can be punished for the unethical behavior of its managers and employees.**

3-2a Who, What, and Why?

Nearly all businesses are covered by the U.S. Sentencing Commission's guidelines. This includes nonprofits, partnerships, labor unions, unincorporated organizations and associations, incorporated organizations, and even pension funds, trusts, and joint stock companies. If your organization can be characterized as a business (remember, nonprofits count, too), then it is subject to the guidelines.[12]

The guidelines cover offenses defined by federal laws such as invasion of privacy, price fixing, fraud, customs violations, antitrust violations, civil rights violations, theft, money laundering, conflicts of interest, embezzlement, dealing in stolen goods, copyright infringements, extortion, and more. But it's not enough merely to stay within the law. The purpose of the guidelines is not just to punish companies *after* they or their employees break the law, but rather to encourage companies to take proactive steps that will discourage or prevent white-collar crime *before* it happens. The guidelines also give companies an incentive to cooperate with and disclose illegal activities to federal authorities.[13]

3-2b Determining the Punishment

The guidelines impose smaller fines on companies that take proactive steps to encourage ethical behavior or voluntarily disclose illegal activities to federal authorities. Essentially, the law uses a carrot-and-stick approach. The stick is the threat of heavy fines that can total millions of dollars. The carrot is a greatly reduced fine, but only if the company has started an effective compliance program (discussed below) to encourage ethical behavior *before* the illegal activity occurs.[14] The method used to determine a company's punishment illustrates the importance of establishing a compliance program, as illustrated in Exhibit 3.1.

The first step is to compute the *base fine* by determining what *level of offense* has occurred. The level of the offense (i.e., its seriousness) varies depending on the kind of crime, the loss incurred by the victims, and how much planning went into the crime. For example, simple fraud is a level 6 offense (there are 38 levels in all). But if the victims of that fraud lost more than $5 million, that level 6 offense becomes a level 22 offense. Moreover, anything beyond minimal planning to commit the fraud results in an increase of two levels to a level 24 offense. How much difference would this make to a company? As Exhibit 3.1 shows, crimes at or below level 6 incur a base fine of $5,000, whereas the base fine for level 24 is $2.1 million, a difference of $2.095 million! The base fine for level 38, the top-level offense, is a hefty $72.5 million.

After assessing a *base fine*, the judge computes a culpability score, which is a way of assigning blame to the company. The culpability score can range from 0.05 to 4.0. The greater the corporate responsibility in conducting, encouraging, or sanctioning illegal or unethical activity, the higher the culpability score. A company that already has a compliance program and voluntarily reports the offense to authorities will incur a culpability score of 0.05. By contrast, a company whose management secretly plans, approves, and participates in illegal or unethical activity will receive the maximum score of 4.0.

The culpability score is critical, because the total fine is computed by multiplying the base fine by the culpability score. Going back to our level 24 fraud offense, the left point of the blue arrow in Exhibit 3.1 shows that a company with a compliance program that turns itself in will be fined only $105,000 ($2,100,000 × 0.05). In contrast, a company that secretly planned, approved, and participated in illegal activity will be fined $8.4 million ($2,100,000 × 4.0), as shown by the right point of the blue arrow. The difference is even greater for level 38 offenses.

Exhibit 3.1

Offense Levels, Base Fines, Culpability Scores, and Possible Total Fines under the U.S. Sentencing Commission Guidelines for Organizations

Offense Level	Base Fine	Culpability Score					
		0.05	0.5	1.0	2.0	3.0	4.0
6 or less	$ 5,000	$ 250	$ 2,500	$ 5,000	$ 10,000	$ 15,000	$ 20,000
7	7,500	375	3,750	7,500	15,000	22,500	30,000
8	10,000	500	5,000	10,000	20,000	30,000	40,000
9	15,000	750	7,500	15,000	30,000	45,000	60,000
10	20,000	1,000	10,000	20,000	40,000	60,000	80,000
11	30,000	1,500	15,000	30,000	60,000	90,000	120,000
12	40,000	2,000	20,000	40,000	80,000	120,000	160,000
13	60,000	3,000	30,000	60,000	120,000	180,000	240,000
14	85,000	4,250	42,500	85,000	170,000	255,000	340,000
15	125,000	6,250	62,500	125,000	250,000	375,000	500,000
16	175,000	8,750	87,500	175,000	350,000	525,000	700,000
17	250,000	12,500	125,000	250,000	500,000	750,000	1,000,000
18	350,000	17,500	175,000	350,000	700,000	1,050,000	1,400,000
19	500,000	25,000	250,000	500,000	1,000,000	1,500,000	2,000,000
20	650,000	32,500	325,000	650,000	1,300,000	1,950,000	2,600,000
21	910,000	45,500	455,000	910,000	1,820,000	2,730,000	3,640,000
22	1,200,000	60,000	600,000	1,200,000	2,400,000	3,600,000	4,800,000
23	1,600,000	80,000	800,000	1,600,000	3,200,000	4,800,000	6,400,000
24	2,100,000	105,000	1,050,000	2,100,000	4,200,000	6,300,000	8,400,000
25	2,800,000	140,000	1,400,000	2,800,000	5,600,000	8,400,000	11,200,000
26	3,700,000	185,000	1,850,000	3,700,000	7,400,000	11,100,000	14,800,000
27	4,800,000	240,000	2,400,000	4,800,000	9,600,000	14,400,000	19,200,000
28	6,300,000	315,000	3,150,000	6,300,000	12,600,000	18,900,000	25,200,000
29	8,100,000	405,000	4,050,000	8,100,000	16,200,000	24,300,000	32,400,000
30	10,500,000	525,000	5,250,000	10,500,000	21,000,000	31,500,000	42,000,000
31	13,500,000	675,000	6,750,000	13,500,000	27,000,000	40,500,000	54,000,000
32	17,500,000	875,000	8,750,000	17,500,000	35,000,000	52,500,000	70,000,000
34	28,500,000	1,425,000	14,250,000	28,500,000	57,000,000	85,500,000	114,000,000
35	36,000,000	1,800,000	18,000,000	36,000,000	72,000,000	108,000,000	144,000,000
36	45,500,000	2,275,000	22,750,000	45,500,000	91,000,000	136,500,000	182,000,000
37	57,500,000	2,875,000	28,750,000	57,500,000	115,000,000	172,500,000	230,000,000
38 or more	72,500,000	3,625,000	36,250,000	72,500,000	145,000,000	217,500,000	290,000,000

Source: "Chapter Eight—Part C—Fines," 2004 Federal Sentencing Guidelines, available at www.ussc.gov/guidelines/2010_guidelines/index.cfm.

As shown by the left point of the orange arrow, a company with a compliance program and a 0.05 culpability score is fined only $3.625 million, whereas a company with the maximum 4.0 culpability score is fined a whopping $290 million, as indicated by the right point of the orange arrow. These differences clearly show the importance of having a compliance program in place. Over the last decade, 1,494 companies have been charged under the U.S. Sentencing Guidelines. Seventy-six percent of those charged were fined, with the average fine exceeding

Exhibit 3.2

Compliance Program Steps for the U.S. Sentencing Guidelines for Organizations

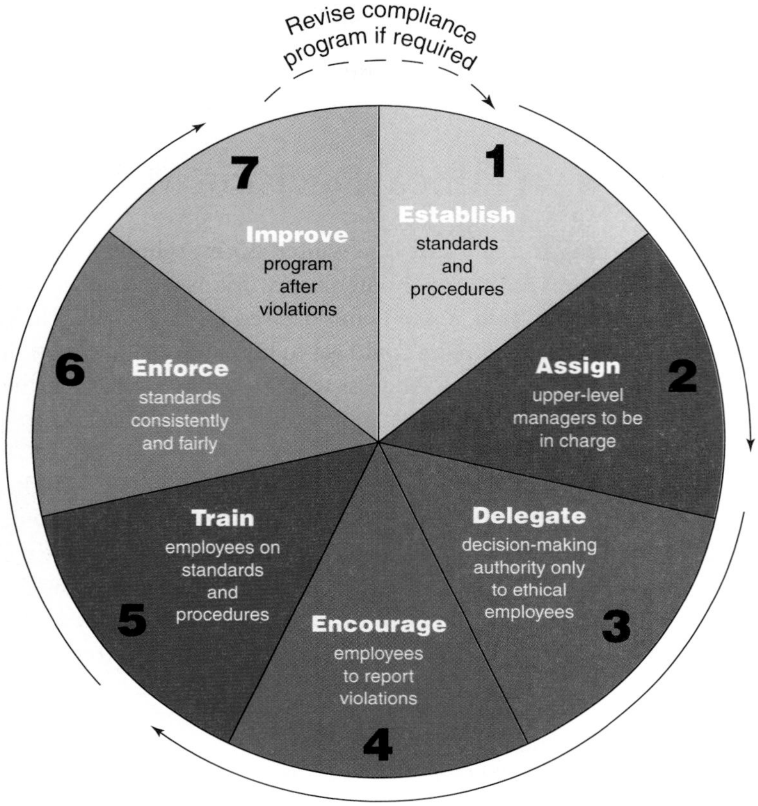

Source: D. R. Dalton, M. B. Metzger, and J. W. Hill, "The 'New' U.S. Sentencing Commission Guidelines: A Wake-up Call for Corporate America," Academy of Management Executive 8 (1994):7–16.

$2 million. Company fines are on average 20 times larger now than before the implementation of the guidelines in 1991.[15]

Fortunately, for companies that want to avoid paying these stiff fines, the U.S. Sentencing Guidelines clearly spell out the seven necessary components of an effective compliance program.[16] Exhibit 3.2 lists those components. For more information, see An Overview of the Organizational Sentencing Guidelines at www.ussc.gov/Guidelines/Organizational_Guidelines/ORGOVER-VIEW.pdf and Sentencing Guidelines Educational Materials at www.ussc.gov/Education_and_Training/Guidelines_Educational_Materials/index.cfm.

REVIEW 3-2

U.S. Sentencing Commission Guidelines for Organizations

Under the U.S. Sentencing Commission Guidelines, companies can be prosecuted and fined up to $300 million for employees' illegal actions. Fines are computed by multiplying the base fine by a culpability score, which ranges from 0.05 to 4.0. Companies that establish compliance programs to encourage ethical behavior can reduce their culpability scores and their fines. Companies without compliance programs can face much heavier fines than companies with established programs. Compliance programs must establish standards and procedures, be run by top managers, encourage hiring and promotion of honest and ethical people, encourage employees to report violations, educate employees about compliance, punish violators, and find ways to improve the program after violations occur.

3-3 Influences on Ethical Decision Making

On a cold morning in the midst of a winter storm, schools were closed and most people had decided to stay home from work. Nevertheless, Richard Addessi had already showered, shaved, and dressed to go to work. He kissed his wife Joan goodbye, but before he could get to his car, he fell dead on the garage floor of a sudden heart attack. Addessi was four months short of his 30-year anniversary with the company. Having begun work at *IBM* at the age of 18, he was just 48 years old.[17]

You're the vice president in charge of benefits at IBM. Given that he was only four months short of full retirement, do you award full retirement benefits to Richard Addessi's wife and daughters? If the answer is "yes," they will receive his full retirement benefits of $1,800 a month and free lifetime medical coverage. If you say no, his widow and two daughters will receive only $340 a month. They will also have to pay $473 a month to continue their current medical coverage. As the VP in charge of benefits at IBM, what would be the ethical thing for you to do?

After reading this section, you should be able to:

3-3 describe what influences ethical decision making.

Although some ethical issues are easily solved, many do not have clearly right or wrong answers. So, what did IBM decide to do? Because Richard Addessi had not completed 30 full years with the company, IBM officials felt they had no choice but to give Joan Addessi and her two daughters the smaller, partial retirement benefits. Do you think IBM's decision was ethical? Probably many of you don't. You may wonder how the company could be so heartless as to deny Richard Addessi's family the full benefits to which you believe they were entitled. Yet others might argue that IBM did the ethical thing by strictly following the rules laid out in its pension benefit plan. After all, being fair means applying the same rules to everyone. Although the answers are rarely clear, managers do need to have a clear sense of how to arrive at an answer in order to manage this ethical ambiguity.

The ethical answers that managers choose depend on **3-3a the ethical intensity of the decision** and **3-3b the moral development of the manager.**

3-3a Ethical Intensity of the Decision

Managers don't treat all ethical decisions the same. The manager who has to decide whether to deny or extend full benefits to Joan Addessi and her family is going to treat that decision much more seriously than the decision of how to deal with an assistant who has been taking paper home for personal use. These decisions differ in their **ethical intensity**, or the degree of concern people have about an ethical issue. When addressing an issue of high ethical intensity, managers are more aware of the impact their decision will have on others. They are more likely to view the decision as an ethical or moral decision rather than as an economic decision. They are also more likely to worry about doing the right thing.

Six factors must be taken into account when determining the ethical intensity of an action. These include

- Magnitude of consequences
- Social consensus
- Probability of effect
- Temporal immediacy
- Proximity of effect
- Concentration of effect.[18]

Magnitude of consequences is the total harm or benefit derived from an ethical decision. The more people who are harmed or the greater the harm to those people, the larger the consequences. **Social consensus** is agreement on whether behavior is bad or good. **Probability of effect** is the chance that something will happen and then result in harm to others. If we combine these factors, we can see the effect they can have on ethical intensity. For example, if there is *clear agreement* (social consensus) that a managerial decision or action is *certain* (probability of effect) to have *large negative consequences* (magnitude of consequences) in some way, then people will be highly concerned about that managerial decision or action, and ethical intensity will be high.

Temporal immediacy is the time between an act and the consequences the act produces. Temporal immediacy is stronger if a manager has to lay off workers next week as opposed to three months from now. **Proximity of effect** is the social, psychological, cultural, or physical distance of a decision maker from those affected by his or her decisions. Thus, proximity of effect is greater when a manager lays off employees he knows than when he lays off employees that he doesn't know. Finally, whereas the magnitude of consequences is the total effect across all people, **concentration of effect** is how much an act affects the average person. Temporarily laying off 100 employees for 10 months without pay is a greater concentration of effect than temporarily laying off 1,000 employees for one month.

Which of these six factors has the greatest impact on ethical intensity? Studies indicate that managers are much more likely to view decisions as ethical issues when the magnitude of consequences (total harm) is high and there is a social consensus (agreement) that a behavior or action is bad.[19] Many people will likely feel IBM was wrong to deny full benefits to Joan Addessi. Why? IBM's decision met five of the six characteristics of ethical intensity. The difference in benefits, more than $23,000 per year, was likely to have serious and immediate consequences for the family, especially in terms of their monthly benefits ($1,800 and free medical coverage if full benefits were awarded versus $340 a month and medical care that costs $473 per month if they weren't). We can closely identify with Joan Addessi and her daughters as opposed to IBM's

ethical intensity
the degree of concern people have about an ethical issue

magnitude of consequences
the total harm or benefit derived from an ethical decision

social consensus
agreement on whether behavior is bad or good

probability of effect
the chance that something will happen and then harm others

temporal immediacy
the time between an act and the consequences the act produces

proximity of effect
the social, psychological, cultural, or physical distance between a decision maker and those affected by his or her decisions

concentration of effect
the total harm or benefit that an act produces on the average person

faceless, nameless corporate identity. The exception, as we will discuss below, is social consensus. Not everyone will agree that IBM's decision was unethical. The judgment also depends on our level of moral development and which ethical principles we use to decide.

3-3b Moral Development

A friend of yours has given you the latest version of Microsoft Office. She forwarded you the download link she received when she bought it and told you to download it yourself before it expires in a couple of days. You're tempted. The Office package costs about $100, which you don't have. Besides, all of your friends have the same version of Microsoft Office, and they didn't pay for it either. Downloading the software to your hard drive without buying your own copy clearly violates copyright laws. But no one would find out. Even if someone does, Microsoft probably isn't going to come after you. Microsoft goes after the big fish—companies that illegally copy and distribute software to their workers and pirates that illegally sell cheap, unauthorized copies.[20] Your computer has booted up, your email is open, and your cursor is hovering over the link in your friend's message. What are you going to do?

In part, according to psychologist Lawrence Kohlberg, your decision will be based on your level of moral development. Kohlberg identified three phases of moral development, with two stages in each phase (see Exhibit 3.3).[21] At the **preconventional level of moral development**, people decide based on selfish reasons. For example, if you are in Stage 1, the punishment and obedience stage, your primary concern will be to avoid trouble for yourself. So you won't copy the software because you are afraid of being caught and punished. Yet, in Stage 2, the instrumental exchange stage, you worry less about punishment and more about doing things that directly advance your wants and needs. So you copy the software.

People at the **conventional level of moral development** make decisions that conform to societal expectations. In other words, they look outside themselves to others for guidance on ethical issues. In Stage 3, the "good boy, nice girl" stage, you normally do what the other "good boys" and "nice girls" are doing. If everyone else is illegally copying software, you will too. But if they aren't, you won't either. In the law and order stage, Stage 4, you again look for external guidance and do whatever the law permits, so you won't copy the software.

People at the **postconventional level of moral development** use internalized ethical principles to solve ethical dilemmas. In Stage 5, the social contract stage, you will refuse to copy the software because, as a whole, society is better off when the rights of others—in this case, the rights of software authors and manufacturers—are not violated. In Stage 6, the universal principle stage, you might or might not copy the software, depending on your principles of right and wrong. Moreover, you will stick to your principles even if your decision conflicts with the law (Stage 4) or what others believe is best for society (Stage 5). For example, those with socialist or communist beliefs would probably choose to copy the software because they believe goods and services should be owned by society rather than by individuals and corporations. (For information about the dos, don'ts, and legal issues concerning software piracy, see the Software & Information Industry Association's website at www.siia.net/piracy/default.asp.)

preconventional level of moral development the first level of moral development in which people make decisions based on selfish reasons

conventional level of moral development the second level of moral development in which people make decisions that conform to societal expectations

postconventional level of moral development the third level of moral development in which people make decisions based on internalized principles

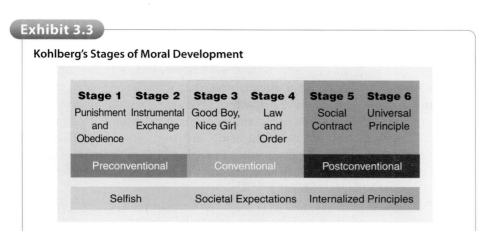

Exhibit 3.3

Kohlberg's Stages of Moral Development

Stage 1	Stage 2	Stage 3	Stage 4	Stage 5	Stage 6
Punishment and Obedience	Instrumental Exchange	Good Boy, Nice Girl	Law and Order	Social Contract	Universal Principle
Preconventional		Conventional		Postconventional	
Selfish		Societal Expectations		Internalized Principles	

Source: W. Davidson III and D. Worrell, "Influencing Managers to Change Unpopular Corporate Behavior through Boycotts and Divestitures," Business & Society 34 (1995): 171–196.

Kohlberg believed that people would progress sequentially from earlier stages to later stages as they became more educated and mature. But only 20 percent of adults ever reach the postconventional stage of moral development, where internal principles guide their decisions. Most adults are in the conventional stage of moral development in which they look outside themselves to others for guidance on ethical issues. This means that most people in the workplace look to and need leadership when it comes to ethical decision making.[22]

REVIEW 3-3

Influences on Ethical Decision Making

Two factors influence ethical decisions: the ethical intensity of the decision and the moral development of the decision maker. Ethical intensity is strong when decisions have large, certain, immediate consequences and when we are physically or psychologically close to those affected by the decision. There are three levels of moral maturity, each with two stages. At the preconventional level, decisions are made for selfish reasons. At the conventional level, decisions conform to societal expectations. At the postconventional level, internalized principles are used to make ethical decisions.

3-4 Practical Steps to Ethical Decision Making

Like the types of decision making we'll explore in Chapter 4, ethical decision making involves a series of steps, and by following them managers can improve the quality of their decisions.

After reading this section, you should be able to:

3-4 explain what practical steps managers can take to improve ethical decision making.

Managers can encourage more ethical decision making in their organizations by **3-4a carefully selecting and hiring ethical employees, 3-4b establishing a specific code of ethics, 3-4c training employees to make ethical decisions,** and **3-4d creating an ethical climate.**

3-4a Selecting and Hiring Ethical Employees

As an employer, you can increase your chances of hiring an honest person if you give job applicants integrity tests. **Overt integrity tests** estimate job applicants' honesty by asking them directly what they think or feel about theft or about punishment of unethical behaviors.[23] For example, an employer might ask an applicant, "Would you ever consider buying something from somebody if you knew the person had stolen the item?" or "Don't most people steal from their companies?" Surprisingly, unethical people will usually answer "yes" to such questions, because they believe that the world is basically dishonest and that dishonest behavior is normal.[24]

Personality-based integrity tests indirectly estimate job applicants' honesty by measuring psychological traits such as dependability and conscientiousness. For example, prison inmates serving time for white-collar crimes (counterfeiting, embezzlement, and fraud) scored much lower than a comparison group of middle-level managers on scales measuring reliability, dependability, honesty, conscientiousness, and abiding by rules.[25] These results show that companies can selectively hire and promote people who will be more ethical.[26] For more on integrity testing, see the What Really Works feature in this chapter.

3-4b Codes of Ethics

Today, almost all large corporations have an ethics code in place. Two things must happen if those codes are to encourage ethical decision making and behavior.[27] First, a company must communicate its code to others both inside and outside the company. Second, in addition to having an ethics code with general guidelines like "do unto others as you would have others do unto you," management must also develop practical ethical standards and procedures specific to the company's line of business. For example, visitors to Nortel's website can download a comprehensive document, the "Code of Business Conduct," that establishes specific ethical standards on topics ranging from bribes and kickbacks to expense vouchers and illegal copying of software.

3-4c Ethics Training

In addition to establishing ethical standards for the company, managers must sponsor and be involved in ethics and compliance training in order to create an ethical company culture.[28] The first objective of ethics training is to develop employees' awareness of ethics.[29] This means helping employees recognize which issues are ethical issues and then avoid rationalizing unethical behavior by thinking, "This isn't really illegal or immoral" or "No one will ever find out." Several companies have created board games to improve awareness of ethical issues.[30] Other ethics-training tools, like the Kew Gardens Principles, examine how ethical decisions can be made in specific scenarios. The Kew Gardens Principles were based on the study of a murder in Kew Gardens, New York, in which witnesses to the attack failed to intervene or seek help. Researchers developed a series of four decision-making factors that are used to help employees determine how they should respond to problems and ethical situations,

overt integrity tests
a written test that estimates job applicants' honesty by directly asking them what they think or feel about theft or about punishment of unethical behaviors

personality-based integrity tests
a written test that indirectly estimates job applicants' honesty by measuring psychological traits, such as dependability and conscientiousness

even when the problems were not of their own doing. These principles are: (1) Need—Greater need, greater responsibility to act; (2) Proximity—How close you are to the problem; (3) Capability—You can intervene only insofar as you are able to; (4) Last Resort—If no one else is able to help, it becomes more important for you to intervene.[31]

The second objective for ethics training programs is to achieve credibility with employees. Not surprisingly, employees can be highly suspicious of management's reasons for offering ethics training. Some companies have hurt the credibility of their ethics programs by having outside instructors and consultants conduct the classes.[32] Employees often complain that outside instructors and consultants are teaching theory that has nothing to do with their jobs and the practical dilemmas they actually face on a daily basis.

Ethics training becomes even more credible when top managers teach the initial ethics classes to their subordinates who in turn teach their subordinates.[33] Michael Hoffman, executive director for the Center for Business Ethics at Bentley College, says that having managers teach ethics courses greatly reinforces the seriousness with which employees treat ethics in the workplace.[34]

The third objective of ethics training is to teach employees a practical model of ethical decision making. A basic model should help them think about the consequences their choices will have on others and consider how they will choose among different solutions. Exhibit 3.4 presents a basic model of ethical decision making.

3-4d Ethical Climate

Organizational culture is key to fostering ethical decision making. The 2009 National Business Ethics Survey reported that only 39 percent of employees who work at companies with a strong ethical culture (where core beliefs are

---

Exhibit 3.4

A Basic Model of Ethical Decision Making

1. **Identify the problem.** What makes it an ethical problem? Think in terms of rights, obligations, fairness, relationships, and integrity. How would you define the problem if you stood on the other side of the fence?

2. **Identify the constituents.** Who has been hurt? Who could be hurt? Who could be helped? Are they willing players, or are they victims? Can you negotiate with them?

3. **Diagnose the situation.** How did it happen in the first place? What could have prevented it? Is it going to get worse or better? Can the damage now be undone?

4. **Analyze your options.** Imagine the range of possibilities. Limit yourself to the two or three most manageable. What are the likely outcomes of each? What are the likely costs? Look to the company mission statement or code of ethics for guidance.

5. **Make your choice.** What is your intention in making this decision? How does it compare with the probable results? Can you discuss the problem with the affected parties before you act? Could you disclose without qualm your decision to your boss, the CEO, the board of directors, your family, or society as a whole?

6. **Act.** Do what you have to do. Don't be afraid to admit errors. Be as bold in confronting a problem as you were in causing it.

Source: L. A. Berger, "Train All Employees to Solve Ethical Dilemmas," Best's Review—Life-Health Insurance Edition 95 (1995): 70–80. Used with permission.

widely shared and strongly held) have observed others engaging in unethical behavior, whereas 76 percent of those who work in organizations with weak ethical cultures (where core beliefs are not widely shared or strongly held) have observed others engage in unethical behavior. Employees in strong ethical cultures are also more likely to report violations, because they expect that management wants them reported and won't retaliate against them for doing so.[35]

We learned in Chapter 2 that leadership is an important factor in creating an organizational culture. So, it's no surprise that in study after study, when researchers ask, "What is the most important influence on your ethical behavior at work?" the answer comes back, "My manager." The first step in establishing an ethical climate is for managers, especially top managers, to act ethically themselves.

A second step in establishing an ethical climate is for top management to be active in and committed to the company ethics program.[36] Top managers who consistently talk about the importance of ethics and back up that talk by participating in their companies' ethics programs send the clear message that ethics matter. Business writer Dayton Fandray says, "You can have ethics offices and officers and training programs and reporting systems, but if the CEO doesn't seem to care, it's all just a sham. It's not surprising to find that the companies that really do care about ethics make a point of including senior management in all of their ethics and compliance programs."[37]

A third step is to put in place a reporting system that encourages managers and employees to report potential ethics violations. **Whistleblowing**, that is, reporting others' ethics violations, is a difficult step for most people to take.[38] Potential whistleblowers often fear that they, and not the ethics violators, will be punished.[39] Managers who have been interviewed about whistleblowing have said, "In every organization, someone's been screwed for standing up." "If anything, I figured that by taking a strong stand I might get myself in trouble. People might look at me as a goody two-shoes. Someone might try to force me out."

Today, many federal and state laws protect the rights of whistleblowers (see www.whistleblowers.org for more information). In particular, the Sarbanes-Oxley Act of 2002 makes it a serious crime for publicly owned companies to retaliate in any way against corporate whistleblowers. Managers who punish whistleblowers can be imprisoned for up to 10 years. The Sarbanes-Oxley Act requires all publicly held companies to establish anonymous hot lines to encourage reporting of unethical and illegal behaviors, so it's not surprising that a recent survey found that 91 percent of companies have an anonymous reporting system whereby employees can report observed misconduct.[40]

REVIEW 3-4
....

Practical Steps to Ethical Decision Making

Employers can increase their chances of hiring ethical employees by administering overt integrity tests and personality-based integrity tests to all job applicants. Most large companies now have corporate codes of ethics. To affect ethical decision making, these codes must be known both inside and outside

whistleblowing
reporting others' ethics violations to management or legal authorities

what *really* works

Integrity Tests

Under the 1991 and 2004 U.S. Sentencing Commission Guidelines, unethical employee behavior can lead to multi-million-dollar fines for corporations, and fraudulent behavior of executives can lead to criminal prosecution. Moreover, workplace deviance like stealing, fraud, and vandalism costs companies an estimated $660 billion a year. One way to reduce workplace deviance and the chances of a large fine for unethical employee behavior is to use overt and personality-based integrity tests to screen job applicants.

One hundred eighty-one studies, with a combined total of 576,460 study participants, have examined how well integrity tests can predict job performance and various kinds of workplace deviance. These studies show that not only can integrity tests help companies reduce workplace deviance, but they also provide the added bonus of helping companies hire workers who are better performers in their jobs.

Workplace Deviance (Counterproductive Behaviors)

Compared with job applicants who score poorly, there is an 82 percent chance that job applicants who score well on overt integrity tests will participate in less illegal activity, unethical behavior, drug abuse, or workplace violence.

Personality-based integrity tests also do a good job of predicting who will engage in workplace deviance. Compared with job applicants who score poorly, there is a 68 percent chance that job applicants who score well on personality-based integrity tests will participate in less illegal activity, unethical behavior, excessive absences, drug abuse, or workplace violence.

Job Performance

In addition to reducing unethical behavior and workplace deviance, integrity tests can help companies hire better performers. Compared with employees who score poorly, there is a 69 percent chance that employees who score well on overt integrity tests will be better performers.

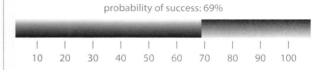

The figures are nearly identical for personality-based integrity tests. Compared with those who score poorly, there is a 70 percent chance that employees who score well on personality-based integrity tests will be better at their jobs.

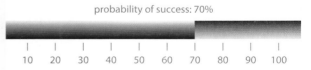

Theft

Although integrity tests can help companies decrease most kinds of workplace deviance and increase employees' job performance, they have a smaller effect on a specific kind of workplace deviance: theft. Compared with employees who score poorly, there is a 57 percent chance that employees who score well on overt integrity tests will be less likely to steal. No theft data were available to assess personality-based integrity tests.

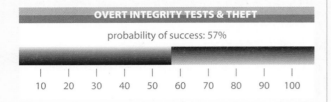

OVERT INTEGRITY TESTS & THEFT

probability of success: 57%

| | | | | | | | | | |
|10|20|30|40|50|60|70|80|90|100|

Faking and Coaching on Integrity Tests

Although overt and personality-based integrity tests do a very good job of helping companies hire people of higher integrity, it is possible to improve scores on these tests through coaching and faking. In coaching, job applicants are taught the underlying rationale of an integrity test or given specific directions for improving their integrity scores. Faking occurs when applicants simply try to "beat the test" or try to fake a good impression. Unfortunately for the companies that use integrity tests, both strategies work.

On average, coaching can improve scores on overt integrity tests by an astounding 1.5 standard deviations and on personality-based integrity tests by a meaningful 0.36 standard deviation. This would be the equivalent of increasing your total SAT score by 150 and 36 points, respectively (the SAT has a mean of 500 and a standard deviation of 100). Likewise, on average, faking can improve scores on overt integrity tests by an impressive 1.02 standard deviations and on personality-based integrity tests by a meaningful 0.59 standard deviation. Again, this would be the equivalent of increasing your SAT score by 102 and 59 points, respectively.

Companies that want to avoid coaching and faking effects must maintain tight security over integrity tests so that applicants have little information regarding them, periodically check the validity of the tests to make sure they're accurately predicting workplace deviance and job performance, or periodically switch tests if they suspect that test security has been compromised.[41]

the organization. In addition to offering general rules, ethics codes must provide specific, practical advice. Ethics training seeks to increase employees' awareness of ethical issues, make ethics a serious and credible factor in organizational decisions, and teach employees a practical model of ethical decision making. The most important factors in creating an ethical business climate are the personal examples set by company managers, involvement of management in the company ethics program, a reporting system that encourages whistleblowers to report potential ethics violations, and fair but consistent punishment of violators.

3-5 To Whom Are Organizations Socially Responsible?

Social responsibility is a business's obligation to pursue policies, make decisions, and take actions that benefit society.[42] Unfortunately, because there are strong disagreements over to whom and for what in society organizations are responsible, it can be difficult for managers to know what is or will be perceived as socially responsible corporate behavior. In a recent McKinsey & Co. study of 1,144 top global executives, 79 percent predicted that at least some responsibility for dealing with future social and political issues would fall on corporations, but only 3 percent said they themselves do a good job of dealing with these issues.[43] So what should managers and corporations do to be socially responsible?

Some say that corporations need to give more to nonprofit organizations. In fact, despite the economic slowdown, annual corporate giving to charities

social responsibility
a business's obligation to pursue policies, make decisions, and take actions that benefit society

has increased to $14.1 billion in cash and in-kind gifts.[44] Checkbook philanthropy, however, isn't enough these days, says Susan Puflea, senior vice president and director of GolinHarris Change.[45] Companies, she says, also need to be socially responsible as they conduct their businesses. Wells Fargo, Bank of America, Morgan Stanley, and Citibank announced they will stop financing companies that search for coal by blasting off mountain tops (and depositing the remains in the rivers and valleys below). HSBC, a London-based bank, announced that it will no longer finance palm oil production, which is blamed for massive deforestation in developing countries.[46]

But those companies weren't socially responsible just out of the goodness of their hearts; they changed their lending policies because of the risk to their business reputations. These examples illustrate the challenges and different motivations of acting in a socially responsible manner: balancing the needs of different groups in the face of limited resources and/or constraints.

Doing the Right Thing

Greenwashing

Many companies brag about how they care about the environment, but most consumers don't believe that companies are committed to being green. According to a Harris Interactive poll, just 16 percent of consumers believe that most companies are committed to improving the environment by practicing sustainable business or offering environmentally responsible products. Forty-eight percent of consumers believe that "some" companies are committed to that goal, whereas 24 percent believe that only a few companies are so committed. So what can managers do? Ron Loch, vice president for greentech and sustainability at Gibbs & Soell, says, "As long as companies are transparent in their communications and don't overstate the social and environmental impact of their efforts, they can avoid being painted with the greenwash brush. It gets back to the need of really taking inventory of what is happening throughout the organization and then weaving that into a compelling, credible, and defensible narrative." So do the right thing—don't talk about "being green" just to get consumers' attention. Make sure that the message you send out to consumers reflects the social responsibility commitments that your company has made.[47]

After reading this section, you should be able to:

3-5 explain to whom organizations are socially responsible.

There are two perspectives regarding to whom organizations are socially responsible: the shareholder model and the stakeholder model. According to the late Nobel Prize–winning economist Milton Friedman, the only social responsibility that organizations have is to satisfy their owners, that is, company shareholders. This view—called the **shareholder model**—holds that the only social responsibility that businesses have is to maximize profits. By maximizing profit, the firm maximizes shareholder wealth and satisfaction. More specifically, as profits rise, the company stock owned by shareholders generally increases in value.

Friedman argued that it is socially irresponsible for companies to divert time, money, and attention from maximizing profits to social causes and charitable organizations. The first problem, he believed, is that organizations cannot act effectively as moral agents for all company shareholders. Although shareholders are likely to agree on investment issues concerning a company, it's highly unlikely that they have common views on what social causes a company should or should not support. For instance, most *Fortune* 500 companies have corporate foundations that support nonprofit organizations. But even corporate leaders support a variety of causes. One could easily ask why Walmart

shareholder model
a view of social responsibility that holds that an organization's overriding goal should be profit maximization for the benefit of shareholders

doesn't support music instruction (as Honda does), or why Honda doesn't support domestic violence prevention (as Verizon Wireless does).[48] Which is why Friedman argued that companies should maximize profits for shareholders. Shareholders can then use their time and increased wealth to contribute to the social causes, charities, or institutions they want, rather than those that companies want.

The second major problem, Friedman said, is that the time, money, and attention diverted to social causes undermine market efficiency.[49] In competitive markets, companies compete for raw materials, talented workers, customers, and investment funds. A company that spends money on social causes will have less money to purchase quality materials or to hire talented workers who can produce a valuable product at a good price. If customers find the company's product less desirable, its sales and profits will fall. If profits fall, the company's stock price will decline, and the company will have difficulty attracting investment funds that could be used to fund long-term growth. In the end, Friedman argues, diverting the firm's money, time, and resources to social causes hurts customers, suppliers, employees, and shareholders.

By contrast, under the **stakeholder model**, management's most important responsibility is the firm's long-term survival (not just maximizing profits), which is achieved by satisfying the interests of multiple corporate stakeholders (not just shareholders).[50] PepsiCo CEO Indra Nooyi says that a company operating under the stakeholder model has to redefine profit; "[we] have to make sure our new P&L (profit & loss statement) actually says revenue, less costs of goods sold, less costs to society—and that's your real profit."[51] **Stakeholders** are persons or groups with a legitimate interest in a company.[52] Because stakeholders are interested in and affected by the organization's actions, they have a "stake" in what those actions are. Consequently, stakeholder groups may try to influence the firm to act in their own interests. Exhibit 3.5 shows the various stakeholder groups that the organization must satisfy to assure its long-term survival.

Being responsible to multiple stakeholders raises two basic questions. First, how does a company identify organizational stakeholders? Second, how does a company balance the needs of different stakeholders? Distinguishing between primary and secondary stakeholders can help answer these questions.[53]

Some stakeholders are more important to the firm's survival than others. **Primary stakeholders** are groups on which the organization depends for its long-term survival; they include shareholders, employees, customers, suppliers, governments, and local communities. When managers are struggling to balance the needs of different stakeholders, the stakeholder model suggests that the needs of primary stakeholders take precedence over the needs of secondary stakeholders. But among primary stakeholders, are some more important than others? According to the life-cycle theory of organizations, the answer is "yes." In practice, though, CEOs typically give somewhat higher priority to shareholders, employees, and customers than to suppliers, governments, and local communities, no matter what stage of the life cycle a company is in.[54]

Addressing the concerns of primary stakeholders is important because, if a stakeholder group becomes dissatisfied and terminates its relationship with

stakeholder model
a theory of corporate responsibility that holds that management's most important responsibility, long-term survival, is achieved by satisfying the interests of multiple corporate stakeholders

stakeholders
persons or groups with a "stake" or legitimate interest in a company's actions

primary stakeholders
any group on which an organization relies for its long-term survival

Exhibit 3.5

Stakeholder Model of Corporate Social Responsibility

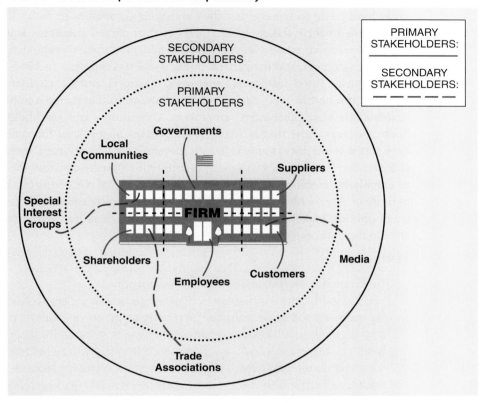

Source: Source: "The Stakeholder Theory of the Corporation: Concepts, Evidence and Implications" (Figure), T. Donaldson & L. E. Preston, Academy of Management Review, 1995, vol. 20. Reproduced by permission of Academy of Management (NY) in the formats Textbook and Other Book via Copyright Clearance Center.

the company, the company could be seriously harmed or go out of business. By creating an environmental index that describes the total environmental impact of a product—from creation to shipping to recycling—WALMART is addressing the environmental concerns of several primary stakeholders. Walmart not only expects the index to affect which products its customers buy; it is already telling its suppliers that products with higher environmental scores will receive preferential shelf space in its stores, which could dramatically affect product sales.[55]

Secondary stakeholders, such as the media and special interest groups, can influence or be influenced by the company. Unlike the primary stakeholders, however, they do not engage in regular transactions with the company and are not critical to its long-term survival. Meeting the needs of primary stakeholders is therefore usually more important than meeting the needs of secondary stakeholders. Nevertheless, secondary stakeholders are still important because they can affect public perceptions and opinions about socially responsible behavior.

secondary stakeholders
any group that can influence or be influenced by a company and can affect public perceptions about the company's socially responsible behavior

So, to whom are organizations socially responsible? Many commentators, especially economists and financial analysts, continue to argue that organizations are responsible only to shareholders. Increasingly, however, top managers have come to believe that they and their companies must be socially responsible to their stakeholders. This view has gained adherents since the Great Depression, when General Electric first identified shareholders, employees, customers, and the general public as its stakeholders. In 1947, Johnson & Johnson listed customers, employees, managers, and shareholders as its stakeholders; and in 1950, Sears Roebuck announced that its most important stakeholders were "customers, employees, community, and stockholders."[56] Today, surveys show that as many as 80 percent of top-level managers believe that it is unethical to focus just on shareholders. Twenty-nine states have changed their laws to allow company boards of directors to consider the needs of employees, creditors, suppliers, customers, and local communities, as well as those of shareholders.[57] Although there is not complete agreement, a majority of opinion makers would argue that companies must be socially responsible to their stakeholders.

REVIEW 3-5

To Whom Are Organizations Socially Responsible?

Social responsibility is a business's obligation to benefit society. To whom are organizations socially responsible? According to the shareholder model, the only social responsibility that organizations have is to maximize shareholder wealth by maximizing company profits. According to the stakeholder model, companies must satisfy the needs and interests of multiple corporate stakeholders, not just shareholders. However, the needs of primary stakeholders, on which the organization relies for its existence, take precedence over those of secondary stakeholders.

3-6 For What Are Organizations Socially Responsible?

If organizations are to be socially responsible to stakeholders, what are they to be socially responsible *for*? As Exhibit 3.6 illustrates, companies can best benefit their stakeholders by fulfilling their economic, legal, ethical, and discretionary responsibilities.[58] Economic and legal responsibilities are at the bottom of the pyramid, because they play a larger part in a company's social responsibility than do ethical and discretionary responsibilities. However, the relative importance of these various responsibilities depends on society's expectations of corporate social responsibility at a particular point in time.[59] A century ago, society expected businesses to meet their economic and legal responsibilities and little else. Today, when society judges whether businesses are socially responsible, ethical and discretionary responsibilities are considerably more important than they used to be.

After reading this section, you should be able to:

3-6 explain for what organizations are socially responsible.

Exhibit 3.6

Social Responsibilities

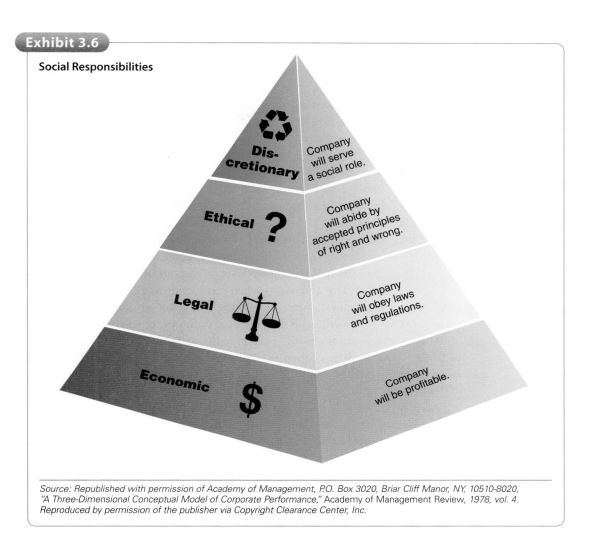

Source: Republished with permission of Academy of Management, P.O. Box 3020, Briar Cliff Manor, NY, 10510-8020, "A Three-Dimensional Conceptual Model of Corporate Performance," Academy of Management Review, 1978, vol. 4. Reproduced by permission of the publisher via Copyright Clearance Center, Inc.

Historically, **economic responsibility**, or making a profit by producing a product or service valued by society, has been a business's most basic social responsibility. Organizations that don't meet their financial and economic expectations come under tremendous pressure. For example, company boards are quick these days to fire CEOs. Owen Van Natta, CEO of *MySpace*, was fired after just eight months on the job. When he started, MySpace had 64 percent of social networking traffic compared to 29 percent for Facebook. When he was fired, Facebook had 68 percent and MySpace had 28 percent.[60] On an annual basis, roughly 4 percent of the CEOs of large companies are fired.[61] Nearly one-third of all CEOs are eventually fired because of their inability to successfully change their companies.[62]

Legal responsibility is a company's social responsibility to obey society's laws and regulations as it tries to meet its economic responsibilities. For instance, companies award stock options so that managers and employees are rewarded when the company does well. Stock options give the right to purchase shares of stock at a set price. Let's say that on June 1, the company awards you

economic responsibility
a company's social responsibility to make a profit by producing a valued product or service

legal responsibility
a company's social responsibility to obey society's laws and regulations

the right (or option) to buy 100 shares of stock that, on that day, sell for $10 a share. If the stock price falls below $10, the options are worthless. But, if the stock price rises above $10, the options have value. Specifically, if the stock price rises to $15 a share, you can exercise your options by paying the company $1,000 (100 shares at $10 a share). But because the stock is selling for $15, you can sell your 100 shares for $1,500 and make $500. But what if you could go back in time to, say, January 1, when the stock was selling for $5? You'd make $1,000 instead of $500. It would be unethical and illegal, however, to "backdate" your options to when the stock sold for a lower price. Doing so would illegally increase the value of your options. But that's exactly what the president and chief operating officer did at Monster Worldwide (which runs Monster.com). By improperly backdating his options, he earned an additional $24 million.[63] At Monster, however, backdating was condoned by the CEO, who routinely backdated options for members of the management team.[64]

Ethical responsibility is a company's social responsibility not to violate accepted principles of right and wrong when conducting its business. Because different stakeholders may disagree about what is or is not ethical, meeting ethical responsibilities is more difficult than meeting economic or legal responsibilities.

Discretionary responsibilities pertain to the social roles that businesses play in society beyond their economic, legal, and ethical responsibilities. After a massive earthquake in Haiti killed 220,000 people and destroyed the homes of 1.9 million more, companies came to aid by partnering with and supporting humanitarian agencies. DIGICEL, the largest mobile telecom company in the Caribbean, used its mobile network to instantly transfer funds to 2 million Haitians whose local banks had been destroyed in the quake. GOOGLE created a specially made missing persons database that helped families and the authorities learn what had happened to their loved ones.[65] Discretionary responsibilities such as these are voluntary. Companies are not considered unethical if they don't perform them. Today, however, corporate stakeholders expect companies to do much more than in the past to meet their discretionary responsibilities.

REVIEW 3-6

For What Are Organizations Socially Responsible?

Companies can best benefit their stakeholders by fulfilling their economic, legal, ethical, and discretionary responsibilities. Being profitable, or meeting one's economic responsibility, is a business's most basic social responsibility. Legal responsibility consists of following a society's laws and regulations. Ethical responsibility means not violating accepted principles of right and wrong when doing business. Discretionary responsibilities are social responsibilities beyond basic economic, legal, and ethical responsibilities.

3-7 Responses to Demands for Social Responsibility

Social responsiveness refers to a company's strategy to respond to stakeholders' economic, legal, ethical, or discretionary expectations concerning social responsibility. A social responsibility problem exists whenever company actions do not

---

ethical responsibility
a company's social responsibility not to violate accepted principles of right and wrong when conducting its business

discretionary responsibilities
the social roles that a company fulfills beyond its economic, legal, and ethical responsibilities

social responsiveness
refers to a company's strategy to respond to stakeholders' economic, legal, ethical, or discretionary expectations concerning social responsibility

Exhibit 3.7

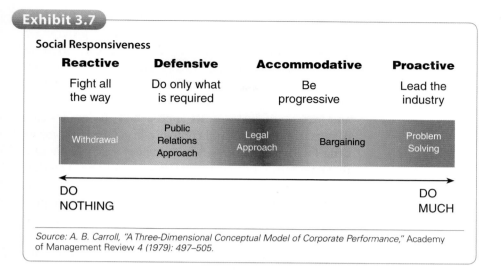

Source: A. B. Carroll, "A Three-Dimensional Conceptual Model of Corporate Performance," Academy of Management Review 4 (1979): 497–505.

meet stakeholder expectations. One model of social responsiveness, shown in Exhibit 3.7, identifies four strategies for responding to social responsibility problems: reactive, defensive, accommodative, and proactive. These strategies differ in the extent to which the company is willing to act to meet or exceed society's expectations.

After reading this section, you should be able to:

3-7 explain how organizations can choose to respond to societal demands for social responsibility.

A company using a **reactive strategy** will do less than society expects. It may deny responsibility for a problem or fight any suggestions that the company should solve a problem. Shortly after APPLE introduced the iPhone 4, consumers started complaining about poor signal quality and dropped calls, a side-effect of the antenna placement. Apple denied the problem and blamed the customers. When complaints grew, Apple reported that the problem was a software problem. Finally, after extensive protests and the threat of government intervention, Apple provided all phone owners a plastic case that solved the problem. Even then, Steve Jobs insisted that only 55 percent of all iPhones had a problem, and that phones from competitors like Nokia, HTC, and Blackberry had the same issues.[66]

By contrast, a company using a **defensive strategy** would admit responsibility for a problem but would do the least required to meet societal expectations. Documents from a pending lawsuit against DELL suggest that the company shipped at least 11.8 million computers that had faulty electrical components and capacitors that broke and leaked fluid. When an internal study helped Dell identify the problem, Dell continued to try to cover up the problem. One internal memo to salespeople said, "Don't bring this to customers' attention proactively." And, in many cases, Dell actually repaired the broken computers with more of the same faulty components. Although Dell took a $300 million charge to fix the computers, and has extended warranties for some customers, it has still not issued a general recall, which means that many customers may not be aware that they had purchased faulty computers. Dell's strategy throughout this process has been defensive.[67]

reactive strategy
a social responsiveness strategy in which a company does less than society expects

defensive strategy
a social responsiveness strategy in which a company admits responsibility for a problem but does the least required to meet societal expectations

A company using an **accommodative strategy** will accept responsibility for a problem and take a progressive approach by doing all that could be expected to solve the problem. Finally, a company using a **proactive strategy** will anticipate responsibility for a problem before it occurs, do more than expected to address the problem, and lead the industry in its approach. Two decades ago, MERCK, a pharmaceutical company, began giving away its drug for river blindness, which thrives and spreads easily along fertile riverbanks in Africa and Latin America. River blindness affects 37 million people worldwide and could infect up to 100 million others.[69] Merck's drug program is the largest, on-going medical donation program in history. Since 1987, Merck has given away 530 million treatments at a cost of $3.75 billion. The World Health Organization now believes that, thanks to Merck's contributions, river blindness is on the verge of being completely eliminated in Africa.[70]

REVIEW 3-7

Responses to Demands for Social Responsibility

Social responsiveness is a company's response to stakeholders' demands for socially responsible behavior. There are four social responsiveness strategies. When a company uses a reactive strategy, it denies responsibility for a problem. When it uses a defensive strategy, it takes responsibility for a problem but does the minimum required to solve it. When a company uses an accommodative strategy, it accepts responsibility for problems and does all that society expects to solve them. Finally, when a company uses a proactive strategy, it does much more than expected to solve social responsibility problems.

3-8 Social Responsibility and Economic Performance

One question that managers often ask is, "Does it pay to be socially responsible?" In previous editions of this textbook, the answer was "no," as early research indicated that there was not an inherent relationship between social responsibility and economic performance.[71] Recent research, however, leads to different conclusions. There is no trade-off between being socially responsible and economic performance.[72] And there is a small, positive relationship between being socially responsible and economic performance that strengthens with corporate reputation.[73] Let's explore what each of these results means.

After reading this section, you should be able to:

3-8 explain whether social responsibility hurts or helps an organization's economic performance.

First, managers don't need to choose between being socially responsible and maximizing economic performance.[74] Being socially responsible usually

accommodative strategy
a social responsiveness strategy in which a company accepts responsibility for a problem and does all that society expects to solve that problem

proactive strategy
a social responsiveness strategy in which a company anticipates responsibility for a problem before it occurs and does more than society expects to address the problem

won't make a business less profitable. What this suggests is that the costs of being socially responsible—and those costs can be high, especially early on—can be offset by a better product or corporate reputation, which results in stronger sales or higher profit margins. For example, HONDA, which introduced the first hybrid car in North America, has long been an industry leader in fuel efficiency and environmentally friendly technology. So when it decided to enter the private plane market with the new Honda Jet, it took the same approach, making a light-weight, fuel-efficient plane. The plane is also faster than competitors and less expensive to operate. Although it seats a pilot and just four passengers, the cost of flying the Honda Jet will be no more expensive on a per mile basis than the common Canadair CRJ-200 regional jet, which transports 40 to 50 passengers. Honda believes that its socially responsible design is the key to making the Honda Jet profitable.[75]

Second, it usually *does* pay to be socially responsible, and that relationship becomes stronger particularly when a company or its products have a strong reputation for social responsibility.[76] For example, *GE*, long one of the most admired and profitable corporations in the world, was one of the first and largest *Fortune* 500 companies to make a strategic commitment to providing environmentally friendly products and service. CEO Jeffrey Immelt wants GE to "develop and drive the technologies of the future that will protect and clean our environment."[77] Is Immelt doing this because of personal beliefs? He says no. "It's no great thrill for me to do this stuff. . . . I never put it in right versus wrong terms." GE calls its strategy "ecoimagination," which it says is "helping to solve the world's biggest environmental challenges while driving profitable growth for GE." Says Immelt, "We invest in the basic strategies that we think are going to fit into [ecoimagination], but make money for our investors at the same time."[78] In just five years, GE has increased the number of ecoimagination products from 17 to 80. As a result, it now sells more than $17 billion of such products and services each year, with annual revenue growth increasing by double digits.[79]

Finally, even if there is generally a small positive relationship between social responsibility and economic performance that becomes stronger when a company or its products have a positive reputation for social responsibility, and even if there is no trade-off between being socially responsible and economic performance, there is no guarantee that socially responsible companies will be profitable. Simply put, socially responsible companies experience the same ups and downs in economic performance that traditional businesses do. A good example is *BEN & JERRY's*, the ice cream company. Ben & Jerry's started in 1978, when founders Ben Cohen and Jerry Greenfield sent away for a $5 course on how to make ice cream. Ben & Jerry's is as famous for its commitment to social responsibility as for its super premium ice cream. The company donates 7.5 percent of its pretax profits to support AIDS patients, homeless people, and the environment.[80] Moreover, customers buy Ben & Jerry's ice cream because it tastes great *and* because they want to support a socially responsible company. As Ben Cohen says, "We see ourselves as somewhat of a social service agency and somewhat of an ice cream company."[81] But—and this is a big "but"— despite its outstanding reputation as a socially responsible company, Ben & Jerry's consistently had financial troubles after going public (selling shares of stock to the public) 15 years ago. In fact, its financial problems became so severe that Ben and Jerry sold the company to British-based Unilever.[82] Being socially responsible may be the right thing to do, and is usually associated with increased profits, but it doesn't guarantee business success.

REVIEW 3-8

Social Responsibility and Economic Performance

Does it pay to be socially responsible? Studies show that there is generally no trade-off between social responsibility and economic performance. In most circumstances, there is generally a small positive relationship between social responsibility and economic performance that becomes stronger when a company or its products have a positive reputation. Social responsibility, however, does not guarantee profitability, as socially responsible companies experience the same ups and downs as other companies.

 # Management Decision

Responding to Tragedy[83]

On April 5, 2010, an explosion at the Upper Big Branch coal mine in Montcoal, West Virginia, killed 29 workers. Over the next several weeks and days, as nationwide attention turned to this tragedy, it was discovered that the mine's operating company, Massey Energy, was cited for numerous safety and regulatory violations. One month prior to the accident, the mine was written up more than 50 times, with 12 of those notices relating to an excessive buildup of coal dust and methane, conditions that can cause explosions like the one that occurred. The very day of the explosion, federal regulators identified two more safety violations, a failure to have updated maps of escape routes in case of an accident and a failure to outfit miners with required communication and tracking equipment that would help them stay in contact with aboveground employees. All told, officials found 1,342 safety violations at Upper Big Branch from 2005 to April 2009. And according to these investigators, miners at Upper Big Branch lost more time to work-site accidents than any other mine in the country.

In spite of the large number of violations, Massey continues to insist that they are committed to safety. On its website, the company proclaims "Safety is the top priority for every Massey member....We work hard to instill a zero-tolerance policy and commitment from all members, whether they work at corporate headquarters or in the mines, to make safety the number one priority—every day." However, the company's reactions to regulators' citations have generally been resistant and confrontational. According to government records, Massey has contested or appealed a good portion of the violations it has received since 2005. By doing so, it has been able to avoid paying the fines and making the safety changes required by regulators.

The question for you, as a manager at Massey Energy, is this: How will you address your company's ethical responsibility? Will you continue to insist that the company is doing everything it can for safety, even as the number of violations skyrockets? Will you insist that all safety violations be addressed immediately and that unsafe mines be closed until they pass inspections, at the cost of hundreds of millions of dollars? What steps could you take to insure that your company is an industry leader in safety, while also remaining profitable?

Questions

1. How would you describe Massey's current approach to its ethical and social responsibility?

2. Which approach to social responsibility would you recommend that Massey take in the future?

3. How might the temporary closure of dangerous mines and the investment of funds into new safety systems be an economic stimulus for Massey?

 ## Practice Being a Manager

Discerning Unethical Behavior

Applying ethical judgment in an organizational setting can be challenging. This exercise offers you the opportunity to consider how you might approach such a situation as a manager in an investment firm.

Read the scenario and prepare your responses to the individual (homework) questions in advance of discussing this exercise in class.

Scenario

Imagine that you are a newly hired portfolio manager at Excalibur Funds. Although you're new to this job, you have eight years' experience in the mutual fund business. You left a larger and more established mutual fund company to join Excalibur because of its reputation as a bright, up-and-coming investment company, a place where someone like yourself could participate in building a new and dynamic investment company.

Your new fund, the Pioneer Fund, is a growth-oriented fund investing in small companies. Typically, the majority of the fund's stock investments is in high-technology companies. Pioneer is moving up fast in its peer group, and if the fund continues to perform well, you stand a good chance of being the manager recognized when it breaks into the top tier of performance.

One of the features that attracted you to this job is the opportunity to work with a seasoned group of traders, analysts, and staff professionals. The Pioneer Fund staff has averaged 10 percent turnover over the past five years, unusual in an industry where turnover commonly reaches 60 to 80 percent. After a month of working with your new team, however, you have noticed some troubling patterns. First, you felt that some of your staff were delaying or stonewalling you on several occasions when you requested more detailed information on particular trades. It took too long to get the information, and when you did receive it, the information looked a little *too* neat and well organized. Second, the analysts have seemed guarded regarding their interaction with some of the technology companies in which the Pioneer Fund invests. On more than one occasion, you've noticed analysts quickly ending phone calls when you entered the office or minimizing computer screens when you walk by their desks. Finally, the group just seems a bit too *nice* when you are around. The investment business is often hectic and stressful. Shouting matches over investment decisions are not uncommon, and grumbling is a second language. But all you get are smiles and charm.

So here you are at your desk on a Saturday evening, finishing off the last of a pot of coffee and planning for Monday morning. One thing is clear—you must begin to scratch below the surface of the Pioneer Fund team. Your gut tells you that something is wrong here, perhaps very wrong. For all you know, you may be sitting on the next big investment scandal. Your head tells you that you have no hard evidence of unethical or illegal behavior and that you'd better tread carefully. If your gut is wrong and you run around making hasty accusations, you may lose what appears to be a very talented investment team.

What steps should you take starting Monday morning?

Preparing for Class Discussion

Complete the following steps individually in preparation for class discussion. Write your responses to the questions in each step.

STEP 1 **Understand the situation and key considerations.** What considerations would be important to you in developing a plan of action in this situation? What resources might you draw upon to determine whether or not particular actions are unethical and/or illegal?

STEP 2 **Develop a plan of action.** What steps would you follow in this scenario? What factors should you consider in planning your timing of these steps?

STEP 3 **Anticipate response(s).** How might the Pioneer Fund employees respond to your plan of action? Develop a few scenarios.

Small Group and Class Discussion

Your professor will assign you to a small discussion group. Your group should discuss the following questions and be prepared to share its thoughts with the class:

1. What are the most difficult aspects of responding to a murky situation—those situations in which you sense the presence of unethical and/or illegal behavior but haven't seen unequivocal proof of wrongdoing?

2. What are the risks of waiting for unequivocal proof before beginning to take action? What are the risks of acting decisively based on your "gut" sense of a situation?

3. What is different about acting ethically/responsibly within an organizational environment/culture like that of the Pioneer Fund versus acting ethically/responsibly as an individual? What are the particular challenges and dynamics associated with ethical and responsible behavior in an organization?

 # Self-Assessment

An Ethical Baseline

Most people think they are ethical, particularly when the right thing to do is seemingly obvious. But as you read in the chapter, 75 percent of the respondents in a nationwide survey indicated that they had witnessed unethical behavior at work. In another study across multiple industries, 48 percent of the respondents admitted to actually committing an unethical or illegal act in the past year! And recall that with so many ways to approach ethical decision making, ethical choices are not always cut-and-dried. To give you an idea of your ethical perspective, take this assessment.[84] Answer each of the questions using the following scale:

1 **Strongly agree**
2 **Agree**
3 **Not sure**
4 **Disagree**
5 **Strongly disagree**

1. Did you ever think about taking money from where you worked, but didn't go through with it?

   1   2   3   4   5

2. Have you ever borrowed something from work without telling anyone?

   1   2   3   4   5

3. There are times I've been provoked into a fistfight.

   1   2   3   4   5

4. Is it okay to get around the law if you don't break it?

   1   2   3   4   5

5. I've had fellow employees show me how to take things from where I work.

   1   2   3   4   5

6. I will usually take someone up on a dare.

   1   2   3   4   5

7. I've always driven insured vehicles.

   1   2   3   4   5

8. If you were sent an extra item with an order, would you send it back?

   1   2   3   4   5

9. Would you say everyone is a little dishonest?

   1   2   3   4   5

10. Most supervisors treat their employees fairly.

    1   2   3   4   5

11. I worry about getting hurt at work.

    1   2   3   4   5

12. People say that I'm a workaholic.

    1   2   3   4   5

13. I like to plan things carefully ahead of time.

    1   2   3   4   5

14. Have you found a way a dishonest person in your job could take things from work?

    1   2   3   4   5

15. I often act quickly without stopping to think things through.

    1   2   3   4   5

16. It doesn't bother me what other people think.

    1   2   3   4   5

17. I have friends who are a little dishonest.

    1   2   3   4   5

18. I am not a thrill seeker.

    1   2   3   4   5

19. I have had my driver's license revoked.

    1   2   3   4   5

20. Are you too honest to steal?

    1   2   3   4   5

21. Do most employees take small items from work?

        1   2   3   4   5

22. Do most employees get along well with their supervisors?

        1   2   3   4   5

23. I'm lucky to avoid having accidents.

        1   2   3   4   5

24. I always finish what I start.

        1   2   3   4   5

25. I make sure everything is in its place before leaving home.

        1   2   3   4   5

SCORING

Determine your average score for each category by entering your response to each survey item below, as follows: In blanks that say *regular score*, simply enter your response for that item. If your response was a 4, place a 4 in the *regular score* blank. In blanks that say *reverse score*, subtract your response from 6 and enter the result. So if your response was a 4, place a 2 (6–4 = 2) in the *reverse score* blank. Total your scores; then compute your average score for each section.

Antisocial Behavior

    1. **regular score** _____

    2. **regular score** _____

    3. **regular score** _____

    4. **regular score** _____

    5. **regular score** _____

    6. **regular score** _____

    7. **reverse score** _____

    8. **reverse score** _____

  14. **regular score** _____

  15. **regular score** _____

  16. **regular score** _____

  17. **regular score** _____

  18. **reverse score** _____

  19. **regular score** _____

  20. **reverse score** _____

         TOTAL = _____ ÷ 15 = _____ **(your average for Antisocial Behavior)**

Orderliness/Diligence

12. regular score _____

13. regular score _____

24. regular score _____

25. regular score _____

     TOTAL = _____ ÷ 14 = _____ (your average for Orderliness/Diligence)

Positive Outlook

9. reverse score _____

10. regular score _____

11. reverse score _____

21. reverse score _____

22. regular score _____

23. regular score _____

     TOTAL = _____ ÷ 6 = _____ (your average for Positive Outlook)

You can find the interpretation for your scores online at www.cengagebrain.com.

MANAGEMENT WORKPLACE

Theo Chocolate: Managing Ethics and Social Responsibility

After a trip to cacao farms in Central America, Joe Whinney decided to build the first organic, fair trade, chocolate factory in the United States. Whinney hoped to help solve social and environmental issues by operating a profitable and ethical business. While Theo Chocolate is finding good success in the organic foods industry, perhaps the most exciting thing for "Theonistas" is that the company is being hailed as a voice for change. Employees say they have gained a loyal following for their efforts in the developing world, and business success has opened up new opportunities for sharing their vision of a better world.

What to Watch For and Ask Yourself

1. Which strategy for responding to social responsibility best reflects Theo Chocolate?

2. How do Theo Chocolate's business practices reflect the stakeholder model of social responsibility?

3. What would happen if fair trade goals conflicted with a company's primary responsibility to be profitable?

Endnotes

1. S. Azfzal, "Smokers Need Not Apply: Is Hiring Ban Trend of the Future?" *The Christian Science Monitor*, November 17, 2010, accessed March 4, 2011, from www.csmonitor.com/Business/2010/1117/Smokers-need-not-apply-Is-hiring-ban-trend-of-the-future; M. Hennessy, "Right to Smoke?" *CFO* (February 2006): 54; M. Janofsky, "Ban on Employees Who Smoke Faces Challenges of Bias," *New York Times*, April 28, 1994, A1; M. Lecker, "The Smoking Penalty: Distributive Justice or Smokism?" *Journal of Business Ethics* 84 (2009): 47–64; K. Maher, "Companies Are Closing Doors on Job Applicants Who Smoke," *Wall Street Journal*, December 21, 2004, B6; and A. Sulzberger, "Hospitals Shift Smoking Bans to Smoker Ban," *New York Times*, 10 February 2011, accessed March 4, 2011, from www.nytimes.com/2011/02/11/us/11smoking.html?_r=1 & hp.

2. J. Schramm, "Perceptions on Ethics," *HR Magazine* 49 (November 2004): 176.

3. M. Jackson, "Workplace Cheating Rampant, Half of Employees Surveyed Admit They Take Unethical Actions," *Peoria Journal Star*, April 5, 1997.

4. C. Smith, "The Ethical Workplace," *Association Management* 52 (2000): 70–73.

5. D. Jones, "Do You Trust Your CEO? More Workers Do Now Than Before Recent Big Scandals," *USA Today*, February 12, 2003, B7.

6. R. Guha and R. Krishna, "Corporate News: India Charges Satyam's Founder, Eight Others," *Wall Street Journal*, April 8, 2009, B4.

7. M. Bordwin, "Don't Ask Employees to Do Your Dirty Work," *Management Review*, 1 (October 1995).

8. M. Schweitzer, L. Ordonez, and B. Douma, "Goal Setting As a Motivator of Unethical Behavior," *Academy of Management Journal* 47 (2004): 422–432.

9. S. Pulliam and M. Rothfield, "Plea Deals Ramp Up Pressure in Galleon," *Wall Street Journal*, January 27, 2011, C1; and G. Zuckerman, D. Clark, and S. Pulliam, "Colleagues Finger Billionaire—Galleon Founder Pushed Hard for Stock-Trading Tips; 'Get an Edge or You're Gone,'" *Wall Street Journal*, October 19, 2009, A1.

10. D. Palmer and A. Zakhem, "Bridging the Gap between Theory and Practice: Using the 1991 Federal Sentencing Guidelines as a Paradigm for Ethics Training," *Journal of Business Ethics* 29, no. 1/2 (2001): 77–84.

11. K. Tyler, "Do the Right Thing: Ethics Training Programs Help Employees Deal with Ethical Dilemmas," *HR Magazine*, February 2005, available online at http://moss07 .shrm.org/Publications/hrmagazine/Editorial Content/Pages/0205tyler .aspx [accessed 13 March 2009].

12. D. R. Dalton, M. B. Metzger, and J. W. Hill, "The 'New' U.S. Sentencing Commission Guidelines: A Wake-Up Call for Corporate America," *Academy of Management Executive* 8 (1994): 7–16.

13. B. Ettore, "Crime and Punishment: A Hard Look at White-Collar Crime," *Management Review* 83 (1994): 10–16.

14. F. Robinson and C. C. Pauze, "What Is a Board's Liability for Not Adopting a Compliance Program?" *Healthcare Financial-Management* 51, no. 9 (1997): 64.

15. D. Murphy, "The Federal Sentencing Guidelines for Organizations: A Decade of Promoting Compliance and Ethics," *Iowa Law Review* 87 (2002): 697–719.

16. Robinson and Pauze, "What Is a Board's Liability?"

17. L. A. Hays, "A Matter of Time: Widow Sues IBM over Death Benefits," *Wall Street Journal*, July 6, 1995, A1.

18. T. M. Jones, "Ethical Decision Making by Individuals in Organizations: An Issue-Contingent Model," *Academy of Management Review* 16 (1991): 366–395.

19. S. Morris and R. McDonald, "The Role of Moral Intensity in Moral Judgments: An Empirical Investigation," *Journal of Business Ethics* 14 (1995): 715–726; and B. Flannery and D. May, "Environmental Ethical Decision Making in the U.S. Metal-Finishing Industry," *Academy of Management Journal* 43 (2000): 642–662.

20. L. Chao, "China Court Issues Rare Piracy Penalty to Windows Copycats," *Wall Street Journal*, August 22, 2009, A9.

21. L. Kohlberg, "Stage and Sequence: The Cognitive-Developmental Approach to Socialization," in *Handbook of Socialization Theory and Research*, ed. D. A. Goslin (Chicago: Rand McNally, 1969); and L. Trevino, "Moral Reasoning and Business Ethics: Implications for Research, Education, and Management," *Journal of Business Ethics* 11 (1992): 445–459.

22. L. Trevino and M. Brown, "Managing to be Ethical: Debunking Five Business Ethics Myths," *Academy of Management Executive* 18 (May 2004): 69–81.

23. M. R. Cunningham, D. T. Wong, and A. P. Barbee, "Self-Presentation Dynamics on Overt Integrity Tests: Experimental Studies of the Reid Report," *Journal of Applied Psychology* 79 (1994): 643–658; and J. Wanek, P. Sackett, and D. Ones, "Toward an Understanding of Integrity Test Similarities and Differences: An Item-Level Analysis of Seven Tests," *Personnel Psychology* 56 (Winter 2003): 873–894.

24. H. J. Bernardin, "Validity of an Honesty Test in Predicting Theft among Convenience Store Employees," *Academy of Management Journal* 36 (1993): 1097–1108.

25. J. M. Collins and F. L. Schmidt, "Personality, Integrity, and White-Collar Crime: A Construct Validity Study," *Personnel Psychology* (1993): 295–311.

26. W. C. Borman, M. A. Hanson, and J. W. Hedge, "Personnel Selection," *Annual Review of Psychology* 48 (1997).

27. P. E. Murphy, "Corporate Ethics Statements: Current Status and Future Prospects," *Journal of Business Ethics* 14 (1995): 727–740.

28. "More Corporate Boards Involved in Ethics Programs; Ethics Training Becoming Standard Practice," *PR Newswire*, October 16, 2006.

29. S. J. Harrington, "What Corporate America Is Teaching about Ethics," *Academy of Management Executive* 5 (1991): 21–30.

30 L. A. Berger, "Train All Employees to Solve Ethical Dilemmas," *Best's Review—Life-Health Insurance Edition* 95 (1995): 70–80.

31 D. Schmidt, "Ethics Can Be Taught," *Inc.*, June 24, 2008, accessed July 10, 2010, from www.inc.com/leadership-blog/2008/06/ethics_can_be_taught_1.html.

32 L. Trevino, G. Weaver, D. Gibson, and B. Toffler, "Managing Ethics and Legal Compliance: What Works and What Hurts," *California Management Review* 41, no. 2 (1999): 131–151.

33 Ibid.

34 E. White, "Theory & Practice: What Would You Do? Ethics Courses Get Context; Beyond Checking Boxes, Some Firms Start Talking About Handling Gray Areas," *Wall Street Journal*, June 12, 2006, B3.

35 Supplemental Research Brief, "2009 National Business Ethics Survey: The Importance of Ethical Culture," Ethics Resource Center, June 2010, accessed February 25, 2011, from www.ethics.org/files/u5/CultureSup4.pdf.

36 G. Weaver and L. Trevino, "Integrated and Decoupled Corporate Social Performance: Management Commitments, External Pressures, and Corporate Ethics Practices," *Academy of Management Journal* 42 (1999): 539–552; and L. Trevino, G. Weaver, D. Gibson, and B. Toffler, "Managing Ethics and Legal Compliance: What Works and What Hurts," *California Management Review* 41, no. 2 (1999): 131–151.

37 J. Salopek, "Do the Right Thing," *Training & Development* 55 (July 2001): 38–44.

38 M. Gundlach, S. Douglas, and M. Martinko, "The Decision to Blow the Whistle: A Social Information Processing Framework," *Academy of Management Executive* 17 (2003): 107–123.

39 M. Schwartz, "Business Ethics: Time to Blow the Whistle?" *Globe & Mail*, March 5, 1998, B2.

40 "More Corporate Boards Involved in Ethics Programs," *PR Newswire*.

41 G. Alliger and S. Dwight, "A Meta-Analytic Investigation of the Susceptibility of Integrity Tests to Faking and Coaching," *Educational and Psychological Measurement* 60 (2000): 59–72; and D. S. Ones, C. Viswesvaran, and F. L. Schmidt, "Comprehensive Meta-Analysis of Integrity Test Validities: Findings and Implications for Personnel Selection and Theories of Job Performance," *Journal of Applied Psychology* 78 (1993): 679–703; and "2004 Report to the Nation on Occupational Fraud and Abuse."

42 H. R. Bower, *Social Responsibilities of the Businessman* (New York: Harper & Row, 1953).

43 "Beyond the Green Corporation," *Businessweek*, January 29, 2007.

44 M. Nichols, "Corrected: Amid Recession, U.S. Companies Boost Non-Cash Giving," *Reuters*, October 27, 2010, accessed February 25, 2010, www.reuters.com/article/2010/10/27/us-philanthropy-corporations-idUSTRE69Q0I020101027.

45 Z. Zuno, "Americans Send the Message: Get Down to Business on Corporate Citizenship: Ben & Jerry's, Target, Patagonia, SC Johnson and Gerber Top the 4th GolinHarris Corporate Citizenship Index in Rating of 152 Brands by 5,000 Americans," *Business Wire*, December 6, 2006.

46 T. Zeller Jr., "Banks Grow Wary of Environmental Risks," *New York Times*, August 30, 2010, accessed October 11, 2010, from www.nytimes.com/2010/08/31/business/energy-environment/31coal.html.

47 M. Dolliver, "Thumbs Down on Corporate Green Efforts," Adweek.com, August 31, 2010, accessed October 10, 2010, from www.adweek.com/aw/content_display/news/client/e3i8426 0d4301c885f91b2cd8a712f323cf.

48 "Honda Partnership with the Detroit Symphony Orchestra," Honda, accessed February 25, 2011, http://corporate.honda.com/america/events.aspx?id=dso; "Domestic Violence," Verizon Communications, accessed February 25, 2011, from http://foundation.verizon.com/core/domestic.shtml.

49 S. L. Wartick and P. L. Cochran, "The Evolution of the Corporate Social Performance Model," *Academy of Management Review* 10 (1985): 758–769.

50 S. Waddock, C. Bodwell, and S. Graves, "Responsibility: The New Business Imperative," *Academy of Management Executive* 16 (2002): 132–148.

51 "PepsiCo CEO: Redefine Profit and Loss," *Marketplace*, January 29, 2010, accessed February 25, 2010, from http://marketplace.publicradio.org/display/web/2010/01/29/pm-davos-pepsi-ceo-q/.

52 T. Donaldson and L. E. Preston, "The Stakeholder Theory of the Corporation: Concepts, Evidence, and Implications," *Academy of Management Review* 20 (1995): 65–91.

53 M. B. E. Clarkson, "A Stakeholder Framework for Analyzing and Evaluating Corporate Social Performance," *Academy of Management Review* 20 (1995): 92–117.

54 B. Agle, R. Mitchell, and J. Sonnenfeld, "Who Matters to CEOs? An Investigation of Stakeholder Attributes and Salience, Corporate Performance, and CEO Values," *Academy of Management Journal* 42 (1999): 507–525.

55 K. Rockwood, "Walmart Shoppers: Clean-up in Aisle Nine," *Fast Company*, February 2010, 30–32.

56 L. E. Preston, "Stakeholder Management and Corporate Performance," *Journal of Behavioral Economics* 19 (1990): 361–375.

57 E. W. Orts, "Beyond Shareholders: Interpreting Corporate Constituency Statutes," *George Washington Law Review* 61 (1992): 14–135.

58 A. B. Carroll, "A Three-Dimensional Conceptual Model of Corporate Performance," *Academy of Management Review* 4 (1979): 497–505.

59 Ibid.

60 M. Bunz, "What Ended Owen Van Natta's Short Reign at MySpace?" guardian.co.uk., February 11, 2010, accessed August 12, 2010, from www.guardian.co.uk/media/pda/2010/feb/11/myspace-murdoch).

61 J. Lublin, "CEO Firings on the Rise as Downturn Gains Steam," *Wall Street Journal*, January 13, 2009, B1.

62 D. Woodruff, "Europe Shows More CEOs the Door," *Wall Street Journal*, July 1, 2002.

63 C. Bray, "Ex-Monster President Found Guilty in Backdating Case," *Wall Street Journal*, May 13, 2009, C4.

64 J. Bandler, "McKelvey Admits Monster Backdating; Ex-CEO to Repay Millions but Avoids Jail Due to Illness," *Wall Street Journal*, January 24, 2008, B4.

65 R. Greenhill, "The Corporate Response to Haiti," *Wall Street Journal*, July 17, 2010, A11.

66 B. X. Chen, "Apple's Answer to Antennagate: Free iPhone 4 Cases," *Wired*, July 16, 2010, accessed September 4, 2010, from www.wired.com/gadgetlab/2010/07/iphone-4/; M. Hachman, "Apple's Jobs: You're Holding the iPhone 4 Wrong," *PC Magazine*, June 25, 2010, accessed September 4, 2010, from www.pcmag.com/article2/0,2817,2365705,00.asp; and M. Helft, "Apple Acknowledges Flaw in iPhone Signal Meter," *New York Times*, July 2, 2010, accessed September 4, 2010, from www.nytimes.com/2010/07/03/technology/03apple.html?src=un & feedurl=http://json8.nytimes.com/pages/technology/index.jsonp.

67 A. Vance, "In Faulty-Computer Suit, Window to Dell Decline," *New York Times*, June 28, 2010, accessed June 28, 2010, from www.nytimes.com/2010/06/29/technology/29dell.html?pagewanted=1 & hp.

68 "Why Make a Better Bag?" accessed December 12, 2010, from www.sunchips.com/resources/pdf/sunchips_bags.pdf.

69 "FACT Sheet—Merck Mectizan® Donation Program—River Blindness (Onchocerciasis)," Merck, accessed February 26, 2011, www.merck.com/cr/docs/River%20Blindness%20Fact%20Sheet.pdf.

70 A. Weintraub, "Will Pfizer's Giveaway Drugs Polish Its Public Image?" *Businessweek*, August 3, 2009, 13.

71 A. McWilliams and D. Siegel, "Corporate Social Responsibility: A Theory of the Firm Perspective," *Academy of Management Review* 26, no.1 (2001): 117–127; H. Haines, "Noah Joins Ranks of Socially Responsible Funds," *Dow Jones News Service*, October 13, 1995. A meta-analysis of 41 different studies also found no relationship between corporate social responsibility and profitability. Though not reported in the meta-analysis, when confidence intervals are placed around its average sample-weighted correlation of 0.06, the lower confidence interval includes zero, leading to the conclusion that there is no relationship between corporate social responsibility and profitability. See M. Orlitzky, "Does Firm Size Confound the Relationship between Corporate Social Responsibility and Firm Performance?" *Journal of Business Ethics* 33 (2001): 167–180; and S. Ambec and P. Lanoie, "Does It Pay to Be Green? A Systematic Overview," *Academy of Management Perspectives*, 22 (2008): 45–62.

72 M. Orlitzky, "Payoffs to Social and Environmental Performance," *Journal of Investing* 14 (2005): 48–51.

73 M. Orlitzky, F. Schmidt, and S. Rynes, "Corporate Social and Financial Performance: A Meta-analysis," *Organization Studies* 24 (2003): 403–441.

74 Orlitzky, "Payoffs to Social and Environmental Performance."

75 G. Reynolds, "Can Honda Bring Corporate-Style Jet Travel to the Masses?" *Popular Mechanics*, March 4, 2010, accessed September 5, 2010, from www.popularmechanics.com/technology/aviation/news/Honda Jet_air_travel.

76 Orlitzky, Schmidt, and Rynes, "Corporate Social and Financial Performance."

77 A. Murray and A. Strassel, "Environment (A Special Report); Ahead of the Pack: GE's Jeffrey Immelt on Why It's Business, Not Personal," *Wall Street Journal*, March 24, 2008, R3.

78 K. Kranhold, "Greener Postures: GE's Environment Push Hits Business Realities; CEO's Quest to Reduce Emissions Irks Clients; The Battle of the Bulbs," *Wall Street Journal*, September 14, 2007, A1.

79 "Ecoimagination Is GE," 2008 Ecoimagination Annual Report, accessed August 20, 2009 from http://ge.ecoimagination.com.

80 D. Kadlec and B. Van Voorst, "The New World of Giving: Companies Are Doing More Good, and Demanding More Back," *Time*, May 5, 1997, 62.

81 P. Carlin, "Will Rapid Growth Stunt Corporate Do-Gooders?" *Business & Society Review* (Spring 1995), 36–43.

82 K. Brown, "Chilling at Ben & Jerry's: Cleaner, Greener," *Wall Street Journal*, April 15, 2004, B1.

83 M. Cooper and I. Urbina, "Mine Operator Escaped Extra Oversight after Warning," *New York Times*, April 9, 2010, accessed September 3, 2010, www.nytimes.com/2010/04/10/us/10westvirginia.html?hp; S. Mufson, J. Markon, and E. O'Keefe, "West Virginia Mine Has Been Cited for Myriad Safety Violations," *Washington Post*, April 7, 2010, accessed September 4, 2010, from www.washingtonpost.com/wp-dyn/content/article/2010/04/05/AR2010040503877.html; "Safety," Massey Energy Company, accessed September 4, 2010, from www.masseyenergyco.com/safety/index.shtml; and I. Urbina and B. Becker, "As Rescue Efforts Continue for Miners, Officials Press for Answers," *New York Times*, April 8, 2010, accessed September 4, 2010, from www.nytimes.com/2010/04/08/us/08westvirginia.html.

84 J. E. Wanek, P. R. Sackett, and D. S. Ones, "Towards an Understanding of Integrity Test Similarities and Differences: An Item-Level Analysis of Seven Tests," *Personnel Psychology* 56 (2003): 873–894.

Planning

Chapter Four

Planning and Decision Making

© AP PHOTOS/
IMAGINECHINA

Chapter 4 examines the benefits and pitfalls of planning, making plans work, and the different plans used in organizations. You'll also learn the steps and limitations of rational decision making and review various group decision techniques.

Chapter Five

Organizational Strategy

© JIM GRAHAM/BLOOMBERG/
GETTY IMAGES

Chapter 5 examines how managers use strategies to obtain a sustainable competitive advantage. Then you learn the strategy-making process and how companies answer these questions: What business should we be in? How should we compete in this industry? How should we compete against a particular firm?

Chapter Six

Innovation and Change

© MARK ASHMAN/DISNEY/
HANDOUT/GETTY IMAGES
ENTERTAINMENT/GETTY
IMAGES

Chapter 6 reviews the issues associated with organizational innovation. The first part of this chapter shows you why innovation matters and how to manage innovation to create and sustain a competitive advantage. In the second part of the chapter, you will learn about organizational change and about the risk of not changing.

Chapter Seven

Global Management

© BROWN ADRIAN/
SIPA/NEWSCOM

Chapter 7 examines the impact of global business on U.S. firms and reviews the basic rules and agreements that govern global trade. You'll learn how and when companies go global. And you'll read how companies decide where to expand globally and confront issues like business climates and cultural differences.

© DIZZO/iSTOCK PHOTO

Planning and Decision Making

REEL TO REAL

Management Workplace is at Plant Fantasies.

SELF-ASSESSMENT

To what extent are you self managing? Find out by doing the Self-Assessment for this chapter in the book or online.

ONLINE QUIZZES

Did you get it? Review the main concepts in the chapter by taking the online quizzes on CourseMate!

VIDEO QUIZZES

Get more out of the videos by taking the multimedia video quizzes online.

What Would You Do?

DuPont Headquarters, Wilmington, Delaware[1]

The DuPont company got its start when Eleuthère Irénée du Pont de Nemours fled France's revolution to come to America, where, in 1802, he built a mill on the Brandywine River in Wilmington, Delaware, to produce blasting powder used in guns and artillery. In 1902, E. I. du Pont's great-grandson, Pierre S. du Pont, along with two cousins, bought out other family members and began transforming DuPont into the world's leading chemical company. In its second century, DuPont Corporation would go on to develop Freon for refrigerators and air conditioners; nylon, which is used in everything from women's hose to car tires; Lucite, a ubiquitous clear plastic used in baths, furniture, car lights, and phone screens; Teflon, famous for its nonstick properties in cookware and coatings; Dacron, a wash-and-wear, wrinkle-free polyester; Lycra, the stretchy, clingy fabric used in activewear and swimwear; Nome, a fire-resistant fiber used by firefighters, race car drivers, and to reduce heat in motors and electrical equipment; Corona, a high-end countertop used in homes and offices; and Kevlar, the "bulletproof" material used in body armor worn by police and soldiers, in helmets, and for vehicle protection.

You became DuPont's CEO right as "the world fell apart" at the height of the world financial crisis. Fortunately, you had early warning from sharply declining sales in DuPont's titanium dioxide division, which makes white pigment used in paints, sunscreen, and food coloring. Sales trends there can be counted on to indicate what will happen next in the general economy, so you and your leadership team began working with the heads of all of DuPont's divisions to make contingency plans in case sales dropped by 5 percent, 10 percent, 20 percent, or more. Many DuPont managers thought you were crazy, until the downturn hit. It was difficult, but with plans to cut 6,500 employees at the ready, you were prepared when sales dropped by 20 percent at the end of the year. But when that wasn't enough, salaried and professional employees were asked to voluntarily take unpaid

© JIM GRAHAM/BLOOMBERG GETTY IMAGES

time off and an additional 2,000 jobs were eliminated. In all, these moves reduced expenses by a billion dollars a year. But one place you refused to cut was DuPont's research budget, which remained at $1.4 billion per year.

One of the ways in which the board of directors measures company performance is by comparing DuPont's total stock returns to 19 peer companies. Over the last quarter century, DuPont has regularly ended up in the bottom third of the list. This makes clear that you have one overriding goal: to restore DuPont's prestige, performance, and competitiveness. The question, of course, is how?

Before deciding how to restore DuPont's edge, there are some big questions to consider. First, given sustained weak performance over the last quarter century, do you need to step back and consider DuPont's purpose, that is, the reason that you're in business? After transitioning from blasting powder to chemicals, DuPont's slogan became, "Better things for better living…through chemistry." Is it time, again, to reconsider what DuPont is all about? Or, instead of an intense focus on DuPont's purpose, would it make

© DIZZO/ISTOCK PHOTO

more sense to make lots of plans and lots of bets so that "a thousand flowers can bloom"? In other words, would it be better to keep options open by making small, simultaneous investments in many alternative plans? Then, when one or a few of these plans emerge as likely winners, you invest even more in these plans while discontinuing or reducing investment in the others. Finally, planning is a double-edged sword. If done right, it brings about tremendous increases in individual and organizational performance. But if done wrong, it can have just the opposite effect and harm individual and organizational performance. With that in mind, what kinds of goals should you set for the company? Should you focus on finances, product development, or people? And should you have an overriding goal, or should you have separate goals for different parts of the company?

If you were the CEO at DuPont, what would you do?

4-1 Benefits and Pitfalls of Planning

This chapter begins by examining the benefits and pitfalls of planning. Next, you will learn how to make a plan that works. Then you will look at the different kinds of plans that are used from the top to the bottom in most companies. In the second part of the chapter, we discuss the steps of rational decision making and consider its limitations. We finish the chapter by discussing how managers can use groups and group decision techniques to improve decisions.

After reading this section, you should be able to:

4-1 discuss the benefits and pitfalls of planning.

Are you one of those naturally organized people who always makes a daily to-do list, writes everything down so you won't forget, and never misses a deadline because you keep track of everything with your handy time-management notebook, iPhone, or PC? Or are you one of those flexible, creative, go-with-the-flow people who dislikes planning and organizing because it restricts your freedom, energy, and performance? Some people are natural planners. They love it and can see only its benefits. Other people dislike planning and can see only its disadvantages. It turns out that *both* views have real value.

Planning has advantages and disadvantages.

Let's learn about **4-1a the benefits** and **4-1b the pitfalls of planning.**

4-1a Benefits of Planning

Planning offers several important benefits: intensified effort, persistence, direction, and creation of task strategies.[2] First, managers and employees put forth greater effort when following a plan. Take two workers; instruct one to "do your best" to increase production, and instruct the other to achieve a 2 percent increase in production each month. Research shows that the one with the specific plan will work harder.[3] Second, planning leads to persistence, that is, working hard for long periods. In fact, planning encourages persistence even when there may be little chance of short-term success.[4] The third benefit of planning is direction. Plans encourage managers and employees to direct their persistent efforts *toward* activities that help accomplish their goals and *away* from activities that don't.[5]

The fourth benefit of planning is that it encourages the development of task strategies. In other words, planning not only encourages people to work hard for extended periods and to engage in behaviors directly related to goal accomplishment, it also encourages them to think of better ways to do their jobs. Finally, perhaps the most compelling benefit of planning is that it has been proved to work for both companies and individuals. On average, companies with plans have larger profits and grow much faster than companies that don't.[6] The same holds true for individual managers and employees: There is no better way to improve the performance of the people who work in a company than to have them set goals and develop strategies for achieving those goals.

4-1b Pitfalls of Planning

Despite the significant benefits associated with planning, it is not a cure-all. Plans won't fix all organizational problems. In fact, many management authors and consultants believe that planning can harm companies in several ways.[7] The first pitfall of planning is that it can impede change and prevent or slow needed adaptation. Sometimes companies become so committed to achieving the goals set forth in their plans, or on following the strategies and tactics spelled out in them, that they fail to see that their plans aren't working or that their goals need to change. When it came to producing environmentally sound cars, GENERAL MOTORS missed its initial opportunity because its culture was "wedded to big cars and horsepower." Whereas Toyota formed its "green group" in the mid-1990s—which led to the development of the Prius—GM killed its electric car program. Today, GM has joined the fray with the Chevy Volt, but faces stiff competition from other electric or plug-in hybrid vehicles, such as the Nissan Leaf.[8]

The second pitfall is that planning can create a false sense of certainty. Planners sometimes feel that they know exactly what the future holds for their competitors, their suppliers, and their companies. However, all plans are based on assumptions: "The price of gasoline will increase by 4 percent per year"; "Exports will continue to rise." For plans to work, the assumptions on which they are based must hold true. If the assumptions turn out to be false, then the plans based on them are likely to fail.

The third potential pitfall of planning is the detachment of planners. In theory, strategic planners and top-level managers are supposed to focus on the big picture and not concern themselves with the details of implementation (i.e., carrying out the plan). According to management professor Henry Mintzberg, detachment leads planners to plan for things they don't understand.[9] Plans are meant to be guidelines for action, not abstract theories. Consequently, planners need to be familiar with the daily details of their businesses if they are to produce plans that can work.

REVIEW 4-1

· ·

Benefits and Pitfalls of Planning

Planning involves choosing a goal and developing a method to achieve that goal. Planning is one of the best ways to improve organizational and individual performance. It encourages people to work harder (intensified effort), work hard for extended periods (persistence), engage in behaviors directly related to goal accomplishment (directed behavior), and think of better ways to do their jobs (task strategies). Most importantly, companies that plan have larger profits and faster growth than companies that don't plan. However, planning also has three potential pitfalls. Companies that are overly committed to their plans may be slow to adapt to changes in their environment. Planning is based on assumptions about the future, and when those assumptions are wrong, the plans are likely to fail. Finally, planning can fail when planners are detached from the implementation of plans.

4-2 How to Make a Plan that Works

Planning is a double-edged sword. If done right, planning brings about tremendous increases in individual and organizational performance. If planning is done wrong, however, it can have just the opposite effect and harm individual and organizational performance.

After reading this section, you should be able to:

4-2 describe how to make a plan that works.

There are several elements involved in making a plan that works.

As depicted in Exhibit 4.1, planning consists of **4-2a setting goals, 4-2b developing commitment to the goals, 4-2c developing effective action plans, 4-2d tracking progress toward goal achievement,** and **4-2e maintaining flexibility in planning.**

4-2a Setting Goals

The first step in planning is to set goals. To direct behavior and increase effort, goals need to be specific and challenging.[10] For example, deciding to "increase

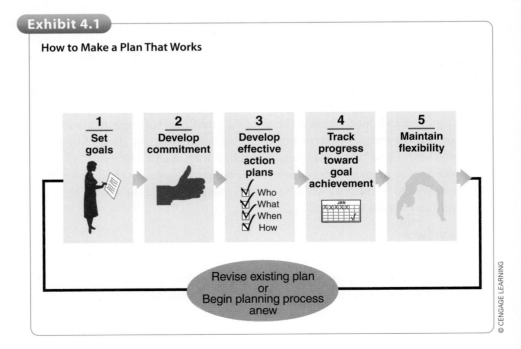

Exhibit 4.1

How to Make a Plan That Works

1	2	3	4	5
Set goals	Develop commitment	Develop effective action plans	Track progress toward goal achievement	Maintain flexibility
		Who / What / When / How		

Revise existing plan
or
Begin planning process
anew

© CENGAGE LEARNING

Part Two *Planning*

sales this year" won't direct and energize workers as much as deciding to "increase North American sales by 4 percent in the next six months." Likewise, deciding to "drop a few pounds" won't motivate you as much as deciding to "lose 15 pounds." Specific, challenging goals provide a target for which to aim and a standard against which to measure success.

One way of writing effective goals for yourself, your job, or your company is to use the SMART guidelines. **SMART goals** are **S**pecific, **M**easurable, **A**ttainable, **R**ealistic, and **T**imely.[11] Let's take a look at *NISSAN's* zero-emissions program, which led to the electric car Leaf, to see how it might measure up to the SMART guidelines for goals.

First, is the goal *Specific*? Yes, because "zero emissions" tells us that Nissan isn't just looking to *reduce* emissions but to eliminate them. And "all-electric" rules out gas-electric hybrids like those produced by competitors. In addition to being specific, the goal is also *Measurable* because Nissan has put a number on the emissions—namely zero. Whether the goal is *Attainable* or not depends on whether the all-electric car performs as expected. Nissan has been researching lithium-ion battery technology for almost 20 years and claims to have developed a battery that can power a car up to 100 miles and recharge in just eight hours. Current trends in government regulation and consumer preferences toward more environmentally friendly vehicles and increasing gasoline prices suggest that an all-electric car is *Realistic* from a business standpoint, but that can't be determined until the Leaf is available to consumers. Finally, the goal is *Timely* because Nissan's goal was to roll out the Leaf in Japan and the United States in 2010, which it achieved, and then to the rest of the world by 2012.[12]

4-2b Developing Commitment to Goals

Just because a company sets a goal doesn't mean that people will try to accomplish it. If workers don't care about a goal, that goal won't encourage them to work harder or smarter. Thus, the second step in planning is to develop commitment to goals.[13]

Goal commitment is the determination to achieve a goal. Commitment to achieve a goal is not automatic. Managers and workers must choose to commit themselves to a goal. Edwin Locke, professor emeritus of management at the University of Maryland and the foremost expert on how, why, and when goals work, tells a story about an overweight friend who lost 75 pounds. Locke says, "I asked him how he did it, knowing how hard it was for most people to lose so much weight." His friend responded, "Actually, it was quite simple. I simply decided that I *really wanted* to do it."[14] Put another way, goal commitment is really wanting to achieve a goal.

So how can managers bring about goal commitment? The most popular approach is to set goals participatively. Rather than assigning goals to workers ("Johnson, you've got till Tuesday of next week to redesign the flux capacitor so it gives us 10 percent more output"), managers and employees choose goals together. The goals are more likely to be realistic and attainable if employees participate in setting them. Another technique for gaining commitment to a goal is to make the goal public. For example, college students who publicly communicated their semester grade goals ("This semester, I'm shooting for a 3.5") to significant

SMART goals
goals that are **S**pecific, **M**easurable, **A**ttainable, **R**ealistic, and **T**imely

goal commitment
the determination to achieve a goal

others (usually a parent or sibling) were much more committed to achieving their grades than those who did not. More important, those students earned grades that were nearly a half-grade higher than the grades of students who did not tell others about their grade goals. So, one way to increase commitment to goals is to go public by having individuals or work units tell others about their goals. Still another way to increase goal commitment is to obtain top management's support. Top management can show support for a plan or program by providing funds, speaking publicly about the plan, or participating in the plan itself.

4-2c Developing Effective Action Plans

The third step in planning is to develop effective action plans. An **action plan** lists the specific steps (how), people (who), resources (what), and time period (when) for accomplishing a goal. Coming out of bankruptcy, corporate reorganization, and a government bailout, *CHRYSLER* presented a detailed plan for returning to profitability. First, it established a time period (*when*) by presenting an outline of what the company would do over the next five years. Second, it clearly identified *who* is behind the company's new strategic plan. CEO Sergio Machionne spearheaded a "painful and difficult" process of assessing Chrysler's strengths and weakness, where "no stone [was] unturned." Third, Chrysler's plan explained *how* it would return to profitability by detailing a thorough makeover of its core brands Jeep, Chrysler, and Dodge. Under this plan, some older models will be redesigned and repackaged, whereas other models that have not sold well will be eliminated (such as the Jeep Commander and Chrysler Sebring). As for the resources (*what*), Chrysler's plan calls for extensive collaboration and borrowing from Italian automaker Fiat (which has a 20 percent stake in Chrysler). Not only will Chrysler sell the Fiat 500, a subcompact city car that has been extremely popular in Europe, but it will also borrow Fiat's technological and design innovations to offer fuel-efficient, stylish vehicles that will attract a new segment of U.S. consumers.[15]

action plan
the specific steps, people, and resources needed to accomplish a goal

Chrysler CEO Sergio Machionne, pictured here, spearheaded the action plans the company needed to return to profitability.

4-2d Tracking Progress

The fourth step in planning is to track progress toward goal achievement. There are two accepted methods of tracking progress. The first is to set proximal goals and distal goals. **Proximal goals** are short-term goals or subgoals, whereas **distal goals** are long-term or primary goals.[16] The idea behind setting proximal goals is that achieving them may be more motivating and rewarding than waiting to reach far-off distal goals.

The second method of tracking progress is to gather and provide performance feedback. Regular, frequent performance feedback allows workers and managers to track their progress toward goal achievement and make adjustments in effort, direction, and strategies.[17] Exhibit 4.2 shows the impact of feedback on safety behavior at a large bakery company with a worker safety record that was two and a half times worse than the industry average. During the baseline period, workers

proximal goals
short-term goals or subgoals

distal goals
long-term or primary goals

Effects of Goal Setting, Training, and Feedback on Safe Behavior in a Bread Factory

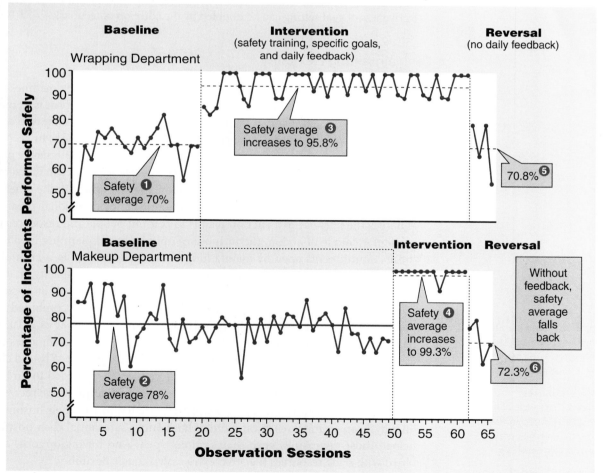

Source: From "A Behavioral Approach to Occupational Safety: Pinpointing and Reinforcing Safe Performance in a Food Manufacturing Plant," J. Komaki, K. D. Barwick, and L. R. Scott, Journal of Applied Psychology, 1978, vol. 63 (1978): 464–445. Copyright © 1978 by the American Psychological Association.

in the wrapping department, who measure and mix ingredients, roll the bread dough, and put it into baking pans, performed their jobs safely about 70 percent of the time (see ❶ in Exhibit 4.2). The baseline safety record for workers in the makeup department, who bag and seal baked bread and assemble, pack, and tape cardboard cartons for shipping, was somewhat better at 78 percent (see ❷). The company then gave workers 30 minutes of safety training, set a goal of 90 percent safe behavior, and then provided daily feedback (such as a chart similar to that in Exhibit 4.2). Performance improved dramatically. During the intervention period, safely performed behaviors rose to an average of 95.8 percent for wrapping workers (see ❸) and 99.3 percent for workers in the makeup department (see ❹), and never fell below 83 percent. Thus, the combination of training, a challenging goal, and feedback led to a dramatic increase in performance. The importance of feedback alone can be seen in the reversal stage, when the company quit posting daily feedback on safe behavior. Without daily feedback, the percentage of safely performed behavior returned to baseline levels—70.8 percent for the wrapping department (see ❺) and 72.3 percent for the makeup department (see ❻). For planning to be effective, workers need both a specific, challenging goal and regular feedback to track their progress. Indeed, additional research indicates that the effectiveness of goal setting can be doubled by the addition of feedback.[18]

4-2e Maintaining Flexibility

Because action plans are sometimes poorly conceived and goals sometimes turn out not to be achievable, the last step in developing an effective plan is to maintain flexibility. One method of maintaining flexibility while planning is to adopt an options-based approach.[19] The goal of **options-based planning** is to keep options open by making small, simultaneous investments in many alternative plans. Then, when one or a few of these plans emerge as likely winners, you invest even more in these plans while discontinuing or reducing investment in the others.

In part, options-based planning is the opposite of traditional planning. Whereas the purpose of an action plan is to commit people and resources to a particular course of action, the purpose of options-based planning is to leave those commitments open by maintaining **slack resources**, that is, a cushion of resources, such as extra time, people, money, or production capacity, that can be used to address and adapt to unanticipated changes, problems, or opportunities.[20] Holding options open gives you choices. And choices, combined with slack resources, give you flexibility. For example, in the summer of 2010, still facing uncertainties surrounding the economic recovery, U.S. companies held $1.84 trillion in cash reserves, up 26 percent from a year earlier. Why did companies have so much cash on hand, much more than they needed to do business? Because when credit markets dried up at the beginning of the recession, most companies could not get the loans they needed to run their businesses. So why keep so much cash on hand? Maintaining substantial cash positions helped those companies keep their options open. And having options, combined with slack resources (i.e., that extra cash), equals flexibility.[21]

Another method of maintaining flexibility while planning is to take a learning-based approach. Traditional planning assumes that initial action plans are correct and will lead to success. By contrast, **learning-based planning**

options-based planning
maintaining planning flexibility by making small, simultaneous investments in many alternative plans

slack resources
a cushion of extra resources that can be used with options-based planning to adapt to unanticipated change, problems, or opportunities

learning-based planning
learning better ways of achieving goals by continually testing, changing, and improving plans and strategies

assumes that action plans need to be continually tested, changed, and improved as companies learn better ways of achieving goals.[22] At 76 million people, baby boomers, born between 1946 and 1964, represent the largest and wealthiest demographic in business history. To appeal to the aging population, companies are adapting products, albeit carefully. For example, Ken Romanzi, chief operating officer at OCEAN SPRAY CRANBERRIES, INC., says, "We don't do anything to remind boomers that they are getting older."[23] So what adjustments have companies made as they learned about aging boomers' preferences? KIMBERLY-CLARK spent two years redesigning its Depend products, making them look more like gender-specific underwear than adult diapers. Mark Cammarota, who manages the Depends brand, says, "Past generations were more accepting that they had a condition, and this was the product that they have to wear. The boomers don't have that attitude. They demand and expect more."[24] Likewise, ARM & HAMMER learned that older customers struggled to read the lettering on its cat-litter packaging, so it increased the font size by 20 percent and made sure there were bright contrasts between the lettering and the background colors.[25]

REVIEW 4-2

How to Make a Plan That Works

There are five steps to making a plan that works: (1) Set SMART goals, or goals that are **S**pecific, **M**easurable, **A**ttainable, **R**ealistic, and **T**imely. (2) Develop commitment to the goals from the people who contribute to goal achievement. Managers can increase workers' goal commitment by encouraging worker participation in goal setting, making goals public, and getting top management to show support for workers' goals. (3) Develop action plans for goal accomplishment. (4) Track progress toward goal achievement by setting both proximal and distal goals and by providing workers with regular performance feedback. (5) Maintain flexibility. Keeping options open through options-based planning and seeking continuous improvement through learning-based planning help organizations maintain flexibility as they plan.

4-3 Planning from Top to Bottom

Planning works best when the goals and action plans at the bottom and middle of the organization support the goals and action plans at the top of the organization. In other words, planning works best when everybody pulls in the same direction.

After reading this section, you should be able to:

    4-3 discuss how companies can use plans at all management levels, from top to bottom.

Exhibit 4.3 illustrates this planning continuity, beginning at the top with a clear definition of the company purpose and ending at the bottom with the execution of operational plans.

Let's see how **4-3a top managers create the organization's purpose statement and strategic objective, 4-3b middle managers develop tactical plans and use management by objectives to motivate employee efforts toward the**

Exhibit 4.3

Planning from Top to Bottom

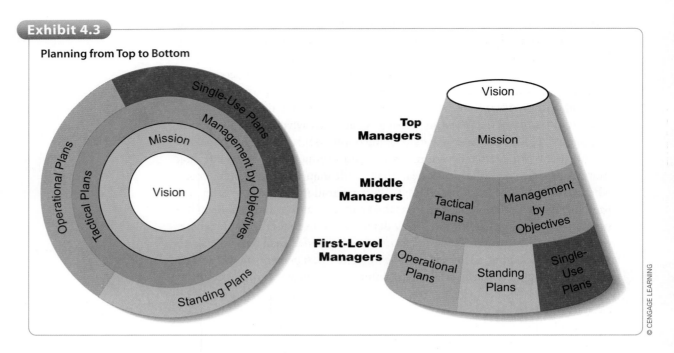

© CENGAGE LEARNING

overall purpose and strategic objective, and **4-3c first-level managers use operational, single-use, and standing plans to implement the tactical plans.**

strategic plans
overall company plans that clarify how the company will serve customers and position itself against competitors over the next two to five years

4-3a Starting at the Top

As shown in Exhibit 4.4, top management is responsible for developing long-term **strategic plans** that make clear how the company will serve customers and

Exhibit 4.4

Time Lines for Strategic, Tactical, and Operational Plans

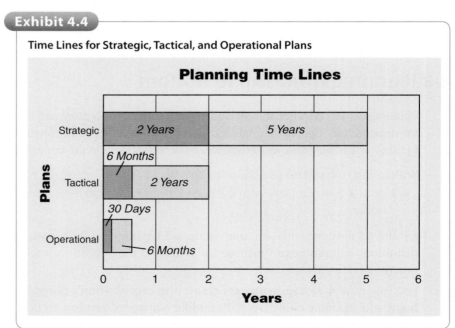

© CENGAGE LEARNING

position itself against competitors in the next two to five years. (The strategic planning and management process is examined in its entirety in Chapter 5.) Strategic planning begins with the creation of an organizational purpose.

A **purpose statement**, which is often referred to as an organizational mission or vision, is a statement of a company's purpose or reason for existing.[26] Purpose statements should be brief—no more than two sentences. They should also be enduring, inspirational, clear, and consistent with widely shared company beliefs and values. An excellent example of a well-crafted purpose statement is that of *Avon*, the cosmetics company: "to be the company that best understands and satisfies the product service and self-fulfillment needs of women globally." This statement guides everyone in the organization and provides a focal point for the delivery of beauty products and services to the customer, women around the world. The purpose is the same whether Avon is selling lipstick to women in India, shampoo packets to women in the Amazon, or jewelry to women in the United States. Despite any regional differences in specific strategy, the overall goal—understanding the needs of women globally—does not change. Other examples of organizational purposes that have been particularly effective include Walt Disney Company's "to make people happy" and Schlage Lock Company's "to make the world more secure."[27]

The **strategic objective**, which flows from the purpose, is a more specific goal that unifies company-wide efforts, stretches and challenges the organization, and possesses a finish line and a time frame.[28] For example, in 1961, President John F. Kennedy established a strategic objective for *NASA* with this simple statement: "Achieving the goal, before this decade is out, of landing a man on the moon and returning him safely to earth."[29] NASA achieved this strategic objective on July 20, 1969, when astronaut Neil Armstrong walked on the moon. Once the strategic objective has been accomplished, a new one should be chosen. However, the new strategic objective must grow out of the organization's purpose, which does not change significantly over time. Consider, for example, NASA's hopes to accomplish its latest strategic goal, or what it calls its "exploration systems mission directorate," between 2015 and 2020. NASA's strategic goal is to "return to the moon, where we will build a sustainable long-term human presence."[30] NASA further explains its strategic goal by saying, "As the space shuttle approaches retirement and the International Space Station nears completion, NASA is building the next fleet of vehicles to bring astronauts back to the moon, and possibly to Mars and beyond."

purpose statement
a statement of a company's purpose or reason for existing

strategic objective
a more specific goal that unifies company-wide efforts, stretches and challenges the organization, and possesses a finish line and a time frame

4-3b Bending in the Middle

Middle management is responsible for developing and carrying out tactical plans to accomplish the

MANAGEMENT FACT

Clean Hands = No Regret?

Your management team recently had to make the difficult choice of cutting 10 percent of the workforce. It was a hard decision, but it would help prevent the permanent closure of the company. Many of the managers, however, are feeling pretty guilty. What to do? Maybe they should wash their hands. Recent research shows that the act of washing hands might help people feel less regret about decisions. In one study, people were given a choice of two jars of jam. One group was allowed to wash their hands with an antiseptic wipe, whereas the other group was allowed only to look at the wipe. Although the group that did not wipe their hands rated the jam they chose 24 percent higher than what they did not choose, the group that did wipe their hands preferred their choice by only a statistically insignificant amount (indicating they didn't feel the need to justify their decision).[31]

organization's strategic objective. **Tactical plans** specify how a company will use resources, budgets, and people to accomplish specific goals related to its strategic objective for the next five years. Whereas strategic plans and objectives are used to focus company efforts over the next two to five years, tactical plans and objectives are used to direct behavior, efforts, and attention over the next six months to two years. Like nearly every other newspaper, *USA Today* has experienced severe losses over the past few years. With subscriptions down by 14 percent, nearly double the industry-wide average, it lost its status as the nation's number one newspaper to the *Wall Street Journal*. Gannett, its parent company, also posted losses of $1.34 billion. To return to profitability, *USA Today* announced that it would de-emphasize print media and focus on delivering digital content to computers and mobile devices. As part of this shift, the newspaper announced a tactical plan to eliminate 9 percent of its staff, spin off the sports division into its own division, and reorganize the newsroom from its traditional four content sections, News, Sports, Money, and Leisure, to Your Life, Travel, Breaking News, Investigative, and National.[32]

Management by objectives is a management technique often used to develop and carry out tactical plans. **Management by objectives (MBO)** is a four-step process in which managers and their employees (1) discuss possible goals; (2) collectively select goals that are challenging, attainable, and consistent with the company's overall goals; (3) jointly develop tactical plans that lead to the accomplishment of tactical goals and objectives; and (4) meet regularly to review progress toward accomplishment of those goals. At *Kindermusik International*, a music education publisher, all 50 employees attend weekly one-hour meetings to review the company's weekly goals and financial results. Half-day review sessions are held each quarter to review results and to discuss how to cut costs and increase revenues. Because they regularly review and discuss goal progress, employees were sensitive to reducing costs, so they proposed replacing the company's five-day sales convention, which costs about $50,000, with a series of meetings. CEO Michael Dougherty said, "If you'd asked me, I would have said, 'We've always done the convention.' But the folks who are closer to the event and closer to the customers know that there were other and better ways to achieve the same goal."[33]

4-3c Finishing at the Bottom

Lower-level managers are responsible for developing and carrying out **operational plans**, which are the day-to-day plans for producing or delivering the organization's products and services. Operational plans direct the behavior, efforts, and priorities of operative employees for periods ranging from 30 days to six months. There are three kinds of operational plans: single-use plans, standing plans, and budgets.

Single-use plans deal with unique, one-time-only events. When one of *Imperial Sugar's* factories in Georgia exploded, killing 14 employees and injuring many more, new CEO John Sheptor quickly put together a plan for identifying missing and injured workers, and establishing a command center

---

tactical plans
plans created and implemented by middle managers that specify how the company will use resources, budgets, and people over the next six months to two years to accomplish specific goals within its mission

management by objectives (MBO)
a four-step process in which managers and employees discuss and select goals, develop tactical plans, and meet regularly to review progress toward goal accomplishment

operational plans
day-to-day plans, developed and implemented by lower-level managers, for producing or delivering the organization's products and services over a 30-day to six-month period

single-use plans
plans that cover unique, one-time-only events

---

what *really* works

Management by Objectives

For years, both managers and management researchers have wondered how much of an effect planning has on organizational performance, or indeed if it has any effect at all. Although proponents argued that planning encourages workers to work hard, persist in their efforts, engage in behaviors directly related to goal accomplishment, and develop better strategies for achieving goals, opponents argued that planning impedes organizational change and adaptation, creates the illusion of managerial control, and artificially separates thinkers and doers.

Now, however, the results from 70 different organizations strongly support the effectiveness of management by objectives (i.e., short-term planning).

Management by Objectives (MBO)

Management by objectives is a process in which managers and subordinates at all levels in a company sit down together to jointly set goals, share information, and discuss strategies that could lead to goal achievement, and then regularly meet to review progress toward accomplishing those goals. Thus, MBO is based on goals, participation, and feedback. On average, companies that effectively use MBO outproduce those that don't use MBO by an incredible 44.6 percent. And in companies where top management is committed to MBO—that is, where objective setting begins at the top—the average increase in performance is an even more astounding 56.5 percent. By contrast, when top management does not participate in or support MBO, the average increase in productivity is only 6.1 percent. In all, there is a 97 percent chance that companies that use MBO will outperform those that don't! Thus, MBO can make a very big difference to the companies that use it.[34]

When done right, MBO is an extremely effective method of tactical planning. Still, MBO is not without disadvantages.[35] Some MBO programs involve excessive paperwork, requiring managers to file annual statements of plans and objectives, plus quarterly or semiannual written reviews assessing goal progress. Today, however, electronic and Web-based management systems and software make it easier for managers and employees to set goals, link them to the organization's strategic direction, and continuously track and evaluate their progress.[36]

Another difficulty is that managers are frequently reluctant to give employees feedback about their performance. A third disadvantage is that managers and employees sometimes have difficulty agreeing on goals. And when employees are forced to accept goals that they don't want, goal commitment and employee effort suffer. Last, because MBO focuses on quantitative, easily measured goals, employees may neglect important but unmeasured parts of their jobs. In other words, if your job performance is judged only by whether you reduce costs by 3 percent or raise revenues by 5 percent, then you are unlikely to give high priority to the unmeasured but still important parts of your job, such as mentoring new employees or sharing knowledge and skills with coworkers.

ISTOCKPHOTO/ISITOX/© VALASHKO VIACHASLAU

to communicate with employees' families, the media, and local government officials.[37]

Unlike single-use plans that are created, carried out once, and then never used again, **standing plans** save managers time because once the plans are created, they can be used repeatedly to handle frequently recurring events. If you encounter a problem that you've seen before, someone in your company has probably written a standing plan that explains how to address it. Using this plan, rather than reinventing the wheel, will save you time. There are three kinds of standing plans: policies, procedures, and rules and regulations.

Policies indicate the general course of action that company managers should take in response to a particular event or situation. A well-written policy will also specify why the policy exists and what outcome the policy is intended to produce. At AMERICAN HONDA, travel expense tracking software sends e-mails to employees and their bosses pointing out that a $1,000 ticket purchased by the employee could have been purchased for $800 a week earlier. This system helps employees adhere to the company's travel policies and expense guidelines.[38]

Procedures are more specific than policies because they indicate the series of steps that should be taken in response to a particular event. A manufacturer's procedure for handling defective products might include the following steps. Step 1: Rejected material is locked in a secure area with "reject" documentation attached. Step 2: Material Review Board (MRB) identifies the defect and how far outside the standard the rejected products are. Step 3: MRB determines the disposition of the defective product as either scrap or rework. Step 4: Scrap is either discarded or recycled, and rework is sent back through the production line to be fixed. Step 5: If delays in delivery will result, MRB member notifies customer.[39]

Rules and regulations are even more specific than procedures because they specify what must happen or not happen. They describe precisely how a particular action should be performed. For instance, many companies have rules and regulations forbidding managers from writing job reference letters for employees who have worked at their firms, because a negative reference may prompt a former employee to sue for defamation of character.[40]

After single-use plans and standing plans, budgets are the third kind of operational plan. **Budgeting** is quantitative planning because it forces managers to decide how to allocate available money to best accomplish company goals. According to Jan King, author of *Business Plans to Game Plans*, "Money sends a clear message about your priorities. Budgets act as a language for communicating your goals to others." Exhibit 4.5 shows the operating budget outlays for the U.S. federal government. Together, social programs (Social Security and income security, or welfare) and health care programs (Medicare and health) account for 62 percent of the federal budget.

REVIEW 4-3
. . . .
Planning from Top to Bottom
Proper planning requires that the goals at the bottom and middle of the organization support the objectives at the top of the organization. Top management develops strategic plans that indicate how a company will serve

---

standing plans
plans used repeatedly to handle frequently recurring events

policies
a standing plan that indicates the general course of action that should be taken in response to a particular event or situation

procedures
a standing plan that indicates the specific steps that should be taken in response to a particular event

rules and regulations
standing plans that describe how a particular action should be performed, or what must happen or not happen in response to a particular event

budgeting
quantitative planning through which managers decide how to allocate available money to best accomplish company goals

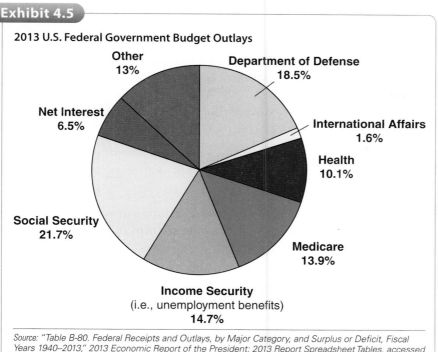

Exhibit 4.5

2013 U.S. Federal Government Budget Outlays

- Other 13%
- Department of Defense 18.5%
- International Affairs 1.6%
- Health 10.1%
- Medicare 13.9%
- Income Security (i.e., unemployment benefits) 14.7%
- Social Security 21.7%
- Net Interest 6.5%

Source: "Table B-80. Federal Receipts and Outlays, by Major Category, and Surplus or Deficit, Fiscal Years 1940–2013," 2013 Economic Report of the President: 2013 Report Spreadsheet Tables, accessed May 10, 2012, from http://www.gpo.gov/fdsys/pkg/ERP-2012/pdf/ERP-2012-table80.pdf.

customers and position itself against competitors over a period of two to five years. Middle managers use techniques like management by objectives to develop tactical plans that direct behavior, efforts, and priorities over the next six months to two years. Finally, lower-level managers develop operational plans that guide daily activities in producing or delivering an organization's products and services. Operational plans typically span periods ranging from 30 days to six months. There are three kinds of operational plans: single-use plans, standing plans (policies, procedures, and rules and regulations), and budgets.

4-4 Steps and Limits to Rational Decision Making

Imagine that your boss asks you for a recommendation on outfitting the sales force, many of whom travel regularly, with new computers. She asks you to prepare a report that details the problems the sales team has been having with its computers and summarizes both current and future needs. You need to come up with at least five plans or options for getting computers to help members of the sales team do their job as efficiently as possible, no matter where they are. When your boss delegates this "computer problem," what she really wants from you is a rational decision. **Decision making** is the process of choosing a solution from available alternatives.[41] **Rational decision making** is a systematic process in which managers define problems, evaluate alternatives, and choose optimal

decision making
the process of choosing a solution from available alternatives

rational decision making
a systematic process of defining problems, evaluating alternatives, and choosing optimal solutions

Exhibit 4.6

Steps of the Rational Decision-Making Process

1 Define the Problem

2 Identify Decision Criteria

3 Weight the Criteria

4 Generate Alternative Courses of Action

5 Evaluate Each Alternative

6 Compute the Optimal Decision

solutions that provide maximum benefits to their organizations. Thus, your boss expects you to define and analyze the computer problem and explore alternatives. Furthermore, your solution has to be optimal, because the department is going to live with the computer equipment you recommend for the next three years. How will you proceed? The second half the chapter will help you figure it out.

After reading this section, you should be able to:

4-4 explain the steps and limits to rational decision making.

The first step involves getting a firm grasp of the process. Exhibit 4.6 shows the six steps of the rational decision-making process.

Let's learn more about each of these steps: **4-4a define the problem, 4-4b identify decision criteria, 4-4c weight the criteria, 4-4d generate alternative courses of action, 4-4e evaluate each alternative**, and **4-4f compute the optimal decision.** Then we'll consider **4-4g limits to rational decision making.**

4-4a Define the Problem

The first step in decision making is identifying and defining the problem. A **problem** exists when there is a gap between a desired state (what is wanted) and an existing state (the situation you are actually facing). For instance, women want to look good and be comfortable in properly fitted clothes. But because the garment industry's size standards were collected 60 years ago on a small group of Caucasian women in their 20s, fit varies tremendously. A size 8 in one brand will be a size 10 in another. As a result, women who can't find well-fitting clothes leave stores without purchasing or are forced to buy poorly fitting clothes that are returned to the store or discarded after several wearings. Either way, the result is the same: Clothing manufacturers have a problem because dissatisfied customers won't buy their brands in the future.[42]

The presence of a gap between an existing state and a desired state (such as selling clothes that should fit, but don't) is no guarantee that managers will make decisions to solve problems. Three things must occur for this to happen.[43] First, managers have to be aware of the gap. They have to know there is a problem before they can begin solving it. For example, after noticing that people were spending more money on their pets, a new dog food company created an expensive, high-quality dog food. To emphasize its quality, the dog food was sold in cans and bags with gold labels, red letters, and detailed information about its benefits and nutrients. Yet the product did not sell very well, and the company went out of business in less than a year. Its founders didn't understand why. When they asked a manager at a competing dog food company what their biggest mistake had been, the answer was, "Simple. You didn't have a picture of a dog on the package."[44] This problem would have been easy to solve if management had only been aware of it.

problem
a gap between a desired state and an existing state

Being aware of a problem isn't enough to begin the decision-making process. Managers also have to be motivated to reduce the gap between a desired and an existing state. During the latest recession, STARBUCKS closed nearly 1,000 stores and laid off over 25,000 employees, to cut expenses by $100 million. But, it wasn't until McDonald's rolled out a national advertising campaign for its lower-priced McCafé mochas, lattes, and cappuccinos that Starbucks was finally motivated to cut product prices. CEO Howard Schultz said, "We know customers are looking for meaningful value, not just a lower price. In the coming days we're going to arm our consumers and partners with the facts about Starbucks coffee."[45] Those facts include lowering the price of basic drinks, such as a "grande" iced coffee, by 45 cents, to less than $2. With profits down 77 percent and same-store sales down 8 percent, and with McDonald's now selling specialty coffee drinks for $3 or less, Starbucks was motivated to take steps to keep customers who might be tempted by McDonald's lower prices.

© Verity Jane Smith/Brand X Pictures/Jupiterimages

Finally, it's not enough to be aware of a problem and be motivated to solve it. Managers must also have the knowledge, skills, abilities, and resources to fix the problem. Product designer Cricket Lee tried to solve the sizing problem in the women's clothing industry by developing FITLOGIC, a sizing standard that takes account of body types and is not intimidating for larger women.[46] Although relatively unknown, Lee has convinced QVC (a home-shopping TV network), Nordstroms, Macy's, and Jones Apparel to license Fitlogic to help women with different body shapes buy better-fitting clothes.[47]

4-4b Identify Decision Criteria

Decision criteria are the standards used to guide judgments and decisions. Typically, the more criteria a potential solution meets, the better that solution will be. Let's return to the employee who was given the responsibility for making a rational decision about the sales team's computer setup. What general factors would be important when purchasing computers for traveling salespeople? Reliability, price, warranty, on-site service, and compatibility with existing software, printers, and computers would all be important, but you must also consider the technical details. What specific factors would you want the computers to have? Well, with technology changing so quickly, you'll probably want to buy computers with as much capability and flexibility as you can afford.

decision criteria
the standards used to guide judgments and decisions

Today, for the first time, laptops now account for over 50 percent of the market.[48] Business laptops come in four distinct model types. There are budget models that are good for routine office work but are usually saddled with a slower processor; workhorse models that are not lightweight but have all the features; slim models for traveling that usually require an external drive to read/write to a DVD/CD; and tablet models like Apple's iPad.[49] What will the users really need? Will they need to burn CDs and DVDs or just read them? How much memory and hard drive space will the users need? Should you pay extra for durability, file encryption, larger screens, and extra-large batteries? Answering questions like these will help you identify the criteria that will guide the purchase of the new equipment.

4-4c Weight the Criteria

After identifying decision criteria, the next step is deciding which criteria are more or less important. Although there are numerous mathematical models for weighting decision criteria, all require the decision maker to provide an initial ranking of the criteria. Some use **absolute comparisons**, in which each criterion is compared with a standard or ranked on its own merits. For example, *Consumer Reports* uses this checklist when it rates and recommends new cars: predicted reliability, previous owners' satisfaction, predicted depreciation (the price you could expect if you sold the car), ability to avoid an accident, fuel economy, crash protection, acceleration, ride, and front seat comfort.[50]

Different individuals will rank these criteria differently, depending on what they value or require in a car. Exhibit 4.7 shows the absolute weights that someone buying a car might use. Because these weights are absolute, each criterion is judged on its own importance, using a five-point scale, with "5" representing "critically important" and "1" representing "completely unimportant." In this instance, predicted reliability, fuel economy, and front seat comfort were rated most important, and acceleration and predicted depreciation were rated least important.

absolute comparisons
a process in which each decision criterion is compared to a standard or ranked on its own merits

---

Exhibit 4.7

Absolute Weighting of Decision Criteria for a Car Purchase

Highlighted numbers indicate how important the particular criterion is to a hypothetical car buyer. Your rankings might be very different.

	CU	NVI	SI	I	CI
1. Predicted reliability	1	2	3	4	⑤
2. Owner satisfaction	1	②	3	4	5
3. Predicted depreciation	①	2	3	4	5
4. Avoiding accidents	1	2	3	④	5
5. Fuel economy	1	2	3	4	⑤
6. Crash protection	1	2	3	④	5
7. Acceleration	①	2	3	4	5
8. Ride	1	2	③	4	5
9. Front seat comfort	1	2	3	4	⑤

© CENGAGE LEARNING

Note: CU: completely unimportant; NVI: not very important; SI: somewhat important; I: important; CI: critically important

Another method uses **relative comparisons**, in which each criterion is compared directly with every other criterion.[51] Exhibit 4.8 shows six criteria that someone might use when buying a house. Moving down the first column of Exhibit 4.8, we see that the time of the daily commute has been rated less important (-1) than school system quality; more important ($+1$) than having an inground pool, sunroom, or a quiet street; and just as important as the house being brand new (0). Total weights, which are obtained by summing the scores in each column, indicate that the daily commute and school system quality are the most important factors to this home buyer, while an inground pool, sun room, and a quiet street are the least important. So with relative comparison, criteria are directly compared with each other.

Exhibit 4.8

Relative Comparison of Home Characteristics

Home Characteristics	DC	SSQ	IP	SR	QS	NBH
Daily commute (DC)		+1	−1	−1	−1	0
School system quality (SSQ)	−1		−1	−1	−1	−1
Inground pool (IP)	+1	+1		0	0	+1
Sun room (SR)	+1	+1	0		0	0
Quiet street (QS)	+1	+1	0	0		0
Newly built house (NBH)	0	+1	−1	0	0	
Total weight	+2	+5	−3	−2	−2	0

© CENGAGE LEARNING

4-4d Generate Alternative Courses of Action

After identifying and weighting the criteria that will guide the decision-making process, the next step is to identify possible courses of action that could solve the problem. In general, at this step the idea is to generate as many alternatives as possible. Let's assume that you're trying to select a city in Europe to be the location of a major office. After meeting with your staff, you generate a list of possible alternatives: Amsterdam, Netherlands; Barcelona or Madrid, Spain; Berlin or Frankfurt, Germany; Brussels, Belgium; London, England; Milan, Italy; Paris, France; and Zurich, Switzerland.

4-4e Evaluate Each Alternative

The next step is to systematically evaluate each alternative against each criterion. Because of the amount of information that must be collected, this step can take much longer and be much more expensive than other steps in the decision-making process. When selecting a European city for your office, you could contact economic development offices in each city, systematically interview businesspeople or executives who operate there, retrieve and use published government data on each location, or rely on published studies such as Cushman & Wakefield's *European Cities Monitor*, which conducts an annual survey of more than 500 senior European executives who rate 34 European cities on 12 business-related criteria.[52]

No matter how you gather the information, once you have it, the key is to systematically use that information to evaluate each alternative against each criterion. Exhibit 4.9 shows how each of the 10 cities on your staff's list fared on each of the 12 criteria (higher scores are better), from qualified staff to freedom from pollution. Although London has the most qualified staff, the best access to markets and telecommunications, and is the easiest city to travel to and from,

relative comparisons
a process in which each decision criterion is compared directly with every other criterion

Exhibit 4.9

Criteria Ratings Used to Determine the Best Location for a New Office

	Access to Markets	Qualified staff	Telecommunications	Travel to/from City	Cost & Value of Office Space	Cost of Staff	Available Office Space	Languages Spoken	Business Climate	Travel within City	Quality of Life	Freedom from pollution	Weighted Average	Ranking
Criteria Weights	0.60	0.53	0.52	0.42	0.33	0.32	0.25	0.21	0.20	0.20	0.16	0.16		
London	1.50	1.36	1.27	1.79	0.27	0.10	0.42	1.48	0.55	1.26	0.46	0.15	4.03	1
Paris	1.09	0.84	0.89	1.36	0.22	0.10	0.37	0.58	0.30	1.07	0.52	0.12	2.83	2
Frankfurt	0.68	0.57	0.70	1.17	0.38	0.11	0.44	0.57	0.38	0.35	0.17	0.18	2.16	3
Amsterdam	0.42	0.40	0.39	0.68	0.30	0.19	0.30	0.96	0.47	0.34	0.44	0.63	1.72	5
Brussels	0.46	0.43	0.37	0.48	0.44	0.17	0.42	0.98	0.37	0.29	0.41	0.27	1.65	7
Berlin	0.44	0.39	0.41	0.35	0.78	0.40	0.79	0.50	0.34	0.78	0.38	0.29	1.85	4
Munich	0.34	0.47	0.48	0.37	0.18	0.03	0.18	0.30	0.22	0.47	0.62	0.57	1.36	9
Madrid	0.45	0.46	0.27	0.41	0.52	0.61	0.67	0.22	0.29	0.53	0.67	0.13	1.70	6
Barcelona	0.23	0.32	0.16	0.29	0.52	0.59	0.52	0.23	0.31	0.47	1.08	0.42	1.45	8
Dusseldorf	0.30	0.30	0.23	0.21	0.37	0.14	0.28	0.18	0.17	0.22	0.20	0.26	0.97	10

Source: "European Cities Monitor," Cushman & Wakefield, 2011, available at www.cushwake.com/cwglobal/docviewer/2120_ECM_2011__FINAL_10Oct.pdf?id=c 50500003p&repositoryKey=CoreRepository&itemDesc=document&cid=c38200001p&crep=Core&cdesc=binaryPubContent&Country=GLOBAL& Language=EN&just_logged_in=1.

it is also one of the most polluted and expensive cities on the list. Paris offers excellent access to markets and clients, but if your staff is multilingual, Amsterdam may be a better choice.

4-4f Compute the Optimal Decision

The final step in the decision-making process is to compute the optimal decision by determining the optimal value of each alternative. This is done by multiplying the rating for each criterion (Step 4.5) by the weight for that criterion (Step 4.3), and then summing those scores for each alternative course of action that you generated (Step 4.4). For example, the 500 executives participating in Cushman & Wakefield's survey of the best European cities for business rated the 12 decision criteria in terms of importance, as shown in the first row of Exhibit 4.9 ("Criteria Weights"). Access to quality staff, markets, telecommunication, and easy travel to and from the city were the four most important factors, and quality of life and freedom from pollution were the least important factors.

To calculate the optimal value for Paris, its score in each category is multiplied by the weight for each category (0..84 × 0.53 in the qualified staff category, e.g.). Then all of these scores are added together to produce the optimal value, as follows:

$$(1.09 \times 0.60) + (0.84 \times 0.53) +$$
$$(0.89 \times 0.52) +$$
$$(1.36 \times 0.42) + (0.22 \times 0.33) + (0.10 \times 0.32) +$$
$$(0.37 \times 0.25) + (.058 \times 0.21) + (0.30 \times 0.20) +$$
$$(1.07 \times 0.20) + (0.52 \times 0.16) + (0.12 \times 0.16) = 2.83$$

Because London has a weighted average of 4.03 compared to 2.83 for Paris and 2.16 for Frankfurt, London clearly ranks as the best location for your company's new European office because of: its large number of qualified staff; easy access to markets; outstanding ease of travel to, from, and within the city; excellent telecommunications; and top-notch business climate.

4-4g Limits to Rational Decision Making

In general, managers who diligently complete all six steps of the rational decision-making model will make better decisions than those who don't. So whenever possible, managers should try to follow the steps in the rational decision-making model, especially for big decisions with long-range consequences.

It's highly doubtful, however, that rational decision making can always help managers choose *optimal* solutions that provide *maximum* benefits to their organizations. The terms *optimal* and *maximum* suggest that rational decision making leads to perfect or near-perfect decisions. Of course, for managers to make perfect decisions, they have to operate in perfect worlds with no real-world constraints. In an optimal world, the manager who asked you to develop a computer strategy for the sales team would be able to define clearly which salespeople needed budget laptops, slim laptops, workhorse laptops, or tablet laptops, and simply ensure that all team members received exactly what they needed to do their jobs effectively. You would not be constrained by price or time as you develop solutions. Furthermore, without any constraints, the manager could identify and weight an extensive list of decision criteria, generate a complete list of possible solutions, and then test and evaluate each computer against each decision criterion. Finally, the manager would have the necessary experience and knowledge with computers to easily make sense of all the sophisticated information. Of course, it never works like that in the real world. Managers face time and money constraints. They often don't have time to make extensive lists of decision criteria. And they often don't have the resources to test all possible solutions against all possible criteria.

The rational decision-making model describes the way decisions *should* be made. In other words, decision makers wanting to make optimal decisions *should not* have to face time and cost constraints. They *should* have unlimited resources and time to generate and test all alternative solutions against all decision criteria. And they *should* be willing to recommend any decision that produces optimal benefits for the company, even if that decision would harm their own jobs or departments. Of course, very few managers actually make rational decisions the way they *should*. The way in which managers actually make decisions is more accurately described as bounded (or limited) rationality. **Bounded rationality** means that managers try to take a rational approach to decision making but are restricted by real-world constraints, incomplete and imperfect information, and their own limited decision-making capabilities.

In theory, fully rational decision makers **maximize** decisions by choosing the optimal solution. In practice, however, limited resources along with attention, memory, and expertise problems make it nearly impossible for managers to maximize decisions. Consequently, most managers don't maximize—they satisfice. Whereas maximizing is choosing the best alternative, **satisficing** is choosing a "good-enough" alternative. With 24 decision criteria, 50 alternative computers to choose from, two computer labs with hundreds of thousands of dollars of equipment, and unlimited time and money, the manager could test all alternatives against all decision criteria and choose the perfect computer. In reality, however, the manager's limited time, money, and expertise mean that only a few alternatives will be assessed against a few decision criteria. In practice, the manager will visit two or three computer or electronic stores, read a couple of recent computer reviews, and get bids from Dell, Lenovo, and Hewlett-Packard as well as some online superstores like CDW or PC Connection. The decision will be complete when the manager finds a good-enough laptop that meets a few decision criteria.

REVIEW 4-4

Steps and Limits to Rational Decision Making

Rational decision making is a six-step process in which managers define problems, evaluate alternatives, and compute optimal solutions. The first step is identifying and defining the problem. Problems exist where there is a gap between desired and existing states. Managers won't begin the decision-making process unless they are aware of the gap, motivated to reduce it, and possess the necessary resources to fix it. The second step is defining the decision criteria that are used when judging alternatives. In Step 3, an absolute or relative comparison process is used to rate the importance of the decision criteria. Step 4 involves generating as many alternative courses of action (i.e., solutions) as possible. Potential solutions are assessed in Step 5 by systematically gathering information and evaluating each alternative against each criterion. In Step 6, criterion ratings and weights are used to compute the optimal value for each alternative course of action. Rational managers then choose the alternative with the highest optimal value.

The rational decision-making model describes how decisions should be made in an ideal world without limits. However, bounded rationality recognizes that in the real world, managers' limited resources, incomplete and imperfect information, and limited decision-making capabilities restrict their decision-making processes. These limitations often prevent managers from being rational decision makers.

bounded rationality
a decision-making process restricted in the real world by limited resources, incomplete and imperfect information, and managers' limited decision-making capabilities

maximize
choosing the best alternative

satisficing
choosing a "good enough" alternative

4-5 Using Groups to Improve Decision Making

According to a study reported in *Fortune* magazine, 91 percent of U.S. companies use teams and groups to solve specific problems (i.e., make decisions).[53] Why so many? Because when done properly, group decision making can lead to much better decisions than those typically made by individuals. In fact, numerous studies show that groups consistently outperform individuals on complex tasks.

After reading this section, you should be able to:

4-5 explain how group decisions and group decision-making techniques can improve decision making.

Let's explore the **4-5a advantages and pitfalls of group decision making** and see how the following group decision-making methods—**4-5b structured conflict, 4-5c the nominal group technique, 4-5d the Delphi technique, 4-5e the stepladder technique,** and **4-5f electronic brainstorming**—can be used to improve decision making.

4-5a Advantages and Pitfalls of Group Decision Making

Groups can do a much better job than individuals in two important steps of the decision-making process: defining the problem and generating alternative solutions. There are four reasons for this. First, groups are able to view problems from multiple perspectives because group members usually possess different knowledge, skills, abilities, and experiences. Being able to view problems from different perspectives, in turn, can help groups perform better on complex tasks and make better decisions than individuals.[54]

Second, groups can find and access much more information than individuals alone. At *1-800-GOT-JUNK?*, a national chain of over 200 locations that provides efficient, timely junk removal, applicants are not interviewed by one person at a time. Instead, each applicant is interviewed by a group of eight people with eight different areas of expertise. Together they assess the candidate immediately following the interview. CEO Brian Scudamore believes there is wisdom in crowds, and relying on groups to conduct interviews has helped his company maintain a remarkably low employee turnover rate of only 1.4 percent.[55]

Third, the increased knowledge and information available to groups make it easier for them to generate more alternative solutions. Studies show that generating lots of alternative solutions is critical to improving the quality of decisions. Finally, if groups are involved in the decision-making process, group members will be more committed to making chosen solutions work.

Although groups can do a better job of defining problems and generating alternative solutions, group decision making is subject to some pitfalls that can quickly erase these gains. One possible pitfall is groupthink. **Groupthink** occurs in highly cohesive groups when group members feel intense pressure to agree with each other so that the group can approve a proposed solution.[56] Because groupthink leads to consideration of a limited number of solutions and restricts discussion of any considered solutions, it

groupthink
a barrier to good decision making caused by pressure within the group for members to agree with each other

usually results in poor decisions. Groupthink is most likely to occur under the following conditions:

- The group is insulated from others with different perspectives.
- The group leader begins by expressing a strong preference for a particular decision.
- The group has no established procedure for systematically defining problems and exploring alternatives.
- Group members have similar backgrounds and experiences.[57]

Groupthink may be one of the key reasons behind the failure of LEHMAN BROTHERS in 2008, one of Wall Street's largest and most storied investment banks, and the second largest bankruptcy of all time. Lehman Brothers was highly leveraged, which is like betting with borrowed money and is a highly risky strategy. Lehman Brothers began to lose money and kept on investing—partly because of groupthink. Lehman's risk management staff kept telling top management that it was too highly leveraged and that economic conditions could quickly lead to huge losses, but Lehman's leadership wouldn't listen.[58] When Lehman's top risk management officer, Madelyn Antoncic, sounded alarms, she was ignored and excluded from big decisions. Eventually she was fired for her dissenting views.

A second potential problem with group decision making is that it takes considerable time. Reconciling schedules so that group members can meet takes time. Furthermore, it's a rare group that consistently holds productive, task-oriented meetings to effectively work through the decision process. Some of the most common complaints about meetings (and thus group decision making) are that the meeting's purpose is unclear, participants are unprepared, critical people are absent or late, conversation doesn't stay focused on the problem, and no one follows up on the decisions that were made.

A third possible pitfall to group decision making is that sometimes one or two people, perhaps the boss or a strong-willed, vocal group member, can dominate group discussion and limit the group's consideration of different problem definitions and alternative solutions. And unlike individual decisions where people feel personally responsible for making a good choice, another potential problem is that group members may not feel accountable for the decisions made and actions taken by the group.

Although these pitfalls can lead to poor decision making, this doesn't mean that managers should avoid using groups to make decisions. When done properly, group decision making can lead to much better decisions. The pitfalls of group decision making are not inevitable. Managers can overcome most of them by using the various techniques described next.

4-5b Structured Conflict

c-type conflict (cognitive conflict)
disagreement that focuses on problem- and issue-related differences of opinion

Most people view conflict negatively. Yet the right kind of conflict can lead to much better group decision making. **C-type conflict**, or **cognitive conflict**, focuses on problem and issue-related differences of opinion.[59] In c-type conflict, group members disagree because their different experiences and expertise lead them to view the problem and its potential solutions differently. C-type conflict is also characterized by a willingness to examine, compare, and reconcile those differences to produce the best possible solution.

By contrast, **a-type conflict**, meaning **affective conflict**, refers to the emotional reactions that can occur when disagreements become personal rather than professional. A-type conflict often results in hostility, anger, resentment, distrust, cynicism, and apathy. Unlike c-type conflict, a-type conflict undermines team effectiveness by preventing teams from engaging in the activities characteristic of c-type conflict that are critical to team effectiveness. Examples of a-type conflict statements are "your idea," "our idea," "my department," "you don't know what you are talking about," or "you don't understand our situation." Rather than focusing on issues and ideas, these statements focus on individuals.[60]

Two methods of introducing structured c-type conflict into the group decision-making process are devil's advocacy and dialectical inquiry. The **devil's advocacy** approach can be used to create c-type conflict by assigning an individual or a subgroup the role of critic. The following five steps establish a devil's advocacy program:

1. Generate a potential solution.
2. Assign a devil's advocate to criticize and question the solution.
3. Present the critique of the potential solution to key decision makers.
4. Gather additional relevant information.
5. Decide whether to use, change, or not use the originally proposed solution.[61]

Dialectical inquiry creates c-type conflict by forcing decision makers to state the assumptions of a proposed solution (a thesis) and then generate a solution that is the opposite (antithesis) of the proposed solution. The following are the five steps of the dialectical inquiry process:

1. Generate a potential solution.
2. Identify the assumptions underlying the potential solution.
3. Generate a conflicting counterproposal based on the opposite assumptions.
4. Have advocates of each position present their arguments and engage in a debate in front of key decision makers.
5. Decide whether to use, change, or not use the originally proposed solution.[62]

BMW uses dialectical inquiry in its design process, typically creating six internal design teams to compete against each other to design a new car. After a front-runner or leading design emerges from one of the teams, another team is assigned to design a car that is diametrically opposed to the leading design (Step 3 of the dialectical inquiry method).[63]

When properly used, both the devil's advocacy and dialectical inquiry approaches introduce c-type conflict into the decision-making process. Contrary to the common belief that conflict is bad, studies show that these methods lead not only to less a-type conflict but also improved decision quality and greater acceptance of decisions once they have been made.[64] See the What Really Works feature for more information on both techniques.

a-type conflict (affective conflict)
disagreement that focuses on individuals or personal issues

devil's advocacy
a decision-making method in which an individual or a subgroup is assigned the role of a critic

dialectical inquiry
a decision-making method in which decision makers state the assumptions of a proposed solution (a thesis) and generate a solution that is the opposite (antithesis) of that solution

4-5c Nominal Group Technique

Nominal means "in name only." Accordingly, the **nominal group technique** received its name because it begins with a quiet time in which group members independently write down as many problem definitions and alternative solutions as possible. In other words, the nominal group technique begins by having group members act as individuals. After the quiet time, the group leader asks each member to share one idea at a time with the group. As they are read aloud, ideas are posted on flip charts or wallboards for all to see. This step continues until all ideas have been shared. In the next step, the group discusses the advantages and disadvantages of the ideas. The nominal group technique closes with a second quiet time in which group members independently rank the ideas presented. Group members then read their rankings aloud, and the idea with the highest average rank is selected.[65]

The nominal group technique improves group decision making by decreasing a-type conflict. But it also restricts c-type conflict. Consequently, the nominal group technique typically produces poorer decisions than the devil's advocacy and dialectical inquiry approaches. Nonetheless, more than 80 studies have found that nominal groups produce better ideas than those produced by traditional groups.[66]

4-5d Delphi Technique

In the **Delphi technique**, the members of a panel of experts respond to questions and to each other until reaching agreement on an issue. The first step is to assemble a panel of experts. Unlike other approaches to group decision making, however, it isn't necessary to bring the panel members together in one place. Because the Delphi technique does not require the experts to leave their offices or disrupt their schedules, they are more likely to participate. For example, a colleague and I were asked by a local government agency to use a Delphi technique to assess the "10 most important steps for small businesses." The first step is to assemble the group. We assembled a panel of local top-level managers and CEOs.

The second step is to create a questionnaire consisting of a series of open-ended questions for the group. We asked our panel of experts to answer questions like these: What is the most common mistake made by small-business owners? Right now, what do you think is the biggest threat to the survival of most small businesses? If you had one piece of advice to give to the owner of a small business, what would it be?

In the third step, the group members' written responses are analyzed, summarized, and fed back to the group for reactions until the members reach agreement. In our Delphi study, it took about a month to get the panel members' written responses to the first three questions. Then we summarized their responses in a brief report (no more than two pages). We sent the summary to the panel members and asked them to explain why they agreed or disagreed with the conclusions from the first round of questions. Asking group members why they agree or disagree is important because it helps uncover their unstated assumptions and beliefs. Again, this process of summarizing panel feedback and obtaining reactions to that feedback continues until the panel members

nominal group technique
a decision-making method that begins and ends by having group members quietly write down and evaluate ideas to be shared with the group

Delphi technique
a decision-making method in which members of a panel of experts respond to questions and to each other until reaching agreement on an issue

reach agreement. For our study, it took just one more round for the panel members to reach a consensus. In all, it took approximately three and a half months to complete our Delphi study.

Managers should not use the Delphi technique for common decisions. Because it is a time-consuming, labor-intensive, and expensive process, the Delphi technique is best reserved for important long-term issues and problems. Nonetheless, the judgments and conclusions obtained from it are typically better than those obtained from one expert.

4-5e Stepladder Technique

The stepladder technique improves group decision making by ensuring that each member's contributions are independent and are considered and discussed by the group. As shown in Exhibit 4.10, the **stepladder technique** begins with discussion between two group members who share their thoughts, ideas, and recommendations before jointly making a tentative decision. Other group members are added to the discussion one at a time at each step, like a stepladder. The existing group members take the time to listen to and understand each new member's thoughts, ideas, and recommendations. Then they share the ideas and suggestions they had already considered. The group discusses the new and old ideas together and makes a tentative decision. This process (new member's ideas are heard, group shares previous ideas and suggestions, discussion is held, tentative group decision is made) continues until each group member's ideas have been discussed.

For the stepladder technique to work, group members must have enough time to consider the problem or decision on their own, present their ideas to the group, and thoroughly discuss all ideas and alternatives with the group at each step. Rushing through a step destroys the advantages of this technique. Also, groups must make sure that subsequent group members are completely unaware of previous discussions and suggestions. This will ensure that each member who joins the group brings truly independent thoughts and suggestions, thus greatly increasing the chances of making better decisions. All members must be present before a final decision is made.

One study found that groups using the stepladder technique produced significantly better decisions than did traditional groups in which all group

Doing the Right Thing

Dos and Don'ts of Conference Calls

Conference calls are a great way to hold meetings. They are an easy way to get people to "check in" no matter where they are, but there are also many challenges for making them effective and efficient. It can be hard to hear what other people are saying. Some people might be watching TV or surfing the Web instead of paying attention. Some people aren't used to talking on the phone with more than one person and can end up talking over each other. David Lavenda, vice president of Mainsoft, offers up 10 tips for making good conference calls:

1. Keep statements short and ask for frequent feedback.
2. Don't use slides if you can avoid it, since reading slides with text is boring, and you can't control what people are looking at.
3. If you must show slides, don't send them ahead of time.
4. Send out an agenda ahead of time and stick to it.
5. Use video if possible. Skype or webcams provide visual cues that help people stay engaged, and off the video games.
6. Let the participants know if you are recording the call.
7. Start on time.
8. Make sure the moderator dials in early.
9. Don't dial in from a mobile phone.
10. Set limits on call duration.[67]

stepladder technique
a decision-making method in which group members are added to a group discussion one at a time (like a stepladder). the existing group members listen to each new member's thoughts, ideas, and recommendations; then the group shares the ideas and suggestions that it had already considered, discusses the new and old ideas, and makes a decision

what *really* works

Devil's Advocacy, Dialectical Inquiry, and Considering Negative Consequences

Ninety percent of the decisions managers face are well-structured problems that recur frequently under conditions of certainty. For example, for most retailers, a customer's request for a refund on a returned item without a receipt is a well-structured problem. It happens every day (recurs frequently), and it's easy to determine whether a customer has a receipt (condition of certainty).

Well-structured problems are solved with programmed decisions in which a policy, procedure, or rule clearly specifies how to solve the problem. Thus, there's no mystery about what to do when someone shows up without a receipt: Allow the item to be exchanged for one of similar value, but don't give a refund.

In some sense, programmed decisions really aren't decisions, because anyone with experience knows what to do. No thought is required. What keeps managers up at night is the other 10 percent of problems. Ill-structured problems that are novel (no one's seen them before) and exist under conditions of uncertainty are solved with nonprogrammed decisions. Nonprogrammed decisions do not involve standard methods of resolution. Every time managers make a nonprogrammed decision, they have to figure out a new way of handling a new problem. That's what makes the decisions so tough.

Both the devil's advocacy and dialectical inquiry approaches to decision making, along with a related approach (considering negative consequences), can be used to improve nonprogrammed decision making. All three work because they force decision makers to identify and criticize the assumptions underlying the nonprogrammed decisions that they hope will solve ill-structured problems.

Devil's Advocacy

There is a 58 percent chance that decision makers who use the devil's advocacy approach to criticize and question their solutions will produce decisions that are better than decisions based on the advice of experts.

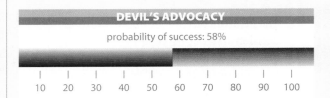

Dialectical Inquiry

There is a 55 percent chance that decision makers who use the dialectical inquiry approach to criticize and question their solutions will produce decisions that are better than decisions based on the advice of experts.

Note that each technique has been compared with decisions obtained by following experts' advice. So, although these probabilities of success (55 percent and 58 percent) seem small, they very likely understate the effects of both techniques. In other words, the probabilities of better decisions would have been much larger if both techniques had been compared with unstructured decision-making processes.

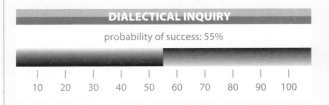

Group Decision Making and Considering Negative Consequences

Considering negative consequences, such as with a devil's advocate or via critical inquiry, means pointing out the potential disadvantages of proposed solutions. There is an 86 percent chance that groups that consider negative consequences will produce better decisions than those that don't.[68]

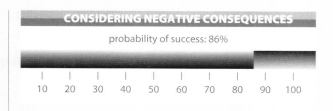

CONSIDERING NEGATIVE CONSEQUENCES

probability of success: 86%

10 20 30 40 50 60 70 80 90 100

Exhibit 4.10

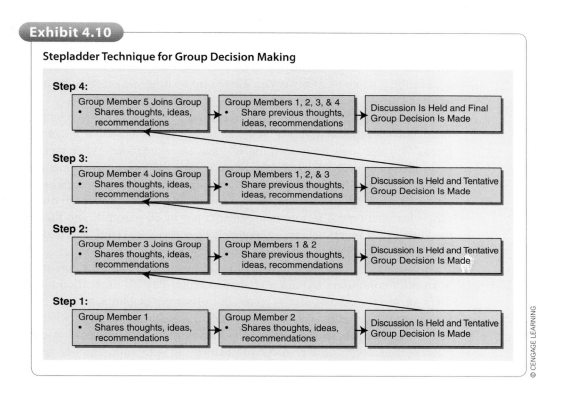

Stepladder Technique for Group Decision Making

Step 4:

| Group Member 5 Joins Group • Shares thoughts, ideas, recommendations | Group Members 1, 2, 3, & 4 • Share previous thoughts, ideas, recommendations | Discussion Is Held and Final Group Decision Is Made |

Step 3:

| Group Member 4 Joins Group • Shares thoughts, ideas, recommendations | Group Members 1, 2, & 3 • Share previous thoughts, ideas, recommendations | Discussion Is Held and Tentative Group Decision Is Made |

Step 2:

| Group Member 3 Joins Group • Shares thoughts, ideas, recommendations | Group Members 1 & 2 • Share previous thoughts, ideas, recommendations | Discussion Is Held and Tentative Group Decision Is Made |

Step 1:

| Group Member 1 • Shares thoughts, ideas, recommendations | Group Member 2 • Shares thoughts, ideas, recommendations | Discussion Is Held and Tentative Group Decision Is Made |

© CENGAGE LEARNING

---

members are present for the entire discussion. Moreover, the stepladder groups performed better than the best individual member of their group 56 percent of the time, whereas traditional groups outperformed the best individual member of their group only 13 percent of the time.[69] Besides better performance, groups using the stepladder technique also generated more ideas and were more satisfied with the decision-making process. This technique also works particularly well with audio conferencing, in which geographically dispersed group members make decisions via a telephone conference call.[70]

4-5f Electronic Brainstorming

Brainstorming, in which group members build on others' ideas, is a technique for generating a large number of alternative solutions. Brainstorming has four rules:

1. The more ideas, the better.
2. All ideas are acceptable, no matter how wild or crazy they might seem.

brainstorming

a technique in which group members build on others' ideas for generating a large number of alternative solutions

3. Other group members' ideas should be used to come up with even more ideas.

4. Criticism or evaluation of ideas is not allowed.

Although brainstorming is great fun and can help managers generate a large number of alternative solutions, it does have a number of disadvantages. Fortunately, **electronic brainstorming**, in which group members use computers to communicate and generate alternative solutions, overcomes the disadvantages associated with face-to-face brainstorming.[71]

The first disadvantage that electronic brainstorming overcomes is **production blocking**, which occurs when you have an idea but have to wait to share it because someone else is already presenting an idea to the group. During this short delay, you may forget your idea or decide that it really wasn't worth sharing. Production blocking doesn't happen with electronic brainstorming. All group members are seated at computers, so everyone can type in ideas whenever they occur. There's no waiting your turn to be heard by the group.

The second disadvantage that electronic brainstorming overcomes is **evaluation apprehension**, that is, being afraid of what others will think of your ideas. With electronic brainstorming, all ideas are anonymous. When you type in an idea and hit the Enter key to share it with the group, group members see only the idea. Furthermore, many brainstorming software programs also protect anonymity by displaying ideas in random order. So if you laugh maniacally when you type "Cut top management's pay by 50 percent!" and then hit the Enter key, it won't show up immediately on everyone's screen. This makes it doubly difficult to determine who is responsible for which comments.

In the typical layout for electronic brainstorming, all participants sit in front of computers around a U-shaped table. This configuration allows them to see their computer screens, the other participants, a large main screen, and a meeting leader or facilitator. Exhibit 4.11 shows what the typical electronic brainstorming group member will see on his or her computer screen. Step 1 in electronic brainstorming is to anonymously generate as many ideas as possible. Groups commonly generate 100 ideas in a half-hour period. Step 2 is to edit the generated ideas, categorize them, and eliminate redundancies. Step 3 is to rank the categorized ideas in terms of quality. Step 4, the last step, has three parts: Generate a series of action steps, decide the best order for accomplishing these steps, and identify who is responsible for each step. All four steps are accomplished with computers and electronic brainstorming software.[72]

Studies show that electronic brainstorming is much more productive than face-to-face brainstorming. Four-person electronic brainstorming groups produce 25 to 50 percent more ideas than four-person regular brainstorming groups, and 12-person electronic brainstorming

electronic brainstorming
a decision-making method in which group members use computers to build on each others' ideas and generate as many alternative solutions as possible

production blocking
a disadvantage of face-to-face brainstorming in which a group member must wait to share an idea because another member is presenting an idea

evaluation apprehension
fear of what others will think of your ideas

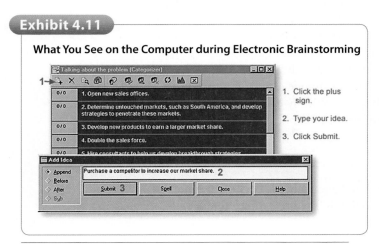

Exhibit 4.11

What You See on the Computer during Electronic Brainstorming

Source: Developing Consensus with GroupSystems. © 2002 GroupSystems.com

groups produce 200 percent more ideas than regular groups of the same size! In fact, because production blocking (having to wait your turn) is not a problem for electronic brainstorming, the number and quality of ideas generally increase with group size.[73]

Even though it works much better than traditional brainstorming, electronic brainstorming has disadvantages, too. An obvious problem is the expense of computers, networks, software, and other equipment. As these costs continue to drop, however, electronic brainstorming will become cheaper.

Another problem is that the anonymity of ideas may bother people who are used to having their ideas accepted by virtue of their position (i.e., the boss). On the other hand, one CEO said, "Because the process is anonymous, the sky's the limit in terms of what you can say, and as a result it is more thought-provoking. As a CEO, you'll probably discover things you might not want to hear but need to be aware of."[74]

A third disadvantage is that outgoing individuals who are more comfortable expressing themselves verbally may find it difficult to express themselves in writing. Finally, the most obvious problem is that participants have to be able to type. Those who can't type, or who type slowly, may be easily frustrated and find themselves at a disadvantage to experienced typists. For example, one meeting facilitator was informed that an especially fast typist was pretending to be more than one person. Says the facilitator, "He'd type 'Oh, I agree' and then 'Ditto, ditto' or 'What a great idea,' all in quick succession, using different variations of uppercase and lowercase letters and punctuation. He tried to make it seem like a lot of people were concurring, but it was just him." Eventually, the person sitting next to him got suspicious and began watching his screen.[75]

REVIEW 4-5

. . . .

Using Groups to Improve Decision Making

When groups view problems from multiple perspectives, use more information, have a diversity of knowledge and experience, and become committed to solutions they help choose, they can produce better solutions than individual decision makers. However, group decisions can suffer from these disadvantages: groupthink, slowness, discussions dominated by just a few individuals, and unfelt responsibility for decisions. Group decisions work best when group members encourage c-type conflict. However, group decisions don't work as well when groups become mired in a-type conflict. The devil's advocacy and dialectical inquiry approaches improve group decisions because they bring structured c-type conflict into the decision-making process. By contrast, the nominal group technique and the Delphi technique both improve decision making by reducing a-type conflict through limited interactions between group members. The stepladder technique improves group decision making by adding each group member's independent contributions to the discussion one at a time. Finally, because it overcomes the problems of production blocking and evaluation apprehension, electronic brainstorming is a more effective method of generating alternatives than face-to-face brainstorming.

Management Team Decision

To Pay or Not to Pay?[76]

Toyota used to sit on top of the world. It basked in the reputation of building high-quality cars efficiently. It enjoyed unprecedented growth, even surpassing General Motors as the largest car manufacturer in the world. But all of that came tumbling down with reports that cars were accelerating out of control, careening down highways, and putting everyone's lives in danger. There was even a recording of a 911 call from an off-duty policeman who lost control of his car and died in the ensuing crash. Toyota responded with a recall of historic proportions—nearly 8 million cars in the United States and 1.8 million in Europe. It even suspended sales of brand new models, including the best-selling Camry and Corolla, until the vehicles could be repaired. But still, there was confusion about what was causing the problems—was it the floor mats, the braking system, the software controlling the engine, or something else? Conspiracy theorists argued that Toyota had no clue what was causing the sudden acceleration and that their recall was basically worthless.

By early 2009, your company was in a situation it had not faced for decades—its sales had dropped by 16 percent. Even General Motors, the bankrupt General Motors, which looked like it could do nothing right for many years, grew 8 percent during the same time. According to some journalists, the recall cost Toyota more than $2 billion. But by March 2010, things seemed to be on the rebound. Sales picked up dramatically, 35 percent from the previous year, and 88 percent from the previous month. Customers were once again buying Toyotas and putting their confidence in its ability to produce reliable cars.

But just as things seemed to be rosy again, Transportation Secretary Ray LaHood announced plans to levy a fine of $16.4 million against your company. The money itself isn't necessarily a problem. Even with losses, Toyota still made $1.8 billion in the fourth quarter of 2009. The fine would be less than 1 percent of what you earned in just three months. So why not just "take the medicine" as it were, pay the fine, and move on from the whole mess? Because the fine comes attached with a statement that Toyota "knowingly hid" safety problems in order to avoid a costly recall. According to LaHood, "We now have proof that Toyota failed to live up to its legal obligations. Worse yet, they knowingly hid a dangerous defect for months from U.S. officials and did not take action to protect millions of drivers and their families."

So, what will you choose to do? You could just pay the fine and admit fault; but if you do, the company's reputation for quality will take a perhaps fatal blow. You wouldn't just be admitting that you made a mistake, but that you deliberately lied about it in order to keep making money. What's more, an admission of covering up would give great support to the hundreds of lawsuits that claim Toyota committed consumer fraud. How much money would those settlements cost? You could, of course, just contest the fine and the admission. But, your company's reputation is already fragile, and fighting the government (and potentially losing) may make things even worse.

Form a group with three or four other students and discuss what decision you would make as a Toyota management team by answering the following questions.

Questions

1. What is your recommendation for how Toyota should approach this situation?

2. What are the decision criteria that should be used in this situation, and how should they be weighted?

3. Under what conditions do you think it is acceptable for Toyota to settle for a "good enough" decision?

Practice Being a Manager

Effective planning and decision making are crucial to the success of organizations. Your success as a manager will be determined in large part by your planning and decision-making capabilities. This exercise highlights some well-tested tools for strengthening your planning and decision-making skills.

Individual Preparation

STEP 1 **Identify your "best company."** Suppose that you are going to develop a plan that will result in your being hired to work for the single *best company* possible. "Best company" has not been defined for you, so you must determine what this might mean. Identify your "best company," and make your plan. You need to consider such aspects as building the right academic and work profile, marketing yourself to the company, and interviewing effectively. Carefully record both your plan and the steps that you took to develop it. In class, you will be asked to share this information with a small discussion group.

Small Group Discussion

STEP 2 **Discuss your plan.** Taking turns, individually share your plan with the members of your discussion group. Members should listen carefully, ask questions, and make notes regarding the similarities and differences of individual plans.

STEP 3 **Create a brochure.** Now suppose that your group has been asked to develop a brochure for distribution in college career centers. The brochure will be titled "Getting a Job with Your Dream Company."

Using what you have learned from sharing your individual plans, work as a group to develop a sketch/outline of this brochure.

Class Discussion

STEP 4 **As a class, discuss the following questions:**

- Did you follow the rational decision-making process in identifying your best company and creating your plan for landing a job with this company? Why or why not?

- What role might bounded rationality have played in your individual and/or team decision-making process?

- Does planning increase the likelihood of success in being hired by a great company? Why or why not?

- If you were an editor assigned the project of developing the brochure "Getting a Job with Your Dream Company," would you be more likely to give the assignment to (1) a qualified individual or (2) a qualified group? Considering your recent experiences in this exercise, what are the trade-offs of each approach (individual versus group decision making)?

Self-Assessment

Self-Management

A key part of planning is setting goals and tracking progress toward their achievement. As a manager, you will be involved in some type of planning in an organization. But the planning process is also used in a personal context, where it is called self-management. Self-management involves setting goals for yourself, developing a method or strategy to achieve them, and then carrying them out. For some people, self-management comes naturally. Everyone seems to know someone who is highly organized, self-motivated, and disciplined. That someone may even be you. If that someone is not you, however, then you will need to develop your self-management skills as a means to becoming a better manager.

A part of planning, and therefore management, is setting goals and tracking progress toward goal achievement.[77] Answer each of the questions using the following scale:

1 Strongly disagree
2 Disagree
3 Not sure
4 Agree
5 Strongly agree

1. I regularly set goals for myself.

    1   2   3   4   5

2. I keep track of how well I've been doing.

    1   2   3   4   5

3. I generally keep the resolutions that I make.

    1   2   3   4   5

4. I often seek feedback about my performance.

    1   2   3   4   5

5. I am able to focus on positive aspects of my work.

    1   2   3   4   5

6. I'll sometimes deny myself something until I've set my goals.

    1   2   3   4   5

7. I use a to-do list to plan my activities.

    1   2   3   4   5

8. I have trouble working without supervision.

    1   2   3   4   5

9. When I set my mind on some goal, I persevere until it's accomplished.

    1   2   3   4   5

10. I'm a self-starter.

    1   2   3   4   5

11. I make lists of things I need to do.

    1   2   3   4   5

12. I'm good at time management.

    1   2   3   4   5

13. I'm usually confident that I can reach my goals.

    1   2   3   4   5

14. I am careful about how I manage my time.

    1   2   3   4   5

15. I always plan my day.

    1   2   3   4   5

16. I often find I spend my time on trivial things and put off doing what's really important.

    1   2   3   4   5

17. Unless someone pushes me a bit, I have trouble getting motivated.

    1   2   3   4   5

18. I reward myself when I meet my goals.

    1   2   3   4   5

19. I tend to dwell on unpleasant aspects of the things I need to do.

    1   2   3   4   5

20. I tend to deal with life as it comes rather than to try to plan things.

    1   2   3   4   5

21. I generally try to find a place to work where I'll be free from interruptions.

    1   2   3   4   5

22. I'm pretty disorganized.

    1   2   3   4   5

23. The goals I set are quite specific.

    1   2   3   4   5

24. Distractions often interfere with my performance.

    1   2   3   4   5

25. I sometimes give myself a treat if I've done something well.

    1   2   3   4   5

26. I am able to focus on positive aspects of my activities.

    1   2   3   4   5

27. I use notes or other prompts to remind myself of schedules and deadlines.

    1   2   3   4   5

28. I seem to waste a lot of time.

    1   2   3   4   5

29. I use a day planner or other aids to keep track of schedules and deadlines.

    1   2   3   4   5

30. I often think about how I can improve my performance.

    1   2   3   4   5

31. I tend to lose track of the goals I've set for myself.

    1   2   3   4   5

32. I tend to set difficult goals for myself.

    1   2   3   4   5

33. I plan things for weeks in advance.

    1   2   3   4   5

34. I try to make a visible commitment to my goals.

    1   2   3   4   5

35. I set aside blocks of time for important activities.

    1   2   3   4   5

SCORING

Determine your score by entering your response to each survey item, as follows. In blanks that say *regular score*, simply enter your response for that item. If your response was a 4, place a 4 in the *regular score* blank. In blanks that say *reverse score*, subtract your response from 6 and enter the result. So if your response was a 4, place a 2 (6 − 4 = 2) in the *reverse score* blank. Add up your total score.

1. regular score _____

2. regular score _____

3. regular score _____

4. regular score _____

5. regular score _____

6. regular score _____

7. regular score _____

8. reverse score _____

9. regular score _____

10. regular score _____

11. regular score _____

12. regular score _____

13. regular score _____

14. regular score _____

15. regular score _____

16. reverse score _____

17. reverse score _____

18. regular score _____

19. reverse score _____

20. reverse score _____

21. regular score _____

22. reverse score _____

23. regular score _____

24. reverse score _____

25. regular score _____

26. regular score _____

27. regular score _____

28. reverse score _____

29. regular score _____

30. regular score _____

31. reverse score _____

32. regular score _____

33. regular score _____

34. regular score _____

35. regular score _____

TOTAL = _____

You can find the interpretation for your score at www.cengagebrain.com.

MANAGEMENT WORKPLACE

© CENGAGE LEARNING

Plant Fantasies: Managerial Decision Making

Teresa Carleo, owner of Plant Fantasies, is the gardener for such well-known New York City properties as the Trump Organization, John Jay College, and Jack Resnick & Sons. In landscaping, success often boils down to big decisions over little details. Although some decisions involve plant colors and types, others involve complex negotiation with people, such as when Plant Fantasies builds designs created by outside landscape architects.

What to Watch For and Ask Yourself

1. Did Plant Fantasies owner Teresa Carleo follow the rational decision-making process to launch Plant Fantasies? Explain.

2. List an example of a programmed decision at Plant Fantasies. Identify a nonprogrammed decision at Plant Fantasies.

Endnotes

1. C. Loomis and D. Burke, "Can Ellen Kullman Make DuPont Great Again?" *Fortune*, May 3, 2010, 156–163; and M. Reisch, "Leading DuPont: After a Difficult First Year as CEO, Ellen Kullman Sets the Stage for Growth," *Chemical & Engineering News*, April 12, 2010, 10–13.

2. E. A. Locke and G. P. Latham, *A Theory of Goal Setting & Task Performance* (Englewood Cliffs, NJ: Prentice Hall, 1990).

3. M. E. Tubbs, "Goal-Setting: A Meta-Analytic Examination of the Empirical Evidence," *Journal of Applied Psychology* 71 (1986): 474–483.

4. J. Bavelas and E. S. Lee, "Effect of Goal Level on Performance: A Trade-Off of Quantity and Quality," *Canadian Journal of Psychology* 32 (1978): 219–240.

5. Harvard Management Update, "Learn by 'Failing Forward,'" *Globe & Mail*, October 31, 2000, B17.

6. C. C. Miller, "Strategic Planning and Firm Performance: A Synthesis of More Than Two Decades of Research," *Academy of Management Performance* 37 (1994): 1649–1665.

7. H. Mintzberg, "Rethinking Strategic Planning: Part I: Pitfalls and Fallacies," *Long Range Planning* 27 (1994): 12–21, and "Part II: New Roles for Planners," 22–30; and H. Mintzberg, "The Pitfalls of Strategic Planning," *California Management Review* 36 (1993): 32–47.

8. J. Stoll, "GM Sees Brighter Future," *Wall Street Journal*, January 18, 2008, A3; D. Welch, "Live Green or Die," *Businessweek*, May 26, 2008, 36–41; L. Greenemeier, "GM's Chevy Volt to Hit the Streets of San Francisco and Washington, D.C.," *60-Second Science Blog*, February 5, 2009, accessed November 30, 2010, from www.scientificamerican.com/blog/post.cfm?id=chevy-volt-to-hit-the-streets-of-sa-2009-02-05; and "Electric Vehicles Expected in the Next Two Years (Photos)," CNET, July 16, 2010, accessed August 15, 2010, from http://news.cnet.com/2300-11128_3-10004136.html?tag=mncol.

9. Mintzberg, "The Pitfalls of Strategic Planning."

10. Locke and Latham, *A Theory of Goal Setting & Task Performance.*

11. A. King, B. Oliver, B. Sloop, and K. Vaverek, *Planning & Goal Setting for Improved Performance: Participant's Guide* (Cincinnati, OH: Thomson Executive Press, 1995).

12. A. Taylor III, "Here Comes the Electric Nissan," *Fortune*, March 1, 2010, 90–98.

13. C. Loomis, J. Schlosser, J. Sung, M. Boyle, and P. Neering, "The 15% Delusion: Brash Predictions about Earnings Growth Often Lead to Missed Targets, Battered Stock, and Creative Accounting—and That's When Times Are Good," *Fortune*, February 5, 2001, 102; H. Paster, "Manager's Journal: Be Prepared," *Wall Street Journal*, September 24, 2001, A24; P. Sellers, "The New Breed: The Latest Crop of CEOs Is Disciplined, Deferential, Even a Bit Dull," *Fortune*, November 18, 2002, 66; and H. Klein and M. Wesson, "Goal and Commitment and the Goal-Setting Process: Conceptual Clarification and Empirical Synthesis," *Journal of Applied Psychology* 84 (1999): 885–896.

14. Locke and Latham, *A Theory of Goal Setting & Task Performance.*

15. K. Linbaugh and N.E. Boudette, "Fiat Models to Drive Chrysler," *Wall Street Journal*, October 27, 2009, accessed September 1, 2010, from http://online.wsj.com/article/SB125659536562909009.html?mg=com-wsj; and B. Vlasic and N. Bunkley, "Party's Over: A New Tone for Chrysler," *New York Times*, November 4, 2009, accessed September 1, 2010, from www.nytimes.com/2009/11/05/business/05auto.html.

16. A. Bandura and D. H. Schunk, "Cultivating Competence, Self-Efficacy, and Intrinsic Interest through Proximal Self-Motivation," *Journal of Personality & Social Psychology* 41 (1981): 586–598.

17. Locke and Latham, *A Theory of Goal Setting & Task Performance.*

18. M. J. Neubert, "The Value of Feedback and Goal Setting over Goal Setting Alone and Potential Moderators of This Effect: A Meta-Analysis," *Human Performance* 11 (1998): 321–335.

19. E. H. Bowman and D. Hurry, "Strategy through the Option Lens: An Integrated View of Resource Investments and the Incremental-Choice Process," *Academy of Management Review* 18 (1993): 760–782.

20. M. Lawson, "In Praise of Slack: Time Is of the Essence," *Academy of Management Executive* 15 (2000): 125–135.

21. J. Lahart, "U.S. Firms Build Up Record Cash Piles," *Wall Street Journal*, June 10, 2010, accessed June 11, 2010, from http://online.wsj.com/article/SB10001424052748704312104575298652567988246.html?mod=WSJ_hps_LEFTWhatsNews.

22. N. A. Wishart, J. J. Elam, and D. Robey, "Redrawing the Portrait of a Learning Organization: Inside Knight-Ridder, Inc.," *Academy of Management Executive* 10 (1996): 7–20.

23. E. Byron, "From Diapers to 'Depends': Marketers Discreetly Retool for Aging Boomers," *Wall Street Journal*, February 5, 2011, accessed March 5, 2011, from http://online.wsj.com/article/SB10001424052748704013604576104394209062996.html.

24. Ibid.

25. Ibid.

26. J. C. Collins and J. I. Porras, "Organizational Vision and Visionary Organizations," *California Management Review* (Fall 1991): 30–52.

27. Ibid.

28. J. C. Collins and J. I. Porras, "Organizational Vision and Visionary Organizations," *California Management Review* (Fall 1991): 30–52; and J. A. Pearce II, "The Company Mission as a Strategic Goal," *Sloan Management Review* (Spring 1982): 15–24. Collins and Porras define an organization's mission: "A mission is a clear and compelling goal that serves to unify an organization's efforts. An effective mission must stretch and challenge the organization, yet be achievable." However, many others define mission as an organization's purpose. In

this edition, to be more specific and avoid confusion, we used Collins and Porras's term *purpose statement*, meaning a clear statement of an organization's purpose or reason for existence. Furthermore, we continued to use Collins and Porras's definition of a mission (i.e., "a clear and compelling goal…,") but instead call it "the strategic objective."

29 "President Bush Announces New Vision for Space Exploration Program," The White House, accessed April 17, 2005, from www.whitehouse.gov/news/releases/2004/01/20040114-1.html.

30 "NASA's Exploration Systems Mission Directorate," Exploration: NASA's Plans to Explore the Moon, Mars, and Beyond, accessed May 29, 2009, from www.nasa.gov.

31 "Clean Hands Appear to Calm the Mind," *Wall Street Journal*, May 18, 2010, accessed August 10, 2010, from http://online.wsj.com/article/SB10001424052748703460404575244823148621434.html.

32 G. Bensinger, "Gannett's USA Today to Cut 130 Jobs, Shuffles Management Posts," Bloomberg.com, August 27, 2010, from www.bloomberg.com/news/2010-08-27/gannett-s-usa-today-to-cut-130-jobs-restructure-as-circulation-declines.html; and M. Liedtke, "USA Today Shaking Up Staff in 'Radical' Overhaul," Associated Press, August 27, 2010, from www.google.com/hostednews/ap/article/ALeqM5j5qqSYmjDdJs6syeIugPf5J50p9AD9HS2JJG0.

33 L. Lorberf, "Running the Show—An Open Book: When Companies Share Their Financial Data with Employees, the Results Can Be Dramatic," *The Wall Street Journal*, February 23, 2009, R8.

34 R. Rodgers and J. E. Hunter, "Impact of Management by Objectives on Organizational Productivity," *Journal of Applied Psychology* 76 (1991): 322–336.

35 E. Marlow and R. Schilhavy, "Expectation Issues in Management by Objectives Programs," *Industrial Management* 33, no. 4 (1991): 29.

36 "Web MBO Teams with Deloitte & Touche to Deliver Innovative Web-Based 'Management-by-Objectives and Performance Management' Solutions," *PR Newswire*, June 19, 2001.

37 "The Issue: Coping with Catastrophe," *Bloomberg Businessweek*, November 20, 2009, accessed January 10, 2010, from www.businessweek.com/managing/content/nov2009/ca20091120_038561.htm.

38 S. McCartney, "Is Your Boss Spying on Your Upgrades?" *Wall Street Journal*, August 12, 2008, D1.

39 Adapted from quality procedure at G&G Manufacturing, Cincinnati, Ohio.

40 N. Humphrey, "References a Tricky Issue for Both Sides," *Nashville Business Journal* 11 (May 8, 1995): 1A.

41 K. R. MacCrimmon, R. N. Taylor, and E. A. Locke, "Decision Making and Problem Solving," in *Handbook of Industrial & Organizational Psychology*, ed. M. D. Dunnette (Chicago: Rand McNally, 1976), 1397–1453.

42 A. Zimmerman, "Cricket Lee Takes on the Fashion Industry," *Wall Street Journal*, March 17, 2008, R1.

43 MacCrimmon, Taylor, and Locke, "Decision Making and Problem Solving."

44 G. Kress, "The Role of Interpretation in the Decision Process," *Industrial Management* 37 (1995): 10–14.

45 J. Jargon, "As Profit Cools, Starbucks Plans Price Campaign," *Wall Street Journal*, April 30, 2009, B3.

46 Zimmerman, "Cricket Lee Takes on the Fashion Industry."

47 Ibid.

48 "Notebook Shipments Surpass Desktops in the U.S. Market for the First Time, According to IDC," BusinessWire, accessed May 30, 2009, from www.businesswire.com/news/home/20081028005575/en/Notebook-Shipments-Surpass-Desktops-U.S.-Market-Time, October 28, 2008.

49 "Computer Buying Guide: Recommended Computers," *Consumer Reports*, www.consumerreports.org, accessed August 29, 2012, *http://www.consumerreports.org/cro/computers.htm*; "Recommended Tablets," *Consumer Reports*, accessed August 29, 2012, http://www.consumerreports.org/cro/tablets.

50 "New-Vehicle Ratings Comparison by Car Category," ConsumerReports.org, accessed February 29, 2005, from www.consumerreports.org/cro/cars/index.htm.

51 P. Djang, "Selecting Personal Computers," *Journal of Research on Computing in Education* 25 (1993): 327.

52 "European Cities Monitor," Cushman & Wakefield, 2010, http://www.europeancitiesmonitor.eu/wp-content/uploads/2010/10/ECM-2010-Full-Version.pdf.

53 B. Dumaine, "The Trouble with Teams," *Fortune*, September 5, 1994, 86–92.

54 L. Pelled, K. Eisenhardt, and K. Xin, "Exploring the Black Box: An Analysis of Work Group Diversity, Conflict, and Performance," *Administrative Science Quarterly* 44, no. 1 (March 1, 1999): 1.

55 B. Scudamore, "Gather Round! For a Group Interview," *Inc.* (August 2006): 94.

56 I. L. Janis, *Groupthink* (Boston: Houghton Mifflin, 1983).

57 C. P. Neck and C. C. Manz, "From Groupthink to Teamthink: Toward the Creation of Constructive Thought Patterns in Self-Managing Work Teams," *Human Relations* 47 (1994): 929–952; and J. Schwartz and M. L. Wald, "'Groupthink' Is 30 Years Old, and Still Going Strong," *New York Times*, March 9, 2003, 5.

58 R. Wartzman, "10 Management Lessons from Lehman's Demise," *Businessweek Online*, September 21, 2009, 13.

59 A. Mason, W. A. Hochwarter, and K. R. Thompson, "Conflict: An Important Dimension in Successful Management Teams," *Organizational Dynamics* 24 (1995): 20.

60 C. Olofson, "So Many Decisions, So Little Time: What's Your Problem?" *Fast Company*, October 1, 1999, 62.

61 R. Cosier and C. R. Schwenk, "Agreement and Thinking Alike: Ingredients for Poor Decisions," *Academy of Management Executive* 4 (1990): 69–74.

62 Ibid.

63 B. Breen, "BMW: Driven by Design," *Fast Company*, September 1, 2002, 123.

64 K. Jenn and E. Mannix, "The Dynamic Nature of Conflict: A Longitudinal Study of Intragroup Conflict and Group

Performance," *Academy of Management Journal* 44, no. 2 (2001): 238–251; and R. L. Priem, D. A. Harrison, and N. K. Muir, "Structured Conflict and Consensus Outcomes in Group Decision Making," *Journal of Management* 21 (1995): 691–710.

65 A. Van De Ven and A. L. Delbecq, "Nominal versus Interacting Group Processes for Committee Decision Making Effectiveness," *Academy of Management Journal* 14 (1971): 203–212.

66 A. R. Dennis and J. S. Valicich, "Group, Sub-Group, and Nominal Group Idea Generation: New Rules for a New Media?" *Journal of Management* 20 (1994): 723–736.

67 D. Lavenda, "10 Rules for Effective Conference Calls" *Fast Company*, May 23, 2010, available online at www.fastcompany.com/1651164/10-rules-for-effective-conference-calls.

68 C. R. Schwenk, "Effects of Devil's Advocacy and Dialectical Inquiry on Decision Making: A Meta-Analysis," *Organizational Behavior & Human Decision Performance* 47 (1990): 161–176; and M. Orlitzky and R. Hirokawa, "To Err Is Human, to Correct for It Divine: A Meta-Analysis of Research Testing the Functional Theory of Group Decision-Making Effectiveness," *Small Group Research* 32, no. 3 (June 2001): 313–341.

69 S. G. Rogelberg, J. L. Barnes-Farrell, and C. A. Lowe, "The Stepladder Technique: An Alternative Group Structure Facilitating Effective Group Decision Making," *Journal of Applied Psychology* 77 (1992): 730–737; and S. G. Rogelberg and M. S. O'Connor, "Extending the Stepladder Technique: An Examination of the Self-Paced Stepladder Groups," *Group Dynamics: Theory, Research, & Practice* 2 (1998): 82–91.

70 S. Rogelberg, M. O'Connor, and M. Sedergurg, "Using the Stepladder Technique to Facilitate the Performance of Audioconferencing Groups," *Journal of Applied Psychology* 87 (2002): 994–1000.

71 R. B. Gallupe, W. H. Cooper, M. L. Grise, and L. M. Bastianutti, "Blocking Electronic Brainstorms," *Journal of Applied Psychology* 79 (1994): 77–86.

72 R. B. Gallupe and W. H. Cooper, "Brainstorming Electronically," *Sloan Management Review* (Fall 1993): 27–36.

73 Ibid.

74 G. Kay, "Effective Meetings through Electronic Brainstorming," *Management Quarterly* 35 (1995): 15.

75 A. LaPlante, "90s Style Brainstorming," *Forbes ASAP*, October 25, 1993, 44.

76 A. Jones, "The Toyota Fine: The $16M Might Not Be Toyota's Biggest Problem," *Wall Street Journal*, April 7, 2010, accessed June 20, 2010, from http://blogs.wsj.com/law/2010/04/07/the-toyota-fine-the-16m-might-not-be-toyotas-biggest-problem/; M. Maynard and H. Tabuchi, "Toyota Sees Sales Rebounding," *New York Times*, March 30, 2010, accessed June 20, 2010, from www.nytimes.com/2010/03/31/business/global/31toyota.html; and "Sizing Up the Damage," *Marketwatch*, January 29, 2010, accessed June 20, 2010, from www.marketwatch.com/story/toyota-faces-grim-january-sales-2010-01-29; and "Toyota Car Recall May Cost $2bn," *BBC*, accessed June 20, 2010, from http://news.bbc.co.uk/2/hi/business/8493414.stm.

77 R.J. Aldag and L. W. Kuzuhara, *Mastering Management Skills: A Manager's Toolkit* (Mason, OH: Thomson South-Western, 2005), 172–173.

Organizational Strategy

OUTLINE

REEL TO REAL

© TETRA IMAGES/CORBIS

Management Workplace is at Theo Chocolate.

SELF-ASSESSMENT

© ISTOCKPHOTO/ALEXANDER KALINA

Want some baseline data on how your attitudes about strategy might affect your management skills? Then do the Self-Assessment for this chapter in the book or online.

ONLINE QUIZZES

© ISTOCKPHOTO/PEARLEYE

Did you get it? Review the main concepts in the chapter by taking the online quizzes on Coursemate!

VIDEO QUIZZES

© ISTOCKPHOTO/DAVID HUGHES

Get more out of the videos by taking the multimedia video quizzes online.

What Would You Do?

Walt Disney Company Headquarters, Burbank, California[1]

Over two decades, your predecessor and boss at the Walt Disney Company, CEO Michael Eisner, accomplished much, starting the Disney Channel, the Disney Stores, and Disneyland Paris, and acquiring ABC television, Starwave Web services (from Microsoft cofounder Paul Allan), and Infoseek (an early Web search engine). But his strong personality and critical management style created conflict with shareholders, creative partners, and board members, including Roy Disney, nephew of founder Walt Disney.

One of your first moves as Disney's new CEO was repairing relationships with Pixar Studios and its then CEO Steve Jobs. Pixar produced computer-animated movies for Disney to distribute and market. Disney also had the right to produce sequels to Pixar Films, such as *Toy Story*, without Pixar's involvement. Jobs argued, however, that Pixar should have total financial and creative control over its films. When Disney CEO Michael Eisner disagreed, relations broke down, with Pixar seeking other partners. On becoming CEO, you approached Jobs about Disney buying Pixar for $7 billion. More important than the price, however, was promising Jobs and Pixar's leadership, President Ed Catmull and creative guru John Lasseter, total creative control of Pixar's films *and* Disney's storied but struggling animation unit. Said Jobs, "I wasn't sure I could get Ed and John to come to Disney unless they had that control."

Although Pixar and Disney animation thrived under the new arrangement, Disney still had a number of critical strategic problems to address. Disney was "too old" and suffering from brand fatigue as its classic but aging characters, Mickey Mouse (created in 1928) and Winnie-the-Pooh (licensed by Disney in 1961), accounted for 80 percent of consumer sales. On the other hand, Disney was also "too young" and suffering from "age compression," meaning it appealed only to young children and not preteens, who gravitated to Nickelodeon, and certainly not to teens at all. Finally, despite its legendary animated films, over time

MARK ASHMAN/DISNEY/HANDOUT/GETTY IMAGES ENTERTAINMENT/GETTY IMAGES

Disney products had developed a reputation for low-quality production, poor acting, and weak scripts. Movies *High School Musical 3: Senior Year*, *Beverly Hills Chihuahua*, *Bolt*, *Confessions of a Shopaholic*, *Race to Witch Mountain*, and *Bedtime Stories* disappointed audiences and failed to meet financial goals. As you told your board of directors, "It's not the marketplace, it's our slate [of TV shows and movies]."

With many of Disney's brands and products clearly suffering, you face a basic decision: Should Disney grow, stabilize, or retrench? Disney is an entertainment conglomerate with Walt Disney Studios (films), parks and resorts (including Disney Cruise lines and vacations), consumer products (e.g., toys, clothing, books, magazines, and merchandise), and media networks such as TV (ABC, ESPN, Disney Channels, ABC Family), radio, and the Disney Interactive Media Group (online, mobile, and video games and products). If Disney should grow, where? Like Pixar, is another strategic acquisition necessary? If so, who? If stable, how do you improve quality to keep doing what Disney has

© DIZZO/ISTOCK PHOTO

been doing, but even better? Finally, retrenchment would mean shrinking Disney's size and scope. If you were to do this, what divisions would you shrink or sell?

Next, given the number of different entertainment areas that Disney has, what business is it really in? Is Disney a content business, creating characters and stories? Or is it a technology/distribution business that simply needs to find ways to buy content wherever it can, for example, by buying Pixar and then delivering that content in ways that customers want (e.g., DVDs, cable channels, iTunes, Netflix, social media, Internet TV)?

Finally, from a strategic perspective, how should Disney's different entertainment areas be managed? Should there be one grand strategy (i.e., growth, stability, retrenchment) that every division follows, or should each division have a focused strategy for its own market and customers? Likewise, how much discretion should division managers have to set and execute their strategies, or should that be controlled and approved centrally by the strategic planning department at Disney headquarters?

If you were CEO at Disney, what would you do?

5-1 Sustainable Competitive Advantage

Just two years ago, there was no market for tablet computers. A number of computer makers sold touch screen laptops, but other than some programs that allowed users to handwrite notes, there was little to distinguish these machines from other, traditional laptops. All of that changed when APPLE released its iPad, a tablet computer that was controlled by a multitouch display and that could run hundreds and thousands of applications that allowed users to read books, watch movies, listen to music, check the weather, or play games. With its innovative product, Apple in effect created a new market for portable, touch-based tablet computers. The iPad is not without its competitors, however. The Amazon Kindle Fire, for example, is a touch screen tablet that runs on Google's Android system. It features a dual-core processor, a 7-inch screen, and enough capacity to store 10 movies, 800 songs, or 6,000 books. The device also allows users to access Amazon's large collection of e-books. In spite of this competition, Apple dominates the tablet computer market. In 2011, Apple sold 40 million iPads and held a dominant 62 percent of the market share. To maintain its dominance, Apple recently announced the release of the new iPad that features a faster processor, 4G network access for faster downloads, as well as voice dictation for e-mails, messages, and other apps that recognize English, French, German, and Japanese. And it has unveiled the new iPad mini, too.[2]

How can a company like Apple, which dominates a particular industry, maintain its competitive advantage as strong, well-financed competitors enter the market? What steps can Apple and other companies take to better manage their strategy-making process?

After reading this section, you should be able to:

5-1 specify the components of sustainable competitive advantage and explain why it is important.

Resources are the assets, capabilities, processes, employee time, information, and knowledge that an organization controls. Firms use their resources to improve organizational effectiveness and efficiency. Resources are critical to

resources
the assets, capabilities, processes, employee time, information, and knowledge that an organization uses to improve its effectiveness and efficiency, create and sustain competitive advantage, and fulfill a need or solve a problem

organizational strategy because they can help companies create and sustain an advantage over competitors.[3] That is, organizations can achieve a **competitive advantage** by using their resources to provide greater value for customers than competitors can. For example, the iPad's competitive advantage came partly from its sleek, attractive design, and partly from the reputation that Apple built producing innovative, easy-to-use products.

The goal of most organizational strategies is to create and then sustain a competitive advantage. A competitive advantage becomes a **sustainable competitive advantage** when other companies cannot duplicate the value a firm is providing to customers. Sustainable competitive advantage is *not* the same as a long-lasting competitive advantage, though companies obviously want a competitive advantage to last a long time. Instead, a competitive advantage is *sustained* if competitors have tried unsuccessfully to duplicate the advantage and have, for the moment, stopped trying to duplicate it. It's the corporate equivalent of your competitors saying, "We give up. You win. We can't do what you do, and we're not even going to try to do it anymore." As Exhibit 5.1 shows, four conditions must be met if a firm's resources are to be used to achieve a sustainable competitive advantage. The resources must be valuable, rare, imperfectly imitable, *and* nonsubstitutable.

Valuable resources allow companies to improve their efficiency and effectiveness. Unfortunately, changes in customer demand and preferences, competitors' actions, and technology can make once-valuable resources much less valuable. For sustained competitive advantage, valuable resources must also be rare resources. Think about it: How can a company sustain a competitive advantage if all of its competitors have similar resources and capabilities? Before the iPad was introduced, netbooks appeared to be the next big thing in mobile computing. They were small and light and very affordable, averaging anywhere from $200 to $500. Users could run basic programs like Web browsing and word processing. Sales were brisk until the iPad came on the market, with its touch-screen, intuitive operating system, and large selection of app software. It took only 28 days for the first iPad to sell 1 million units. The sales of netbooks fell by 40 percent in one year.[4]

Consequently, **rare resources**, resources that are not controlled or possessed by many competing firms, are necessary to sustain a competitive advantage. One of Apple's truly rare resources is its ability to reconfigure existing technology into a package that is easy to use, elegantly designed, and therefore highly desired by customers. Apple used its wealth of experience from developing the iPod, iPod touch, and iPhone to create an operating system for the iPad that was easy to use, and more importantly, basically identical to what was found on its other products. Its single platform gave users the same experience across multiple devices. An iPhone user who just purchased an iPad will have little difficulty learning how to use it. This is not the case with the iPad's chief competitors, tablets powered by Google's Android. Because Android is open source, manufacturers can alter the basic operating system

competitive advantage
providing greater value for customers than competitors can

sustainable competitive advantage
a competitive advantage that other companies have tried unsuccessfully to duplicate and have, for the moment, stopped trying to duplicate

valuable resources
resources that allow companies to improve their efficiency and effectiveness

rare resource
a resource that is not controlled or possessed by many competing firms

Exhibit 5.1

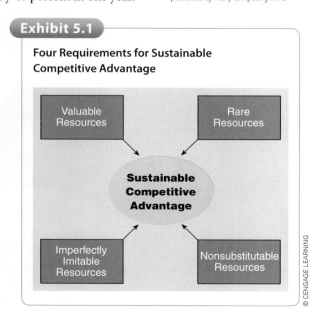

Four Requirements for Sustainable Competitive Advantage

Valuable Resources

Rare Resources

Sustainable Competitive Advantage

Imperfectly Imitable Resources

Nonsubstitutable Resources

© CENGAGE LEARNING

in different ways; so, there is little uniformity across various Android devices. Simply put, one Android tablet might look, and work, differently than another, and one company might offer an app that will not work on another Android device.[5]

As this example shows, valuable and rare resources can create temporary competitive advantage. For sustained competitive advantage, however, other firms must be unable to imitate or find substitutes for those valuable, rare resources. **Imperfectly imitable resources** are those resources that are impossible or extremely costly or difficult to duplicate. Both GOOGLE and AMAZON operate online app stores that are in some way similar to Apple's App Store. Users can log on to the sites, browse around for programs, and purchase and download them to their devices. The big difference, however, is in security. Apple's App Store is a closed platform, meaning that if a software developer wants to sell an app on Apple's site, the company first puts it through a review process to check for content and security issues. As noted above, however, Android is an open platform, and in the case of apps, it means that Google does not pre-screen apps before publishing them. This makes it far easier for developers with bad intentions to create and sell applications that can harm devices or steal personal information. According to a study by Juniper Networks, the number of such malware applications for Android climbed to 28,000 in 2011, a 3,325 percent increase from the previous year.[6]

Valuable, rare, imperfectly imitable resources can produce sustainable competitive advantage only if they are also **nonsubstitutable resources**, meaning that no other resources can replace them and produce similar value or competitive advantage. This is most evident in the dominance of Apple's iTunes software. The industry has tried to produce equivalent substitutes for iTunes, but competitors have had to experiment with different business models in order to get customers to accept them. For example, AMAZON MP3 not only gives consumers access to 18 million digital songs, but it also allows them to store their files on Amazon's cloud servers and stream them to any device they own. Google's music service, called appropriately enough GOOGLE MUSIC, also allows users to store their music on Google's cloud servers and stream to whatever device they want. Google, however, was able to reach licensing agreements with only two record companies, so the selection of songs that Google Music has for sale is quite limited.

Apple has responded to these competitors by introducing its own cloud-based service called iCloud. The software essentially provides consumers with an online locker, in which they can store music, video, or photo files, as well as apps, to access from multiple devices. In addition, iCloud lets users synchronize other data, like appointments, e-mail, and documents, between their iPhone, iPad, and Macintosh computers.[7]

In summary, Apple has reaped the rewards of a first-mover advantage when it introduced the iPad. The company's history of developing customer-friendly software, the innovative capabilities of the iPad, the uniformity of experience, and the security of the App Store provide customers with a service that has been valuable, rare, relatively nonsubstitutable, and, in the past, imperfectly imitable. Past success is, however, no guarantee of future success: Apple needs to continually change and develop its offerings or risk being unseated by a

imperfectly imitable resource
a resource that is impossible or extremely costly or difficult for other firms to duplicate

nonsubstitutable resource
a resource that produces value or competitive advantage and has no equivalent substitutes or replacements

more nimble competitor whose products are more relevant and have higher perceived value to the consumer.

REVIEW 5-1

Sustainable Competitive Advantage

Firms can use their resources to create and sustain a competitive advantage, that is, to provide greater value for customers than competitors can. A competitive advantage becomes sustainable when other companies cannot duplicate the benefits it provides and have, for now, stopped trying. To provide a sustainable competitive advantage, the firm's resources must be valuable (capable of improving efficiency and effectiveness), rare (not possessed by many competing firms), imperfectly imitable (extremely costly or difficult to duplicate), and nonsubstitutable (competitors cannot substitute other resources to produce similar value).

5-2 Strategy-Making Process

To create a sustainable competitive advantage, a company must have a strategy.[8]

After reading this section, you should be able to:

5-2 describe the steps involved in the strategy-making process.

Exhibit 5.2 displays the three steps of the strategy-making process: **5-2a assess the need for strategic change, 5-2b conduct a situational analysis,** and then **5-2c choose strategic alternatives.** Let's examine each of these steps in more detail.

5-2a Assessing the Need for Strategic Change

The external business environment is much more turbulent than it used to be. With customers' needs constantly growing and changing, and with competitors working harder, faster, and smarter to meet those needs, the first step in creating a strategy is determining the need for strategic change. In other words, the company should determine whether it needs to change its strategy to sustain a competitive advantage.[9]

Determining the need for strategic change might seem easy to do, but it's really not. There's a great deal of uncertainty in strategic business environments. Furthermore, top-level managers are often slow to recognize the need for strategic change, especially at successful companies that have created and sustained competitive advantages. Because they are acutely aware of the strategies that made their companies successful, they continue to rely on those strategies, even as the competition changes. In other words, success often leads to **competitive inertia**—a reluctance to change strategies or competitive practices that have been successful in the past.

CARREFOUR, the French retail giant that invented hypermarket stores (combination grocery and department stores under one roof) half a century ago, is a prime example of a company suffering from competitive inertia. Carrefour has lost market share in its hypermarket stores for five straight years.[10] Carrefour's "quality for all" approach, which focused on high-quality goods and food, relied on frequent price increases to keep profits strong. European customers, however, realized they could get cheaper prices and better service at specialized stores, such as electronics stores. The company's new CEO Lars Olofsson has attacked

competitive inertia
a reluctance to change strategies or competitive practices that have been successful in the past

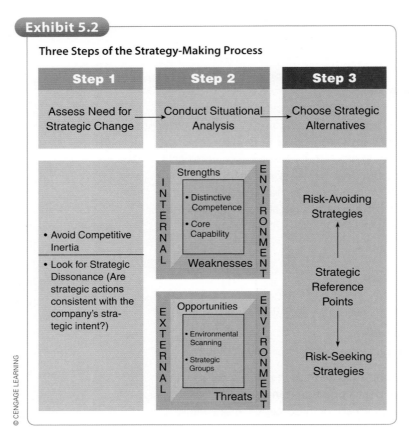

Exhibit 5.2

Three Steps of the Strategy-Making Process

Step 1	Step 2	Step 3
Assess Need for Strategic Change	Conduct Situational Analysis	Choose Strategic Alternatives

Step 1:
- Avoid Competitive Inertia
- Look for Strategic Dissonance (Are strategic actions consistent with the company's strategic intent?)

Step 2:

INTERNAL ENVIRONMENT
Strengths
- Distinctive Competence
- Core Capability
Weaknesses

EXTERNAL ENVIRONMENT
Opportunities
- Environmental Scanning
- Strategic Groups
Threats

Step 3:
Risk-Avoiding Strategies
Strategic Reference Points
Risk-Seeking Strategies

© CENGAGE LEARNING

Carrefour's competitive inertia by replacing the entire top-management team with outsiders from other companies. He's also declared that Carrefour will follow a low-price strategy that relies on selling its own house brands rather than those of other companies. Says Olofsson, "What's very important is price image. If I'm the No. 1 preferred retailer…I'm the most likely to be the most profitable."[11]

Besides being aware of the dangers of competitive inertia, what can managers do to improve the speed and accuracy with which they determine the need for strategic change? One method is to actively look for signs of strategic dissonance. **Strategic dissonance** is a discrepancy between a company's intended strategy and the strategic actions managers take when actually implementing that strategy.[12] While most toy and game makers make big profits during the holidays, *HASBRO*, the maker of games like Monopoly and Scrabble, saw profits fall 15 percent during one disastrous Christmas season. The sharp decline was due primarily to Hasbro's strategy of focusing on movies and television. Rather than producing innovative board-game offerings, or investing in the rapidly growing online gaming market, Hasbro had spent most of its resources on trying to develop movies and TV shows based on their toys and games, such as the *Transformers* movie franchise and *Battleship*.[13]

Note, however, that strategic dissonance is not the same thing as when a strategy does not produce the results that it's supposed to. It can also mean that the intended strategy is out of date and needs to be changed.

5-2b Situational Analysis

A situational analysis can also help managers determine the need for strategic change. A **situational analysis**, also called a **SWOT analysis** for *strengths, weaknesses, opportunities*, and *threats*, is an assessment of the strengths and weaknesses in an organization's internal environment and the opportunities and threats in its external environment.[14] Ideally, as shown in Step 2 of Exhibit 5.2, a SWOT analysis helps a company determine how to increase internal strengths and minimize internal weaknesses while maximizing external opportunities and minimizing external threats.

When *MEMORIAL HOSPITAL* of Fremont, Ohio, decided that the process it used to order all the necessary medical and administrative supplies was out of control, managers asked all the departments to work together to conduct

strategic dissonance
a discrepancy between a company's intended strategy and the strategic actions managers take when implementing that strategy

situational (SWOT) analysis
an assessment of the strengths and weaknesses in an organization's internal environment and the opportunities and threats in its external environment

a SWOT analysis. The process helped the hospital identify its strengths, such as the experience of the materials management group, and its weaknesses, which included allowing anyone in the organization to order anything he or she wanted from any vendor. Departments outlined opportunities to dramatically improve the quality and flow of supplies while controlling costs and determined that one of the biggest threats was expired medical supplies. Using the SWOT analysis as a map, the hospital began requiring all vendors to register when they entered the building, wear a visitor's badge while on hospital premises, and process all orders through the central purchasing department. Soon, the hospital staff developed the right mix of products and product inventories required for each area of the hospital and at the same time dramatically reduced the number of staff involved in purchasing and stocking supplies. Over two years, the hospital saved more than $1 million, and administrators won praise from hospital departments for their ability to improve services.[15]

As this example illustrates, a SWOT analysis can be used to evaluate entire companies or individual operations within an organization. All companies' competitive advantages can erode over time if internal strengths eventually become weaknesses. Consequently, an analysis of an organization's internal environment, that is, a company's strengths and weaknesses, often begins with an assessment of its distinctive competencies and core capabilities. A **distinctive competence** is something that a company can make, do, or perform better than its competitors. For example, *Consumer Reports* magazine consistently ranks Honda and Subaru cars as tops in quality and reliability.[16] Similarly, *PC Magazine* readers ranked Apple's desktop and laptop computers best in terms of service and reliability.[17]

Whereas distinctive competencies are tangible—for example, a product or service is faster, cheaper, or better—the core capabilities that produce distinctive competencies are not. **Core capabilities** are the less visible, internal, decision-making routines, problem-solving processes, and organizational cultures that determine how efficiently inputs can be turned into outputs. Distinctive competencies cannot be sustained for long without superior core capabilities. Offering gourmet, environmentally conscious food products at a low cost is the distinctive competence of TRADER JOE'S. One can find 10 kinds of hummus and every kind of dried fruit imaginable. Most of the products sold at Trader Joe's have no artificial colors, artificial flavors, or preservatives. The core capabilities the company uses to execute this strategy are to buy in large quantities and to find great, new products for its stores. While a typical grocery store will sell 40 different kinds of peanut butter, Trader Joe's sells just 10, and sells out of each kind quicker. In turn, suppliers sell higher volumes of products to Trader Joe's for lower prices. The key to making that work, however, is for Trader Joe's customers to know its products are excellent. A former employee put it this way, if customers are "going to get behind only one jar of Greek olives, then they're sure as heck going to make sure it's the most fabulous jar of Greek olives they can find for the price."[18] Most grocery chains rely on trade shows for their research, but Trader Joe's core capability is sending its four best buyers, also known as product developers, around the world in search of new, high-quality, great-tasting products. This results in high travel expenses, but with great results. Stores feature 15 or more new products each week, bringing curious customers back to find out what's new.[19]

After examining internal strengths and weaknesses, the second part of a situational analysis is to look outside the company and assess the opportunities

distinctive competence
what a company can make, do, or perform better than its competitors

core capabilities
the internal decision-making routines, problem-solving processes, and organizational cultures that determine how efficiently inputs can be turned into outputs

and threats in the external environment. In Chapter 2, you learned that *environmental scanning* involves searching the environment for important events or issues that might affect the organization, such as pricing trends or new products and technology. In a situational analysis, however, managers use environmental scanning to identify specific opportunities and threats that can either improve or harm the company's ability to sustain its competitive advantage. Identification of strategic groups and formation of shadow-strategy task forces are two ways to do this.

Strategic groups are not groups that actually work together. They are companies—usually competitors—that managers closely follow. More specifically, a **strategic group** is a group of other companies within an industry against which top managers compare, evaluate, and benchmark their company's strategic threats and opportunities.[20] (*Benchmarking* involves identifying outstanding practices, processes, and standards at other companies and adapting them to your own company.) Typically, managers include companies as part of their strategic group if they compete directly with those companies for customers or if those companies use strategies similar to theirs. The U.S. home improvement industry has annual sales in excess of $290 billion.[22] It's likely that the managers at *Home Depot*, the largest U.S. home improvement and hardware retailer, assess strategic threats and opportunities by comparing their company to a strategic group consisting of the other major home improvement supply companies.

In fact, when scanning the environment for strategic threats and opportunities, managers tend to categorize the different companies in their industries as core, secondary, and transient firms.[23] **Core firms** are the central companies in a strategic group. Among home improvement stores, Lowe's is the closest competitor to Home Depot and is the core firm in Home Depot's strategic group. When most managers scan their environments for strategic threats and opportunities, they concentrate on the strategic actions of core firms, not unrelated firms like Aubuchon. For example, unlike Lowe's, Home Depot's management probably doesn't include Aubuchon Hardware in its core strategic group, because it has only 130 stores in New England and upstate New York.

Secondary firms are firms that use strategies related to but somewhat different from those of core firms. 84 Lumber has 265 stores in 35 states, but even though its stores are open to the public, the company focuses on supplying professional contractors, to whom it sells 95 percent of its products. Home Depot would most likely classify 84 Lumber as a secondary firm in its strategic group analysis.[24] Managers need to be aware of the potential threats and opportunities posed by secondary firms, but they usually spend more time assessing the threats and opportunities associated with core firms.

In short, a situational analysis has two basic parts. The first is to examine internal strengths and weaknesses by focusing on distinctive competencies and core capabilities. The second is to examine external opportunities and threats by focusing on environmental scanning and strategic groups.

strategic group
a group of companies within an industry against which top managers compare, evaluate, and benchmark strategic threats and opportunities

core firms
the central companies in a strategic group

secondary firms
the firms in a strategic group that follow strategies related to but somewhat different from those of the core firms

5-2c Choosing Strategic Alternatives

After determining the need for strategic change and conducting a situational analysis, the last step in the strategy-making process is to choose strategic alternatives that will help the company create or maintain a sustainable competitive advantage. According to strategic reference point theory, managers choose between two basic alternative strategies. They can choose a conservative, *risk-avoiding strategy* that aims to protect an existing competitive advantage, or they can choose an aggressive, *risk-seeking strategy* that aims to extend or create a sustainable competitive advantage. Menards is a hardware store chain with 40,000 employees and 210 locations throughout the Midwest.[25] When hardware giant Home Depot entered the Midwest, Menards faced a choice: Avoid risk by continuing with the strategy it had in place before Home Depot's arrival, or seek risk by trying to establish a competitive advantage against Home Depot, which is six times its size. Some of its competitors decided to fold. Kmart closed all of its Builders Square hardware stores when Home Depot came to Minneapolis. Handy Andy liquidated its 74 stores when Home Depot came to the Midwest. But Menards decided to fight, spending millions to open 35 new stores at the same time that Home Depot was opening 44 of its own.[26]

The choice to seek or avoid risk typically depends on whether top management views the company as falling above or below strategic reference points. **Strategic reference points** are the targets that managers use to measure whether their firm has developed the core competencies that it needs to achieve a sustainable competitive advantage. If a hotel chain decides to compete by providing superior quality and service, then top management will track the success of this strategy through customer surveys or published hotel ratings such as those provided by the prestigious Mobil Travel Guide. If a hotel chain decides to compete on price, it will regularly conduct market surveys to check the prices of other hotels. The competitors' prices are the hotel managers' strategic reference points against which to compare their own pricing strategy. If competitors can consistently underprice them, then the managers need to determine whether their staff and resources have the core competencies to compete on price.

As shown in Exhibit 5.3, when a company is performing above or better than its strategic reference points, top management will typically be satisfied with the company's strategy. Ironically, this satisfaction tends to make top management conservative and averse to risk. Because the company already has a sustainable competitive advantage, the worst thing that could happen would be to lose it, so new issues or changes in the company's external environments are viewed as threats. By contrast, when a company is performing below or worse than its strategic reference points, top management will typically be dissatisfied with the company's strategy. In this instance, managers are much more likely to choose a daring, risk-taking strategy. If the current strategy is producing substandard results, the company has nothing to lose by switching to risky new strategies in the hopes that it can create a sustainable competitive advantage. Managers of companies in this situation view new issues or changes in external environments as opportunities for potential gain.

Strategic reference point theory is not deterministic, however. Managers are not predestined to choose risk-averse or risk-seeking strategies for their

strategic reference points the strategic targets managers use to measure whether a firm has developed the core competencies it needs to achieve a sustainable competitive advantage

Exhibit 5.3

Strategic Reference Points

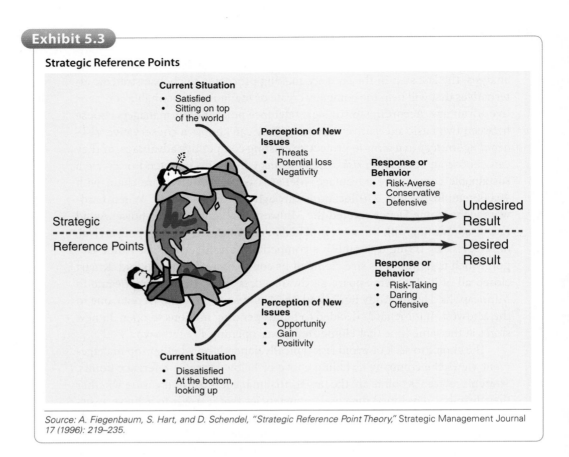

Source: A. Fiegenbaum, S. Hart, and D. Schendel, "Strategic Reference Point Theory," Strategic Management Journal 17 (1996): 219–235.

companies. Indeed, one of the most important elements of the theory is that managers *can* influence the strategies chosen by their company by *actively changing and adjusting* the strategic reference points they use to judge strategic performance. If a company has become complacent after consistently surpassing its strategic reference points, then top management can change from a risk-averse to a risk-taking orientation by raising the standards of performance (i.e., the strategic reference points). This is just what happened at MENARDS.

Instead of being satisfied with merely protecting its existing stores (a risk-averse strategy), founder John Menard changed the strategic reference points the company had been using to assess strategic performance. To encourage a daring, offensive-minded strategy that would allow the company to open nearly as many new stores as Home Depot, he determined that Menards would have to beat Home Depot on not one or two, but four, strategic reference points: price, products, sales per square foot, and "friendly accessibility." The strategy appears to be succeeding. In terms of price, market research indicates that a 100-item shopping cart of goods is consistently cheaper at Menards. In terms of products, Menards sells 50,000 products per store, the same as Home Depot. In terms of sales per square foot, Menards ($407 per square foot) outsells Home Depot ($300 per square foot).[27] Finally, unlike Home Depot's warehouse-like stores, Menards' stores are built to resemble grocery stores. Shiny tiled floors, wide aisles, and easy-to-reach products all make Menards a "friendlier" place for shoppers. And now with Lowe's, the second-largest hardware store chain in the nation, also entering

what *really* works

Strategy Making for Firms, Big and Small

Companies create strategies that produce sustainable competitive advantage by using the strategy-making process (assessing the need for strategic change, conducting a situational analysis, and choosing strategic alternatives). For years, it had been thought that strategy making was something that only large firms could do well. It was believed that small firms did not have the time, knowledge, or staff to do a good job of strategy making. However, two meta-analyses indicate that strategy making can improve the profits, sales growth, and return on investment of both big *and* small firms.

Strategy Making for Big Firms

There is a 72 percent chance that big companies that engage in the strategy-making process will be more profitable than big companies that don't. Not only does strategy making improve profits, but it also helps companies grow. Specifically, there is a 75 percent chance that big companies that engage in the strategy-making process will have greater sales and earnings growth than big companies that don't.

Thus, in practical terms, the strategy-making process can make a significant difference in a big company's profits and growth.

Strategy Making for Small Firms

Strategy making can also improve the performance of small firms. There is a 61 percent chance that small firms that engage in the strategy-making process will have more sales growth than small firms that don't. Likewise, there is a 62 percent chance that small firms that engage in the strategy-making process will have a larger return on investment than small companies that don't. Thus, in practical terms, the strategy-making process can make a significant difference in a small company's profits and growth too.

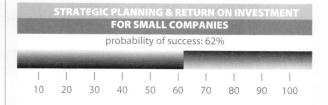

External Growth through Acquisitions

One way to grow a company is through external growth, or buying other companies (see Section 3.1 on portfolio strategy). However, researchers have long debated whether buying other companies actually adds value to the acquiring company. A meta-analysis based on 103 studies and a sample of 25,205 companies indicates that, on average, acquiring other companies actually *hurts* the value of the acquiring firm. In other words, there is only a 45 percent chance that growing a company through external acquisitions will work![28]

its markets, Menards has added a fifth strategic reference point: store size. At 225,000 square feet, most new Menards stores are more than double the size of Home Depot's stores and 100,000 square feet larger than Lowe's biggest stores.[29]

So even when (perhaps *especially* when) companies have achieved a sustainable competitive advantage, top managers must adjust or change strategic reference points to challenge themselves and their employees to develop new core competencies for the future. In the long run, effective organizations will frequently revise their strategic reference points to better focus managers' attention on the new challenges and opportunities that occur in their ever-changing business environments.

REVIEW 5-2

Strategy-Making Process

The first step in the strategy-making process is determining whether a strategy needs to be changed to sustain a competitive advantage. Because uncertainty and competitive inertia make this difficult to determine, managers can improve the speed and accuracy of this step by looking for differences between top management's intended strategy and the strategy actually implemented by lower-level managers (i.e., looking for strategic dissonance). The second step is to conduct a situational analysis that examines internal strengths and weaknesses (distinctive competencies and core capabilities), as well as external threats and opportunities (environmental scanning and strategic groups). In the third step of the strategy-making process, strategic reference point theory suggests that when companies are performing better than their strategic reference points, top management will typically choose a risk-averse strategy. When performance is below strategic reference points, it is more likely to choose risk-seeking strategies. Importantly, however, managers can influence the choice of strategic alternatives by actively changing and adjusting the strategic reference points they use to judge strategic performance.

5-3 Corporate-Level Strategies

To formulate effective strategies, companies must be able to answer these three basic questions:

- What business are we in or should we be in?
- How should we compete in this industry?
- Who are our competitors, and how should we respond to them?

These simple but powerful questions are at the heart of corporate-, industry-, and firm-level strategies, which is the focus of the second half of this chapter.

After reading this section, you should be able to:

5-3 explain the different kinds of corporate-level strategies.

Corporate-level strategy is the overall organizational strategy that addresses the question "What business or businesses are we in or should we be in?"

Exhibit 5.4 shows the two major approaches to corporate-level strategy that companies use to decide which businesses they should be in: **5-3a portfolio strategy** and **5-3b grand strategies**.

Exhibit 5.4

Corporate-Level Strategies

Portfolio Strategy	Grand Strategies
• Acquisitions, unrelated diversification, related diversification, single businese	• Growth
• Boston Consulting Group matrix	• Stability
• Stars	• Retrenchment/recovery
• Question mark	
• Cash cow	
• Dogs	

© CENGAGE LEARNING

5-3a Portfolio Strategy

One of the standard strategies for stock market investors is **diversification**, or owning stocks in a variety of companies in different industries. The purpose of this strategy is to reduce risk in the overall stock portfolio (the entire collection of stocks). The basic idea is simple: If you invest in 10 companies in 10 different industries, you won't lose your entire investment if one company performs poorly. Furthermore, because they're in different industries, one company's losses are likely to be offset by another company's gains. Portfolio strategy is based on these same ideas.

Portfolio strategy is a corporate-level strategy that minimizes risk by diversifying investment among various businesses or product lines.[30] Just as a diversification strategy guides an investor who invests in a variety of stocks, portfolio strategy guides the strategic decisions of corporations that compete in a variety of businesses. For example, portfolio strategy could be used to guide the strategy of a company like *3M*, which makes 55,000 products for six different businesses.[31] Just as investors consider the mix of stocks in their stock portfolio when deciding which stocks to buy or sell, managers following portfolio strategy try to acquire companies that fit well with the rest of their corporate portfolio and to sell those that don't. Portfolio strategy provides the following guidelines to help companies make these difficult decisions.

First, according to portfolio strategy, the more businesses in which a corporation competes, the smaller its overall chances of failing. Think of a corporation as a stool and its businesses as the legs of the stool. The more legs or businesses added to the stool, the less likely it is to tip over. Using this analogy, portfolio strategy reduces 3M's risk of failing because the corporation's survival depends on essentially six different business sectors. Managers employing portfolio strategy can either develop new businesses internally or look for **acquisitions**, that is, other companies to buy. Either way, the goal is to add legs to the stool.

corporate-level strategy
the overall organizational strategy that addresses the question "what business or businesses are we in or should we be in?"

diversification
a strategy for reducing risk by buying a variety of items (stocks or, in the case of a corporation, types of businesses) so that the failure of one stock or one business does not doom the entire portfolio

portfolio strategy
a corporate-level strategy that minimizes risk by diversifying investment among various businesses or product lines

acquisition
the purchase of a company by another company

unrelated diversification
creating or acquiring companies in completely unrelated businesses

BCG matrix
a portfolio strategy, developed by the boston consulting group, that categorizes a corporation's businesses by growth rate and relative market share, and helps managers decide how to invest corporate funds

star
a company with a large share of a fast-growing market

question mark
a company with a small share of a fast-growing market

cash cow
a company with a large share of a slow-growing market

dog
a company with a small share of a slow-growing market

Second, beyond adding new businesses to the corporate portfolio, portfolio strategy predicts that companies can reduce risk even more through **unrelated diversification**—creating or acquiring companies in completely unrelated businesses (more on the accuracy of this prediction later). According to portfolio strategy, when businesses are unrelated, losses in one business or industry should have minimal effect on the performance of other companies in the corporate portfolio. One of the best examples of unrelated diversification is *Samsung* of Korea. Samsung has five businesses in electronics, five in machinery and heavy industries, two in chemicals, three in financial services, and other businesses ranging from automobiles to hotels and entertainment.[32] Because most internally grown businesses tend to be related to existing products or services, portfolio strategy suggests that acquiring new businesses is the preferred method of unrelated diversification.[33]

Third, investing the profits and cash flows from mature, slow-growth businesses into newer, faster-growing businesses can reduce long-term risk. The best-known portfolio strategy for guiding investment in a corporation's businesses is the Boston Consulting Group (BCG) matrix.[34] The **BCG matrix** is a portfolio strategy that managers use to categorize their corporation's businesses by growth rate and relative market share, helping them decide how to invest corporate funds. The matrix, shown in Exhibit 5.5, separates businesses into four categories based on how fast the market is growing (high growth or low growth) and the size of the business's share of that market (small or large). **Stars** are companies that have a large share of a fast-growing market. To take advantage of a star's fast-growing market and its strength in that market (large share), the corporation must invest substantially in it. The investment is usually worthwhile, however, because many stars produce sizable future profits. **Question marks** are companies that have a small share of a fast-growing market. If the corporation invests in these companies, they may eventually become stars, but their relative weakness in the market (small share) makes investing in question marks more risky than investing in stars. **Cash cows** are companies that have a large share of a slow-growing market. Companies in this situation are often highly profitable, hence the name "cash cow." Finally, **dogs** are companies that have a small share of a slow-growing market. As the name suggests, having a small share of a slow-growth market is often not profitable.

Exhibit 5.5

Boston Consulting Group Matrix

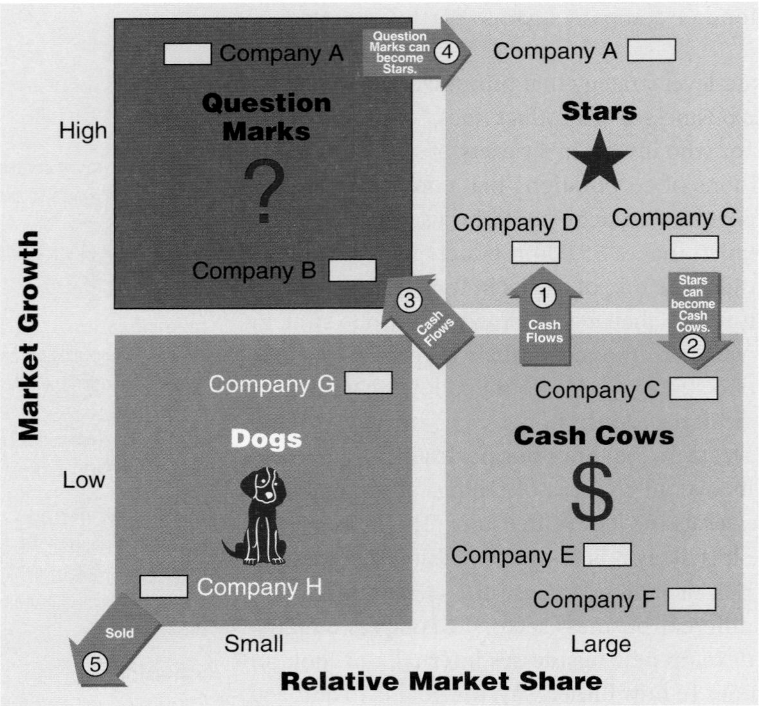

Because the idea is to redirect investment from slow-growing to fast-growing companies, the BCG matrix starts by recommending that while the substantial cash flows from cash cows last, they should be reinvested in stars (see ① in Exhibit 5.5) to help them grow even faster and obtain even more market share. Using this strategy, current profits help produce future profits. Over time, as their market growth slows, some stars may turn into cash cows (see ②). Cash flows should also be directed to some question marks (see ③). Though riskier than stars, question marks have great potential because of their fast-growing market. Managers must decide which question marks are most likely to turn into stars (and therefore warrant further investment) and which ones are too risky and should be sold. Over time, managers hope some question marks will become stars as their small markets become large ones (see ④). Finally, because dogs lose money, the corporation should "find them new owners" or "take them to the pound." In other words, dogs should either be sold to other companies or closed down and liquidated for their assets (see ⑤).

Although the BCG matrix and other forms of portfolio strategy are relatively popular among managers, portfolio strategy has some drawbacks. The most significant? Contrary to the predictions of portfolio strategy, the evidence suggests that acquiring unrelated businesses is *not* useful. As shown in Exhibit 5.6, there is a U-shaped relationship between diversification and risk. The left side of the curve shows that single businesses with no diversification are extremely risky (if the single business fails, the entire business fails). So, in part, the portfolio strategy of diversifying is correct—competing in a variety of different businesses can lower risk. However, portfolio strategy is partly wrong, too—the right side of the curve shows that conglomerates composed of completely unrelated businesses are even riskier than single, undiversified businesses.[35]

A second set of problems with portfolio strategy has to do with the dysfunctional consequences that can occur when companies are categorized as stars, cash cows, question marks, or dogs. Contrary to expectations, the BCG matrix often yields incorrect judgments about a company's potential. In other words, managers using the BCG matrix aren't very good at accurately determining which companies should be categorized as stars, cash cows, questions marks, or dogs. The most common mistake is simply miscategorizing highly profitable companies as dogs.[36] In part, this is because the BCG

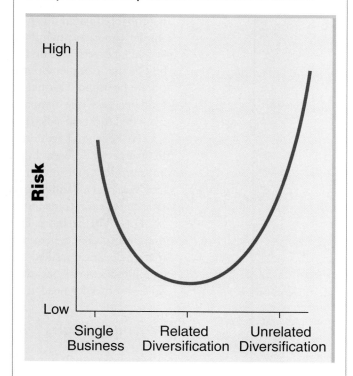

Exhibit 5.6

U-Shaped Relationship Between Diversification and Risk

Source: From M. Lubatkin and P. J. Lane, "Psst…The Merger Mavens Still Have It Wrong!" Academy of Management Executive 10 (1996): 21–39. Reproduced with permission of Academy of Management (NY) in the formats Textbook and Other Book via Copyright Clearance Center.

relies on past performance, which is a notoriously poor predictor of future company performance. More worrisome, however, is research that indicates that the BCG matrix actually makes managers worse at judging the future profitability of a business. A study conducted in six countries over five years gave managers and business students clear information about the current and future profits of three companies and asked them to select the one that would be most successful in the future. Although not labeled this way, one company was clearly a star, another was a dog, and the last was a cash cow. Just exposing people to the ideas in the BCG matrix led them to incorrectly categorize less profitable businesses as the most successful businesses 64 percent of the time, while actually *using* the BCG matrix led to making the same mistake 87 percent of the time.[37]

Furthermore, using the BCG matrix can also weaken the strongest performer in the corporate portfolio, the cash cow. As funds are redirected from cash cows to stars, corporate managers essentially take away the resources needed to take advantage of the cash cow's new business opportunities. As a result, the cash cow becomes less aggressive in seeking new business or in defending its present business. Finally, labeling a top performer as a cash cow can harm employee morale. Cash-cow employees realize that they have inferior status and that instead of working for themselves, they are now working to fund the growth of stars and question marks.

So, what kind of portfolio strategy does the best job of helping managers decide which companies to buy or sell? The U-shaped curve in Exhibit 5.6 indicates that, contrary to the predictions of portfolio strategy, the best approach is probably **related diversification**, in which the different business units share similar products, manufacturing, marketing, technology, or cultures. The key to related diversification is to acquire or create new companies with core capabilities that complement the core capabilities of businesses already in the corporate portfolio. Hormel Foods is an example of related diversification in the food business. The company both manufactures and markets a variety of foods, from deli meats to salsa, to the infamous SPAM.

We began this section with the example of 3M and its 55,000 products sold in over seven different business sectors. Although seemingly different, most of 3M's product divisions are based in some fashion on its distinctive competencies in adhesives and tape (e.g., wet or dry sandpaper, Post-it notes, Scotchgard fabric protector, transdermal skin patches, and reflective material used in traffic signs). Furthermore, all of 3M's divisions share its strong corporate culture that promotes and encourages risk taking and innovation. In sum, in contrast to a single, undiversified business or unrelated diversification, related diversification reduces risk because the different businesses can work as a team, relying on each other for needed experience, expertise, and support.

5-3b Grand Strategies

A **grand strategy** is a broad strategic plan used to help an organization achieve its strategic goals.[38] Grand strategies guide the strategic alternatives that managers of individual businesses or subunits may use in deciding what businesses they should be in. There are three kinds of grand strategies: growth, stability, and retrenchment/recovery.

related diversification
creating or acquiring companies that share similar products, manufacturing, marketing, technology, or cultures

grand strategy
a broad corporate-level strategic plan used to achieve strategic goals and guide the strategic alternatives that managers of individual businesses or subunits may use

The purpose of a **growth strategy** is to increase profits, revenues, market share, or the number of places (stores, offices, locations) in which the company does business. Companies can grow in several ways. They can grow externally by merging with or acquiring other companies in the same or different businesses. Some of the largest mergers and acquisitions of recent years include Roche acquiring Genentech (pharmaceuticals), Pfizer acquiring Wyeth (pharmaceuticals), Mars acquiring Wrigley (gum and candy), and InBev acquiring Anheuser-Busch (beer and alcoholic beverages).

Another way to grow is internally, directly expanding the company's existing business or creating and growing new businesses. NESTLÉ, the world's largest food company, had to find a way to grow while dealing with record-high prices for cocoa and sugar, two key ingredients for its chocolate products. To boost growth, Nestlé spent $24 million to promote its Aero, a chocolate bar that is filled with bubbles of air. While the bubbles give the chocolate a creamier texture, it also bulks up the candy bar without adding more ingredients, quite helpful at a time of high commodity costs. Thanks to the company's promotional emphasis, sales of Aero helped the company earn a profit of $10.3 billion on growth of sales of 7.5 percent.[40]

The purpose of a **stability strategy** is to continue doing what the company has been doing, just doing it better. Companies following a stability strategy try to improve the way in which they sell the same products or services to the same customers. Since its inception in 1938, *REI* has never strayed from its focus on the outdoors. Its Mountain Safety Research division designs and makes mountaineering equipment, clothing, and camping products. REI Adventures offers adventure travel packages (e.g., kayaking, climbing, and backpacking), with hand-picked local guides on all seven continents. Finally, in addition to its website, REI has 80 stores in 27 states, selling high-quality outdoor gear, clothing, and footwear.[41] And today, with 3.5 million members whose membership entitles them to discounts and expert advice, REI is one of the largest retail co-ops in the world. Companies often choose a stability strategy when their external environment doesn't change much or after they have struggled with periods of explosive growth.

The purpose of a **retrenchment strategy** is to turn around very poor company performance by shrinking the size or scope of the business or, if a company is in multiple businesses, by closing or shutting down different lines of the business. The first step of a typical retrenchment strategy might include: making significant cost reductions; laying off employees; closing poorly performing stores, offices, or manufacturing plants; or closing or selling entire lines of products or services.[42]

AP PHOTO/PRNEWSFOTO/PEPSICO

After Coca-Cola acquired Glaceau Vitaminwater, PepsiCo realized that its SoBe line of beverages would face much stiffer competition. To spur growth, PepsiCo cut prices, started a new marketing campaign, and offered a no-calorie version of its drinks. As a result, SoBe's market share doubled, and sales of its leading product, Lifewater, rose 85 percent.[39]

growth strategy
a strategy that focuses on increasing profits, revenues, market share, or the number of places in which the company does business

stability strategy
a strategy that focuses on improving the way in which the company sells the same products or services to the same customers

retrenchment strategy
a strategy that focuses on turning around very poor company performance by shrinking the size or scope of the business

Doing the Right Thing

Accentuate the Positive

During an economic downturn, it is hard for managers and employees to stay positive. If it's not the threat of lay-offs, it's the near-constant barrage of news about how entire industries are struggling to stay afloat. Research shows, however, that optimism in the workplace helps companies grow even during difficult times. By measuring workplace engagement with questions like "Does your boss support you?" and "Do you have a best friend at work?" researchers found that increased employee engagement led to increased company performance. So, in down times, do the right thing—resist the urge to spread bad news and don't let a pessimistic culture develop. Instead, accentuate the positive, be optimistic, and make sure that your employees feel supported, rewarded, and engaged at work. Not only will they be happier, but their performance will likely be better too.[43]

After cutting costs and reducing a business's size or scope, the second step in a retrenchment strategy is recovery. **Recovery** consists of the strategic actions that a company takes to return to a growth strategy. This two-step process of cutting and recovery is analogous to pruning roses. Prior to each growing season, roses should be cut back to two-thirds their normal size. Pruning doesn't damage the roses; it makes them stronger and more likely to produce beautiful, fragrant flowers. The retrenchment-and-recovery process is similar. Cost reductions, layoffs, and plant closings are sometimes necessary to restore companies to good health. When company performance drops significantly, a strategy of retrenchment and recovery may help the company return to a successful growth strategy.

REVIEW 5-3

Corporate-Level Strategies

Corporate-level strategies, such as portfolio strategy and grand strategies, help managers determine what businesses they should be in. Portfolio strategy focuses on lowering business risk by being in multiple, unrelated businesses and by investing the cash flows from slow-growth businesses into faster-growing businesses. One portfolio strategy, the BCG matrix, suggests that cash flows from cash cows should be reinvested in stars and in carefully chosen question marks. Dogs should be sold or liquidated. Portfolio strategy has several problems, however. Acquiring unrelated businesses actually increases risk rather than lowering it. The BCG matrix is often wrong when predicting companies' futures (e.g., as dogs or cash cows). And redirecting cash flows can seriously weaken cash cows. The most successful way to use the portfolio approach to corporate strategy is to reduce risk through related diversification.

The three kinds of grand strategies are growth, stability, and retrenchment/recovery. Companies can grow externally by merging with or acquiring other companies, or they can grow internally through direct expansion or creating new businesses. Companies choose a stability strategy—selling the same products or services to the same customers—when their external environment changes very little or after they have dealt with periods of explosive growth. Retrenchment strategy, shrinking the size or scope of a business, is used to turn around poor performance. If retrenchment works, it is often followed by a recovery strategy that focuses on growing the business again.

recovery
the strategic actions taken after retrenchment to return to a growth strategy

5-4 Industry-Level Strategies

Industry-level strategy addresses the question: How should we compete in this industry?

After reading this section, you should be able to:

5-4 describe the different kinds of industry-level strategies.

Let's find out more about industry-level strategies, by discussing **5-4a the five industry forces that determine overall levels of competition in an industry,** as well as **5-4b the positioning strategies** and **5-4c adaptive strategies that companies can use to achieve sustained competitive advantage and above-average profits.**

5-4a Five Industry Forces

According to Harvard professor Michael Porter, five industry forces determine an industry's overall attractiveness and potential for long-term profitability. These include the character of the rivalry, the threat of new entrants, the threat of substitute products or services, the bargaining power of suppliers, and the bargaining power of buyers. The stronger these forces, the less attractive the industry becomes to corporate investors, because it is more difficult for companies to be profitable. Porter's industry forces are illustrated in Exhibit 5.7. Let's examine how these forces are bringing changes to several kinds of industries.

Character of the rivalry is a measure of the intensity of competitive behavior among companies in an industry. Is the competition among firms aggressive and cutthroat, or do competitors focus more on serving customers than on attacking each other? Both industry attractiveness and profitability decrease when rivalry is cutthroat. For example, selling cars is a highly competitive business. Pick up a local newspaper on Friday, Saturday, or Sunday morning, and you'll find dozens of pages of car advertising. In fact, competition in new car sales is so intense that if it weren't for used-car sales, repair work, and replacement parts, many auto dealers would actually lose money.

The **threat of new entrants** is a measure of the degree to which barriers to

industry-level strategy
corporate strategy that addresses the question "how should we compete in this industry?"

character of the rivalry
measure of the intensity of competitive behavior between companies in an industry

threat of new entrants
measure of the degree to which barriers to entry make it easy or difficult for new companies to get started in an industry

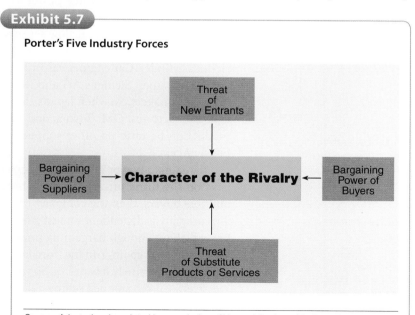

Exhibit 5.7

Porter's Five Industry Forces

Source: Adapted and reprinted by permission of Harvard Business Review. From "How Competitive Forces Shape Strategy," by Michael E. Porter, Harvard Business Review (March/April 1979), copyright © 1979 by the President and Fellows of Harvard College. All rights reserved.

entry make it easy or difficult for new companies to get started in an industry. If new companies can enter the industry easily, then competition will increase, and prices and profits will fall. On the other hand, if there are sufficient barriers to entry, such as large capital requirements to buy expensive equipment or plant facilities, or the need for specialized knowledge, then competition will be weaker, and prices and profits will generally be higher. For instance, high costs make it very difficult to enter the natural gas business. ANADARKO PETROLEUM has discovered three immense natural gas sites off the coast of Mozambique, which are estimated to yield 6 to 8 trillion cubic feet of gas. At a minimum, it will take $2 billion and six years, two for planning and four for construction, before any gas can be extracted and shipped to customers.[44]

The **threat of substitute products or services** is a measure of the ease with which customers can find substitutes for an industry's products or services. If customers can easily find substitute products or services, the competition will be greater and profits will be lower. If there are few or no substitutes, competition will be weaker and profits will be higher. Generic medicines are some of the best-known examples of substitute products.

Bargaining power of suppliers is a measure of the influence that suppliers of parts, materials, and services to firms in an industry have on the prices of these inputs. When companies can buy parts, materials, and services from numerous suppliers, the companies will be able to bargain with the suppliers to keep prices low. On the other hand, if there are few suppliers, or if a company is dependent on a supplier with specialized skills and knowledge, then the suppliers will have the bargaining power to dictate price levels. With 60 percent of the global market, HITACHI AUTOMOTIVE SYSTEMS dominates the production and supply of automotive airflow sensors that measure how much air has been drawn into an engine so that the proper amount of fuel is injected into the engine's cylinder. Car engines can't run correctly without this device. Only two other companies, Siemens AG and Robert Bosch GmbH, make them, but not for all automakers. So when Japan's catastrophic earthquake damaged Hitachi's Japanese factories, GM, Toyota, and PSA Peugeot-Citroen had to shut down production because no other suppliers produced the airflow sensors needed for their cars.[45]

Bargaining power of buyers is a measure of the influence that customers have on the firm's prices. If a company sells a popular product or service to multiple buyers, then the company has more power to set prices. By contrast, if a company is dependent on just a few high-volume buyers, those buyers will typically have enough bargaining power to dictate prices. COSTCO, a membership warehouse chain, and the third largest retailer in the United States, focuses on offering extremely low prices. So when Coca-Cola wanted to raise prices aggressively, Costco stopped selling Coca-Cola products. According to a message on Costco's website, "At this time, Coca-Cola has not provided Costco with competitive pricing so that we may pass along the value our members deserve." After three weeks of negotiations, Coca-Cola lowered its prices, and its products were back on Costco shelves.[46]

threat of substitute products or services measure of the ease with which customers can find substitutes for an industry's products or services

bargaining power of suppliers measure of the influence that suppliers of parts, materials, and services to firms in an industry have on the prices of these inputs

bargaining power of buyers measure of the influence that customers have on a firm's prices

5-4b Positioning Strategies

After analyzing industry forces, the next step in industry-level strategy is to protect your company from the negative effects of industry-wide competition and to create a sustainable competitive advantage. According to Michael Porter, there are three positioning strategies: cost leadership, differentiation, and focus.

Cost leadership means producing a product or service of acceptable quality at consistently lower production costs than competitors so that the firm can offer the product or service at the lowest price in the industry. Cost leadership protects companies from industry forces by deterring new entrants, who will have to match low costs and prices. Cost leadership also forces down the prices of substitute products and services, attracts bargain-seeking buyers, and increases bargaining power with suppliers, who have to keep their prices low if they want to do business with the cost leader.

Differentiation means making your product or service sufficiently different from competitors' offerings so that customers are willing to pay a premium price for the extra value or performance that it provides. Differentiation protects companies from industry forces by reducing the threat of substitute products. It also protects companies by making it easier to retain customers and more difficult for new entrants trying to attract new customers. The starting price of the hybrid cars is $22,000 for a Toyota Prius, $26,000 for a Honda Civic, and $28,000 for a Ford Fusion. With these lower-priced options, why would anyone spend $40,000 on a Chevy Volt hybrid? Hopefully because the Volt's innovative gas-electric hybrid goes 40 miles before the gas engine kicks in, making the Volt the most fuel efficient car on the market.

With a **focus strategy**, a company uses either cost leadership or differentiation to produce a specialized product or service for a limited, specially targeted group of customers in a particular geographic region or market segment. Focus strategies typically work in market niches that competitors have overlooked or have difficulty serving. From newspapers to magazines to books, the publishing industry finds falling sales, reduced revenues, and no clear idea what to do about it. One area in publishing, however, is growing $100 million a year, nearly 8 percent per year on average. Romance novels account for just 14 percent of all books sold. But this book segment is the top-performing category on the *New York Times, USA Today,* and *Publishers Weekly* best-seller lists. One of the most popular subject areas, according to sales figures, is Mennonite and Amish-themed romances. A highly anticipated novel, for example, tells the story of a young woman whose parents have died in a horse-drawn-carriage accident and who meets a suitor who will test the limits of her Amish faith. So, although most people don't read romance novels, catering to those who do with micro-themed books (i.e., a focus strategy) is one of the few successful strategies in publishing today.[47]

5-4c Adaptive Strategies

Adaptive strategies are another set of industry-level strategies. Whereas the aim of positioning strategies is to minimize the effects of industry competition and build a sustainable competitive advantage, the purpose of adaptive strategies

cost leadership
the positioning strategy of producing a product or service of acceptable quality at consistently lower production costs than competitors can, so that the firm can offer the product or service at the lowest price in the industry

differentiation
the positioning strategy of providing a product or service that is sufficiently different from competitors' offerings that customers are willing to pay a premium price for it

focus strategy
the positioning strategy of using cost leadership or differentiation to produce a specialized product or service for a limited, specially targeted group of customers in a particular geographic region or market segment

is to choose an industry-level strategy that is best suited to changes in the organization's external environment. There are four kinds of adaptive strategies: defenders, prospectors, analyzers, and reactors.[48]

Defenders seek moderate, steady growth by offering a limited range of products and services to a well-defined set of customers. In other words, defenders aggressively "defend" their current strategic position by doing the best job they can to hold on to customers in a particular market segment. In the home security market, contracts for 24-hour monitoring for break-ins and fire generally last three years, after which time most consumers shop around for the best deal and change companies. At BROADVIEW SECURITY, formerly known as Brink's Home Security, however, the average customer stays for 12 years. Broadview's defender strategy is even more impressive because they target only customers with good credit records. Ian Zaffino, a business analyst at Oppenheimer Funds, says Broadview "isn't really into adding [subscribers] for the heck of it. They are concerned with adding high-quality subs [subscribers]."[49] As a result, the company has zero debt.

Prospectors seek fast growth by searching for new market opportunities, encouraging risk taking, and being the first to bring innovative new products to market. Prospectors are analogous to gold miners who "prospect" for gold nuggets (i.e., new products) in hopes that the nuggets will lead them to a rich deposit of gold (i.e., fast growth).

Analyzers are a blend of the defender and prospector strategies. They seek moderate, steady growth *and* limited opportunities for fast growth. Analyzers are rarely first to market with new products or services. Instead, they try to simultaneously minimize risk and maximize profits by following or imitating the proven successes of prospectors.

Finally, unlike defenders, prospectors, or analyzers, **reactors** do not follow a consistent strategy. Rather than anticipating and preparing for external opportunities and threats, reactors tend to "react" to changes in their external environment after they occur. Not surprisingly, reactors tend to be poorer performers than defenders, prospectors, or analyzers. A reactor approach is inherently unstable, and firms that fall into this mode of operation must change their approach or face almost certain failure.

REVIEW 5-4

. . . .

Industry-Level Strategies

Industry-level strategies focus on how companies choose to compete in their industry. Five industry forces determine an industry's overall attractiveness to corporate investors and its potential for long-term profitability. Together, a high level of new entrants, substitute products or services, bargaining power of suppliers, bargaining power of buyers, and rivalry among competitors combine to increase competition and decrease profits. Three positioning strategies can help companies protect themselves from the negative effects of industry-wide competition. Under a cost leadership strategy, firms try to keep production costs low so that they can sell products at prices lower than competitors. Differentiation is a strategy aimed at making a product or service sufficiently different from competitors' products so that it can command a premium price. Using a focus strategy, firms seek to produce a specialized product or service

---

defenders
companies using an adaptive strategy aimed at defending strategic positions by seeking moderate, steady growth and by offering a limited range of high-quality products and services to a well-defined set of customer

prospectors
companies using an adaptive strategy that seeks fast growth by searching for new market opportunities, encouraging risk taking, and being the first to bring innovative new products to market

analyzers
companies using an adaptive strategy that seeks to minimize risk and maximize profits by following or imitating the proven successes of prospectors

reactors
companies using an adaptive strategy of not following a consistent strategy, but instead reacting to changes in the external environment after they occur

for a limited, specially targeted group of customers. The four adaptive strategies help companies adapt to changes in the external environment. Defenders want to "defend" their current strategic positions. Prospectors look for new market opportunities by bringing innovative new products to market. Analyzers minimize risk by following the proven successes of prospectors. Reactors do not follow a consistent strategy, but instead react to changes in their external environment after they occur.

5-5 Firm-Level Strategies

Microsoft brings out its Xbox 360 video-game console; Sony counters with its PlayStation 3. Sprint Nextel drops prices and increases monthly cell phone minutes; Verizon strikes back with better reception and even lower prices and more minutes. Starbucks Coffee opens a store, and nearby locally run coffeehouses respond by improving service, increasing portions, and holding the line on prices. Attack and respond, respond and attack.

After reading this section, you should be able to:

5-5 explain the components and kinds of firm-level strategies.

Firm-level strategy addresses the question: How should we compete against a particular firm?

Let's find out more about the firm-level strategies (direct competition between companies) by reading about **5-5a the basics of direct competition**, and **5-5b the strategic moves involved in direct competition between companies.**

5-5a Direct Competition

Although Porter's five industry forces indicate the overall level of competition in an industry, most companies do not compete directly with all the firms in their industry. For example, McDonald's and Red Lobster are both in the restaurant business, but no one would characterize them as competitors. McDonald's offers low-cost, convenient fast food in a seat-yourself restaurant, whereas Red Lobster offers mid-priced, sit-down seafood dinners complete with servers and a bar.

Instead of competing with an industry, most firms compete directly with just a few companies within it. **Direct competition** is the rivalry between two companies offering similar products and services that acknowledge each other as rivals and take offensive and defensive positions as they act and react to each other's strategic actions.[50] Two factors determine the extent to which firms will be in direct competition with each other: market commonality and resource similarity. **Market commonality** is the degree to which two companies have overlapping products, services, or customers in multiple markets. The more markets in which there is product, service, or customer overlap, the more intense the direct competition between the two companies. **Resource similarity** is the extent to which a competitor has similar amounts and kinds of resources, that is, similar assets, capabilities, processes, information, and knowledge used to create and sustain an advantage over competitors. From a competitive

firm-level strategy
a corporate strategy that addresses the question "how should we compete against a particular firm?"

direct competition
the rivalry between two companies that offer similar products and services, acknowledge each other as rivals, and act and react to each other's strategic actions

market commonality
the degree to which two companies have overlapping products, services, or customers in multiple markets

resource similarity
the extent to which a competitor has similar amounts and kinds of resources

standpoint, resource similarity means that your direct competitors can probably match the strategic actions that your company takes.

Exhibit 5.8 shows how market commonality and resource similarity interact to determine when and where companies are in direct competition.[51] The overlapping area in each quadrant (between the triangle and the rectangle, or between the differently colored rectangles) depicts market commonality. The larger the overlap, the greater the market commonality. Shapes depict resource similarity, with rectangles representing one set of competitive resources and triangles representing another. Quadrant I shows two companies in direct competition because they have similar resources at their disposal and a high degree of market commonality. These companies try to sell similar products and services to similar customers. McDonald's and Burger King would clearly fit here as direct competitors.

In Quadrant II, the overlapping parts of the triangle and rectangle show two companies going after similar customers with some similar products or services, but with different competitive resources. McDonald's and Wendy's restaurants would fit here. Wendy's is after the same lunchtime and dinner crowds that McDonald's is. Nevertheless, with its more expensive hamburgers, fries, shakes, and salads, Wendy's is less of a direct competitor to McDonald's than Burger King is. Wendy's Garden Sensation salads (using fancy lettuce varieties, grape tomatoes, and mandarin oranges) bring in customers who would have eaten at more expensive casual dining restaurants like Applebee's.[52]

In Quadrant III, the very small overlap shows two companies with different competitive resources and little market commonality. McDonald's and Luby's cafeterias fit here. Although both are in the fast-food business, there's almost no overlap in terms of products and customers. Luby's sells baked chicken, turkey, roasts, meat loaf, and vegetables, none of which are available at McDonald's. Furthermore, Luby's customers aren't likely to eat at McDonald's. In fact, Luby's is not really competing with other fast-food restaurants at all, but with eating at home.

Finally, in Quadrant IV, the small overlap between the two rectangles shows that McDonald's and Subway compete with similar resources but with little market commonality. In terms of resources, sales at McDonald's are much larger, but Subway has grown substantially in the last decade and now has 33,749 stores worldwide, compared to 32,737

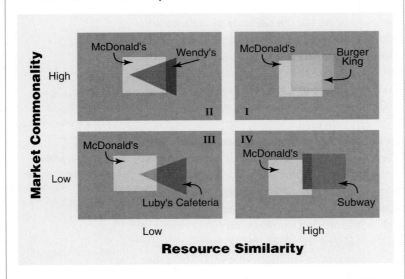

Exhibit 5.8

A Framework of Direct Competition

Source: From M. Chen, "Competitor Analysis and Interfirm Rivalry: Toward a Theoretical Integration," Academy of Management Review 21 (1996): 21–39. Reproduced by permission of Academy of Management (NY) in the formats Textbook and Other Book via Copyright Clearance Center.

worldwide at McDonald's (just 14,027 in the United States).[53] Although Subway and McDonald's compete, they aren't direct competitors in terms of market commonality in the way that McDonald's and Burger King are, because Subway, unlike McDonald's, sells itself as a provider of healthy fast food.

5-5b Strategic Moves of Direct Competition

Whereas corporate-level strategies help managers decide what business to be in and industry-level strategies help them determine how to compete within an industry, firm-level strategies help managers determine when, where, and what strategic actions should be taken against a direct competitor. Firms in direct competition can make two basic strategic moves: attack and response.

An **attack** is a competitive move designed to reduce a rival's market share or profits. For example, the two leaders in the e-reader market, AMAZON and BARNES & NOBLE, have been engaged in a lengthy battle over prices. In order to reduce sales of Barnes & Noble's Nook readers, Amazon introduced the Kindle with Special Offers model, an e-reader that periodically showed ads, and was priced at $114, $35 dollars less than the cheapest Nook model. A few months later, Amazon dropped the price to just $79.[54]

A **response** is a countermove, prompted by a rival's attack, that is designed to defend or improve a company's market share or profit. There are two kinds of responses.[55] The first is to match or mirror your competitor's move, as Barnes & Noble did when it lowered the price of its Nook Simple Touch, which had been selling for $139, to $99.[56]

The second kind of response, however, is to respond along a different dimension from your competitor's move or attack. Rather than cutting prices, Amazon responded to Barnes & Noble's moves by letting customers get rid of advertisements. For a fee of $30, users of ad-supported Kindles could now use their e-readers without seeing the pop-up advertisements.[57]

Market commonality and resource similarity determine the likelihood of an attack or response, that is, whether a company is likely to attack a direct competitor or to strike back with a strong response when attacked. When market commonality is large and companies have overlapping products, services, or customers in multiple markets, there is less motivation to attack and more motivation to respond to an attack. The reason for this is straightforward: When firms are direct competitors in a large number of markets, as Amazon and Barnes & Noble are, they have a great deal at stake.

Whereas market commonality affects the likelihood of an attack or a response to an attack, resource similarity largely affects response capability, that is, how quickly and forcefully a company can respond to an attack. When resource similarity is strong, the responding firm will generally be able to match the strategic moves of the attacking firm. Consequently, a firm is less likely to attack firms with similar levels of resources because it is unlikely to gain any sustained advantage when the responding firms strike back. On the other hand, if one firm is substantially stronger than another (i.e., there is low resource similarity), then a competitive attack is more likely to produce sustained competitive advantage.

Regardless of who wins, it often happens that price wars ends up hurting both companies' profits.

attack
a competitive move designed to reduce a rival's market share or profits

response
a competitive countermove, prompted by a rival's attack, to defend or improve a company's market share or profit

In general, the more moves (i.e., attacks) a company initiates against direct competitors, and the greater a company's tendency to respond when attacked, the better its performance. More specifically, attackers and early responders (companies that are quick to launch a retaliatory attack) tend to gain market share and profits at the expense of late responders. This is not to suggest that a full-attack strategy always works best. In fact, attacks can provoke harsh retaliatory responses. When it first came on the market, SONY'S PLAYSTATION 3 (PS3) cost $599, but it came with an 80-GB hard drive and a then-rare Blu-ray drive. Sales lagged. However, Nintendo's Wii game console cost $249 and Microsoft's Xbox 360 game console cost $400. So Sony cut the price of the 80-GB PS3 to $499 and introduced a 40-GB PS3 for $399.[58] Microsoft responded over the next four years with a combination of price cuts.[59] Today, with a 320-GB PS3 costing $400 and a 160-GB PS3 costing $300, Sony is now priced more competitively with 250-GB Xbox 360, which costs $300. As a result, global sales of the PS3 now total 43.4 million units compared to the Xbox 360's 42.9 million.[60] Consequently, when deciding when, where, and what strategic actions to take against a direct competitor, managers should always consider the possibility of retaliation.

REVIEW 5-5

Firm-Level Strategies

Firm-level strategies are concerned with direct competition between firms. Market commonality and resource similarity determine whether firms are in direct competition and thus likely to attack each other or respond to each other's attacks. In general, the more markets in which there is product, service, or customer overlap, and the greater the resource similarity between two firms, the more intense the direct competition between them. When firms are direct competitors in a large number of markets, attacks are less likely because responding firms are highly motivated to quickly and forcefully defend their profits and market share. By contrast, resource similarity affects response capability, meaning how quickly and forcefully a company responds to an attack. When resource similarity is strong, attacks are much less likely to produce a sustained advantage, because the responding firm is capable of striking back with equal force.

Market entries and exits are the most important kinds of attacks and responses. Entering a new market is a clear offensive signal, whereas exiting a market is a clear signal that a company is retreating. Market entry is perhaps the most forceful attack or response because it sends the clear signal that the company is committed to gaining or defending market share and profits at a direct competitor's expense. In general, attackers and early responders gain market share and profits at the expense of late responders. Attacks must be carefully planned and carried out, however, because they can provoke harsh retaliatory responses.

Management Decision

Dealing with Competition[61]

You are an executive at Pepsi, and you've just made what feels like a great decision. For many years, various health and children's groups have been calling for reductions of high-calorie and high-fat foods in U.S. schools. Even if schools provided nutritious, fresh, and healthy food, they argued, it was no competition for the salty and sugary treats available in vending machines. These groups even had First Lady Michelle Obama lead a nationwide campaign.

In response, you've made a monumental decision, the first by any soft-drink producer—to remove full-calorie beverages from all schools in over 200 countries by 2012. Your decision is being hailed by numerous organizations, from the World Heart Federation and the American Heart Association to the William J. Clinton Foundation. Not only do they credit your company for taking an important first step in the fight against childhood obesity, but they also celebrate your willingness to take initiative instead of waiting for government regulations.

Some of your colleagues, however, are not in a celebratory mood. Though your company has received some great publicity, they've read numerous reports that Coca-Cola will take a different course. Although all soft-drink producers agreed not to sell full-calorie products in primary/elementary schools, Coca-Cola recently revised its sales policy to allow sales in schools if parents or school officials request it. What is more, Coca-Cola has decided that it will continue to sell full-calorie beverages to secondary schools, as they argue that parents and school officials "should have the right to choose what is best for their schools."

Your colleagues worry that Coca-Cola's policy could give them a huge competitive advantage. Even though Pepsi will still have a presence in primary and secondary schools, their offerings will be limited to low-calorie diet drinks, bottled water, low-fat milk, and juice with no added sugar. These products may have to compete with Coca-Cola's lineup of full-calorie, sugar-loaded drinks. There doesn't seem to be much doubt about what the students will choose. After all, if students opted for diet drinks or water in the first place, the sale of full-calorie drinks would not have turned into a public health issue.

Your colleagues fear that Pepsi's commitment to public health will give Coca-Cola an insurmountable competitive edge. So, late in one business day, a group of colleagues comes to your office. "You're the one that came up with this great plan," they say. "How are we going to respond?"

Questions

1. Using Porter's Five Industry Forces, map the soft-drink industry.

2. What are the risks and opportunities of the strategies followed by Pepsi? Of Coca-Cola?

3. How would you respond to Coca-Cola's change in sales policy? How would you ensure Pepsi's board that this response will allow you to remain competitive and profitable?

Practice Being a Manager

Most Likely to Succeed

Organizational strategy is aimed at achieving sustainable competitive advantage over rivals in a particular market. This exercise will offer you the opportunity to consider how companies in the restaurant industry might develop a strategy and attempt to gain sustainable competitive advantage.

For purposes of this exercise, your professor will organize your class into small teams. Each team will be competing for the title of "Most Likely to Succeed." One team will be designated as judges for this competition.

STEP 1 (15 minutes): **Develop a concept for a new restaurant business.** You may choose to develop your concept as a local, regional, or national company—but in all cases, you must plan to open a restaurant in your local area. Your concept should include the following: (1) a name for your restaurant/chain; (2) a description of your menu, layout, and any other distinguishing features; and (3) likely direct competitors of your new concept. Prepare an informal presentation of not more than two minutes.

STEP 2 (20 minutes): **Present the concepts.** Each team will make an informal two-minute presentation of the restaurant concepts.

STEP 3 (5 minutes): **Judge the presentations.** Judges will confer and reach a decision regarding the top concepts on the basis of "Most Likely to Succeed." Judges should apply the sustainable competitive advantage concept/factors in making their selections. While the judges are conferring, each team should discuss and evaluate the concepts presented by the competing teams. Teams should apply the tools and concepts in this chapter in evaluating these concepts.

STEP 4 **Discuss as a class.**

- What are the challenges of achieving sustainable competitive advantage in the restaurant business? Consider cases of failure and success in your local market—what factors seemed to play a role in determining success or failure?

- What *strategic groups*, or clusters of direct competitors (e.g., fast-food burgers) were identified in the team presentations? Which strategic groups might be tougher to enter in your local area? Which might be easier to enter?

- Do major restaurant chains have a built-in sustainable competitive advantage over local competition in your area? If you think so, what is the source of this advantage, and is it more pronounced in some strategic groups than in others (e.g., greater in tacos than in fine dining)? If not, what strategies have the "locals" used to successfully compete with larger restaurant chains?

Self-Assessment

Strategy Questionnaire

Generally speaking, a strategy is a plan of action that is designed to help you achieve a goal. Strategies are not limited to grand plans that help you accomplish grand goals. You probably use strategies every day in simple ways. For example, think of a route you regularly drive. Do you know how fast (or slow) you need to go to catch all the lights on green? Or where to swerve to avoid a pothole? Or even when to take a side street to shave a few minutes off your commute? Speeding up for one block in order to catch the green lights at the next five intersections is a strategy. Strategy, then, involves thinking about how you are going to accomplish what you set out (i.e., have planned) to do.

This assessment will provide some baseline information on attitudes you might have that will relate to your management skills.[62] Answer each of the questions as either "True" or "False." Try not to spend too much time on any one item, and be sure to answer all the questions.

_____ 1. I get satisfaction from competing with others.

_____ 2. It's usually not important to me to be the best.

_____ 3. Competition destroys friendships.

_____ 4. Games with no clear-cut winners are boring.

_____ 5. I am a competitive individual.

_____ 6. I will do almost anything to avoid an argument.

_____ 7. I try to avoid competing with others.

_____ 8. I would like to be on a debating team.

_____ 9. I often remain quiet rather than risk hurting another person.

_____ 10. I find competitive situations unpleasant.

_____ 11. I try to avoid arguments.

_____ 12. In general, I will go along with the group rather than create conflict.

_____ 13. I don't like competing against other people.

_____ 14. I don't like games that are winner-take-all.

_____ 15. I dread competing against other people.

_____ 16. I enjoy competing against an opponent.

_____ 17. When I play a game, I like to keep score.

_____ 18. I often try to outperform others.

_____ 19. I like competition.

_____ 20. I don't enjoy challenging others even when I think they are wrong.

SCORING

To determine your score, count the number of responses marked "True" and enter it here _____. You can find the interpretation for your score at www.cengagebrain.com.

MANAGEMENT WORKPLACE

Theo Chocolate: Strategy Formulation and Execution

At first, Theo Chocolate offered an exotic line of dark-chocolate and milk-chocolate bars and truffles. These early treats had unusual names such as the 3400 Phinney Bar, and they were wrapped in artistic watercolor packaging with whimsical cover designs. The chocolate was well received by critics and organic food enthusiasts but was not popular with mainstream consumers. Founder Joe Whinney began working on a new strategy, creating classic milk chocolate bars as a gateway product that would attract consumers more easily. Theo now offers two distinct product lines for two different market segments—a Classic line of milk-chocolate bars for mainstream customers, and Fantasy Flavors for more adventurous eaters.

What to Watch For and Ask Yourself

1. Evaluate Theo's new strategy in light of the company's strengths, weaknesses, opportunities, and threats.

2. Using the BCG Matrix, explain Theo's decision to offer a Classic line of chocolate bars after having limited success with Fantasy Flavor chocolates.

3. Is a differentiation, cost leadership, or focus strategy right for Theo Chocolate? Explain.

Endnotes

1. D. Fonda, L. Locke, J. Ressner, and R. Corliss, "When Woody Met Mickey," *Time*, February 6, 2006, 46–47; R. Grover, "How Bob Iger Unchained Disney," *Businessweek*, February 5, 2007, 74–79; M. Marr, "Better Mousetrap: In Shakeup, Disney Rethinks How It Reaches Audiences; Iger Seeks High-Tech Delivery of Movies, TV Shows; Theater Owners Worry; 'Housewives' on a Handheld," *Wall Street Journal*, October 1, 2005, A1; R. Siklos, "Q & A, The Iger Difference," *Fortune*, April 28, 2008, 90–94; R. Siklos, "Bob Iger Rocks Disney," *Fortune*, January 19, 2009, 80–86; and T. Stanley, "Iger Needs Superpowers for Quick Fix at Disney," *Advertising Age*, March 21, 2005, 33–34.

2. www.washingtonpost.com/business/technology/apples-ipad-3-faces-stiffer-competition-than-ipad-2/2012/02/29/gIQAGhzKkR_story.html; www.pcmag.com/article2/0,2817,2400378,00.asp; www.informationweek.com/news/hardware/mac/232602197; www.isuppli.com/Display-Materials-and-Systems/News/Pages/Apples-Toughest-Competition-in-the-Fourth-Quarter-Tablet-Market-Was-Apple.aspx; P. Gupta and N. Randewich, "Apple Unwraps Mini-iPad to Take on Amazon, Google," Yahoo! News, October 23, 2012, http://news.yahoo.com/apple-unwraps-mini-ipad-amazon-google-005515849.html?utm_source=dlvr.it&utm_medium=twitter.

3. J. Barney, "Firm Resources and Sustained Competitive Advantage," *Journal of Management* 17 (1991): 99–120; and J. Barney, "Looking Inside for Competitive Advantage," *Academy of Management Executive* 9 (1995): 49–61.

4. D. Bailey, "Is It Time to Say Goodbye to Netbooks?" *The Motley Fool*, April 30, 2011, accessed March 1, 2012, www.fool.com/investing/general/2011/04/30/is-it-time-to-say-goodbye-to-netbooks.aspx; S. Lohr, "Netbooks Lose Status as Tablets Like the iPad Rise," *New York Times*, February 13, 2011, accessed March 1, 2012, www.nytimes.com/2011/02/14/technology/14netbook.html?pagewanted=all.

5. D. Pogue, "Just How Many Android Tablet Apps Are There?" *New York Times*, July 1, 2011, accessed March 2, 2012, http://pogue.blogs.nytimes.com/2011/07/01/mystery-how-many-android-tablet-apps/.

6. Juniper Networks "2011 Mobile Threats Report" accessed March 1, 2012, www.juniper.net/us/en/local/pdf/additional-resources/jnpr-2011-mobile-threats-report.pdf?utm_source=promo & utm_medium=right_promo&utm_campaign=mobile_threat_report_0212.

7. J. Newman, "In Defense of Google Music," *Time*, February 24, 2012, accessed March 1, 2012, http://techland.time.com/2012/02/24/in-defense-of-google-music/; D. Pogue "A Look at Apple's iCloud," *New York Times*, October 13, 2011, accessed March 1, 2012, http://pogue.blogs.nytimes.com/2011/10/13/a-look-at-icloud/; B. Stone, "Will Amazon's Cloud Music Service Fly?" *BloombergBusinessweek*, March 31, 2011, accessed March 1, 2012, www.businessweek.com/magazine/content/11_15/b4223043644684.htm.

8. S. Hart and C. Banbury, "How Strategy-Making Processes Can Make a Difference," *Strategic Management Journal* 15 (1994): 251–269.

9. R. A. Burgelman, "Fading Memories: A Process Theory of Strategic Business Exit in Dynamic Environments," *Administrative Science Quarterly* 39 (1994): 24–56; and R. A. Burgelman and A. S. Grove, "Strategic Dissonance," *California Management Review* 38 (Winter 1996): 8–28.

10. C. Passariello, "Carrefour's Makeover Plan: Become IKEA of Groceries," *Wall Street Journal*, September 16, 2010, B1.

11. C. Passariello, "Olofsson's Fight against the Status Quo at Carrefour," *Wall Street Journal*, September 16, 2010, accessed March 29, 2011, from http://online.wsj.com/article/SB10001424052748703743504575493813065751290.html.

12. Burgelman and Grove, "Strategic Dissonance."

13. A. Zimmerman, "Hasbro Falls Prey to 'Angry Birds,'" *Wall Street Journal,* December 15, 2011, accessed March 1, 2012. http://online.wsj.com/article/SB100014240529702048445045770987780656830196.html.

14. A. Fiegenbaum, S. Hart, and D. Schendel, "Strategic Reference Point Theory," *Strategic Management Journal* 17 (1996): 219–235.

15. D. Carpenter, "SWOT Team Solves Supply Chain Issues," *Materials Management in Health Care* (April 2006): 40–42.

16. "Consumer Reports Automaker Report Cards 2012: Subaru Drives into Top Spot as Honda Slips," *Sacramento Bee*, March 1, 2012, accessed March 1, 2012. www.sacbee.com/2012/02/28/4297509/consumer-reports-automaker-report.html.

17. B. Gottesman, "The Tech Brands You Trust Most," *PC Magazine*, October 2011, 30–43.

18. B. Kowitt, "Inside Trader Joe's," *Fortune*, September 6, 2010, 86–96.

19. C. Palmieri, "Inside Tesco's New U.S. Stores," *Businessweek Online*, December 4, 2007, accessed 9 April 2011, from www.businessweek.com/globalbiz/content/dec2007/gb2007123_870617_page_2.htm; "Unique Products, Reasonable Prices Spell Success for Trader Joe's," *Food Institute Report* 81 (March 3, 2008): 4; and "Trader Joe's: Why the Hype?" *Bulletin* (Bend, Oregon), March 27, 2008.

20. A. Fiegenbaum and H. Thomas, "Strategic Groups as Reference Groups: Theory, Modeling and Empirical Examination of Industry and Competitive Strategy," *Strategic Management Journal* 16 (1995): 461–476.

21. J. B. White, "Ford's New Pickup Line: Like My Tough V-6?" *Wall Street Journal*, August 18, 2010, accessed November 20, 2010, from http://online.wsj.com/article/SB10001424052748704554104575435343519425512.html.

22. "Continued Weaknesses in Housing and the Overall Economy Are Now Foreseen to Result in Three Consecutive Years of Market Declines," *Home Improvement Research Institute*, accessed June 5, 2009, from www.hiri.org.

23. R. K. Reger and A. S. Huff, "Strategic Groups: A Cognitive Perspective," *Strategic Management Journal* 14 (1993): 103–124.

24 84 Lumber, accessed July 29, 2008, www.84lumber.com.

25 "Menard, Inc.," *Hoover's Company Profiles*, May 8, 2003.

26 J. Samuelson, "Tough Guy Billionaire," *Forbes*, February 24, 1997, 64–66.

27 S. Bucksot, C. Jensen, & D. Tratensek, "Where Are We Headed?" *2005 Market Measure: The Industry's Annual Report*, www.nrha.org/MM2004.pdf, March 6, 2005.

28 Hart and Banbury, "How Strategy-Making Processes Can Make a Difference"; C. C. Miller and L. B. Cardinal, "Strategic Planning and Firm Performance: A Synthesis of More Than Two Decades of Research," *Academy of Management Journal* 37 (1994): 1649–1665; D. King, D. Dalton, C. Daily, and J. Covin, "Meta-Analyses of Post-Acquisition Performance: Indications of Unidentified Moderators," *Strategic Management Journal* 25 (2004): 187–200; and C. R. Schwenk, "Effects of Formal Strategic Planning on Financial Performance in Small Firms: A Meta Analysis," *Entrepreneurship Theory & Practice* (Spring 1993): 53–64.

29 H. Murphy, "Menard's Tool in Retail Battle: Gigantic Stores," *Crain's Chicago Business*, August 12, 2002, 3.

30 M. Lubatkin, "Value-Creating Mergers: Fact or Folklore?" *Academy of Management Executive* 2 (1988): 295–302; M. Lubatkin and S. Chatterjee, "Extending Modern Portfolio Theory into the Domain of Corporate Diversification: Does It Apply?" *Academy of Management Journal* 37 (1994): 109–136; and M. H. Lubatkin and P. J. Lane, "Psst … The Merger Mavens Still Have It Wrong!" *Academy of Management Executive* 10 (1996): 21–39.

31 "Who We Are," 3M, accessed April 7, 2009, from http://solutions.3m.com/wps/portal/3M/en_US/about-3M/information/about/us/.

32 "About Samsung," Samsung, accessed July 29, 2008, from www.samsung.com/us/aboutsamsung/index.html.

33 "Affiliated Companies," Samsung, April 7, 2011, from www.samsung.com/hk_en/aboutsamsung/samsunggroup/affiliatedcompanies/SAMSUNGGroup_AffiliatedCompanies.html.

34 www.bcg.com/this_is_BCG/bcg_history/bcg_history_2005.html; and www.wikipedia.org/wiki/Boston_Consulting_Group_Matrix.

35 D. Hambrick, I. MacMillan, and D. Day, "Strategic Attributes and Performance in the BCG Matrix—A PIMS-based Analysis of Industrial Product Businesses," *Academy of Management Journal* 25 (1982): 510–531.

36 J. Armstrong and R. Brodie, "Effects of Portfolio Planning Methods on Decision Making: Experimental Results," *International Journal of Research in Marketing* 11 (1994): 73–84.

37 K. Brooker, "Plugging the Leaks at P & G: A First-Year Report Card for CEO Durk Jager," *Fortune*, February 21, 2000, 44; and "R & D's Formula for Success," Procter & Gamble, accessed March 17, 2009, from www.pg.com/science/rd_formula_success.shtml.

38 J. A. Pearce II, "Selecting among Alternative Grand Strategies," *California Management Review* (Spring 1982): 23–31.

39 "How PepsiCo Reversed Its SoBe Water Brand," *Bloomberg Businessweek*, June 28, 2010, 15–16.

40 M. Laycock, "Aero Sales Help York Nestlé Factory in Tough Year," *The Press*, December 31, 2011, accessed March 2, 2012, http://www.yorkpress.co.uk/news/9446032.Aero_sales_help_York_factory_in_tough_year/; T. Mulier, "Breathing More Profit into Chocolate Bars," *BloombergBusinessweek*, February 24, 2011, accessed March 2, 2012, www.businessweek.com/magazine/content/11_10/b4218021563564.htm; "Nestlé Reports £6.5 bn Annual Profit," *The Independent*, February 16, 2012, accessed March 2, 2012, www.independent.co.uk/news/business/news/nestle-reports-65bn-annual-profit-6977817.html.

41 "About REI," REI, accessed June 7, 2009, from www.rei.com/aboutrei/about_rei.html; and "Recreational Equipment, Inc.," Hoover, accessed June 7, 2009, from www.hoovers.com/company/Recreational_Equipment_Inc/hcxjji-1.html.

42 J. A. Pearce II, "Retrenchment Remains the Foundation of Business Turnaround," *Strategic Management Journal* 15 (1994): 407–417.

43 M. Conlin, "Is Optimism a Competitive Advantage," *Bloomberg Businessweek*, August 13, 2009, accessed February 1, 2011, from www.businessweek.com/magazine/content/09_34/b4144052828198.htm.

44 D. Winning, "Anadarko Considers Mozambique Gas Site," *Wall Street Journal*, November 30, 2010, accessed April 8, 2011, from http://online.wsj.com/article/SB10001424052748704584804575645190168232732.html.

45 M. Ramsey and S. Moffett, "Japan Parts Shortage Hits Auto Makers—Hard-to-Find Electronic Component Made by Hitachi Causes U.S., European Production Cutbacks by GM and Peugeot," *Wall Street Journal*, March 24, 2011, B1.

46 E. Fredrix and S. Skidmore, "Costco Nixes Coke Products over Pricing Dispute," ABCNews.com, November 17, 2009, from http://abcnews.go.com/Business/wireStory?id=9103485; and "Update1—Costco to Resume Stocking Coca-Cola Drinks," Reuters.com, December 10, 2009, from www.reuters.com/article/idUSN1020190520091210.

47 S. Morgan, "Getting Dirty in Dutch Country," *Bloomberg Businessweek*, July 26–August 1, 2010, 69–71.

48 R. E. Miles and C. C. Snow, *Organizational Strategy, Structure, & Process* (New York: McGraw-Hill, 1978); S. Zahra and J. A. Pearce, "Research Evidence on the Miles-Snow Typology," *Journal of Management* 16 (1990): 751–768; and W. L. James and K. J. Hatten, "Further Evidence on the Validity of the Self-Typing Paragraph Approach: Miles and Snow Strategic Archetypes in Banking," *Strategic Management Journal* 16 (1995): 161–168.

49 D. Benoit, "Losing Its Brink's Name, Broadview Feels Secure—Home-Alarm Company, Spun Off From Parent, Looks to Expand Stable Customer Base during Transition," *Wall Street Journal*, July 22, 2009, page no. n/a.

50 M. Chen, "Competitor Analysis and Interfirm Rivalry: Toward a Theoretical Integration," *Academy of Management Review* 21 (1996): 100–134; and J. C. Baum and H. J. Korn, "Competitive Dynamics of Interfirm Rivalry," *Academy of Management Journal* 39 (1996): 255–291.

51 Ibid.

52 S. Leung, "Wendy's Sees Green in Salad Offerings—More Sophistication, Ethnic Flavors Appeal to Women, Crucial to Building Market Share," *Wall Street Journal*, April 24, 2003, B2.

53 J. Jargon, "Subway Runs Past McDonald's Chain," *Wall Street Journal*, March 8, 2011, accessed April 9, 2011 from http://online.wsj.com/article/SB1000142405274870338670457618 6432177464052.html; "2010 Annual Report," McDonald's, accessed April 9, 2011, from www.aboutmcdonalds.com/etc/medialib/aboutMcDonalds/investor_relations3.Par.56096.File.dat/2010.

54 C. C. Miller, "Amazon to Sell the Kindle Reader at a Lower Price, but with Advertising Added," *New York Times*, April 11, 2011,accessed March 5, 2012, www.nytimes.com/2011/04/12/technology/12amazon.html; J. Pepitone, "Amazon Pushes Hard on Ad-Supported Kindle Line" CNNMoney, October 3, 2011, accessed March 5, 2012, http://money.cnn.com/2011/10/03/technology/amazon_kindle_ads/index.htm.

55 D. Ketchen Jr., C. Snow, and V. Street, "Improving Firm Performance by Matching Strategic Decision-Making Processes to Competitive Dynamics," *Academy of Management Executive* 18 (2004): 29–43.

56 N. Olivarez-Giles, "Barnes & Noble Nook Simple Touch e-Reader Drops to $99," *Los Angeles Times*, November 7, 2011, accessed March 5, 2012, http://latimesblogs.latimes.com/technology/2011/11/barnes-noble-drops-nook-simple-touch-ereader-to-99-dollars.html.

57 C. Sorrel, "Remove Ads from 'Special Offers' Kindle for $30," Wired.com, October, 7, 2011, accessed March 5, 2012, www.wired.com/gadgetlab/2011/10/remove-ads-from-special-offers-kindle-for-30/.

58 Y. Kane, "Sony Price Cut Helps Its PS3 Gain Traction; Move Boosts Sales of Game Consoles in Time for Holidays," *Wall Street Journal*, November 26, 2007, B4.

59 D. Wakabayashi, "Hope Fades for PS3 as a Comeback Player—In Battle of the Game Consoles, Nintendo Wii and Microsoft Xbox Widen Leads over Sony's PlayStation," *Wall Street Journal*, December 29, 2008, B1; N. Wingfield, "Microsoft Cuts Xbox to $199," *Wall Street Journal*, September 4, 2008, B9; and N. Wingfield, "Microsoft to Cut Xbox 360 Pro Price," *Wall Street Journal*, July 11 2008, B6.

60 B. Strauss, "PS3 Surpasses Xbox 360 in Worldwide Sales," *Business Insider*, March 31, 2011, accessed April 9, 2011, from www.businessinsider.com/ps3-surpasses-xbox-360-in-world-wide-sales-2011-3.

61 B. McKay, "Soft-Drink Sales Drop in Schools, Group Says," *Wall Street Journal*, March 8, 2010, B3; and "Pepsi Says No to Soda Sales at Schools," *Wall Street Journal*, March 17, 2010, D3.

62 J. M. Houston and R. D. Smither, "The Nature of Competitiveness: The Development and Validation of the Competitiveness Index," *Educational and Psychological Measurement* 52 (1992): 407–418.

Innovation and Change

REEL TO REAL

Management Workplace is at Holden Outerwear.

SELF-ASSESSMENT

How creative are you? What do you think of creative endeavors? Do the Self-Assessment for this chapter in the book or online to find out.

ONLINE QUIZZES

Did you get it? Review the main concepts in the chapter by taking the online quizzes on CourseMate!

VIDEO QUIZZES

Get more out of the videos by taking the multimedia video quizzes online.

© TETRA IMAGES/ CORBIS

© ISTOCKPHOTO/ ALEXANDER KALINA

© ISTOCKPHOTO/ PEARLEYE

© ISTOCKPHOTO/DAVID HUGHES

What Would You Do?

3M Headquarters, Minneapolis, MN[1]

With 40,000 global patents and patent applications, 3M, maker of Post-it notes, reflective materials (Scotch lite), and 55,000 products in numerous industries (displays and graphics, electronics and communications, health care, safety and security, transportation, manufacturing, office products, and home and leisure), has long been one of the most innovative companies in the world. 3M codified its focus on innovation into a specific goal, "30/5," which meant that 30 percent of its sales each year must come from products no more than five years old. The logic was simple but powerful. Each year, five-year-old products become six years old and would not be counted toward the 30 percent of sales. Thus, the 30/5 goal encouraged everyone at 3M to be on the lookout for and open to new ideas and products. Furthermore, 3M allowed its engineers and scientists to spend 5 percent of their time, roughly two hours per week, doing whatever they wanted as long as it was related to innovation and new product development.

And it worked, for a while. A decade ago, the Boston Consulting Group, one of the premier consulting companies in the world, ranked 3M as **the** most innovative company in the world. In subsequent years, it dropped to second, third, and then seventh. Today, 3M doesn't even crack the top 50. Dev Patnaik, of Jump Associates, an innovation consulting firm, says, "People have kind of forgotten about those guys [3M]. When was the last time you saw something innovative or experimental coming out of there?" So, what happened?

When your predecessor became CEO 10 years ago, he found a struggling, inefficient, oversized company in need of change. He cut costs by laying off 8,000 people. Marketing and research and development funds, which had been allocated to divisions independent of performance (all divisions got the same increase each year), were now distributed based on past performance and growth potential. Perform poorly, and your funds would shrink the next year. Likewise, with U.S. sales stagnating

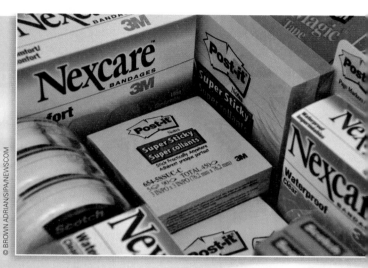

and Asia sales rising, management decreased headcount, hiring, and capital expenditures in the United States, while significantly increasing all three in fast-growing Asian markets. Six Sigma processes, popularized at Motorola and GE, were introduced to analyze how things got done, to remove unnecessary steps, and to change procedures that caused defects. Thousands of 3M managers and employees became trained as Six Sigma "black belts" and returned to their divisions and departments to root out inefficiencies, reduce production times, and decrease waste and product errors. And it worked incredibly well, in part. Costs and capital spending dropped, while profits surged 35 percent to record levels. But, product innovation, as compared to the 30/5 goal, sank dramatically, as only 21 percent of profits were generated by products that were no more than five years old.

So, what should 3M do? From inception, 3M has been an innovator, bringing a stream of new products and services to market, creating value for customers, sustainable advantage over competitors, and sizable returns for investors. Thanks to your predecessor, 3M has lower costs, is highly efficient, and much more profitable. But it no longer ranks among the most innovative firms in the world. In fact, the use of Six Sigma procedures appears to be inversely related to product innovation. If that's the case, should 3M continue to focus on using Six Sigma procedures to reduce costs and increase efficiencies, or should it strive again to encourage its scientists and managers to focus on innovation? Which will make 3M more competitive in the long run?

When people think of innovation, they tend to think of game-changing advances that render current products obsolete, for example, comparing the iPhone to text-based "smartphones." Innovation, however, also occurs with lots of incremental changes over time. What are the advantages and disadvantages for 3M of each approach, and when and where would each be more likely to work? Finally, some companies innovate from within by successfully implementing creative ideas in their products or services. Sometimes, though, innovation is acquired by purchasing other companies that have made innovative advances. For example, Google bought YouTube to combine its search expertise with YouTube's online video capabilities. Over time, how much should companies like 3M rely on acquisitions for innovation? Should 3M acquire half, one-third, 10 percent, or 5 percent of its new products through acquisitions? What makes the most sense and why?

If you were in charge at 3M, what would you do?

6-1 Organizational Innovation

We begin this chapter by reviewing the issues associated with organizational innovation, the problem facing 3M. **Organizational innovation** is the successful implementation of creative ideas in an organization.[2] **Creativity**, which is a form of organizational innovation, is the production of novel and useful ideas.[3] In the first part of this chapter, you will learn why innovation matters and how to manage innovation to create and sustain a competitive advantage. In the second part, you will learn about **organizational change**, which is a difference in the form, quality, or condition of an organization over time.[4] You will also learn about the risk of not changing and the ways in which companies can manage change. Let's begin by looking at innovation.

After reading this section, you should be able to:

6-1 explain why innovation matters to companies.

JERNHUSEN AB, a Swedish property-administration firm, is building a new 13-story office and retail building near Stockholm's Central Station. How should the company heat it? Problem number two: How should it get rid of excess heat in the train station, generated by the 250,000 people who pass through it every day? As Karl Sundholm, representative of Jernhusen, puts it, "All people produce heat, and that heat is in fact fairly difficult to get rid of. Instead of opening windows and letting all that heat go to waste we want to harness it through the ventilation system."[5] The innovative solution to both problems? Convert the heat in the station to hot water and pump it through the heating system of the new building, using pipes that connect the building to the station. Sundholm estimates the system will cost about 300,000 kronor (32,000 euros; US\$47,000) to install, and it is likely to reduce energy consumption by 15 percent. Per Berggren, Jernhusen's managing director, notes, "It's more like thinking out of the box, being environmentally smart."[6] The successful implementation of creative ideas, like using the heat generated by train terminal passengers to heat a nearby office building, is organizational innovation at work.[7]

organizational innovation
the successful implementation of creative ideas in organizations

creativity
the production of novel and useful ideas

organizational change
a difference in the form, quality, or condition of an organization over time

We can only guess what changes technological innovations will bring in the next 20 years. Will we carry computers in our pockets? Today's iPhones and Android, Android, and Windows 8 phones are a step in that direction. Will solar power and wind power get cheap and efficient enough so that your home has a stand-alone power source off the main electrical grid? And will HD TVs, now the standard, be replaced by lifelike HD holographic pictures (think of R2D2 projecting Princess Leia in *Star Wars*) that project lifelike 3-D images?[8] Who knows? The only thing we do know about the next 20 years is that innovation will continue to change our lives.

Let's begin our discussion of innovation by learning about **6-1a technology cycles** and **6-1b innovation streams.**

6-1a Technology Cycles

Technology consists of the knowledge, tools, and techniques used to transform inputs (raw materials and information) into outputs (products and services). A **technology cycle** begins with the birth of a new technology and ends when that technology reaches its limits and dies as it is replaced by a newer, substantially better technology.[9] For example, technology cycles occurred when air conditioners supplanted fans, when Henry Ford's Model T replaced horse-drawn carriages, and when battery-powered wristwatches replaced mechanically powered, stem-wound wristwatches.

From Gutenberg's invention of the printing press in the 1400s to the rapid advance of the Internet, studies of hundreds of technological innovations have shown that nearly all technology cycles follow the typical **S-curve pattern of innovation,** shown in Exhibit 6.1.[10] Early in a technology cycle, there is still much to learn, so progress is slow, as depicted by point A on the S-curve. The flat slope indicates that increased effort (in terms of money or research and development) brings only small improvements in technological performance.

INTEL's technology cycles have followed this pattern. Intel spends billions to develop new computer chips and to build new production facilities. Intel has found that the technology cycle for its integrated circuits is about three years. In each three-year cycle, Intel introduces a new chip, improves the chip by making it a little bit faster each year, and then replaces that chip at the end of the cycle with a brand-new, substantially faster chip. At first, though, the billions Intel spends typically produce only small improvements in performance. For instance, Intel's first 60-megahertz (MHz) Pentium processors ran at a speed of 51 based on the iComp Index, as shown in Exhibit 6.2. (The iComp Index is a benchmark test for measuring relative computer speed. For example, a computer with an iComp score of 200 is twice as fast as a computer with an iComp score

technology
the knowledge, tools, and techniques used to transform inputs into outputs

technology cycle
a cycle that begins with the "birth" of a new technology and ends when that technology reaches its limits and is replaced by a newer, substantially better technology

S-curve pattern of innovation
a pattern of technological innovation characterized by slow initial progress, then rapid progress, and then slow progress again as a technology matures and reaches its limits

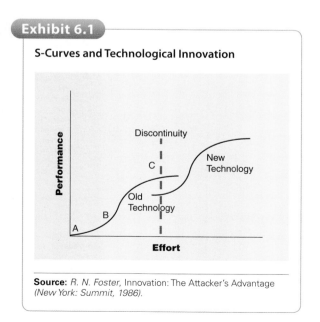

Exhibit 6.1

S-Curves and Technological Innovation

Source: *R. N. Foster, Innovation: The Attacker's Advantage (New York: Summit, 1986).*

of 100.) Six months later, Intel's new 75-MHz Pentium was only slightly faster, with an iComp speed of 67.

Fortunately, as the new technology matures, researchers figure out how to get better performance from it. This is represented by point B of the S-curve in Exhibit 6.1. The steeper slope indicates that small amounts of effort will result in significant increases in performance. Again, Intel's technology cycles have followed this pattern. After six months to a year with a new chip design, Intel's engineering and production people typically figure out how to make the new chips much faster. Despite slow progress at point A in the first six months, Intel soon rolled out 100-MHz, 120-MHz, 133-MHz, 150-MHz, and 166-MHz Pentium chips that, based on the iComp Index, were 76 percent, 96 percent, 117 percent, 124 percent, and 149 percent, respectively, faster than the original 60-MHz speed (see Exhibit 6.2).

Exhibit 6.2

iComp Index 2.0 Comparing the Relative Performance of Different Intel Microprocessors

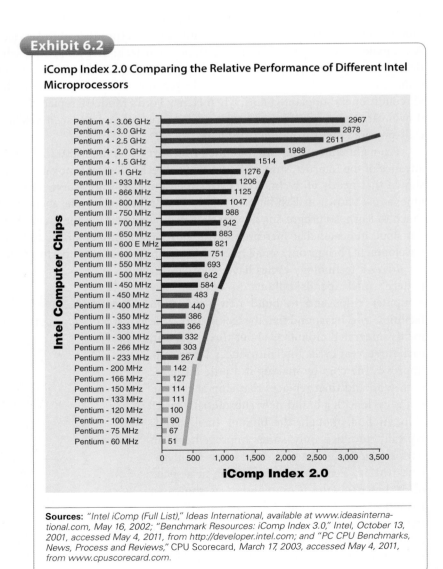

Sources: "Intel iComp (Full List)," Ideas International, available at www.ideasinternational.com, May 16, 2002; "Benchmark Resources: iComp Index 3.0," Intel, October 13, 2001, accessed May 4, 2011, from http://developer.intel.com; and "PC CPU Benchmarks, News, Process and Reviews," CPU Scorecard, March 17, 2003, accessed May 4, 2011, from www.cpuscorecard.com.

At point C in Exhibit 6.1, the flat slope again indicates that further efforts to develop this particular technology will result in only small increases in performance. More importantly, however, point C indicates that the performance limits of that particular technology are being reached. In other words, additional significant improvements in performance are highly unlikely. Exhibit 6.2 shows that with iComp speeds of 127 and 142, Intel's 166-MHz and 200-MHz Pentiums were 2.49 and 2.78 times as fast as its original 60-MHz Pentiums. Yet, despite these impressive gains in performance, Intel was unable to make its Pentium chips run any faster because the basic design had reached its limits.

After a technology has reached its limits at the top of the S-curve, significant improvements in performance usually come from radical new designs or new performance-enhancing materials. In Exhibit 6.1, that new technology is represented by the second S-curve. The changeover or discontinuity between the old and new technologies is represented by the dotted line. At first, the old and new technologies will likely coexist. Eventually, however, the new technology will replace the old technology. When that happens, the old technology cycle will be complete, and a new one will have started.

The changeover between Intel's Pentium processors, the old technology, and its Pentium II processors, the new technology (despite their similar names, these chips used significantly different technologies) took approximately one year. Exhibit 6.2 shows the changeover or discontinuity between the two technologies. With an iComp speed of 267, the first Pentium II (233 MHz) was 88 percent faster than the last Pentium processor. And because their design and performance were significantly different from (and faster than) Pentium II chips, Intel's Pentium III chips represented the beginning of yet another S-curve technology cycle—a 450-MHz Pentium III chip was 21 percent faster than a 450-MHz Pentium II chip. Over time, improving existing technology (tweaking the performance of the current technology cycle), combined with replacing old technology with new technology cycles (the Pentium 4 replacing the Pentium III replacing the Pentium II replacing the Pentium), has increased the speed of Pentium computer processors by a factor of 58 in just 17 years, and all computer processors by a factor of 300! Intel continues to improve the speed and capability of its processors. For example, today's super-powerful 64-bit processors have 592 million transistors compared to 3.1 million transistors for 1990s 32-bit processors, or just 4,500 transistors for the 8-bit processors, which began personal computing in the 1970s.[11]

Though the evolution of Intel's Pentium chips has been used to illustrate S-curves and technology cycles, it's important to note that technology cycles and technological innovation don't necessarily involve faster computer chips or cleaner-burning automobile engines. Remember, *technology* is simply the knowledge, tools, and techniques used to transform inputs into outputs. So a technology cycle occurs whenever there are major advances or changes in the *knowledge, tools*, and *techniques* of a field or discipline, whatever they may be.

For example, most cities could benefit from commuter rail transportation systems, but the cost is prohibitive relative to the benefits except in the most highly populated cities, like Boston, New York, or Chicago. Even aboveground light rail systems, which are supposed to be less expensive, cost $5 million a mile. This is why the self-powered rail cars made by US RAIL CAR are

US Railcar's self-propelled engines don't require expensive rail systems or locomotive engines.

so innovative. Where typical passenger trains are pulled by a locomotive, US Rail's cars are self-propelled by two built-in diesel engines and can pull up to two other passenger cars. As a result, passenger loads are 18 percent higher, fuel costs are half of normal passenger car systems, and pollution is reduced by 72 percent. And because they are engineered to use existing rail lines, no new rail has to be laid. Ulimately, the only cost is new stations and parking lots. Finally, initial capital outlays are small because cities can begin by buying one or two self-propelled cars and have them pull one or two passenger cars. As ridership slowly grows, simply add more self-propelled cars.[12]

So, when you think about technology cycles, don't automatically think "high technology." Instead, broaden your perspective by considering advances or changes in any kind of knowledge, tools, and techniques.

6-1b Innovation Streams

In Chapter 5, you learned that organizations can create *competitive advantage* for themselves if they have a *distinctive competence* that allows them to make, do, or perform something better than their competitors. A competitive advantage becomes sustainable if other companies cannot duplicate the benefits obtained from that distinctive competence. Technological innovation, however, can enable competitors to duplicate the benefits obtained from a company's distinctive advantage. It can also quickly turn a company's competitive advantage into a competitive disadvantage.

Companies that want to sustain a competitive advantage must understand and protect themselves from the strategic threats of innovation. Over the long run, the best way for a company to do that is to create a stream of its own innovative ideas and products year after year. Consequently, we define **innovation streams** as patterns of innovation over time that can create sustainable competitive advantage.[13] Exhibit 6.3 shows a typical innovation consisting of a series of technology cycles. Recall that a technology cycle begins with a new technology and ends when it is replaced by a newer, substantially better technology. The innovation stream in Exhibit 6.3 shows three such technology cycles.

An innovation stream begins with a **technological discontinuity**, in which a scientific advance or a unique combination of existing technologies creates a significant breakthrough in performance or function. For example, minimally invasive techniques are revolutionizing brain surgery. When Douglas Baptist had a golf ball-sized tumor, his surgeon cut a tiny opening through his eyebrow, removed the tumor, and sewed up the opening, leaving practically no trace of the operation. Dr. John Mangiardi, who did the procedure, says, "We used to have to shave off half the head. We don't do that anymore."[14] Further advances in technology are now being used to remove brain tumors via an endoscope inserted through the patient's nose.[15] As a result of these advances, the cost

innovation streams
patterns of innovation over time that can create sustainable competitive advantage

technological discontinuity
the phase of an innovation stream in which a scientific advance or unique combination of existing technologies creates a significant breakthrough in performance or function

Part Two *Planning*

Exhibit 6.3

Innovation Streams: Technology Cycles over Time

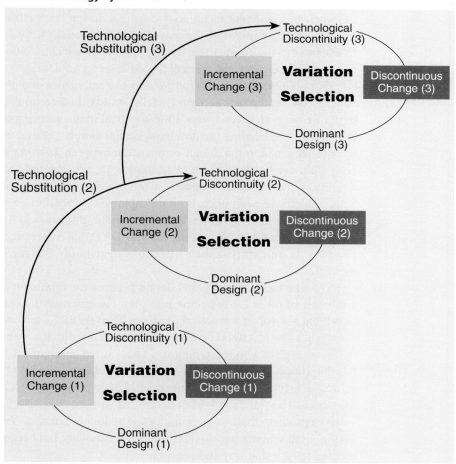

Source: *Adapted from M. L. Tushman, P. C. Anderson, and C. O'Reilly, "Technology Cycles, Innovation Streams, and Ambidextrous Organizations," in* Managing Strategic Innovation and Change, *M. L. Tushman & P. Anderson, eds., (1997), 3–23. © 1997 by Oxford University Press, Inc. Used by permission of Oxford University Press, Inc.*

and length of hospital stays associated with these surgeries have been cut in half.

Technological discontinuities are followed by a **discontinuous change**, which is characterized by technological substitution and design competition. **technological substitution** occurs when customers purchase new technologies to replace older technologies. In the past, people who wanted to rent movies had to drive to stores like Blockbuster. Today, mail service and on-demand streaming services from NetFlix and Amazon enable users to watch movies. Not surprisingly, video-rental store sales have declined. Movie Gallery, the second largest video rental chain, shut its doors for good in early 2010, while Blockbuster declared bankruptcy as it struggles to deal with $1 billion in debt.[16]

Discontinuous change is also characterized by **design competition**, in which the old technology and several different new technologies compete to

discontinuous change
the phase of a technology cycle characterized by techn=ological substitution and design competition

technological substitution
the purchase of new technologies to replace older ones

design competition
competition between old and new technologies to establish a new technological standard or dominant design

establish a new technological standard or dominant design. Because of large investments in old technology, and because the new and old technologies are often incompatible with each other, companies and consumers are reluctant to switch to a different technology during a design competition. In addition, during design competition, the older technology usually improves significantly in response to the competitive threat from the new technologies; this response also slows the changeover from older to newer technologies.

Discontinuous change is followed by the emergence of a **dominant design**, which becomes the new accepted market standard for technology.[17] Dominant designs emerge in several ways. One is critical mass, meaning that a particular technology can become the dominant design simply because most people use it. This happened in the design competition between TOSHIBA's HD DVD and Sony's Blu-ray for dominance in establishing a new standard format for high-definition home video. Toshiba lost the design competition because Warner Bros., which had been using both technologies, decided to go exclusively with Blu-ray. At the time of Warner's announcement, Blu-ray held 64 percent of the market, compared to 36 percent for HD DVD.[18] Retailers soon joined Warner Bros. in announcing their intentions to sell only Blu-ray equipment and movies.

The best technology doesn't always become the dominant design, because a number of other factors come into play. For instance, a design can become dominant if it solves a practical problem. The QWERTY keyboard (named for the top left line of letters) became the dominant design for typewriters because it slowed typists who, by typing too fast, caused mechanical typewriter keys to jam. Though computers can easily be switched to the DVORAK keyboard layout, which doubles typing speed and cuts typing errors in half, QWERTY lives on as the standard keyboard. In this instance, the QWERTY keyboard solved a problem that, with computers, is no longer relevant. Yet it remains the dominant design not because it is the best technology, but because most people learned to type that way and continue to use it.

Dominant designs can also emerge through independent standards bodies. The International Telecommunication Union (ITU) (www.itu.ch) is an independent organization that establishes standards for the communications industry. Various standards are proposed, discussed, negotiated, and changed until agreement is reached on a final set of standards that communication industries (Internet, telephone, satellites, radio) will follow worldwide.

No matter how it happens, the emergence of a dominant design is a key event in an innovation stream. First, the emergence of a dominant design indicates that there are winners and losers. Technological innovation is both competence enhancing and competence destroying. Companies that bet on the now-dominant design usually prosper. By contrast, when companies bet on the wrong design or the old technology, they may experience **technological lockout**, which occurs when a new dominant design (i.e., a significantly better technology) makes it difficult for a company to competitively sell its products.[19] Second, the emergence of a dominant design signals a shift from design experimentation and competition to **incremental change**, a phase in which companies innovate by lowering the cost and improving the functioning and performance of the dominant design. For example, manufacturing

dominant design
a new technological design or process that becomes the accepted market standard

technological lockout
the inability of a company to competitively sell its products because it relied on old technology or a nondominant design

incremental change
the phase of a technology cycle in which companies innovate by lowering costs and improving the functioning and performance of the dominant technological design

efficiencies enable Intel to cut the cost of its chips by one-half to two-thirds during a technology cycle, while doubling or tripling their speed. This focus on improving the dominant design continues until the next technological discontinuity occurs.

REVIEW 6-1

. . . .

Organizational Innovation

Technology cycles typically follow an S-curve pattern of innovation. Early in the cycle, technological progress is slow and improvements in technological performance are small. As a technology matures, however, performance improves quickly. Finally, as the limits of a technology are reached, only small improvements occur. At this point, significant improvements in performance must come from new technologies.

The best way to protect a competitive advantage is to create a stream of innovative ideas and products. Innovation streams begin with technological discontinuities that create significant breakthroughs in performance or function. Technological discontinuities are followed by discontinuous change, in which customers purchase new technologies (technological substitution) and companies compete to establish the new dominant design (design competition). Dominant designs emerge because of critical mass, because they solve a practical problem, or because of the negotiations of independent standards bodies. Because technological innovation is both competence enhancing and competence destroying, companies that bet on the wrong design often struggle (technological lockout), whereas companies that bet on the eventual dominant design usually prosper. Emergence of a dominant design leads to a focus on incremental change, lowering costs, and making small, but steady improvements in the dominant design. This focus continues until the next technological discontinuity occurs.

6-2 Managing Innovation

One consequence of technology cycles and innovation streams is that managers must be equally good at managing innovation in two very different circumstances. First, during discontinuous change, companies must find a way to anticipate and survive the technological changes that can suddenly transform industry leaders into losers and industry unknowns into powerhouses. Companies that can't manage innovation following technological discontinuities risk quick organizational decline and dissolution. Second, after a new dominant design emerges following discontinuous change, companies must manage the very different process of incremental improvement and innovation. Companies that can't manage incremental innovation slowly deteriorate as they fall farther behind industry leaders.

After reading this section, you should be able to:

6-2 discuss the different methods that managers can use to effectively manage innovation in their organizations.

Unfortunately, what works well when managing innovation during discontinuous change doesn't work well when managing innovation during periods of incremental change (and vice versa).

Consequently, to successfully manage innovation streams, companies need to be good at three things: **6-2a managing sources of innovation, 6-2b managing innovation during discontinuous change**, and **6-2c managing innovation during incremental change.**

6-2a Managing Sources of Innovation

Innovation comes from great ideas. So a starting point for managing innovation is to manage the sources of innovation, that is, where new ideas come from. One place that new ideas originate is with brilliant inventors. Do you know who invented the telephone, the light bulb, a way to collect and store electricity, air conditioning, radio, television, automobiles, the jet engine, computers, and the Internet? These innovations were created by Alexander Graham Bell, Thomas Edison, Pieter van Musschenbroek, Willis Carrier, Guglielmo Marconi, John Baird and Philo T. Farnsworth, Gottlieb Daimler and Wilhelm Maybach, Sir Frank Whittle, Charles Babbage, and Vint Cerf and Robert Kahn, respectively. These innovators and their innovations forever changed the course of modern life. But only a few companies have the likes of an Edison, Marconi, or Bell working for them. Given that great thinkers and inventors are in short supply, what might companies do to ensure a steady flow of good ideas?

Well, when we say that innovation begins with great ideas, we're really saying that innovation begins with creativity. As we defined it at the beginning of this chapter, creativity is the production of novel and useful ideas.[20] Although companies can't command employees to be creative ("You *will* be more creative!"), they can jump-start innovation by building **creative work environments**, in which workers perceive that creative thoughts and ideas are welcomed and valued. As Exhibit 6.4 shows, creative

creative work environments
workplace cultures in which workers perceive that new ideas are welcomed, valued, and encouraged

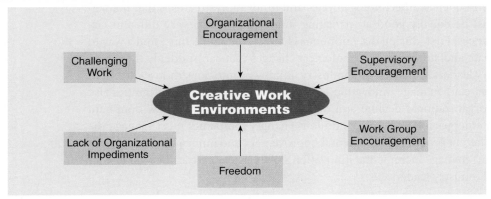

work environments have six components that encourage creativity: challenging work, organizational encouragement, supervisory encouragement, work group encouragement, freedom, and a lack of organizational impediments.[21]

Work is *challenging* when it requires effort, demands attention and focus, and is perceived as important to others in the organization. According to researcher Mihaly Csikszentmihalyi (pronounced "ME-high-ee CHICK-sent-me-high-ee"), challenging work promotes creativity because it creates a rewarding psychological experience known as "flow." **Flow** is a psychological state of effortlessness, in which you become completely absorbed in what you're doing and time seems to fly. When flow occurs, who you are and what you're doing become one. Csikszentmihalyi first encountered flow when studying artists: "What struck me by looking at artists at work was their tremendous focus on the work, this enormous involvement, this forgetting of time and body. It wasn't justified by expectation of rewards, like, 'Aha, I'm going to sell this painting.'"[22] Csikszentmihalyi has found that chess players, rock climbers, dancers, surgeons, and athletes regularly experience flow, too. A key part of creating flow experiences, and thus creative work environments, is to achieve a balance between skills and task challenge. Workers become bored when they can do more than is required of them and anxious when their skills aren't sufficient to accomplish a task. When skills and task challenge are balanced, however, flow and creativity can occur.

A creative work environment requires three kinds of encouragement: organizational, supervisory, and work group encouragement. *Organizational encouragement* of creativity occurs when management encourages risk taking and new ideas, supports and fairly evaluates new ideas, rewards and recognizes creativity, and encourages the sharing of new ideas throughout different parts of the company. *Supervisory encouragement* of creativity occurs when supervisors provide clear goals, encourage open interaction with subordinates, and actively support development teams' work and ideas. *Work group encouragement* occurs when group members have diverse experience, education, and backgrounds, and the group fosters: mutual openness to ideas; positive, constructive challenge to ideas; and shared commitment to ideas. For further discussion of these factors, see Chapter 9 on managing teams.

Freedom means having autonomy over one's day-to-day work and a sense of ownership and control over one's ideas. Numerous studies have indicated that creative ideas thrive under conditions of freedom. At the TATA GROUP, a conglomerate based in India that produces everything from coffee to cars, every employee is allowed to spend five hours a week on personal projects. Then, through its in-house social media network, called IdeaMax, employees propose, comment, and vote on ideas, some 12,000 of which have been proposed within the last year.[23]

To foster creativity, companies may also have to *remove impediments* to creativity from their work environments. Internal conflict and power struggles, rigid management structures, and a conservative bias toward the status quo can all discourage creativity. They create the perception that others in the organization will decide which ideas are acceptable and deserve support.

flow
a psychological state of effortlessness in which you become completely absorbed in what you're doing and time seems to pass quickly

Doing the Right Thing

Don't Steal Ideas

Stealing ideas is never a good idea. By taking credit for other people's great work, you're disregarding the efforts that they put into thinking of and developing the next great idea that will fuel your company's success. But did you know that stealing ideas is also bad for the entire organization? When you steal ideas from others, it actually squelches the creative powers in your company. After all, if someone else is just going to take credit for all of your creative work and get all of the benefits, then what's the point? Why even bother thinking of anything innovative? So do the right thing, and don't steal others' ideas. It will help keep the creative juices flowing.[24]

6-2b Experiential Approach: Managing Innovation during Discontinuous Change

A study of 72 product-development projects (i.e., innovation) in 36 computer companies across the United States, Europe, and Asia sheds light on how to manage innovation. Companies that succeeded in periods of discontinuous change (characterized by technological substitution and design competition, as described earlier) typically followed an experiential approach to innovation.[25] The **experiential approach to innovation** assumes that innovation is occurring within a highly uncertain environment and that the key to fast product innovation is to use intuition, flexible options, and hands-on experience to reduce uncertainty and accelerate learning and understanding. The experiential approach to innovation has five aspects: design iterations, testing, milestones, multifunctional teams, and powerful leaders.[26]

An iteration is a repetition. So a **design iteration** is a cycle of repetition in which a company tests a prototype of a new product or service, improves on the design, and then builds and tests the improved product or service prototype. A **product prototype** is a full-scale working model that is being tested for design, function, and reliability. **Testing** is a systematic comparison of different product designs or design iterations. Companies that want to create a new dominant design following a technological discontinuity quickly build, test, improve, and retest a series of different product prototypes.

By trying a number of very different designs or making successive improvements and changes in the same design, frequent design iterations reduce uncertainty and improve understanding. Simply put, the more prototypes you build, the more likely you are to learn what works and what doesn't. Also, when designers and engineers build a number of prototypes, they are less likely to fall in love with a particular prototype. Instead, they'll be more concerned with improving the product or technology as much as they can. Testing speeds up and improves the innovation process too. When two very different design prototypes are tested against each other, or the new design iteration is tested against the previous iteration, product design strengths and weaknesses quickly become apparent. Likewise, testing uncovers errors early in the design process, when they are easiest to correct. Finally, testing accelerates learning and understanding by forcing engineers and product designers to examine hard data about product performance. When there's hard evidence that prototypes are testing well, the confidence of the design team grows. Also, personal conflict between design team members is less likely when testing focuses on hard measurements and facts rather than personal hunches and preferences.

Milestones are formal project review points used to assess progress and performance. For example, a company that has put itself on a 12-month

experiential approach to innovation
an approach to innovation that assumes a highly uncertain environment and uses intuition, flexible options, and hands-on experience to reduce uncertainty and accelerate learning and understanding

design iteration
a cycle of repetition in which a company tests a prototype of a new product or service, improves on that design, and then builds and tests the improved prototype

product prototype
a full-scale working model that is being tested for design, function, and reliability

testing
the systematic comparison of different product designs or design iterations

milestones
formal project review points used to assess progress and performance

schedule to complete a project might schedule milestones at the 3-month, 6-month, and 9-month points on the schedule. By making people regularly assess what they're doing, how well they're performing, and whether they need to take corrective action, milestones provide structure to the general chaos that follows technological discontinuities. Milestones also shorten the innovation process by creating a sense of urgency that keeps everyone on task. Finally, milestones are beneficial for innovation because meeting regular milestones builds momentum by giving people a sense of accomplishment.

Multifunctional teams are work teams composed of people from different departments. Multifunctional teams accelerate learning and understanding by mixing and integrating technical, marketing, and manufacturing activities. By involving all key departments in development from the start, multifunctional teams speed innovation through early identification of new ideas or problems that would typically not have been generated or addressed until much later.

Powerful leaders provide the vision, discipline, and motivation to keep the innovation process focused, on time, and on target. Powerful leaders are able to get resources when they are needed, are typically more experienced, have high status in the company, and are held directly responsible for the products' success or failure. On average, powerful leaders can get innovation-related projects done nine months faster than leaders with little power or influence.

MANAGEMENT TREND

Reverse Innovation

For large multinational companies, innovation often flows "downward": products or services are created in a developed economy, such as the United States, and then adapted for sale in emerging economies. *General Electric* uses "reverse innovation," where new products are first developed in emerging economies and then adapted for and distributed to developed countries. For example, GE's researchers in India created a handheld electrocardiogram device (a machine that records heart activity), while GE teams in China came up with a portable ultrasound scanner that is slightly larger than an iPod. Both devices were developed to meet the needs of local doctors who needed affordable, light, and portable diagnostic tools that they could take to service patients in rural areas. However, both devices also help GE offer lower prices than its competitors in the United States and other developed markets. Rethinking the direction of innovation has allowed GE to be more competitive at home and abroad.[27]

6-2c Compression Approach: Managing Innovation during Incremental Change

Whereas the experiential approach is used to manage innovation in highly uncertain environments during periods of discontinuous change, the compression approach is used to manage innovation in more certain environments during periods of incremental change. Whereas the goals of the experiential approach are significant improvements in performance and the establishment of a *new* dominant design, the goals of the compression approach are lower costs and incremental improvements in the performance and function of the *existing* dominant design.

The general strategies in each approach are different too. With the experiential approach, the general strategy is to build something new, different, and substantially better. Because there's so much uncertainty—no one knows which technology will become the market leader—companies adopt a winner-take-all approach by trying to create the market-leading, dominant design. With the compression approach, the general strategy is to compress

multifunctional teams
work teams composed of people from different departments

the time and steps needed to bring about small, consistent improvements in performance and functionality. Because a dominant technology design already exists, the general strategy is to continue improving the existing technology as rapidly as possible.

In short, a **compression approach to innovation** assumes that innovation is a predictable process, that incremental innovation can be planned using a series of steps, and that compressing the time it takes to complete those steps can speed up innovation. The compression approach to innovation has five aspects: planning, supplier involvement, shortening the time of individual steps, overlapping steps, and multifunctional teams.[28]

In Chapter 4, *planning* was defined as choosing a goal and a method or strategy to achieve that goal. When *planning for incremental innovation*, the goal is to squeeze or compress development time as much as possible, and the general strategy is to create a series of planned steps to accomplish that goal. Planning for incremental innovation helps avoid unnecessary steps and enables developers to sequence steps in the right order to avoid wasted time and delays between steps. Planning also reduces misunderstandings and improves coordination.

Most planning for incremental innovation is based on the idea of generational change. **Generational change** occurs when incremental improvements are made to a dominant technological design such that the improved version of the technology is fully backward compatible with the older version.[29] Software is backward compatible if a new version of the software will work with files created by older versions. One of the expected and important features of video game consoles is their ability to play games purchased for earlier machines. When developing its PlayStation 3 (PS3), Sony decided to reduce the game machine's backward compatibility with its predecessor, the PlayStation 2 (PS2), because of production costs. As you can imagine, Sony paid the price in reduced sales and angry consumers.[30]

Because the compression approach assumes that innovation can follow a series of preplanned steps, one of the ways to shorten development time is *supplier involvement*. Delegating some of the preplanned steps in the innovation process to outside suppliers reduces the amount of work that internal development teams must do. Plus, suppliers provide an alternative source of ideas and expertise that can lead to better designs. Sysco, the largest foodservice distributor in North America, not only supplies restaurants and chefs with the ingredients they need, but also helps them find ways to improve their business through a free consulting service called Business Review. In this program, Sysco employees help restaurateurs select and use ingredients to maximize profitability, design menus so that the most profitable items catch customers' attention, and train waitstaff to provide excellent customer service.

Another way to shorten development time is simply to *shorten the time of individual steps* in the innovation process. A common way to do that is through computer-aided design (CAD). CAD speeds up the design process by allowing designers and engineers to make and test design changes using computer models rather than physically testing expensive prototypes. CAD also speeds innovation by making it easy to see how design changes affect engineering, purchasing, and production.

compression approach to innovation
an approach to innovation that assumes that incremental innovation can be planned using a series of steps and that compressing those steps can speed innovation

generational change
change based on incremental improvements to a dominant technological design such that the improved technology is fully backward compatible with the older technology

In a sequential design process, each step must be completed before the next step begins. But sometimes multiple development steps can be performed at the same time. *Overlapping steps* shorten the development process by reducing delays or waiting time between steps. SUMMIT ENTERTAINMENT used overlapping steps to great success in producing the *Twilight* movie franchise. Although it used the same actors and screenwriter throughout the series, by using new directors and production crews for each film, Summit was able to begin production on each film while the previous film was in postproduction. This allowed the studio to release films at regular intervals in order to capitalize on the surprising success of the first film in a timely manner.[31]

REVIEW 6-2

Managing Innovation

To successfully manage innovation streams, companies must manage the sources of innovation and learn to manage innovation during both discontinuous and incremental change. Because innovation begins with creativity, companies can manage the sources of innovation by supporting a creative work environment in which creative thoughts and ideas are encouraged. Creative work environments provide challenging work; offer organizational, supervisory, and work group encouragement; allow significant freedom; and remove organizational impediments to creativity.

Companies that succeed in periods of discontinuous change typically follow an experiential approach to innovation. The experiential approach assumes that intuition, flexible options, and hands-on experience can reduce uncertainty and accelerate learning and understanding. This approach involves frequent design iterations, frequent testing, regular milestones, creation of multifunctional teams, and use of powerful leaders to guide the innovation process. A compression approach to innovation works best during periods of incremental change. This approach assumes that innovation can be planned using a series of steps and that compressing the time it takes to complete those steps can speed up innovation. The five aspects of the compression approach are planning (generational change), supplier involvement, shortening the time of individual steps (computer-aided design), overlapping steps, and multifunctional teams.

6-3 Managing Organizational Change

Five years ago, sales of BlackBerry phones, made by Canadian-based RESEARCH IN MOTION (RIM), dominated corporate and consumer markets, and were growing faster than any other cell phone maker. Today, however, with the surging sales and growth of Apple's iPhones and Google's Android phones, RIM holds only 16 percent of the market, a figure that is steadily declining. Sales of the BlackBerry Torch, RIM's answer to the iPhone and Android phones, have been disappointing. So have sales of BlackBerry apps. Although there are nearly 370,000 apps available for the iPhone and 260,000 available for Android phones, only 26,000 apps are available for BlackBerries.[32] Also, buying and installing BlackBerry apps is often cumbersome, requiring multiple download, installation, and payment steps. App developers also find writing apps for BlackBerry phones frustrating. Andrew Stein, director of mobile business development for PopCap Games, which sells popular games like *Bejeweled* and *Plants vs. Zombies*, says, "RIM today is not really on our radar."[33]

While RIM has responded by courting app developers, simplifying its app website, cutting phone prices, and by giving away its enterprise server software (needed to link BlackBerry phones to corporate e-mail servers) to small companies, company leadership might be better served to figure out why, after spending $1.35 billion a year on research, the company can't come up with competitive products.[34] How is it that RIM can't seem to change? What could it do differently?

After reading this section on organizational change, you should be able to:

6-3 discuss the different methods that managers can use to better manage change as it occurs.

According to social psychologist Kurt Lewin, change is a function of the forces that promote change and the opposing forces that slow or resist change.[35] **Change forces** lead to differences in the form, quality, or condition of an organization over time. By contrast, **resistance forces** support the status quo, that is, the existing conditions in an organization. Change is difficult under any circumstances. In a study of heart bypass patients, doctors told participants straightforwardly to change their eating and health habits or they would die. Unbelievably, a full 90 percent of participants did *not* change their habits at all![36] This fierce resistance to change also applies to organizations (such as RIM).

Resistance to change is caused by self-interest, misunderstanding and distrust, and a general intolerance for change.[37] People resist change out of *self-interest* because they fear that change will cost or deprive them of something they value. Resistance might stem from a fear that the changes will result in a loss of pay, power, responsibility, or even perhaps one's job. People also resist change because of *misunderstanding* and *distrust*; they don't understand the change or the reasons for it, or they distrust the people—typically management—behind

change forces
forces that produce differences in the form, quality, or condition of an organization over time

resistance forces
forces that support the existing state of conditions in organizations

resistance to change
opposition to change resulting from self-interest, misunderstanding and distrust, or a general intolerance for change

© YURI ARCURS/SHUTTERSTOCK.COM

the change. Resistance isn't always visible at first. In fact, some of the strongest resisters may initially support the changes in public, nodding and smiling their agreement, but then ignore the changes in private and do their jobs as they always have. Management consultant Michael Hammer calls this deadly form of resistance the "Kiss of Yes."[38]

Resistance may also come from a generally low tolerance for change. Some people are simply less capable of handling change than others. People with a *low tolerance for change* feel threatened by the uncertainty associated with change and worry that they won't be able to learn the new skills and behaviors needed to successfully negotiate change in their companies.

Because resistance to change is inevitable, successful change efforts require careful management. In this section, you will learn about **6-3a managing resistance to change, 6-3b what not to do when leading organizational change**, and **6-3c different change tools and techniques.**

6-3a Managing Resistance to Change

According to Kurt Lewin, managing organizational change is a basic process of unfreezing, change intervention, and refreezing. **Unfreezing** is getting the people affected by change to believe that change is needed. During the **change intervention** itself, workers and managers change their behavior and work practices. **Refreezing** is supporting and reinforcing the new changes so that they stick.

Resistance to change is an example of frozen behavior. Given the choice between changing and not changing, most people would rather not change. Because resistance to change is natural and inevitable, managers need to unfreeze resistance to change to create successful change programs. The following methods can be used to manage resistance to change: education and communication, participation, negotiation, top-management support, and coercion.[39]

When resistance to change is based on insufficient, incorrect, or misleading information, managers should *educate* employees about the need for change and *communicate* change-related information to them. Managers must also supply the information and funding or other support employees need to make changes. For example, resistance to change can be particularly strong when one company buys another company. This is because one company in the merger usually has a higher status due to its size, or higher profitability, or the fact that it is the acquiring company. These status differences are important to managers and employees, particularly if they're in the lower-status company, because they may worry about retaining their jobs or influence after the merger. That fear or concern can greatly increase resistance to change.[40]

Another way to reduce resistance to change is to have those affected by the change *participate in planning and implementing the change process*. Employees who participate have a better understanding of the change and the need for it. Furthermore, employee concerns about change can be addressed as they occur if employees participate in the planning and implementation process.

Employees are also less likely to resist change if they are allowed *to discuss and agree on who will do what* after change occurs. When *DEGW*, an architectural firm, was working with the CANADIAN BROADCASTING COMPANY to determine

unfreezing
getting the people affected by change to believe that change is needed

change intervention
the process used to get workers and managers to change their behavior and work practices

refreezing
supporting and reinforcing new changes so that they "stick"

how to redesign its 1.5 million square foot headquarters in Toronto, it used a software game called "The Sandbox" to help solve problems on getting company teams, leaders, and real estate managers to agree on what the redesigned space should look like. When playing the game, employees must talk about and make decisions regarding furniture and desk configurations, office privacy, noise, and lounge and public spaces. A finalized design usually emerges after three two-hour game sessions. Game developer Scott Francisco says, "The Sandbox allowed us to address underperforming space by tapping into the knowledge and skills of staff at all levels, turning an intractable problem into a creative outcome. It's designed to elicit interest and engagement."[41] The Sandbox works so well at generating discussions and leading to consensus that DEGW uses it worldwide with its clients.

Resistance to change also decreases when change efforts receive *significant managerial support*. Managers must do more than talk about the importance of change, though. They must provide the training, resources, and autonomy needed to make change happen. The telemarketing industry averages a yearly turnover rate of 43 percent. RYLA TELESERVICES, however, has a much lower rate of turnover, 27 percent, because of its caring environment and the training it invests in its workers. Founder Mark Wilson says, "The industry has a bad stereotype of sweatshops and high turnover. We're proving you can overcome that if you take a creative approach."[42]

Finally, resistance to change can be managed through coercion, or the use of formal power and authority to force others to change. Because of the intense negative reactions it can create (e.g., fear, stress, resentment, sabotage of company products), coercion should be used only when a crisis exists or when all other attempts to reduce resistance to change have failed. Exhibit 6.5 summarizes some additional suggestions for what managers can do when employees resist change.

coercion
the use of formal power and authority to force others to change

---

Exhibit 6.5

What to Do When Employees Resist Change

Unfreezing

Share reasons	Share the reasons for change with employees.
Empathize	Be empathetic to the difficulties that change will create for managers and employees.
Communicate	Communicate the details simply, clearly, extensively, verbally, and in writing.

Change

Explain benefits	Explain the benefits, "what's in it for them."
Champion	Identify a highly respected manager to manage the change effort.
Seek input	Allow the people who will be affected by change to express their needs and offer their input.
Choose timing	Don't begin change at a bad time, for example, during the busiest part of the year or month.
Maintain security	If possible, maintain employees' job security to minimize fear of change.
Offer training	Offer training to ensure that employees are both confident and competent to handle new requirements.
Pace yourself	Change at a manageable pace. Don't rush.

Source: G. J. Iskat and J. Liebowitz, "What to Do When Employees Resist Change," Supervision, August 1, 1996.

Part Two *Planning*

6-3b What *Not* to Do When Leading Change

So far, you've learned about the basic change process (unfreezing, change, refreezing) and managing resistance to change. Harvard Business School professor John Kotter argues that knowing what *not* to do is just as important as knowing what to do when it comes to achieving successful organizational change.[43]

Exhibit 6.6 shows the most common errors that managers make when they lead change. The first two errors occur during the unfreezing phase, when managers try to get the people affected by change to believe that change is really needed. The first and potentially most serious error is *not establishing a great enough sense of urgency*. Indeed, Kotter estimates that more than half of all change efforts fail because the people affected are not convinced that change is necessary. People will feel a greater sense of urgency if a leader in the company makes a public, candid assessment of the company's problems and weaknesses. CELESTICA, INC., located in Toronto, Canada, is an electronics manufacturing services company that produces complex printed circuit assemblies, such as PC motherboards and networking cards, flat-screen TVs, and Xbox video game systems for Microsoft. When Craig Muhlhauser took over as president and CEO, Celestica, Inc. was losing money and market share. Muhlhauser went to work right away. He informed employees that the company couldn't survive if it didn't change. Within his first 30 days as CEO, he reduced staff by 35 percent, moved new people into important positions, and had the attention of everyone in the company.[44]

The second mistake that occurs in the unfreezing process is *not creating a powerful enough coalition*. Change often starts with one or two people, but it has to be supported by a critical and growing group of people if an entire department, division, or company is to be affected. Besides top management, Kotter recommends that key employees, managers, board members, customers, and even union leaders be members of a *core change coalition* that guides and supports organizational change. "In a turnaround, there are three kinds of employees," said Muhlhauser—those on your side, those on the fence, and those who will never buy in. The latter have to be let go and those on the fence should be persuaded to contribute or leave. Says Muhlhauser, "We have to make change, change is difficult and as we make change, it is important to realize that there are people who are going to resist that change. In talking to those people, the objective is to move everybody into the column of supporters. But that is probably unachievable."[45] It's also important to strengthen this core change coalition's resolve by periodically bringing its members together for off-site retreats.

The next four errors that managers make occur during the change phase, when a change intervention is used to try to get workers and managers to change

Exhibit 6.6

Errors Managers Make When Leading Change

Unfreezing

1. Not establishing a great enough sense of urgency.
2. Not creating a powerful enough guiding coalition.

Change

3. Lacking a vision.
4. Undercommunicating the vision by a factor of 10.
5. Not removing obstacles to the new vision.
6. Not systematically planning for and creating short-term wins.

Refreezing

7. Declaring victory too soon.
8. Not anchoring changes in the corporation's culture.

Source: *J. P. Kotter, "Leading Change: Why Transformation Efforts Fail,"* Harvard Business Review *73, no. 2 (March–April 1995): 59.*

their behavior and work practices. *Lacking a vision* for change is a significant error at this point. As you learned in Chapter 5, a *vision* (defined as a *purpose statement* in Chapter 5) is a statement of a company's purpose or reason for existing. A vision for change makes clear where a company or department is headed and why the change is occurring. Change efforts that lack vision tend to be confused, chaotic, and contradictory. By contrast, change efforts guided by visions are clear and easy to understand and can be effectively explained in five minutes or less.

Undercommunicating the vision by a factor of 10 is another mistake in the change phase. According to Kotter, companies mistakenly hold just one meeting to announce the vision. Or, if the new vision receives heavy emphasis in executive speeches or company newsletters, senior management then undercuts the vision by behaving in ways contrary to it. Successful communication of the vision requires that top managers link everything the company does to the new vision and that they "walk the talk" by behaving in ways consistent with the vision. Furthermore, even companies that begin change with a clear vision sometimes make the mistake of *not removing obstacles to the new vision*. They leave formidable barriers to change in place by failing to redesign jobs, pay plans, and technology to support the new way of doing things. One of Celestica's key obstacles was efficiently and effectively managing a complex supply chain. CEO Craig Muhlhauser and his management team reduced shipping speeds and kept costs low by implementing Liveshare, an information system that gave it and its suppliers real-time data on sales, production, inventory, and shipping for all of its products. With Liveshare, Best Buy can see live, up-to-date numbers, indicating how many of those video games are rolling off Celestica's production lines or are now on trucks in route to Best Buy trucking depots.[46]

Another error in the change phase is *not systematically planning for and creating short-term wins*. Most people don't have the discipline and patience to wait two years to see if the new change effort works. Change is threatening and uncomfortable, so people need to see an immediate payoff if they are to continue to support it. Kotter recommends that managers create short-term wins by actively picking people and projects that are likely to work extremely well early in the change process. Celestica's Craig Muhlhauser understood the importance of short-term wins. Said Muhlhauser, "My approach was to look at the first 30 days, then at the first 3 months, then at the first 12 months; and then I took a look at the three years. In a turnaround, you have to take hold very quickly. You have to show relatively quick hits [i.e., short-term wins]—to show your turnaround strategy is working—and then you deal with a multitude of issues in a very focused way that will allow you to continue to show improvement."[47]

The last two errors that managers make occur during the refreezing phase, when attempts are made to support and reinforce changes so that they stick. *Declaring victory too soon* is a tempting mistake in the refreezing phase. Managers typically declare victory right after the first large-scale success in the change process. Declaring success too early has the same effect as draining the gasoline out of a car: It stops change efforts dead in their tracks. With success declared, supporters of the change process stop pushing to make change happen. After all, why push when success has been achieved? Rather than declaring victory, managers should use the momentum from short-term wins to push for even bigger or faster changes. This maintains urgency and prevents change supporters from slacking off before the changes are frozen into the company's culture.

The last mistake that managers make is *not anchoring changes in the organization's culture*. An *organization's culture* is the set of key values, beliefs, and attitudes shared by organizational members, which determines the accepted way of doing things in a company. As you learned in Chapter 2, changing cultures is extremely difficult and time consuming. According to Kotter, two things help anchor changes in a corporation's culture. The first is showing people directly that changes have actually improved performance. At Celestica, this was demonstrated by the quick increase in quarterly profits, which led to a 60 percent increase in its stock price.[48] The second is to make sure that the people who get promoted fit the new culture. If they don't, it's a clear sign that the changes were only temporary. To anchor this change, Muhlhauser created a culture of meritocracy that rewarded managers and employees for their contributions. The rewards came in the form of promotions, pay increases, and huge bonuses. Customer satisfaction has improved. With the increasing demand for consumer products, such as smartphones, employees are excited about the prospects for Celestica. "We've got some new programs in the pipeline so we're optimistic about our ability to compete in and win in that market," said Muhlhauser.[49]

6-3c Change Tools and Techniques

Imagine that your boss came to you and said, "All right, genius, you wanted it. You're in charge of turning around the division." Where would you begin? How would you encourage change-resistant managers to change? What would you do to include others in the change process? How would you get the change process off to a quick start? Finally, what approach would you use to promote long-term effectiveness and performance? Results-driven change, the General Electric workout, transition management teams, and organizational development are different change tools and techniques that can be used to address these issues.

One of the reasons that organizational change efforts fail is that they are activity-oriented rather than results-oriented. In other words, they focus primarily on changing company procedures, management philosophy, or employee behavior. Typically, there is much buildup and preparation as consultants are brought in, presentations are made, books are read, and employees and managers are trained. There's a tremendous emphasis on doing things the new way. But, with all the focus on "doing," almost no attention is paid to *results*, to seeing if all this activity has actually made a difference.

By contrast, **results-driven change** supplants the emphasis on activity with a laserlike focus on quickly measuring and improving results.[50] Top managers at *HYUNDAI* knew that if they were to compete successfully against the likes of Honda and Toyota, they would have to improve the quality of their cars substantially. So top managers guided the company's results-driven change process by, first, increasing the number of quality teams from 100 to 865. Then, all employees were required to attend seminars on quality improvement and use the results of industry quality studies, like those published annually by J. D. Power

results-driven change
change created quickly by focusing on the measurement and improvement of results

and Associates, as their benchmark. Hyundai then measured the effects of the focus on quality. Before the change, a new Hyundai averaged 23.4 initial quality problems; after the results-driven change efforts, that number dropped to 9.6.[51] Today, according to J. D. Power and Associates, Hyundai ranks seventh overall out of 33 automakers in initial car quality behind Porsche, Acura, Mercedes-Benz, and Lexus, Ford, and Honda.[52]

An advantage of results-driven change is that quick, visible improvements motivate employees to continue to make additional changes to improve measured performance. Exhibit 6.7 describes the basic steps of results-driven change.

The **General Electric workout** is a special kind of results-driven change. The "workout" involves a three-day meeting that brings together managers and employees from different levels of an organization to generate and act quickly on solutions to specific business problems.[53] On the first morning, the boss discusses the agenda and targets specific business problems that the group will solve. Then, the boss leaves and an outside facilitator breaks the group (typically 30 to 40 people) into five or six teams and helps them spend the next day and a half discussing and debating solutions.

On day three, in what GE calls a "town meeting," the teams present specific solutions to their boss, who has been gone since day one. As each team's spokesperson makes specific suggestions, the boss has only three options: agree on the spot, say no, or ask for more information so that a decision can be made by a specific, agreed-on date. GE boss Armand Lauzon sweated his way through a town meeting. To encourage him to say yes, his workers set up the meeting room to put pressure on Lauzon. He says, "I was wringing wet within half an hour. They had 108 proposals, I had about a minute to say yes or no to each one, and I couldn't make eye contact with my boss without turning around, which would show everyone in the room that I was chicken."[54] In the end, Lauzon agreed to all but eight suggestions. Furthermore, once those decisions were made, no one at GE was allowed to overrule them.

While the GE workout clearly speeds up change, it may also fragment change if different managers approve conflicting suggestions in separate town meetings across a company. By contrast, a transition management team provides a way to coordinate change throughout an organization. A **transition management team (TMT)** is a group of 8 to 12 people whose full-time job is to manage and coordinate a company's change process.[55] One member of the TMT is assigned to anticipate and manage the emotions and behaviors related to resistance to change. Despite their importance, many companies overlook the impact that negative emotions and resistant behaviors can have on the change process. TMT members report to the CEO every day, decide which change projects are approved and funded, select and evaluate the people in charge of different change projects, and make sure that different change projects complement one another.

General Electric workout
a three-day meeting in which managers and employees from different levels and parts of an organization quickly generate and act on solutions to specific business problems

transition management team (TMT)
a group of 8 to 12 people whose full-time job is to manage and coordinate a company's change process

It is also important to say what a TMT is *not*. A TMT is not an extra layer of management further separating upper management from lower managers and employees. A TMT is not a steering committee that creates plans for others to carry out. Instead, the members of the TMT are fully involved with making change happen on a daily basis. Furthermore, it's not the TMT's job to determine how and why the company will change. That responsibility belongs to the CEO and upper management. Finally, a TMT is not permanent. Once the company has successfully changed, the TMT is disbanded. Exhibit 6.8 lists the primary responsibilities of TMTs.

Organizational development is a philosophy and collection of planned change interventions designed to improve an organization's long-term health and performance. Organizational development takes a long-range approach to change; it assumes that top-management support is necessary for change to succeed; it creates change by educating workers and managers to change ideas, beliefs, and behaviors so that problems can be solved in new ways; and it emphasizes employee participation in diagnosing, solving, and evaluating problems.[56] As shown in Exhibit 6.9, organizational development interventions begin with the recognition of a problem. Then, the company designates a **change agent** to be formally in charge of guiding the change effort. This person can be someone from the company or a professional consultant. The change agent clarifies the problem, gathers information, works with decision makers to create and implement an action plan, helps to evaluate

organizational development
a philosophy and collection of planned change interventions designed to improve an organization's long-term health and performance

change agent
the person formally in charge of guiding a change effort

Exhibit 6.8

Primary Responsibilities of Transition Management Teams

1. Establish a context for change and provide guidance.
2. Stimulate conversation.
3. Provide appropriate resources.
4. Coordinate and align projects.
5. Ensure congruence of messages, activities, policies, and behaviors.
6. Provide opportunities for joint creation.
7. Anticipate, identify, and address people problems.
8. Prepare the critical mass.

Source: J. D. Duck, "Managing Change: The Art of Balancing," Harvard Business Review on Change (Boston: Harvard Business School Press, 1998), 55–81.

Exhibit 6.9

General Steps for Organizational Development Interventions

1. **Entry** A problem is discovered and the need for change becomes apparent. A search begins for someone to deal with the problem and facilitate change.
2. **Startup** A change agent enters the picture and works to clarify the problem and gain commitment to a change effort.
3. **Assessment & feedback** The change agent gathers information about the problem and provides feedback about it to decision makers and those affected by it.
4. **Action planning** The change agent works with decision makers to develop an action plan.
5. **Intervention** The action plan, or organizational development intervention, is carried out.
6. **Evaluation** The change agent helps decision makers assess the effectiveness of the intervention.
7. **Adoption** Organizational members accept ownership and responsibility for the change, which is then carried out through the entire organization.
8. **Separation** The change agent leaves the organization after first ensuring that the change intervention will continue to work.

Source: W. J. Rothwell, R. Sullivan, and G. M. McLean, Practicing Organizational Development: A Guide for Consultants (San Diego: Pfeiffer & Co., 1995).

what *really* works

Change the Work Setting or Change the People? Do Both!

Let's assume that you believe that your company needs to change. Congratulations! Just recognizing the need for change puts you ahead of 80 percent of the companies in your industry. But now that you've recognized the need for change, how do you make change happen? Should you focus on changing the work setting or the behavior of the people who work in that setting? It's a classic chicken-or-egg type of question. Which would you do?

A recent meta-analysis based on 52 studies and a combined total of 29,611 study participants indicated that it's probably best to do both!

Changing the Work Setting

An organizational work setting has four parts: organizing arrangements (control and reward systems, organizational structure), social factors (people, culture, patterns of interaction), technology (how inputs are transformed into outputs), and the physical setting (the actual physical space in which people work). Overall, there is a 55 percent chance that organizational change efforts will successfully bring changes to a company's work setting. Although the odds are 55–45 in your favor, this is a much lower probability of success than you've seen with the management techniques discussed in other chapters. This simply reflects how strong resistance to change is in most companies.

CHANGE THE SETTING
probability of success: 55%

| 10 | 20 | 30 | 40 | 50 | 60 | 70 | 80 | 90 | 100 |

Changing the People

Changing people means changing individual work behavior. The idea is powerful. Change the decisions people make.

Change the activities they perform. Change the information they share with others. And change the initiatives they take on their own. Change these individual behaviors and collectively you change the entire company. Overall, there is a 57 percent chance that organizational change efforts will successfully change people's individual work behavior. If you're wondering why the odds aren't higher, consider how difficult it is to change personal behavior. It's incredibly difficult to quit smoking, change your diet, or maintain a daily exercise program. Not surprisingly, changing personal behavior at work is also difficult. Viewed in this context, a 57 percent chance of success is a notable achievement.

CHANGE THE PEOPLE
probability of success: 57%

| 10 | 20 | 30 | 40 | 50 | 60 | 70 | 80 | 90 | 100 |

Changing Individual Behavior and

Organizational Performance

The point of changing individual behavior is to improve organizational performance (increase profits, market share, and productivity, and lower costs). Overall, there is a 76 percent chance that changes in individual behavior will produce changes in organizational outcomes. So, if you want to improve your company's profits, market share, or productivity, focus on changing the way that your people behave at work.[57]

CHANGE INDIVIDUAL BEHAVIOR
probability of success: 76%

| 10 | 20 | 30 | 40 | 50 | 60 | 70 | 80 | 90 | 100 |

the plan's effectiveness, implements the plan throughout the company, and then leaves (if from outside the company) after making sure the change intervention will continue to work.

REVIEW 6-3

Managing Change

The basic change process involves unfreezing, change, and refreezing. Resistance to change, which stems from self-interest, misunderstanding and distrust, and a general intolerance for change, can be managed through education and communication, participation, negotiation, top-management support, and coercion. Knowing what *not* to do is as important as knowing what to do to achieve successful change. Managers should avoid these errors when leading change: not establishing urgency, not creating a guiding coalition, lacking a vision, undercommunicating the vision, not removing obstacles to the vision, not creating short-term wins, declaring victory too soon, and not anchoring changes in the corporation's culture.

Finally, managers can use a number of change techniques. Results-driven change and the GE workout reduce resistance to change by getting change efforts off to a fast start. Transition management teams, which manage a company's change process, coordinate change efforts throughout an organization. Organizational development is a collection of planned change interventions (large system, small group, person-focused), guided by a change agent, that are designed to improve an organization's long-term health and performance.

 # Management Team Decision

Face the Future[58]

Times don't seem to be much better to be in the oil business. Sure, there have been some bumps in the road the past few years—the tragic oil spill in the Gulf of Mexico and unstable prices and supply due to political situations. But there's one piece of news that makes all those obstacles easier to deal with—profits are up, and not just a little bit, either. Profits are positively soaring. Exxon announced that its earnings for the most recent quarter were up 69 percent from the previous year, to $10.65 billion. Royal Dutch Shell posted an increase of 30 percent to $6.29 billion, even while experiencing a 2.5 percent decrease in production, and Occidental Petroleum's earnings jumped 46 percent to $1.55 billion.

Times certainly seem to be great, but there are many executives in your company who are pushing for big changes. Sure, they argue, revenues and earnings and profits are sky-high

right now. But what about the future? Consumers and governments around the world are growing more concerned about oil—about how it impacts the environment and about whether there will be enough to meet fuel demands. In response to these concerns, there has been much research and development dedicated to alternative fuel vehicles, from all-electric cars like the Nissan Leaf, to gas-electric hybrids like the Chevy Volt or hydrogen-powered cars like the Honda FCX Clarity. And consumers have responded quite favorably. In just four short months, GM sold over 2,000 Volts and Nissan sold over 1,000 Leafs. Furthermore, nearly 20,000 customers have already paid a deposit to be put on a waiting list for the Leaf, and almost 54,000 are on the Volt waiting list.

The executives pushing for change point to these figures as a sign that the auto industry will soon experience a dramatic shift. They're arguing that the age of the gasoline engine (along with gas stations and gas companies) will soon be over, replaced by a more environmentally friendly method of fueling cars. In their view, the company should act now, and quickly, to take advantage of this shift by investing in a nation wide network of electric-charging stations, where consumers recharge their all-electric or plug-in hybrid cars. That way, when gas-engine technology is eventually surpassed, your company will be in prime position to provide recharging infrastructure to the entire country.

There are others in the company, however, who doubt that this is the right step to take. Although they recognize that gas engines may not last forever, they're not convinced that it's a technology in decline. They recognize as well that sales of electric cars and hybrids are on the rise, but these are still microscopic compared to the 11.5 million conventional cars sold in the United States or the 18 million sold in China last year. They are also concerned that all-electric cars are just one choice among many alternative fuels; there are also hydrogen-powered cars, natural gas-powered cars,

biofuels, and who knows what else will be developed in the future. Their great worry is that the company will spend huge amounts of time and money to develop a recharging network only to have another alternative fuel rise as the dominant design.

So what should the company do? Should it look to the future right now, even as its earnings from oil are near record highs? Or should it stay the course?

For this Management Team Decision, form a group with three or four other students and answer the questions on the next page.

Questions

1. What is your recommendation for how the company should proceed? Should it take action on developing an alternative fuel network or wait until a dominant design arises?

2. What are the advantages and disadvantages of choosing a technology format before a dominant design arises?

3. What steps could the company take to help ensure that electric engines become the dominant design?

 ## Practice Being a Manager

Supporting Creativity

Successfully managing innovation is challenging. Companies must find ways to support creativity and invention while screening their investments in support of innovation. This exercise will give you an opportunity to experience a bit of the organizational dynamic regarding innovation and investment.

STEP 1 **Assign roles.** Your professor will assign you to a pair or small group and give your team a role as either "Inventors" or "Investors." Regardless of role, assume that you work for a large clothing and accessories company that targets college students. Your company makes some traditional clothing and gear (such as backpacks and folios) but also prides itself on developing new and innovative products. And recently there has been some interest in

considering new services that the company might offer to the college market, things like event or trip planning.

STEP 2 **Work with your partner(s) on the following tasks, depending on your assigned role.** *Inventors:* Brainstorm and work to develop a new product or service concept. Be prepared to explain your concept to those inside the company who screen ideas and recommend investments.

Investors: Discuss and agree upon some criteria that your company should use to screen new-product and service concepts and to identify which ones to recommend to senior management. Be prepared to listen to one or more concept presentations, ask questions, and then use your criteria to evaluate the concept(s).

STEP 3 **Pair up.** As instructed by your professor, Inventor and Investor groups should pair up. Inventors will now present their new concept, and investors will ask questions and then use their criteria to rate the concept.

STEP 4 **Change roles.** As time allows, your professor will rotate Inventor and Investor pairings through a few rounds of concept presentation and investor evaluation.

STEP 5 **Debrief.** Return to your original Inventor or Investor pair or group, and discuss your experiences in this role-playing. What are some of the challenges of playing this role? What was it like to interact with the "other side" of the presentation/evaluation process?

STEP 6 **Discuss challenges.** As a class, discuss the challenges likely faced by companies as they try to successfully manage innovation. Some items for discussion might include:

1. What is the impact of an "evaluation/rating" on the creative process?

2. Do you think that "inventor units" (such as product development and R&D) and "investor units" (finance) often clash over new-product investment decisions? Why or why not?

3. What role might organizational culture (and subculture) play in the innovation and investment processes?

4. How might managers support healthy innovation and wise investment?

 ## Self-Assessment

Mind Benders

Innovation is a key to corporate success. Companies that innovate and embrace the changes in their business environment tend to outperform those that stand still. Even so, innovative companies don't simply rely on the creativity of their own workforce. They often contract with outside providers to generate new ideas for everything from operations to new products. In other words, innovative companies fill gaps in their own creativity by looking outside the organization.

As a manager, you will benefit from understanding how you are creative (not *whether* you are creative). And just as important as your own creativity is your attitude toward creative endeavors.

This assessment will provide some baseline information you can use as you develop your managerial skills.[59] Indicate the extent to which each of the following statements is true of either your actual behavior or your intentions at work. That is, describe the way you are or the way you intend to be on the job. Use this scale for your responses:

1 Almost never true

2 Seldom true

3 Not applicable

4 Often true

5 Almost always true

1. I openly discuss with my supervisor how to get ahead.
   1   2   3   4   5

2. I try new ideas and approaches to problems.
   1   2   3   4   5

3. I take things or situations apart to find out how they work.
   1   2   3   4   5

4. I welcome uncertainty and unusual circumstances related to my tasks.
   1   2   3   4   5

5. I negotiate my salary openly with my supervisor.

    1   2   3   4   5

6. I can be counted on to find a new use for existing methods or equipment.

    1   2   3   4   5

7. Among my colleagues and coworkers, I will be the first or nearly the first to try out a new idea or method.

    1   2   3   4   5

8. I take the opportunity to translate communications from other departments for my work group.

    1   2   3   4   5

9. I demonstrate originality.

    1   2   3   4   5

10. I will work on a problem that has caused others great difficulty.

    1   2   3   4   5

11. I provide critical input toward a new solution.

    1   2   3   4   5

12. I provide written evaluations of proposed ideas.

    1   2   3   4   5

13. I develop contacts with experts outside my firm.

    1   2   3   4   5

14. I use personal contacts to maneuver into choice work assignments.

    1   2   3   4   5

15. I make time to pursue my own pet ideas or projects.

    1   2   3   4   5

16. I set aside resources for the pursuit of a risky project.

    1   2   3   4   5

17. I tolerate people who depart from organizational routine.

    1   2   3   4   5

18. I speak out in staff meetings.

    1   2   3   4   5

19. I work in teams to try to solve complex problems.

    1   2   3   4   5

20. If my coworkers are asked, they will say I am a wit.

    1   2   3   4   5

TOTAL = ____

SCORING

Determine your score by adding up all the numbers you circled.

    You can find an interpretation of your score at www.cengagebrain.com.

REEL TO REAL

▶ MANAGEMENT WORKPLACE

Holden Outerwear: Managing Change and Innovation

Founded in 2002 by professional snowboarder Mikey LeBlanc, Holden Outerwear has given traditional baggy outerwear a complete style makeover. Unlike ski-apparel brands that focus on utility at the expense of looking good, Holden pants and jackets possess features that are inspired by runway brands like Marc Jacobs and G-Star, as Holden is always looking to bring new elements of style to the slopes. Holden has the attention of everyone in its industry. Retailers wait anxiously to see Le Blanc's newest collections, and competitors from Burton and Salomon to Bonfire and Walmart borrow heavily from Holden's collections. LeBlanc doesn't worry too much about the rampant plagiarism that goes on in his industry. As he sees it, imitation is the highest form of flattery. Plus, Holden's business is based on finding the next big thing. When it comes to style, Holden is the leader, never the follower.

What to Watch For and Ask Yourself

1. Identify the type of change that Holden's leaders are managing on a daily basis.

2. What resistance has Holden encountered while introducing innovative garment designs? How was it able to overcome that resistance?

Endnotes

1. "The 50 Most Innovative Companies 2010," *Bloomberg Businessweek*, accessed May 4, 2011, from www.businessweek.com/interactive_reports/innovative_companies_2010.html; M. Arndt and D. Brady, "3M's Rising Star," *Businessweek*, April 12, 2004, 62–74; M. Gunther, M. Adamo, and B. Feldman, "3M'S Innovation Revival," *Fortune*, September 27, 2010, 73–76; and B. Hindo, "3M: Struggle between Efficiency and Creativity," *Businessweek Online*, September 17, 2007, 36.

2. T. M. Amabile, R. Conti, H. Coon, J. Lazenby, and M. Herron, "Assessing the Work Environment for Creativity," *Academy of Management Journal* 39 (1996): 1154–1184.

3. Ibid.

4. A. H. Van de Ven and M. S. Poole, "Explaining Development and Change in Organizations," *Academy of Management Review* 20 (1995): 510–540.

5. "Swedes to Use Body Heat to Warm Offices," ABC News, accessed September 17, 2008, from http://abcnews.go.com/International/wireStory?id=410819; E. Yerger, "Company in Sweden Uses Body Heat to Warm Office Building," *Unusual Things*, accessed September 17, 2008, from www.popfi.com/2008/01/14/company-to-use-body-heat-to-warmoffice-building-2; and D. Chazan, "Office Block Warmed by Body Heat," BBC News, accessed September 17, 2008, from http://news.bbc.co.uk/2/hi/science/nature/7233123.stm.

6. Ibid.

7. Amabile et al., "Assessing the Work Environment for Creativity."

8. S. McBride, "Thinking About Tomorrow: How We Watch Movies and TV," *Wall Street Journal*, January 28, 2008, R1.

9. P. Anderson and M. L. Tushman, "Managing through Cycles of Technological Change," *Research/Technology Management* (May–June 1991): 26–31.

10. R. N. Foster, *Innovation: The Attacker's Advantage* (New York: Summit, 1986).

11. "The Silicon Engine: A Timeline of Semiconductors in Computers," Computer History Museum, accessed April 22, 2011, from www.computerhistory.org/semiconductor/.

12. A. Otis, "The Impetus for Vermont Buying Colorado Railcar DMU's," *TrainRiders/Northeast*, January 1, 2007, accessed November 11, 2009, from www.railivemont.org/passenger/the-colorado-railcar-dmu-purchase/new-dmus-the-impitus-for-their-purchase.html; and www.usrailcar.com.

13. M. L. Tushman, P. C. Anderson, and C. O'Reilly, "Technology Cycles, Innovation Streams, and Ambidextrous Organizations: Organization Renewal through Innovation Streams and Strategic Change," in *Managing Strategic Innovation and Change*, M. L. Tushman and P. Anderson, eds. (New York: Oxford Press, 1997), 3–23.

14. P. Landers, "Brain Surgery Made Simple—New Less-Invasive Procedures Reduce Pain, Recovery Time; Sending in the Tiny Robots," *Wall Street Journal*, October 31, 2002, D1.

15. "Breakthrough Brain Surgery: Neurosurgeons Can Now Remove Brain Cancer Endoscopically," *Science Daily*, August 1, 2005, accessed November 8, 2009, from www.sciencedaily.com.

16. D. Lieberman, "Blockbuster Files for Chapter 11 Bankruptcy, Will Reorganize," *USA Today*, September 23, 2010, accessed May 4, 2011, from www.usatoday.com/money/media/2010-09-23-blockbuster23_ST_N.htm

17. W. Abernathy and J. Utterback, "Patterns of Industrial Innovation," *Technology Review* 2 (1978): 40–47.

18. "Blu Capabilities Still Up in the Air," *Home Media Magazine*.

19. M. Schilling, "Technological Lockout: An Integrative Model of the Economic and Strategic Factors Driving Technology Success and Failure," *Academy of Management Review* 23 (1998): 267–284; and M. Schilling, "Technology Success and Failure in Winner-Take-All Markets: The Impact of Learning Orientation, Timing, and Network Externalities," *Academy of Management Journal* 45 (2002): 387–398.

20. Amabile et al., "Assessing the Work Environment for Creativity."

21. Ibid.

22. M. Csikszentmihalyi, *Flow: The Psychology of Optimal Experience* (New York: Harper & Row, 1990).

23. B. Kowitt, "Dunkin' Brands' Kitchen Crew," *Fortune*, May 24, 2010. 72–74.

24. S. Carson, "Plagiarism and Its Effect on Creative Work," *Psychology Today*, October 16, 2010, accessed 4 May 2011 from www.psychologytoday.com/blog/life-art/201010/plagiarism-and-its-effect-creative-work.

25. K. M. Eisenhardt, "Accelerating Adaptive Processes: Product Innovation in the Global Computer Industry," *Administrative Science Quarterly* 40 (1995): 84–110.

26. Ibid.

27. K. Shwiff, "GE CEO Touts 'Reverse Innovation' Model," *Wall Street Journal*, September 23, 2009, accessed 4 May 2011 from http://online.wsj.com/article/NA_WSJ_PUB:SB125364544835231531.html.

28. L. Kraar, "25 Who Help the U.S. Win: Innovators Everywhere Are Generating Ideas to Make America a Stronger Competitor. They Range from a Boss Who Demands the Impossible to a Mathematician with a Mop," *Fortune*, March 22, 1991.

29. M. W. Lawless and P. C. Anderson, "Generational Technological Change: Effects of Innovation and Local Rivalry on Performance," *Academy of Management Journal* 39 (1996): 1185–1217.

30. B. Kuchera, "Sony Confirms 40GB PS3 for Europe, Removes Backwards Compatibility," *Ars Technica*, October 5, 2007, accessed August 20, 2011, from http://arstechnica.com/gaming/news/2007/10/sony-confirms-40gb-ps3-for-europe-removes-all-backwards-compatibility.ars.

31. J. Rich, "Twilight Exclusive: Chris Weitz Will Not Direct Third Film, 'Eclipse,'" *Hollywood Insider*, February 21, 2009, accessed July 23, 2010, from http://hollywoodinsider.ew.com/2009/02/21/twilight-chris/; G. McIntyre, "On the Set: 'New Moon' on the Rise," *Los Angeles Times*, July 19, 2009,

accessed July 23, 2010, from www.latimes.com/entertainment/news/la-ca-newmoon19-2009jul19,0,3312678,full.story; N. Sperling, "It's Official: Bill Condon Will Direct Twilight's Final Chapter 'Breaking Dawn,'" *Hollywood Insider*, April 28, 2010, accessed July 23, 2010, from http://hollywoodinsider.ew.com/2010/04/28/bill-condon-will-direct-twilights-final-chapter-breaking-dawn/.

32 "No. of Apps: Apple vs. BlackBerry vs. Windows!" Gadget Fan Site, April 4, 2011, accessed April 23, 2011, from http://gadgetfansite.com/no-of-apps-apple-vs-android-vs-blackberry-vs-windows.html.

33 P. Dvorak, "Digital Media: RIM Tries Harder on Apps—Blackberry Maker Hopes New Tools Lure Customers from iPhone, Other Devices," *Wall Street Journal*, October 15, 2010, B5.

34 S. Weinberg, "Corporate News: BlackBerry Gets Squeezed by Rivals," *Wall Street Journal*, September 17, 2010, B3. By contrast, Apple, which leads the industry innovative products, spends just 2.7 percent of sales on research. M. Peers, "RIM: Less Research = More Motion," *Wall Street Journal*, March 30, 2011, C16.

35 K. Lewin, *Field Theory in Social Science: Selected Theoretical Papers* (New York: Harper & Brothers, 1951).

36 A. Deutschman, "Making Change: Why Is It So Darn Hard to Change Our Ways?" *Fast Company*, May 2005, 52–62.

37 Lewin, *Field Theory in Social Science*.

38 A. B. Fisher, "Making Change Stick," *Fortune*, April 17, 1995, 121.

39 J. P. Kotter and L. A. Schlesinger, "Choosing Strategies for Change," *Harvard Business Review* (March–April 1979): 106–114.

40 S. Giessner, G. Viki, T. Otten, S. Terry, and D. Tauber, "The Challenge of Merging: Merger Patterns, Premerger Status, and Merger Support," *Personality and Social Psychology Bulletin* 32, no. 3 (2006): 339–352.

41 H. Schwarz, "A Game Can Change the Office," TFM Facility Blog, July 16, 2008, accessed April 23, 2011, from www.todaysfacilitymanager.com/facilityblog/2008/07/a-game-can-change-the-office.html.

42 S. Covel, "Small Business Link: Telemarketer Bucks High Turnover Trend; Communication, Promotions and Financial Perks Help Employees Stay Loyal," *Wall Street Journal*, November 19, 2007, B6.

43 J. P. Kotter, "Leading Change: Why Transformation Efforts Fail," *Harvard Business Review* 73 (March–April 1995): 59.

44 G. Pitts, "A Classic Turnaround—With Some Twists," *Globe and Mail*, July 7, 2008, B1.

45 Ibid.

46 P. Engardio and J. McGregor, "Lean and Mean Gets Extreme," *Businessweek*, March 23, 2009, 60.

47 Pitts, "A Classic Turnaround."

48 R. Carrick, "Rising from the Stock Market Rubble," *Globe and Mail (Canada)*, June 21, 2008, B15; and W. Dabrowski, "Celestica Buoyed by Smartphone Market Potential: Electronics Maker's CEO Optimistic about Ability to 'Compete and Win' Despite Fall in Profit, Revenue," *The Toronto Star*, April 24, 2009, B04.

49 Ibid.

50 S. Cramm, "A Change of Hearts," *CIO*, April 1, 2003, accessed May 20, 2003, from www.cio.com/archive/040103/hs_leadership.html.

51 M. Ihlwan, L. Armstrong, and M. Eidam, "Hyundai: Kissing Clunkers Goodbye," *Businessweek*, May 17, 2004, 46.

52 J. D. Power and Associates, "J. D. Power and Associates Reports: Domestic Brands Surpass Imports in Initial Quality for the First Time in IQS History," Autoblog, June 17, 2010, accessed April 23, 2011, from www.autoblog.com/2010/06/17/jd-power-2010-initial-quality-study-domestics-lead-imports/.

53 R. N. Ashkenas and T. D. Jick, "From Dialogue to Action in GE WorkOut: Developmental Learning in a Change Process," in W. A. Pasmore and R. W. Woodman (eds.), *Research in Organizational Change and Development*, vol. 6 (Greenwich, CT: JAI Press, 1992), 267–287.

54 T. Stewart, "GE Keeps Those Ideas Coming," *Fortune*, August 12, 1991, 40.

55 J. D. Duck, "Managing Change: The Art of Balancing," *Harvard Business Review on Change* (Boston: Harvard Business School Press, 1998), 55–81.

56 W. J. Rothwell, R. Sullivan, and G. M. McLean, *Practicing Organizational Development: A Guide for Consultants* (San Diego, CA: Pfeiffer & Co., 1995).

57 P. J. Robertson, D. R. Roberts, and J. I. Porras, "Dynamics of Planned Organizational Change: Assessing Empirical Support for a Theoretical Model," *Academy of Management Journal* 36 (1993): 619–634.

58 N. Batiwalla, "Nissan's Leaf Sales Spike in April," *Nashville Business Journal*, May 3, 2011, accessed May 9, 2011, from www.bizjournals.com/nashville/news/2011/05/03/nissan-leaf-sales-spike.html; "China 2010 Auto Sales Reach 18 million, Extend Lead," *Bloomberg Businessweek*, January 10, 2011, accessed May 9, 2011, from www.bloomberg.com/news/2011-01-10/china-2010-auto-sales-reach-18-million-extend-lead-update1-.html; C. Trudell ,"U.S. Auto Sales Probably Rose, Completed 2010 Rebound," *Bloomberg Businessweek*, January 3, 2011, accessed May 9, 2011, from www.bloomberg.com/news/2011-01-03/u-s-auto-sales-may-match-2010-high-complete-first-annual-gain-in-5-years.html; GM Volt Wait List Data, accessed May 9, 2011, from http://gm-volt.com/wait-list-data/; I. Ordonez, "Exxon, Shell Profits Soar on Higher Oil Prices," *Wall Street Journal*, April 29, 2011, accessed May 9, 2011, from http://online.wsj.com/article/SB10001424052748704330404576291350999515650.html; and "Sales Update: Nissan Leaf Hits 573, Chevy Volt at 493 in April," Autoblog.com, May 3, 2011, accessed May 9, 2011, from www.autoblog.com/2011/05/03/sales-update-nissan-leaf-hits-573-chevy-volt-at-493-in-april/.

59 J. E. Ettlie and R. D. O'Keefe, "Innovative Attitudes, Values, and Intentions in Organizations," *Journal of Management Studies* 19 (1982): 163–182.

Global Management

OUTLINE

REEL TO REAL

Management Workplace is at Holden Outerwear.

SELF-ASSESSMENT

Are you nation minded or world minded? Find out by doing the Self-Assessment for this chapter in the book or online.

ONLINE QUIZZES

Did you get it? Review the main concepts in the chapter by taking the online quizzes on CourseMate!

VIDEO QUIZZES

Get more out of the videos by taking the multimedia video quizzes online.

What Would You Do?

Groupon Headquarters, Chicago, Illinois[1]

From 400 subscribers and 30 daily deals in 30 cities in December 2008 to 35 million subscribers and 900 daily deals in 550 markets today, Groupon got to $1 billion in sales faster than any other company. Starbucks CEO Howard Schultz, who was an eBay board member and is now a Groupon investor and board member, said, "Starbucks and eBay were standing still compared to what is happening with Groupon. I candidly haven't witnessed anything quite like this. They have cracked the code on a very significant opportunity." Eric Lefkofsky, who chairs Groupon's board said, "The numbers got crazy a long time ago, and they keep getting crazier." So, what is propelling Groupon's astronomical growth? How does it work?

Groupon sends a daily e-mail to its 35 million subscribers, offering a discount to a restaurant, museum, store, or service provider in their city. This "coupon" becomes a "groupon" because the company offering the discount specifies how many people (i.e., a group) must buy before the deal "tips." For example, a local restaurant may require 100 people to buy. If only 90 do, then no one gets the discount. Daily deals go viral as those who buy send the discount to others who might be interested. When the deal tips (and 95% do), the company and Groupon split the revenue.

Why would companies sign up, especially since half of the money goes to Groupon? Nearly all of Groupon's clients are local companies, which have few cost-effective ways of advertising. Radio, newspapers, and online advertising all require upfront payment (whether they work or not). By contrast, local companies pay Groupon only after the daily deal attracts enough customers to be successful. Another problem with traditional ads is that they are broadcast to a wide group of people, many of whom have little interest in what's being advertised. The viral nature of Groupon's coupons, however, along with tailoring deals based on subscribers' ages, interests, and discretionary dollars, lets companies target Groupon's daily deals to customers who are more likely to buy. Groupon's CEO, Andrew Mason, said, "We think the Internet has the potential to change the way people discover and buy from local businesses."

Because there are few barriers to entry and the basic Web platform is easy to copy, Groupon's record growth and 80 percent U.S. market share has attracted start-up competitors like Living Social, Tippr, Bloomspot, Scoutmob, and BuyWithMe, along with offerings from Google, Facebook, and Walmart. Globally, Groupon's business has been copied in 50 countries. China alone has 1,000 Groupon-type businesses, including one that has copied Groupon's website down to the www.groupon.com. Likewise, Taobao, which is part of Alibaba Group Holdings, one of China's largest Internet companies, has a group buying service call "Ju Hua Suan," which translates to "Group Bargain."

So although Groupon has grown to $1 billion in sales faster than any other company, competitors threaten to take much of that business, especially in international markets, which Groupon is just starting to enter. As Groupon goes global, should it adapt its business to different cultures? For example, it relies on a large Chicago-based sales force to build and retain business with merchants, and 70 comedy writers to write ad copy. Similarly, who should make key decisions—managers at headquarters or managers in each country? In short, should Groupon run its business the same way all around the world? How should Groupon expand internationally? Should it license its Web services to businesses in each area, form a strategic alliance with key foreign business partners (it rejected Google's $6 billion offer in the United States), or should it completely own and control each Groupon business throughout the world? Finally, deciding where to go global is always important, but with so many foreign markets already heavy with competitors, the question for Groupon isn't where to expand, but how to expand successfully in so many different places at the same time.

If you were in charge at Groupon, what would you do?

7-1 Global Business, Trade Rules, and Trade Agreements

Groupon's challenge regarding international expansion is an example of the central issue in global business: How can you be sure that the way you run your business in one country is the right way to run that business in another? This chapter discusses how organizations answer that question. We start by examining global business in two ways: first by exploring its impact on U.S. businesses and then by reviewing the basic rules and agreements that govern global trade. Next, we examine how and when companies go global by examining the trade-off between consistency and adaptation and by discussing how to organize a global company. Finally, we look at how companies decide where to expand globally and consider how to find the best business climate, how to adapt to cultural differences, and how to prepare employees for international assignments.

After reading this section, you should be able to:

7-1 discuss the impact of global business and the trade rules and agreements that govern it.

Business is the buying and selling of goods or services. Buying this textbook was a business transaction. So was selling your first car. So was getting paid for babysitting or for mowing lawns. **Global business** is the buying and selling of goods and services by people from different countries. The Timex watch that I wore while I was writing this chapter was purchased at a Walmart in Texas. But because it was made in the Philippines, I participated in global business when I wrote Walmart a check. Walmart, for its part, had already paid Timex, which had paid the company that employs the Filipino managers and workers who made my watch. Of course, there is more to global business than buying imported products at Walmart.

If you want a simple demonstration of the impact of global business, look at the tag on your shirt, the inside of your shoes, and the inside of your cell phone (take out your battery). Chances are all of these items were made in different places around the world. As I write this, my shirt, shoes, and cell phone were made in Thailand, China, and Korea. Where were yours made?

Let's learn more about **7-1a the impact of global business, 7-1b how tariff and nontariff trade barriers have historically restricted global business, 7-1c how**

global business
the buying and selling of goods and services by people from different countries

today global and regional trade agreements are reducing those trade barriers worldwide, and **7-1d how consumers are responding to those changes in trade rules and agreements.**

7-1a The Impact of Global Business

Thomas Friedman, author and columnist for the *New York Times*, observed global business in action when he visited *INFOSYS*, a consulting and information technology company, in India. When Infosys CEO Nandan Nilekani showed Friedman the company's global videoconference room, the journalist was immediately struck by the wall-sized flat-screen TV that the CEO claimed to be the biggest in Asia. Eight clocks on the wall above the giant screen (one each for the eastern United States, western United States, Greenwich Mean Time, India, Singapore, Hong Kong, Japan, and Australia) are a reminder that the Infosys workday runs 24/7/365. The sizeable virtual meeting room can bring together key players from the company's entire global supply chain for any project at any moment. According to Nikelani, "That's what globalization is all about today."[2]

Infosys does global business by selling products and services worldwide, with managers and employees from different continents working together as seamlessly as if they were next door to each other. But Infosys isn't unique. There are thousands of other multinational companies just like it.

Multinational corporations are corporations that own businesses in two or more countries. In 1970, more than half of the world's 7,000 multinational corporations were headquartered in just two countries: the United States and the United Kingdom. Today, there are nearly 104,000 multinational corporations, almost 15 times as many as in 1970, and only 9,692, or 9.3 percent, are based in the United States.[3] Today, 73,144 multinationals, or 70.5 percent, are based in other developed countries (e.g., Germany, Italy, Canada, and Japan), whereas 30,209, or 29.1 percent, are based in developing countries (e.g., Colombia, South Africa). So, today multinational companies can be found by the thousands all over the world!

Another way to appreciate the impact of global business is by considering direct foreign investment. Direct foreign investment occurs when a company builds a new business or buys an existing business in a foreign country. *NOKIA-SIEMENS NETWORKS*, operated jointly by Finland-based Nokia and Germany-based Siemens, made a direct foreign investment in the United States when it paid $1.2 billion to buy Motorola's network equipment business, to add new customers in Japan and North America.[4] Of course, companies from many other countries also own businesses in the United States. As Exhibit 7.1 shows, companies from the United Kingdom, Japan, the Netherlands, Germany, Canada, Switzerland, France, and Luxembourg have the largest direct foreign investment in the United States. Overall, foreign companies invest more than $2.3 trillion a year to do business in the United States.

But direct foreign investment in the United States is only half the picture. U.S. companies also have made large direct foreign investments in countries throughout the world. For example, *HERSHEY CO.*, a Pennsylvania-based candy company, purchased Barry Callebaut AG's Van Houten consumer chocolate

multinational corporation
a corporation that owns businesses in two or more countries

direct foreign investment
a method of investment in which a company builds a new business or buys an existing business in a foreign country

Exhibit 7.1

Direct Foreign Investment in the United States

- Other (19.5%)
- United Kingdom (18.5%)
- Japan (11%)
- Netherlands (9.3%)
- Germany (9.1%)
- Switzerland (8.2%)
- Canada (8.8%)
- France (8.2%)
- Luxembourg (7.7%)

Source: K. Barefoot and M. Ibarra-Caton, "Direct Investment Positions for 2010: Country and Industry Detail," Bureau of Economic Analysis, July 2011, accessed September 3, 2012, from http://www.bea.gov/scb/pdf/2011/07%20July/0711_direct.pdf.

Exhibit 7.2

U.S. Direct Foreign Investment Abroad

- Netherlands (13.3%)
- Other (33.6%)
- United Kingdom (13.0%)
- Canada (7.6%)
- Luxembourg (7.0%)
- Bermuda (6.8%)
- Ireland (4.9%)
- United Kingdom Islands, Caribbean (3.8%)
- Switzerland (3.7%)
- Australia (3.4%)
- Japan (2.9%)

Source: K. Barefoot and M. Ibarra-Caton, "Direct Investment Positions for 2010: Country and Industry Detail," Bureau of Economic Analysis, July 2011, accessed September 3, 2012, from http://www.bea.gov/scb/pdf/2011/07%20July/0711_direct.pdf

business in Asia, allowing Hershey, which gets most of its growth from North America, to expand internationally.[5] As Exhibit 7.2 shows, U.S. companies have made their largest direct foreign investments in the Netherlands, the United Kingdom, and Canada. Overall, U.S. companies invest more than $3.9 trillion a year to do business in other countries.

So, whether foreign companies invest in the United States or U.S. companies invest abroad, direct foreign investment is an increasingly important and common method of conducting global business.

7-1b Trade Barriers

Although today's consumers usually don't care where the products they buy come from (more on this in Section 7-1d), national governments have traditionally preferred that consumers buy domestically made products in hopes that such purchases would increase the number of domestic businesses and workers. Indeed, governments have done much more than hope that you will buy from domestic companies. Historically, governments have actively used **trade barriers** to make it much more expensive or difficult (or sometimes impossible) for consumers to buy or consume imported goods. For example, the Chinese government adds a 105 percent tariff to the price of chickens imported from the United States. The U.S. government, in turn, imposes a 35 percent tariff on tires imported from China.[6] By establishing these restrictions and taxes, the Chinese and U.S. governments are engaging in **protectionism**, which is the use of trade barriers to protect local companies and their workers from foreign competition.

Governments have used two general kinds of trade barriers: tariff and nontariff barriers. A **tariff** is a direct tax on imported goods. Tariffs increase the cost of imported goods relative to that of domestic goods. For example, the

trade barriers
government-imposed regulations that increase the cost and restrict the number of imported goods

protectionism
a government's use of trade barriers to shield domestic companies and their workers from foreign competition

tariff
a direct tax on imported goods

U.S. import tax on trucks is 25 percent. This means that U.S. buyers must pay $25,000 for an imported truck valued at $20,000, with $5,000 going to the U.S. government. As a result, fewer than 10,000 pickup trucks are imported by the United States each year.[7] **Nontariff barriers** are nontax methods of increasing the cost or reducing the volume of imported goods. There are five types of nontariff barriers: quotas, voluntary export restraints, government import standards, government subsidies, and customs valuation/classification. Because there are so many different kinds of nontariff barriers, they can be an even more potent method of shielding domestic industries from foreign competition.

Quotas are specific limits on the number or volume of imported products. For example, China allows only 20 foreign films to be released in Chinese movie theaters each year.[8] Like quotas, **voluntary export restraints** limit the amount of a product that can be imported annually. The difference is that the exporting country rather than the importing country imposes restraints. Usually, however, the "voluntary" offer to limit exports occurs because the importing country has implicitly threatened to impose quotas. For example, to protect South African textile manufacturers from cheap and plentiful Chinese textile products, the South African government convinced China to "voluntarily" restrict the textiles it exports to South Africa each year.[9] According to the World Trade Organization (see the discussion in Section 7-1c), however, voluntary export restraints are illegal and should not be used to restrict imports.[10]

In theory, **government import standards** are established to protect the health and safety of citizens. In reality, such standards are often used to restrict or ban imported goods. For example, Taiwan restricts both the age and type of beef that can be imported from the United States. According to Taiwanese government and health officials, this is to prevent the spread of mad cow disease among Taiwanese cattle, and protect Taiwanese consumers from developing Creutzfeldt-Jakob disease. However, the ban, which essentially blocks any U.S. beef from entering Taiwan, is being used to protect the Taiwanese beef industry. Kie-Duck Park, of South Korea's independent Sejong Institute, agreed, saying, "We [in Asia] see the agricultural industry as a kind of strategic industry, and people want to keep that industry safe."[11]

Many nations also use **subsidies**, such as long-term, low-interest loans, cash grants, and tax deferments, to develop and protect companies in special industries. Not surprisingly, businesses complain about unfair trade practices when foreign companies receive government subsidies.

The last type of nontariff barrier is **customs classification**. As products are imported into a country, they are examined by customs agents, who must decide into which of nearly 9,000 categories they should classify a product. Classification is important because the category assigned by customs agents can greatly affect the size of the tariff and whether the item is subject to import quotas. For example, the U.S. Customs Service has several customs classifications for imported shoes. Tariffs on imported leather or "nonrubber" shoes are about 10 percent, whereas tariffs on imported rubber shoes, such as athletic footwear or waterproof shoes, range from 20 to 84 percent. (See www.usitc.gov for full information on tariffs.) The difference is large enough that some importers try to make their rubber shoes look like leather in hopes of receiving the nonrubber customs classification and lower tariff.

nontariff barriers
nontax methods of increasing the cost or reducing the volume of imported goods

quota
a limit on the number or volume of imported products

voluntary export restraints
voluntarily imposed limits on the number or volume of products exported to a particular country

government import standard
a standard ostensibly established to protect the health and safety of citizens, but, in reality, often used to restrict imports

subsidies
government loans, grants, and tax deferments given to domestic companies to protect them from foreign competition

customs classification
a classification assigned to imported products by government officials that affects the size of the tariff and imposition of import quotas

7-1c Trade Agreements

Thanks to the trade barriers described above, buying imported goods has often been much more expensive and difficult than buying domestic goods. During the 1990s, however, the regulations governing global trade were transformed. The most significant change was that 124 countries agreed to adopt the Uruguay Round of the **General Agreement on Tariffs and Trade (GATT)**. GATT, which existed from 1947 to 1995, was an agreement to regulate trade among (eventually) more than 120 countries, the purpose of which was "substantial reduction of tariffs and other trade barriers and the elimination of preferences."[12] GATT members engaged in eight rounds of trade negotiations, with the Uruguay Round signed in 1994 and going into effect in 1995. Although GATT itself was replaced by the **World Trade Organization (WTO)** in 1995, the changes that it made continue to encourage international trade. Today, the WTO and its member countries are negotiating what's known as the Doha Round, which seeks to advance trade opportunities for developing countries in areas ranging from agriculture to services to intellectual property rights.

The WTO, headquartered in Geneva, Switzerland, administers trade agreements, provides a forum for trade negotiations, handles trade disputes, monitors national trade policies, and offers technical assistance and training for developing countries for its 155 member countries. Through tremendous decreases in tariff and nontariff barriers, the Uruguay round of GATT made it much easier and cheaper for consumers in all countries to buy foreign products. GATT also established stricter limits on government subsidies. For example, the Uruguay round of GATT put limits on how much national governments can subsidize private research in electronic and high-technology industries. The Uruguay round of GATT also established protections for intellectual property, such as trademarks, patents, and copyrights.

Finally, trade disputes between countries now are fully settled by arbitration panels from the WTO. In the past, countries could use their veto power to cancel a panel's decision. Now, however, countries that are members of the WTO no longer have veto power. Thus, WTO rulings are complete and final. Exhibit 7.3 provides a brief overview of the WTO and its functions.

The second major development that has reduced trade barriers has been the creation of **regional trading zones**, or zones in which tariff and nontariff barriers are reduced or eliminated for countries within the trading zone (see Exhibit 7.4). The largest and most important trading zones are in Europe (the Maastricht Treaty), North America (the North American Free Trade Agreement, or NAFTA), Central America (Central America Free Trade Agreement, or CAFTA-DR), South America (Union of South American Nations, or UNASUR), and Asia (the Association of Southeast Asian Nations, or ASEAN, and Asia-Pacific Economic Cooperation, or APEC).

The **Maastricht Treaty** transformed 12 different economies and 12 currencies into one common economic market, the European Union (EU), with one common currency. By 2007, with the entry of Bulgaria and Romania, the total number of member countries reached 27.[13] Croatia, Macedonia, and Turkey have applied and are being considered for membership.[14] On January 1, 2002, a single common currency, the euro, went into circulation, and today 17 of the

General Agreement on Tariffs and Trade (GATT)
a worldwide trade agreement that reduced and eliminated tariffs, limited government subsidies, and established protections for intellectual property

World Trade Organization (WTO)
the successor to GATT; the only international organization dealing with the global rules of trade between nations Its main function is to ensure that trade flows as smoothly, predictably, and freely as possible

regional trading zones
areas in which tariff and nontariff barriers on trade between countries are reduced or eliminated

Maastricht Treaty of Europe
a regional trade agreement between most European countries

Exhibit 7.3

The World Trade Organization

✓ **FACT FILE**

WORLD TRADE
ORGANIZATION

Location: Geneva, Switzerland
Established: January 1, 1995
Created by: Uruguay Round
negotiations (1986–1994)
Membership: 155 countries
on May 10, 2012
Budget: 196 million Swiss
francs for 2011
Secretariat staff: 637
Head: Pascal Lamy
(Director-General)

Functions:
• Administering WTO trade
  agreements
• Forum for trade negotiations
• Handling trade disputes
• Monitoring national trade
  policies
• Technical assistance and
  training for developing countries
• Cooperation with other
  international organizations

Source: Accessed May 8, 2012, from www.wto.org/english/thewto_e/whatis_e/whatis_e.htm.

EU's members circulate it (Austria, Belgium, Cyprus, Estonia, Finland, France, Germany, Greece, Ireland, Italy, Luxembourg, Malta, the Netherlands, Portugal, Slovenia, Slovakia, and Spain).[15]

NAFTA, the **North American Free Trade Agreement** between the United States, Canada, and Mexico, went into effect on January 1, 1994. More than any other regional trade agreement, NAFTA has liberalized trade between countries so that businesses can plan for one market (North America) rather than for three separate markets (the United States, Canada, and Mexico). One of NAFTA's most important achievements was to eliminate most product tariffs *and* prevent the three countries from increasing existing tariffs or introducing new ones. Overall, Mexican and Canadian exports to the United States are up 247 percent since NAFTA went into effect. U.S. exports to Mexico and Canada are up 171 percent too, growing twice as fast as U.S. exports to any other part of the world.[16] In fact, Mexico and Canada now account for 40 percent of all U.S. exports.[17] (For more information about NAFTA, see the Office of NAFTA & Inter-American Affairs at www.ustr.gov/trade-agreements/free-trade-agreements/north-american-free-trade-agreement-nafta.)

CAFTA-DR, the new **Central America Free Trade Agreement** between the United States and the Central American countries of Costa Rica, El Salvador, Guatemala, Honduras, Nicaragua, and the Dominican Republic went into effect in August 2005.[18] With a combined population of 48.2 million, the CAFTA-DR countries together are the seventh-largest U.S. export market in the world and the third-largest U.S. export market in Latin America, after Mexico and Brazil.[19] (For more information about CAFTA-DR, see www.fas.usda.gov/itp/CAFTA/cafta.asp.)

North American Free Trade Agreement (NAFTA)
a regional trade agreement between the United States, Canada, and Mexico

Central America Free Trade Agreement (CAFTA-DR)
a regional trade agreement between Costa Rica, the Dominican Republic, El Salvador, Guatemala, Honduras, Nicaragua, and the United States

Exhibit 7.4

Global Map of Regional Trade Agreements

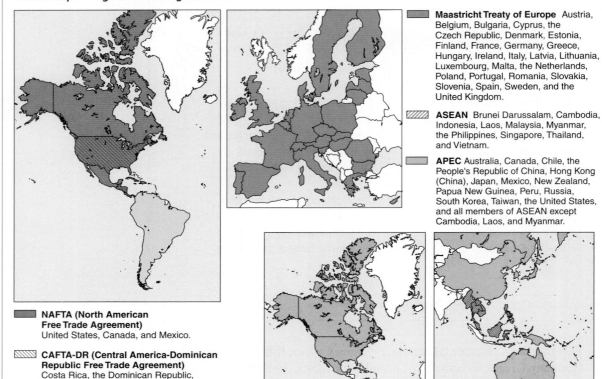

Maastricht Treaty of Europe Austria, Belgium, Bulgaria, Cyprus, the Czech Republic, Denmark, Estonia, Finland, France, Germany, Greece, Hungary, Ireland, Italy, Latvia, Lithuania, Luxembourg, Malta, the Netherlands, Poland, Portugal, Romania, Slovakia, Slovenia, Spain, Sweden, and the United Kingdom.

ASEAN Brunei Darussalam, Cambodia, Indonesia, Laos, Malaysia, Myanmar, the Philippines, Singapore, Thailand, and Vietnam.

APEC Australia, Canada, Chile, the People's Republic of China, Hong Kong (China), Japan, Mexico, New Zealand, Papua New Guinea, Peru, Russia, South Korea, Taiwan, the United States, and all members of ASEAN except Cambodia, Laos, and Myanmar.

NAFTA (North American Free Trade Agreement) United States, Canada, and Mexico.

CAFTA-DR (Central America-Dominican Republic Free Trade Agreement) Costa Rica, the Dominican Republic, El Salvador, Guatemala, Honduras, Nicaragua, and the United States.

UNASUR (Union of South American Nations) Argentina, Bolivia, Brazil, Chile, Colombia, Ecuador, Guyana, Paraguay, Peru, Suriname, Uruguay, and Venezuela.

© CENGAGE LEARNING

Union of South American Nations (UNASUR)

a regional trade agreement between the former Mercosur nations, the Andean Community, and Guyana, Suriname, and Chile.

Association of Southeast Asian Nations (ASEAN)

a regional trade agreement between Brunei Darussalam, Cambodia, Indonesia, Laos, Malaysia, Myanmar, the Philippines, Singapore, Thailand, and Vietnam

On May 23, 2008, 12 South American countries signed the Union of South American Nations (UNASUR) Constitutive Treaty, which united the former Mercosur (Argentina, Brazil, Paraguay, Uruguay, and Venezuela) and Andean Community (Bolivia, Colombia, Ecuador, and Peru) alliances along with Guyana, Suriname, and Chile. UNASUR aims to create a unified South America by permitting free movement between nations, creating a common infrastructure that includes an interoceanic highway, and establishing the region as a single market by eliminating all tariffs by 2019.[20] (For more about UNASUR see www.comunidadandina.org/ingles/sudamerican.htm.)

ASEAN, the Association of Southeast Asian Nations, and APEC, the Asia-Pacific Economic Cooperation, are the two largest and most important regional trading groups in Asia. ASEAN is a trade agreement between Brunei Darussalam, Cambodia, Indonesia, Lao PDR, Malaysia, Myanmar, the Philippines, Singapore, Thailand, and Vietnam, which form a market of more than 591 million people. An ASEAN free trade area will begin in 2015 for the six original countries (Brunei Darussalam, Indonesia, Malaysia, the Philippines, Singapore, and Thailand) and in 2018 for the newer member countries (Cambodia, Lao PDR, Myanmar, and Vietnam).[21] (For more information about ASEAN, see www.aseansec.org.)

APEC is a broad agreement that includes Australia, Canada, Chile, the People's Republic of China, Hong Kong, Japan, Mexico, New Zealand, Papua New Guinea, Peru, Russia, South Korea, Taiwan, the United States, and all the members of ASEAN except Cambodia, Lao PDR, and Myanmar. APEC's 21 member countries contain 2.75 billion people, account for 44 percent of all global trade, and have a combined gross domestic product of over $34 trillion.[22] APEC countries began reducing trade barriers in 2000, though all the reductions will not be completely phased in until 2020.[23] (For more information about APEC, see www.apec.org.)

7-1d Consumers, Trade Barriers, and Trade Agreements

In Tokyo, a 12-ounce Coke costs $1.49.[24] A cup of regular coffee costs $10.19 in Moscow, $6.77 in Paris, and $6.62 in Athens.[25] In the United States, each of these items costs about a dollar.[26] A Big Mac from McDonald's costs an average of $4.21 in the United States, $4.63 in Canada, and $6.81 in Switzerland. Although not all products are more expensive in other countries (in some, they are cheaper; e.g., a Big Mac averages $2.44 in China and $2.45 in South Africa), international studies find that American consumers get much more for their money than consumers in the rest of the world.[27] For example, the average worker earns nearly $71,520 a year in Switzerland, $87,350 in Norway, $41,850 in Japan, and $46,360 in America.[28] Yet, after adjusting these incomes for how much they can buy, the Swiss income is equivalent to just $49,960, the Norwegian income to $58,570, and the Japanese income to $34,610.[29] This is the same as saying that $1 of income can buy you only 72 cents' worth of goods in Switzerland, 65 cents in Norway, and 88 cents' worth in Japan. In other words, Americans can buy much more with their incomes than those in other countries.

One reason that Americans get more for their money is that the U.S. marketplace is the most competitive in the world and has been one of the easiest for foreign companies to enter.[30] Although some U.S. industries, such as textiles, have been heavily protected from foreign competition by trade barriers, for the most part, American consumers (and businesses) have had plentiful choices among American-made and foreign-made products. More important, the high level of competition between foreign and domestic companies that creates these choices helps keep prices low in the United States. Furthermore, it is precisely the lack of choice and the low level of competition that keep prices higher in countries that have not been as open to foreign companies and products. For example, Japanese trade barriers are estimated to cost Japanese consumers more

Asia-Pacific Economic Cooperation (APEC)
a regional trade agreement between Australia, Canada, Chile, the People's Republic of China, Hong Kong, Japan, Mexico, New Zealand, Papua New Guinea, Peru, Russia, South Korea, Taiwan, the United States, and all the members of ASEAN except Cambodia, Laos, and Myanmar

© ERIKO SUGITA/REUTERS/LANDOV

than $100 billion a year. In fact, Japanese trade barriers amount to a 51 percent tax on food for the average Japanese family.[31]

So why do trade barriers and free trade agreements matter to consumers? They're important because free trade agreements increase choices, competition, and purchasing power and thus decrease what people pay for food, clothing, necessities, and luxuries. Accordingly, today's consumers rarely care where their products and services come from.

REVIEW 7-1

Global Business, Trade Rules, and Trade Agreements

Today, there are more than 104,000 multinational corporations worldwide; just 9 percent are based in the United States. Global business affects the United States in two ways: through direct foreign investment in the United States by foreign companies and through U.S. companies' investment in business in other countries. United States direct foreign investment throughout the world typically amounts to about $3.9 trillion per year, whereas direct foreign investment by foreign companies in the United States amounts to $2.3 trillion per year. Historically, tariffs and nontariff trade barriers, such as quotas, voluntary export restraints, government import standards, government subsidies, and customs classifications, have made buying foreign goods much harder or more expensive than buying domestically produced products. In recent years, however, worldwide trade agreements such as GATT, along with regional trading agreements like the Maastricht Treaty of Europe, NAFTA, CAFTA-DR, USAN, ASEAN, and APEC, have substantially reduced tariff and nontariff barriers to international trade. Companies have responded by investing in growing markets in Asia, Eastern Europe, and Latin America. Consumers have responded by purchasing products based on value, rather than geography.

7-2 Consistency or Adaptation?

Once a company has decided that it *will* go global, it must decide *how* to go global. For example, if you decide to sell in Singapore, should you try to find a local business partner who speaks the language, knows the laws, and understands the customs and norms of Singapore's culture? Or should you simply export your products from your home country? What do you do if you are also entering Eastern Europe, perhaps starting in Hungary? Should you use the same approach in Hungary that you used in Singapore?

After reading this section, you should be able to:

7-2 explain why companies choose to standardize or adapt their business procedures.

In this section, we turn to a key issue: How can you be sure that the way you run your business in one country is the right way to run that business in another? In other words, how can you strike the right balance between global consistency and local adaptation?

Global consistency means that a multinational company with offices, manufacturing plants, and distribution facilities in different countries uses the same rules, guidelines, policies, and procedures to run those offices, plants,

global consistency
when a multinational company has offices, manufacturing plants, and distribution facilities in different countries and runs them all using the same rules, guidelines, policies, and procedures

and facilities. Managers at company headquarters value global consistency because it simplifies decisions. By contrast, a company following a policy of **local adaptation** modifies its standard operating procedures to adapt to differences in foreign customers, governments, and regulatory agencies. Local adaptation is typically preferred by local managers who are charged with making the international business successful in their countries.

If companies lean too much toward global consistency, they run the risk of using management procedures poorly suited to particular countries' markets, cultures, and employees (i.e., a lack of local adaptation). Swedish-based *H & M* is a large clothing retailer that offers the same products in stores in 37 countries. However, because most of its clothes are designed for climates with long cold winters and short summers, H & M has been unable to enter markets that have drastically different climates. Thus, although H & M has stores in Toledo, Ohio, it has only a minimal presence in Los Angeles, and no presence at all in Dallas, Texas. If it is to continue to grow, H & M must adapt its product selection to warmer climates.[32]

If, however, companies focus too much on local adaptation, they run the risk of losing the cost effectiveness and productivity that result from using standardized rules and procedures throughout the world. Consider the case of *TUPPERWARE* in India. Since it first entered India in 1996, Tupperware has grown by nearly 30 percent each year. Much of the company's success is due to adapting and changing its product line to suit local food habits. For example, even though one of Tupperware's bestselling products worldwide is a square bread container, perfect for storing slices from bread loaves, in India it created a new round bread container that could store *roti* and *chapati*, round flatbreads that are integral to Indian cuisine.[33]

REVIEW 7-2

. . . .

Consistency or Adaptation?

Global business requires a balance between global consistency and local adaptation. Global consistency means using the same rules, guidelines, policies, and procedures in each location. Managers at company headquarters like global consistency because it simplifies decisions. Local adaptation means adapting standard procedures to individual markets. Local managers prefer a policy of local adaptation because it gives them more control. Not all businesses need the same combinations of global consistency and local adaptation. Some thrive by emphasizing global consistency and ignoring local adaptation. Others succeed by ignoring global consistency and emphasizing local adaptation.

7-3 Forms for Global Business

Besides determining whether to adapt organizational policies and procedures, a company must also determine how to organize itself for successful entry into foreign markets.

After reading this section, you should be able to:

    7-3 explain the different ways that companies can organize to do business globally.

local adaptation
modifying rules, guidelines, policies, and procedures to adapt to differences in foreign customers, governments, and regulatory agencies

Historically, companies have generally followed the *phase model of globalization*, in which a company makes the transition from a domestic company to a global company in the following sequential phases: **7-3a exporting, 7-3b cooperative contracts, 7-3c strategic alliances,** and **7-3d wholly owned affiliates**.

At each step, the company grows much larger, uses those resources to enter more global markets, is less dependent on home country sales, and is more committed in its orientation to global business. Some companies, however, do not follow the phase model of globalization.[34] Some skip phases on their way to becoming more global and less domestic. Others don't follow the phase model at all.

These are known as **7-3e global new ventures**. This section reviews these forms of global business.[35]

7-3a Exporting

When companies produce products in their home countries and sell those products to customers in foreign countries, they are exporting. *A-POWER ENERGY GENERATION SYSTEMS*, a Chinese alternative energy company, runs a production and assembly plant in Nevada. Although the facility produces wind turbines that are sold in the United States, A-Power also exports wind turbines from Nevada to Mexico, Canada, and Central and South America.[36]

Exporting as a form of global business offers many advantages. It makes the company less dependent on sales in its home market and provides a greater degree of control over research, design, and production decisions. *American Idol* has been America's No. 1 television show for nearly a decade. But did you know that there are 42 other versions of *American Idol* around the world? And did you know that *FREMANTLE MEDIA*, which owns and exports those different versions of *American Idol*, produces global versions of *Family Feud* (48 countries), *The Price Is Right* (30 countries), and *Got Talent* (27 countries)?[37] What makes this work in so many different countries is Fremantle Media's tight control of production. CEO Tony Cohen says, "It's not just about the licensing of formats but the brilliance with which you execute it. You've got to do it well. These things have been through evolution and are pretty well perfect. You can't tamper with it; we're very possessive about that."[38]

Though advantageous in a number of ways, exporting also has its disadvantages. The primary disadvantage is that many exported goods are subject to tariff and nontariff barriers that can substantially increase their final cost to consumers. A second disadvantage is that transportation costs can significantly increase the price of an exported product. There is yet a third disadvantage of exporting: Companies that export depend on foreign importers for product distribution. If, for example, the foreign importer makes a mistake on the paperwork that accompanies a shipment of imported goods, those goods can be returned to the foreign manufacturer at the manufacturer's expense.

7-3b Cooperative Contracts

When an organization wants to expand its business globally without making a large financial commitment to do so, it may sign a **cooperative contract** with a foreign business owner who pays the company a fee for the right to conduct

exporting
selling domestically produced products to customers in foreign countries

cooperative contract
an agreement in which a foreign business owner pays a company a fee for the right to conduct that business in his or her country

that business in his or her country. There are two kinds of cooperative contracts: licensing and franchising.

Under a **licensing** agreement, a domestic company, the *licensor*, receives royalty payments for allowing another company, the *licensee*, to produce its product, sell its service, or use its brand name in a particular foreign market. BIODELIVERY SCIENCES INTERNATIONAL (BDSI), a pharmaceutical company in North Carolina, reached a licensing agreement with TTY Biopharm, a Taiwanese drug company. TTY Biopharm paid BDSI a $1.3 million licensing fee in exchange for the right to manufacture and sell BDSI's Onsolis painkilling drug for cancer patients in Taiwan.[39]

One of the most important advantages of licensing is that it allows companies to earn additional profits without investing more money. As foreign sales increase, the royalties paid to the licensor by the foreign licensee increase. Moreover, the licensee, not the licensor, invests in production equipment and facilities to produce the product. Licensing also helps companies avoid tariff and nontariff barriers. Because the licensee manufactures the product within the foreign country, tariff and nontariff barriers don't apply.

The biggest disadvantage associated with licensing is that the licensor gives up control over the quality of the product or service sold by the foreign licensee. Unless the licensing agreement contains specific restrictions, the licensee controls the entire business from production to marketing, to final sales. Many licensors include inspection clauses in their license contracts, but closely monitoring product or service quality from thousands of miles away can be difficult. An additional disadvantage is that licensees can eventually become competitors, especially when a licensing agreement includes access to important technology or proprietary business knowledge.

A **franchise** is a collection of networked firms in which the manufacturer or marketer of a product or service, the *franchisor*, licenses the entire business to another person or organization, the *franchisee*. For the price of an initial franchise fee plus royalties, franchisors provide franchisees with training, assistance with marketing and advertising, and an exclusive right to conduct business in a particular location. Most franchise fees run between $5,000 and $35,000. Franchisees pay MCDONALD'S, one of the largest franchisors in the world, an initial fee of $45,000. Another $950,900 to $1,797,700 is needed beyond that to pay for food inventory, kitchen equipment, construction, landscaping, and other expenses (the cost varies per country). Although franchisees typically borrow part of this cost from a bank, McDonald's requires franchisees to put down 40 percent in cash for the initial investment.[40] Because typical royalties range from 2 to 12.5 percent of gross sales, franchisors are well rewarded for the help they provide to franchisees. More than 400 U.S. companies franchise their businesses to foreign franchise partners.

Overall, franchising is a fast way to enter foreign markets. Over the last 20 years, U.S. franchisors have more than doubled their number of global franchises, for a total of more than 100,000 global franchise units. Because it gives the franchisor additional cash flows from franchise fees and royalties, franchising can be a good strategy when a company's domestic sales have slowed. Despite the many advantages of franchising, franchisors face a loss of control when they sell businesses to franchisees who are thousands of miles away.

licensing
an agreement in which a domestic company, the licensor, receives royalty payments for allowing another company, the licensee, to produce the licensor's product, sell its service, or use its brand name in a specified foreign market

franchise
a collection of networked firms in which the manufacturer or marketer of a product or service, the franchisor, licenses the entire business to another person or organization, the franchisee

Although there are exceptions, franchising success may be somewhat culture bound. Because most global franchisors begin by franchising their businesses in similar countries or regions, and because 65 percent of franchisors make absolutely no change in their business for overseas franchisees, that success may not generalize to cultures with different lifestyles, values, preferences, and technological infrastructures. Customizing menus to local tastes is one of the primary ways that fast-food companies can succeed in international markets. When Taco Bell went to India, its menu was adapted to Indian tastes and included potato tacos and burritos filled with paneer, an Indian cheese. It also hired employees to explain burritos, tacos, and quesadillas to customers. KFC succeeds in China by selling congee (rice porridge) and a chicken wrap inspired by Peking duck. Pizza Hut sells Asian-inspired products like a salmon roll seasoned with lemon and a seafood pizza with crab sticks, green pepper, and pineapple.[41]

7-3c Strategic Alliances

Companies forming **strategic alliances** combine key resources, costs, risks, technology, and people. GARMIN, which produces satellite navigation devices, and VOLVO PENTA, which makes leisure and commercial boat engines and propulsion systems, have formed a strategic alliance to jointly develop and market marine instrumentation, navigation, and communication equipment.[42] The most common strategic alliance is a **joint venture**, which occurs when two existing companies collaborate to form a third company. The two founding companies remain intact and unchanged except that together they now own the newly created joint venture.

One of the advantages of global joint ventures is that, like licensing and franchising, they help companies avoid tariff and nontariff barriers to entry. Another advantage is that companies participating in a joint venture bear only part of the costs and the risks of that business. Many companies find this attractive because of the expense of entering foreign markets or developing new products. Global joint ventures can be especially advantageous to smaller local partners who link up with larger, more experienced foreign firms that can bring advanced management, resources, and business skills to the joint venture. For example, DAIMLER AG, the Germany-based automaker, recently agreed to a joint venture with China-based BEIQI FOTON MOTOR COMPANY to manufacture and sell large trucks in China. While Daimler will benefit from establishing a presence in China's quickly growing market, Beiqi Foton will benefit from having access to Daimler's expertise in diesel engines and exhaust systems.[43]

Managing global joint ventures can also be difficult because they represent a merging of four cultures: the country and the organizational cultures of the first partner, and the country and the organizational cultures of the second partner. Because of these problems, companies forming global joint ventures should carefully develop detailed contracts that specify the obligations of each party. The joint venture contract specifies how much each company will invest, what its rights and responsibilities are, and what it is entitled to if the joint venture does not work out. These steps are important because the rate of failure for global joint ventures is estimated to be as high as 70 percent.[44]

strategic alliance
an agreement in which companies combine key resources, costs, risk, technology, and people

joint venture
a strategic alliance in which two existing companies collaborate to form a third, independent company

7-3d Wholly Owned Affiliates (Build or Buy)

Approximately one-third of multinational companies enter foreign markets through wholly owned affiliates. Unlike licensing arrangements, franchises, or joint ventures, **wholly owned affiliates** are 100 percent owned by the parent company.

The primary advantage of wholly owned businesses is that the parent company receives all of the profits and has complete control over the foreign facilities. The biggest disadvantage is the expense of building new operations or buying existing businesses. Although the payoff can be enormous if wholly owned affiliates succeed, the losses can be immense if they fail, because the parent company assumes all of the risk. DEUTSCHE TELEKOM, the largest telecommunications company in Europe, established a presence in the United States through its affiliate T-Mobile USA. T-Mobile had decent performance for almost a decade, but more recently, T-Mobile has begun losing customers because it does not carry the iPhone. In 2010 alone, the company lost 390,000 fixed-contract customers, and had twice as many customers *not* renew their contracts as its nearest competitor. These struggles in the United States contributed to a 37 percent drop in profits for Deutsche Telekom, which in turn led Deutsche Telekom to sell T-Mobile USA to AT&T for $39 billion.[45]

7-3e Global New Ventures

Companies used to evolve slowly from small operations selling in their home markets to large businesses selling to foreign markets. Furthermore, as companies went global, they usually followed the phase model of globalization. Recently, however, three trends have combined to allow companies to skip the phase model when going global. First, quick, reliable air travel can transport people to nearly any point in the world within one day. Second, low-cost communication technologies, such as e-mail, teleconferencing, phone conferencing, and the Internet, make it easier to communicate with global customers, suppliers, managers, and employees. Third, there is now a critical mass of businesspeople with extensive personal experience in all aspects of global business.[46] This combination of developments has made it possible to start companies that are global from inception. With sales, employees, and financing in different countries, **global new ventures** are companies that are founded with an active global strategy.[47]

Although there are several different kinds of global new ventures, all share two common factors. First, the company founders successfully develop and communicate the company's global vision from inception. Second, rather than going global one country at a time, new global ventures bring a product or service to market in several foreign markets at the same time. Founded by longtime airline executives Steven Udvar-Hazy and John L. Plueger, AIR LEASE CORPORATION is a company that provides aircraft to commercial airlines through lease agreements. Although based in Los Angeles, its mission is to provide equipment and financing to airlines all over the world. CEO Udvar-Hazy says, "We look forward to working with the leading global airlines as they modernize their fleets." Within a year of start-up, Air Lease expects to have a fleet of over 100 commercial jets leased to airlines throughout the world.[48]

wholly owned affiliates
foreign offices, facilities, and manufacturing plants that are 100 percent owned by the parent company

global new ventures
new companies that are founded with an active global strategy and have sales, employees, and financing in different countries

Forms for Global Business
The phase model of globalization says that as companies move from a domestic to a global orientation, they use these organizational forms in sequence: exporting, cooperative contracts (licensing and franchising), strategic alliances, and wholly owned affiliates. Yet not all companies follow the phase model. For example, global new ventures are global from their inception.

7-4 Finding the Best Business Climate

Deciding *where* to go global is just as important as deciding *how* your company will go global.

After reading this section, you should be able to:

7-4 explain how to find a favorable business climate.

When making this decision, companies try to find countries or regions with promising business climates.

An attractive global business climate **7-4a positions the company for easy access to growing markets, 7-4b is an effective but cost-efficient place to build an office or manufacturing facility**, and **7-4c minimizes the political risk to the company.**

7-4a Growing Markets

The most important factor in an attractive business climate is access to a growing market. For example, no product is known and purchased by as many people throughout the world as COCA-COLA. Yet even Coke, which is available in over 200 countries, still has tremendous potential for further global growth. Coca-Cola gets 78 percent of its sales outside of North America, and emerging markets, where it has seen its fastest growth, now account for half of Coke's sales worldwide.[49]

Two factors help companies determine the growth potential of foreign markets: purchasing power and foreign competitors. **Purchasing power** is measured by comparing the relative cost of a standard set of goods and services in different countries. Earlier in the chapter, we noted that a Coke costs $1.49 cents in Tokyo. Because a 12-ounce Coke costs only about 75 cents in the United States, the average American would have more purchasing power than the average Japanese. Purchasing power is growing in countries like India and China, which have low average levels of income. This is because basic living expenses such as food, shelter, and transportation are very inexpensive in those countries, so consumers still have money to spend after paying for necessities, especially as salaries increase thanks to demand from international trade.

Consequently, countries with high and growing levels of purchasing power are good choices for companies looking for attractive global markets. Coke has found that the per capita consumption of Coca-Cola, or the number of Cokes a person drinks per year, rises directly with purchasing power. For example, in China, Brazil, and Australia, where the average person earns, respectively,

purchasing power
the relative cost of a standard set of goods and services in different countries

$7,400, $10,900, and $41,300 annually, the number of Coca-Cola soft drinks consumed per year increases, respectively, from 34 to 229 to 319. The more purchasing power people have, the more likely they are to purchase soft drinks.

The second part of assessing the growth potential of global markets involves analyzing the degree of global competition, which is determined by the number and quality of companies that already compete in a foreign market. For example, MARCOPOLO, Brazil's biggest bus maker, with $1.1 billion in annual sales, focuses on selling buses in emerging-market countries like Argentina, Mexico, Colombia, and South Africa, where there's strong demand and little competition. EMBRAER, Brazil's leading airplane manufacturer, gets one-third of its sales from emerging markets (compared to 1 percent in 2005). Unlike Marcopolo, however, Embraer is seeing increased competition from Russia's Sukhio and the Commercial Aircraft Corporation of China for sales in these markets.[50]

7-4b Choosing an Office/Manufacturing Location

Companies do not have to establish an office or manufacturing location in each country they enter. They can license, franchise, or export to foreign markets, or they can serve a larger region from one country. But there are many reasons why a company might choose to establish a location in a foreign country.

The criteria for choosing an office or manufacturing location are different from the criteria for entering a foreign market. Rather than focusing on costs alone, companies should consider both qualitative and quantitative factors. Two key qualitative factors are workforce quality and company strategy. Workforce quality is important because it is often difficult to find workers with the specific skills, abilities, and experience that a company needs to run its business. Workforce quality is one reason that many companies doing business in Europe locate their customer call centers in the Netherlands. Workers in the Netherlands are the most linguistically gifted in Europe, with 73 percent speaking two languages, 44 percent speaking three languages, and 12 percent speaking more than three. Of course, with employees who speak several languages, call centers located in the Netherlands can handle calls from more countries and generally employ 30 to 50 percent fewer employees than those located in other parts of Europe.[51]

A company's strategy is also important when choosing a location. For example, a company pursuing a low-cost strategy may need plentiful raw materials, low-cost transportation, and low-cost labor. A company pursuing a differentiation strategy (typically a higher-priced, better product or service) may need access to high-quality materials and a highly skilled and educated workforce.

Quantitative factors such as the kind of facility being built, tariff and nontariff barriers, exchange rates, and transportation and labor costs should also be considered when choosing an office or manufacturing location.

7-4c Minimizing Political Risk

When managers think about political risk in global business, they envision burning factories and riots in the streets. Although political events such as these receive dramatic and extended coverage from the media, the political

Doing the Right Thing

Obey the Laws

In 1997, the member countries of the Organisation for Economic Co-operation and Development (OECD) adopted the OECD Anti-Bribery Convention. Each country that ratified the convention (38 in total, covering the world's largest economies) agreed to enact and enforce legislation that makes it illegal to bribe a foreign business or government official. The convention has required a number of countries to create new laws against bribery or enhance laws that were already written. In a recent survey, however, the anticorruption agency Transparency International reveals that more than half of OECD convention members are failing to enforce antibribery laws. This puts more pressure on you, as a manager. Even though your competitors may use bribes to try to get ahead, do the right thing and stay within the boundaries of the law.[55]

risks that most companies face usually are not covered as breaking stories on Fox News or CNN. Nonetheless, the negative consequences of ordinary political risk can be just as devastating to companies that fail to identify and minimize that risk.[52]

When conducting global business, companies should attempt to identify two types of political risk: political uncertainty and policy uncertainty.[53] **Political uncertainty** is associated with the risk of major changes in political regimes that can result from war, revolution, death of political leaders, social unrest, or other influential events. **Policy uncertainty** refers to the risk associated with changes in laws and government policies that directly affect the way foreign companies conduct business.

Policy uncertainty is the more common—and perhaps more frustrating—form of political risk in global business, especially when changes in laws and government policies directly undercut sizable investments made by foreign companies. BlackBerry smart phones, made by the Canadian-based *RESEARCH IN MOTION (RIM)*, are extraordinarily popular in Saudi Arabia because they offer secure, encrypted, electronic communication. Saudi Arabia's Communication and Information Technology Commission, however, worries that RIM's encryption systems will prevent security officials from monitoring terrorist groups that use BlackBerries for communication. As a result, the Saudi government announced that BlackBerry phones would be prohibited. Because of this policy change, RIM was suddenly at risk of losing 750,000 users. After intense negotiations, RIM Research agreed to install computer servers, giving the Saudi government unencrypted access to monitor user communications and activities.[54]

Several strategies can be used to minimize or adapt to the political risk inherent in global business. An *avoidance strategy* is used when the political risks associated with a foreign country or region are viewed as too great. If firms are already invested in high-risk areas, they may divest or sell their businesses. If they have not yet invested, they will likely postpone their investment until the risk shrinks.

Control is an active strategy to prevent or reduce political risks. Firms using a control strategy lobby foreign governments or international trade agencies to change laws, regulations, or trade barriers that hurt their business in that country. Another method for dealing with political risk is *cooperation*, which involves using joint ventures and collaborative contracts, such as franchising

policy uncertainty
the risk associated with changes in laws and government policies that directly affect the way foreign companies conduct business

political uncertainty
the risk of major changes in political regimes that can result from war, revolution, death of political leaders, social unrest, or other influential events

and licensing. Although cooperation does not eliminate the political risk of doing business in a country, it can limit the risk associated with foreign ownership of a business. For example, a German company forming a joint venture with a Chinese company to do business in China may structure the joint venture contract so that the Chinese company owns 51 percent or more of the joint venture. Doing so qualifies the joint venture as a Chinese company and exempts it from Chinese laws that apply to foreign-owned businesses. However, cooperation cannot always protect against *policy risk* if a foreign government changes its laws and policies to directly affect the way foreign companies conduct business.

REVIEW 7-4

Finding the Best Business Climate

The first step in deciding where to take your company globally is finding an attractive business climate. Look for a growing market where consumers have strong purchasing power and foreign competitors are weak. When locating an office or manufacturing facility, consider both qualitative and quantitative factors. In assessing political risk, be sure to examine political uncertainty and policy uncertainty. If the location you choose has considerable political risk, you can avoid it, try to control the risk, or use a cooperation strategy.

7-5 Becoming Aware of Cultural Differences

Some of the more interesting and amusing aspects of global business are the unexpected confrontations that people have with cultural differences, "the way they do things over there." *Wall Street Journal* columnist Geoffrey Fowler wrote of an incident in Hong Kong where a Chinese colleague casually observed that he had gained weight and three others had simply told him he was fat.[56] Uttered in the United States, such comments would be considered rude. Fowler indicates that in China, however, where people openly talk about people's weight, body shapes, and salaries, such comments are probably just friendliness. So what does Fowler say when his friendly Chinese colleagues tell him he's fat? "There's so much good food here."

After reading this section, you should be able to:

7-5 discuss the importance of identifying and adapting to cultural differences.

National culture is the set of shared values and beliefs that affects the perceptions, decisions, and behavior of the people from a particular country. The first step in dealing with culture is to recognize that there are meaningful differences. Professor Geert Hofstede spent 20 years studying cultural differences in 53 different countries. His research shows that there are five consistent cultural dimensions across countries: power distance, individualism, masculinity/femininity, uncertainty avoidance, and short-term versus long-term orientation.[57]

Power distance is the extent to which people in a country accept that power is distributed unequally in society and organizations. In countries where power distance is weak, such as Denmark and Sweden, employees don't like their organization or their boss to have power over them or tell them what to do. They want to have a say in decisions that affect them.

national culture
the set of shared values and beliefs that affects the perceptions, decisions, and behavior of the people from a particular country

Individualism is the degree to which societies believe that individuals should be self-sufficient. In individualistic societies, employees put loyalty to themselves first and loyalty to their company and work group second.

Masculinity and *femininity* capture the difference between highly assertive and highly nurturing cultures. Masculine cultures emphasize assertiveness, competition, material success, and achievement, whereas feminine cultures emphasize the importance of relationships, modesty, caring for the weak, and quality of life.

The cultural difference of *uncertainty avoidance* is the degree to which people in a country are uncomfortable with unstructured, ambiguous, unpredictable situations. In countries with strong uncertainty avoidance, like Greece and Portugal, people tend to be aggressive and emotional and seek security rather than uncertainty.

Short-term/long-term orientation addresses whether cultures are oriented to the present and seek immediate gratification or to the future and defer gratification. Not surprisingly, countries with short-term orientations are consumer driven, whereas countries with long-term orientations are savings driven. Cultural differences affect perceptions, understanding, and behavior. Recognizing cultural differences is critical to succeeding in global business. Nevertheless, as Hofstede pointed out, descriptions of cultural differences are based on averages—the average level of uncertainty avoidance in Portugal, the average level of power distance in Argentina, and so forth. Accordingly, says Hofstede, "If you are going to spend time with a Japanese colleague, you shouldn't assume that all cultural statements about Japanese society automatically apply to this person."[58] Similarly, cultural beliefs may differ significantly from one part of a country to another.[59]

After becoming aware of cultural differences, the second step is deciding how to adapt your company to those differences. Unfortunately, studies investigating the effects of cultural differences on management practices point more to difficulties than to easy solutions. One problem is that different cultures will probably perceive management policies and practices differently.

Another difficulty is that cultural values are changing, albeit slowly, in many parts of the world. The fall of communism in Eastern Europe and the former Soviet Union and the broad economic reforms in China have produced sweeping changes on two continents in the last two decades. Thanks to increased global trade resulting from free trade agreements, major economic transformations are also under way in India, China, Central America, and South America. Consequently, when trying to adapt management practices to cultural differences, companies must ensure that they are not basing their adaptations on outdated and incorrect assumptions about a country's culture.

REVIEW 7-5
. . . .

Becoming Aware of Cultural Differences

National culture is the set of shared values and beliefs that affects the perceptions, decisions, and behavior of the people from a particular country. The first step in dealing with culture is to recognize meaningful differences such as power distance, individualism, masculinity, uncertainty avoidance, and short-term/long-term orientation. Cultural differences should be carefully interpreted because they are based on averages, not individuals. Adapting managerial practices to cultural differences is difficult because policies and practices can be perceived differently in different cultures. Another difficulty is that cultural values may be changing in many parts of the world. Consequently, when companies try to adapt management practices to cultural differences, they need to be sure that they are not using outdated assumptions about a country's culture.

7-6 Preparing for an International Assignment

Tom Bonkenburg is director of European operations for St. Onge Company, a supply-chain consulting firm in York, Pennsylvania. Bonkenburg went to Moscow for a first-time meeting with the director of a Russian firm with which his company hoped to do business. He said that when he met the Russian director, "I gave my best smile, handshake and friendly joke . . . only to be met with a dreary and unhappy look." Afterward, though, he received a friendly e-mail from the Russian director, indicating that the meeting had been very positive. Subsequently, Bonkenburg learned that Russians save smiling and friendliness for personal meetings and are expected to be serious at business meetings. Says, Bonkenburg, "He was working as hard to impress me as I was to impress him."[60]

After reading this section, you should be able to:

7-6 explain how to successfully prepare workers for international assignments.

If you become an **expatriate**, someone who lives and works outside his or her native country, chances are you'll run into cultural surprises like Tom Bonkenburg did. The difficulty of adjusting to linguistical, cultural, and social differences is the primary reason for expatriate failure in overseas assignments. For example, although there have recently been disagreements among researchers about these numbers, it is probably safe to say that 5 to 20 percent of American expatriates sent abroad by their companies will return to the United States before they have successfully completed their assignments.[61] Of those who do complete their international assignments, about one-third are judged by their companies to be no better than marginally effective.[62] Because the average cost of sending an employee on a three-year international assignment is $1 million, failure in those assignments can be extraordinarily expensive.[63]

The chances for a successful international assignment can be increased through **7-6a language and cross-cultural training** and **7-6b consideration of spouse, family, and dual-career issues.**

7-6a Language and Cross-Cultural Training

Predeparture language and cross-cultural training can reduce the uncertainty that expatriates feel, the misunderstandings that take place between expatriates and natives, and the inappropriate behaviors that expatriates unknowingly commit when they travel to a foreign country. Indeed, simple things like using a phone, locating a public toilet, asking for directions, finding out how much things cost, exchanging greetings, or understanding what people want can

expatriate
someone who lives and works outside his or her native country

become tremendously complex when expatriates don't know a foreign language or a country's customs and cultures. In his book *Blunders in International Business*, David Ricks tells the story of an American manager working in the South Pacific who, by hiring too many local workers from one native group, unknowingly upset the balance of power in the island's traditional status system. The islanders met on their own and quickly worked out a solution to the problem. After concluding their meeting at 3 A.M., they calmly went to the manager's home to discuss their solution with him (time was not important in their culture). But because the American didn't speak their language and didn't understand why they had shown up en masse outside his home at 3 A.M., he called in the Marines, who were stationed nearby, to disperse what he thought was a riot.

Expatriates who receive predeparture language and cross-cultural training make faster adjustments to foreign cultures and perform better on their international assignments.[64] Unfortunately, only a third of the managers who go on international assignments are offered any kind of predeparture training, and only half of those actually participate in the training![65] This is somewhat surprising given the failure rates for expatriates and the high cost of those failures. Furthermore, with the exception of some language courses, predeparture training is not particularly expensive or difficult to provide. Three methods can be used to prepare workers for international assignments: documentary training, cultural simulations, and field experiences.

Documentary training focuses on identifying specific, critical differences between cultures. For example, when 60 workers at AXCELIS TECHNOLOGIES in Beverly, Massachusetts, were preparing to do business in India, they learned that while Americans make eye contact and shake hands firmly when greeting others, Indians, as a sign of respect, do just the opposite, avoiding eye contact and shaking hands limply.[66]

After learning specific, critical differences through documentary training, trainees can then participate in *cultural simulations*, in which they practice adapting to cultural differences. *EMC*, a global provider of information storage solutions, uses cultural simulations to train its people. EMC's cultural simulations use photos and audio and video clips to present real-world situations. EMC employees must decide what to do and then learn what happened as a result of their choices. Whether it's interacting with customers or dealing with EMC employees from other countries, at every step they have the opportunity to learn good and bad methods of responding to cultural differences.[67]

Finally, *field simulation* training, a technique made popular by the U.S. Peace Corps, places trainees in an ethnic neighborhood for three to four hours to talk to residents about cultural differences. For example, a U.S. electronics manufacturer prepared workers for assignments in South Korea by having trainees explore a nearby South Korean neighborhood and talk to shopkeepers and people on the street about South Korean politics, family orientation, and day-to-day living practices.

MANAGEMENT FACT

Wanted: International Experience

Working as an expat has always had an appeal to those who love experiencing other cultures. And, it's helped companies find a place in markets all over the world. Research has found, however, that overseas experience also makes for better managers. A research study at Northwestern's Kellogg School of Management found that 60 percent of students who lived abroad were able to solve a creative-thinking problem, compared to just 42 percent of students who did not live abroad. In another study, conducted at Sorbonne University in Paris, researchers showed students three words and were asked to come up with another word that linked all of them. Those who studied abroad were able to give more correct answers than those who did not. So what's a great way to develop great managers? Send them overseas![68]

7-6b Spouse, Family, and Dual-Career Issues

Not all international assignments are difficult for expatriates and their families, but the evidence clearly shows that how well an expatriate's spouse and family adjust to the foreign culture is the most important factor in determining the success or failure of an international assignment. A number of companies, however, have found that adaptability screening and intercultural training for families can lead to more successful overseas adjustment.

Adaptability screening is used to assess how well managers and their families are likely to adjust to foreign cultures. For example, PRUDENTIAL RELOCATION MANAGEMENT's international division has developed an Overseas Assignment Inventory (OAI) to assess a spouse and family's open-mindedness, respect for others' beliefs, sense of humor, and marital communication. But adaptability screening does not just involve a company assessing an employee; it can also involve an employee screening international assignments for desirability. Because more employees are becoming aware of the costs of international assignments (spouses having to give up or change jobs, children having to change schools, everyone having to learn a new language), some companies are willing to pay for a preassignment trip so the employee and his or her spouse can investigate the country *before* accepting the international assignment.[69]

Only 40 percent of expatriates' families receive language and cross-cultural training, yet such training is just as important for the families of expatriates as for the expatriates themselves.[70] In fact, it may be more important because, unlike expatriates whose professional jobs often shield them from the full force of a country's culture, spouses and children are fully immersed in foreign neighborhoods and schools. Households must be run, shopping must be done, and bills must be paid. Expatriates' children must deal with different cultural beliefs and practices, too. In addition to helping families prepare for the cultural differences they will encounter, language and cross-cultural training can help reduce uncertainty about how to act and decrease misunderstandings between expatriates and their families and locals.

REVIEW 7-6

Preparing for an International Assignment

Many expatriates return prematurely from international assignments because of poor performance. However, premature return is much less likely to happen if employees receive language and cross-cultural training, such as documentary training, cultural simulations, or field experiences, before going on assignment. Adjustment of expatriates' spouses and families, which is the most important determinant of success in international assignments, can be improved through adaptability screening and intercultural training.

what *really* works

Cross-Cultural Training

Most expatriates will tell you that cross-cultural training helped them adjust to foreign cultures. Such anecdotal data, however, are not as convincing as systematic studies. Twenty-one studies, with a combined total of 1,611 participants, have examined whether cross-cultural training affects the self-development, relationships, perceptions, adjustment, and job performance of expatriates. Overall, they show that cross-cultural training works extremely well in most instances.

Self-Development

When you first arrive in another country, you must learn how to make decisions that you took for granted in your home country: how to get to work, how to get to the grocery, how to pay your bills, and so on. If you've generally been confident about yourself and your abilities, an overseas assignment can challenge that sense of self. Cross-cultural training helps expatriates deal with these and other challenges. Expatriates who receive cross-cultural training are 79 percent more likely to report healthy psychological well-being and self-development than those who don't receive training.

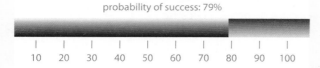

Fostering Relationships

One of the most important aspects of an overseas assignment is establishing and maintaining relationships with host nationals. If you're in Brazil, you need to make friends with Brazilians. Many expatriates, however, make the mistake of making friends only with other expatriates from their home country. In effect, they become social isolates in a foreign country. They work and live there, but as much as they can, they speak their native language, eat their native foods, and socialize with other expatriates from their home country. Cross-cultural training makes a big difference in whether expatriates establish relationships with host nationals. Expatriates who receive cross-cultural training are 74 percent more likely to establish such relationships.

Accurate Perceptions of Culture

Another characteristic of successful expatriates is that they understand the cultural norms and practices of the host country. For example, many Americans do not understand the famous pictures of Japanese troops turning their backs to American military commanders on V-J Day, when Japan surrendered to the United States at the end of World War II. Americans viewed this as a lack of respect, when, in fact, in Japan, turning one's back in this way is a sign of respect. Cross-cultural training makes a big difference in the accuracy of perceptions concerning host country norms and practices. Expatriates who receive cross-cultural training are 74 percent more likely to have accurate perceptions.

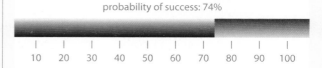

Rapid Adjustment

New employees are most likely to quit in the first six months because this initial period requires the most adjustment: learning new names, new faces, new procedures, and new information.

It's tough. Of course, expatriates have a much harder time adjusting to their new jobs because they are also learning new languages, new foods, new customs, and often new lifestyles. Expatriates who receive cross-cultural training are 74 percent more likely to make a rapid adjustment to a foreign country.

RAPID ADJUSTMENT TO FOREIGN CULTURES AND COUNTRIES

probability of success: 74%

| 10 | 20 | 30 | 40 | 50 | 60 | 70 | 80 | 90 | 100 |

Job Performance

It's good that cross-cultural training improves self-development, fosters relationships, improves the accuracy of perceptions, and helps expatriates make rapid adjustments to foreign cultures. From an organizational standpoint, however, the ultimate test of cross-cultural training is whether it improves expatriates' job performance. The evidence shows that cross-cultural training makes a significant difference in expatriates' job performance, although the difference is not quite as large as for the other factors. Nonetheless, it is estimated that cross-cultural training for 100 managers could bring about $390,000 worth of benefits to a company, or nearly $4,000 per manager. This is an outstanding return on investment, especially when you consider the high rate of failure for expatriates. Expatriates who have received cross-cultural training are 71 percent more likely to have better on-the-job performance than those who did not receive cross-cultural training.[71]

ON-THE-JOB PERFORMANCE
probability of success: 74%

| 10 | 20 | 30 | 40 | 50 | 60 | 70 | 80 | 90 | 100 |

Management Decision

Cultural Backlash in India[72]

As you look at the latest quarterly earnings report of your clothing and accessories company, you think to yourself: "You are a genius!" It was your idea to move manufacturing to India last year, and it was your idea to partner with a local retail chain to get your products to Indian consumers. So even though your U.S. sales fell 5 percent, much in part due to the recession, your company's profits actually rose 35 percent, thanks to all the money you made in India. Almost every day, you walk through the city and you see young, affluent Indians wearing your jeans, clutching your purses, donning your sunglasses, and you are unbelievably glad that you decided to come into this dynamic, fast-growing market that really likes Western fashion styles.

There are many people, however, who aren't so fond of your styles, and of Western culture in general. Various religious and political conservative groups have recently been protesting the growing influence of Western culture in India, sometimes in quite violent ways. During a recent Valentine's Day, a group of men publicly beat young couples who were holding hands or having a romantic dinner. In another city, a group of people attacked women who were at bars and dance clubs. And just the other day, you saw a crowd of people throwing your jeans, purses, and sunglasses into a big bonfire as a statement against Western fashion. Even businesses are getting into the anti-American sentiment; a local beverage company announced that they would take on the popularity of Coke and Pepsi by selling a beverage based on cow urine, which is considered a holy, medicinal drink by Hindus.

When you came up with the idea of expanding into India, you certainly didn't think that you would find yourself in the middle of a cultural clash. "I'm just here to sell jeans," you think, "not to tell people how to live." But clearly, many people view companies like yours as a threat to their culture and heritage.

Questions

1. How would you, as the manager of this company, deal with the risk associated with doing business in countries that feel threatened by American culture?

2. How might your company use an alliance with local companies to adapt to local concerns about American culture?

 ## Practice Being a Manager

Hometown Culture

One of the major dilemmas in global management concerns the degree to which a multinational firm should adapt its business practices to particular locations and cultures versus the degree to which it should maintain consistency across all its operations. In general, firms prefer consistency because it streamlines operations and may result in global economies of scale. At the same time, multinational firms cannot gloss over differences without running the risk of losing a particular market to more responsive (local) competition. In this exercise, you will interpret your "hometown" culture for a large multinational company.

Suppose that a large multinational equipment company (based outside your country of origin) is planning to open a major production facility and retail dealership in your hometown. This company has hired you as a consultant to help it successfully establish operations in your hometown.

STEP 1 **Describe your hometown.** Write a brief sketch (one or two pages, using bullet points, will suffice) in which you describe the important cultural features of your hometown, including such aspects as language, dress, courtesy and customs, and attitudes toward "foreignness" and newcomers. Try as much as possible to capture aspects of the location and culture of your hometown that would be important for newcomers to recognize and respect.

STEP 2 **Form a team.** Your professor will assign you to small discussion groups of three to five students.

STEP 3 **Share your description.** Take turns in your discussion groups introducing yourselves, identifying your hometown, and sharing the highlights of your brief sketch of your hometown. Listen for similarities and differences across your hometowns.

STEP 4 **Make recommendations.** As a group, agree on some recommendations to the multinational company. Assume that the company is planning to enter all of your hometowns simultaneously. To what degree might the company use a consistent (same) approach in entering your hometowns? Is one or more of your hometowns likely to require a foreign multinational to make more particular adaptations?

STEP 5 **Share findings with class.** Each group should share its list of hometowns and its recommendations with the class.

STEP 6 **Consider challenges.** As a class, discuss the challenges of entering global markets, particularly in regard to achieving the appropriate mix of consistency and adaptation.

Self-Assessment

Are You Nation-Minded or World-Minded?

Attitudes about global business are as varied as managers are numerous. It seems that the business press can always find someone who is for globalization and someone who is against it. But regardless of your opinion on the subject, managers will increasingly confront issues related to the globalization of the business environment. It is probable that, as a manager, you will need to develop global sensibilities (if you don't already have them). Understanding your own cultural perspective is the first step in doing so.

This assessment has two parts: Step 1, complete the questionnaire shown below; Step 2, determine your score.[73]

STEP 1 Use the 6-point rating scale to complete the 32-question inventory shown below.

1 **Strongly disagree**

2 **Disagree**

3 **Mildly disagree**

4 **Mildly agree**

5 **Agree**

6 **Strongly agree**

1. Our country should have the right to prohibit certain racial and religious groups from entering it to live.

   1   2   3   4   5   6

2. Immigrants should not be permitted to come into our country if they compete with our own workers.

   1   2   3   4   5   6

3. It would set a dangerous precedent if every person in the world had equal rights that were guaranteed by an international charter.

   1   2   3   4   5   6

4. All prices for exported food and manufactured goods should be set by an international trade committee.

   1   2   3   4   5   6

5. Our country is probably no better than many others.

   1   2   3   4   5   6

6. Race prejudice may be a good thing for us because it keeps many undesirable foreigners from coming into this country.

   1   2   3   4   5   6

7. It would be a mistake for us to encourage certain racial groups to become well educated because they might use their knowledge against us.

   1   2   3   4   5   6

8. We should be willing to fight for our country without questioning whether it is right or wrong.

   1   2   3   4   5   6

9. Foreigners are particularly obnoxious because of their religious beliefs.

   1   2   3   4   5   6

10. Immigration should be controlled by a global organization rather than by each country on its own.

      1   2   3   4   5   6

11. We ought to have a world government to guarantee the welfare of all nations irrespective of the rights of any one.

      1   2   3   4   5   6

12. Our country should not cooperate in any global trade agreements that attempt to better world economic conditions at our expense.

      1   2   3   4   5   6

13. It would be better to be a citizen of the world than of any particular country.

      1   2   3   4   5   6

14. Our responsibility to people of other races ought to be as great as our responsibility to people of our own race.

      1   2   3   4   5   6

15. A global committee on education should have full control over what is taught in all countries about history and politics.

      1   2   3   4   5   6

16. Our country should refuse to cooperate in a total disarmament program even if some other nations agree to it.

      1   2   3   4   5   6

17. It would be dangerous for our country to make international agreements with nations whose religious beliefs are antagonistic to ours.

      1   2   3   4   5   6

18. Any healthy individual, regardless of race or religion, should be allowed to live wherever he or she wants to in the world.

      1   2   3   4   5   6

19. Our country should not participate in any global organization that requires that we give up any of our national rights or freedom of action.

      1   2   3   4   5   6

20. If necessary, we ought to be willing to lower our standard of living to cooperate with other countries in getting an equal standard for every person in the world.

      1   2   3   4   5   6

21. We should strive for loyalty to our country before we can afford to consider world brotherhood.

      1   2   3   4   5   6

22. Some races ought to be considered naturally less intelligent than ours.

      1   2   3   4   5   6

23. Our schools should teach the history of the whole world rather than of our own country.

      1   2   3   4   5   6

24. A global police force ought to be the only group in the world allowed to have armaments.

      1   2   3   4   5   6

25. It would be dangerous for us to guarantee by international agreement that every person in the world should have complete religious freedom.

     1   2   3   4   5   6

26. Our country should permit the immigration of foreign peoples, even if it lowers our standard of living.

     1   2   3   4   5   6

27. All national governments ought to be abolished and replaced by one, central, world government.

     1   2   3   4   5   6

28. It would not be wise for us to agree that working conditions in all countries should be subject to international control.

     1   2   3   4   5   6

29. Patriotism should be a primary aim of education so that our children will believe our country is the best in the world.

     1   2   3   4   5   6

30. It would be a good idea if all the races were to intermarry until there was only one race in the world.

     1   2   3   4   5   6

31. We should teach our children to uphold the welfare of all people everywhere, even though it may be against the best interests of our own country.

     1   2   3   4   5   6

32. War should never be justifiable, even if it is the only way to protect our national rights and honor.

     1   2   3   4   5   6

STEP 2 Determine your score by entering your response to each survey item below, as follows. In blanks that say *regular score*, simply enter your response for that item. If your response was a 4, place a 4 in the *regular score* blank. In blanks that say *reverse score*, subtract your response from 7 and enter the result. So if your response was a 4, place a 3 (7–4 = 3) in the *reverse score* blank.

   1. reverse score   _____

   2. reverse score   _____

   3. reverse score   _____

   4. regular score   _____

   5. regular score   _____

   6. reverse score   _____

   7. reverse score   _____

   8. reverse score   _____

   9. reverse score   _____

  10. regular score   _____

  11. regular score   _____

  12. reverse score   _____

  13. regular score   _____

  SUBTOTAL = _____

14. regular score _____

15. regular score _____

16. reverse score _____

17. reverse score _____

18. regular score _____

19. reverse score _____

20. regular score _____

21. reverse score _____

22. reverse score _____

23. regular score _____

24. regular score _____

25. reverse score _____

26. regular score _____

27. regular score _____

28. reverse score _____

29. reverse score _____

30. regular score _____

31. regular score _____

32. regular score _____

SUBTOTAL = _____

SCORING

Total your scores from items 1–13 _____

Total your scores from items 14–32 _____

Add together to compute TOTAL = _____

Find the interpretation to your score at www.cengagebrain.com

REEL TO REAL

 MANAGEMENT WORKPLACE

Holden Outerwear: Managing in a Global Environment

Although an American brand, Holden apparel is made in China. The company would like to manufacture in the United States, but government regulations, labor costs, and high corporate tax rates are too heavy a burden. Availability of materials is another factor, as many of the pieces that Holden needs, like buttons, snaps, and fabrics, would still have to be brought in from Asia even if the garment were made domestically. In addition, garment making requires skilled laborers, and founder Mikey LeBlanc says that the United States lacks a manufacturing base to do the job. For any company that sources materials and labor overseas, shipping is a vital, ongoing concern, and over time, LeBlanc has consolidated his shipping by using a single distribution hub in China to increase efficiency and reduce costs.

What to Watch For and Ask Yourself

1. Which stage of globalization characterizes Holden Outerwear's international involvement?
2. Identify Holden's primary approach to entering the international market. What are the benefits of this entry strategy?
3. What are the challenges of international management for leaders at Holden?

Endnotes

1   L. Chao, "Taobao to Launch Local Deals on Group-Buying Website," *Wall Street Journal*, February 23, 2011, accessed May 15, 2011, from http://online.wsj.com/article/SB100014240527870377570457616134083998996.html; B. Stone and D. MacMillan, "Groupon's $6 billion Snub," *Bloomberg Businessweek*, December 13, 2010, 6–7; B. Stone and D. MacMillan, "Are Four Words Worth $25 billion?" *Bloomberg Businessweek*, March 21, 2011, 70–75; and R. Underwood, "Groupon versus the World," *Inc.*, October 2010, 116–118; and B. Weiss, "The Weekend Interview with Andrew Mason: Groupon's $6 billion Gambler," *Wall Street Journal*, December 18, 2010, A15.

2   T. Friedman, "It's a Flat World, After All," *New York Times*, April 3, 2005, 33.

3   "Web table 34. Number of parent corporations and foreign affiliates, by region and economy, latest available year (Number)," World Investment Report 2010, United Nations Conference on Trade and Development, accessed May 11, 2012, at www.unctad.org/Sections/dite_dir/docs/WIR11_web%20tab%2034.pdf.

4   T. Virki, "Nokia Siemens buys Motorola Network Ops for $1.2 billion," Reuters, July 19, 2010, accessed July 23, 2010, from www.reuters.com/article/idUSTRE66I24P20100719.

5   A. Cordeiro, "Hershey to Expand in Asia," *Wall Street Journal*, March 12, 2009, B5.

6   E. L. Andrews, "U.S. Adds Tariffs on Chinese Tires," *Wall Street Journal*, September 11, 2009, accessed June 9, 2010, from www.nytimes.com/2009/09/12/business/global/12tires.html?_r=1 & scp=1& sq=tariff & st=cse; and M. Kitchen, "China to Set Anti-Dumping Measures on U.S. Chicken," Market Watch, February 5, 2010, accessed August 3, 2010, from www.marketwatch.com/story/china-to-set-anti-dumping-measures-on-us-chicken-2010-02-05.

7   G. Williams III, "News on the Road Column," *San Antonio Express–News*, March 3, 2006.

8   K. Bradsher, "W.T.O. Rules Against China's Limits on Imports," *New York Times*, August 12, 2009, accessed June 9, 2010, from www.nytimes.com/2009/08/13/business/global/13trade.html?scp=3 & sq=trade%20quota&st=cse.

9   R. Geldenhuys, "China Import Quotas Illegal under WTO Law?" Floor, Inc. Attorneys, September 18, 2006, accessed May 13, 2011 from www.tradelaw.co.za/news/article.asp?newsID_101.

10 "Understanding the WTO," *World Trade Organization*, accessed August 5, 2008, from www.wto.org/english/thewto_e/whatis_e/tif_e/agrm9_e.htm.

11 J. Adams, "Taiwan Curbs U.S. Beef Imports in Latest Asia Trade Frictions," *Christian Science Monitor*, January 5, 2010, accessed July 23, 2010, from www.csmonitor.com/World/Asia-Pacific/2010/0105/Taiwan-curbs-US-beef-imports-in-latest-Asia-trade-frictions.

12 "GATT/WTO," Duke Law: Library & Technology, accessed June 12, 2009, from www.law.duke.edu/lib/researchguides/gatt.html.

13 "The History of the European Union," *Europa—European Union Online,* accessed August 6, 2008, from http://europa.eu/abc/european_countries/index_en.htm; and "Member States of the EU," Europa: The EU at a Glance, accessed May 12, 2012, from http://europa.eu/abc/european_countries/candidate_countries/index_en.htm.

14 "Candidate Countries," Europa: The EU at a Glance, accessed May 12, 2012, from http://europa.eu/abc/european_countries/candidate_countries/index_en.htm.

15 "Map of Euro Area 1999–2011," European Central Bank, accessed May 10, 2012 from http://www.ecb.int/euro/intro/html/map.en.html.

16 "Testimony of Under Secretary of Commerce for International Trade Grant D. Aldona: The Impact of NAFTA on the United States Economy," Senate Foreign Relations Committee, Subcommittee on International Economic Policy, Export & Trade Promotion, February 7, 2007.

17 "Top U.S. Export Markets: Free Trade Agreement and Country Fact Sheets," International Trade Administration, U.S. Department of Commerce, 2009, accessed May 8, 2011, from http://trade.gov/publications/pdfs/top-us-export-markets-2009.pdf.

18 "CAFTA-DR (Dominican Republic-Central America FTA)," Office of the United States Trade Representative, accessed May 12, 2012, from www.ustr.gov/trade-agreements/free-trade-agreements/cafta-dr-dominican-republic-central-america-fta.

19 "US Trade with the CAFTA-DR Countries," Office of the United States Trade Representative (July 2007), accessed August 6, 2008, from www.ustr.gov/assets/Trade_Agreements/Bilateral/CAFTA/Briefing_Book/asset_upload_file601_13191.pdf.

20 UNASUR, Union of South American Nations, accessed May 12, 2012, from www.comunidadandina.org/ingles/sudamerican.htm.

21 "Selected Basic ASEAN Indicators, 2011," *Association of Southeast Nations,* February 15, 2011, accessed May 8, 2011, from www.aseansec.org/stat/Table1.pdf; "Selected Basic ASEAN Indicators, 2005," Association of Southeast Nations, accessed August 6, 2008, from www.aseansec.org/stat/Table1.pdf; "Top Ten ASEAN Trade Partner Countries/Regions, 2005," Association of Southeast Nations, accessed August 6, 2008, from www.aseansec.org/Stat/Table20.pdf; "ASEAN Free Trade Area (AFTA)," Association of Southeast Nations, accessed August 6, 2008, www.aseansec.org/12021.htm.

22 "Frequently Asked Questions (FAQs)" *Asia—PacificEconomic Cooperation,* accessed May 8, 2011, from www.apec.org/FAQ.aspx.

23 "Member Economies," Asia Pacific Economic Cooperation, accessed May 12, 2012, from www.apec.org/apec/ member_economies/key_websites.html; "Frequently Asked Questions (FAQs)," Asia-Pacific Economic Cooperation, accessed August 6, 2008, from www.apec.org/apec/tools/faqs.html.

24 www.tokyoprices.com/category/food-prices/.

25 Z. Greenburg, "World's Most Expensive Cups of Coffee," *Forbes*, July 24, 2008, accessed June 13, 2009, from www.forbes.com/2008/07/23/cities-coffee-expensive-forbeslife-cx_zg_0724expensivecoffee.html.

26 Z. Greenburg, "Moscow Tops Most Expensive Cup of Coffee List," *Forbes* on MSNBC.com, August 13, 2008, from www.msnbc.msn.com/id/26062313/ns/business-forbes com/t/moscow-tops-most-expensive-cup-coffee-list/.

27 "The Big Mac Index: An Indigestible Problem," *Economist*, January 12, 2012, accessed May 12, 2012, from www.economist.com/blogs/graphicdetail/2012/01/daily-chart-3?page=1

28 "2010 GNI per capita, Atlas method (current US$)," The World Bank, accessed May 11, 2012, from http://search.worldbank.org/data?qterm=2011%20gni%20per%20capita & language=EN.

29 "2010 GNI per capita, PPP (current US$)," The World Bank, accessed May 11, 2012, from http://search.worldbank.org/data?qterm=2011%20gni%20per%20capita & language=EN.

30 "The Global Competitiveness Report: 2008–2009," World Economic Forum, accessed June 14, 2009, from www.weforum.org/documents/GCR0809/index.html.

31 "Freer Trade Cuts the Cost of Living," *World Trade Organization*, accessed August 6, 2008, from www.wto.org/english/thewto_e/whatis_e/10ben_e/10b04_e.htm.

32 E. Holmes, "How H and M Keeps Its Cool," *Wall Street Journal*, May 10, 2010, accessed September 9, 2010, from http://online.wsj.com/article/SB10001424052748703338004575230493697911432.html?mod=dist_smartbrief.

33 A. Singh and S. Shankar, "Tupperware Parties Help Reshape India's Kitchens," Bloomberg.com, July 13 2010, accessed July 23, 2010, from www.Businessweek.com/globalbiz/content/jul2010/gb20100713_165186.htm; and A. Singh and S. Shankar, "Tupperware Story Throws up Some Success Mantras for Indian Market," *Economic Times*, June 11, 2010, accessed July 23, 2010, from http://economictimes.indiatimes.com/Features/Corporate-Dossier/Tupperware-story-throws-up-some-success-mantras-for-Indian-market/articleshow/6034418.cms?curpg=1.

34 A. Sundaram and J. S. Black, "The Environment and Internal-Organization of Multinational Enterprises," *Academy of Management Review* 17 (1992): 729–757.

35 H. S. James Jr., and M. Weidenbaum, *When Businesses Cross International Borders: Strategic Alliances & Their Alternatives* (Westport, CT: Praeger Publishers, 1993).

36 W. Sedgwick, "Nevada Lands First Chinese Wind Turbine Factory in US," Greentechnologydaily.com, March 11, 2010, accessed August 8, 2010, from www.greentechnologydaily.com/solar-wind/661-nevada-lands-first-chinese-wind-turbine-factory-in-us.

37 "Fast Facts about FremantleMedia," Fremantle Media, accessed May 9, 2011, from www.fremantlemedia.com/About_Us/Fast_Facts_About_Us.aspx.

38 A. Davidson, "TV Boss with the X Factor," *Sunday Times*, September 23, 2007, Business 9.

39 F. Vinulan, "BDSI Strikes $1.3 Million Licensing Deal for Onsolis Cancer Patch in Taiwan," *Triangle Business Journal*, October 7, 2010, accessed October 7, 2010, from www.bizjournals.com/triangle/stories/2010/10/04/daily41.html?q=licensing.

40 "New Restaurants," McDonald's, accessed March 18, 2009, from www.aboutmcdonalds.com/mcd/franchising/us_franchising/purchasing_your_franchise/new_restaurants.html.

41 K. Chu, "Fast-Food Chains in Asia Cater Menus to Customers," *USA Today*, September 7, 2010, accessed October 8, 2010, from www.usatoday.com/money/world/2010-09-07.asiatastes07_ST_N.htm; and S. Stern "Fast-Food Chains Adapt to Local Tastes," CNN, April 8, 2010, accessed October 8, 2010, from http://articles.cnn.com/2010-04-08/living/fast.food_1_taco-bell-burger-burritos-and-quesadillas?_s=PM:LIVING.

42 Press Release, "Garmin and Volvo Penta Form Strategic Alliance to Create Marine Instrumentation, Navigation and Communication Equipment," Garmin, February 18, 2011, accessed May 9, 2011, from http://garmin.blogs.com/my_weblog/2011/02/garmin-and-volvo-penta-form-strategic-alliance-to-create-marine-instrumentation-navigation-and-commu.html.

43 C. Rauwald, "Daimler, Beiqi Foton Ink Deal on China Truck Joint Venture," *Wall Street Journal*, July 16, 2010, accessed September 10, 2010, from http://online.wsj.com/article/SB10001424052748704682604575370061075262570.html.

44 B. R. Schlender, "How Toshiba Makes Alliances Work," *Fortune*, October 4, 1993, 116–120; and "Joint Ventures," *Encyclopedia of Business*, 2nd ed., accessed August 6, 2008, from www.referenceforbusiness.com/encyclopedia/Int-Jun/Joint-Ventures.html#WHY_JOINT_VENTURES_FAIL.

45 "Deutsche Telekom Profit down 37 Percent to $696 million," *Yahoo! News*, May 6, 2011, accessed May 14, 2011, from http://news.yahoo.com/s/ap/20110506/ap_on_bi_ge/eu_germany_earns_deutsche_telekom_1; and K. J. O'Brien, "How the iPhone Led to the Sale of T-Mobile USA," *New York Times*, March 21, 2011, accessed May 14, 2011, from http://dealbook.nytimes.com/2011/03/21/how-the-iphone-led-to-the-sale-of-t-mobile-usa/.

46 W. Hordes, J. A. Clancy, and J. Baddaley, "A Primer for Global Start-Ups," *Academy of Management Executive*, May 1995, 7–11.

47 D. Pavlos, J. Johnson, J. Slow, and S. Young, "Micromultinationals: New Types of Firms for the Global Competitive Landscape," *European Management Journal* 21, no. 2 (April 2003): 164; B. M. Oviatt and P. P. McDougall, "Toward a Theory of International New Ventures," *Journal of International Business Studies* (Spring 1994): 45–64; and S. Zahra, "A Theory of International New Ventures: A Decade of Research," *Journal of International Business Studies* (January 2005): 20–28.

48 Newswire, "Air Lease Corporation, the New Global Aviation Venture, Is Ready for Take-Off with Substantial Financing and a Top-Flight Senior Management Team," *PR Newswire*, July 15, 2010, accessed July 23, 2010, from www.prnewswire.com/news-releases/air-lease-corporation-the-new-global-aviation-venture-is-ready-for-take-off-with-substantial-financing-and-a-top-flight-senior-management-team-98529409.html.

49 "2010 Annual Report," The Coca-Cola Company, accessed May 11, 2011, from www.thecoca-colacompany.com/ourcompany/ar/pdf/TCCC_2010_Annual_Review.pdf.

50 S. Kennedy, M. Bristow, and S. Adam, "There's a New Silk Road, and It Doesn't Lead to the U.S.," *Bloomberg Business-week*, August 9–15, 2010, 13–14.

51 "Customer Care in the Netherlands," The Netherlands Foreign Investment Agency, accessed February 13, 2007, from www.nfia.com/customer_care.html.

52 J. Oetzel, R. Bettis, and M. Zenner, "How Risky Are They?" *Journal of World Business* 36, no. 2 (Summer 2001): 128–145.

53 K. D. Miller, "A Framework for Integrated Risk Management in International Business," *Journal of International Business Studies*, 2nd Quarter 1992, 311.

54 A. Al-Shihri "Blackberry-Saudi Arabia to Share User Data in Deal That Could Set Precedent," *Huffington Post*, August 7, 2010, accessed October 15, 2010, from www.huffingtonpost.com/2010/08/07/blackberrysaudi-arabia-de_n_674621.html.

55 V. Kortekaas, "OECD Nations 'Failing to Enforce Anti-Bribery Rules,'" *Financial Times*, October 26, 2010, accessed 13 May 2011X, from www.ft.com/cms/s/0/06704206-e0e3-11df-87da-00144feabdc0.html#axzz1DNqVGvkv

56 G. Fowler, "In China's Offices, Foreign Colleagues Might Get an Earful," *Wall Street Journal*, 13 February 2007, B1.

57 G. Hofstede, "The Cultural Relativity of the Quality of Life Concept," *Academy of Management Review* 9 (1984): 389–398; G. Hofstede, "The Cultural Relativity of Organizational Practices and Theories," *Journal of International Business Studies*, Fall 1983, 75–89; G. Hofstede, "The Interaction between National and Organizational Value Systems," *Journal of Management Studies*, July 1985, 347–357; and M. Hoppe, "An Interview with Geert Hofstede," *Academy of Management Executive*, February 2004, 75–79.

58 R. Hodgetts, "A Conversation with Geert Hofstede," *Organizational Dynamics*, Spring 1993, 53–61.

59 T. Lenartowicz and K. Roth, "Does Subculture within a Country Matter? A Cross-Cultural Study of Motivational Domains and Business Performance in Brazil," *Journal of International Business Studies* 32 (2001): 305–325.

60 E. Maltby, "Expanding Abroad? Avoid Cultural Gaffes—Entrepreneurs Looking Overseas Often Neglect to Learn Local Business Etiquette; In Britain, a 'Scheme' Carries No Taint," *Wall Street Journal*, January 19, 2010, B5.

61 J. S. Black, M. Mendenhall, and G. Oddou, "Toward a Comprehensive Model of International Adjustment: An Integration of Multiple Theoretical Perspectives," *Academy of Management Review* 16 (1991): 291–317; R. L. Tung, "American Expatriates Abroad: From Neophytes to Cosmopolitans," *Columbia Journal of World Business*, 22 June 1998, 125; A. Harzing, "The Persistent Myth of High Expatriate Failure Rates," *International Journal of Human Resource Management* 6 (1995): 457–475; A. Harzing, "Are Our Referencing Errors Undermining Our Scholarship and Credibility? The Case of Expatriate Failure Rates," *Journal of Organizational Behavior* 23 (2002): 127–148; and N. Forster, "The Persistent Myth of High Expatriate Failure Rates: A Reappraisal," *International Journal of Human Resource Management* 8 (1997): 414–433.

62 J. Black, "The Right Way to Manage Expats," *Harvard Business Review* 77 (March–April 1999): 52; and C. Joinson, "No Returns," *HR Magazine*, November 1, 2002, 70.

63 C. Joinson, "No Returns."

64 J. S. Black and M. Mendenhall, "Cross-Cultural Training Effectiveness: A Review and Theoretical Framework for Future Research," *Academy of Management Review* 15 (1990): 113–136.

65 K. Essick, "Executive Education: Transferees Prep for Life, Work in Far-Flung Lands," *Wall Street Journal*, November 12, 2004, A6.

66 P. W. Tam, "Culture Course—'Awareness Training' Helps U.S. Workers Better Know Their Counterparts in India," *Wall Street Journal*, May 25, 2004, B1.

67 S. Hamm, "Aperian: Helping Companies Bridge Cultures," *BusinessWeek*, September 8, 2008, 16.

68 W. W. Maddux, A. D. Galinsky, and C. T. Tadmor, "Be a Better Manager: Live Abroad," *Harvard Business Review*, September 9, 2010, accessed November 20, 20-10, from http://hbr.org/2010/09/be-a-better-manager-live-abroad/ar/1.

69 W. Arthur Jr., and W. Bennett Jr., "The International Assignee: The Relative Importance of Factors Perceived to Contribute to Success," *Personnel Psychology* 48 (1995): 99–114; and B. Cheng, "Home Truths about Foreign Postings; To Make an Overseas Assignment Work, Employers Need More Than an Eager Exec with a Suitcase. They Must Also Motivate the Staffer's Spouse," *Businessweek Online*, accessed March 20, 2009, from www.Businessweek.com/careers/content/jul2002/ca20020715_9110.htm.

70 D. Eschbach, G. Parker, and P. Stoeberl, "American Repatriate Employees' Retrospective Assessments of the Effects of Cross-Cultural Training on Their Adaptation to International Assignments," *International Journal of Human Resource Management* 12 (2001): 270–287; and "Culture Training: How to Prepare Your Expatriate Employees for Cross-Cultural Work Environments," *Managing Training & Development*, February 1, 2005.

71 S. P. Deshpande and C. Viswesvaran, "Is Cross-Cultural Training of Expatriate Managers Effective? A Meta-Analysis," *International Journal of Intercultural Relations* 16, no. 3 (1992): 295–310.

72 M. Srivastava, "Business Caught in Middle of India's Culture War," *Bloomberg Businessweek*, February 18, 2009, accessed September 10, 2010, from www.Businessweek.com/globalbiz/content/feb2009/gb20090218_783926_page_2.htm.

73 R. W. Boatler, "Study Abroad: Impact on Student World-mindedness," *Journal of Teaching in International Business* 2, no. 2 (1990): 13–17; R. W. Boatler, "Worldminded Attitude Change in a Study Abroad Program: Contact and Content Issues," *Journal of Teaching in International Business* 3, no. 4 (1992): 59–68; H. Lancaster, "Learning to Manage in a Global Workplace (You're on Your Own)," *Wall Street Journal*, June 2, 1998, B1; and D. L. Sampson and H. P. Smith, "A Scale to Measure Worldminded Attitudes," *Journal of Social Psychology* 45 (1957): 99–106.

Organizing

Chapter Eight

Designing Adaptive Organizations

© AP IMAGES/DARRAON CUMMING

Chapter 8 shows you the traditional organizational structure approach to organizational design (the vertical and horizontal configuration of departments, authority, and jobs within a company), as well as how contemporary organizations are redesigning their processes to better transform inputs into outputs.

Chapter Nine

Managing Teams

© ANTONY NETTLE/ALAMY

Chapter 9 reviews the advantages and disadvantages of teams and explores when companies should use them. You'll also read about the different types of work teams and the characteristics common to all teams, and learn practical steps to managing teams—team goals and priorities, and organizing, training, and compensating teams.

Chapter Ten

Managing Human Resources

JANI BRYSON/ISTOCKPHOTO.COM

Chapter 10 covers the key aspects of human resource systems: understanding human resource legislation; finding qualified employees; developing the knowledge, skills, and abilities of the workforce; implementing effective compensation practices; and effectively managing separation.

© DIZZO/ISTOCK PHOTO

Designing Adaptive Organizations

REEL TO REAL

Management Workplace is at Modern Shed.

SELF-ASSESSMENT

Do you prefer flexibility or structure? Do the Self-Assessment for this chapter in the book or online to find out how much of each is the right proportion for you.

ONLINE QUIZZES

Did you get it? Review the main concepts in the chapter by taking the online quizzes on CourseMate!

VIDEO QUIZZES

Get more out of the videos by taking the multimedia video quizzes online.

What Would You Do?

Eli Lilly Headquarters, Indianapolis, Indiana[1]

Tick-tock. After being named Lilly's new CEO, you sent each top executive a digital clock counting down the time to October 23, 2011, the day that Lilly's 20-year patent runs out on Zyprexa, a schizophrenia drug that generates $5 billion a year in revenue. On that day, Eli Lilly loses the exclusive right to sell Zyprexa, and other drug manufacturers will begin selling generic versions for much lower prices. Lilly has seven other major drugs that will fall off the "patent cliff" in the next seven years, and stands to lose 75 percent of its annual revenue if it doesn't generate new "blockbuster" drugs. Like a Hollywood studio, Lilly needs to keep coming up with "blockbusters" in order to sustain profitability and market share. Hence, the message inscribed on the clocks, "Do what we do," that is, discover and develop new drugs at Lilly. Tick-tock.

© AP IMAGES/DARRON CUMMING

Lilly isn't the only pharmaceutical company in this situation. Over the next three years, the entire industry will see half of its revenues fall off patent as three dozen major drugs become eligible to be sold as generics. When that happens, the company that held the patent typically sees sales of that drug drop by 80 percent. Pfizer will lose an estimated $13 billion a year when Lipitor, the top-selling statin, a cholesterol-lowering drug, loses its patent. By 2012, Merck will lose patent protection on its three top-selling drugs, Fosamax (osteoporosis), Singulair (asthma), and Cozaar (blood pressure), which account for 44 percent of its sales.

Unfortunately, Lilly has been here before, when its patent expired on Prozac, a drug for depression, taken daily by 40 million people. Then-CEO Sidney Taurel said, "The situation we had in the mid-1990s, of having 35 percent of our sales dependent on Prozac, won't repeat itself." Taurel took steps to energize Lilly's drug development by increasing the research and development (R & D) budget by 30 percent, hiring 700 new scientists, and instructing Lilly's 7,000 researchers to focus on drugs that could produce $500 million a year in sales.

This time, however, expanding headcount and increasing R & D budgets aren't options. With the potential loss of so much revenue, you had to lower costs. Accordingly, you laid off 5,500 workers and cut $1 billion in annual expenses. Les Funtleyder, an analyst at Miller Tabak & Co. in New York, said, "It's been another tough year for Big Pharma [cutting 37,000 jobs]. Lilly is not in this boat alone, by any means. But they probably have the biggest immediate challenge, because their patent cliff is so steep."

With those short-term steps behind you, the long-term challenge is to grow Lilly's drug pipeline. But how? You need to encourage faster, less expensive innovation, which is never easy. Some think that large budgets, centralized approval for allocating research dollars, and siloed research (where few know and understand what others in the company are working on) stifle innovation and slow the decision-making process. If that's the case, what might Lilly do internally to restructure itself to improve communication in product-development teams and speed up the entire drug-development process? Also, if the traditional company structure used by pharmaceutical firms (typically functional, product, or matrix structures) hasn't been

© DIZZO/ISTOCK PHOTO

successful at encouraging drug development, are there non-traditional organizational structures that Lilly could use to help to speed development and lower costs? Finally, to what extent should Lilly outsource parts of its drug-development process to outside vendors and companies? Because you risk creating new competitors with your own dollars when you outsource, a general guideline is to outsource only noncore business activities. But when you're a pharmaceutical firm, drug development is the core of your business.

Is there a way for Lilly to effectively outsource drug development that gets around those risks? Tick-tock. Tick-tock. The clock is running.

If you were Lilly's CEO, what would you do?

8-1 Designing Organizational Structures

No one builds a house without first looking at the design. Put a window there. Take out a wall here. Soon you've got the design you want. Only then do you start building. These days, the design of a company is just as important as the design of a house. Even successful companies, such as Lilly, must constantly examine their organizational design.

After reading this section, you'll be able to:

8-1 describe the difference between organizational structure and organizational process.

This chapter begins by reviewing the traditional organizational structure approach to organizational design. **Organizational structure** is the vertical and horizontal configuration of departments, authority, and jobs within a company. Organizational structure is concerned with questions such as Who reports to whom? and Who does what? and Where is the work done? For example, SONY CORPORATION OF AMERICA was headed by Chairman and CEO Howard Stringer, who was based in New York City. But Sony has a number of divisions to handle different sectors of the company's business, each headed by its own president or CEO. PlayStations are developed and managed in Foster City, California, by Sony Computer Entertainment, which is part of the Consumer Products and Services Group.[2] Sony camcorders, home theater equipment, LCD TVs, VAIO computers, Blu-ray players, and the Walkman are handled in San Diego by Sony Electronics. The Spider-Man films, *Jeopardy!* and *Seinfeld* were brought to you by Sony Pictures, a division of Sony Entertainment in Culver City, California, and the music of Foo Fighters, Pink, Shakira, and Avril Lavigne comes courtesy of Sony Music Entertainment in New York City.[3] Companies like Sony use organizational structure to set up departments and relationships among employees in order to make business happen. You can see Sony's organizational structure in Exhibit 8.1. In the first half of the chapter, you will learn about the traditional vertical and horizontal approaches to organizational structure, including departmentalization, organizational authority, and job design.

organizational structure
the vertical and horizontal configuration of departments, authority, and jobs within a company

Exhibit 8.1

Sony's Organizational Structure

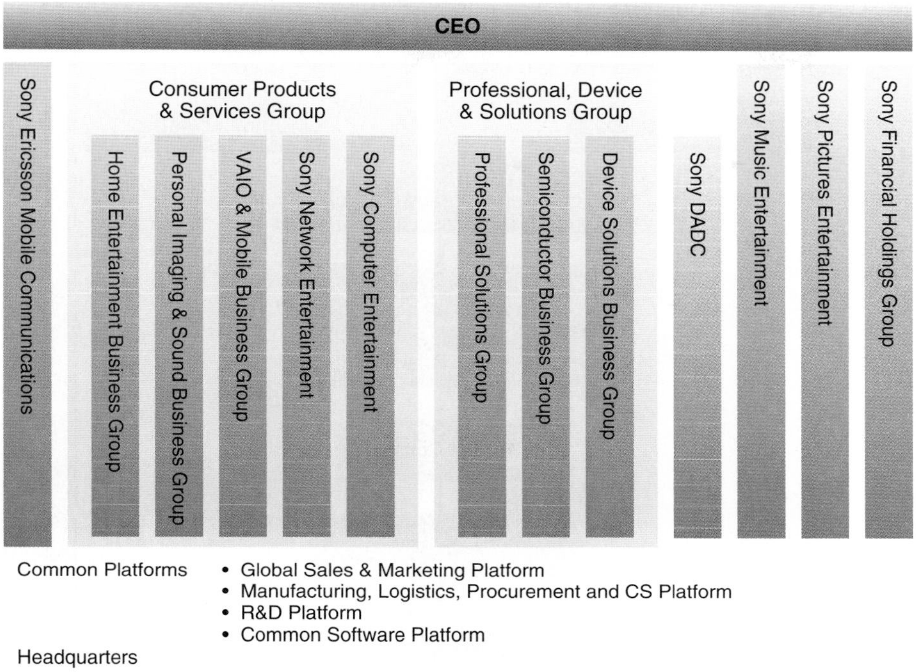

CEO

Sony Ericsson Mobile Communications

Consumer Products & Services Group
- Home Entertainment Business Group
- Personal Imaging & Sound Business Group
- VAIO & Mobile Business Group
- Sony Network Entertainment
- Sony Computer Entertainment

Professional, Device & Solutions Group
- Professional Solutions Group
- Semiconductor Business Group
- Device Solutions Business Group

Sony DADC

Sony Music Entertainment

Sony Pictures Entertainment

Sony Financial Holdings Group

Common Platforms
- Global Sales & Marketing Platform
- Manufacturing, Logistics, Procurement and CS Platform
- R&D Platform
- Common Software Platform

Headquarters

Source: Sony Organizational Chart available online at http://www.sony.net/SonyInfo/CorporateInfo/Data/ organization.html, [accessed 10 September 2008].

In the second half of the chapter, you will learn how contemporary organizations are becoming more adaptive by redesigning their internal and external processes. An **organizational process** is the collection of activities that transforms inputs into outputs that customers value.[4] Organizational process asks, How do things get done? For example, MICROSOFT uses basic internal and external processes, shown in Exhibit 8.2, to write computer software. The process starts when Microsoft gets feedback from customers through Internet newsgroups, e-mail, phone calls, or letters. This information helps Microsoft understand customers' needs and problems, and identify important software issues and needed changes and functions. Microsoft then rewrites the software, testing it internally at the company, and then externally through its beta-testing process, in which customers who volunteer or are selected by Microsoft give the company extensive feedback. The feedback is then used to make improvements to the software. The beta-testing process may take as long as a year and involve thousands of knowledgeable people. After final corrections are made to the software, the company distributes and sells it to customers. They start the process again by giving Microsoft more feedback. Indeed, Microsoft's advertising campaign for the kickoff of Windows 7, which was developed through extensive beta testing, was "I'm a PC, and Windows 7 was my idea."

organizational process
the collection of activities that transform inputs into outputs that customers value

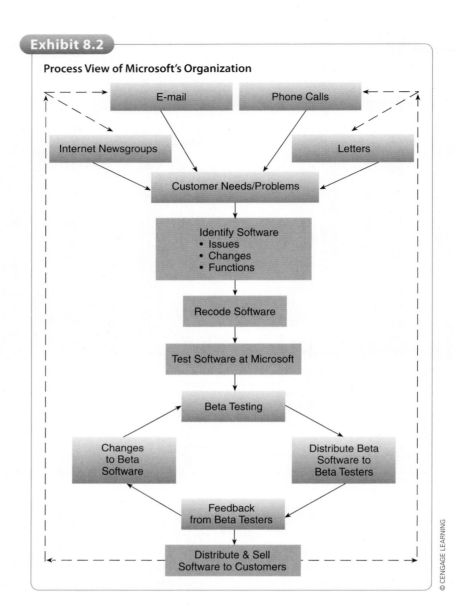

Exhibit 8.2

Process View of Microsoft's Organization

- E-mail
- Phone Calls
- Internet Newsgroups
- Letters
- Customer Needs/Problems
- Identify Software
  - Issues
  - Changes
  - Functions
- Recode Software
- Test Software at Microsoft
- Beta Testing
- Changes to Beta Software
- Distribute Beta Software to Beta Testers
- Feedback from Beta Testers
- Distribute & Sell Software to Customers

© CENGAGE LEARNING

This process view of Microsoft, which focuses on how things get done, is very different from the hierarchical view of Sony, which focuses on accountability, responsibility, and positions within the chain of command. In the second half of the chapter, you will learn how companies use reengineering, empowerment, and behavioral informality to redesign their internal organizational processes. The chapter ends with a discussion about the ways in which companies are redesigning their external processes, that is, how they are changing to improve their interactions with those outside the company. In that discussion, you will explore the basics of modular and virtual organizations.

Designing Organizational Structures

Like a successful architect, a successful company must constantly examine its organizational design. Organizational structure is the vertical and horizontal configuration of departments, authority, and jobs within a company. Organizational structure is concerned with questions such as Who reports to whom? and Who does what? and Where is the work done? That is, companies use organizational structure to set up departments and relationships among employees in order to make business happen. Contemporary organizations are becoming more adaptive by redesigning their internal and external processes. An organizational process is the collection of activities that transforms inputs into outputs that customers value. Organizational process asks, How do things get done?

8-2 Departmentalization

With 15,700 patents, 13,000 products, and 17 manufacturing facilities worldwide, BOSTON SCIENTIFIC is one of the largest medical device companies in the world. To improve company performance, Boston Scientific changed its organizational structure to focus on four product areas: the cardiology, rhythm and vascular group (for treating coronary artery disease, irregular heart rhythms, and vascular blockages), the endoscopy division (for treating the digestive system and the lungs), the urology and women's health division (for treating kidney and bladder stones, as well as incontinence), and the neuromodulation division (for treating chronic pain). Furthermore, the headquarters for international business will be eliminated. The presidents of the Japan group, Europe group, and the newly formed Emerging Markets Group (India, China, Brazil, Russia, Eastern Europe, and parts of the Middle East, Asia, and Latin America) will instead report directly to the CEO.[5] Why would a large company like Boston Scientific, with 25,000 employees and $7.8 billion in annual revenues, completely restructure its organizational design? What does it expect to gain from this change?

After reading this section, you'll have a better understanding of the importance of organizational structure because you should be able to:

8-2 describe the departmentalization approach to organizational structure.

Traditionally, organizational structures have been based on some form of departmentalization. **Departmentalization** is a method of subdividing work and workers into separate organizational units that take responsibility for completing particular tasks.[6] Bayer, a Germany-based company, has separate departments or divisions for health care, crop science, material science, and services.[7]

Traditionally, organizational structures have been created by departmentalizing work according to five methods: **8-2a functional, 8-2b product, 8-2c customer, 8-2d geographic,** and **8-2e matrix.**

departmentalization
subdividing work and workers into separate organizational units responsible for completing particular tasks

Exhibit 8.3

Functional Departmentalization

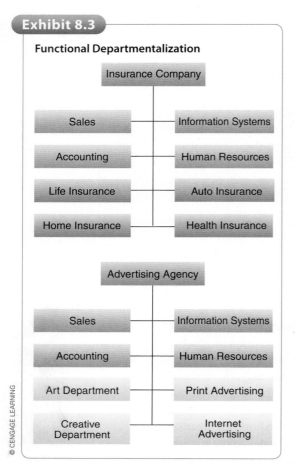

Insurance Company

Sales	Information Systems
Accounting	Human Resources
Life Insurance	Auto Insurance
Home Insurance	Health Insurance

Advertising Agency

Sales	Information Systems
Accounting	Human Resources
Art Department	Print Advertising
Creative Department	Internet Advertising

functional departmentalization
organizing work and workers into separate units responsible for particular business functions or areas of expertise

8-2a Functional Departmentalization

The most common organizational structure is functional departmentalization. Companies tend to use this structure when they are small or just starting out. **Functional departmentalization** organizes work and workers into separate units responsible for particular business functions or areas of expertise. A common functional structure might have individuals organized into accounting, sales, marketing, production, and human resources departments.

Not all functionally departmentalized companies have the same functions. The insurance company and the advertising agency shown in Exhibit 8.3 both have sales, accounting, human resources, and information systems departments, as indicated by the green boxes. The blue and khaki boxes indicate the functions that are different. As would be expected, the insurance company has separate departments for life, auto, home, and health insurance. The advertising agency has departments for artwork, creative work, print advertising, and Internet advertising. So the departments in a company that uses functional structure depend in part on the business or industry a company is in.

Functional departmentalization has some advantages. First, it allows work to be done by highly qualified specialists. Although the accountants in the accounting department take responsibility for producing accurate revenue and expense figures, the engineers in R & D can focus their efforts on designing a product that is reliable and simple to manufacture. Second, it lowers costs by reducing duplication. When the engineers in R & D come up with a fantastic new product, they don't have to worry about creating an aggressive advertising campaign to sell it. That task belongs to the advertising experts and sales representatives in marketing. Third, with everyone in the same department having similar work experience or training, communication and coordination are less problematic for departmental managers.

At the same time, functional departmentalization has a number of disadvantages. To start, cross-department coordination can be difficult. Managers and employees are often more interested in doing what's right for their function than in doing what's right for the entire organization. A good example is the traditional conflict between marketing and manufacturing. Marketing typically pushes for spending more money to make more products with more capabilities to meet customer needs. By contrast, manufacturing pushes for fewer products with simpler designs so that manufacturing facilities can ship finished products on time and keep costs within expense budgets. As companies grow, functional departmentalization may also lead to slower decision making and produce managers and workers with narrow experience and expertise.

8-2b Product Departmentalization

Product departmentalization organizes work and workers into separate units responsible for producing particular products or services. Exhibit 8.4 shows the product departmentalization structure used by UNITED TECHNOLOGIES CORPORATION (UTC), which is organized along six different product lines: Carrier (heating, ventilating, and air conditioning), Hamilton Sundstrand (aircraft electrical power generation and distribution systems), Otis (design, manufacture, installation, maintenance, and servicing of elevators and escalators), Pratt & Whitney (commercial and military jet aircraft engines), Sikorsky (military and commercial helicopters), and UTC Fire & Security (fire safety and security products and services).[8]

One of the advantages of product departmentalization is that, like functional departmentalization, it allows managers and workers to specialize in one area of expertise. Unlike the narrow expertise and experiences in functional departmentalization, however, managers and workers develop a broader set of experiences and expertise related to an entire product line. Likewise, product departmentalization makes it easier for top managers to assess work-unit performance. Because of the clear separation of their six different product divisions, United Technologies' top managers can easily compare the performance of the Otis elevators division and the Pratt & Whitney aircraft engines. The divisions had similar revenues—almost $11.8 billion for Otis and $12.6 billion for Pratt & Whitney—but Otis had a profit of $2.4 billion (a 20.3% profit margin) compared with just $1.8 billion (a 14.3% profit margin) for Pratt & Whitney.[9] Finally, decision making should be faster because managers and workers are responsible for the entire product line rather than for separate functional departments; in other words, there are fewer conflicts compared to functional departmentalization.

The primary disadvantage of product departmentalization is duplication. You can see in Exhibit 8.4 that UTC's Otis elevators and Pratt

product departmentalization organizing work and workers into separate units responsible for producing particular products or services

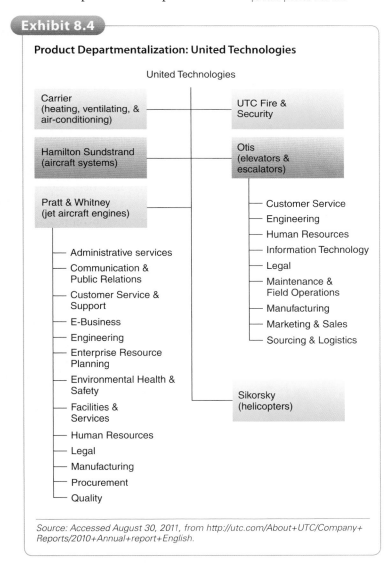

Exhibit 8.4

Product Departmentalization: United Technologies

United Technologies

- Carrier (heating, ventilating, & air-conditioning)
- Hamilton Sundstrand (aircraft systems)
- Pratt & Whitney (jet aircraft engines)
  - Administrative services
  - Communication & Public Relations
  - Customer Service & Support
  - E-Business
  - Engineering
  - Enterprise Resource Planning
  - Environmental Health & Safety
  - Facilities & Services
  - Human Resources
  - Legal
  - Manufacturing
  - Procurement
  - Quality
- UTC Fire & Security
- Otis (elevators & escalators)
  - Customer Service
  - Engineering
  - Human Resources
  - Information Technology
  - Legal
  - Maintenance & Field Operations
  - Manufacturing
  - Marketing & Sales
  - Sourcing & Logistics
- Sikorsky (helicopters)

Source: Accessed August 30, 2011, from http://utc.com/About+UTC/Company+Reports/2010+Annual+report+English.

The S-92 helicopter built by UTC's Sikorsky helicopter division.

& Whitney aircraft engines divisions both have customer service, engineering, human resources, legal, manufacturing, and procurement (similar to sourcing and logistics) departments. Duplication like this often results in higher costs. If United Technologies were instead organized by function, one lawyer could handle matters related to both elevators and aircraft engines rather than working on only one or the other.

A second disadvantage is the challenge of coordinating across the different product departments. United Technologies would probably have difficulty standardizing its policies and procedures in product departments as different as the Carrier (heating, ventilating, and air conditioning) and Sikorsky (military and commercial helicopters) divisions.

8-2c Customer Departmentalization

Customer departmentalization organizes work and workers into separate units responsible for particular kinds of customers. For example, as Exhibit 8.5 shows, *Swisscom AG*, Switzerland's leading telecommunications provider, is organized into departments by type of customer: residential, small- and medium-sized businesses, larger corporations, and network and IT customers.[10]

The primary advantage of customer departmentalization is that it focuses the organization on customer needs rather than on products or business functions. Furthermore, creating separate departments to serve specific kinds of customers allows companies to specialize and adapt their products and services to customer needs and problems. The primary disadvantage of customer departmentalization is that, like product departmentalization, it leads to duplication of resources. It can be difficult to achieve coordination across different customer departments, as is also the case with product departmentalization. Finally, the emphasis on meeting customers' needs may lead workers to make decisions that please customers but hurt the business.

8-2d Geographic Departmentalization

customer departmentalization
organizing work and workers into separate units responsible for particular kinds of customers

geographic departmentalization
organizing work and workers into separate units responsible for doing business in particular geographic areas

Geographic departmentalization organizes work and workers into separate units responsible for doing business in particular geographic areas. Exhibit 8.6 shows the geographic departmentalization used by *AB InBev*, the largest beer brewer in the world. AB InBev has 133 brewing facilities in 23 countries, 114,000 employees, and annual revenue of $36.3 billion.[11]

As shown in Exhibit 8.6, AB InBev has operations in six regional groups, each with a regional headquarters: North America, Latin America North, Latin America South, Western Europe, Central and Eastern Europe, and Asia Pacific.

Exhibit 8.5

Customer Departmentalization: Swisscom AG

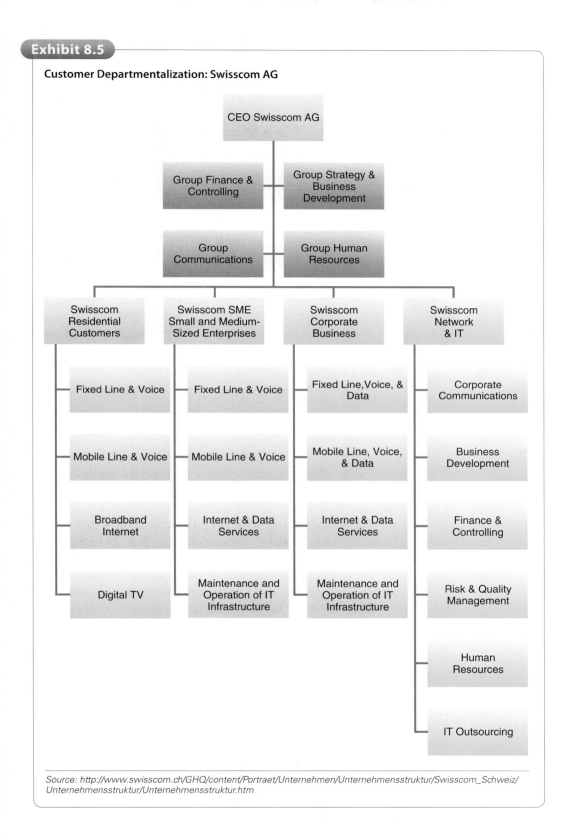

Source: http://www.swisscom.ch/GHQ/content/Portraet/Unternehmen/Unternehmensstruktur/Swisscom_Schweiz/
Unternehmensstruktur/Unternehmensstruktur.htm

Exhibit 8.6

Geographic Departmentalization: AB InBev Company

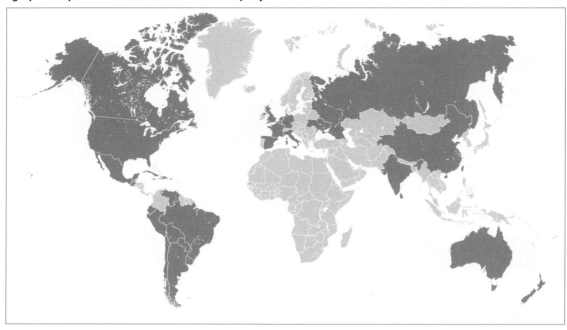

Source: http://www.ab-inbev.com/go/investors/overview/anheuser_busch_inbev_company_profile.cfm.

Each of these regions would be a sizable company by itself. The smallest region, Asia Pacific, for instance, sold 55.6 million hectoliters of beer for annual revenue of $2.3 billion.

The primary advantage of geographic departmentalization is that it helps companies respond to the demands of different markets. This can be especially important when the company sells in different countries. For example, although AB InBev has three global brands (Budweiser, Stella Artois, and Beck's) sold worldwide and two (Hoegaarden and Leffe) sold in multiple countries, most of its brands are local. You'll find the Antarctica and Bohemia brands in Brazil, the Bell-Vue and Jupiler brands in Belgium, and the Sibirskaya Korona and T. Tolstiak brands in Russia.[12] Another advantage is that geographic departmentalization can reduce costs by locating unique organizational resources closer to customers. For instance, it is cheaper in the long run for AB InBev to build bottling plants in each region than to, for example, transport beer to Belgium, after it has been brewed and bottled in Russia.[13]

The primary disadvantage of geographic departmentalization is that it can lead to duplication of resources. For example, while it may be necessary to adapt products and marketing to different geographic locations, it's doubtful that AB InBev needs significantly different inventory tracking systems from location to location. Also, even more than with the other forms of departmentalization, it can be difficult to coordinate departments that are literally thousands of miles from each other and whose managers have very limited contact with each other.

Exhibit 8.7

Matrix Departmentalization: Procter & Gamble

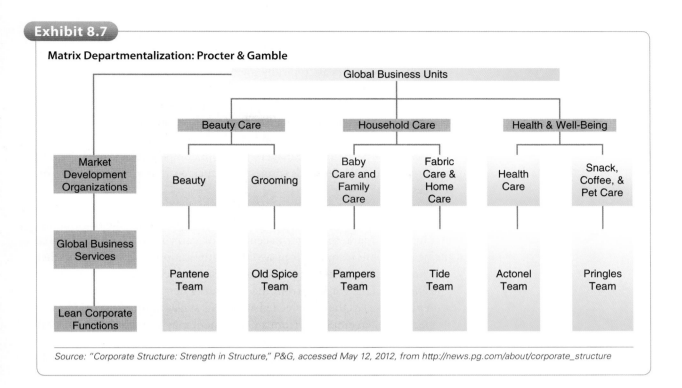

Source: "Corporate Structure: Strength in Structure," P&G, accessed May 12, 2012, from http://news.pg.com/about/corporate_structure

8-2e Matrix Departmentalization

Matrix departmentalization is a hybrid structure in which two or more forms of departmentalization are used together. The most common matrix combines the product and functional forms of departmentalization, but other forms may also be used. Exhibit 8.7 shows the matrix structure used by *Procter & Gamble*, which has 127,000 employees working in 80 different countries.[14] Across the top of Exhibit 8.7, you can see that the company uses a product unit structure where it groups its billion-dollar brands into three global business units, each of which has two segments. The left side of the figure, however, shows that the company is also using a functional structure based on three functions: market development, global business services, and lean corporate functions.[15]

The boxes in the figure represent the matrix structure, created by the combination of the product and functional structures. For example, the Pantene Team (Pantene is a set of hair care products within the beauty segment of the beauty-care global-business unit) would work with market development to adapt and sell Pantene products worldwide, use global-business services to work with suppliers and keep costs down, and then rely on corporate functions for assistance in hiring employees, billing customers, and paying suppliers.

Several things distinguish matrix departmentalization from the other traditional forms of departmentalization.[16] First, most employees report to two bosses, one from each core part of the matrix. For example, as shown in Exhibit 8.7, a manager on the Pampers team responsible for marketing would report to a boss in the baby-care and family-care segment of the household-care global-business unit as well as to a boss in the market-development unit.

matrix departmentalization
a hybrid organizational structure in which two or more forms of departmentalization, most often product and functional, are used together

Second, by virtue of their hybrid design, matrix structures lead to much more cross-functional interaction than other forms of departmentalization. In fact, although matrix workers are typically members of only one functional department (based on their work experience and expertise), they are also commonly members of several ongoing project, product, or customer groups. Third, because of the high level of cross-functional interaction, matrix departmentalization requires significant coordination between managers in the different parts of the matrix. In particular, managers have the complex job of tracking and managing the multiple demands (project, product, customer, or functional) on employees' time.

The primary advantage of matrix departmentalization is that it allows companies to manage in an efficient manner large, complex tasks like researching, developing, and marketing pharmaceuticals or carrying out complex global businesses. Efficiency comes from avoiding duplication. For example, rather than having an entire marketing function for each project, the company simply assigns and reassigns workers from the marketing department (or market development at P&G) as they are needed at various stages of product completion. More specifically, an employee from a department may simultaneously be part of five different ongoing projects but may be actively completing work on only a few projects at a time. Another advantage is the pool of resources available to carry out large, complex tasks. Because of the ability to pull in expert help from all the functional areas of the company quickly, matrix project managers have a much more diverse set of expertise and experience at their disposal than managers in the other forms of departmentalization.

The primary disadvantage of matrix departmentalization is the high level of coordination required to manage the complexity involved in running large, ongoing projects at various levels of completion. Matrix structures are notorious for confusion and conflict between project bosses in different parts of the matrix. Disagreements or misunderstandings about schedules, budgets, available resources, and the availability of employees with particular functional expertise are common in matrix structures. Another disadvantage is that matrix structures require much more management skill than the other forms of departmentalization.

Because of these problems, many matrix structures evolve from a **simple matrix**, in which managers in different parts of the matrix negotiate conflicts and resources directly, to a **complex matrix**, in which specialized matrix managers and departments are added to the organizational structure. In a complex matrix, managers from different parts of the matrix might report to the same matrix manager, who helps them sort out conflicts and problems.

Sometimes, however, even these steps aren't enough to alleviate the problems that can occur in matrix structures. Europe-based *UNILEVER* is the maker and marketer of such well-known products as Dove soap, Lipton teas, and Lawry's seasonings. Unilever was run using a complex matrix structure. The company even had dual headquarters in Rotterdam, the Netherlands, and London, England. The confusion and conflict associated with having two sets of management located in two headquarters were so great that Unilever has now switched to just one CEO and one headquarters and has moved to a simpler structure.[17]

simple matrix
a form of matrix departmentalization in which managers in different parts of the matrix negotiate conflicts and resources

complex matrix
a form of matrix departmentalization in which managers in different parts of the matrix report to matrix managers, who help them sort out conflicts and problems

Departmentalization

The five traditional departmental structures are functional, product, customer, geographic, and matrix. Functional departmentalization is based on the different business functions or expertise used to run a business. Product departmentalization is organized according to the different products or services a company sells. Customer departmentalization focuses its divisions on the different kinds of customers a company has. Geographic departmentalization is based on the different geographic areas or markets in which the company does business. Matrix departmentalization is a hybrid form that combines two or more forms of departmentalization, the most common being the product and functional forms. There is no single best departmental structure. Each structure has advantages and disadvantages.

8-3 Organizational Authority

The second part of traditional organizational structures is authority.

After reading this section, you should be able to:

8-3 explain organizational authority.

Authority is the right to give commands, take action, and make decisions to achieve organizational objectives.[18]

Traditionally, organizational authority has been characterized by the following dimensions: **8-3a chain of command, 8-3b line versus staff authority, 8-3c delegation of authority,** and **8-3d degree of centralization.**

8-3a Chain of Command

Turn back a few pages to Sony's organizational chart in Exhibit 8.1. If you place your finger on any position in the chart, say, VAIO & Mobile Business Group (under Consumer Products & Services Group), you can visualize the line upward to the company's CEO, Howard Stringer. This line, which vertically connects every job in the company to higher levels of management, represents the chain of command. The **chain of command** is the vertical line of authority that clarifies who reports to whom throughout the organization. People higher in the chain of command have the right, *if they so choose*, to give commands, take action, and make decisions concerning activities occurring anywhere below them in the chain. In the following discussion about delegation and decentralization, you will learn that managers don't always choose to exercise their authority directly.[19]

One of the key assumptions underlying the chain of command is **unity of command,** which means that workers should report to just one boss.[20] In practical terms, this means that only one person can be in charge at a time. Matrix organizations, in which employees have two bosses, automatically violate this principle. This is one of the primary reasons that matrix organizations are difficult to manage. Unity of command serves an important purpose: to prevent the

authority
the right to give commands, take action, and make decisions to achieve organizational objectives

chain of command
the vertical line of authority that clarifies who reports to whom throughout the organization

unity of command
a management principle that workers should report to just one boss

confusion that might arise when an employee receives conflicting commands from two different bosses. Robert Steinberg and John Scharffenberger founded SCHARFFEN BERGER CHOCOLATE MAKER, a producer of high-end, gourmet chocolate. Early on, they served as coleaders, which hurt company performance because subordinates weren't sure who reported to whom. And because there wasn't one clear vision of how the company would operate, employees were often confused about priorities and goals. Eventually, Scharffenberger bought out his partner. Revenues reached $10 million in just a few years and the company proved so successful that it was sold to Hershey for $50 million.[21]

8-3b Line versus Staff Authority

A second dimension of authority is the distinction between line and staff authority. **Line authority** is the right to command immediate subordinates in the chain of command. For example, Sony's CEO has line authority over the head of Sony's Professional, Device & Solutions Group, which includes Sony's Semiconductor Business Group. Stringer can issue orders to that division president and expect them to be carried out. In turn, the head of Sony Professional, Device & Solutions can issue orders to his subordinates and expect them to be carried out. **Staff authority** is the right to *advise*, but not command, others who are not subordinates in the chain of command. For example, a manager in human resources at Sony might advise the manager in charge of Sony's Home Entertainment Business Group on a hiring decision but cannot give orders to hire a certain applicant.

The terms "line" and "staff" are also used to describe different functions within the organization. A **line function** is an activity that contributes directly to creating or selling the company's products. So, for example, activities that take place within the manufacturing and marketing departments would be considered line functions. A **staff function**, such as accounting, human resources, or legal services, does not contribute directly to creating or selling the company's products, but instead supports line activities. For example, marketing managers might consult with the legal staff to make sure the wording of a particular advertisement is legal.

8-3c Delegation of Authority

Managers can exercise their authority directly by completing tasks themselves, or they can choose to pass on some of their authority to subordinates. **Delegation of authority** is the assignment of direct authority and responsibility to a subordinate to complete tasks for which the manager is normally responsible.

When a manager delegates work, three transfers occur, as illustrated in Exhibit 8.8. First, the manager transfers full responsibility for the assignment to the subordinate. Many managers, however, find giving up full responsibility somewhat difficult. However, one CEO says, "If you can delegate a task to somebody who can do it 75 percent to 80 percent as

---

line authority
the right to command immediate subordinates in the chain of command

staff authority
the right to advise, but not command, others who are not subordinates in the chain of command

line function
an activity that contributes directly to creating or selling the company's products

staff function
an activity that does not contribute directly to creating or selling the company's products, but instead supports line activities

delegation of authority
the assignment of direct authority and responsibility to a subordinate to complete tasks for which the manager is normally responsible

---

Exhibit 8.8

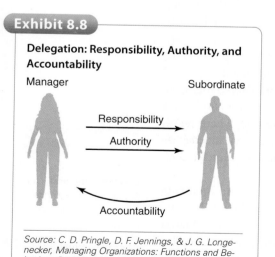

Delegation: Responsibility, Authority, and Accountability

Manager   Subordinate

Responsibility →

Authority →

← Accountability

Source: C. D. Pringle, D. F. Jennings, & J. G. Longenecker, Managing Organizations: Functions and Behaviors © 1990. Adapted by permission of Pearson Education, Inc., Upper Saddle River, NJ.

well as you can today, you delegate it immediately." Why? The reason is that many tasks don't need to be done perfectly; they just need to be *done*. And delegating tasks that someone else can do frees managers to assume other important responsibilities. Delegating authority can generate a related problem: micromanaging. Sometimes managers delegate, only to interfere later with how the employee is performing the task. But delegating full responsibility means that the employee—not the manager—is now completely responsible for task completion.

The second transfer that occurs with delegation is that the manager gives the subordinate full authority over the budget, resources, and personnel needed to do the job. To do the job effectively, subordinates must have the same tools and information at their disposal that managers had when they were responsible for the same task. In other words, for delegation to work, delegated authority must be commensurate with delegated responsibility. The third transfer that occurs with delegation is the transfer of accountability. The subordinate now has the authority and responsibility to do the job and, in return, is accountable for getting the job done. In other words, managers delegate their managerial authority and responsibility to subordinates in exchange for results. Exhibit 8.9 gives some tips on how to be an effective delegator.

Exhibit 8.9

How to Be a More Effective Delegator

1. Trust your staff to do a good job. Recognize that others have the talent and ability to complete projects.
2. Avoid seeking perfection. Establish a standard of quality and provide a time frame for reaching it.
3. Give effective job instructions. Make sure employees have enough information to complete the job successfully.
4. Know your true interests. Delegation is difficult for some people who actually prefer doing the work themselves rather than managing it.
5. Follow up on progress. Build in checkpoints to help identify potential problems.
6. Praise the efforts of your staff
7. Don't wait to the last minute to delegate. Avoid crisis management by routinely delegating work.
8. Ask questions, expect answers, and assist employees to help them complete the work assignments as expected.
9. Provide the resources you would expect if you were doing an assignment yourself.
10. Delegate to the lowest possible level to make the best possible use of organizational resources, energy, and knowledge.

Source: S. B. Wilton, "Are You an Effective Delegator?" Female Executive, 1 November, 1994, 19.

8-3d Degree of Centralization

If you've ever called a company's toll-free number with a complaint or a special request and been told by the customer service representative, "I'll have to ask my manager" or "I'm not authorized to do that," you know that centralization of authority exists in that company. **Centralization of authority** is the location of most authority at the upper levels of the organization. In a centralized organization, managers make most decisions, even the relatively small ones. That's why the customer service representative you called couldn't make a decision without first asking the manager.

If you are lucky, however, you may have talked to a customer service representative at another company who said, "I can take care of that for you right now." In other words, the person was able to handle your problem without any input from or consultation with management. **Decentralization** is the location

centralization of authority
the location of most authority at the upper levels of the organization

decentralization
the location of a significant amount of authority in the lower levels of the organization

of a significant amount of authority in the lower levels of the organization. An organization is decentralized if it has a high degree of delegation at all levels. In a decentralized organization, workers closest to problems are authorized to make the decisions necessary to solve the problems on their own.

Decentralization has a number of advantages. It develops employee capabilities throughout the company and leads to faster decision making and more satisfied customers and employees. Furthermore, a study of 1,000 large companies found that companies with a high degree of decentralization outperformed those with a low degree of decentralization in terms of return on assets (6.9% vs. 4.7%), return on investment (14.6% vs. 9.0%), return on equity (22.8% vs. 16.6%), and return on sales (10.3% vs. 6.3%). Surprisingly, the same study found that few large companies actually are decentralized. Specifically, only 31 percent of employees in these 1,000 companies were responsible for recommending improvements to management. Overall, just 10 percent of employees received the training and information needed to support a truly decentralized approach to management.[22]

With results like these, the key question is no longer *whether* companies should decentralize, but *where* they should decentralize. One rule of thumb is to stay centralized where standardization is important and to decentralize where standardization is unimportant. **Standardization** is solving problems by consistently applying the same rules, procedures, and processes.

REVIEW 8-3
. . . .

Organizational Authority

Organizational authority is determined by the chain of command, line versus staff authority, delegation, and the degree of centralization in a company. The chain of command vertically connects every job in the company to higher levels of management and makes clear who reports to whom. Managers have line authority to command employees below them in the chain of command but have only staff, or advisory, authority over employees not below them in the chain of command. Managers delegate authority by transferring to subordinates the authority and responsibility needed to do a task; in exchange, subordinates become accountable for task completion. In centralized companies, most authority to make decisions lies with managers in the upper levels of the company. In decentralized companies, much of the authority is delegated to the workers closest to problems, workers who can then make the decisions necessary for solving the problems themselves. Centralization works best for tasks that require standardized decision making. When standardization isn't important, decentralization can lead to faster decisions, greater employee and customer satisfaction, and significantly better financial performance.

8-4 Job Design

standardization
solving problems by consistently applying the same rules, procedures, and processes

Imagine that McDonald's decided to pay $75,000 a year to its drive-through window cashiers. That's $75,000 for saying, "Welcome to McDonald's. May I have your order please?" Would you take the job? Sure you would. Work a couple of years; make a hundred and fifty grand. Why not? Let's assume, however, that to get this salary, you have to be a full-time McDonald's drive-through window cashier for the next 10 years. Would you still take the job? Just imagine, 40 to 60 times an hour, you'd repeat the same basic process:

1. "Welcome to McDonald's. May I have your order please?"
2. Listen to the order. Repeat it for accuracy. State the total cost. "Please drive to the second window."
3. Take the money. Make change.
4. Give customers drinks, straws, and napkins.
5. Give customers food.
6. "Thank you for coming to McDonald's."

Could you stand to do the same simple tasks an average of 50 times per hour, 400 times per day, 2,000 times per week, 8,000 times per month? Few can. Fast-food workers rarely stay on the job more than six months. Indeed, McDonald's and other fast-food restaurants have well over 100 percent employee turnover each year.[23]

After reading this section, you should be able to:

8-4 discuss the different methods for job design.

In this next section, you will learn about **job design**—the number, kind, and variety of tasks that individual workers perform in doing their jobs.

You will learn **8-4a why companies continue to use specialized jobs like the McDonald's drive-through job** and **8-4b how job rotation, job enlargement, job enrichment,** and **8-4c the job characteristics model** are being used to overcome the problems associated with job specialization.

8-4a Job Specialization

Job specialization occurs when a job comprises a small part of a larger task or process. Specialized jobs are characterized by simple, easy-to-learn steps, low variety, and high repetition, like the McDonald's drive-through window job just described. One of the clear disadvantages of specialized jobs is that, being so easy to learn, they quickly become boring. This, in turn, can lead to low job satisfaction and high absenteeism and employee turnover, all of which are very costly to organizations.

Why, then, do companies continue to create and use specialized jobs? The primary reason is that specialized jobs are very economical. Once a job has been specialized, it takes little time to learn and master. Consequently, when experienced workers quit or are absent, the company can replace them with new employees and lose little productivity. For example, next time you're at McDonald's, notice the pictures of the food on the cash registers. These pictures make it easy for McDonald's trainees to quickly learn to take orders. Likewise, to simplify and speed operations, the drink dispensers behind the counter are set to automatically fill drink cups. Put a medium cup below the dispenser. Punch the medium drink button. The soft-drink machine then fills the cup to within a half-inch of the top, while that same worker goes to get your fries. At

job design
the number, kind, and variety of tasks that individual workers perform in doing their jobs

job specialization
a job composed of a small part of a larger task or process

McDonald's, every task has been simplified in this way. Because the work is designed to be simple, wages can remain low because it isn't necessary to pay high salaries to attract highly experienced, educated, or trained workers.

8-4b Job Rotation, Enlargement, and Enrichment

Because of the efficiency of specialized jobs, companies are often reluctant to eliminate them. Consequently, job-redesign efforts have focused on modifying jobs to keep the benefits of specialized jobs while reducing their obvious costs and disadvantages. Three methods—job rotation, job enlargement, and job enrichment—have been used to try to improve specialized jobs.[24]

In factory work or even some office jobs, many workers perform the same task all day long. If you attach side mirrors in an auto factory, you probably complete this task 45 to 60 times an hour. If you work as the cashier at a grocery store, you check out a different customer every two to three minutes. And if you work as an office receptionist, you may answer and direct phone calls up to 200 times an hour. **Job rotation** attempts to overcome the disadvantages of job specialization by periodically moving workers from one specialized job to another to give them more variety and the opportunity to use different skills. For example, an office receptionist who does nothing but answer phones could be systematically rotated to a different job, such as typing, filing, or data entry, every day or two. Because employees simply switch from one specialized job to another, job rotation allows companies to retain the economic benefits of specialized work. At the same time, the greater variety of tasks makes the work less boring and more satisfying for workers.

Another way to counter the disadvantages of specialization is to enlarge the job. **Job enlargement** increases the number of different tasks that a worker performs within one particular job. Instead of being assigned just one task, workers with enlarged jobs are given several tasks to perform. For example, an enlarged "mirror attacher" job might include attaching the mirror, checking to see that the mirror's power adjustment controls work, and then cleaning the mirror's surface. Though job enlargement increases variety, many workers report feeling more stress when their jobs are enlarged. Consequently, many workers view enlarged jobs as simply more work, especially if they are not given additional time to complete the additional tasks.

Job enrichment attempts to overcome the deficiencies in specialized work by increasing the number of tasks *and* by giving workers the authority and control to make meaningful decisions about their work.[25] At AES, an independent power company that sells electricity to public utilities and steam (for power) to industrial organizations, workers are given an extraordinary level of authority and control. For example, with his hands still blackened after unloading coal from a barge, employee Jeff Hatch calls a broker to determine which Treasury bills the company should buy to maximize the short-term return on its available cash. Hatch asks his broker, "What kind of rate can you give me for $10 million at 30 days?" When the broker tells him, "6.09 percent," he responds, "But I just got a 6.13 percent quote from Chase."[26] Indeed, ordinary plant technicians at AES are given budgets worth several million dollars and are trusted to purchase everything from mops to gas turbines.

job rotation
periodically moving workers from one specialized job to another to give them more variety and the opportunity to use different skills

job enlargement
increasing the number of different tasks that a worker performs within one particular job

job enrichment
increasing the number of tasks in a particular job and giving workers the authority and control to make meaningful decisions about their work

8-4c Job Characteristics Model

In contrast to job rotation, job enlargement, and job enrichment, which focus on providing variety in job tasks, the **Job Characteristics Model (JCM)** is an approach to job redesign that seeks to formulate jobs in ways that motivate workers and lead to positive work outcomes.[27]

As shown in Exhibit 8.10, the primary goal of the model is to create jobs that result in positive personal and work outcomes, such as internal work motivation, satisfaction with one's job, and work effectiveness. Of these, the central concern of the JCM is internal motivation. **Internal motivation** is motivation that comes from the job itself rather than from outside rewards such as a raise or praise from the boss. If workers feel that performing the job well is itself rewarding, then the job has internal motivation. Statements such as "I get a nice sense of accomplishment" or "I feel good about myself and what I'm producing" are examples of internal motivation.

Moving to the left in Exhibit 8.10, you can see that the JCM specifies three critical psychological states that must occur for work to be internally motivating. First, workers must *experience the work as meaningful*; that is, they must view their job as being important. Second, they must *experience responsibility*

Job Characteristics Model (JCM)
an approach to job redesign that seeks to formulate jobs in ways that motivate workers and lead to positive work outcomes

internal motivation
motivation that comes from the job itself rather than from outside rewards

---

Exhibit 8.10

Job Characteristics Model

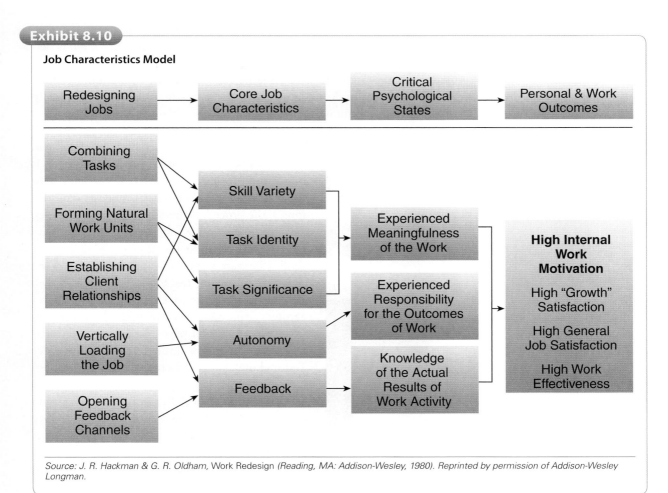

Source: J. R. Hackman & G. R. Oldham, Work Redesign (Reading, MA: Addison-Wesley, 1980). Reprinted by permission of Addison-Wesley Longman.

for work outcomes—they must feel personally responsible for the work being done well. Third, workers must have *knowledge of results*; that is, they must know how well they are performing their jobs. All three critical psychological states must occur for work to be internally motivating.

Let's return to our grocery store cashier. Cashiers usually have knowledge of results. When you're slow, your checkout line grows long. If you make a mistake, customers point it out. Likewise, cashiers experience responsibility for work outcomes. At the end of the day, the register is totaled, the money is counted, and, if the money in the till is less than what's recorded in the register, most stores make the cashier pay the difference. Nonetheless, despite knowing the results and experiencing responsibility for work outcomes, most grocery store cashiers (at least where I shop) aren't internally motivated because they don't experience the work as meaningful. With scanners, it takes little skill to learn or do the job. Anyone can do it. In addition, cashiers have few decisions to make, and the job is highly repetitive.

What kinds of jobs produce the three critical psychological states? Moving another step to the left in Exhibit 8.10, you can see that these psychological states arise from jobs that are strong on five core job characteristics: skill variety, task identity, task significance, autonomy, and feedback. **Skill variety** is the number of different activities performed in a job. **Task identity** is the degree to which a job, from beginning to end, requires completion of a whole and identifiable piece of work. **Task significance** is the degree to which a job is perceived to have a substantial impact on others inside or outside the organization. **Autonomy** is the degree to which a job gives workers the discretion, freedom, and independence to decide how and when to accomplish the work. Finally, **feedback** is the amount of information the job provides to workers about their work performance.

To illustrate how the core job characteristics work together, let's use them to assess more thoroughly why the McDonald's drive-through window job is not particularly satisfying or motivating. To start, skill variety is low. Except for the size of an order or special requests ("no onions"), the process is the same for each customer. At best, task identity is moderate. Although you take the order, handle the money, and deliver the food, others are responsible for a larger part of the process—preparing the food. Task identity will be even lower if the McDonald's has two drive-through windows, because each drive-through window worker will have an even more specialized task. The first is limited to taking the order and making change, whereas the second just delivers the food.

Task significance, the impact you have on others, is probably low. Autonomy is also very low: McDonald's has strict rules about dress, cleanliness, and procedures. But the job does provide immediate feedback such as positive and negative customer comments, car horns honking,

skill variety
the number of different activities performed in a job

task identity
the degree to which a job, from beginning to end, requires the completion of a whole and identifiable piece of work

task significance
the degree to which a job is perceived to have a substantial impact on others inside or outside the organization

autonomy
the degree to which a job gives workers the discretion, freedom, and independence to decide how and when to accomplish the job

feedback
the amount of information the job provides to workers about their work performance

This two-window, multi-lane drive-through in Monroe, Washington, is typical of McDonald's (and other fast-food restaurants) around the country. But even though this way of organizing the work is extremely efficient, it can be less than stimulating for employees.

what *really* works

The Job Characteristics Model: Making Jobs More Interesting and Motivating

Think of the worst job you ever had. Was it factory work where you repeated the same task every few minutes? Was it an office job requiring a lot of meaningless paperwork? Or was it a job so specialized that it took no effort or thinking whatsoever to do?

The job characteristics model reviewed in this chapter suggests that workers will be more motivated or satisfied with their work if their jobs have greater task identity, task significance, skill variety, autonomy, and feedback. Eighty-four studies, with a combined total of 22,472 participants, found that, on average, these core job characteristics make jobs more satisfying for most workers. In addition, jobs rich with the five core job characteristics are especially satisfying for workers who possess an individual characteristic called *growth need strength*. Read on to see how well the JCM really increases job satisfaction and reduces workplace absenteeism.

Job Satisfaction

There is a 66 percent chance that workers will be more satisfied with their work when their jobs have task identity, the chance to complete an entire job from beginning to end, than when they don't.

On average, there is a 69 percent chance that workers will be more satisfied with their work when their jobs have task significance—a substantial impact on others—than when they don't.

On average, there is a 70 percent chance that workers will be more satisfied with their work when their jobs have skill variety—a variety of activities, skills, and talents—than when they don't.

On average, there is a 73 percent chance that workers will be more satisfied with their work when their jobs have autonomy—the discretion to decide how and when to accomplish the work—than when they don't.

On average, there is a 70 percent chance that workers will be more satisfied with their work when their jobs provide feedback—information about their work performance—than when they don't.

These statistics indicate that, on average, the JCM has, at worst, a 66 percent chance of improving workers' job satisfaction. In all, this is impressive evidence that the model works. In general, you can expect these results when redesigning jobs based on the model.

We can be more accurate about the effects of the JCM, however, if we split workers into two groups: those with high growth need strength and those with low growth need strength.

Growth need strength is the need or desire to achieve personal growth and development through one's job. Workers high in growth need strength respond well to jobs designed according to the JCM because they enjoy work that challenges them and allows them to learn new skills and knowledge. In fact, there is an 84 percent chance that workers with high growth need strength will be more satisfied with their work when their jobs are redesigned according to the JCM.

By comparison, because they aren't as interested in being challenged or learning new things at work, there is only a 69 percent chance that workers low in growth need strength will be satisfied with jobs that have been redesigned according to the principles of the JCM. This is still a favorable percentage, but it is weaker than the 84 percent chance of job satisfaction that occurs for workers high in growth need strength.

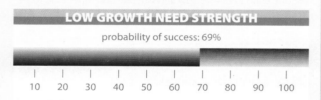

Workplace Absenteeism

Although not shown in the job characteristics model displayed in Exhibit 8.10, workplace absenteeism is an important personal or work outcome affected by a job's core characteristics. In general, the "richer" your job is with task identity, task significance, skill variety, autonomy, and feedback, the more likely you are to show up for work every day.

Workers are 63 percent more likely to attend work when their jobs have task identity than when they don't.

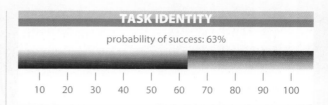

Workers are 68 percent more likely to attend work when their jobs have task significance than when they don't.

Workers are 72 percent more likely to attend work when their jobs have skill variety than when they don't.

Workers are 74 percent more likely to attend work when their jobs have autonomy than when they don't.

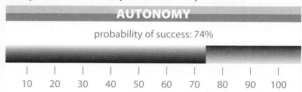

Workers are 72 percent more likely to attend work when their jobs provide feedback than when they don't.[28]

the amount of time it takes to process orders, and the number of cars in the drive-through. With the exception of feedback, the low levels of the core job characteristics show why the drive-through window job is not internally motivating for many workers.

What can managers do when jobs aren't internally motivating? The far left column of Exhibit 8.10 lists five job-redesign techniques that managers can use to strengthen a job's core characteristics. *Combining tasks* increases skill variety and task identity by joining separate, specialized tasks into larger work modules. Work can be formed into *natural work units* by arranging tasks according to logical or meaningful groups. *Establishing client relationships* increases skill variety, autonomy, and feedback by giving employees direct contact with clients and customers. In some companies, truck drivers are expected to establish business relationships with their regular customers. When something goes wrong with a shipment, customers are told to call drivers directly. *Vertical loading* means pushing some managerial authority down to workers.

The last job-redesign technique offered by the model, *opening feedback channels*, means finding additional ways to give employees direct, frequent feedback about their job performance. For additional information on the JCM, see this chapter's What Really Works feature.

REVIEW 8-4

Job Design

Companies use specialized jobs because they are economical and easy to learn and don't require highly paid workers. But specialized jobs aren't motivating or particularly satisfying for employees. Companies have used job rotation, job enlargement, job enrichment, and the job characteristics model to make specialized jobs more interesting and motivating. With job rotation, workers move from one specialized job to another. Job enlargement simply increases the number of different tasks within a particular job. Job enrichment increases the number of tasks in a job and gives workers authority and control over their work. The goal of the job characteristics model is to make jobs intrinsically motivating. For this to happen, jobs must be strong on five core job characteristics (skill variety, task identity, task significance, autonomy, and feedback), and workers must experience three critical psychological states (knowledge of results, responsibility for work outcomes, and meaningful work). If jobs aren't internally motivating, they can be redesigned by combining tasks, forming natural work units, establishing client relationships, vertical loading, and opening feedback channels.

8-5 Designing Organizational Processes

After reading this section, you should be able to:

8-5 differentiate between mechanistic and organic organizations and identify which design technique is appropriate for each.

More than 40 years ago, Tom Burns and G. M. Stalker described how two kinds of organizational designs, mechanistic and organic, are appropriate for different kinds of organizational environments.[29] **Mechanistic organizations** are characterized by: specialized jobs and responsibilities; precisely defined, unchanging roles; and a rigid chain of command based on centralized authority and vertical communication. This type of organization works best in stable, unchanging business environments. By contrast, **organic organizations** are characterized by: broadly defined jobs and responsibility; loosely defined, frequently changing roles; and decentralized authority and horizontal communication based on

mechanistic organization
an organization characterized by specialized jobs and responsibilities; precisely defined, unchanging roles; and a rigid chain of command based on centralized authority and vertical communication

organic organization
an organization characterized by broadly defined jobs and responsibility; loosely defined, frequently changing roles; and decentralized authority and horizontal communication based on task knowledge

task knowledge. This type of organization works best in dynamic, changing business environments.

The organizational design techniques described in the first half of this chapter—departmentalization, authority, and job design—are better suited for mechanistic organizations and the stable business environments that were more prevalent before 1980. By contrast, the organizational design techniques discussed next, in the second part of the chapter, are more appropriate for organic organizations and the increasingly dynamic environments in which today's businesses compete. The key difference between these approaches is that mechanistic organizational designs focus on organizational structure, whereas organic organizational designs are concerned with organizational process, or the collection of activities that transform inputs into outputs valued by customers.

REVIEW 8-5

. . . .

Designing Organizational Processes

Mechanistic organizational structures work best in stable, unchanging business environments, whereas, by contrast, organic organizational structures work best in dynamic, changing business environments.

8-6 Intraorganizational Processes

An **intraorganizational process** is the collection of activities that take place within an organization to transform inputs into outputs that customers value.

After reading the following section, you should be able to:

8-6 explain the methods that companies are using to redesign internal organizational processes (i.e., intraorganizational processes).

The steps involved in an automobile insurance claim are a good example of an intraorganizational process:

1. Document the loss (the accident).
2. Assign an appraiser to determine the dollar amount of damage.
3. Make an appointment to inspect the vehicle.
4. Inspect the vehicle.
5. Write an appraisal and get the repair shop to agree to the damage estimate.
6. Pay for the repair work.
7. Return the repaired car to the customer.

Let's take a look at how companies are using **8-6a reengineering, 8-6b empowerment,** and **8-6c behavioral informality** to redesign intraorganizational processes like these.

8-6a Reengineering

In their best-selling book *Reengineering the Corporation*, Michael Hammer and James Champy define **reengineering** as "the *fundamental* rethinking and *radical* redesign of business *processes* to achieve *dramatic* improvements in critical,

intraorganizational process
the collection of activities that take place within an organization to transform inputs into outputs that customers value

reengineering
fundamental rethinking and radical redesign of business processes to achieve dramatic improvements in critical measures of performance, such as cost, quality, service, and speed

contemporary measures of performance, such as cost, quality, service and speed."[30] Hammer and Champy further explained the four key words shown in italics in this definition. The first key word is *fundamental*. When reengineering organizational designs, managers must ask themselves, Why do we do what we do? and Why do we do it the way we do? The usual answer is: Because that's the way we've always done it. The second key word is *radical*. Reengineering is about significant change, about starting over by throwing out the old ways of getting work done. The third key word is *processes*. Hammer and Champy noted that "most business people are not process oriented; they are focused on tasks, on jobs, on people, on structures, but not on processes." The fourth key word is *dramatic*. Reengineering is about achieving quantum improvements in company performance.

An example from IBM Credit's operation illustrates how work can be reengineered.[31] *IBM Credit* lends businesses money to buy IBM computers. Previously, the loan application bounced around five departments over six days before being approved or denied. Of course, this delay cost IBM business. Some customers got their loans elsewhere. Others, frustrated by the wait, simply canceled their orders.

Finally, two IBM managers decided to walk a loan straight through each of the departments involved in the process. At each step, they asked the workers to stop what they were doing and immediately process their loan application. They were shocked by what they found. From start to finish, the entire process took just 90 minutes! The six-day turnaround time was almost entirely due to delays in handing off the work from one department to another. The solution: IBM redesigned the process so that one person, not five people in five separate departments, would handle the entire loan-approval process without any handoffs. The results were indeed dramatic. Reengineering the credit process reduced approval time from six days to four hours and allowed IBM Credit to increase the number of loans it handled by a factor of 100![32]

Reengineering changes an organization's orientation from vertical to horizontal. Instead of taking orders from upper management, lower- and middle-level managers and workers take orders from a customer who is at the beginning and end of each process. Instead of running independent functional departments, managers and workers in different departments take ownership of cross-functional processes. Instead of simplifying work so that it becomes increasingly specialized, reengineering complicates work by giving workers increased autonomy and responsibility for complete processes.

In essence, reengineering changes work by changing **task interdependence**, the extent to which collective action is required to complete an entire piece of work. As shown in Exhibit 8.11, there are three kinds of task interdependence.[33] In **pooled interdependence**, each job or department contributes to the whole independently. In **sequential interdependence**, work must be performed in succession, as one group's or job's outputs become the inputs for the next group or job. Finally, in **reciprocal interdependence**, different jobs or groups work together in a back-and-forth manner to complete the process. By reducing the handoffs between different jobs or groups, reengineering decreases sequential interdependence. Likewise, reengineering decreases pooled interdependence by redesigning work so that formerly independent jobs or

task interdependence
the extent to which collective action is required to complete an entire piece of work

pooled interdependence
work completed by having each job or department independently contribute to the whole

sequential interdependence
work completed in succession, with one group's or job's outputs becoming the inputs for the next group or job

reciprocal interdependence
work completed by different jobs or groups working together in a back-and-forth manner

Exhibit 8.11

Reengineering and Task Interdependence

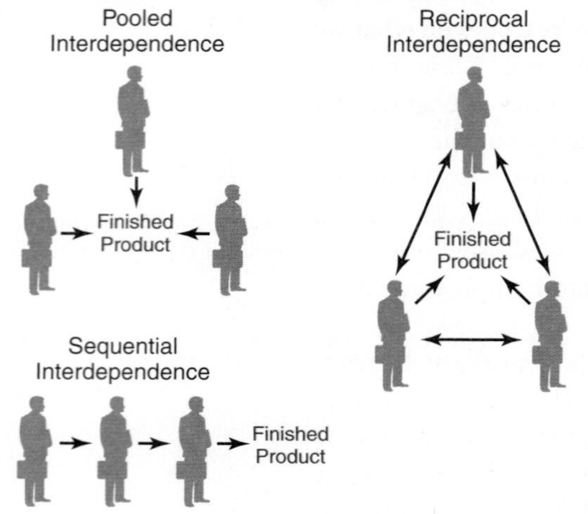

Pooled Interdependence

Finished Product

Reciprocal Interdependence

Finished Product

Sequential Interdependence

Finished Product

departments now work together to complete processes. Finally, reengineering increases reciprocal interdependence by making groups or individuals responsible for larger, more complete processes in which several steps may be accomplished at the same time.

As an organizational design tool, reengineering promises big rewards, but it has also come under severe criticism. The most serious complaint is that because it allows a few workers to do the work formerly done by many, reengineering is simply a corporate code word for cost cutting and worker layoffs.[34] For this reason, detractors claim that reengineering hurts morale and performance. Even though ordering times were reduced from three weeks to three days, *LEVI STRAUSS* ended an $850 million reengineering project because of the fear and turmoil it created in the company's workforce. One low point occurred when Levi management, encouraged by its reengineering consultants, told 4,000 workers that they would have to "reapply for their jobs" as the company shifted from its traditional vertical structure to a process-based form of organizing. Today, even reengineering gurus Hammer and Champy admit that roughly 70 percent of all reengineering projects fail because of how they affect people in the workplace. Says Hammer, "I wasn't smart enough about [the people issues]. I was reflecting my engineering background and was insufficiently appreciative of the human dimension. I've [now] learned that's critical."[35]

8-6b Empowerment

Another way of redesigning intraorganizational processes is through empowerment. **Empowering workers** means permanently passing decision-making authority and responsibility from managers to workers. For workers to be fully empowered, companies must give them the information and resources they need to make and carry out good decisions and then reward them for taking individual initiative.[36]

When workers are given the proper information and resources and are allowed to make good decisions, they experience strong feelings of empowerment. **Empowerment** is a feeling of intrinsic motivation, in which workers perceive their work to have meaning and perceive themselves to be competent, have an impact, and be capable of self-determination.[37] Work has meaning when it is consistent with personal standards and beliefs. Workers feel competent when they believe they can perform an activity with skill. The belief that they are having an impact comes from a feeling that they can affect work outcomes. A feeling of self-determination arises from workers' belief that they have the autonomy to choose how best to do their work.

Empowerment can lead to changes in organizational processes because meaning, competence, impact, and self-determination produce empowered employees who take active rather than passive roles in their work. At *SOUTHWEST AIRLINES*, employees are given freedom to address customers' needs even before they make

empowering workers
permanently passing decision-making authority and responsibility from managers to workers by giving them the information and resources they need to make and carry out good decisions

empowerment
feelings of intrinsic motivation, in which workers perceive their work to have impact and meaning and perceive themselves to be competent and capable of self-determination

a complaint. Passenger Mark Dickinson arrived at the airport two hours before the flight he would take to see his two-year-old grandson who was about to be taken off life support. Long lines at security, however, made Dickinson late for his flight, and even though he ran through the terminal in his socks, he got to the gate 12 minutes late for the departure. But the plane was still there. As it turns out, the pilot found out about Dickinson's situation from the agent who sold the ticket and decided to hold the plane at the gate until he was ready to go.[38]

8-6c Behavioral Informality

How would you describe the atmosphere in the office where you last worked? Was it a formal, by-the-book, follow-the-rules, address-each-other-by-last-names atmosphere? Or was it more informal, with an emphasis on results rather than rules, casual business dress rather than suits, and first names rather than last names and titles? Or was it somewhere in between?

Behavioral informality (or formality) is a third influence on intraorganizational processes. **Behavioral informality** refers to workplace atmospheres characterized by spontaneity, casualness, and interpersonal familiarity. By contrast, **behavioral formality** refers to workplace atmospheres characterized by routine and regimen, specific rules about how to behave, and impersonal detachment. Dress codes and office layouts are two of the key factors that influence behavioral informality.

Casual dress policies and open office systems are two of the most popular methods for increasing behavioral informality. In fact, a survey conducted by the Society for Human Resource Management indicates that casual dress policies (no suits, ties, jackets, dresses, or formal clothing required) are extremely popular.[39] Today, 84 percent of companies have some form of casual dress code, up from 63 percent 11 years ago and 24 percent 16 years ago.[40] Still, companies such as retailer Target have instituted formal dress codes that ban business casual based on the idea that a more professional workplace will lead to better results.[41] However, 85 percent of human resources directors believe that casual dress can improve office morale, and 79 percent say that employees are very satisfied with casual dress codes.[42] Moreover, nearly two-thirds of the human resources directors believe that casual dress policies are an important tool for attracting qualified employees in tight labor markets.

Although casual dress increases behavioral informality by having managers and workers at all levels dress in a more relaxed manner, open office systems increase behavioral informality by significantly increasing the level of communication and interaction among employees. By definition, **open office systems** try to increase interaction by removing physical barriers that separate workers. One characteristic of open office systems is that they have much more shared space than private space. **Shared spaces** are areas used by and open to all employees. Cubicles with low-to-the-ground partitions (used by 75 percent of office workers); offices with no doors or with glass walls; collections of comfortable furniture that encourage people to congregate; and common areas with tables and chairs that encourage people to meet, work, or eat together are examples of shared space.[43] In contrast, **private spaces**, such as private offices with doors, are used by and open to just one employee.

behavioral informality a workplace atmosphere characterized by spontaneity, casualness, and interpersonal familiarity

behavioral formality a workplace atmosphere characterized by routine and regimen, specific rules about how to behave, and impersonal detachment

open office systems offices in which the physical barriers that separate workers have been removed in order to increase communication and interaction

shared spaces spaces used by and open to all employees

private spaces spaces used by and open to just one employee

Doing the Right Thing

Don't Scavenge That Office If Somebody Is Still in It

It's like road kill in the animal kingdom. As soon as the word gets out that someone is leaving the company, coworkers start scheming to scavenge the office leftovers—chairs, computer monitors, filing cabinets, even staplers. "This issue is practically everywhere," says Mary Wong, president of a human resources consulting company. "Professionals—anyone you and I would normally consider to be very adult—turn into children" over the prospect of picking an empty office clean of its "goodies." Sometimes—and this is where it gets disrespectful—office scavengers move in even before the employee, who's often been laid off, has left. Ethics consultant Steve Lawler tells the story of a laid-off manager who, just hours after hearing the bad news, was already getting requests for the expensive Herman Miller Aeron chair in which he was still sitting. Office scavenging is a strange and predictable aspect of office life. It happens everywhere. But if you're going to scavenge, and you probably will, do the right thing by maintaining the dignity of departing coworkers: Wait until the office is empty before you strike.[48]

The advantage of an open office with extensive shared space is that it dramatically increases the amount of unplanned, spontaneous, and chance communication among employees.[44] People are much more likely to plan meetings and work together when numerous collaboration spaces with conference tables, white boards, and computers are readily available. With no office walls, inviting common areas, and different departments mixed together in large open spaces, spontaneous communication occurs more often.

SIGMA-ALADRICH, a biotechnology firm, built a new office with a three-story open staircase at the center of the building. The open staircase is complemented by benches and expansive landings on each story so people can sit and talk. Indeed, soon after the move to the new office, two scientists from opposite sides of the building ran into each other on the stairs, stopped to talk, and ended up generating a significant new reagent for scientific testing.[45]

Not everyone is enthusiastic about open offices, however. For example, Ingrid Tischer, who sits in a cubicle next to the kitchen in her office, says she can't help being distracted by others' conversations, and frequently joins in. Because of the location of her cubicle, "I know things about my colleagues' lives, and they know things about mine."[46] In fact, cubicle dwellers are interrupted by "noise, visual distractions, and chatty visitors" up to 21 times a day. And, because it takes about three minutes each time to refocus on what they were doing, cubicle workers can lose an hour a day to these interruptions. For this reason, Sun Microsystems and Microsoft give their employees private offices. William Agnello, Sun's vice president of real estate and the workplace, says, "We have researched the heck out of this. Our studies show that, for our engineers, there are just too many distractions and interruptions."[47]

Indeed, because there is so much shared space and so little private space, companies with open systems have to take steps to give employees privacy when they need to concentrate on individual work.

REVIEW 8-6

Intraorganizational Processes

Today, companies are using reengineering, empowerment, and behavioral informality to change their intraorganizational processes. Through fundamental rethinking and radical redesign of business processes, reengineering changes an organization's orientation from vertical to horizontal. Reengineering changes work processes by decreasing sequential and pooled interdependence and by increasing reciprocal interdependence. Reengineering promises dramatic increases in productivity and customer satisfaction, but it has been criticized as simply an excuse to cut costs and lay off workers.

Empowering workers means taking decision-making authority and responsibility from managers and giving it to workers. Empowered workers develop feelings of competence and self-determination and believe that their work has meaning and impact. Workplaces characterized by behavioral informality are spontaneous and casual. Casual dress policies and open office systems are two of the most popular methods for increasing behavioral informality.

8-7 Interorganizational Processes

An **interorganizational process** is a collection of activities that occur *among companies* to transform inputs into outputs that customers value. In other words, many companies work together to create a product or service that keeps customers happy.

After reading the following section, you should be able to:

8-7 describe the methods that companies are using to redesign external organizational processes (i.e., interorganizational processes).

From soundtracks to staging, to locations, to postproduction and marketing, dozens of different firms worked with WARNER BROS. PICTURES to create the last two films in the *Harry Potter* movies series, *Harry Potter and the Deathly Hallows*, parts 1 and 2. Part 1 was filmed at Leavesden Film Studios, owned by Warner Brothers and located in Hertfordshire, England. Part 2 was filmed at Pinewood Studios, also located in England. The visual effects of both movies were handled by two companies, Double Negative, which won an Oscar for its special effects work in *Inception,* and Framestore, which won an Oscar for its work on *The Golden Compass.* The music for both films was composed by Alexander Desplat and performed by the London Symphony Orchestra.[49]

In this section, you'll explore interorganizational processes by learning about **8-7a modular organizations** and **8-7b virtual organizations**.[50]

8-7a Modular Organizations

Except for the core business activities that they can perform better, faster, and cheaper than others, **modular organizations** outsource all remaining business activities to outside companies, suppliers, specialists, or consultants. The term *modular* is used because the business activities purchased from outside companies can be added and dropped as needed, much like adding pieces to a three-dimensional puzzle. Exhibit 8.12 depicts a modular organization in which the company has chosen to keep training, human resources, sales, product design, manufacturing, customer service, R & D, and information technology as core business activities but has outsourced the noncore activities of product distribution, Web page design, advertising, payroll, accounting, and packaging.

interorganizational process
a collection of activities that take place among companies to transform inputs into outputs that customers value

modular organization
an organization that outsources noncore business activities to outside companies, suppliers, specialists, or consultants

Exhibit 8.12

Modular Organization

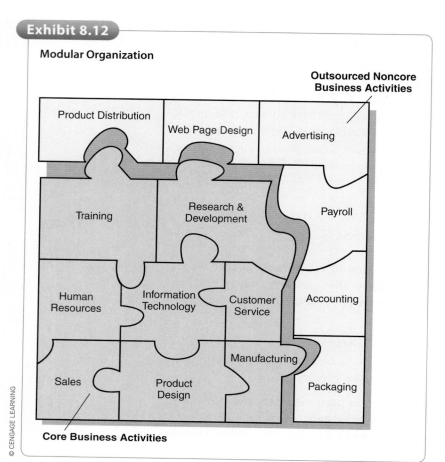

Product Distribution

Web Page Design

Outsourced Noncore Business Activities

Advertising

Training

Research & Development

Payroll

Human Resources

Information Technology

Customer Service

Accounting

Sales

Product Design

Manufacturing

Packaging

Core Business Activities

Modular organizations have several advantages. First, because modular organizations pay for outsourced labor, expertise, or manufacturing capabilities only when needed, they can cost significantly less to run than traditional organizations. For example, most of the design and marketing work for Apple's iPad 2 is run out of company headquarters in Cupertino, California. Most of the components for the device, however, are outsourced to other companies. LG and Samsung, Korean firms, make the iPad 2's LCD panels, and the touch panel that goes on top of the screen comes from TPK and Wintek, both based in China.[51]

Modular organizations have disadvantages too. The primary disadvantage is the loss of control that occurs when key business activities are outsourced to other companies. Also, companies may reduce their competitive advantage in two ways if they mistakenly outsource a core business activity. First, as a result of competitive and technological change, the noncore business activities a company has outsourced may suddenly become the basis for competitive advantage. Second, related to that point, suppliers to whom work is outsourced can sometimes become competitors.

8-7b Virtual Organizations

In contrast to modular organizations in which the interorganizational process revolves around a central company, a **virtual organization** is part of a network in which many companies share skills, costs, capabilities, markets, and customers with each other. Exhibit 8.13 shows a virtual organization in which, for "today," the parts of a virtual company consist of product design, purchasing, manufacturing, advertising, and information technology. Unlike modular organizations, in which the outside organizations are tightly linked to one central company, virtual organizations work with some companies in the network alliance, but not with all. So, whereas a puzzle with various pieces is a fitting metaphor for a modular organization, a potluck dinner is an appropriate metaphor for a virtual organization. All participants bring their finest food dish but eat only what they want.

virtual organization
an organization that is part of a network in which many companies share skills, costs, capabilities, markets, and customers to collectively solve customer problems or provide specific products or services

Another difference is that the working relationships between modular organizations and outside companies tend to be more stable and longer lasting than the shorter, often temporary relationships found among the virtual companies in a network alliance. The composition of a virtual organization is always changing. The combination of network partners that a virtual corporation has at any one time depends on the expertise needed to solve a particular problem or provide a specific product or service. This is why the businessperson in the network organization shown in Exhibit 8.13 is saying, "Today, I'll have...." Tomorrow, the business could want something completely different. In this sense, the term "virtual organization" means the organization that exists "at the moment."

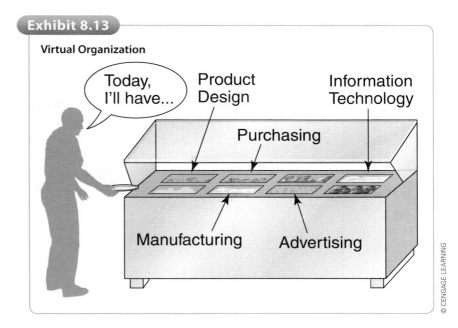

Exhibit 8.13

Virtual Organization

For example, 21 carton manufacturers have formed a network of virtual organizations called the *INDEPENDENT CARTON GROUP (ICG)*.[52] The original network that brought five independent carton companies together was designed so that each of the five companies could help each other in case a catastrophe occurred at one of their production facilities. For instance, if an ICG company ever experienced a catastrophe at a production facility, the other four members of the ICG would be there to temporarily provide alternative production arrangements so the affected company wouldn't lose its customers. However, as the group grew, they realized they could trade off manufacturing capacities with each other to better serve customers' needs, so they combined their efforts to provide carton packaging in 16 different industries, from automotive to biotech to food to electronics. ICG customers benefit from competitive pricing, uninterrupted supplies, and group purchasing power.

Virtual organizations have a number of advantages. They let companies share costs. And because members of virtual organizations can quickly combine their efforts to meet customers' needs, they are fast and flexible. Finally, because each member of the network alliance is the best at what it does, virtual organizations should in theory provide better products and services in all respects.

As with modular organizations, a disadvantage of virtual organizations is that once work has been outsourced, it can be difficult to control the quality of work done by network partners. The greatest disadvantage, however, is that tremendous managerial skills are required to make a network of independent organizations work well together, especially because their relationships tend to be short and based on a single task or project.

Virtual organizations are using two methods to solve this problem. The first is to use a *broker*. In traditional, hierarchical organizations, managers plan, organize, and control. But with the horizontal, interorganizational processes that characterize virtual organizations, the job of a broker is to create and assemble the knowledge, skills, and resources from different companies for outside parties, such as customers.[53] The second way to make networks of virtual organizations more manageable is to use a *virtual organization agreement* that, somewhat like a contract, specifies the schedules, responsibilities, costs, payouts, and liabilities for participating organizations.[54] For more information on how a virtual organizations works, see www.independentcartongroup.com.

REVIEW 8-7

Interorganizational Processes

Organizations are using modular and virtual organizations to change interorganizational processes. Because modular organizations outsource all noncore activities to other businesses, they are less expensive to run than traditional companies. However, modular organizations require extremely close relationships with suppliers. They may result in a loss of control, and could create new competitors if the wrong business activities are outsourced. Virtual organizations participate in a network in which they share skills, costs, capabilities, markets, and customers. As customer problems, products, or services change, the combination of virtual organizations that work together changes. Virtual organizations can reduce costs, respond quickly, and, if they can successfully coordinate their efforts, produce outstanding products and service.

 ## Management Team Decision

China—The Future of General Motors?[55]

It's been a rough ride for General Motors. In 2008, GM's remarkable run of 77 years as the world's largest automaker came to a crashing halt. In 2009, after a decade of mismanagement and declining sales, the company declared bankruptcy and needed a massive government bailout and thorough reorganization to stay afloat. During that time, more than 2,000 dealers were closed for good, and almost 23,000 employees were released. There is some hope that the new, streamlined GM, featuring new models, will regain its once-dominant position in the U.S. auto market. However, it is becoming increasingly clear that GM's future may lie in China.

In 2009, there were 13.6 million cars sold in China, an increase of 46 percent from 2008, and nearly 3 million more cars than were sold in the United States at the same time. In 1977, there were just 1 million cars in China; as of 2008, there were 51 million, and it's conservatively expected that the Chinese auto market will grow 10 percent to 15 percent every year. Unlike in the United States, GM hasn't been stuck on the sidelines in China. It sold 1.83 million cars in 2009, an increase of 67 percent over the previous year, and has a solid record of 15 consecutive months in which its sales have grown by double digits. By 2015, GM hopes to sell 3 million cars per year in China. This would not only make GM the largest auto seller in China, but it would make China GM's largest and most lucrative market.

Currently, GM operates in China as part of a joint venture with the SAIC Motor Corporation. Through the partnership, GM owns a minority stake in two companies,

SAIC-GM-Wuling and Shanghai General Motors. Increasingly, however, you've heard your GM colleagues argue that new organizational design is needed, one that will give the company a stronger presence in China, and decrease its dependence on the U.S. market. A group of these managers has come to you to seek out your opinion on how GM can organize to best take advantage of shifting conditions in the global auto market.

Questions

1. The text describes a number of different approaches concerning organizational structure. Which do you think would be ideal for GM's success in China? Which of the structures would help GM expand to other foreign markets?

2. What are the advantages and disadvantages of promoting decentralization in GM's operations in China?

 ## Practice Being a Manager

Work Dynamics

Effective organization is vital to the accomplishment of company objectives. Two critical aspects of effective organization are departmentalization and the design of jobs. In this role-play exercise, you will have the opportunity to experience some of the work dynamics surrounding the grouping of workers and the design of jobs.

STEP 1 **Form work groups.** Your professor will form groups and give you a role assignment.

STEP 2 **Review your role.** Read your role assignment carefully, and prepare to begin working per your role assignment.

STEP 3 (10–20 minutes): **Begin acting.** When your professor directs you to begin, you should start working as assigned by your role.

STEP 4 **Compile your results.** Total your results by work group, and compare across the teams.

STEP 5 **Debrief as a class.** Discuss the results as a class. What factors seemed to play a role in the efficiency and effectiveness of the work groups? What role did organization and job design play? If this were an actual organizational work group, what might you do to improve performance and worker satisfaction?

Self-Assessment

Flexibility and Structure

Every organization needs some degree of flexibility and standardization. In other words, companies need to have enough flexibility in their organizations to respond to changes in their business environment, but firms also must have certain structures in place to ensure smooth operations. For example, if someone gets hurt on company property, clear procedures about what to do in the case of an accident help managers respond quickly and confidently. But being overly committed to following rules can hamstring an organization and keep it from growing. As a manager, you will probably encounter both types of situations, and to respond appropriately, you will need to have an idea of how comfortable you are in a formal environment versus a more loosely structured workplace. Every organization needs some degree of flexibility to adapt to new situations and some degree of standardization to make routine tasks and decisions as efficient and effective as possible.[56] In this assessment, indicate the extent to which you agree or disagree with the following statements. Use this scale for your responses:

1   Strongly disagree

2   Disagree

3   Slightly disagree

4   Neutral

5   Slightly agree

6   Agree

7   Strongly agree

1. If a written rule does not cover some situation, we make up informal rules for doing things as we go along.

    1   2   3   4   5   6   7

2. I feel that I am my own boss in most matters.

    1   2   3   4   5   6   7

3. There are many things in my business that are not covered by some formal procedure.

    1   2   3   4   5   6   7

4. A person can make his or her own decisions without checking with somebody else.

    1   2   3   4   5   6   7

5. Usually, my contact with my company and its representatives involves doing things "by the rule book."

    1   2   3   4   5   6   7

6. How things are done here is left up to the person doing the work.

    1   2   3   4   5   6   7

7. Contacts with my company and its representatives are on a formal, preplanned basis.

    1   2   3   4   5   6   7

8. People here are allowed to do almost anything as they please.

    1   2   3   4   5   6   7

9. I ignore the rules and reach informal agreements to handle some situations.

    1   2   3   4   5   6   7

10. Most people here make their own rules on the job.

    1   2   3   4   5   6   7

11. When rules and procedures exist in my company, they are usually written agreements.

    1   2   3   4   5   6   7

12. The employees are constantly being checked on for rule violations.

    1   2   3   4   5   6   7

13. People here feel as though they are constantly being watched, to see that they obey all the rules.

    1   2   3   4   5   6   7

SCORING

Determine your score by entering your response to each survey item, as follows. In blanks that say *regular score*, simply enter your response for that item. If your response was a 6, place a 6 in the *regular* score blank. In blanks that say *reverse score*, subtract your response from 8 and enter the result. So if your response was a 6, place a 2 ($8 - 6 = 2$) in the *reverse score* blank.

1. reverse score ___
2. reverse score ___
3. reverse score ___
4. reverse score ___
5. regular score ___
6. reverse score ___
7. regular score ___
8. reverse score ___
9. reverse score ___
10. reverse score ___
11. regular score ___
12. regular score ___
13. regular score ___

TOTAL = ___

You can see where you fall on the formality continuum and find the interpretation of your score at: www.cengagebrain.com.

▶ MANAGEMENT WORKPLACE

Modern Shed: Designing Adaptive Organizations

Modern Shed, based in Seattle, builds paneled dwellings for use as studio spaces, home offices, pool houses, project sheds, guesthouses, and more. Like the sheds, the company is built to be adaptive, scalable, and suited to the needs of the environment. Modern Shed counts only 12 to 14 full-time employees. But at times, its output rivals that of a large builder, thanks to collaboration with outside sales reps and a dealer network comprising 35 independent contractors. According to managers at Modern Shed, the logical process of building sheds from smaller scale structures to larger ones is a metaphor for how modern organizations should be built.

What to Watch For and Ask Yourself

1. Describe how Modern Shed functions as a modular organization.

2. What are the advantages and disadvantages of Modern Shed's organizational structure?

Endnotes

1. M. Arndt, "Eli Lilly: Life after Prozac," *Businessweek*, July 23, 2001, 80–82; P. Loftus, "Patent Expirations Loom for Lilly," *Wall Street Journal*, August 12, 2009, no page number available; P. Loftus, "Corporate News: Lilly Set to Cut Jobs as Patents Expire," *Wall Street Journal*, September 15, 2009, B3; P. Loftus, "Boss Talk: With Patents Expiring, Eli Lilly Retools," *Wall Street Journal*, July 6, 2010, B5; B. Martinez and J. Goldstein, "Big Pharma Faces Grim Prognosis; Industry Fails to Find New Drugs to Replace Wonders Like Lipitor," *Wall Street Journal*, December 6, 2007, A1; J. Russell, "Cuts at Lilly Yield Painful Progress," *Indianapolis Star*, October 2, 2010, A1; and A. Weintrub & M. Tirrell, "Eli Lilly's Drug Assembly Line," *Businessweek*, March 8, 2010, 56–57.

2. "Sony Group Organizational Chart Summary," Sony, April 1, 2011, accessed May 15, 2011, from www.sony.net/SonyInfo/CorporateInfo/Data/organization.html.

3. "Corporate Fact Sheet," Sony Pictures, accessed May 12, 2012, from www.sonypictures.com/corp/corporatefact.html; and "Facts and Figures," Sony Music, accessed May 12, 2012, from www.sonymusic.com/page/facts-and-figures.

4. M. Hammer and J. Champy, *Reengineering the Corporation: A Manifesto for Business Revolution* (New York: Harper & Row, 1993).

5. "Boston Scientific Announces Management Changes and Restructuring Initiatives," *Boston Scientific*, February 10, 2010, accessed May 15, 2011, from http://bostonscientific.mediaroom.com/index.php?s=43 & item=895.

6. J. G. March and H. A. Simon, *Organizations* (New York: John Wiley & Sons, 1958).

7. "Bayer Group: Profile and Organization," Bayer AG, accessed March 20, 2009, from www.bayer.com/bayer-group/profileand-organization/page2351.htm.

8. "Company Overview: 2010 " UTC, accessed May 15, 2010, from www.utc.com/StaticFiles/UTC/StaticFiles/utc_overview.pdf.

9. "Company Overview: 2010," UTC, accessed May 15, 2010, from www.utc.com/StaticFiles/UTC/StaticFiles/utc_overview.pdf.

10. "Company Structure," Swisscom AG, accessed May 15, 2011, from www.swisscom.ch/GHQ/content/Portraet/Unternehmen/Unternehmensstruktur/?lang=en.

11. "About AB InBev: In a Few Facts," AB InBev, accessed May 16, 2011, from www.ab-inbev.com/go/about_abinbev/our_company/in_a_few_facts.cfm.

12. "Our Top 10 Markets," AB InBev, accessed May 16, 2011, from https://docs.google.com/viewer?url=http://www.ab-inbev.com/pdf/AB_InBev_AR10_OurTopTenMarkets.pdf.

13. "Anheuser Busch InBev in Russia Key Facts & Figures," AB InBev, accessed May 16, 2011, from https://docs.google.com/viewer?url=http://www.ab-inbev.com/pdf/factsheets/Russia2010.pdf; and "Anheuser Busch InBev in Belgium Key Facts and Figures," AB InBev, accessed May 16, 2011, from www.ab-inbev.com/pdf/factsheets/Belgium2010.pdf.

14. "Who We Are," P&G, accessed November 14, 2009, from www.pg.com.

15. "Corporate Info: Corporate Structure," Procter & Gamble, accessed May 12, 2012, from http://news.pg.com/about/corporate_structure.

16. L. R. Burns, "Adoption and Abandonment of Matrix Management Programs: Effects of Organizational Characteristics and Interorganizational Networks," *Academy of Management Journal* 36 (1993): 106–138.

17. D. Ball, "Unilever Shakes Up Its Management to Spur Growth," *Wall Street Journal*, February 11, 2005, A2.

18. H. Fayol, *General and Industrial Management*, trans. C. Storrs (London: Pitman Publishing, 1949).

19. M. Weber, *The Theory of Social and Economic Organization*, trans. and ed. A. M. Henderson and T. Parsons (New York: Free Press, 1947).

20. Fayol, *General and Industrial Management*.

21. "John Scharffenberger, "The Tastemaker," Inc.com, May 1, 2009, accessed October 25, 2010, from www.inc.com/magazine/20090501/john-scharffenberger-the-tastemaker.html.

22. E. E. Lawler, S. A. Mohrman, and G. E. Ledford, *Creating High Performance Organizations: Practices and Results of Employee Involvement and Quality Management in Fortune 1000 Companies* (San Francisco: Jossey-Bass, 1995).

23. S. Curry, "Retention Getters," *Incentive*, 1 April 2005.

24. R. W. Griffin, *Task Design* (Glenview, IL: Scott, Foresman, 1982).

25. F. Herzberg, *Work and the Nature of Man* (Cleveland, OH: World Press, 1966).

26. A. Markels, "Team Approach: A Power Producer Is Intent on Giving Power to Its People—Groups of AES Employees Do Complex Tasks Ranging from Hiring to Investing—Making Sure Work Is 'Fun,'" *Wall Street Journal*, July 3, 1995, A1.

27. R. Hackman and G. R. Oldham, *Work Redesign* (Reading, MA: Addison-Wesley, 1980).

28. Y. Fried and G. R. Ferris, "The Validity of the Job Characteristics Model: A Review and Meta-Analysis," *Personnel Psychology* 40 (1987): 287–322; and B. T. Loher, R. A. Noe, N. L. Moeller, and M. P. Fitzgerald, "A Meta-Analysis of the Relation of Job Characteristics to Job Satisfaction," *Journal of Applied Psychology* 70 (1985): 280–289.

29. T. Burns and G. M. Stalker, *The Management of Innovation* (London: Tavistock, 1961).

30. Hammer and Champy, *Reengineering the Corporation*.

31. Ibid.

32. C. Tuna, "Remembrances: Champion of 'Re-Engineering' Saved Companies, Challenged Thinking," *Wall Street Journal*, September 6, 2008, A12.

33. J. D. Thompson, *Organizations in Action* (New York: McGraw-Hill, 1967).

34 D. Pink, "Who Has the Next Big Idea?" *Fast Company*, September 1, 2001, 108.

35 C. Tuna, "Remembrances: Champion of 'Re-Engineering' Saved Companies, Challenged Thinking."

36 G. M. Spreitzer, "Individual Empowerment in the Workplace: Dimensions, Measurement, and Validation," *Academy of Management Journal* 38 (1995): 1442–1465.

37 K. W. Thomas and B. A. Velthouse, "Cognitive Elements of Empowerment," *Academy of Management Review* 15 (1990): 666–681.

38 D. Stanley, "Southwest Holds Plane for Grandfather of Slain Boy," The Denver Channel.com, January 13, 2011, accessed February 3, 2011, from www.thedenverchannel .com/news/26483696/detail.html.

39 L. Munoz, "The Suit Is Back—Or Is It? As Dot-Coms Die, So Should Business Casual. But the Numbers Don't Lie," *Fortune*, June 25, 2001, 202; and F. Swoboda, "Casual Dress Becomes the Rule," *Las Vegas Review-Journal*, March 3, 1996.

40 C. Lu-Lien Tan, "Business Attire: The Office Coverup," *Wall Street Journal*, August 5, 2006, P1.

41 Ibid.

42 "SHRM Online Poll Results," Society for Human Resource Management, www.shrm.org/poll/results.asp?Question#89, 21 May 2003.

43 W. Bounds, "Phone Calls Are Public Affairs for Open-Plan Office Dwellers," *Wall Street Journal*, July 10, 2002, B1.

44 "Designing the Ever-Changing Workplace," *Architectural Record* (September 1995): 32–37.

45 A. Frangos, "Property Report: See You on the Way Up! Office Stairs Get 'Aspirational,'" *Wall Street Journal*, May 19, 2004, B1.

46 J. Sandberg, "Cookies, Gossip, Cubes: It's a Wonder Any Work Gets Done at the Office," *Wall Street Journal*, April 28, 2004, B1.

47 L. Gallagher, "At Work: Get Out of My Face: Open Offices Were Hailed as the Answer to Hierarchical, Rigid Organizations. Employees Would Rather Have Privacy," *Forbes*, October 18, 1999, 105.

48 S. Hwang, "Cubicle Culture: Office Vultures Circle Still-Warm Desks Left Empty by Layoffs," *The Wall Street Journal*, August 14, 2001, B1.

49 "Harry Potter," Wikipedia, accessed May 18, 2011, from http://en.wikipedia.org/wiki/Harry_Potter_and_the_Deathly_ Hallows_(film)#Production.

50 G. G. Dess, A. M. A. Rasheed, K. J. McLaughlin, and R. L. Priem, "The New Corporate Architecture," *Academy of Management Executive* 9 (1995): 7–18.

51 D. E. Diliger, "Report Details iPad 2 Components, 5 million Unit Supply," Apple Insider, www.appleinsider.com/ articles/11/01/30/report_details_ipad_2_components_5_ million_unit_supply.html.

52 "About the ICG," Independent Carton Group, accessed May 18, 2011, from www.independentcartongroup.com/ about.htm.

53 C. C. Snow, R. E. Miles, and H. J. Coleman Jr., "Managing 21st Century Network Organizations," *Organizational Dynamics*, Winter 1992, 5–20.

54 J. H. Sheridan, "The Agile Web: A Model for the Future?" *Industry Week*, March 4, 1996, 31.

55 "China Ends U.S's Reign as Largest Auto Market," *Bloomberg News*, January 11, 2010, accessed November 15, 201, from www.bloomberg.com/apps/news?pid=20601087 & sid=aE.x_r_l9NZE; "GM's China Sales Exceed U.S. for Third Straight Month," *Businessweek*, April 2, 2010, accessed November 15, 2010, from www.Businessweek.com/news/2010-04-02/ gm-sales-gain-in-china-on-government-stimulus-update1-. html; and E. Fung, "GM Sees Chain Sales Exceeding 3 Mln Units in 2015," *Wall Street Journal*, April 12, 2010, accessed November 15, 2010, from http://online.wsj.com/ article/BT-CO-20100412-701317.html?mod=WSJ_World_ MIDDLEHeadlinesAsia.

56 G. Bruner, K. James, and P. Hensel, *Marketing Scales Handbook* (Chicago: American Marketing Association, 2001), vol. 3: 931–934.

Managing Teams

OUTLINE

REEL TO REAL

Management Workplace is at Holden Outerwear.

SELF-ASSESSMENT

What do you *really* think of working in teams? Do the Self-Assessment for this chapter in the book or online to find out.

ONLINE QUIZZES

Did you get it? Review the main concepts in the chapter by taking the online quizzes on CourseMate!

VIDEO QUIZZES

Get more out of the videos by taking the multimedia video quizzes online.

What Would You Do?

Cessna Headquarters, Wichita, Kansas[1]

The words "Cessna Skyhawk" have special meaning for anyone who has ever wanted to learn to fly. At 27 feet long and 8 feet tall, with a 36-foot wingspan, a 140 mph cruising speed, and room for two adults and their luggage, more people have learned to fly with a Cessna Skyhawk than with any other plane in aviation history. In fact, the Cessna Skyhawk is the best-selling plane of all time. Clyde Cessna built his first plane in 1911, and Cessna became a storied name in aviation. Cessna built 750 gliders for the army in World War II, introduced the Skyhawk in 1956, produced the first turbo-charged and cabin-pressurized single-engine planes in the 1960s, delivered its first business jet in the 1970s, topped $1 billion in sales in the 1980s, and then, in one of the worst downturns in the history of aviation business, nearly went out of business over the next decade and a half.

Sales of general aviation aircraft, which had topped out at 17,000 planes per year, dropped to 12,000 planes within a year, and over the next decade finally hit rock bottom at 928 planes for the entire industry. During the same time, Cessna's sales of piston-engine planes, like the Skyhawk, dropped from 8,000 per year to just 600. Cessna was forced to lay off 75 percent of the employees at its piston-engine plane factories (Cessna also makes business jets and larger planes) and eventually stopped making piston-engine planes altogether. However, after the economy improved and the U.S. government approved the General Aviation Revitalization Act (barring product liability lawsuits on any plane over 18 years old), Cessna decided to start building its legendary Skyhawks again.

This is where you come in. With nearly 20 years in the company, your first job with Cessna was teaching Cessna dealers how to service and maintain single-engine planes. But now, with profits flowing again and the company's legal risk greatly reduced thanks to the Revitalization Act, you've been made the vice president of Cessna's "new" single-engine business. It's your job to rebuild this part of the business from the ground up. And because

© ANTONY NETTLE/ALAMY

pilots tend to remain loyal to the kind of airplane on which they learned to fly, much depends on your success or failure. If you can rebuild Cessna's single-engine business, the pilots who learn to fly on today's Cessna Skyhawks will be buying Cessna business jets 20 years from now.

One of the advantages of starting completely over is that you get to design the entire production facility—from its location, to the new workers, to the suppliers—everything is up for grabs. For instance, Cessna does most of its production in Wichita, Kansas. But since it left the single-engine plane business, Wichita mostly produces a small number of highly customized jets each year, just the opposite of your business, which is a high number of standardized, single-engine planes. So, given the differences, you locate the new single-engine plane factory in Independence, Kansas, two hours away by car, and only 40 minutes away in one of Cessna's small planes. Along with a new location, you're debating taking a new approach to manufacturing planes by using production teams. This decision may strike some colleagues as radical, particularly at conservative-minded Cessna where one of your fellow managers admitted, "We probably got into a mode of doing things for the future based on how we'd always done things in the past." But the more you think about it, the more

© DIZZO/ISTOCK PHOTO

you are convinced that it is the right decision. Instead of using a standard production line where each worker does just one task, you are thinking about using teams to assemble Skyhawks and other single-engine planes. In an incredible departure from the engineering-based standards in which the motions of every worker on the assembly line are studied for time, cost, and efficiency implications, production teams would be completely responsible for assembling the planes and for costs and quality.

You expect to see several benefits from a team-based approach: increased customer satisfaction from improved product quality; faster, more efficient production; and higher employee job satisfaction. A few things worry you, however. Despite all of their promise, teams and teamwork are also prone to significant disadvantages. They're expensive to implement. They require significant training. And they work only about a third of the time they're used. So, despite their promise, you can't ignore the reality that using teams would be quite risky for Cessna.

Still, you can't help thinking that teams could pay off and that there might be ways for you to minimize the risk of failure. For example, because the plant will be in a new location, Independence, Kansas, you get to start with a brand new workforce. What kinds of people should you hire for teamwork? What kinds of skills and experience will they need to succeed in a team environment? If you decide to take the plunge and use teams, how much authority and responsibility should you give them? Should they be limited to just advising management, or should you make them totally responsible for quality, costs, and productivity? Finally, while you're considering using teams on the assembly line, are there other places in which you might use teams? Not all teams are alike. Maybe there are other places in which teams could contribute to the success of Cessna's "new" single-engine plane-manufacturing facility?

If you were in charge of Cessna's "new" single-engine factory, what would you do?

9-1 The Good and Bad of Using Teams

We begin this chapter by reviewing the advantages and disadvantages of teams and exploring when companies should use teams instead of more traditional approaches. Next, we discuss the different types of work teams and the characteristics that all teams share. The chapter ends by focusing on the practical steps to managing teams: team goals and priorities; and organizing, training, and compensating teams.

Work teams consist of a small number of people with complementary skills who hold themselves mutually accountable for pursuing a common purpose, achieving performance goals, and improving interdependent work processes.[2] By this definition, computer programmers working on separate projects in the same department of a company would not be considered a team. To be a team, the programmers would have to be interdependent and share responsibility and accountability for the quality and amount of computer code they produced.[3] Teams are becoming more important in many industries because they help organizations respond to specific problems and challenges. Though work teams are not the answer for every situation or organization, if the right teams are used properly and in the right settings, teams can dramatically improve company performance over more traditional management approaches while also instilling a sense of vitality in the workplace that is otherwise difficult to achieve.

work team
a small number of people with complementary skills who hold themselves mutually accountable for pursuing a common purpose, achieving performance goals, and improving interdependent work processes

Part Three *Organizing*

After reading this section, you should be able to:

9-1 explain the good and bad of using teams.

Ninety-one percent of organizations are significantly improving their effectiveness by using work teams.[4] Procter & Gamble and Cummins Engine began using teams in 1962 and 1973, respectively, while companies like Boeing, Caterpillar, and General Electric established work teams in the mid- to late 1980s. Today, most companies use teams to tackle a variety of issues.[5] "Teams are ubiquitous. Whether we are talking about software development, Olympic hockey, disease outbreak response, or urban warfare, teams represent the critical unit that 'gets things done' in today's world."[6]

Let's continue our discussion of teams by learning about **9-1a the advantages of teams, 9-1b the disadvantages of teams**, and **9-1c when to use and not use teams.**

9-1a The Advantages of Teams

Companies are making greater use of teams because teams have been shown to improve customer satisfaction, product and service quality, speed and efficiency in product development, employee job satisfaction, and decision making.[7] Teams help businesses increase *customer satisfaction* in several ways. One way is to create work teams that are trained to meet the needs of specific customers. For example, STAFF MANAGEMENT, which hires temporary workers for companies, was asked by a leading online retailer to hire 10,000 people for the 2010 holiday season. Staff Management's hiring team used social media, such as Facebook, job fairs, and other hiring events to generate the applicants.[8]

Businesses also create problem-solving teams and employee involvement teams to study ways to improve overall customer satisfaction and make recommendations for improvements. Teams like these typically meet on a weekly or monthly basis.

Teams also help firms improve *product and service quality* in several ways.[9] In contrast to traditional organizational structures where management is responsible for organizational outcomes and performance, teams take direct responsibility for the quality of the products and service they produce and sell.

As you learned in Chapter 6, companies that are slow to innovate or integrate new features and technologies into their products are at a competitive disadvantage. Therefore, a third reason that teams are increasingly popular is that they can increase *speed and efficiency when designing and manufacturing products.*[10] LOUIS VUITTON, the French-based world-renowned fashion house, designs and makes some of the most expensive, best-selling purses, shoulder bags, tote bags, and luggage in the world. It used to take 30 craftspeople eight days to produce just one bag! Each worker completed just one task, such as cutting leather, gluing and sewing, or stitching the lining, and bottlenecks would form as the slower workers forced faster workers to wait for the next purse to come to them for work. Louis Vuitton fixed the problem by switching to teams of 6 to 12 workers who learned to complete four different production steps. Teams were then positioned in U-shaped workstations with sewing machines and assembly tables so that team members could pass bags back and forth without waiting. The result? It now takes just one day and 6 to 12 workers to produce a bag. Furthermore, because team members complete multiple tasks, teams can now work on different kinds of bags, which allows the company to switch production quickly to its best-selling items. Finally, with quality up significantly, returns of defective bags have dropped by two-thirds.[11]

Another reason for using teams is that teamwork often leads to increased *job satisfaction*.[12] One reason that teamwork can be more satisfying than traditional work is that it gives workers a chance to improve their skills. This is often accomplished through **cross-training**, in which team members are taught how to do all or most of the jobs performed by the other team members. The advantage for the organization is that cross-training allows a team to function normally when one member is absent, quits, or is transferred.

A second reason that teamwork is satisfying is that work teams often receive proprietary business information that is available only to managers at most companies. For example, WHOLE FOODS has an "open books, open door, open people" philosophy. Team members are given full access to their store's financial information and everyone's salaries, including those of the store manager and the CEO.[13] Each day, next to the time clock, Whole Foods employees can see the previous day's sales for each team as well as the sales on the same day from the previous year. Each week, team members can examine the same information, broken down by team, for all of the Whole Foods stores in their region.

Team members also gain job satisfaction from unique leadership responsibilities that are not typically available in traditional organizations. Furthermore, rotating leadership among team members can lead to more participation and cooperation in team decision making and improved team performance.

Finally, teams share many of the advantages of group decision making discussed in Chapter 4. For instance, because team members possess different knowledge, skills, abilities, and experiences, a team is able to view problems from multiple perspectives. This diversity of viewpoints increases the odds that team decisions will solve the underlying causes of problems and not just address the symptoms. The increased knowledge and information available to teams also make it easier for them to generate more alternative solutions, a critical part of improving the quality of decisions. Because team members are involved in decision-making processes, they are also likely to be more committed to making those decisions work. In short, teams can do a much better job than individuals in two important steps of the decision-making process: defining the problem and generating alternative solutions.

9-1b The Disadvantages of Teams

Although teams can significantly improve customer satisfaction, product and service quality, speed and efficiency in product development, employee job satisfaction, and decision making, using teams does not guarantee these positive outcomes. In fact, if you've ever participated in team projects in your classes, you're probably already aware of some of the problems inherent in work teams. Despite all of their promise, teams and teamwork are also prone to these significant disadvantages: initially high turnover, social loafing, and the problems associated with group decision making.

cross-training
training team members to do all or most of the jobs performed by the other team members

The first disadvantage of work teams is *initially high turnover*. Teams aren't for everyone, and some workers balk at the responsibility, effort, and learning required in team settings. Some people may quit because they object to the way team members closely scrutinize each other's job performance, particularly when teams are small. Beverly Reynolds, who quit Eaton Corporation's team-based system after nine months, says her coworkers "weren't standing watching me, but from afar, they were watching me." And even though her teammates were willing to help her improve her job performance, she concludes, "As it turns out, it just wasn't for me at all."[14]

Social loafing is another disadvantage of work teams. Social loafing occurs when workers withhold their efforts and fail to perform their share of the work.[15] A nineteenth-century French engineer named Maximilian Ringlemann first documented social loafing when he found that one person pulling on a rope alone exerted an average of 139 pounds of force on the rope. In groups of three, the average force dropped to 117 pounds per person. In groups of eight, the average dropped to just 68 pounds per person. Ringlemann concluded that the larger the team, the smaller the individual effort. In fact, social loafing is more likely to occur in larger groups where identifying and monitoring the efforts of individual team members can be difficult.[16] In other words, social loafers count on being able to blend into the background where their lack of effort isn't easily spotted. From team-based class projects, most students already know about social loafers, or "slackers," who contribute poor, little, or no work whatsoever. Not surprisingly, a study of 250 student teams found that the most talented students are typically the least satisfied with teamwork because of having to carry slackers and do a disproportionate share of their team's work.[17] Perceptions of fairness are negatively related to the extent of social loafing within teams.[18]

How prevalent is social loafing on teams? One study found that when team activities were not mandatory, only 25 percent of manufacturing workers volunteered to join problem-solving teams; 70 percent were quiet, passive supporters (i.e., they didn't put forth effort); and 5 percent were actively opposed to these activities.[19] Another study found that on management teams, 56 percent of the managers, or more than half, withheld their effort in one way or another. Exhibit 9.1 lists the factors that encourage people to withhold effort in teams.

Finally, teams share many of the *disadvantages of group decision making* discussed in Chapter 4, such as groupthink. In *groupthink*, members of highly cohesive groups feel intense pressure not to

social loafing
behavior in which team members withhold their efforts and fail to perform their share of the work

Exhibit 9.1

Factors That Encourage People to Withhold Effort in Teams

1. **The presence of someone with expertise.** Team members will withhold effort when another team member is highly qualified to make a decision or comment on an issue.

2. **The presentation of a compelling argument.** Team members will withhold effort if the arguments for a course of action are very persuasive or similar to their own thinking.

3. **The lack of confidence in one's ability to contribute.** Team members will withhold effort if they are unsure about their ability to contribute to discussions, activities, or decisions. This is especially so for high-profile decisions.

4. **An unimportant or meaningless decision.** Team members will withhold effort by mentally withdrawing or adopting a "who cares" attitude if decisions don't affect them or their units, or if they don't see a connection between their efforts and their team's successes or failures.

5. **A dysfunctional decision-making climate.** Team members will withhold effort if other team members are frustrated or indifferent or if a team is floundering or disorganized.

Source: P. W. Mulvey, J. F. Veiga, and P. M. Elsass, "When Teammates Raise a White Flag," Academy of Management Executive 10, no. 1 (1996): 40–49.

disagree with each other so that the group can approve a proposed solution. Because groupthink restricts discussion and leads to consideration of a limited number of alternative solutions, it usually results in poor decisions. Also, team decision making takes considerable time, and team meetings can often be unproductive and inefficient. Another possible pitfall is *minority domination*, where just one or two people dominate team discussions, restricting consideration of different problem definitions and alternative solutions. Finally, team members may not feel accountable for the decisions and actions taken by the team.

9-1c When to Use Teams

As the two previous subsections made clear, teams have significant advantages *and* disadvantages. Therefore, the question is not whether to use teams, but *when* and *where* to use teams for maximum benefit and minimum cost. As Doug Johnson, associate director at the Center for Collaborative Organizations at the University of North Texas, puts it, "Teams are a means to an end, not an end in themselves. You have to ask yourself questions first. Does the work require interdependence? Will the team philosophy fit company strategy? Will management make a long-term commitment to this process?"[20] Exhibit 9.2 provides some additional guidelines on when to use or not use teams.[21]

First, teams should be used when there is a clear, engaging reason or purpose for using them. Too many companies use teams because they're popular or because the companies assume that teams can fix all problems. Teams are much more likely to succeed if they know why they exist and what they are supposed to accomplish, and more likely to fail if they don't. Johan Bruyneel has won the *Tour de France* nine times. No other team director has even come close to his record. What accounts for his teams' successes? Clear purposes and goals. Bruyneel plans out the entire year before the race, mixing in the right combination of training, racing, and rest. Then, for each of the nine members of his riding teams, he develops daily, weekly, monthly, and annual goals to prepare them to fulfill their team roles.[22]

Second, teams should be used when the job can't be done unless people work together. This typically means that teams are needed when tasks are complex, require multiple perspectives, or require repeated interaction with others to complete.

If tasks are simple and don't require multiple perspectives or repeated interaction with others, however, teams should not be used.[23] Consultant Jeff Palfini says, "Managers confronted with a new task should always consider whether pulling

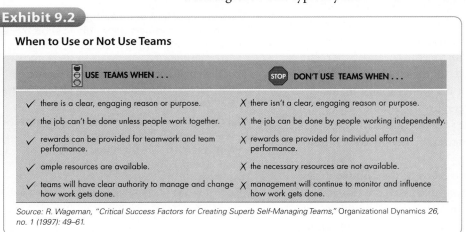

Exhibit 9.2

When to Use or Not Use Teams

🚦 USE TEAMS WHEN . . .	🛑 DON'T USE TEAMS WHEN . . .
✓ there is a clear, engaging reason or purpose.	✗ there isn't a clear, engaging reason or purpose.
✓ the job can't be done unless people work together.	✗ the job can be done by people working independently.
✓ rewards can be provided for teamwork and team performance.	✗ rewards are provided for individual effort and performance.
✓ ample resources are available.	✗ the necessary resources are not available.
✓ teams will have clear authority to manage and change how work gets done.	✗ management will continue to monitor and influence how work gets done.

Source: R. Wageman, "Critical Success Factors for Creating Superb Self-Managing Teams," Organizational Dynamics 26, no. 1 (1997): 49–61.

together a team will be the most efficient way to complete the task. Sometimes it's faster and less complicated to parcel it out or delegate it to one or two people, especially if the task is fairly routine."[24]

Third, teams should be used when rewards can be provided for teamwork and team performance. Rewards that depend on team performance rather than individual performance are the key to rewarding team behaviors and efforts. You'll read more about team rewards later in the chapter, but for now it's enough to know that if the type of reward

Johan Bruyneel understands his team needs to plan well in advance. Here, he's pictured with his team in Albuquerque, New Mexico, a full six months before the start of the Tour de France.

(individual vs. team) is not matched to the type of performance (individual vs. team), teams won't work. This was the case at SAVILLS a London-based global real estate advising and consulting firm. Director Mark Ridley realized that the company's incentive structure was encouraging individual, but not group, effort. Says Ridley, "We were only rewarding one element of behavior—[individual] financial performance. It was difficult to get someone in Scotland to pass work to Birmingham or to get someone in London to help in Scotland." While the old system was based on 81 different profit and loss statements and only rewarded individuals, the new reward system is based on individual performance plus the performance of their overall division, their local team, and their contributions to the team, such as cross-selling with other Savills' salespeople. Behavior has already begun to change.[25] Systems that reward individual performance but hope for high team-level performance are sure to fail.[26]

REVIEW 9-1

. . . .

The Good and Bad of Using Teams

In many industries, teams are growing in importance because they help organizations respond to specific problems and challenges. Teams have been shown to increase customer satisfaction (specific customer teams), product and service quality (direct responsibility), speed and efficiency in product development (overlapping development phases), and employee job satisfaction (cross-training, unique opportunities, and leadership responsibilities). Although teams can produce significant improvements in these areas, using teams does not guarantee these positive outcomes. Teams and teamwork have the disadvantages of initially high turnover and social loafing (especially in large groups). Teams also share many of the advantages (multiple perspectives, generation of more alternatives, and more commitment) and disadvantages (groupthink, time consuming, poorly run meetings, domination by a few team members, and weak accountability) of group decision making. Finally, teams should be used for a clear purpose, when the work requires that people work together, when rewards can be provided for both teamwork and team performance, when ample resources can be provided, and when teams can be given clear authority over their work.

9-2 Kinds of Teams

Companies use different kinds of teams for different purposes.

After reading this section, you should be able to:

9-2 recognize and understand the different kinds of teams.

GOOGLE uses teams to innovate and develop new products as well as tweak and improve its search algorithms and functions.[27] JCPENNEY uses teams to execute its "door to floor" strategy, which aims to get the right merchandise to the right store at the right time so that Penney's customers find what they want when they want it.[28]

Let's continue our discussion of teams by learning about the different kinds of teams that companies like Google and JCPenney use to make themselves more competitive. We look first at **9-2a how teams differ in terms of autonomy, which is the key dimension that makes one team different from another**, and then at **9-2b some special kinds of teams**.

9-2a Autonomy, the Key Dimension

Teams can be classified in a number of ways, such as permanent or temporary, or functional or cross-functional. However, studies indicate that the amount of autonomy possessed by a team is the key difference among teams.[29] *Autonomy* is the degree to which workers have the discretion, freedom, and independence to decide how and when to accomplish their jobs. Exhibit 9.3 shows how five kinds of teams differ in terms of autonomy. Moving left to right across the autonomy continuum at the top of the exhibit, traditional work groups and employee involvement groups have the least autonomy; semiautonomous work groups have more autonomy; and, finally, self-managing teams and self-designing teams have the most autonomy. Moving from bottom to top along the left side of the exhibit, note that the number of responsibilities given to each kind of team increases directly with its autonomy. Let's review each of these kinds of teams and their autonomy and responsibilities in more detail.

The smallest amount of autonomy is found in **traditional work groups**, where two or more people work together to achieve a shared goal. In these groups, workers are responsible for doing the work or "executing the task," but they do not have direct responsibility or control over their work. Workers report to managers, who are responsible for their performance and have the authority to hire and fire them, make job assignments, and control resources.

Employee involvement teams, which have somewhat more autonomy, meet on company time on a weekly or monthly basis to provide advice or make

traditional work group
a group composed of two or more people who work together to achieve a shared goal

employee involvement team
team that provides advice or makes suggestions to management concerning specific issues

Exhibit 9.3

Team Authority Continuum

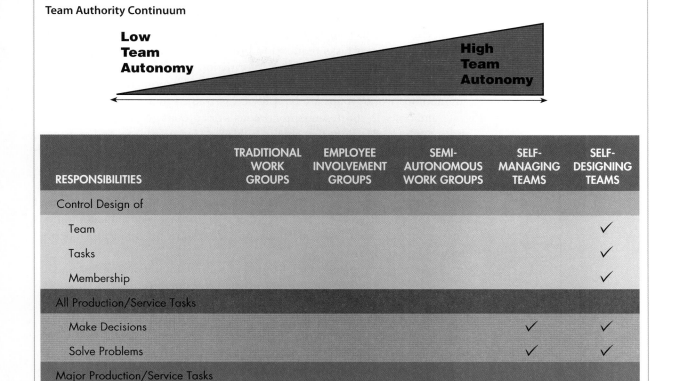

RESPONSIBILITIES	TRADITIONAL WORK GROUPS	EMPLOYEE INVOLVEMENT GROUPS	SEMI-AUTONOMOUS WORK GROUPS	SELF-MANAGING TEAMS	SELF-DESIGNING TEAMS
Control Design of					
Team					✓
Tasks					✓
Membership					✓
All Production/Service Tasks					
Make Decisions				✓	✓
Solve Problems				✓	✓
Major Production/Service Tasks					
Make Decisions			✓	✓	✓
Solve Problems			✓	✓	✓
Receive Information			✓	✓	✓
Give Advice/Make Suggestions		✓	✓	✓	✓
Execute Task	✓	✓	✓	✓	✓

Sources: R. D. Banker, J. M. Field, R. G. Schroeder, and K. K. Sinha, "Impact of Work Teams on Manufacturing Performance: A Longitudinal Field Study," Academy of Management Journal 39 (1996): 867–890; and J. R. Hackman, "The Psychology of Self-Management in Organizations," in Psychology and Work: Productivity, Change, and Employment, M. S. Pallak & R. Perlof, eds. (Washington, DC: American Psychological Association), 85–136.

suggestions to management concerning specific issues such as plant safety, customer relations, or product quality.[30] Though they offer advice and suggestions, they do not have the authority to make decisions. Membership on these teams is often voluntary, but members may be selected because of their expertise. The idea behind employee involvement teams is that the people closest to the problem or situation are best able to recommend solutions. At EICHSTAEDT, a San Francisco–based accounting firm, employee involvement teams serve as developmental opportunities for junior accountants. For example, Cynthia Bonavia led the "rewards" team charged with studying employee perceptions of the firm's rewards and benefits system, nonmonetary rewards, work/life balance, and employee satisfaction. Likewise, Tracy Hom led a team that studied how to improve employee mentoring.[31]

Semiautonomous work groups not only provide advice and suggestions to management but also have the authority to make decisions and solve problems related to the major tasks required to produce a product or service. Semiautonomous groups regularly receive information about budgets, work quality and performance, and competitors' products. Furthermore, members of semiautonomous work groups are typically cross-trained in a number of different skills and tasks. In short, semiautonomous work groups give employees the authority to make decisions that are typically made by supervisors and managers.

That authority is not complete, however. Managers still play a role, though one that is much reduced compared with traditional work groups, in supporting the work of semiautonomous work groups. The role a manager plays on a team usually evolves over time. Managers have to adjust what they do based on the sophistication of the team. A lot of what managers of semiautonomous work groups do is ask good questions, provide resources, and facilitate performance of group goals.

Self-managing teams differ from semiautonomous work groups in that team members manage and control *all* of the major tasks *directly related* to production of a product or service without first getting approval from management. This includes managing and controlling the acquisition of materials, making a product or providing a service, and ensuring timely delivery. **Self-designing teams** have all the characteristics of self-managing teams, but they can also control and change the design of the teams themselves, the tasks they do and how and when they do them, and the membership of the teams.

9-2b Special Kinds of Teams

Cross-functional teams are intentionally composed of employees from different functional areas of the organization.[32] Because their members have different functional backgrounds, education, and experience, cross-functional teams usually attack problems from multiple perspectives and generate more ideas and alternative solutions, all of which are especially important when trying to innovate or do creative problem solving.[33] Cross-functional teams can be used almost anywhere in an organization and are often used in conjunction with matrix and product organizational structures (see Chapter 8). They can also be used either with part-time or temporary team assignments or with full-time, long-term teams.

Virtual teams are groups of geographically and/or organizationally dispersed coworkers who use a combination of telecommunications and information technologies to accomplish an organizational task.[34] Members of virtual teams rarely meet face-to-face; instead, they use e-mail, videoconferencing, and group communication software. *CHARTER*, the magazine of the Institute of Chartered Accountants in Australia, describes the prevalence of virtual teams in Sydney's local cafés: "Dateline: 4pm at a Surry Hills café in Sydney. The lunch crowd has long gone but the room is bustling, a sea of laptops, vibrating Black-Berrys and iPhones. . . . You will find this growing modern workforce prolifically sprouting in every industrialized groove of the globe. Most of them are

semiautonomous work group
a group that has the authority to make decisions and solve problems related to the major tasks of producing a product or service

self-managing team
a team that manages and controls all of the major tasks of producing a product or service

self-designing team
a team that has the characteristics of self-managing teams but also controls team design, work tasks, and team membership

cross-functional team
a team composed of employees from different functional areas of the organization

virtual team
a team composed of geographically and/or organizationally dispersed coworkers who use telecommunication and information technologies to accomplish an organizational task

logged in to a morning meeting in Dubai, going over a spreadsheet with a colleague lunching in Singapore, or waiting for London to wake up."[35]

The principal advantage of virtual teams is their flexibility. Employees can work with each other, regardless of physical location, time zone, or organizational affiliation.[36] Because the team members don't meet in a physical location, virtual teams also find it much easier to include other key stakeholders such as suppliers and customers. Plus, virtual teams have certain efficiency advantages over traditional team structures. Because the teammates do not meet face-to-face, a virtual team typically requires a smaller time commitment than a traditional team does. Moreover, employees can fulfill the responsibilities of their virtual team membership from the comfort of their own offices without the travel time or downtime typically required for face-to-face meetings.[37]

project team
a team created to complete specific, one-time projects or tasks within a limited time

A drawback of virtual teams is that the team members must learn to express themselves in new contexts.[38] The give-and-take that naturally occurs in face-to-face meetings is more difficult to achieve through videoconferencing or other methods of virtual teaming. Similarly, several studies have also shown that physical proximity enhances information processing.[39] Therefore, some companies bring virtual team members together on a regular basis to try to minimize these problems. Exhibit 9.4 provides a number of tips for successfully managing virtual teams.

Project teams are created to complete specific, one-time projects or tasks within a limited time.[40] Project teams are often used to develop new products, significantly improve existing products, roll out new information systems, or build new factories or offices. The project team is typically led by a project manager who has the overall responsibility for planning, staffing, and managing the team, which usually includes employees from different functional areas. One advantage of project teams is that drawing employees from different functional areas can reduce or eliminate communication barriers. In turn, as long as team members feel free to express their ideas, thoughts, and concerns, free-flowing communication encourages cooperation among separate departments and typically speeds up the design process.[41] Another advantage of project teams is their flexibility. When projects are finished, project team members either move on to the next project or return to their functional units. For example, publication of this book required designers, editors, page compositors, and Web designers, among others. When the task was finished, these

---

Exhibit 9.4

Tips for Managing Successful Virtual Teams

- Select people who are self-starters and strong communicators.

- Keep the team focused by establishing clear, specific goals and by explaining the consequences and importance of meeting these goals.

- Provide frequent feedback so that team members can measure their progress.

- Keep team interactions upbeat and action-oriented by expressing appreciation for good work and completed tasks.

- "Personalize" the virtual team by periodically bringing team members together and by encouraging team members to share information with each other about their personal lives. This is especially important when the virtual team first forms.

- Improve communication through increased telephone calls, e-mails, and Internet messaging and videoconference sessions.

- Periodically ask team members how well the team is working and what can be done to improve performance.

- Empower virtual teams so they have the discretion, freedom, and independence to decide how and when to accomplish their jobs.

Sources: W. F. Cascio, "Managing a Virtual Workplace," Academy of Management Executive 14 (2000): 81–90; B. Kirkman, B. Rosen, P. Tesluk, and C. Gibson, "The Impact of Team Empowerment on Virtual Team Performance: The Moderating Role of Face-to-Face Interaction," Academy of Management Journal 47 (2004): 175–192; S. Furst, M. Reeves, B. Rosen, and R. Blackburn, "Managing the Life Cycle of Virtual Teams," Academy of Management Executive (May 2004): 6–20; and C. Solomon, "Managing Virtual Teams," Workforce 80 (June 2001), 60.

---

people applied their skills to other textbook projects. Because of this flexibility, project teams are often used with the matrix organizational designs discussed in Chapter 8.

REVIEW 9-2

Kinds of Teams

Companies use different kinds of teams to make themselves more competitive. Autonomy is the key dimension that makes teams different. Traditional work groups (which execute tasks) and employee involvement groups (which make suggestions) have the lowest levels of autonomy. Semiautonomous work groups (which control major direct tasks) have more autonomy, whereas self-managing teams (which control all direct tasks) and self-designing teams (which control membership and how tasks are done) have the highest levels of autonomy. Cross-functional, virtual, and project teams are common but are not easily categorized in terms of autonomy. Cross-functional teams combine employees from different functional areas to help teams attack problems from multiple perspectives and generate more ideas and solutions. Virtual teams use telecommunications and information technologies to bring coworkers together, regardless of physical location or time zone. Virtual teams reduce travel and work time, but communication may suffer because team members don't work face-to-face. Finally, project teams are used for specific, one-time projects or tasks that must be completed within a limited time. Project teams reduce communication barriers and promote flexibility; teams and team members are reassigned to their department or new projects as old projects are completed.

9-3 Work Team Characteristics

"Why did I ever let you talk me into teams? They're nothing but trouble."[42] Lots of managers have this reaction after making the move to teams. Many don't realize that this reaction is normal, both for them and for workers. In fact, such a reaction is characteristic of the *storming* stage of team development (discussed in Section 9-3e). Understanding the characteristics of work teams is essential for making teams an effective part of an organization.

After reading this section, you should be able to:

9-3 describe the general characteristics of work teams.

Managers who are familiar with the important characteristics of teams will be better prepared to manage the predictable changes that occur when companies make the switch to team-based structures, as well as any problems that may arise.

In this section, you'll learn about **9-3a team norms, 9-3b team cohesiveness, 9-3c team size, 9-3d team conflict**, and **9-3e the stages of team development.**

9-3a Team Norms

norms
informally agreed-on standards that regulate team behavior

Over time, teams develop **norms**, which are informally agreed-on standards that regulate team behavior.[43] Norms are valuable because they let team members know what is expected of them. Studies indicate that norms are one of the most powerful influences on work behavior because they regulate the everyday actions that allow teams to function effectively. Team norms are often associated with positive outcomes such as stronger organizational commitment, more trust in management, and stronger job and organizational satisfaction.[44] Effective work teams develop norms about the quality and timeliness of job performance, absenteeism, safety, and honest expression of ideas and opinions. Surgeon Atul Gawande, author of *The Checklist Manifesto*, contends that, "The complexity of what we [in modern medicine] have to deliver on exceeds our abilities as experts partly because the volume of knowledge has exceeded what training can possibly provide."[45] So, in his operating rooms, Gawande and his surgical teams use and review checklists to make sure each small but critical step is completed by each member of the surgical team following agreed-on standards of behavior or norms.

Norms can also influence team behavior in negative ways. For example, most people would agree that the following are negative behaviors: damaging organizational property; saying or doing something to hurt someone at work; intentionally doing one's work badly, incorrectly, or slowly; griping about coworkers; deliberately bending or breaking rules; or doing something to harm the company or boss. A study of workers from 34 teams in 20 different organizations found that teams with negative norms strongly influenced their team members to engage in these negative behaviors. In fact, the longer individuals were members of a team with negative norms, and the more frequently they interacted with their teammates, the more likely they were to perform negative behaviors. Because team norms typically develop early in the life of a team, these results indicate how important it is for teams to establish positive norms from the outset.[46]

9-3b Team Cohesiveness

Cohesiveness is another important characteristic of work teams. Cohesiveness is the extent to which team members are attracted to a team and motivated to remain in it.[47] The level of cohesiveness in a group is important for several reasons. To start, cohesive groups have a better chance of retaining their members. As a result, cohesive groups typically experience lower turnover.[48] In addition, team cohesiveness promotes cooperative behavior, generosity, and a willingness on the part of team members to assist each other.[49] When team cohesiveness is high, team members are more motivated to contribute to the team because they want to gain the approval of other team members. For these reasons and others, studies have clearly established that cohesive teams consistently perform better.[50] Furthermore, cohesive teams quickly achieve high levels of performance. By contrast, teams low in cohesion take much longer to reach the same levels of performance.[51]

What can be done to promote team cohesiveness? First, make sure that all team members are present at team meetings and activities. Team cohesiveness suffers when members are allowed to withdraw from the team and miss team meetings and events.[52] Second, create additional opportunities for teammates

cohesiveness
the extent to which team members are attracted to a team and motivated to remain in it

what *really* works

Cohesion and Team Performance

Have you ever worked in a really cohesive group where everyone liked and enjoyed each other and was glad to be part of the group? It's great. By contrast, have you ever worked in a group where everyone really disliked each other and was unhappy to be part of the group? It's terrible. Anyone who has had either of these experiences can appreciate how important group cohesion is and the effect it can have on team performance. Indeed, 46 studies based on 1,279 groups confirm that cohesion does matter.

Team Performance
On average, there is a 66 percent chance that cohesive teams will outperform less cohesive teams.

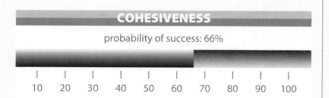

Team Performance with Interdependent Tasks
Teams work best for interdependent tasks that require people to work together to get the job done. When teams perform interdependent tasks, there is a 73 percent chance that cohesive teams will outperform less cohesive teams.

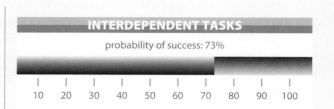

Team Performance with Independent Tasks
Teams generally are not suited for independent tasks that people can accomplish by themselves. When teams perform independent tasks, there is only a 60 percent chance that cohesive teams will outperform less cohesive teams.

Some caution is warranted in interpreting these results. For example, there is always the possibility that a team could become so cohesive that its team goals become more important than organizational goals. Also, teams sometimes unite around negative goals and norms that are harmful rather than helpful to organizations. Nonetheless, there is also room for even more optimism about cohesive teams. Teams that are cohesive *and* committed to the goals they are asked to achieve should have an even higher probability of success than the numbers shown here.[53]

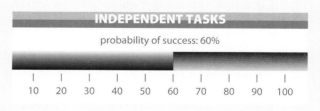

to work together by rearranging work schedules and creating common workspaces. When task interdependence is high and team members have lots of chances to work together, team cohesiveness tends to increase.[54] Third, engaging in nonwork activities as a team can help build cohesion. Finally, companies build team cohesiveness by making employees feel that they are part of an organization.

9-3c Team Size

The relationship between team size and performance appears to be curvilinear. Very small or very large teams may not perform as well as moderately sized teams. For most teams, the right size is somewhere between six and nine members.[55] A team of this size is small enough for the team members to get to know each other and for each member to have an opportunity to contribute in a meaningful way to the success of the team. At the same time, the team is also large enough to take advantage of team members' diverse skills, knowledge, and perspectives. It is also easier to instill a sense of responsibility and mutual accountability in teams of this size.[56]

When teams get too large, team members find it difficult to get to know one another, and the team may splinter into smaller subgroups. When this occurs, subgroups sometimes argue and disagree, weakening overall team cohesion. As teams grow, there is also a greater chance of *minority domination*, where just a few team members dominate team discussions. Even if minority domination doesn't occur, larger groups may not have time for all team members to share their input. And when team members feel that their contributions are unimportant or not needed, the result is less involvement, effort, and accountability to the team.[57] Large teams also face logistical problems such as finding an appropriate time or place to meet. Finally, the incidence of social loafing, discussed earlier in the chapter, is much higher in large teams.

Just as team performance can suffer when a team is too large, it can also be negatively affected when a team is too small. Teams with just a few people may lack the diversity of skills and knowledge found in larger teams. Also, teams that are too small are unlikely to gain the advantages of team decision making (multiple perspectives, generating more ideas and alternative solutions, and stronger commitment) found in larger teams.

What signs indicate that a team's size needs to be changed? If decisions are taking too long, the team has difficulty making decisions or taking action, a few members dominate the team, or the commitment or efforts of team members are weak, chances are the team is too big. In contrast, if a team is having difficulty coming up with ideas or generating solutions, or the team does not have the expertise to address a specific problem, chances are the team is too small.

9-3d Team Conflict

Conflict and disagreement are inevitable in most teams. But this shouldn't surprise anyone. From time to time, people who work together are going to disagree about what and how things get done. What causes conflict in teams? Although almost anything can lead to conflict—casual remarks that unintentionally offend a team member or fighting over scarce resources—the primary cause of team conflict is disagreement over team goals and priorities.[58] Other common causes of team conflict include disagreements over task-related issues, interpersonal incompatibilities, and simple fatigue.

Though most people view conflict negatively, the key to dealing with team conflict is not avoiding it, but rather making sure that the team experiences the right kind of conflict. In Chapter 4, you learned about *c-type conflict*, or

cognitive conflict, which focuses on problem-related differences of opinion, and *a-type conflict*, or *affective conflict*, which refers to the emotional reactions that can occur when disagreements become personal rather than professional.[59] Cognitive conflict is strongly associated with improvements in team performance, whereas affective conflict is strongly associated with decreases in team performance.[60] Why does this happen? With cognitive conflict, team members disagree because their different experiences and expertise lead them to different views of the problem and solutions. Indeed, managers who participated on teams that emphasized cognitive conflict described their teammates as "smart," "team players," and "best in the business." They described their teams as "open," "fun," and "productive." One manager summed up the positive attitude that team members had about cognitive conflict by saying, "We scream a lot, then laugh, and then resolve the issue."[61] Thus, cognitive conflict is also characterized by a willingness to examine, compare, and reconcile differences to produce the best possible solution.

By contrast, affective conflict often results in hostility, anger, resentment, distrust, cynicism, and apathy. Managers who participated on teams that experienced affective conflict described their teammates as "manipulative," "secretive," "burned out," and "political."[62] Not surprisingly, affective conflict can make people uncomfortable and cause them to withdraw and decrease their commitment to a team.[63] Affective conflict also lowers the satisfaction of team members, may lead to personal hostility between coworkers, and can decrease team cohesiveness.[64] So, unlike cognitive conflict, affective conflict undermines team performance by preventing teams from engaging in the kinds of activities that are critical to team effectiveness.

So, what can managers do to manage team conflict? First, they need to realize that emphasizing cognitive conflict alone won't be enough. Studies show that cognitive and affective conflicts often occur together in a given team activity! Sincere attempts to reach agreement on a difficult issue can quickly deteriorate from cognitive to affective conflict if the discussion turns personal and tempers and emotions flare. Although cognitive conflict is clearly the better approach to take, efforts to engage in cognitive conflict should be managed well and checked before they deteriorate and the team becomes unproductive.

Can teams disagree and still get along? Fortunately, they can. In an attempt to study this issue, researchers examined team conflict in 12 high-tech companies. In four of the companies, work teams used cognitive conflict to address work problems but did so in a way that minimized the occurrence of affective conflict.[65]

9-3e Stages of Team Development

As teams develop and grow, they pass through four stages of development. As shown in Exhibit 9.5, those stages are forming, storming, norming, and performing.[66] Although not every team passes through each of these stages, teams that do tend to be better performers.[67] This holds true even for teams composed of seasoned executives. After a period of time, however, if a team is not managed well, its performance may start to deteriorate as the team begins a process of decline and progresses through the stages of de-norming, de-storming, and de-forming.[68]

Forming is the initial stage of team development. This is the getting-acquainted stage in which team members first meet each other, form initial impressions, and try to get a sense of what it will be like to be part of the team. Some of the first team norms will be established during this stage as team members begin to find out what behaviors will and won't be accepted by the team. During this stage, team leaders should allow time for team members to get to know each other, set early ground rules, and begin to set up a preliminary team structure.

Conflicts and disagreements often characterize the second stage of team development, **storming**. As team members begin working together, different personalities and work styles may clash. Team members become more assertive at this stage and more willing to state opinions. This is also the stage when team members jockey for position and try to establish a favorable role for themselves

---

Exhibit 9.5

Stages of Team Development

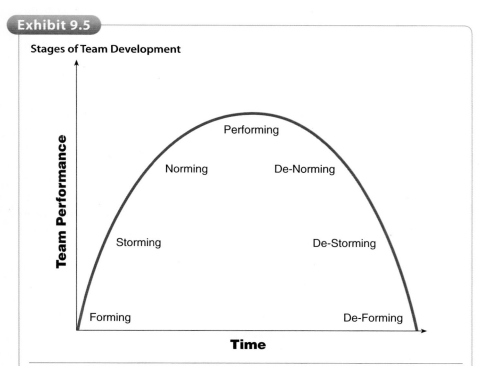

Sources: J. F. McGrew, J. G. Bilotta, and J. M. Deeney, "Software Team Formation and Decay: Extending the Standard Model for Small Groups," *Small Group Research 30, no. 2 (1999): 209–234;* and B. W. Tuckman, "Development Sequence in Small Groups," *Psychological Bulletin 63, no. 6 (1965); 384–399.*

forming
the first stage of team development, in which team members meet each other, form initial impressions, and begin to establish team norms

storming
the second stage of development, characterized by conflict and disagreement, in which team members disagree over what the team should do and how it should do it

on the team. In addition, team members are likely to disagree about what the group should do and how it should do it. Team performance is still relatively low, given that team cohesion is weak and team members are still reluctant to support each other. Because teams that get stuck in the storming stage are almost always ineffective, it is important for team leaders to focus the team on team goals and on improving team performance. Team members need to be particularly patient and tolerant with each other in this stage.

During **norming**, the third stage of team development, team members begin to settle into their roles as team members. Positive team norms will have developed by this stage, and teammates should know what to expect from each other. Petty differences should have been resolved, friendships will have developed, and group cohesion will be relatively strong. At this point, team members will have accepted team goals, be operating as a unit, and, as indicated by the increase in performance, be working together effectively. This stage can be very short and is often characterized by someone on the team saying, "I think things are finally coming together." Note, however, that teams may also cycle back and forth between storming and norming several times before finally settling into norming.

In the last stage of team development, **performing**, performance improves because the team has finally matured into an effective, fully functioning team. At this point, members should be fully committed to the team and think of themselves as members of a team and not just employees. Team members often become intensely loyal to one another at this stage and feel mutual accountability for team successes and failures. Trivial disagreements, which can take time and energy away from the work of the team, should be rare. At this stage, teams get a lot of work done, and it is fun to be a team member.

The team should not become complacent, however. Without effective management, its performance may begin to decline as the team passes through the stages of de-norming, de-storming, and de-forming.[69] Indeed, John Puckett, manufacturing vice president for circuit-board manufacturer XEL Communications, says, "The books all say you start in this state of chaos and march through these various stages, and you end up in this state of ultimate self-direction, where everything is going just great. They never tell you it can go back in the other direction, sometimes just as quickly."[70]

In **de-norming**, which is a reversal of the norming stage, team performance begins to decline as the size, scope, goal, or members of the team change. With new members joining the group, older members may become defensive as established ways of doing things are questioned and challenged. Expression of ideas and opinions becomes less open. New members change team norms by actively rejecting or passively neglecting previously established team roles and behaviors.

In **de-storming**, which is a reversal of the storming phase, the team's comfort level decreases. Team cohesion weakens as more group members resist conforming to team norms and quit participating in team activities. Angry emotions flare as the group explodes in conflict and moves into the final stage of de-forming.

In **de-forming**, which is a reversal of the forming stage, team members position themselves to gain control of pieces of the team. Team members begin

norming
the third stage of team development, in which team members begin to settle into their roles, group cohesion grows, and positive team norms develop

performing
the fourth and final stage of team development, in which performance improves because the team has matured into an effective, fully functioning team

de-norming
a reversal of the norming stage, in which team performance begins to decline as the size, scope, goal, or members of the team change

de-storming
a reversal of the storming phase, in which the team's comfort level decreases, team cohesion weakens, and angry emotions and conflict may flare

de-forming
a reversal of the forming stage, in which team members position themselves to control pieces of the team, avoid each other, and isolate themselves from team leaders

306

to avoid each other and isolate themselves from team leaders. Team performance rapidly declines as the members quit caring about even minimal requirements of team performance.

If teams are actively managed, decline is not inevitable. However, managers need to recognize that the forces at work in the de-norming, de-storming, and de-forming stages represent a powerful, disruptive, and real threat to teams that have finally made it to the performing stage. Getting to the performing stage is half the battle. Staying there is the second half.

REVIEW 9-3
. . . .

Work Team Characteristics

The most important characteristics of work teams are team norms, cohesiveness, size, conflict, and development. Norms let team members know what is expected of them and can influence team behavior in positive and negative ways. Positive team norms are associated with organizational commitment, trust, and job satisfaction. Team cohesiveness helps teams retain members, promotes cooperative behavior, increases motivation, and facilitates team performance. Attending team meetings and activities, creating opportunities to work together, and engaging in nonwork activities can increase cohesiveness. Team size has a curvilinear relationship with team performance: Teams that are very small or very large do not perform as well as moderate-sized teams of six to nine members. Teams of this size are cohesive and small enough for team members to get to know each other and contribute in a meaningful way, but are large enough to take advantage of team members' diverse skills, knowledge, and perspectives. Conflict and disagreement are inevitable in most teams. The key to dealing with team conflict is to maximize cognitive conflict, which focuses on issue-related differences, and minimize affective conflict, the emotional reactions that occur when disagreements become personal rather than professional. As teams develop and grow, they pass through four stages of development: forming, storming, norming, and performing. After a period of time, however, if a team is not managed well, its performance may decline as the team regresses through the stages of de-norming, de-storming, and de-forming.

9-4 Enhancing Work Team Effectiveness

Making teams work is a challenging and difficult process, yet one that managers need to understand.

After reading this section, you should be able to:

9-4 explain how to enhance work team effectiveness.

Despite the difficulties working with teams, companies can increase the likelihood that teams will succeed by carefully managing **9-4a the setting of team goals and priorities** and **9-4b how work team members are selected, 9-4c trained,** and **9-4d compensated.**[71]

9-4a Setting Team Goals and Priorities

In Chapter 4, you learned that having specific, measurable, attainable, realistic, and timely (SMART) goals is one of the most effective means for improving individual job performance. Fortunately, team goals also improve team performance. In fact, team goals lead to much higher team performance 93 percent of the time.[72] For example, BEST BUY, the electronic retailer, assembled four groups of young salespeople and had them live together in a Los Angeles apartment for 10 weeks. Jeremy Sevush, a sales floor supervisor, said, "My friends joked and said I was joining 'Real World: Best Buy Edition.'" Their goal—to generate quick, easy-to-start business ideas for Best Buy. Because they had a clear goal and limited time, everyone was focused. And it worked. Sevush and his team came up with Best Buy Studio, Web-design consulting for small businesses. It was up and running just a few weeks after moving out of the apartments.[73]

Why is setting *specific* team goals so critical to team success? One reason is that increasing a team's performance is inherently more complex than just increasing one individual's job performance. For instance, consider that any team is likely to involve at least four different kinds of goals: each member's goal for the team, each member's goal for himself or herself on the team, the team's goal for each member, and the team's goal for itself.[74] In other words, without a specific goal for the team itself (the last of the four goals listed), team members may head off in all directions at once pursuing these other goals. Consequently, setting a specific goal *for the team* clarifies team priorities by providing a clear focus and purpose.

Challenging team goals affect how hard team members work. In particular, they greatly reduce the incidence of social loafing. When faced with difficult goals, team members necessarily expect everyone to contribute. Consequently, they are much more likely to notice and complain if a teammate isn't doing his or her share. In fact, when teammates know each other well, when team goals are specific, when team communication is good, and when teams are rewarded for team performance (discussed below), there is only a 1 in 16 chance that teammates will be social loafers.[75]

What can companies and teams do to ensure that team goals lead to superior team performance? One increasingly popular approach is to give teams stretch goals. *Stretch goals* are extremely ambitious goals that workers don't know how to reach.[76] Four things must occur for stretch goals to effectively motivate teams.[77] First, teams must have a high degree of autonomy or control over how they achieve their goals. Second, teams must be empowered with control resources, such as budgets, workspaces, computers, or whatever else they need to do their jobs. Steve Kerr, Goldman Sachs' chief learning officer, says, "We have a moral obligation to try to give people the tools to meet tough goals. I think it's totally wrong if you don't give employees the tools to succeed, then punish them when they fail."[78]

Third, teams need structural accommodation. **Structural accommodation** means giving teams the ability to change organizational structures, policies, and practices if doing so helps them meet their stretch goals. Finally, teams need bureaucratic immunity. **Bureaucratic immunity** means that teams

structural accommodation
the ability to change organizational structures, policies, and practices in order to meet stretch goals

bureaucratic immunity
the ability to make changes without first getting approval from managers or other parts of an organization

no longer have to go through the frustratingly slow process of multilevel reviews and sign-offs to get management approval before making changes. Once granted bureaucratic immunity, teams are immune from the influence of various organizational groups and are accountable only to top management. Therefore, teams can act quickly, and even experiment, with little fear of failure.

9-4b Selecting People for Teamwork

University of Southern California management professor Edward Lawler says, "People are very naive about how easy it is to create a team. Teams are the Ferraris of work design. They're high performance but high maintenance and expensive."[79] It's almost impossible to have an effective work team without carefully selecting people who are suited for teamwork or for working on a particular team. A focus on teamwork (individualism–collectivism), team level, and team diversity can help companies choose the right team members.[80]

Are you more comfortable working alone or with others? If you strongly prefer to work alone, you may not be well suited for teamwork. Indeed, studies show that job satisfaction is higher in teams when team members prefer working with others.[81] An indirect way to measure someone's *preference for teamwork* is to assess the person's degree of individualism or collectivism. **Individualism–collectivism** is the degree to which a person believes that people should be self-sufficient and that loyalty to one's self is more important than loyalty to one's team or company.[82] *Individualists*, who put their own welfare and interests first, generally prefer independent tasks in which they work alone. In contrast, *collectivists*, who put group or team interests ahead of self-interests, generally prefer interdependent tasks in which they work with others. Collectivists would also rather cooperate than compete and are fearful of disappointing team members or of being ostracized from teams. Given these differences, it makes sense to select team members who are collectivists rather than individualists. Indeed, many companies use individualism–collectivism as an initial screening device for team members.

Although many people think of golf as the ultimate individual game, team play, where individual players work together, can be found at the highest level of the professional game in the *Ryder Cup*, where, for eight decades, European and American players have squared off every other year in team-based competition. Instead of selecting players based on their golf records alone (i.e., individualism), Browne and U.S. coach Paul Azinger selected players based on their ability to fit into the overall U.S. team of 12 players and into smaller "pods" of four players (i.e., collectivism). If team diversity is desired, however, individualists may also be appropriate, as discussed below. To determine your preference for teamwork, take the Team Player Inventory shown in Exhibit 9.6.

Team level is the average level of ability, experience, personality, or any other factor on a team. For example, a high level of team experience means that a team has particularly experienced team members. This does not mean that every member of the team has considerable experience, but that enough team members do to significantly raise the average level of experience on the team.

individualism–collectivism
the degree to which a person believes that people should be self-sufficient and that loyalty to one's self is more important than loyalty to team or company

team level
the average level of ability, experience, personality, or any other factor on a team

Exhibit 9.6

The Team Player Inventory

	STRONGLY DISAGREE				STRONGLY AGREE
1. I enjoy working on team/group projects.	1	2	3	4	5
2. Team/group project work easily allows others to not pull their weight.	1	2	3	4	5
3. Work that is done as a team/group is better than the work done individually.	1	2	3	4	5
4. I do my best work alone rather than in a team/group.	1	2	3	4	5
5. Team/group work is overrated in terms of the actual results produced.	1	2	3	4	5
6. Working in a team/group gets me to think more creatively.	1	2	3	4	5
7. Teams/groups are used too often, when individual work would be more effective.	1	2	3	4	5
8. My own work is enhanced when I am in a team/group situation.	1	2	3	4	5
9. My experiences working in team/group situations have been primarily negative.	1	2	3	4	5
10. More solutions/ideas are generated when working in a team/group situation than when working alone.	1	2	3	4	5

Reverse score items 2, 4, 5, 7, and 9. Then add the scores for items 1 to 10. Higher scores indicate a preference for teamwork, whereas lower total scores indicate a preference for individual work.

Source: T. J. B. Kline, "The Team Player Inventory: Reliability and Validity of a Measure of Predisposition toward Organizational Team-Working Environments," Journal for Specialists in Group Work 24, no. 1 (1999): 102–112.

Team level is used to guide selection of teammates when teams need a particular set of skills or capabilities to do their jobs well.

Whereas team level represents the average level or capability on a team, **team diversity** represents the variances or differences in ability, experience, personality, or any other factor on a team.[83] From a practical perspective, why is team diversity important? Professor John Hollenbeck explains, "Imagine if you put all the extroverts together. Everyone is talking, but nobody is listening. [By contrast,] with a team of [nothing but] introverts, you can hear the clock ticking on the wall."[84] Not only do strong teams have talented members (i.e., a high team level), but those talented members are also different in terms of ability, experience, or personality. Team diversity is often used to guide the selection of team members when teams must complete a wide range of different tasks or when tasks are particularly complex.

Once the right team has been put together in terms of individualism–collectivism, team level, and team diversity, it's important to keep the team together as long as practically possible. Interesting research by the National Transportation Safety Board shows that 73 percent of serious mistakes made by jet cockpit crews are made the very first day that a crew flies together as a team and that 44 percent of serious mistakes occur on their very first flight together that day (pilot teams fly two to three flights per day). Moreover, research has

team diversity
the variances or differences in ability, experience, personality, or any other factor on a team

shown that fatigued pilot crews who have worked together before make significantly fewer errors than rested crews who have never worked together.[85] Their experience working together helps them overcome their fatigue and outperform new teams that have not worked together before. So, once you've created effective teams, keep them together as long as possible.

9-4c Team Training

After selecting the right people for teamwork, you need to train them. To be successful, teams need significant training, particularly in interpersonal skills, decision-making and problem-solving skills, conflict resolution skills, and technical training. Organizations that create work teams *often underestimate the amount of training* required to make teams effective. This mistake occurs frequently in successful organizations where managers assume that if employees can work effectively on their own, they can work effectively in teams. In reality, companies that use teams successfully provide thousands of hours of training to make sure that teams work.

Most commonly, members of work teams receive training in interpersonal skills. Interpersonal skills such as listening, communicating, questioning, and providing feedback enable people to have effective working relationships with others. Because of teams' autonomy and responsibility, many companies also give team members training in *decision-making* and *problem-solving skills* to help them do a better job of cutting costs and improving quality and customer service. Many organizations also teach teams *conflict resolution skills*. People approach problems through diverse perspectives, so when working toward a common goal, conflicts are bound to arise. Taine Moufarrige, executive director of Servcorp, a global company hosting serviced and virtual offices for about 12,000 clients, says, "It's not just about disagreements, it's about working through problems, managing differences of opinion, and that's vital for moving forward."[86]

Firms must also provide team members with the *technical training* they need to do their jobs, particularly if they are being cross-trained to perform all of the different jobs on the team, as was described earlier in the chapter in the example about the craftsmen from Louis Vuitton. Cross-training is less appropriate for teams of highly skilled workers. For instance, it is unlikely that a group of engineers, computer programmers, and systems analysts would be cross-trained for each other's jobs.

Team leaders need training too, as they often feel unprepared for their new duties. Exhibit 9.7 lists the top 10 problems team leaders face. The solution

interpersonal skills skills, such as listening, communicating, questioning, and providing feedback, that enable people to have effective working relationships with others

Exhibit 9.7

Top 10 Problems Reported by Team Leaders

1. Confusion about their new roles and about what they should be doing differently
2. Feeling they've lost control
3. Not knowing what it means to coach or empower
4. Having personal doubts about whether the team concept will really work
5. Uncertainty about how to deal with employees' doubts about the team concept
6. Confusion about when a team is ready for more responsibility
7. Confusion about how to share responsibility and accountability with the team
8. Concern about promotional opportunities, especially about whether the "team leader" title carries any prestige
9. Uncertainty about the strategic aspects of the leader's role as the team matures
10. Not knowing where to turn for help with team problems, as few, if any, of their organization's leaders have led teams

Source: B. Filipczak, M. Hequet, C. Lee, M. Picard, & D. Stamps, "More Trouble with Teams," *Training*, October 1996, 21.

is extensive training. Overall, does team training work? One recent study found that across a wide variety of setting, tasks, team types, and 2,650 teams in different organizations, team training was positively related to team performance outcomes.[87]

9-4d Team Compensation and Recognition

Compensating teams correctly is very difficult. For instance, one survey found that only 37 percent of companies were satisfied with their team compensation plans and even fewer, just 10 percent, reported being "very positive."[88] One of the problems, according to Susan Mohrman of the Center for Effective Organizations at the University of Southern California, is that "there is a very strong set of beliefs in most organizations that people should be paid for how well they do. So when people first get put into team-based organizations, they really balk at being paid for how well the team does. It sounds illogical to them. It sounds like their individuality and their sense of self-worth are being threatened."[89] Consequently, companies need to carefully choose a team compensation plan and then fully explain how teams will be rewarded. One basic requirement for team compensation to work is that the level of rewards (individual vs. team) must match the level of performance (individual vs. team).

Employees can be compensated for team participation and accomplishments in three ways: skill-based pay, gainsharing, and nonfinancial rewards. **Skill-based pay** programs pay employees for learning additional skills or knowledge.[90] These programs encourage employees to acquire the additional skills they will need to perform multiple jobs within a team and to share knowledge with others within their work groups.[91]

In **gainsharing** programs, companies share the financial value of performance gains, such as productivity increases, cost savings, or quality improvements, with their workers.[92] *Nonfinancial rewards* are another way to reward teams for their performance. These rewards, which can range from vacations to T-shirts, plaques, and coffee mugs, are especially effective when coupled with management recognition, such as awards, certificates, and praise.[93] Nonfinancial awards tend to be most effective when teams or team-based interventions, such as total quality management (see Chapter 18), are first introduced.[94]

Which team compensation plan should your company use? In general, skill-based pay is most effective for self-managing and self-directing teams performing complex tasks. In these situations, the more each team member knows and can do, the better the whole team performs. By contrast, gainsharing works best in relatively stable environments where employees can focus on improving the productivity, cost savings, or quality of their current work system.

Finally, given the level of dissatisfaction with most team compensation systems, what compensation plans would today's managers like to use with the teams in their companies? Among managers, 40.5 percent would directly link merit-pay increases to team performance but allow adjustments within teams for differences in individual performance. By contrast, 13.7 percent would also link merit-based increases directly to team performance but give each team member an equal share of the team's merit-based reward. And 19.1 percent would use gainsharing plans based on quality, delivery, productivity, or cost

skill-based pay
compensation system that pays employees for learning additional skills or knowledge

gainsharing
a compensation system in which companies share the financial value of performance gains, such as productivity, cost savings, or quality, with their workers

reduction and then provide equal payouts to all teams and team members. Another 14.5 percent would also use gainsharing, but they would vary the team gainsharing award, depending on how much money the team saved the company. Payouts would still be equally distributed within teams. Finally, 12.2 percent of managers would opt for plant-wide profit-sharing plans tied to overall company or division performance.[95] In this case, there would be no payout distinctions between or within teams.

REVIEW 9-4

Enhancing Work Team Effectiveness

Companies can make teams more effective by setting team goals and managing how team members are selected, trained, and compensated. Team goals provide a clear focus and purpose, reduce the incidence of social loafing, and lead to higher team performance 93 percent of the time. Extremely difficult stretch goals can be used to motivate teams as long as teams have autonomy, control over resources, structural accommodation, and bureaucratic immunity. Not everyone is suited for teamwork. When selecting team members, companies should select people who have a preference for teamwork (individualism-collectivism) and should consider team level (average ability on a team) and team diversity (different abilities on a team). Organizations that successfully use teams provide thousands of hours of training to make sure that teams work. The most common types of team training are for interpersonal skills, decision-making and problem-solving skills, conflict resolution, technical training to help team members learn multiple jobs (i.e., cross-training), and training for team leaders. Employees can be compensated for team participation and accomplishments in three ways: skill-based pay, gainsharing, and nonfinancial rewards.

 # Management Team Decision

Getting Along

Nine months ago, the executives running your design firm decided to start using teams. Before that, all of the work was done on an individual basis. Ron, the marketing guy, would run some consumer surveys to try to identify new fads. He would pass this information on to Susie in the art department, who would come up with some sketches of new products based on the surveys. She would then pass this on to production, where Maury would look at the sketches and see what kind of materials would have to be ordered so that Sharon could have a chance to work up some prototypes. Finally, about five months later, Marcus in sales would have some samples that he could take around to potential customers. But after switching to one team where all these people could work together and share their ideas at each step of the process, that time was cut down to just six weeks.

The executives of your company were thrilled with these results, and no doubt they patted themselves on the back for coming up with the brilliant idea of using teams. There is, though, just one thing that they didn't take into consideration—the team members hate each other! Marcus thinks that Ron talks too much and dominates every single team meeting. Maury, who hates sports, thinks that Susie wastes all of her time following the University of Michigan football team. Susie, meanwhile, hates it that Sharon won't stop it with stories about her kids. As for Marcus, nobody can quite figure him out, but almost everyone on the team thinks that he is bigoted.

With all of these negative emotions floating around, your project team has become stagnant. The meetings are uncomfortable, to say the least, and the interaction between the members has become toxic. It's been virtually impossible to get people to share ideas, reflect on others' ideas, or even just look each other in the eyes. Most meetings, it's plainly obvious that the only reason people are in the meetings is because they have to be.

A few weeks ago, Ron and Maury went to senior managers and asked what they would need to do to not have to work in teams anymore. The managers, in turn, told them to tell everyone else that, in effect, they were stuck with what they got. The managers are unwilling to give up the gains in productivity and speed, so the team is just going to have to learn how to work together.

So, here you sit, a dysfunctional team, with a directive from your bosses to learn how to get along. How do you do it?

Questions

1. In your opinion, do the interpersonal conflicts in this group make it impossible for team members to work together?

2. What are some ways that this group can decrease interpersonal conflicts and increase its cohesiveness?

 ## Practice Being a Manager

Campus Improvement

Teamwork is vital to the success of organizations. And this makes creating high-performance teams an important management challenge. In this exercise, you will work with fellow students to brainstorm the creation of a high-performing team. Pay particular attention to the assumptions that you and your peers bring to this process regarding what works and what doesn't work in creating a high-performance team. At the conclusion of the exercise, you will have an opportunity to discuss the theory and common assumptions regarding effective team building.

STEP 1 **Get into groups.** Your professor will organize small groups.

STEP 2 **Review the situation.** Assume that your group has been handpicked by the president of your college or university to work for one semester as a "campus improvement" team. At the end of the year, you will submit your recommendations to the president and the board of your institution. These leaders have assured you that they will make every effort to implement your recommendations.

STEP 3 **Develop a plan.** Brainstorm to develop a plan for working as a team to achieve the objective of delivering a set of quality recommendations to the president and the board. You should consider the following in developing your plan:

- Working well together as a team
- Establishing criteria for "quality recommendations" (such as representing the various important constituencies and interests on campus)
- Outlining steps, areas and types of work, and assignments for each member that are most likely to take full advantage of the capabilities and resources in your team

STEP 4 **Discuss your plans as a class.** Is this the sort of project that is well suited to using a work team? Why or why not? How might work team characteristics such as norms, cohesiveness, and team size play a role in this team effort? What conflicts might be likely down the road, and at what stage of the process are these conflicts most likely to occur?

Self-Assessment

Working in Groups

From sports to school, to work, to civic involvement, working in teams is increasingly part of our experience. Even though teams are frequently used to get work done, people still have widely varying opinions of their value. Think of your own situation. When a professor divides the class into groups to complete a project, do you respond with an inward smile or a heavy sigh? Do you enjoy team projects, or would you rather just do your own work? The following 20-question survey assesses your thoughts about working in teams.[96] Indicate the extent to which you agree with each of the following statements. Try not to spend too much time on any one item, and be sure to answer all the questions. Use this scale for your responses:

1 **Strongly disagree**
2 **Disagree**
3 **Slightly disagree**
4 **Neutral**
5 **Slightly agree**
6 **Agree**
7 **Strongly agree**

1. Only those who depend on themselves get ahead in life.

   1   2   3   4   5   6   7

2. To be superior, a person must stand alone.

   1   2   3   4   5   6   7

3. If you want something done right, you've got to do it yourself.

   1   2   3   4   5   6   7

4. What happens to me is my own doing.

   1   2   3   4   5   6   7

5. In the long run, the only person you can count on is yourself.

   1   2   3   4   5   6   7

6. Winning is everything.

   1   2   3   4   5   6   7

7. I feel that winning is important in both work and games.

   1   2   3   4   5   6   7

8. Success is the most important thing in life.

   1   2   3   4   5   6   7

9. It annoys me when other people perform better than I do.

   1   2   3   4   5   6   7

10. Doing your best isn't enough; it is important to win.

   1   2   3   4   5   6   7

11. I prefer to work with others in a group rather than working alone.

   1   2   3   4   5   6   7

12. Given the choice, I would rather do a job where I can work alone than do a job where I have to work with others in a group.

   1   2   3   4   5   6   7

13. Working with a group is better than working alone.

    1   2   3   4   5   6   7

14. People should be made aware that if they are going to be part of a group, then they are sometimes going to have to do things they don't want to do.

    1   2   3   4   5   6   7

15. People who belong to a group should realize that they're not always going to get what they personally want.

    1   2   3   4   5   6   7

16. People in a group should realize that they sometimes are going to have to make sacrifices for the sake of the group as a whole.

    1   2   3   4   5   6   7

17. People in a group should be willing to make sacrifices for the sake of the group's well-being.

    1   2   3   4   5   6   7

18. A group is more productive when its members do what they want to do rather than what the group wants them to do.

    1   2   3   4   5   6   7

19. A group is most efficient when its members do what they think is best rather than doing what the group wants them to do.

    1   2   3   4   5   6   7

20. A group is more productive when its members follow their own interests and desires.

    1   2   3   4   5   6   7

SCORING

Determine your score by entering your response to each survey item below, as follows. In blanks that say *regular score*, simply enter your response for that item. If your response was a 3, place a 3 in the *regular score* blank. In blanks that say *reverse score*, subtract your response from 8 and enter the result. So if your response was a 3, place a 5 (8−3 = 5) in the *reverse score* blank.

1.	reverse score _____		11.	regular score _____
2.	reverse score _____		12.	reverse score _____
3.	reverse score _____		13.	regular score _____
4.	reverse score _____		14.	regular score _____
5.	reverse score _____		15.	regular score _____
6.	reverse score _____		16.	regular score _____
7.	reverse score _____		17.	regular score _____
8.	reverse score _____		18.	reverse score _____
9.	reverse score _____		19.	reverse score _____
10.	reverse score _____		20.	reverse score _____

TOTAL = _____

You can find the interpretation of your score at www.cengagebrain.com.

REEL TO REAL

▶ MANAGEMENT WORKPLACE

© CENGAGE LEARNING 2013

Holden Outerwear: Leading Teams

At Holden Outerwear, it's all about teamwork. Founder Mikey LeBlanc believes that teamwork is critical to the company's position as an innovation leader. Holden's use of teams is something that emerged out of necessity. For much of the company's brief history, managers worked independently on design projects. But as the company grew, LeBlanc needed more designers, and he began looking to outside freelancers for help. Nikki Brush, a design and development manager at Holden, remembers when she was first brought on as a freelancer. Today she is a full-time manager at the company. The switch from freelancer to in-house manager has been positive for Nikki Brush, although her role on the team has changed.

What to Watch For and Ask Yourself

1. What type of team did Nikki Brush participate in when she was a freelancer? What type of team does she participate in as a full-time employee at Holden?

2. What are the advantages and disadvantages of using teams at Holden? What can managers do to help avoid the disadvantages?

3. What steps do the leaders of Holden take to insure that their workgroups have high levels of cohesion?

► Endnotes

1. "You. Happy. You. Learning to Fly," Cessna. [Online], accessed May 22, 2011, from www.cessna.com/learn-to-fly. html; T. Greenwood, M. Bradford, and B. Greene, "Becoming a Lean Enterprise: A Tale of Two Firms," *Strategic Finance*, November 1, 2002, 32; B. Milligan, "Cessna Uses Baldrige Process to Identify Best Suppliers," *Purchasing*, April 6, 2000, 75; J. Morgan, "Cessna Charts a Supply Chain Flight Strategy," *Purchasing*, September 7, 2000, 42; J. Morgan, "Cross-Functional Buying: Why Teams Are Hot," *Purchasing*, April 5, 2001, 27; J. Morgan, "Cessna Aims to Drive SCM to Its Very Core: Here Are 21 Steps and Tools It's Using to Make This Happen," *Purchasing*, June 6, 2002, 31; P. Siekman, "Cessna Tackles Lean Manufacturing," *Fortune*, May 1, 2000, I222 B+; and P. Siekman, "The Snap-Together Business Jet; Bombardier's New Recipe: A Dozen Big Pieces, Four Days to Assemble Them, and It's Ready to Fly," *Fortune*, January 21, 2002, 104A.

2. J. R. Katzenbach and D. K. Smith, *The Wisdom of Teams* (Boston: Harvard Business School Press, 1993).

3. S. G. Cohen and D. E. Bailey, "What Makes Teams Work: Group Effectiveness Research from the Shop Floor to the Executive Suite," *Journal of Management* 23, no. 3 (1997): 239–290.

4. B. Dumaine, "The Trouble with Teams," *Fortune*, September 5, 1994, 86–92.

5. K. C. Stag, E. Salas, and S. M. Fiore, "Best Practices in Cross-Training Teams," in *Workforce Cross-Training Handbook*, D. A. Nembhard, ed. (Boca Raton, FL: CRC Press), 156–175.

6. M. Marks, "The Science of Team Effectiveness," *Psychological Science in the Public Interest* (December 2006): pi–i.

7. S. E. Gross, *Compensation for Teams* (New York: American Management Association, 1995); B. L. Kirkman and B. Rosen, "Beyond Self-Management: Antecedents and Consequences of Team Empowerment," *Academy of Management Journal* 42 (1999): 58–74; G. Stalk and T. M. Hout, *Competing against Time: How Time-Based Competition Is Reshaping Global Markets* (New York: Free Press, 1990); and S. C. Wheelwright and K. B. Clark, *Revolutionizing New Product Development* (New York: Free Press, 1992).

8. PRWeb, "Staff Management|SMX Named a Finalist in the 2011 American Business Awards," *Yahoo! News*, May 18, 2011, accessed May 21, 2011, from http://news.yahoo.com/s/prweb/20110518/bs_prweb/prweb8455166_2; and "Staff Management's Expertise in Large-Scale Seasonal Hiring Projects Featured in Several Major Online Publications," Staff Management, December 10, 2010, accessed May 21, 2011, from www.staffmanagement.com/News-Story/Staff-Management-Expertise-Large-Scale-Hiring.aspx.

9. R. D. Banker, J. M. Field, R. G. Schroeder, and K. K. Sinha, "Impact of Work Teams on Manufacturing Performance: A Longitudinal Field Study," *Academy of Management Journal* 39 (1996): 867–890.

10. Stalk and Hout, *Competing against Time*.

11. C. Passariello, "Brand-New Bag: Louis Vuitton Tries Modern Methods on Factory Lines; For Craftsmen, Multitasking Replaces Specialization; Inspiration from Japan; 'What Do Our Clients Want?'" *Wall Street Journal*, October 9, 2006, A1.

12. J. L. Cordery, W. S. Mueller, and L. M. Smith, "Attitudinal and Behavioral Effects of Autonomous Group Working: A Longitudinal Field Study," *Academy of Management Journal* 34 (1991): 464–476; and T. D. Wall, N. J. Kemp, P. R. Jackson, and C. W. Clegg, "Outcomes of Autonomous Workgroups: A Long-Term Field Experiment," *Academy of Management Journal* 29 (1986): 280–304.

13. "Declaration of Interdependence," Whole Foods Market, accessed August 12, 2008, from www.wholefoodsmarket.com/company/declaration.html.

14. T. Aeppel, "Missing the Boss: Not All Workers Find Idea of Empowerment as Neat as It Sounds—Some Hate Fixing Machines, Apologizing for Errors, Disciplining Teammates—Rah-Rah Types Do the Best," *Wall Street Journal*, September 8, 1997, A1.

15. R. Liden, S. Wayne, R. Jaworski, and N. Bennett, "Social Loafing: A Field Investigation," *Journal of Management* 30 (2004): 285–304.

16. J. George, "Extrinsic and Intrinsic Origins of Perceived Social Loafing in Organizations," *Academy of Management Journal* 35 (1992): 191–202.

17. T. T. Baldwin, M. D. Bedell, and J. L. Johnson, "The Social Fabric of a Team-Based M.B.A. Program: Network Effects on Student Satisfaction and Performance," *Academy of Management Journal* 40 (1997): 1369–1397.

18. K. H. Price, D. A. Harrison, and J. H. Gavin, "Withholding Inputs in Team Contexts: Member Composition, Interaction Processes, Evaluation Structure and Social Loafing," *Journal of Applied Psychology* 91(6) (2006): 1375–1384.

19. J. Hoerr, "The Payoff from Teamwork—The Gains in Quality Are Substantial—So Why Isn't It Spreading Faster?" *Businessweek*, July 10, 1989, 56.

20. C. Joinson, "Teams at Work," *HR Magazine*, May 1, 1999, 30.

21. R. Wageman, "Critical Success Factors for Creating Superb Self-Managing Teams," *Organizational Dynamics* 26, no. 1 (1997): 49–61.

22. R. Karlgaard, "Leadership Lessons from the Tour de France," *Forbes*, July 31, 2009, accessed November 16, 2009, from www.forbes.com/2009/07/31/karlgaard-leadership-sports-intelligent-technology-sports.html.

23. D. A. Harrison, S. Mohammed, J. E. McGrath, A. T. Florey, and S. W. Vanderstoep, "Time Matters in Team Performance: Effects of Member Familiarity, Entrainment, and Task Discontinuity on Speed and Quality," *Personnel Psychology* 56(3) (2003, August): 633–669.

24. J. Palfini, "Forget What You Learned in Grade School: Five Teamwork Myths," BNET: The CBS Interactive Business Network, August 1, 2007, www.bnet.com/blog/teamwork/

forget-what-you-learned-in-grade-school-five-teamwork-myths/103.

25 "Ridley's Reforms Reward Team Effort," *Estates Gazette*, March 20, 2010, 35.

26 M. Bolch, "Rewarding the Team: Make Sure Team-Oriented Compensation Plans Are Designed Carefully," *HR Magazine*, February 2007, 52(2).

27 J. Vascellaro, "Google Searches for Ways to Keep Big Ideas at Home—Giant Speeds Access to Bosses in Effort to Transform More Projects into Products," *Wall Street Journal*, June 18, 2009, B1.

28 "'Mission Almost Complete,' JLife: JC Penney Associates Winning Together," September 2009, accessed May 21, 2011, http://jcpenney.net/jlife/2009/09/Door_to_floor.html.

29 Kirkman and Rosen, "Beyond Self-Management: Antecedents and Consequences of Team Empowerment."

30 S. Easton and G. Porter, "Selecting the Right Team Structure to Work in Your Organization," in *Handbook of Best Practices for Teams*, vol. 1, G. M. Parker, ed. (Amherst, MA: Irwin, 1996).

31 C. Kaufmann, "Employee Involvement: A New Blueprint for Success," *Journal of Acountancy* 209 (2010):46–49.

32 R. J. Recardo, D. Wade, C. A. Mention, and J. Jolly, *Teams* (Houston: Gulf Publishing Co., 1996).

33 D. R. Denison, S. L. Hart, and J. A. Kahn, "From Chimneys to Cross-Functional Teams: Developing and Validating a Diagnostic Model," *Academy of Management Journal* 39, no. 4 (1996): 1005–1023.

34 A. M. Townsend, S. M. DeMarie, and A. R. Hendrickson, "Virtual Teams: Technology and the Workplace of the Future," *Academy of Management Executive* 13, no. 3 (1998): 17–29.

35 N. Apostolou, "Making Virtual Teams a Reality," *Charter* 81, no. 8 (2010): 52–53.

36 R. S. Wellins, W. C. Byham, and G. R. Dixon, *Inside Teams* (San Francisco: Jossey-Bass, 1994).

37 Townsend, DeMarie, and Hendrickson, "Virtual Teams."

38 W. F. Cascio, "Managing a Virtual Workplace," *Academy of Management Executive* 14 (2000): 81–90.

39 R. Katz, "The Effects of Group Longevity on Project Communication and Performance," *Administrative Science Quarterly* 27 (1982): 245–282.

40 D. Mankin, S. G. Cohen, & T. K. Bikson, *Teams and Technology: Fulfilling the Promise of the New Organization* (Boston: Harvard Business School Press, 1996).

41 K. Lovelace, D. Shapiro, and L. Weingart, "Maximizing Cross-Functional New Product Teams' Innovativeness and Constraint Adherence: A Conflict Communications Perspective," *Academy of Management Journal* 44 (2001): 779–793.

42 L. Holpp and H. P. Phillips, "When Is a Team Its Own Worst Enemy?" *Training*, September 1, 1995, 71.

43 S. Asche, "Opinions and Social Pressure," *Scientific American* 193 (1995): 31–35.

44 S. G. Cohen, G. E. Ledford, and G. M. Spreitzer, "A Predictive Model of Self-Managing Work Team Effectiveness," *Human Relations* 49, no. 5 (1996): 643–676.

45 R. Collett, "How to Improve Product Development Productivity—Lessons from the Checklist Manifesto," The EE Compendium: The Home of Electronic Engineering and Embedded Systems Programming, accessed May 22, 2011, from http://ee.cleversoul.com/news/lessons-from-the-checklist-manifesto.html.

46 K. Bettenhausen and J. K. Murnighan, "The Emergence of Norms in Competitive Decision-Making Groups," *Administrative Science Quarterly* 30 (1985): 350–372.

47 M. E. Shaw, *Group Dynamics* (New York: McGraw-Hill, 1981).

48 S. E. Jackson, "The Consequences of Diversity in Multidisciplinary Work Teams," in *Handbook of Work Group Psychology*, M. A. West, ed. (Chichester, UK: Wiley, 1996).

49 A. M. Isen and R. A. Baron, "Positive Affect as a Factor in Organizational Behavior," in *Research in Organizational Behavior* 13, L. L. Cummings and B. M. Staw, eds. (Greenwich, CT: JAI Press, 1991): 1–53.

50 C. R. Evans and K. L. Dion, "Group Cohesion and Performance: A Meta-Analysis," *Small Group Research* 22, no. 2 (1991): 175–186.

51 R. Stankiewicsz, "The Effectiveness of Research Groups in Six Countries," in *Scientific Productivity*, F. M. Andrews, ed. (Cambridge: Cambridge University Press, 1979), 191–221.

52 F. Rees, *Teamwork from Start to Finish* (San Francisco: Jossey-Bass, 1997).

53 S. M. Gully, D. S. Devine, and D. J. Whitney, "A Meta-Analysis of Cohesion and Performance: Effects of Level of Analysis and Task Interdependence," *Small Group Research* 26, no. 4 (1995): 497–520.

54 Gully, Devine, and Whitney, "A Meta-Analysis of Cohesion and Performance."

55 F. Tschan and M. V. Cranach, "Group Task Structure, Processes and Outcomes," in *Handbook of Work Group Psychology*, M. A. West, ed. (Chichester, UK: Wiley, 1996).

56 D. E. Yeatts and C. Hyten, *High Performance Self-Managed Teams* (Thousand Oaks, CA: Sage Publications, 1998); and H. M. Guttman and R. S. Hawkes, "New Rules for Strategic Development," *Journal of Business Strategy* 25, no. 1 (2004): 34–39.

57 Ibid; J. Colquitt, R. Noe, & C. Jackson, "Justice in Teams: Antecedents and Consequences of Procedural Justice Climate," *Personnel Psychology*, April 1, 2002, 83.

58 D. S. Kezsbom, "Re-Opening Pandora's Box: Sources of Project Team Conflict in the '90s," *Industrial Engineering* 24, no. 5 (1992): 54–59.

59 A. C. Amason, W. A. Hochwarter, and K. R. Thompson, "Conflict: An Important Dimension in Successful Management Teams," *Organizational Dynamics* 24 (1995): 20.

60 A. C. Amason, "Distinguishing the Effects of Functional and Dysfunctional Conflict on Strategic Decision Making: Resolving a Paradox for Top Management Teams," *Academy of Management Journal* 39, no. 1 (1996): 123–148.

61 K. M. Eisenhardt, J. L. Kahwajy, and L. J. Bourgeois III, "How Management Teams Can Have a Good Fight," *Harvard Business Review* 75, no. 4 (July–August 1997): 77–85.

62 Ibid.

63 C. Nemeth and P. Owens, "Making Work Groups More Effective: The Value of Minority Dissent," in *Handbook of Work Group Psychology*, M. A. West, ed. (Chichester, UK: Wiley, 1996).

64 J. M. Levin and R. L. Moreland, "Progress in Small Group Research," *Annual Review of Psychology* 9 (1990): 72–78; and S. E. Jackson, "Team Composition in Organizational Settings: Issues in Managing a Diverse Work Force," in *Group Processes and Productivity*, S. Worchel, W. Wood, and J. Simpson, eds. (Beverly Hills, CA: Sage, 1992).

65 Eisenhardt, Kahwajy, & Bourgeois, "How Management Teams Can Have a Good Fight."

66 B. W. Tuckman, "Development Sequence in Small Groups," *Psychological Bulletin* 63, no. 6 (1965): 384–399.

67 Gross, *Compensation for Teams.*

68 J. F. McGrew, J. G. Bilotta, & J. M. Deeney, "Software Team Formation and Decay: Extending the Standard Model for Small Groups," *Small Group Research* 30, no. 2 (1999): 209–234.

69 Ibid.

70 J. Case, "What the Experts Forgot to Mention: Management Teams Create New Difficulties, but Succeed for XEL Communication," *Inc.*, September 1, 1993, 66.

71 J. R. Hackman, "The Psychology of Self-Management in Organizations," in *Psychology and Work: Productivity, Change, and Employment*, M. S. Pallak and R. Perloff, eds. (Washington, DC: American Psychological Association, 1986), 85–136.

72 A. O 'Leary-Kelly, J. J. Martocchio, and D. D. Frink, "A Review of the Influence of Group Goals on Group Performance," *Academy of Management Journal* 37, no. 5 (1994): 1285–1301.

73 R. Jana, "Real Life Imitates Real World," *Businessweek*, March 23, 2009, 42.

74 A. Zander, "The Origins and Consequences of Group Goals," in *Retrospections on Social Psychology*, L. Festinger, ed. (New York: Oxford University Press, 1980), 205–235.

75 M. Erez and A. Somech, "Is Group Productivity Loss the Rule or the Exception? Effects of Culture and Group-Based Motivation," *Academy of Management Journal* 39, no. 6 (1996): 1513–1537.

76 S. Sherman, "Stretch Goals: The Dark Side of Asking for Miracles," *Fortune*, November 13, 1995.

77 K. R. Thompson, W. A. Hochwarter, and N. J. Mathys, "Stretch Targets: What Makes Them Effective?" *Academy of Management Executive* 11, no. 3 (1997): 48–60.

78 Sherman, "Stretch Goals."

79 Dumaine, "The Trouble with Teams."

80 G. A. Neuman, S. H. Wagner, and N. D. Christiansen, "The Relationship between Work-Team Personality Composition and the Job Performance of Teams," *Group & Organization Management* 24, no. 1 (1999): 28–45.

81 M. A. Campion, G. J. Medsker, and A. C. Higgs, "Relations between Work Group Characteristics and Effectiveness: Implications for Designing Effective Work Groups," *Personnel Psychology* 46, no. 4 (1993): 823–850.

82 B. L. Kirkman and D. L. Shapiro, "The Impact of Cultural Values on Employee Resistance to Teams: Toward a Model of Globalized Self-Managing Work Team Effectiveness," *Academy of Management Review* 22, no. 3 (1997): 730–757.

83 J. Bunderson and K. Sutcliffe, "Comparing Alternative Conceptualizations of Functional Diversity in Management Teams: Process and Performance Effects," *Academy of Management Journal* 45 (2002): 875–893.

84 J. Barbian, "Getting to Know You," *Training*, June 2001, 60–63.

85 J. Hackman, "New Rules for Team Building—The Times Are Changing—and So Are the Guidelines for Maximizing Team Performance," *Optimize*, July 1, 2002, 50.

86 P. Nicholas, "It's All about Flight or Fight," *Weekend Australian*, March 14, 2009, 1.

87 E. Salas, D. DiazGranados, C. Klein, C. Burke, K. Stagl, G. Goodwin, and S. Halpin, "Does Team Training Improve Team Performance? A Meta-Analysis," *Human Factors* 50, no. 6 (2008): 903–933.

88 S. Caudron, "Tie Individual Pay to Team Success," *Personnel Journal* 73, no. 10 (October 1994): 40.

89 Ibid.

90 Gross, *Compensation for Teams.*

91 G. Ledford, "Three Case Studies on Skill-Based Pay: An Overview," *Compensation & Benefits Review* 23, no. 2 (1991): 11–24.

92 J. R. Schuster and P. K. Zingheim, *The New Pay: Linking Employee and Organizational Performance* (New York: Lexington Books, 1992).

93 Cohen and Bailey, "What Makes Teams Work."

94 R. Allen and R. Kilmann, "Aligning Reward Practices in Support of Total Quality Management," *Business Horizons* 44 (May 2001): 77–85.

95 J. H. Sheridan, " 'Yes' to Team Incentives," *Industry Week*, March 4, 1996, 63.

96 J. A. Wagner, "Studies of Individualism-Collectivism: Effects on Cooperation in Groups," *Academy of Management Journal* 38, no. 1 (1995): 152–172.

Managing Human Resources

REEL TO REAL

© TETRA IMAGES/ CORBIS

Management Workplace is at Barcelona Restaurant Group.

SELF-ASSESSMENT

© ISTOCKPHOTO/ ALEXANDER KALINA

How anxious do you become during interviews? Do the Self-Assessment for this chapter in the book or online to establish a baseline reading before you begin job hunting.

ONLINE QUIZZES

© ISTOCKPHOTO/ PEARLEYE

Did you get it? Review the main concepts in the chapter by taking the online quizzes on CourseMate!

VIDEO QUIZZES

© ISTOCKPHOTO/DAVID HUGHES

Get more out of the videos by taking the multimedia video quizzes online.

What Would You Do?

Nick's Pizza & Pub, Crystal Lake, Illinois[1]

Your start in the pizza business came in the eighth grade, when your father opened the Village Pizza restaurant. After graduation, you entered the construction business, building homes for more than a decade. But, then, something drew you back. So, you took the family recipes and started your own restaurant, Nick's Pizza & Pub (far enough away to avoid competing with Dad).

Your goal was simple: to build a fun, family restaurant. Nick's Pizza & Pubs—there are now two—have 26-foot high, floor-to-ceiling stone fireplaces, stuffed bears and moose, antler chandeliers, huge aquariums separating the bar and the restaurant, and wood everywhere—oak floors and huge beams recycled from century-old barns. And they're huge, each seating 320 guests. On a Friday night, 1,500 customers will eat at Nick's, most waiting an hour for their tables, while having a drink and eating free peanuts at the bar. Those 1,500 customers will eat 600 pizzas, and carryout customers order another 200. Why do they come? Beyond the great pizza, they come for the value. A medium cheese pizza is $11; soft drinks are $1.75, with free refills; and the popular Italian beef sandwich is under $6.00. Nick's is really affordable, especially for a sit-down restaurant.

With things going so well, you decided to open three more restaurants in the next five years. Unfortunately, the recession changed your plans. Guest counts dropped by 20 percent, or 100,000 people per year, decreasing revenues by nearly $1 million. On top of that, your managers were having difficulty controlling costs. Each week they conducted a physical count, comparing food inventories (tomato sauce, flour, cheese, beef, liquor, etc.) to the previous week, and then adjusted for this week's sales. But beverage and food costs were still above goal, 22 percent of revenues for beverages and 20 percent of revenues for food. The problem, as you discovered, was your management, all hired externally because of their extensive experience at established well-known restaurant chains. Their idea

of leadership, learned in the "command and control" cultures of other restaurants, was telling people what to do. So, they had someone else put in the inventory numbers, and when the numbers came out wrong, they didn't dig deeper or ask questions to discover why.

In the end, with costs up, revenues down, and lending standards tightening, the bank didn't approve the new construction loans. So rather than expanding, your immediate challenge is to fix and grow the two Nick's restaurants that you've got. Frustrated with your managers, you gave responsibility for reducing costs to a 24-year-old who had worked for you since she was 16. She fixed the problem in four weeks by discussing the problem with the kitchen, wait, and bar staffs, who suggested immediate solutions to reduce costs.

Sensing that she was onto something, you pulled together the staffs in both restaurants to make a financial presentation that showed in detail how and where Nick's was earning revenue and incurring expenses. After answering their questions, you asked for their help on three key issues: pay, hiring, and training. Of course, everyone wants to be paid more, but with costs being an issue, are there ways to pay people more but link those increases to the company's profitability and workers doing their jobs better

and staying with the company longer? If so, how? Next, because hiring talented workers is key in the restaurant business, how should Nick's redesign its interview and selection process to do a better job of finding and keeping the best kitchen, wait, and bar staff? What is it about interviews that doesn't work and should be abandoned? If so, what should be done instead, and why? Finally, at most restaurants, training is simply shadowing experienced workers to see what they do. So, what could be done at Nick's to improve training that would help them do their jobs better and to continue learning and improving over time?

If you were in charge at Nick's, what would you do?

10-1 Employment Legislation

The chapter begins by reviewing the major federal laws that affect human resource practice. Next, we explore how companies use recruiting and selection techniques to attract and hire qualified employees to fulfill those needs. The third part of the chapter discusses how training and performance appraisal can develop the knowledge, skills, and abilities of the workforce. The chapter concludes with a review of compensation and employee separation and how companies can manage the separation process when employees leave the organization.

Human resource management (HRM), or the process of finding, developing, and keeping the right people to form a qualified workforce, is one of the most difficult and important of all management tasks. Understanding how employment legislation affects business is a critical first step in human resource planning and management. This is because there are employment laws that govern each stage of the human resource process, from how employees are recruited and selected, to how employees are terminated, and nearly every stage in between.

After reading the next section, you should be able to:

10-1 explain how different employment laws affect human resource practice.

Since their inception, *HOOTERS* restaurants have hired only female servers. Moreover, consistent with the company's marketing theme, the servers wear short nylon shorts and cutoff T-shirts that show their midriffs. The Equal Employment Opportunity Commission (EEOC) began an investigation of Hooters when a Chicago man filed a sex-based discrimination charge. The man alleged that he had applied for a server's job at a Hooters restaurant and was rejected because of his sex. The dispute between Hooters and the EEOC quickly

human resource management (HRM)
the process of finding, developing, and keeping the right people to form a qualified workforce

gained national attention. One sarcastic letter to the EEOC printed in *Fortune* magazine read as follows:

> Dear EEOC:
>
> Hi! I just wanted to thank you for investigating those Hooters restaurants, where the waitresses wear those shorty shorts and midriffy T-shirts. I think it's a great idea that you have decided to make Hooters hire men as—how do you say it?—waitpersons. Gee, I never knew so many men wanted to be waitpersons at Hooters. No reason to let them sue on their own either. You're right, the government needs to take the lead on this one.[2]

This letter characterized public sentiment at the time. Given its backlog of 100,000 job discrimination cases, many wondered if the EEOC didn't have better things to do with its scarce resources.

Three years after the initial complaint, the EEOC ruled that Hooters had violated antidiscrimination laws and offered to settle the case if the company would agree to pay $22 million to the EEOC for distribution to male victims of the "Hooters Girl" hiring policy, establish a scholarship fund to enhance opportunities or education for men, and provide sensitivity training to teach Hooters' employees how to be more sensitive to men's needs. Hooters responded with a $1 million publicity campaign criticizing the EEOC's investigation. Billboards featuring "Vince," a man dressed in a Hooters Girl uniform and blond wig, sprang up all over the country. Hooters customers were given postcards to send complaints to the EEOC. Of course, Hooters paid the postage. As a result of the publicity campaign, restaurant sales increased by 10 percent. Soon thereafter, the EEOC announced that it would not pursue discriminatory hiring charges against Hooters.[3] Nonetheless, the company ended up paying $3.75 million to settle a class-action suit brought by seven men who claimed that their inability to get a job at Hooters violated federal law.[4] Under the settlement, Hooters maintained its women-only policy for server jobs but had to create additional support jobs, such as hosts and bartenders, that would also be open to men. The story doesn't end there, however, as a male applicant who wants to be a Hooters waitperson has sued Hooters, seeking to overturn the prior settlement, which would allow him to be only a host or bartender.[5]

As the Hooters example illustrates, the human resource planning process occurs in a very complicated legal environment.

Let's explore employment legislation by reviewing **10-1a the major federal employment laws that affect human resource practice, 10-1b2 how the concept of adverse impact is related to employment discrimination**, and **10-1c the laws regarding sexual harassment in the workplace.**

Should Hooter's give men the same opportunity as women to work as waitstaff?

© ZUMA PRESS/NEWSCOM

Exhibit 10.1 lists the major federal employment laws and their websites, where you can find more detailed information. Except for the Family and Medical Leave Act and the Uniformed Services Employment and Reemployment Rights Act that are administered by the Department of Labor (www.dol.gov), all of these laws are administered by the EEOC (www.eeoc.gov). The general effect of this body of law, which is still evolving through court decisions, is that employers may not discriminate in employment decisions on the basis of sex, age, religion, color, national origin, race, or disability. The intent is to make these factors irrelevant in employment decisions. Stated another way, employment decisions should be based on factors that are "job related," "reasonably necessary," or a "business necessity" for successful job performance. The only time that sex, age, religion, and the like can be used to make employment decisions is when they are considered a bona fide occupational qualification.[6] Title VII of the 1964 Civil Rights Act says that it is legal to hire and employ someone on the basis of sex, religion, or national origin when there is a **bona fide occupational qualification (BFOQ)** that is "reasonably necessary to the normal operation of that particular business." A Baptist church hiring a new minister can reasonably specify that being a Baptist rather than a Catholic or Presbyterian is a BFOQ for the position. However, it's unlikely that the church could specify race or national origin as a BFOQ. In general, the courts and the EEOC take a hard look when a business claims that sex, age, religion, color, national origin, race, or disability is a BFOQ. For instance, the EEOC disagreed with Hooters' claim that it was "in the business of providing vicarious sexual recreation" and that "female sexuality is a bona fide occupational qualification."[7]

Employers who use sex, age, race, or religion to make employment-related decisions when those factors are unrelated to an applicant's or employee's ability to perform a job may face charges of discrimination from employee lawsuits or the EEOC. When *MASSEY ENERGY COMPANY*, the fourth largest coal company in the United States, bought a shuttered mine from Horizon Natural Resources, it reportedly refused to hire anyone over the age of 40. After a group of more than 200 miners sued, Massey settled the age discrimination suit for $8.75 million.[8] In addition to the laws presented in Exhibit 10.1, there are two other important sets of federal laws: labor laws and laws and regulations governing safety standards. Labor laws regulate the interaction between management and labor unions that represent groups of employees. These laws guarantee employees the right to form and join unions of their own choosing. For more information about labor laws, see the National Labor Relations Board at www.nlrb.gov.

The Occupational Safety and Health Act (OSHA) requires that employers provide employees with a workplace that is "free from recognized hazards that are causing or are likely to cause death or serious physical harm." This law is administered by the Occupational Safety and Health Administration (which, like the act, is referred to as OSHA). OSHA sets safety and health standards for employers and conducts inspections to determine whether those standards are being met. Employers who do not meet OSHA standards may be fined.[9] For more information about OSHA, see www.osha.gov.

bona fide occupational qualification (BFOQ) an exception in employment law that permits sex, age, religion, and the like to be used when making employment decisions, but only if they are "reasonably necessary to the normal operation of that particular business"; BFOQs are strictly monitored by the equal employment opportunity commission

Exhibit 10.1

Summary of Major Federal Employment Laws

Equal Pay Act of 1963	(http://www.eeoc.gov/laws/statutes/epa.cfm)	Prohibits unequal pay for males and females doing substantially similar work.
Civil Rights Act of 1964	(http://www.eeoc.gov/laws/statutes/titlevii.cfm)	Prohibits discrimination on the basis of race, color, religion, sex, or national origin.
Age Discrimination in Employment Act of 1967	(http://www.eeoc.gov/laws/statutes/adea.cfm)	Prohibits discrimination in employment decisions against persons age 40 and over.
Pregnancy Discrimination Act of 1978	(http://www.eeoc.gov/laws/statutes/pregnancy.cfm)	Prohibits discrimination in employment against pregnant women.
Americans with Disabilities Act of 1990	(http://www.eeoc.gov/laws/statutes/ada.cfm)	Prohibits discrimination on the basis of physical or mental disabilities.
Civil Rights Act of 1991	(http://www.eeoc.gov/laws/statutes/cra-1991.cfm)	Strengthened the provisions of the Civil Rights Act of 1964 by providing for jury trials and punitive damages.
Family and Medical Leave Act of 1993	(http://www.dol.gov/dol/topic/benefits-leave/fmla.htm)	Permits workers to take up to 12 weeks of unpaid leave for pregnancy and/or birth of a new child, adoption or foster care of a new child, illness of an immediate family member, or personal medical leave.
Uniformed Services Employment and Reemployment Rights Act of 1994	(http://www.osc.gov/userra.htm)	Prohibits discrimination against those serving in the Armed Forces Reserve, the National Guard, or other uniformed services; guarantees that civilian employers will hold and then restore civilian jobs and benefits for those who have completed uniformed service.

© CENGAGE LEARNING

10-1b Adverse Impact and Employment Discrimination

The EEOC has investigatory, enforcement, and informational responsibilities. Therefore, it investigates charges of discrimination, enforces the employment discrimination laws in federal court, and publishes guidelines that organizations can use to ensure they are in compliance with the law. One of the most important guidelines, jointly issued by the EEOC, the Department of Labor, the U.S. Justice Department, and the federal Office of Personnel Management, is the *Uniform Guidelines on Employee Selection Procedures*, which can be read in their entirety at www.ipacweb.org/files/ug.pdf. These guidelines define two important criteria, disparate treatment and adverse impact, which are used in determining whether companies have engaged in discriminatory hiring and promotion practices.

Disparate treatment, which is *intentional* discrimination, occurs when people, despite being qualified, are *intentionally* not given the same hiring, promotion, or membership opportunities as other employees because of their race, color, age, sex, ethnic group, national origin, or religious beliefs. [10] Legally, a key element of discrimination lawsuits is establishing motive, meaning that the employer intended to discriminate. If no motive can be established, then a claim of disparate treatment may actually be a case of adverse impact. Adverse impact, which is *unintentional* discrimination, occurs when members of a particular race, sex, or ethnic group are *unintentionally* harmed or disadvantaged because they are hired, promoted, or trained (or any other employment decision) at substantially lower rates than others. The courts and federal agencies use the four-fifths (or 80 percent) rule to determine whether adverse impact has occurred. Adverse impact occurs if the decision rate for a protected group of people is less than four-fifths (or 80%) of the decision rate for a nonprotected group (usually white males). So, if 100 white applicants and 100 black applicants apply for entry-level jobs, and 60 white applicants are hired (60/100 = 60%), but only 20 black applicants are hired (20/100 = 20%), adverse impact has occurred (0.20/0.60 = 0.33). The criterion for the four-fifths rule in this situation is 0.48 (0.60 × 0.80 = 0.48). Because 0.33 is less than 0.48, the four-fifths rule has been violated.

Violation of the four-fifths rule is not an automatic indication of discrimination, however. If an employer can demonstrate that a selection procedure or test is valid, meaning that the test accurately predicts job performance or that the test is job related because it assesses applicants on specific tasks actually used in the job, then the organization may continue to use the test. If validity cannot be established, however, then a violation of the four-fifths rule may likely result in a lawsuit brought by employees, job applicants, or the EEOC itself.

10-1c Sexual Harassment

According to the EEOC, sexual harassment is a form of discrimination in which unwelcome sexual advances, requests for sexual favors, or other verbal or physical conduct of a sexual nature occur. From a legal perspective, there are two kinds of sexual harassment, quid pro quo and hostile work environment. [11]

Quid pro quo sexual harassment occurs when employment outcomes, such as hiring, promotion, or simply keeping one's job, depend on whether an individual submits to being sexually harassed. A hostile work environment occurs when unwelcome and demeaning sexually related behavior creates an intimidating, hostile, and offensive work environment. In contrast to quid pro quo cases, a hostile work environment may not result in economic injury. However, it can lead to psychological injury from a stressful work environment.

What common mistakes do managers make when it comes to sexual harassment laws? [12] First, many assume that the victim and harasser must be of opposite sexes. According to the courts, they do not. Sexual harassment can also occur between people of the same sex. Second, managers often assume that sexual harassment can occur only between coworkers or between supervisors and subordinates. Not so. Agents of employers, such as consultants, and even nonemployees can be sexual harassers.

disparate treatment
intentional discrimination that occurs when people are purposely not given the same hiring, promotion, or membership opportunities because of their race, color, sex, age, ethnic group, national origin, or religious beliefs

adverse impact
unintentional discrimination that occurs when members of a particular race, sex, or ethnic group are unintentionally harmed or disadvantaged because they are hired, promoted, or trained (or any other employment decision) at substantially lower rates than others

four-fifths (or 80 percent) rule
a rule of thumb used by the courts and the eeoc to determine whether there is evidence of adverse impact; a violation of this rule occurs when the selection rate for a protected group is less than 80 percent or four-fifths of the selection rate for a nonprotected group

sexual harassment
a form of discrimination in which unwelcome sexual advances, requests for sexual favors, or other verbal or physical conduct of a sexual nature occurs while performing one's job

quid pro quo sexual harassment
a form of sexual harassment in which employment outcomes, such as hiring, promotion, or simply keeping one's job, depend on whether an individual submits to sexual harassment

hostile work environment
a form of sexual harassment in which unwelcome and demeaning sexually related behavior creates an intimidating and offensive work environment

The key is not employee status, but whether the harassment takes place while company business is being conducted. Third, it is often assumed that only people who have themselves been harassed can file complaints or lawsuits. In fact, especially in hostile work environments, anyone affected by offensive conduct can file a complaint or lawsuit.

Finally, what should companies do to make sure that sexual harassment laws are followed and not violated?[13] First, respond immediately when sexual harassment is reported. A quick response encourages victims of sexual harassment to report problems to management rather than to lawyers or the EEOC. Furthermore, a quick and fair investigation may serve as a deterrent to future harassment. A lawyer for the EEOC says, "Worse than having no sexual harassment policy is a policy that is not followed. It's merely window dressing. You wind up with destroyed morale when people who come forward are ignored, ridiculed, retaliated against, or nothing happens to the harasser."[14] Next, take the time to write a clear, understandable sexual harassment policy that is strongly worded, gives specific examples of what constitutes sexual harassment, spells out sanctions and punishments, and is widely publicized within the company. This lets potential harassers and victims know what will not be tolerated and how the firm will deal with harassment should it occur.

At DuPont, Avon, and Texas Industries, employees can call a confidential hotline 24 hours a day, 365 days a year, to report sexual harassment.

Next, establish clear reporting procedures that indicate how, where, and to whom incidents of sexual harassment can be reported. The best procedures ensure that a complaint will receive a quick response, that impartial parties will handle the complaint, and that the privacy of the accused and accuser will be protected.

Finally, managers should also be aware that most states and many cities or local governments have their own employment-related laws and enforcement agencies. So compliance with federal law is often not enough. In fact, organizations can be in full compliance with federal law and at the same time be in violation of state or local sexual harassment laws.

REVIEW 10-1
. . . .

Employment Legislation

Human resource management is subject to the following major federal employment laws: Equal Pay Act, Civil Rights Acts of 1964 and 1991, Age Discrimination in Employment Act, Pregnancy Discrimination Act, Americans with Disabilities Act, Family and Medical Leave Act, and Uniformed Services Employment and Reemployment Rights Act. Human resource management is also subject to review by these federal agencies: Equal Employment Opportunity Commission, Department of Labor, Occupational Safety and Health Administration, and National Labor Relations Board. In general, these laws state that sex, age, religion, color, national origin, race, disability, and pregnancy may not be considered in employment decisions unless these factors reasonably qualify as

BFOQs. Two important criteria, disparate treatment (intentional discrimination) and adverse impact (unintentional discrimination), are used to decide whether companies have wrongly discriminated against someone. Motive is a key part of determining disparate treatment; the courts and federal enforcement agencies use the four-fifths rule to determine whether adverse impact has occurred. The two kinds of sexual harassment are quid pro quo and hostile work environment. Managers often wrongly assume that the victim and harasser must be of the opposite sex, that sexual harassment can occur only between coworkers or between supervisors and their employees, and that only people who have themselves been harassed can file complaints or lawsuits. To ensure compliance with sexual harassment laws, companies should: respond immediately when harassment is reported; write a clear, understandable sexual harassment policy; establish clear reporting procedures; and be aware of and follow city and state laws concerning sexual harassment.

10-2 Recruiting

Recruiting is the process of developing a pool of qualified job applicants. Despite the highest average wages in the country, Australia's mining companies are finding it nearly impossible to find the workers they need. David Knox, CEO of *Santos, Ltd.*, an oil and gas exploration and production company, said, "One of the real challenges in Australia is continuing to get a really high-quality, high-skilled labor force."[15] With some estimating that the industry needs as many as 70,000 to 100,000 more skilled workers, Australian mining companies have had to go as far as India to find and recruit applicants.

After reading this section, you should be able to:

10-2 explain how companies use recruiting to find qualified job applicants.

Finding qualified workers can be an increasingly difficult—but increasingly important—task. Gail Hyland-Savage, CEO of real estate and marketing firm *Michaelson, Connor & Boul*, says, "Staffing is absolutely critical to the success of every company. To be competitive in today's economy, companies need the best people to create ideas and execute them for the organization. Without a competent and talented workforce, organizations will stagnate and eventually perish. The right employees are the most important resources of companies today."[16]

Let's examine **10-2a what job analysis is and how it is used in recruiting, and 10-2b how companies use internal and external recruiting to find qualified job applicants**.

10-2a Job Analysis and Recruiting

Job analysis is a "purposeful, systematic process for collecting information on the important work-related aspects of a job."[17] A job analysis typically collects four kinds of information:

- Work activities such as what workers do and how, when, and why they do it
- The tools and equipment used to do the job

recruiting
the process of developing a pool of qualified job applicants

job analysis
a "purposeful, systematic process for collecting information on the important work-related aspects of a job"[24]

- The context in which the job is performed, such as the actual working conditions or schedule
- The personnel requirements for performing the job, meaning the knowledge, skills, and abilities needed to do a job well[18]

Job analysis information can be collected by having job incumbents and/or supervisors complete questionnaires about their jobs or by direct observation, interviews, or filming employees as they perform their jobs.

Job descriptions and job specifications are two of the most important results of a job analysis. A **job description** is a written description of the basic tasks, duties, and responsibilities required of an employee holding a particular job. **Job specifications**, which are often included as a separate section of a job description, are a summary of the qualifications needed to successfully perform the job. Exhibit 10.2 shows a job description and the job specifications for a helicopter pilot for the city of Little Rock, Arkansas.

Because a job analysis specifies what a job entails as well as the knowledge, skills, and abilities that are needed to do the job well, companies must complete a job analysis *before* beginning to recruit job applicants. Exhibit 10.3 shows that job analysis, job descriptions, and job specifications are the foundation on which all critical human resource activities are built. They are used during recruiting and selection to match applicant qualifications with the requirements of the job. Job descriptions are also used throughout the staffing process to ensure that selection

job description
a written description of the basic tasks, duties, and responsibilities required of an employee holding a particular job

job specifications
a written summary of the qualifications needed to successfully perform a particular job

---

Exhibit 10.2

Job Description and Job Specifications for a Helicopter Pilot for the City of Little Rock, Arkansas

Description For Helicopter Pilot

To provide assistance for air searches, river rescues, high-rise building rescues, and other assignments, by providing air survey and aviation response. Pilots a rotary-wing aircraft, serving as pilot or copilot, to assist in air searches, river rescues, high-rise building rescues, and other assignments. Ensures that aircraft is properly outfitted for each assignment (equipment, rigging tools, supplies, etc.). Performs preflight inspection of aircraft; checks rotors, fuel, lubricants, controls, etc. Prepares written reports on assignments; maintains flight logs. Obtains weather reports; determines to proceed with assignments given forecasted weather conditions. Operates a radio to maintain contact with and to report information to airport personnel and police department personnel.

Job Specifications For Helicopter Pilot

Must possess a valid Commercial Pilot's License for rotary-wing aircraft before employment and maintain licensure for the duration of employment in this position. Must have considerable knowledge of Federal Aviation Administration (FAA) laws and regulations, rotary-wing aircraft operating procedures, air traffic safety, flying procedures and navigational techniques, and FAA and police radio operation and procedures. Must have some knowledge of preventive maintenance methods, repair practices, safety requirements, and inspection procedures. Must have skill in the operation of a rotary-wing aircraft and radio equipment and the ability to conduct safety inspections of aircraft, to maintain aircraft maintenance logs and prepare reports, to detect and identify aircraft malfunction symptoms, to detect and recognize ground conditions and characteristics (utility line breaks, river currents, etc.), to read maps and air navigation charts, and to communicate effectively, both orally and in writing. Must have completed high school; at least one thousand hours of flight time experience in piloting rotary-wing aircraft; OR any equivalent combination of experience and training that provides the required knowledge, skills, and abilities.

Source: "Job Description: Helicopter Pilot," City of Little Rock, Arkansas, www.littlerock.org, May 31, 2003.

Exhibit 10.3

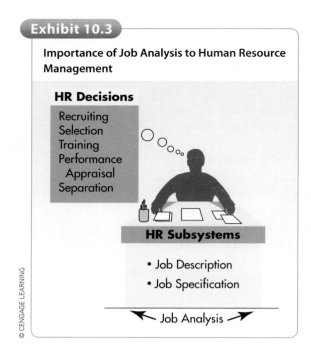

Importance of Job Analysis to Human Resource Management

HR Decisions

Recruiting
Selection
Training
Performance
   Appraisal
Separation

HR Subsystems

- Job Description
- Job Specification

← Job Analysis →

© CENGAGE LEARNING

devices and the decisions based on these devices are job related. For example, the questions asked in an interview should be based on the most important work activities identified by a job analysis. Likewise, during performance appraisals, employees should be evaluated in areas that a job analysis has identified as the most important in a job.

Job analyses, job descriptions, and job specifications also help companies meet the legal requirement that their human resource decisions be job related. To be judged "job related," recruitment, selection, training, performance appraisals, and employee separations must be valid and be directly related to the important aspects of the job as identified by a careful job analysis. In fact, in *Griggs v. Duke Power Co.* and *Albemarle Paper Co. v. Moody*, the U.S. Supreme Court stated that companies should use job analyses to help establish the job relatedness of their human resource procedures.[19] The EEOC's *Uniform Guidelines on Employee Selection Procedures* also recommend that companies base their human resource procedures on job analysis.

10-2b Internal Recruiting and External Recruiting

Internal recruiting is the process of developing a pool of qualified job applicants from people who already work in the company. Internal recruiting, sometimes called "promotion from within," improves employee commitment, morale, and motivation. Recruiting current employees also reduces recruitment start-up time and costs, and because employees are already familiar with the company's culture and procedures, they are more likely to succeed in new jobs.

Job posting is a procedure for advertising job openings within the company to existing employees. A job description and requirements are typically posted on a bulletin board, in a company newsletter, or in an internal computerized job bank that is accessible only to employees. Job posting helps organizations discover hidden talent, allows employees to take responsibility for career planning, and makes it easier for companies to retain talented workers who are dissatisfied in their current jobs and would otherwise leave the company.[20] A *career path* is a planned sequence of jobs through which employees may advance within an organization.

External recruiting is the process of developing a pool of qualified job applicants from outside the company. External recruitment methods include advertising (newspapers, magazines, direct mail, radio, or television), employee referrals (asking current employees to recommend possible job applicants), walk-ins (people who apply on their own), outside organizations (universities, technical/trade schools, professional societies), employment services (state or private employment agencies, temporary help agencies, and professional search firms), special events (career conferences or job fairs), and Internet job sites. Which external recruiting method should you use? Studies show that employee referrals, walk-ins, newspaper advertisements, and state employment agencies tend to be used most frequently for office/clerical and production/service employees. By contrast, newspaper advertisements and college/university

internal recruiting
the process of developing a pool of qualified job applicants from people who already work in the company

external recruiting
the process of developing a pool of qualified job applicants from outside the company

recruiting are used most frequently for professional/technical employees. When recruiting managers, organizations tend to rely most heavily on newspaper advertisements, employee referrals, and search firms.[21]

In the last decade, the biggest change in external recruiting has been the increased use of the Internet. Because these sites attract so many applicants and offer so many services, companies save by finding qualified applicants without having to use more expensive recruitment and search firms, which typically charge one-third or more of a new hire's salary.[22]

Despite their many benefits, however, job websites have a significant drawback: Companies may receive hundreds, if not thousands, of applications from *unqualified* applicants. The sheer volume increases the importance of proper screening and selection. Today, between 82 percent and 92 percent of companies use the Internet to fill job openings. In fact, Internet recruiting is now second to newspaper advertising in terms of the number of applicants it generates.[23] A recent survey conducted by the Society for Human Resource Management (SHRM) indicates that companies that leverage the .jobs domain have more effective recruiting practices across a range of areas and that the domain provides job seekers with a simple, fast, and convenient destination when job hunting.[24]

REVIEW 10-2

. . . .

Recruiting

Recruiting is the process of finding qualified job applicants. The first step in recruiting is to conduct a job analysis to collect information about the important work-related aspects of the job. The job analysis is then used to write a job description of basic tasks, duties, and responsibilities and to write job specifications indicating the knowledge, skills, and abilities needed to perform the job. Job analyses, descriptions, and specifications help companies meet the legal requirement that their human resource decisions be job related. Internal recruiting, or finding qualified job applicants from inside the company, can be done through job posting and career paths. External recruiting, or finding qualified job applicants from outside the company, is done through advertising, employee referrals, walk-ins, outside organizations, employment services, special events, and Internet job sites. The Internet is a particularly promising method of external recruiting because of its low cost, wide reach, and ability to communicate and receive unlimited information.

10-3 Selection

Once the recruitment process has produced a pool of qualified applicants, the selection process is used to determine which applicants have the best chance of performing well on the job.

After reading this section, you should be able to:

10-3 describe the selection techniques and procedures that companies use when deciding which applicants should receive job offers.

At BOSTON CONSULTING GROUP (BCG), one of the world's premiere consulting firms, a team of three recruiters examines résumés from 30 universities. Mel

Wolfgang, a partner who heads America's recruiting for BCG, says, "We look for well-rounded individuals whose interests and life experiences suggest that they would adapt well. We look for evidence that they have led and been empathic with a team or challenging situations." Only six applicants are chosen for a 40-minute interview with two BCG consultants. From there, three applicants go on to second-round interviews with four BCG partners. After consulting with the consultants and partners who conducted interviews, the hiring manager makes the final decision.[25]

As this example illustrates, **selection** is the process of gathering information about job applicants to decide who should be offered a job. To make sure that selection decisions are accurate and legally defensible, the EEOC's *Uniform Guidelines on Employee Selection Procedures* recommend that all selection procedures be validated. **Validation** is the process of determining how well a selection test or procedure predicts future job performance. The better or more accurate the prediction of future job performance, the more valid a test is said to be. See the What Really Works feature later in this chapter for more on the validity of common selection tests and procedures.

Let's examine common selection procedures such as **10-3a application forms and résumés, 10-3b references and background checks, 10-3c selection tests,** and **10-3d interviews**.

10-3a Application Forms and Résumés

The first selection devices that most job applicants encounter when they seek a job are application forms and résumés. Both contain similar information about an applicant, such as name, address, job and educational history, and so forth. Though an organization's application form often asks for information already provided by the applicant's résumé, most organizations prefer to collect this information in their own format for entry into a human resource information system.

Employment laws apply to application forms just as they do to all selection devices. Application forms may ask applicants only for valid, job-related information. Nonetheless, application forms commonly ask applicants for non-job-related information such as marital status, maiden name, age, or date of high school graduation. Indeed, one study found that 73 percent of organizations had application forms that violated at least one federal or state law.[26] Exhibit 10.4 lists the kinds of information that companies may *not* request in application forms, during job interviews, or in any other part of the selection process. Courts will assume that you consider all of the information you request of applicants even if you actually don't. Be sure to ask only those questions that directly relate to the candidate's ability and motivation to perform the job.

Companies should also be aware that employment laws in other countries may differ from U.S. laws. For instance, employers in France may ask applicants for non-job-related personal information such as their age or the number of children. And most French employers expect applicants to include a picture with their résumé.[27] Consequently, companies should closely examine their application forms, interview questions, and other selection procedures for compliance with the law wherever they do business.

selection
the process of gathering information about job applicants to decide who should be offered a job

validation
the process of determining how well a selection test or procedure predicts future job performance. the better or more accurate the prediction of future job performance, the more valid a test is said to be

Exhibit 10.4

Topics That Employers Should Avoid in Application Forms, Interviews, or Other Parts of the Selection Process

1. *Children.* Don't ask applicants if they have children, plan to have them, or have or need child care. Questions about children can unintentionally single out women.

2. *Age.* Because of the Age Discrimination in Employment Act, employers cannot ask job applicants their age during the hiring process. Since most people graduate high school at the age of 18, even asking for high school graduation dates could violate the law.

3. *Disabilities.* Don't ask if applicants have physical or mental disabilities. According to the Americans with Disabilities Act, disabilities (and reasonable accommodations for them) cannot be discussed until a job offer has been made.

4. *Physical characteristics.* Don't ask for information about height, weight, or other physical characteristics. Questions about weight could be construed as leading to discrimination toward overweight people, who studies show are less likely to be hired in general.

5. *Name.* Yes, you can ask an applicant's name, but you cannot ask a female applicant for her maiden name because it indicates marital status. Asking for a maiden name could also lead to charges that the organization was trying to establish a candidate's ethnic background.

6. *Citizenship.* Asking applicants about citizenship could lead to claims of discrimination on the basis of national origin. However, according to the Immigration Reform and Control Act, companies may ask applicants if they have a legal right to work in the United States.

7. *Lawsuits.* Applicants may not be asked if they have ever filed a lawsuit against an employer. Federal and state laws prevent this to protect whistleblowers from retaliation by future employers.

8. *Arrest records.* Applicants cannot be asked about their arrest records. Arrests don't have legal standing. However, applicants can be asked whether they have been convicted of a crime.

9. *Smoking.* Applicants cannot be asked if they smoke. Smokers might be able to claim that they weren't hired because of fears of higher absenteeism and medical costs. However, they can be asked if they are aware of company policies that restrict smoking at work.

10. *AIDS/HIV.* Applicants can't be asked about AIDS, HIV, or any other medical condition. Questions of this nature would violate the Americans with Disabilities Act, as well as federal and state civil rights laws.

Source: J. S. Pouliot, "Topics to Avoid with Applicants," Nation's Business 80, no. 7 (1992): 57.

Résumés also pose problems for companies, but in a different way. Accu-Screen Inc. has kept records for 14 years on résumé falsification data and reports that approximately 43 percent of résumés and job applications contain false information. According to a study conducted by J. J. Keller & Associates, Inc., the nation's leading provider of risk and regulatory management solutions, 55 percent of human resource professionals have discovered lies on résumés or applications when conducting pre-employment background or reference checks.[28] Therefore, managers should verify the information collected via résumés and application forms by comparing it with additional information collected during interviews and other stages of the selection process, such as references and background checks, which are discussed next.

10-3b References and Background Checks

Nearly all companies ask an applicant to provide **employment references**, such as previous employers or coworkers, whom they can contact to learn more about the candidate. **Background checks** are used to verify the truthfulness and accuracy of information that applicants provide about themselves and to uncover negative, job-related background information not provided by

employment references
sources such as previous employers or coworkers who can provide job-related information about job candidates

background checks
procedures used to verify the truthfulness and accuracy of information that applicants provide about themselves and to uncover negative, job-related background information not provided by applicants

applicants. Background checks are conducted by contacting "educational institutions, prior employers, court records, police and governmental agencies, and other informational sources, either by telephone, mail, remote computer access, or through in-person investigations."[29]

Unfortunately, previous employers are increasingly reluctant to provide references or background check information for fear of being sued by previous employees for defamation.[30] If former employers provide potential employers with unsubstantiated information that damages applicants' chances of being hired, applicants can (and do) sue for defamation. As a result, 54 percent of employers will not provide information about previous employees.[31] Many provide only dates of employment, positions held, and date of separation.

10-3c Selection Tests

We're all aware that some people do well in jobs, whereas other people do poorly, but how do you determine into which category an applicant falls? Selection tests give organizational decision makers a chance to know who will likely do well in a job and who won't. The basic idea behind selection testing is to have applicants take a test that measures something directly or indirectly related to doing well on the job. The selection tests discussed here are specific ability tests, cognitive ability tests, biographical data, personality tests, work sample tests, and assessment centers.

Specific ability tests measure the extent to which an applicant possesses the particular kind of ability needed to do a job well. Specific ability tests are also called **aptitude tests** because they measure aptitude for doing a particular task well. For example, if you took the SAT to get into college, then you've taken the aptly named Scholastic Aptitude Test, which is one of the best predictors of how well students will do in college (i.e., scholastic performance). Specific ability tests also exist for mechanical, clerical, sales, and physical work. For example, clerical workers have to be good at accurately reading and scanning numbers as they type or enter data.

Cognitive ability tests measure the extent to which applicants have abilities in perceptual speed, verbal comprehension, numerical aptitude, general reasoning, and spatial aptitude. In other words, these tests indicate how quickly and how well people understand words, numbers, logic, and spatial dimensions. Whereas specific ability tests predict job performance in only particular types of jobs, cognitive ability tests accurately predict job performance in almost all kinds of jobs.[32] Why is this so? The reason is that people with strong cognitive or mental abilities are usually good at learning new things, processing complex information, solving problems, and making decisions, and these abilities are important in almost all jobs.[33] In fact, cognitive ability tests are almost always the best predictors of job performance. Consequently, if you were allowed to use just one selection test, a cognitive ability test would be the one to use.[34] (In practice, though, companies use a battery of different tests because doing so leads to much more accurate selection decisions.)

Biographical data, or **biodata**, are extensive surveys that ask applicants questions about their personal backgrounds and life experiences. The basic idea behind biodata is that past behavior (personal background and life experience)

specific ability tests (aptitude tests)
tests that measure the extent to which an applicant possesses the particular kind of ability needed to do a job well

cognitive ability tests
tests that measure the extent to which applicants have abilities in perceptual speed, verbal comprehension, numerical aptitude, general reasoning, and spatial aptitude

biographical data (biodata)
extensive surveys that ask applicants questions about their personal backgrounds and life experiences

is the best predictor of future behavior. For example, during World War II, the U.S. AIR FORCE had to test tens of thousands of men without flying experience to determine who was likely to be a good pilot. Because flight training took several months and was very expensive, quickly selecting the right people for training was important. After examining extensive biodata, it found that one of the best predictors of success in flight school was whether students had ever built model airplanes that actually flew. This one biodata item was almost as good a predictor as the entire set of selection tests that the Air Force was using at the time.[35]

Most biodata questionnaires have over 100 items that gather information about habits and attitudes, health, interpersonal relations, money, what it was like growing up in your family (parents, siblings, childhood years, teen years), personal habits, current home (spouse, children), hobbies, education and training, values, preferences, and work.[36] In general, biodata are very good predictors of future job performance, especially in entry-level jobs.

You may have noticed that some of the information requested in biodata surveys also appears in Exhibit 10.4 as topics employers should avoid in applications, interviews, or other parts of the selection process. This information can be requested in biodata questionnaires provided that the company can demonstrate that the information is job related (i.e., valid) and does not result in adverse impact against protected groups of job applicants. Biodata surveys should be validated and tested for adverse impact before they are used to make selection decisions.[37]

Personality is the relatively stable set of behaviors, attitudes, and emotions displayed over time, which makes people different from each other. **Personality tests** measure the extent to which applicants possess different kinds of job-related personality dimensions. Of these, only conscientiousness, the degree to which someone is organized, hardworking, responsible, persevering, thorough, and achievement oriented, predicts job performance across a wide variety of jobs.[38] Conscientiousness works especially well in combination with cognitive ability tests, allowing companies to select applicants who are organized, hardworking, responsible, and smart!

Work sample tests, also called "performance tests," require applicants to perform tasks that are actually done on the job. So, unlike specific ability, cognitive ability, biographical data, and personality tests, which are indirect predictors of job performance, work sample tests directly measure job applicants' capability to do the job. Work sample tests are generally very good at predicting future job performance; however, they can be expensive to administer and can be used for only one kind of job. For example, an auto dealership could not use a work sample test for mechanics as a selection test for sales representatives.

Are tests perfect predictors of job performance? No, they aren't. Some people who do well on selection tests will do poorly in their jobs. Likewise, some people who do poorly on selection tests (and therefore weren't hired) would have been very good performers. Nonetheless, valid tests will minimize selection errors (hiring people who should not have been hired and not hiring people who should have been hired), while maximizing correct selection decisions (hiring people who should have been hired and not hiring people who should not have been hired). In short, tests increase the chances that you'll

personality tests
tests that measure the extent to which applicants possess different kinds of job-related personality dimensions

work sample tests
tests that require applicants to perform tasks that are actually done on the job

hire the right person for the job, that is, someone who turns out to be a good performer. So, although tests aren't perfect, almost nothing predicts future job performance as well as the selection tests discussed here. For more on how well selection tests increase the odds of hiring the right person for the job, see the What Really Works feature.

10-3d Interviews

In **interviews**, company representatives ask job applicants job-related questions to determine whether they are qualified for the job. Interviews are probably the most frequently used and relied on selection device. There are several basic kinds of interviews: unstructured, structured, and semistructured. In **unstructured interviews**, interviewers are free to ask applicants anything they want, and studies show that they do. Because interviewers often disagree about which questions should be asked during interviews, different interviewers tend to ask applicants very different questions.[39] Furthermore, individual interviewers even seem to have a tough time asking the same questions from one interview to the next. This high level of variety can make things difficult. As a result, although unstructured interviews do predict job performance with some success, they are about half as accurate as structured interviews at predicting which job applicants should be hired.[40]

By contrast, with **structured interviews**, standardized interview questions are prepared ahead of time so that all applicants are asked the same job-related questions.[41] Four kinds of questions are typically asked in structured interviews:

- Situational questions ask applicants how they would respond in a hypothetical situation ("What would you do if . . .?"). These questions are more appropriate for hiring new graduates, who are unlikely to have encountered real-work situations because of their limited work experience.
- Behavioral questions ask applicants what they did in previous jobs that were similar to the job for which they are applying ("In your previous jobs, tell me about . . .,"). These questions are more appropriate for hiring experienced individuals.
- Background questions ask applicants about their work experience, education, and other qualifications ("Tell me about the training you received at . . . .").
- Job-knowledge questions ask applicants to demonstrate their job knowledge (e.g., nurses might be asked, "Give me an example of a time when one of your patients had a severe reaction to a medication. How did you handle it?").[42]

The primary advantage of structured interviews is that comparing applicants is much easier because they are all asked the same questions. Structuring interviews also ensures that interviewers ask only for important, job-related information. Not only are the accuracy, usefulness, and validity of the interview improved, but the chances that interviewers will ask questions about topics that violate employment laws are reduced (go back to Exhibit 10.4 for a list of these topics).

interviews
a selection tool in which company representatives ask job applicants job-related questions to determine whether they are qualified for the job

unstructured interviews
interviews in which interviewers are free to ask the applicants anything they want

structured interviews
interviews in which all applicants are asked the same set of standardized questions, usually including situational, behavioral, background, and job-knowledge questions

what *really* works

Using Selection Tests to Hire Good Workers

Hiring new employees is always something of a gamble. When you say, "We'd like to offer you the job," you never know how it's going to turn out. Nonetheless, the selection tests discussed in this chapter can go a long way toward taking the gambling aspect out of the hiring process. Indeed, more than 1,000 studies based on over 100,000 study participants strongly indicate that selection tests can give employers a much better than average (50–50) chance of hiring the right workers. If you had odds like these working for you in Las Vegas, you'd make so much money the casinos wouldn't let you in the door.

Cognitive Ability Tests

There is a 76 percent chance that applicants who do well on cognitive ability tests will be much better performers in their jobs than applicants who do not do well on such tests.

Work Sample Tests

There is a 77 percent chance that applicants who do well on work sample tests will be much better performers in their jobs than applicants who do not do well on such tests.

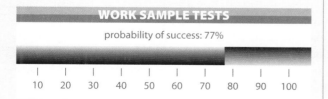

Assessment Centers

There is a 69 percent chance that applicants who do well on assessment center exercises will be much better managers than applicants who do not do well on such exercises.

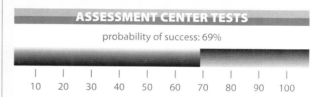

Structured Interviews

There is a 76 percent chance that applicants who do well in structured interviews will be much better performers in their jobs than applicants who do not do well in such interviews.

Cognitive Ability–Work Sample Tests

When deciding whom to hire, most companies use a number of tests to make even more accurate selection decisions. There is an 82 percent chance that applicants who do well on a combination of cognitive ability tests and work sample tests will be much better performers in their jobs than applicants who do not do well on both tests.

Cognitive Ability—Integrity Tests

There is an 83 percent chance that applicants who do well on a combination of cognitive ability tests and integrity tests (see Chapter 4 for a discussion of integrity tests) will be much better performers in their jobs than applicants who do not do well on both tests.

Cognitive Ability—Structured Interviews

There is an 82 percent chance that applicants who do well on a combination of cognitive ability tests and structured interviews will be much better performers in their jobs than applicants who do not do well on both tests.[43]

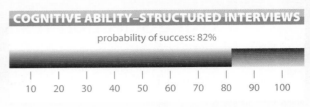

Semistructured interviews lie between structured and unstructured interviews. A major part of the semistructured interview (perhaps as much as 80 percent) is based on structured questions, but some time is set aside for unstructured interviewing to allow the interviewer to probe into ambiguous or missing information uncovered during the structured portion of the interview.

How well do interviews predict future job performance? Contrary to what you've probably heard, recent evidence indicates that even unstructured interviews do a fairly good job.[44] When conducted properly, however, structured interviews can lead to much more accurate hiring decisions than unstructured interviews. In some cases, the validity of structured interviews can rival that of cognitive ability tests.

But even more important, because interviews are especially good at assessing applicants' interpersonal skills, they work particularly well with cognitive ability tests. Combining the two—using structured interviews together with cognitive ability tests to identify smart people who work well in conjunction with others—leads to even better selection decisions than using either alone.[45] Exhibit 10.5 provides a set of guidelines for conducting effective, structured employment interviews.

REVIEW 10-3

Selection

Selection is the process of gathering information about job applicants to decide who should be offered a job. Accurate selection procedures are valid, are legally defendable, and improve organizational performance. Application forms and résumés are the most common selection devices. Because many application forms request illegal, non-job-related information, and as many as one-third of job applicants falsify information on résumés, these procedures are often of little value in making hiring decisions. References and background checks can also be problematic, given that previous employers are reluctant to provide such information for fear of being sued for defamation. Unfortunately, without this information, other employers are at risk of negligent hiring lawsuits. Selection tests generally do the best job of predicting applicants' future job performance. In general, cognitive ability tests, work sample tests,

Exhibit 10.5

Guidelines for Conducting Effective Structural Interviews

Interview Stage	What to Do

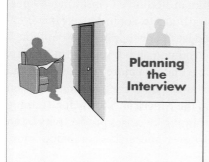

Planning the Interview

- Identify and define the knowledge, skills, abilities, and other (KSAO) characteristics needed for successful job performance.
- For each essential KSAO, develop key behavioral questions that will elicit examples of past accomplishments, activities, and performance.
- For each KSAO, develop a list of things to look for in the applicant's responses to key questions.

Conducting the Interview

- Create a relaxed, nonstressful interview atmosphere.
- Review the applicant's application form, résumé, and other information.
- Allocate enough time to complete the interview without interruption.
- Put the applicant at ease; don't jump right into heavy questioning.
- Tell the applicant what to expect. Explain the interview process.
- Obtain job-related information from the applicant by asking those questions prepared for each KSAO.
- Describe the job and the organization to the applicant. Applicants need adequate information to make a selection decision about the organization.

After the Interview

- Immediately after the interview, review your notes and make sure they are complete.
- Evaluate the applicant on each essential KSAO.
- Determine each applicant's probability of success and make a hiring decision.

Source: B. M. Farrell, "The Art and Science of Employment Interviews," Personnel Journal 65 (1986): 91–94.

biographical data, and assessment centers are the most valid tests, followed by personality tests and specific ability tests, which are still good predictors. Selection tests aren't perfect predictors of job performance, but almost nothing predicts future job performance as well as selection tests. The three kinds of job interviews are unstructured, structured, and semistructured interviews. Of these, structured interviews work best because they ensure that all applicants are consistently asked the same situational, behavioral, background, or job-knowledge questions, in the same order.

10-4 Training

Training means providing opportunities for employees to develop the job-specific skills, experience, and knowledge they need to do their jobs or improve their performance.

training
developing the skills, experience, and knowledge employees need to perform their jobs or improve their performance

After reading this section, you should be able to:

10-4 describe how to select appropriate training methods and evaluate the effectiveness of that training.

Currently, American companies spend more than $60 billion a year on training. According to a recent survey by Mercer Human Resource Consulting, 49 percent of companies are increasing their training budgets. For instance, *Hewlett-Packard* recently increased its training budget to a whopping $300 million.[46] What is driving the infusion of dollars into training and development budgets of companies? Companies like HP recognize that it is more cost-efficient and competitive to develop talent from within rather than compete for talent on the open market.[47] In addition, according to the American Society for Training and Development, a typical investment in training increases productivity by an average of 17 percent, reduces employee turnover, and makes companies more profitable.[48]

Still, to make sure training dollars are well spent, companies need to **10-4a select appropriate training methods**, and **10-4b evaluate training**.

10-4a Training Methods

Assume that you're a training director for a major oil company and that you're in charge of making sure all employees know how to respond effectively in case of an oil spill.[49] Exhibit 10.6 lists a number of training methods you could use: films and videos, lectures, planned readings, case studies, coaching and mentoring, group discussions, on-the-job training, role-playing, simulations and games, vestibule training, and computer-based learning. Which method would be best?

To choose the best method, you should consider a number of factors, such as the number of people to be trained, the cost of training, and the objectives of the training. For instance, if the training objective is to impart information or knowledge to trainees, then you should use films and videos, lectures, and planned readings. In our example, trainees might read a manual or attend a lecture about how to protect a shoreline to keep it from being affected by the spill.

If developing analytical and problem-solving skills is the objective, then use case studies, coaching and mentoring, and group discussions. In our example, trainees might view a video documenting how a team handled exposure to hazardous substances, talk with first responders, and discuss what they would do in a similar situation.

If practicing, learning, or changing job behaviors is the objective, then use on-the-job training, role-playing, simulations and games, and vestibule training. In our example, trainees might participate in a mock shoreline cleanup to learn what to do in the event oil comes to shore. This simulation could take place on an actual shoreline or on a video game-like virtual shoreline.

If training is supposed to meet more than one of these objectives, then your best choice may be to combine one of the previous methods with computer-based training. When *UPS* found that 30 percent of its driver candidates were not passing its traditional classroom-based training program, it introduced Integrad, a simulation featuring "Clarksville," a simulated town in which the driver operates a virtual truck and has to deal with simulations of real-world situations like kids playing in the street and customers confusing UPS with other delivery services. Since switching to Integrad, UPS has seen the failure rate of its trainees drop to just 10 percent.[50]

These days, many companies are adopting Internet training, or "e-learning." E-learning can offer several advantages. Because employees don't need to leave their jobs, travel costs are greatly reduced. Also, because employees can take training modules when it is convenient (i.e., they don't have to fall behind at their jobs to attend weeklong training courses), workplace productivity

Exhibit 10.6

Training Objective Training Method

Impart Information and Knowledge

- **Films and videos.** Films and videos share information, illustrate problems and solutions, and effectively hold trainees' attention.
- **Lectures.** Trainees listen to instructors' oral presentations.
- **Planned readings.** Trainees read about concepts or ideas before attending training.

Develop Analytical and Problem-Solving Skills

- **Case studies.** Cases are analyzed and discussed in small groups. The cases present a specific problem or decision, and trainees develop methods for solving the problem or making the decision.
- **Coaching and mentoring.** Coaching and mentoring of trainees by managers involves informal advice, suggestions, and guidance. This method is helpful for reinforcing other kinds of training and for trainees who benefit from support and personal encouragement.
- **Group discussions.** Small groups of trainees actively discuss specific topics. The instructor may perform the role of discussion leader.

Practice, Learn, or Change Job Behaviors

- **On-the-job training (OJT).** New employees are assigned to experienced employees. The trainee learns by watching the experienced employee perform the job and eventually by working alongside the experienced employee. Gradually, the trainee is left on his or her own to perform the job.
- **Role-playing.** Trainees assume job-related roles and practice new behaviors by acting out what they would do in job-related situations.
- **Simulations and games.** Experiential exercises place trainees in realistic job-related situations and give them the opportunity to experience a job-related condition in a relatively low-cost setting. The trainee benefits from "hands-on experience" before actually performing the job where mistakes may be more costly.
- **Vestibule training.** Procedures and equipment similar to those used in the actual job are set up in a special area called a vestibule. The trainee is then taught how to perform the job at his or her own pace without disrupting the actual flow of work, making costly mistakes, or exposing the trainee and others to dangerous conditions.

Impart Information and Knowledge; Develop Analytical and Problem-Solving Skills; and Practice, Learn, or Change Job Behaviors

- **Computer-based learning.** Interactive videos, software, CD-ROMs, personal computers, teleconferencing, and the Internet may be combined to present multimedia-based training.

Source: A. Fowler, "How to Decide on Training Methods," People Management 25, no. 1 (1995): 36.

should increase and employee stress should decrease. And, if a company's technology infrastructure can support it, e-learning can be much faster than traditional training methods. There are, however, several disadvantages to e-learning. First, despite its increasing popularity, it's not always the appropriate training method. E-learning can be a good way to impart information, but it isn't always as effective for changing job behaviors or developing problem-solving and analytical skills. Second, e-learning requires a significant investment in computers and high-speed Internet and network connections for all employees. Finally, though e-learning can be faster, many employees find it so boring and unengaging that they may choose to do their jobs rather than complete e-learning courses when sitting alone at their desks. E-learning may become more interesting, however, as more companies incorporate gamelike features such as avatars and competition into their e-learning courses.

10-4b Evaluating Training

After selecting a training method and conducting the training, the last step is to evaluate the training. Training can be evaluated in four ways: on *reactions* (how satisfied trainees were with the program), on *learning* (how much employees improved their knowledge or skills), on *behavior* (how much employees actually changed their on-the-job behavior because of training), or on *results* (how much training improved job performance, such as increased sales or quality, or decreased costs).[51] In general, training provides meaningful benefits for most companies if it is done well. For example, a study by the American Society for Training and Development shows that a training budget as small as $680 per employee can increase a company's total return on investment by 6 percent.[52]

REVIEW 10-4
. . . .

Training

Training is used to give employees the job-specific skills, experience, and knowledge they need to do their jobs or improve their job performance. To make sure training dollars are well spent, companies need to determine specific training needs, select appropriate training methods, and then evaluate the training. Selection of an appropriate training method depends on a number of factors, including the number of people to be trained, the cost of training, and the objectives of the training. If training is supposed to meet more than one of these objectives, then it may be best to combine one of the previous methods with computer-based training. Training can be evaluated on reactions, learning, behavior, or results.

10-5 Performance Appraisal

Giving employees the knowledge and skills they need to improve their performance is just the first step in developing employees. The second step—and not enough companies do this—is giving employees formal feedback about their actual job performance. A CEO of a large telecommunications company hired an outside consultant to assess and coach (provide feedback to) the company's top 50 managers. To the CEO's surprise, 75 percent of those managers indicated that the feedback they received from the consultant regarding their strengths and weaknesses was the only substantial feedback they had received about their performance in the last five years. As a result of that feedback, two-thirds of the managers then took positive steps to improve their skills, knowledge, and job performance and expressed a clear desire for more feedback, especially from their boss, the CEO.[53] So, in today's competitive business environment, even top managers understand the importance of formal performance feedback to their growth and development.

After reading this section, you should be able to:

10-5 discuss how to use performance appraisal to give meaningful performance feedback.

Performance appraisal is the process of assessing how well employees are doing their jobs. Most employees and managers intensely dislike the performance appraisal process. *Yahoo!*'s former CEO Carol Bartz said, "If I had my way, I wouldn't do annual reviews. I think the annual review process is so antiquated. I almost would rather ask each employee to tell us if they've had a meaningful conversation with their manager this quarter. Yes or no. And if they say no, they ought to have one."[54]

Unfortunately, attitudes like this are all too common. In fact, 70 percent of employees are dissatisfied with the performance appraisal process in their companies. Likewise, according to the Society for Human Resource Management, 90 percent of human resource managers are dissatisfied with the performance appraisal systems used by their companies.[55]

Performance appraisals are used for four broad purposes: making administrative decisions (e.g., pay increase, promotion, retention), providing feedback for employee development (e.g., performance feedback, developing career plans), evaluating human resource programs (e.g., validating selection systems), and for documentation purposes (e.g., documenting performance ratings and decisions based on those ratings).[56]

Let's explore how companies can avoid some of these problems with performance appraisals by **10-5a accurately measuring job performance** and **10-5b effectively sharing performance feedback with employees**.

10-5a Accurately Measuring Job Performance

Workers often have strong doubts about the accuracy of their performance appraisals—and they may be right. For example, it's widely known that assessors are prone to errors when rating worker performance. Three of the most common rating errors are central tendency, halo, and leniency. *Central tendency error* occurs when assessors rate all workers as average or in the middle of the scale. *Halo error* occurs when assessors rate all workers as performing at the same level (good, bad, or average) in all parts of their jobs. *Leniency error* occurs when assessors rate all workers as performing particularly well. One of the reasons managers make these errors is that they often don't spend enough time gathering or reviewing performance data.

performance appraisal
the process of assessing how well employees are doing their jobs

One of the ways companies try to improve performance appraisal measures is to use as many objective performance measures as possible. **Objective performance measures** are measures of performance that are easily and directly counted or quantified. Common objective performance measures include output, scrap, waste, sales, customer complaints, and rejection rates. But when objective performance measures aren't available (and frequently they aren't), subjective performance measures have to be used instead. **Subjective performance measures** require that someone judge or assess a worker's performance. The most common kind of subjective performance measure is the graphic rating scale (GRS) shown in Exhibit 10.7. Graphic rating scales are most widely used because they are easy to construct, but they are very susceptible to rating errors.

A popular alternative to graphic rating scales is the **behavior observation scale (BOS)**. BOS requires raters to rate the frequency with which workers perform specific behaviors representative of the job dimensions that are critical to successful job performance. Exhibit 10.7 shows a BOS for two important job dimensions for a retail salesperson: customer service and money handling. Notice that each dimension lists several specific behaviors characteristic of a worker who excels in that dimension of job performance. (Normally, the scale would list 7 to 12 items per dimension, not 3, as in the exhibit.) Notice also that the behaviors are good behaviors, meaning they indicate good performance, and the rater is asked to judge how frequently an employee engaged in those good behaviors. The logic behind the BOS is that better performers engage in good behaviors more often.

Not only do BOSs work well for rating critical dimensions of performance, but studies also show that managers strongly prefer BOSs for the following reasons: giving performance feedback; accurately differentiating between poor, average, and good workers; identifying training needs; and accurately measuring performance.[57]

The second approach to improving the measurement of workers' job performance is **rater training**. The most effective is frame-of-reference training, in which a group of trainees learn how to do performance appraisals by watching a videotape of an employee at work. Next, they evaluate the performance of the person in the videotape. A trainer (an expert in the subject matter) then shares his or her evaluations, and trainees' evaluations are compared with the expert's. The expert then explains the rationales behind his or her evaluations. This process is repeated until the difference in evaluations given by trainees and evaluations by the expert are minimized. The underlying logic behind the frame-of-reference training is that by adopting the frame of reference used by an expert, trainees will be able to accurately observe, judge, and use the scale to evaluate performance of others.[58]

10-5b Sharing Performance Feedback

After gathering accurate performance data, the next step is to share performance feedback with employees. Unfortunately, even when performance appraisal ratings are accurate, the appraisal process often breaks down at the feedback stage. Employees become defensive and dislike hearing any negative assessments of their work, no matter how small. Managers become defensive too, and dislike giving appraisal feedback as much as employees dislike receiving it.

objective performance measures
measures of job performance that are easily and directly counted or quantified

subjective performance measures
measures of job performance that require someone to judge or assess a worker's performance

behavior observation scale (BOS)
rating scales that indicate the frequency with which workers perform specific behaviors that are representative of the job dimensions critical to successful job performance

rater training
training performance appraisal raters in how to avoid rating errors and increase rating accuracy

Exhibit 10.7

Subjective Performance Appraisal Scales

Graphic Rating Scale

Example 1:

	Very Poor	Poor	Average	Good	Very Good
1. Quality of work performed is........	1	2	3	4	5

Example 2:

	Very Poor (20% errors)	Poor (15% errors)	Average (10% errors)	Good (5% errors)	Very Good (less than 5% errors)
2. Quality of work performed is........	1	2	3	4	5

Behavioral Observation Scale

Dimension: Customer Service

	Almost Never				Almost Always
1. Greets customers with a smile and a "hello."	1	2	3	4	5
2. Calls other stores to help customers find merchandise that is not in stock.	1	2	3	4	5
3. Promptly handles customer concerns and complaints.	1	2	3	4	5

Dimension: Money Handling

	Almost Never				Almost Always
1. Accurately makes change from customer transactions.	1	2	3	4	5
2. Accounts balance at the end of the day, no shortages or surpluses.	1	2	3	4	5
3. Accurately records transactions in computer system.	1	2	3	4	5

What can be done to overcome the inherent difficulties in performance appraisal feedback sessions? Because performance appraisal ratings have traditionally been the judgments of just one person, the boss, one possibility is to use **360-degree feedback**. In this approach, feedback comes from four sources: the boss, subordinates, peers and coworkers, and the employees themselves. The data, which are obtained anonymously (except for the boss's), are compiled into a feedback report comparing the employee's self-ratings with those

360-degree feedback
a performance appraisal process in which feedback is obtained from the boss, subordinates, peers and coworkers, and the employees themselves

of the boss, subordinates, and peers and coworkers. Usually, a consultant or human resource specialist discusses the results with the employee. The advantage of 360-degree programs is that negative feedback ("You don't listen") is often more credible when it comes from several people.

A word of caution, though: About half of the companies using 360-degree feedback for performance appraisal now use the feedback only for developmental purposes. They found that sometimes when raises and promotions were on the line, peers and subordinates would give high ratings in order to get high ratings from others. Conversely, in some situations, employees distorted ratings to harm competitors or help people they liked. A senior manager at a New York City marketing company agrees, saying that 360-degree feedback "also allows people to vent their frustrations and anger on bosses and colleagues in an insensitive way."[59] On the other hand, studies clearly show that ratees prefer to receive feedback from multiple raters, so 360-degree feedback is likely to continue to grow in popularity.[60]

Herbert Meyer, who has been studying performance appraisal feedback for more than 30 years, recommends a list of topics to discuss in performance appraisal feedback sessions.[61] Furthermore, managers can do three different things to make performance reviews more comfortable and productive. First, they should separate developmental feedback, which is designed to improve future performance, from administrative feedback, which is used as a reward for past performance, such as for raises. When managers give developmental feedback, they're acting as coaches, but when they give administrative feedback, they're acting as judges. These roles, coaches and judges, are clearly incompatible. As coaches, managers encourage, point out opportunities for growth and improvement, and employees are typically open and receptive to feedback. But as judges, managers are evaluative, and employees are typically defensive and closed to feedback.

Second, Meyer suggests that performance appraisal feedback sessions be based on self-appraisals, in which employees carefully assess their own strengths, weaknesses, successes, and failures in writing. Because employees play an active role in the review of their performance, managers can be coaches rather than judges. Also, because the focus is on future goals and development, both employees and managers are likely to be more satisfied with the process and more committed to future plans and changes. And because the focus is on development and not administrative assessment, studies show that self-appraisals lead to more candid self-assessments than traditional supervisory reviews.[62]

Finally, what people do with the performance feedback they receive really matters. A study of 1,361 senior managers found that managers who reviewed their 360-degree feedback with an executive coach (hired by the company) were more likely to set specific goals for improvement, ask their bosses for ways to improve, and subsequently improve their performance.[63]

REVIEW 10-5

. . . .

Performance Appraisal

Most employees and managers intensely dislike the performance appraisal process. Some of the problems associated with appraisals can be avoided, however, by accurately measuring job performance and effectively sharing performance feedback with employees. Organizations should develop good performance appraisal scales and preferably use behavior observation scales (BOSs). They should train raters to accurately evaluate performance, perhaps by providing frame-of-reference training. They should impress upon managers the value of providing feedback in a clear, consistent, and fair manner and of setting goals and monitoring progress toward those goals.

One way to overcome the inherent difficulties in performance appraisal feedback is to provide 360-degree feedback, in which feedback is obtained from four sources: the boss, subordinates, peers and coworkers, and the employees themselves. Feedback tends to be more credible if it is heard from several sources. Finally, especially for managers, it's helpful to have people discuss the feedback they received with executive coaches or the people who provided it.

10-6 Compensation

At PENSKE AUTOMOTIVE GROUP, which has 300 car dealerships worldwide, 8 percent of CEO Roger Penske's bonus is tied to keeping employee turnover below 31 percent. Similar provisions are in place at Pep Boys, a car parts retail chain, and ExlService Holdings, an India-based outsourcing company. Why link managers' pay to employee turnover? According to Tony Pordon, senior vice president at Penske Automotive, "We believe that employee turnover is a symptom of bigger problems at the dealership level."[64] Mark Royal, a consultant for the Hay Group, which specializes in employee compensation, further explains that linking managers' pay to turnover, "is a recognition, on the one hand, of people as a driver of business success. It also reflects a recognition that turnover is costly."[65]

After reading this section, you should be able to:

10-6 describe basic compensation strategies and explain how they affect human resource practice.

Compensation includes both the financial and the nonfinancial rewards that organizations give employees in exchange for their work.

Let's learn more about compensation by examining the **10-6a compensation decisions that managers must make** and **10-6b the role that employment benefits play in compensating today's employees**.

10-6a Compensation Decisions

There are four basic kinds of compensation decisions: pay level, pay variability, pay structure, and employment benefits. We'll discuss employment benefits in the next subsection.[66]

Pay-level decisions are decisions about whether to pay workers at a level that is below, above, or at current market wages. Companies use job evaluation to set their pay structures. **Job evaluation** determines the worth of each job by determining the market value of the knowledge, skills, and requirements needed to perform it. After conducting a job evaluation, most companies try to pay the going rate, meaning the current market wage. There are always companies, however, whose financial situation causes them to pay considerably less than current market wages.

Some companies choose to pay above-average wages to attract and keep employees. *Above-market wages* can attract a larger, more qualified pool of job

compensation
the financial and nonfinancial rewards that organizations give employees in exchange for their work

job evaluation
a process that determines the worth of each job in a company by evaluating the market value of the knowledge, skills, and requirements needed to perform it

applicants, increase the rate of job acceptance, decrease the time it takes to fill positions, and increase the time that employees stay.[67]

Pay-variability decisions concern the extent to which employees' pay varies with individual and organizational performance. Linking pay to performance is intended to increase employee motivation, effort, and job performance. Piecework, sales commissions, profit sharing, employee stock ownership plans, and stock options are common pay-variability options. For instance, under piecework pay plans, employees are paid a set rate for each item produced up to some standard (e.g., 35 cents per item produced for output up to 100 units per day). Once productivity exceeds the standard, employees are paid a set amount for each unit of output over the standard (e.g., 45 cents for each unit above 100 units). Under a sales commission plan, salespeople are paid a percentage of the purchase price of items they sell. The more they sell, the more they earn.

Because pay plans such as piecework and commissions are based on individual performance, they can reduce the incentive that people have to work together. Therefore, companies also use group incentives (discussed in Chapter 8) and organizational incentives, such as profit sharing, employee stock ownership plans, and stock options, to encourage teamwork and cooperation.

With profit sharing, employees receive a portion of the organization's profits over and above their regular compensation. After posting a surprise $2.7 billion profit for 2009—its first in four years—Ford announced it would be issuing profit-sharing checks of about $450 to each of its hourly workers.[68]

Employee stock ownership plans (ESOPs) compensate employees by awarding them shares of the company stock in addition to their regular compensation. Stock options give employees the right to purchase shares of stock at a set price. Options work like this: Let's say you are awarded the right (or option) to buy 100 shares of stock from the company for $5 a share. If the company's stock price rises to $15 a share, you can exercise your options, sell the stock for $15 a share, and come out with $1,000. When you exercise your options, you pay the company $500 (100 shares at $5 a share), but, because the stock is selling for $15 in the stock market, you can sell your 100 shares for $1,500 and make $1,000. Of course, as the company's profits and share values increase, stock options become even more valuable to employees. Stock options have no value, however, if the company's stock falls below the option "grant price," the price at which the options have been issued to you. To learn more about ESOPs and stock options, see the National Center for Employee Ownership (www.nceo.org).

Pay-structure decisions are concerned with internal pay distributions, meaning the extent to which people in the company receive very different levels of pay.[69] With *hierarchical pay structures*, there are big differences from one pay level to another. The highest pay levels are for people near the top of the pay

piecework
a compensation system in which employees are paid a set rate for each item they produce

commission
a compensation system in which employees earn a percentage of each sale they make

profit sharing
a compensation system in which a company pays a percentage of its profits to employees in addition to their regular compensation

employee stock ownership plan (ESOP)
a compensation system that awards employees shares of company stock in addition to their regular compensation

stock options
a compensation system that gives employees the right to purchase shares of stock at a set price, even if the value of the stock increases above that price

distribution. The basic idea behind hierarchical pay structures is that large differences in pay between jobs or organizational levels should motivate people to work harder to obtain those higher-paying jobs. Many publicly owned companies have hierarchical pay structures, paying huge salaries to their top managers and CEOs. For example, the average CEO makes $9.25 million per year ($4,625 per hour), while average workers earn just $41,340 ($20.67 per hour). This huge difference can have a significant detrimental impact on employee morale.[70]

By contrast, *compressed pay structures* typically have fewer pay levels and smaller differences in pay between levels. Pay is less dispersed and more similar across jobs in the company. The basic idea behind compressed pay structures is that similar pay levels should lead to higher levels of cooperation, feelings of fairness and a common purpose, and better group and team performance.

So, should companies choose hierarchical or compressed pay structures? The evidence isn't straightforward, but studies seem to indicate that there are significant problems with the hierarchical approach. The most damaging finding is that there appears to be little link between organizational performance and the pay of top managers.[71] Furthermore, studies of professional athletes indicate that hierarchical pay structures (e.g., paying superstars 40 to 50 times as much as the lowest-paid athlete on the team) hurt the performance of teams and individual players.[72] For now, it seems that hierarchical pay structures work best for independent work, where it's easy to determine the contributions of individual performers and little coordination with others is needed to get the job done. In other words, hierarchical pay structures work best when clear links can be drawn between individual performance and individual rewards. By contrast, compressed pay structures, in which everyone receives similar pay, seem to work best for interdependent work, which requires employees to work together. Some companies are pursuing a middle ground: combining hierarchical and compressed pay structures by giving ordinary workers the chance to earn more through ESOPs, stock options, and profit sharing.

10-6b Employment Benefits

Employment benefits include virtually any kind of compensation other than direct wages paid to employees.[73] Three employee benefits are mandated by law: Social Security, workers' compensation insurance, and unemployment insurance. To attract and retain a good workforce, however, most organizations offer a wide variety of benefits, including retirement plans and pensions, paid holidays, paid vacations, sick leave, health insurance, life insurance, dental care, eye care, day-care facilities, paid personal days, legal assistance, physical fitness facilities, educational assistance, and discounts on company products and services. Although the cost of employee benefits varies by company and by industry, according to the Bureau of Labor Statistics, on average, benefits cost organizations about 29.3 percent of their payroll.[74] Managers should understand that although benefits are unlikely to improve employee motivation and performance, they do affect job satisfaction, employee decisions about staying or leaving the company, and the company's attractiveness to job applicants.[75] One way that organizations make their benefit plans more attractive is by offering **cafeteria benefit plans** or **flexible benefit plans**, that allow employees to choose which benefits they receive,

employment benefits
a method of rewarding employees that includes virtually any kind of compensation other than wages or salaries

cafeteria benefit plans (flexible benefit plans)
plans that allow employees to choose which benefits they receive, up to a certain dollar value

up to a certain dollar value.[76] Many cafeteria or flexible benefit plans start with a core of benefits, such as health insurance and life insurance, that are available to all employees. Then employees are allowed to select the other benefits that best fit their needs, up to a predetermined dollar amount. Some organizations allow employees to choose from several packages of benefits. The packages are of equivalent value but offer a different mix of benefits. For example, older employees may prefer more benefit dollars spent on retirement plans, whereas younger employees may prefer additional vacation days. The drawback to flexible benefit plans has been the high cost of administering them. With advances in information processing technology and Human Resource Information Systems (HRIS), however, the cost has begun to drop in recent years.

REVIEW 10-6

Compensation

Compensation includes both the financial and the nonfinancial rewards that organizations give employees in exchange for their work. There are four basic kinds of compensation decisions: pay level, pay variability, pay structure, and employment benefits. Pay-level decisions determine whether workers will receive wages below, above, or at current market levels. Pay-variability decisions concern the extent to which pay varies with individual and organizational performance. Piecework, sales commissions, profit sharing, employee stock ownership plans, and stock options are common pay-variability options. Pay-structure decisions concern the extent to which people in the company receive very different levels of pay. Hierarchical pay structures work best for independent work, whereas compressed pay structures work best for interdependent work.

Employee benefits include virtually any kind of compensation other than direct wages paid to employees. Flexible or cafeteria benefit plans offer employees a wide variety of benefits, improve job satisfaction, increase the chances that employees will stay with companies, and make organizations more attractive to job applicants. The cost of administering flexible benefit plans has begun to drop in recent years.

10-7 Employee Separations

Employee separation is a broad term covering the loss of an employee for any reason. *Involuntary separation* occurs when employers terminate or lay off employees. *Voluntary separation* occurs when employees quit or retire.

After reading this section, you should be able to:

10-7 discuss three kinds of employee separations: termination, downsizing, and turnover.

Because employee separations affect recruiting, selection, training, and compensation, organizations should forecast the number of employees they expect to lose through terminations, layoffs, turnover, or retirements when doing human resource planning.

Let's explore employee separation by examining **10-7a terminations, 10-7b downsizing, 10-7c turnover.**

employee separation
the voluntary or involuntary loss of an employee

The words "You're fired!" may have never been directed at you, but lots of people hear them, as more than 400,000 people a year get fired from their jobs. Getting fired is a terrible thing, but many managers make it even worse by bungling the firing process. How would you feel if you had been fired by e-mail, or after traveling cross-country to meet your manager? (As awful as that sounds, people have, indeed, been fired in those ways.) Though firing is never pleasant (and managers hate firings nearly as much as employees do), managers can do several things to minimize the problems inherent in firing employees.

To start, in most situations, firing should not be the first option. Instead, employees should be given a chance to change their behavior. When problems arise, employees should have ample warning and must be specifically informed as to the nature and seriousness of the trouble they're in. After being notified, they should be given sufficient time to change their behavior. If problems continue, the employees should again be counseled about their job performance, what could be done to improve it, and the possible consequences if things don't change (such as a written reprimand, suspension without pay, or firing). Sometimes this is enough to solve the problem. If the problem isn't corrected after several rounds of warnings and discussions, however, the employee may be terminated.[77]

Second, employees should be fired only for a good reason. Employers used to hire and fire employees under the legal principle of employment at will, which allowed them to fire employees for a good reason, a bad reason, or no reason at all. (Employees could also quit for a good reason, a bad reason, or no reason whenever they desired.) As employees began contesting their firings in court, however, the principle of wrongful discharge emerged. **Wrongful discharge** is a legal doctrine that requires employers to have a job-related reason to terminate employees. In other words, like other major human resource decisions, termination decisions should be made on the basis of job-related factors such as violating company rules or consistently poor performance. And with former employees winning 68 percent of wrongful discharge cases and the average wrongful termination award at $532,000 and climbing, managers should record the job-related reasons for the termination, document-specific instances of rule violations or continued poor performance, and keep notes and documents from the counseling sessions held with employees.[78]

Finally, to reduce the chances of a wrongful discharge suit, employees should always be fired in private. State the reason for discharge, but don't go into detail or engage in a lengthy discussion with the employee. Make every attempt to be as kind and respectful as possible when informing someone that he or she is being fired. It is permissible and sometimes a good idea to have a witness present. This person should be from human resources or part of the employee's chain of command, such as the supervisor's boss. Company security may be nearby but should not be in the room unless the employee has made direct threats toward others. Finally, managers should be careful not to publicly criticize the employee who has just been fired, as this can also lead to a wrongful discharge lawsuit. In general, unless someone has a "business reason to know" why an employee was fired, the reasons and details related to the firing should remain confidential.[79]

wrongful discharge
a legal doctrine that requires employers to have a job-related reason to terminate employees

10-7b Downsizing

Downsizing is the planned elimination of jobs in a company. Whether it's because of cost cutting, declining market share, previous overaggressive hiring and growth, or outsourcing, companies typically eliminate 1 million to 1.9 million jobs a year.[80] Two-thirds of companies that downsize will downsize a second time within a year.

Does downsizing work? In theory, downsizing is supposed to lead to higher productivity and profits, better stock performance, and increased organizational flexibility. However, numerous studies demonstrate that it doesn't. For instance, a 15-year study found that downsizing 10 percent of a company's workforce produced only a 1.5 percent decrease in costs; that firms that downsized increased their stock price by only 4.7 percent over three years, compared with 34.3 percent for firms that didn't; and that profitability and productivity were generally not improved by downsizing.[81] Downsizing can also result in the loss of skilled workers who would be expensive to replace when the company grows again.[82] These results make it clear that the best strategy is to conduct effective human resource planning and avoid downsizing altogether. Indeed, downsizing should always be a last resort.

If companies do find themselves in financial or strategic situations where downsizing is required for survival, however, they should train managers in how to break the news to downsized employees, have senior managers explain in detail why downsizing is necessary, and time the announcement so that employees hear it from the company and not from other sources, such as TV or newspaper reports.[83] Finally, companies should do everything they can to help downsized employees find other jobs. One of the best ways to do this is to use **outplacement services** that provide employment counseling for people faced with downsizing. Outplacement services often include advice and training in preparing résumés, getting ready for job interviews, and even identifying job opportunities in other companies. Fifty-five percent of companies provide outplacement services for laid-off employees, 76 percent provide extended health coverage, and 45 percent offer extended access to employee assistance programs.[84] Exhibit 10.8 provides additional guidelines for conducting layoffs.

Companies also need to pay attention to the survivors, the employees remaining after layoffs have occurred. University of Pennsylvania management professor Peter Cappelli says that survivors "may feel like they could just as easily be the next person laid off."[85] Lori Stewart Coletti, director of client services at Elaine Construction, a Newton, Massachusetts–based firm, said, "The general feeling is, 'Could I be next?' That's the level of uncertainty that you really have to combat."[86]

downsizing
the planned elimination of jobs in a company

outplacement services
employment-counseling services offered to employees who are losing their jobs because of downsizing

Exhibit 10.8

Guidelines for Conducting Layoffs

1. Provide clear reasons and explanations for the layoffs.

2. To avoid laying off employees with critical or irreplaceable skills, knowledge, and expertise, get input from human resources, the legal department, and several levels of management.

3. Train managers in how to tell employees that they are being laid off (stay calm; make the meeting short; explain why, but don't be personal; and provide information about immediate concerns, such as benefits, job search, and collecting personal goods).

4. Give employees the bad news early in the day, and try to avoid laying off employees just before holidays.

5. Provide outplacement services and counseling to help laid-off employees find new jobs.

6. Communicate with survivors to explain how the company and their jobs will change.

Source: M. Boyle, "The Not-So-Fine Art of the Layoff," Fortune, March 19, 2001, 209.

Employee turnover is the loss of employees who voluntarily choose to leave the company. In general, most companies try to keep the rate of employee turnover low to reduce recruiting, hiring, training, and replacement costs. Not all kinds of employee turnover are bad for organizations, however. In fact, some turnover can actually be good. **Functional turnover** is the loss of poor-performing employees who choose to leave the organization.[87] Functional turnover gives the organization a chance to replace poor performers with better workers. In fact, one study found that simply replacing poor-performing leavers with average workers would increase the revenues produced by retail salespeople in an upscale department store by $112,000 per person per year.[88] By contrast, **dysfunctional turnover**, the loss of high performers who choose to leave, is a costly loss to the organization.

Employee turnover should be carefully analyzed to determine whether good or poor performers are choosing to leave the organization. If the company is losing too many high performers, managers should determine the reasons and find ways to reduce the loss of valuable employees. The company may have to raise salary levels, offer enhanced benefits, or improve working conditions to retain skilled workers. One of the best ways to influence functional and dysfunctional turnover is to link pay directly to performance. A study of four sales forces found that when pay was strongly linked to performance via sales commissions and bonuses, poor performers were much more likely to leave (i.e., functional turnover). By contrast, poor performers were much more likely to stay when paid large, guaranteed monthly salaries and small sales commissions and bonuses.[89]

REVIEW 10-7
. . . .

Employee Separations

Employee separation is the loss of an employee; separation can occur voluntarily or involuntarily. Before firing or terminating employees, managers should give employees a chance to improve. If firing becomes necessary, it should be done because of job-related factors, such as violating company rules or consistently performing poorly. Downsizing is supposed to lead to higher productivity and profits, better stock performance, and increased organizational flexibility, but studies show that it doesn't. The best strategy is to downsize only as a last resort. Companies that do downsize should offer outplacement services to help employees find other jobs. Companies generally try to keep the rate of employee turnover low to reduce costs. Functional turnover can be good for organizations, however, because it offers the chance to replace poor performers with better workers. Managers should analyze employee turnover to determine who is resigning and take steps to reduce the loss of good performers.

employee turnover
loss of employees who voluntarily choose to leave the company

functional turnover
loss of poor-performing employees who voluntarily choose to leave a company

dysfunctional turnover
loss of high-performing employees who voluntarily choose to leave a company

Management Decision

To Facebook or Not to Facebook

For the past six months, you've been heading a hiring committee in charge of hiring a new division manager. It's been a grueling process—filtering through thousands of applications, seemingly endless meetings and discussions debating people's qualifications, so many interviews in different cities that it's hard to remember whom you met and where, and even more debates about who should be flown to your headquarters for a day of final interviews.

But it's almost all over now. After so many interviews and meetings and discussions, the committee has settled on a candidate who everyone thinks is ideal for the job—Ivy-league educated, lots of management experience, a great personality, driven to succeed, willing to learn. . . . He was near the top of your list when you began this process six months ago, and here he is now, in first place at the finish line.

You head into the last hiring committee meeting with lots of relief. Not only are you happy that you found the right person for the job, but you're really glad that this meeting is just going to be a formality. No more debates or arguments about applicants' work experiences, education, or hobbies. Just walk on in, take a quick vote, and then make a call with the job offer.

But as you walk into the committee meeting, there's a strange vibe. Some people look quite worried, whereas others are just angry. When you ask what's going on, one of the committee members responds that in the past few days, she added the final candidate as a friend on Facebook, and what she found on his profile was quite disturbing. There were several photos of him passed out on the sidewalk after drinking too much. Other photos showed him smoking marijuana at a friend's apartment. Another photo shows him wearing a Nazi costume for what you assume is a Halloween party. And there's the language—almost all of his posts are filled with obscenities.

After seeing all of this, half the committee wants to go with another candidate. They can't imagine that this is the kind of person they want leading your company's most important division. The other half of the committee thinks it's not a big deal at all. They believe that how he spends his personal time has absolutely no reflection on his ability to manage, and they're angry that committee members would try to use it against him.

So, here you are, faced with a split (and angry) committee. They're looking to you to break the deadlock—should we hire this guy or move on to someone else?

Questions

1. What decision would you make? Would you hire this person or reopen the search?

2. In your opinion, are companies justified in using an applicant's Facebook or Twitter accounts when considering them for a job?

3. Do you believe that a company should be concerned with how a potential employee spends his or her personal time?

Practice Being a Manager

Legal Recruiting

Managing human resources in today's complex business and legal environment is not easy. Not only must companies hire the creative and hard-working employees who will fuel growth and competitive advantage, but they must also be careful to do so legally and ethically. Unfair discrimination in any HR process will result in poor placement, turnover, and legal woes. This exercise will give you some practice in navigating the challenges of legal and effective recruitment and selection of employees.

STEP 1 **Get into groups.** Your professor will assign you to groups of four or five students.

One student will be given the role of HR attorney for the applicants, two students the role of nursing shift (day/night) managers at Montclair Hospital, and the remaining student(s) will be assigned the role of senior hospital administrator at Montclair Hospital.

Scenario: Montclair Hospital needs to hire new nurses. In fact, the hospital is in a bit of a crisis. Three nurses were recently fired for using drugs while on duty. In the ensuing publicity, a journalist uncovered that two of these nurses were convicted felons. As if these problems were not enough, nurse turnover is up 20 percent this year over last, and productivity of the remaining staff is substandard. Absences are also up lately, particularly those related to child care or elder-care issues.

Both the day and the night nursing-shift managers need to hire some quality nurses—and fast. Hospital administrators have made it abundantly clear that they do not want a repeat of the headline "Felons and Drug Users among Montclair Nursing Staff." Your compensation and benefits are competitive, and, with the exception of the recent news coverage, your hospital enjoys a strong reputation. The nursing labor market is tight (there are fewer nurses than openings), and most new hires are recent nursing school graduates.

Nursing-shift managers need to work together to develop a plan to achieve the following:

1. Hire top-flight nurses to fill vacancies left by recent firings and resignations.

2. Stem the turnover of quality nurses already employed by Montclair.

3. Reduce absenteeism, especially unplanned "emergency" absences that wreak havoc with planning the work of an upcoming shift.

STEP 2A **Outline a plan.** The day and the night nursing-shift managers should work together to sketch out a plan for making progress on the three concerns of Montclair Hospital administration (hiring, turnover, absenteeism). Some elements of this plan might include the following:

- Deciding where and how to recruit top nursing candidates

- Screening applicants to reduce risks of turnover, criminal/behavioral problems, and disruptive absenteeism

- Dealing with the turnover, absenteeism, and productivity problems of existing nursing staff

STEP 2B **Review the plan.** Students in the roles of hospital administrator and HR attorney should listen to the nursing managers as they sketch out their plans. Do not offer comments unless one of the managers asks you for your input. Take careful notes regarding what you hear, with particular attention to concerns and questions. Those in the HR attorney role should consider what you hear from the perspective of both potential applicants (and litigants) and Montclair Hospital (defense of HR practices).

Are the nursing managers developing a plan likely to successfully address the three concerns related to hiring, turnover, and absenteeism? Why or why not? Do you hear anything that might raise a legal concern (such as inappropriate interview questions, possible discrimination)?

STEP 3 **Debrief as a class.** Students should open with comments from each perspective: (1) HR attorneys, (2) hospital administrators, and (3) nursing-shift managers. What are some of the specific concerns or questions that arose in your mind as you played your particular role? What are some of the tensions that face the managers and administrators in this situation? How might the HR system of a hospital be improved? Why might nurses represent a particularly challenging set of HR concerns?

360-Degree Feedback

Whereas most performance appraisal ratings have traditionally come from just one person, the boss, 360-degree feedback is obtained from four sources: the boss, subordinates, peers and coworkers, and the employees themselves. In this assignment, you will be gathering 360-degree feedback from people whom you work with or from a team or group that you're a member of for a class.

Here are some guidelines for obtaining your 360-degree feedback:

- *Carefully select respondents.* One of the keys to good 360-degree feedback is getting feedback from the right people. In general, the people you ask for feedback should interact with you on a regular basis and should have the chance to regularly observe your behavior. Also, be sure to get a representative sample of opinions from a similar number of coworkers and subordinates (assuming you have some).

- *Get a large enough number of responses.* In addition to your boss, you should have a minimum of three peers and three subordinates giving you feedback. Five or six respondents in each of those categories are even better.

- *Ensure confidentiality.* Respondents are much more likely to be honest if they know that their comments are confidential and anonymous. So, when you ask respondents for feedback, have them return their comments to someone other than yourself. This person, your "feedback facilitator," will remove the names and any other information that would identify who made particular comments.

- *Explain how the 360-degree feedback will be used.* In this case, explain that the feedback is for a class assignment, that the results will be used for your own personal growth and development, and that the feedback they give you will not affect your grade or formal assessment at work.

- *Ask respondents to make their feedback as specific as possible.* For instance, "bad attitude" isn't very good feedback. "Won't listen to others' suggestions" is much better because it would let you know how to improve your behavior. Have your respondents use the feedback form below to provide your feedback.

Here's what you need to turn in for this assignment:

1. The names and relationships (boss, peers, subordinates, classmates, teammates) of those whom you've asked for feedback

2. The name of the person you've asked to be your feedback facilitator

3. Copies of all written feedback that was returned to you

4. A one-page summary of the written feedback

5. A one-page description of your specific goals and action plans for responding to the feedback you received

 ## Self-Assessment

Interview Anxiety

How would you feel if you got a call to interview for your dream job? Excited? Nervous? Or downright panicked? It's not uncommon to get butterflies in your stomach at the prospect of a job interview, but some candidates have more than weak knees and sweaty palms. Complete the assessment below by indicating the extent to which you agree with each of the following statements.[90] Your score will be a baseline as you begin working on the skills you'll need during your job hunt. Try not to spend too much time on any one item, and be sure to answer all the questions. Use this scale for your responses:

1 Strongly disagree

2 Disagree

3 Neutral

4 Agree

5 Strongly agree

1. I become so apprehensive in job interviews that I am unable to express my thoughts clearly.

    1   2   3   4   5

2. I often feel uneasy about my appearance when I am being interviewed for a job.

    1   2   3   4   5

3. While taking a job interview, I become concerned that the interviewer will perceive me as socially awkward.

    1   2   3   4   5

4. In job interviews, I get very nervous about whether my performance is good enough.

    1   2   3   4   5

5. During job interviews, my hands shake.

    1   2   3   4   5

6. I get so anxious while taking job interviews that I have trouble answering questions that I know.

    1   2   3   4   5

7. Before a job interview, I am so nervous that I spend an excessive amount of time on my appearance.

    1   2   3   4   5

8. I become very uptight about having to socially interact with a job interviewer.

    1   2   3   4   5

9. I am overwhelmed by thoughts of doing poorly when I am in job interview situations.

    1   2   3   4   5

10. My heartbeat is faster than usual during job interviews.

    1   2   3   4   5

11. During job interviews, I often can't think of a thing to say.

    1   2   3   4   5

12. In job interviews, I worry that the interviewer will focus on what I consider to be my least attractive physical features.

    1   2   3   4   5

13. I get afraid about what kind of personal impression I am making on job interviews.

    1   2   3   4   5

14. I worry that my job interview performance will be lower than that of other applicants.

    1   2   3   4   5

15. It is hard for me to avoid fidgeting during a job interview.

    1   2   3   4   5

16. I feel that my verbal communication skills are strong.

    1   2   3   4   5

17. If I do not look my absolute best in a job interview, I find it very hard to be relaxed.

    1   2   3   4   5

18. During a job interview, I worry that my actions will not be considered socially appropriate.

    1   2   3   4   5

19. During a job interview, I am so troubled by thoughts of failing that my performance is reduced.

    1   2   3   4   5

20. Job interviews often make me perspire (e.g., sweaty palms and underarms).

    1   2   3   4   5

21. During job interviews, I find it hard to understand what the interviewer is asking me.

    1   2   3   4   5

22. I feel uneasy if my hair is not perfect when I walk into a job interview.

    1   2   3   4   5

23. I worry about whether job interviewers will like me as a person.

    1   2   3   4   5

24. During a job interview, I worry about what will happen if I don't get the job.

    1   2   3   4   5

25. My mouth gets very dry during job interviews.

    1   2   3   4   5

26. I find it easy to communicate my personal accomplishments during a job interview.

    1   2   3   4   5

27. During a job interview, I worry about whether I have dressed appropriately.

    1   2   3   4   5

28. When meeting a job interviewer, I worry that my handshake will not be correct.

    1   2   3   4   5

29. While taking a job interview, I worry about whether I am a good candidate for the job.

    1   2   3   4   5

30. I often feel sick to my stomach when I am interviewed for a job.

    1   2   3   4   5

SCORING

Reverse your score on items 16 and 26. That is, if you wrote in a "5," change it to a "1" and vice versa; if you wrote in a "4," change it to a "2" and vice versa.

TOTAL = _____

You can find the interpretation of your score at: www.cengagebrain.com.

MANAGEMENT WORKPLACE

Barcelona Restaurant Group: Managing Human Resources

At the Barcelona Restaurant Group, turnover among waitstaff is 60 percent to 70 percent. One way that Barcelona tries to reduce turnover is to select the right people, using a three-stage recruitment process. First, leaders conduct 20-minute interviews with dozens of candidates. Next, applicants are asked to spend $100 at a Barcelona restaurant and write an essay about the event. The third step is "the trail," when job candidates command the floor, interact with waitstaff and customers, and demonstrate job skills. Approximately one-fourth of the candidates who go on a trail can expect to be hired. According to Scott Lawton, people either possess the necessary intelligence and skills to run a restaurant or they don't.

What to Watch For and Ask Yourself

1. List the three main activities of human resource management (HRM), and identify which activity is examined at length in the video.

2. Of the various steps in Barcelona's employee selection process, the job interview is the most brief. Do you agree with the company's approach to interviewing? Why or why not?

3. How well does Barcelona's three-stage process for matching job applicants with its organizational objectives help the restaurant fit job applicants to the needs of the restaurant?

Endnotes

1. B. Burlingham, "Lessons From a Blue-Collar Millionaire," *Inc.*, February 2010, 56–63; N. Sarillo, "How to Tap Your Staff for Brilliant Ideas," Owner, Nick's Pizza & Pub, Crystal Lake, IL, May 24, 2011, accessed May 26, 2011, from www.bnet.com/blog/smb/how-to-tap-your-staff-for-brilliant-ideas/4628?tag=sec-river2; and K. Springen, "Building A Perfect Pizzeria; How a Construction Worker from Chicago Built His $9 million Pizza Business—One Weathered Beam at a Time," *Newsweek*, July 6, 2005, accessed May 26, 2011, from www.newsweek.com/2005/07/05/building-a-perfect-pizzeria.html.

2. S. Bing, "The Feds Make a Pass at Hooters," *Fortune*, January 15, 1996, 82.

3. J. Helyar, "Hooters: A Case Study," *Fortune*, September 1, 2003, 140.

4. A. Samuels, "Pushing Hot Buttons and Wings," *St. Petersburg (FL) Times*, March 10, 2003, 1A.

5. J. Casale, R. Ceniceros, and M. Hofmann, "Hooters Wannabe Resists Girls-Only Policy," *Business Insurance* 43, no. 4 (2009), 23.

6. P. S. Greenlaw and J. P. Kohl, "Employer 'Business' and 'Job' Defenses in Civil Rights Actions," *Public Personnel Management* 23, no. 4 (1994): 573.

7. Associated Press, "Hooters Settles Suit, Won't Hire Waiters," *Denver Post*, October 1, 1997, A11.

8. "Massey Settles Age Discrimination Suit for $8.75 million," Cleveland.com., October 30, 2009, accessed September 5, 2010, from www.cleveland.com/business/index.ssf/2009/10/massey_settles_age_discriminat.html.

9. J. L. Ledvinka, *Federal Regulation of Personnel and Human Resource Management* (Boston: Kent Publishing Co., 1982), 137–198.

10. Greenlaw and Kohl, "Employer 'Business' and 'Job' Defenses in Civil Rights Actions."

11. W. Peirce, C. A. Smolinski, and B. Rosen, "Why Sexual Harassment Complaints Fall on Deaf Ears," *Academy of Management Executive* 12, no. 3 (1998): 41–54.

12. "Facts about Sexual Harassment," U.S. Equal Employment Opportunity Commission, accessed March 23, 2009, www.eeoc.gov/facts/fs-sex.html.

13. Peirce, Smolinski, and Rosen, "Why Sexual Harassment Complaints Fall on Deaf Ears."

14. Ibid.

15. C. Koons, "Australia's Recovering Mining Industry Struggles to Fill Jobs," *Wall Street Journal*, September 21, 2009, A15.

16. G. Hyland-Savage, "General Management Perspective on Staffing: The Staffing Commandments," in *On Staffing*, N. C. Bukholder, P. J. Edwards Jr., and L. Sartain, eds. (Hoboken, NJ: Wiley, 2004), 280.

17. R. D. Gatewood and H. S. Field, *Human Resource Selection* (Fort Worth, TX: Dryden Press, 1998).

18. Ibid.

19. *Griggs v. Duke Power Co.*, 401 U.S. 424, 436 (1971); *Albemarle Paper Co. v. Moody*, 422 U.S. 405 (1975).

20. J. A. Breaugh, *Recruitment: Science and Practice* (Boston: PWSKent, 1992).

21. J. Breaugh and M. Starke, "Research on Employee Recruitment: So Many Studies, So Many Remaining Questions," *Journal of Management* 26 (2000): 405–434.

22. K. Maher, "Corporations Cut Middlemen and Do Their Own Recruiting," *Wall Street Journal*, January 14, 2003, B10.

23. "Research Demonstrates the Success of Internet Recruiting," *HR Focus*, April 2003, 7.

24. S. Fegley, "2007 Advances in E-Recruiting: Leveraging the .jobs Domain," a survey report published by the Society for Human Resource Management, 2007.

25. S. E. Needleman, "Lifting the Curtain on the Hiring Process," *Wall Street Journal*, January 26, 2010, accessed March 4, 2011, from http://online.wsj.com/article/SB10001424052748703808904575025250789355156.html.

26. C. Camden and B. Wallace, "Job Application Forms: A Hazardous Employment Practice," *Personnel Administrator* 28 (1983): 31–32.

27. J. Kennedy, "Europeans Expect Different Type of Résumé," *Chicago Sun-Times*, June 3, 1999, 73.

28. T. Minton-Eversole, "Background Screens Even More Crucial during Economic Slump," Society of Human Resource Management, 30 July 2008, accessed March 4, 2011, from www.**shrm**.org/ema/library_published/nonIC/CMS_026257.asp.

29. S. Adler, "Verifying a Job Candidate's Background: The State of Practice in a Vital Human Resources Activity," *Review of Business* 15, no. 2 (1993/1994): 3–8.

30. W. Woska, "Legal Issues for HR Professionals: Reference Checking/Background Investigations," *Public Personnel Management* 36 (Spring 2007): 79–89.

31. "More Than 70 Percent of HR Professionals Say Reference Checking Is Effective in Identifying Poor Performers," Society for Human Resource Management, accessed February 3, 2005, www.shrm.org/press_published/CMS_011240.asp.

32. J. Hunter, "Cognitive Ability, Cognitive Aptitudes, Job Knowledge, and Job Performance," *Journal of Vocational Behavior* 29 (1986): 340–362.

33. F. L. Schmidt, "The Role of General Cognitive Ability and Job Performance: Why There Cannot Be a Debate," *Human Performance* 15 (2002): 187–210.

34. K. Murphy, "Can Conflicting Perspectives on the Role of *g* in Personnel Selection Be Resolved?" *Human Performance* 15 (2002): 173–186.

35. E. E. Cureton, "Comment," in *Research Conference on the Use of Autobiographical Data as Psychological Predictors*, E. R. Henry, ed. (Greensboro, NC: The Richardson Foundation, 1965), 13.

36 J. R. Glennon, L. E. Albright, and W. A. Owens, *A Catalog of Life History Items* (Greensboro, NC: The Richardson Foundation, 1966).

37 Gatewood and Field, *Human Resource Selection.*

38 N. Schmitt, "Beyond the Big Five: Increases in Understanding and Practical Utility," *Human Performance* 17 (2004): 347–357.

39 M. S. Taylor and J. A. Sniezek, "The College Recruitment Interview: Topical Content and Applicant Reactions," *Journal of Occupational Psychology* 57 (1984): 157–168.

40 M. Harris, "Reconsidering the Employment Interview: A Review of Recent Literature and Suggestions for Future Research," *Personnel Psychology* (Winter 1989): 691–726.

41 Taylor and Sniezek, "The College Recruitment Interview."

42 R. Burnett, C. Fan, S. J. Motowidlo, and T. DeGroot, "Interview Notes and Validity," *Personnel Psychology* 51, (1998): 375–396; and M. A. Campion, D. K. Palmer, and J. E. Campion, "A Review of Structure in the Selection Interview," *Personnel Psychology* 50, no. 3 (1997): 655–702.

43 J. Cortina, N. Goldstein, S. Payne, K. Davison, and S. Gilliland, "The Incremental Validity of Interview Scores Over and Above Cognitive Ability and Conscientiousness Scores," *Personnel Psychology* 53, no. 2 (2000): 325–351; and F. L. Schmidt and J. E. Hunter, "The Validity and Utility of Selection Methods in Personnel Psychology: Practical and Theoretical Implications of 85 years of Research Findings," *Psychological Bulletin* 124, no. 2 (1998): 262–274.

44 T. Judge, "The Employment Interview: A Review of Recent Research and Recommendations for Future Research," *Human Resource Management Review* 10, no. 4 (2000): 383–406.

45 Cortina, Goldstein, Payne, Davison, and Gilliland, "The Incremental Validity of Interview Scores."

46 K. Tyler, "Training Revs Up," *HR Magazine* (April 2005), Society for Human Resource Management, accessed March 23, 2009, from www.shrm.org/Publications/hrmagazine/EditorialContent/Pages/0405tyler.aspx.

47 Ibid.

48 S. Livingston, T. W. Gerdel, M. Hill, B. Yerak, C. Melvin, and B. Lubinger, "Ohio's Strongest Companies All Agree That Training Is Vital to Their Success," *Cleveland Plain Dealer*, May 21, 1997, 30S.

49 The Oil Spill Training Company, accessed August 14, 2008, from http://oilspilltraining.com/home/index.asp.

50 J. Levitz, "UPS Thinks Out of the Box on Driver Training," *Wall Street Journal*, April 6, 2010, accessed June 10, 2010, from http://online.wsj.com/article/SB10001424052702303912104575164573823418844.html.

51 D. L. Kirkpatrick, "Four Steps to Measuring Training Effectiveness," *Personnel Administrator* 28 (1983): 19–25.

52 L. Bassi, J. Ludwig, D. McMurrer, and M. Van Buren, "Profiting from Learning: Do Firms' Investments in Education and Training Pay Off?" American Society for Training and Development, accessed August 14, 2008, from www.astd.org/NR/rdonlyres/91956A5E-6E57-44DDAE5D-FCFFCDC11C3F/0/ASTD_Profiting_From_Learning.pdf.

53 G. Kesler, "Why the Leadership Bench Never Gets Deeper: Ten Insights about Executive Talent Development," *Human Resource Planning*, January 1, 2002, 32.

54 C. Bartz, "Corner Office: Imagining a World of No Annual Reviews," interview by A. Bryant, *New York Times*, October 17, 2009, accessed July 30, 2010, from www.nytimes.com/2009/10/18/business/18corner.html?_r=1.

55 D. Murphy, "Are Performance Appraisals Worse Than a Waste of Time? Book Derides Unintended Consequences," *San Francisco Chronicle*, September 8, 2001, W1.

56 K. R. Murphy and J. N. Cleveland, *Understanding Performance Appraisal: Social, Organizational and Goal-Based Perspectives* (Thousand Oaks, CA: Sage, 1995).

57 U. J. Wiersma and G. P. Latham, "The Practicality of Behavioral Observation Scales, Behavioral Expectation Scales, and Trait Scales," *Personnel Psychology* 39 (1986): 619–628; and U. J. Wiersma, P. T. Van Den Berg, and G. P. Latham, "Dutch Reactions to Behavioral Observation, Behavioral Expectation, and Trait Scales," *Group & Organization Management* 20 (1995): 297–309.

58 D. J. Schleicher, D. V. Day, B. T. Mayes, and R. E. Riggio, "A New Frame for Frame-of-Reference Training: Enhancing the Construct Validity of Assessment Centers," *Journal of Applied Psychology* (August 2002): 735–746.

59 C. Hymowitz, "Do '360' Job Reviews by Colleagues Promote Honesty or Insults?" *Wall Street Journal*, December 12, 2000, B1.

60 D. A. Waldman, L. E. Atwater, and D. Antonioni, "Has 360 Feedback Gone Amok?" *Academy of Management Executive* 12, no. 2 (1998): 86–94.

61 H. H. Meyer, "A Solution to the Performance Appraisal Feedback Enigma," *Academy of Management Executive* 5, no. 1 (1991): 68–76; G. C. Thornton, "Psychometric Properties of Self-Appraisals of Job Performance," *Personnel Psychology* 33 (1980): 263–271.

62 G. C. Thornton, "Psychometric Properties of Self-Appraisals of Job Performance," *Personnel Psychology* 33 (1980): 263–271.

63 J. Smither, M. London, R. Flautt, Y. Vargas, and I. Kucine, "Can Working with an Executive Coach Improve Multisource Feedback Ratings over Time? A Quasi-Experimental Field Study," *Personnel Psychology* (Spring 2003): 21–43.

64 C. Tuna, "In Some Offices, Keeping Workers Earns a Bonus; More Firms Like Penske Tie Top Managers' Pay to Employee Retention," *Wall Street Journal*, June 30, 2008, B6.

65 Ibid.

66 G. T. Milkovich and J. M. Newman, *Compensation*, 4th ed. (Homewood, IL: Irwin, 1993).

67 M. L. Williams and G. F. Dreher, "Compensation System Attributes and Applicant Pool Characteristics," *Academy of Management Journal* 35, no. 3 (1992): 571–595.

68 N. Bunkley, "Ford Profit Comes as Toyota Hits a Bump," *Wall Street Journal*, January 28, 2010, accessed June 15, 2010, from www.nytimes.com/2010/01/29/business/29ford.html?scp=3&sq=profit-sharing&st=cse.

69 M. Bloom, "The Performance Effects of Pay Dispersion on Individuals and Organizations," *Academy of Management Journal* 42, no. 1 (1999): 25–40.

70 "Trends in CEO Pay," AFL-CIO, accessed August 11, 2011, from www.aflcio.org/corporatewatch/paywatch/pay/index.cfm; and "Employer Costs for Employee Compensation," *Economic News Release*, Bureau of Labor Statistics, June 9, 2010, accessed August 11, 2010, from www.bls.gov/news.release/ecec.nr0.htm.

71 W. Grossman and R. E. Hoskisson, "CEO Pay at the Crossroads of Wall Street and Main: Toward the Strategic Design of Executive Compensation," *Academy of Management Executive* 12, no. 1 (1998): 43–57.

72 Bloom, "The Performance Effects of Pay Dispersion."

73 J. S. Rosenbloom, "The Environment of Employee Benefit Plans," in *The Handbook of Employee Benefits*, J. S. Rosenbloom, ed. (Chicago: Irwin, 1996), 3–13.

74 "Employer Costs for Employee Compensation Summary," Bureau of Labor Statistics, accessed March 11, 2011, from www.bls.gov/news.release/ecec.nr0.htm.

75 A. E. Barber, R. B. Dunham, and R. A. Formisano, "The Impact of Flexible Benefits on Employee Satisfaction: A Field Study," *Personnel Psychology* 45 (1992): 55–75; B. Heshizer, "The Impact of Flexible Benefits on Job Satisfaction and Turnover Intentions," *Benefits Quarterly* 4 (1994): 84–90; and D. M. Cable and T. A. Judge, "Pay Preferences and Job Search Decisions: A Person-Organization Fit Perspective," *Personnel Psychology* 47 (1994): 317–348.

76 B. T. Beam and J. J. McFadden, *Employee Benefits* (Chicago: Dearborn Financial Publishing, 1996).

77 P. Michal-Johnson, *Saying Good-Bye: A Manager's Guide to Employee Dismissal* (Glenview, IL: Scott, Foresman and Co., 1985).

78 M. Bordwin, "Employment Law: Beware of Time Bombs and Shark-Infested Waters," *HR Focus*, April 1, 1995, 19; and D. Jones, "Fired Workers Fight Back . . . and Win; Laws, Juries Shift Protection to Terminated Employees," *USA Today*, April 2, 1998, B1.

79 T. Bland, "Fire at Will, Repent at Leisure," *Security Management* 44 (May 2000): 64.

80 "Mass Layoffs in December 2007 and Annual Totals for 2007," Bureau of Labor Statistics News, January 24, 2008, accessed August 15, 2008, from www.bls.gov/news.release/archives/mmls_01242008.pdf.

81 J. R. Morris, W. F. Cascio, and C. E. Young, "Downsizing after All These Years: Questions and Answers about Who Did It, How Many Did It, and Who Benefited from It," *Organizational Dynamics* 27, no. 3 (1999): 78–87.

82 K. Maher, "Hiring Freezes Cushion New Layoffs," *Wall Street Journal,* January 24, 2008, A13.

83 K. E. Mishra, G. M. Spreitzer, and A. K. Mishra, "Preserving Employee Morale during Downsizing," *Sloan Management Review* 39, no. 2 (1998): 83–95.

84 K. Frieswick, "Until We Meet Again?" *CFO*, October 1, 2001, 41.

85 J. Hilsenrath, "Adventures in Cost Cutting," *Wall Street Journal*, May 10, 2004, R1.

86 M. Jackson, "Downsized, but Still in the Game: Keeping Up Morale Crucial after Job Cuts," *Boston Globe*, January 11, 2009, G1.

87 D. R. Dalton, W. D. Todor, and D. M. Krackhardt, "Turnover Overstated: The Functional Taxonomy," *Academy of Management Review* 7 (1982): 117–123.

88 J. R. Hollenbeck and C. R. Williams, "Turnover Functionality versus Turnover Frequency: A Note on Work Attitudes and Organizational Effectiveness," *Journal of Applied Psychology* 71 (1986): 606–611.

89 C. R. Williams, "Reward Contingency, Unemployment, and Functional Turnover," *Human Resource Management Review* 9 (1999): 549–576.

90 J. McCarthy and R. Goffin, "Measuring Job Interview Anxiety: Beyond Weak Knees and Sweaty Palms," *Personnel Psychology* 54, no. 3 (2004): 31.

Leading

Chapter Eleven

Motivation

DAVE & LES JACOBS/BLEND IMAGES/JUPITER IMAGES

Chapter 11 covers the basics of motivation—effort, needs, and intrinsic and extrinsic rewards. As we progress through the chapter, we build on that basic model of motivation by adding concepts of equity, expectancy, reinforcement, and goal-setting theories. There's also a summary of practical, theory-based actions that managers can take to motivate their workers.

Chapter Twelve

Leadership

© LUAY BAHOORA/ALAMY

Chapter 12 discusses what leadership is, what characteristics are common of leaders, and what leaders do that makes them different from people who aren't leaders. We examine major contingency theories of leadership and review strategic leadership issues, such as charismatic and transformational leadership.

Chapter Thirteen

Communication

© FELIPE TRUEBA/ZUMA PRESS/NEWSCOM

Chapter 13 examines perception in communication, the communication process, and the kinds of organizational communication. You'll also learn about effective one-on-one communication as well as techniques for organization-wide communication.

© DIZZO/ISTOCK PHOTO

Motivation

REEL TO REAL

© TETRA IMAGES/ CORBIS

Management Workplace is at LivingSocial Escapes.

SELF-ASSESSMENT

© ISTOCKPHOTO/ ALEXANDER KALINA

What do you need and want from a job? Do the Self-Assessment for this chapter in the book or online to find out what motivates you.

ONLINE QUIZZES

© ISTOCKPHOTO/ PEARLEYE

Did you get it? Review the main concepts in the chapter by taking the online quizzes on CourseMate!

VIDEO QUIZZES

© ISTOCKPHOTO/DAVID HUGHES

Get more out of the videos by taking the multimedia video quizzes online.

What Would You Do?

SAS World Headquarters, Cary, North Carolina[1]

SAS (pronounced "sass"), which is short for Statistical Analysis System, began when it set out to create statistical software to help agricultural researchers who were studying the effects of soil, seeds, and the weather on crop yields. In 1970, researchers had to write new computer programs every time they analyzed data. SAS standardized that process and made it faster. Because the statistics faculty who wrote SAS needed to generate funds to cover the expiring grant money that paid their salaries, they started leasing SAS to universities and pharmaceutical companies. By 1976, they had 100 customers. However, it wasn't until the first SAS Users Conference later that year, when 300 people showed up, that they realized their business opportunity. As they tell people now, that was pretty much the "aha moment."

From website traffic to credit cards replacing cash, to genome sequencing, to sentiment analysis (analyzing every tweet, blog, and discussion group comment about your company and its products), the amount of digital data that a company has to go through is increasing at exponential rates. As a result, 79 percent of *Fortune* 500 companies use SAS. Shell Oil uses it to analyze data to predict how long the pumps will run on its North Sea oil-drilling platforms. Kohl's department store maximizes profits by using SAS to analyze which products to mark down for sale. Credit card companies use SAS to reduce fraud by identifying unusual credit card purchases in real time. Finally, telecom companies offer great deals to customers who, via SAS, they've determined are more likely to switch to competitors.

Although SAS has been profitable every year since inception, there are threats to its highly successful business model. First, says Gareth Doherty, an industry analyst, "Most organizations aren't in a position to be able to leverage some of the sophisticated applications that SAS offers because the No. 1 constraint when you're working with a tool this sophisticated is the user.

If you don't have a rocket scientist sitting behind the desk, it doesn't matter what you have running on the desktop." Second, SAS products are expensive, starting at $1 million for industry-specific products (i.e., banking or retail), followed by subscription renewals that are 20 percent to 30 percent of the purchase price. Although SAS spends 22 percent of its revenue on research and development each year, larger firms are buying business intelligence companies to compete directly with SAS. SAP paid $6.8 billion for Business Objects, and Oracle paid $3.3 billion for Hyperion. The largest threat may come, however, from IBM, which paid $4.9 billion for Cognos and $1.2 billion for SPSS. IBM combined those firms into its business analytics group, which will employ 200 scientists and 4,000 consultants and analysts. Industry analyst Bill Hostmann says, "It will be a dogfight. SAS has never faced a competitor like IBM. And I do think IBM sees SAS as a big, fatted cow."

With competition intensifying, SAS is shortening its product development cycle from 24 to 36 months to 12 to 18 months. Change like that can't be achieved without attracting and retaining a highly motivated workforce. That's increasingly difficult with tech job openings up 62 percent and a 22 percent average turnover rate in the software industry. That's why Google gave all of its employees a 10 percent raise and a $1,000 bonus. So, the first step in maintaining your competitiveness is figuring out what motivates people to join SAS. Second, getting people to join SAS is one thing, but how do you get them to work hard and maximize their efforts? Should you be egalitarian and pay everyone the same, or should you closely link pay and performance? Finally, how do you get your most talented managers and software engineers to stay? Does SAS need to "go public" like its competitors and issue stock and stock options to its employees? Or are there other ways for SAS to reward people and remain competitive in the talent market?

If you were in charge at SAS, what would you do?

11-1 Basics of Motivation

What makes people happiest and most productive at work? Is it money, benefits, opportunities for growth, interesting work, or something else altogether? And if people desire different things, how can a company keep everyone motivated?

This chapter begins by reviewing the basics of motivation—effort, needs, and intrinsic and extrinsic rewards. We will start with a basic model of motivation and add to it as we progress through each section in the chapter. Next, we will explore how employees' equity perceptions and reward expectations affect their motivation. If you're familiar with the phrase "perception is reality," you're off to a good start in understanding the importance of perceptions and expectations in motivation. The third part of the chapter reviews the role that rewards and goals play in motivating employees. You'll see that finding the right combination of goals and rewards is much harder in practice than it looks. The chapter finishes with a summary of practical, theory-based actions that managers can take to motivate their workers.

After reading this section, you should be able to:

11-1 explain the basics of motivation.

Motivation is the set of forces that initiates, directs, and makes people persist in their efforts to accomplish a goal.[2] *Initiation of effort* is concerned with the choices that people make about how much effort to put forth in their jobs. ("Do I really knock myself out for these performance appraisals or just do a decent job?") *Direction of effort* is concerned with the choices that people make in deciding where to put forth effort in their jobs. ("I should be spending time with my high-dollar accounts instead of learning this new computer system!") *Persistence of effort* is concerned with the choices that people make about how long they will put forth effort in their jobs before reducing or eliminating those efforts. ("I'm only halfway through the project, and I'm exhausted. Do I plow through to the end, or just call it quits?") As Exhibit 11.1 shows, initiation, direction, and persistence are at the heart of motivation.

Jenny Miller manages 170 engineers who design and build computer systems for aircraft carrier flight decks. Despite long hours each week, they were at risk of not meeting a December 1 deadline for their project. So, with the overtime

motivation
the set of forces that initiates, directs, and makes people persist in their efforts to accomplish a goal

budget already spent, she asked for volunteers to work Friday, Saturday, or Sunday of Thanksgiving weekend, without pay or compensatory time off. Still, 20 engineers showed up, the deadline was met, and Miller thanked those who volunteered with $100 gift cards.[3]

It takes insight and hard work to motivate workers to join the company, perform well, and then stay with the company. Would you be motivated to volunteer to work over a holiday weekend if it helped your company meet a key deadline? Which would motivate you more? The chance to become a master craftsperson or the opportunity for promotion and management responsibilities? Answering questions like these is at the heart of figuring out how best to motivate people at work.

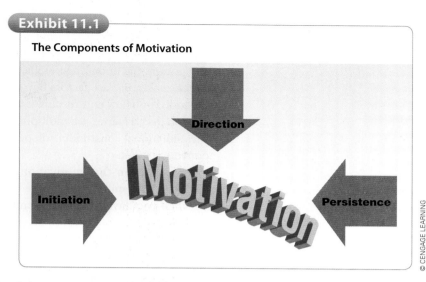

Exhibit 11.1

The Components of Motivation

© CENGAGE LEARNING

Let's learn more about motivation by building a basic model of motivation out of **11-1a effort and performance, 11-1b need satisfaction**, and **11-1c extrinsic and intrinsic rewards** and then discussing **11-1d how to motivate people with this basic model of motivation.**

11-1a Effort and Performance

When most people think of work motivation, they think that working hard (effort) should lead to a good job (performance). Exhibit 11.2 shows a basic model of work motivation and performance, displaying this process. The first thing to notice about Exhibit 11.2 is that this is a basic model of work motivation *and* performance. In practice, it's almost impossible to talk about one without mentioning the other. Not surprisingly, managers often assume motivation to be the only determinant of performance, saying things such as "Your performance was really terrible last quarter. What's the matter? Aren't you as motivated as you used to be?" In fact, motivation is just one of three primary determinants of job performance. In industrial psychology, job performance is frequently represented by this equation:

$$\text{Job Performance} = \text{Motivation} \times \text{Ability} \times \text{Situational Constraints}$$

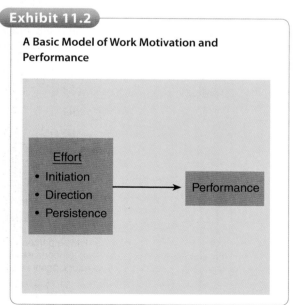

Exhibit 11.2

A Basic Model of Work Motivation and Performance

© CENGAGE LEARNING

In this formula, *job performance* is how well someone performs the requirements of the job. *Motivation*, as defined previously, is effort, the degree to which someone works hard to do the job well. *Ability* is the degree to which workers possess the knowledge, skills, and talent needed to do a job well. And *situational constraints* are factors beyond the control of individual employees, such as tools, policies, and resources that have an effect on job performance. Because job performance is a multiplicative function of motivation times ability times situational constraints, job performance will suffer if any one of these components is weak.

Does this mean that motivation doesn't matter? No, not at all. It just means that all the motivation in the world won't translate into high performance when you have little ability and high situational constraints.

11-1b Need Satisfaction

In Exhibit 11.2, we started with a very basic model of motivation in which effort leads to job performance. But managers want to know, "What leads to effort?" and they will try almost anything they can to find the answer. Employees at S.C. Johnson, a manufacturer of cleaning products, can use a concierge service to mail packages, send flowers, pick up groceries, and even take their car in for an oil change. Amgen, a biotech company, gives its employees three weeks of paid vacation per year, as well as 17 paid holidays, nearly double other businesses. As you can see, employers will do almost anything to motivate employees to put extra effort into their jobs.

Needs are the physical or psychological requirements that must be met to ensure survival and well-being.[4] As shown on the left side of Exhibit 11.3, a person's unmet need creates an uncomfortable, internal state of tension that must be resolved. For example, if you normally skip breakfast but then have to work through lunch, chances are you'll be so hungry by late afternoon that the only thing you'll be motivated to do is find something to eat. So, according to needs theories, people are motivated by unmet needs. But a need no longer motivates once it is met. When this occurs, people become satisfied, as shown on the right side of Exhibit 11.3.

needs
the physical or psychological requirements that must be met to ensure survival and well-being

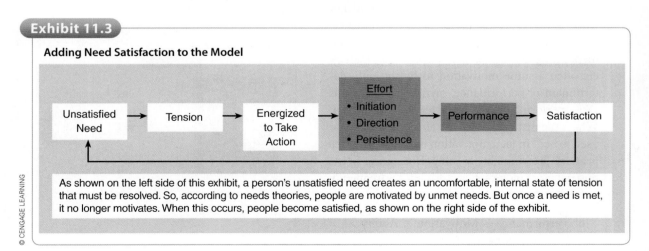

Exhibit 11.3

Adding Need Satisfaction to the Model

As shown on the left side of this exhibit, a person's unsatisfied need creates an uncomfortable, internal state of tension that must be resolved. So, according to needs theories, people are motivated by unmet needs. But once a need is met, it no longer motivates. When this occurs, people become satisfied, as shown on the right side of the exhibit.

© CENGAGE LEARNING

Note: Throughout the chapter, as we build on this basic model, the parts of the model that we've already discussed will appear shaded in color. For example, because we've already discussed the effort → performance part of the model, those components are shown with a colored background. When we add new parts to the model, they will have a white background. Because we're adding need satisfaction to the model at this step, the need–satisfaction components of unsatisfied need, tension, energized to take action, and satisfaction are shown with a white background. This shading convention should make it easier to understand the work motivation model as we add to it in each section of the chapter.

Because people are motivated by unmet needs, managers must learn what those unmet needs are and address them. This is not always a straightforward task, however, because different needs theories suggest different categories of needs. Exhibit 11.4 shows needs from three well-known needs theories. Maslow's Hierarchy of Needs suggests that people are motivated by *physiological* (food and water), *safety* (physical and economic), *belongingness* (friendship, love, and social interaction), *esteem* (achievement and recognition), and *self-actualization* (realizing your full potential) needs.[5] Alderfer's ERG Theory collapses Maslow's five needs into three: *existence* (safety and physiological needs), *relatedness* (belongingness), and *growth* (esteem and self-actualization).[6] McClelland's Learned Needs Theory suggests that people are motivated by the need for *affiliation* (to be liked and accepted), the need for *achievement* (to accomplish challenging goals), or the need for *power* (to influence others).[7]

Things become even more complicated when we consider the different predictions made by these theories. According to Maslow, needs are arranged in a hierarchy from low (physiological) to high (self-actualization). Within this hierarchy, people are motivated by their lowest unsatisfied need. As each need is met, they work their way up the hierarchy from physiological to self-actualization needs. By contrast, Alderfer says that people can be motivated by more than one need at a time. Furthermore, he suggests that people are just as likely to move down the needs hierarchy as up, particularly when they are unable to achieve satisfaction at the next higher need level. McClelland argues that the degree to which particular needs motivate varies tremendously from person to person. Some people are motivated primarily by achievement and others by power or affiliation. Moreover, McClelland says that needs are learned, not innate. For instance, studies show that children whose parents own a small business or hold a managerial position are much more likely to have a high need for achievement.[8]

Exhibit 11.4

Needs Classification of Different Theories

	Maslow's Hierarchy	Alderfer's Erg	McClelland's Learned Needs
Higher-Order Needs	Self-Actualization Esteem Belongingness	Growth Relatedness	Power Achievement Affiliation
Lower-Order Needs	Safety Physiological	Existence	

© CENGAGE LEARNING

So, with three different sets of needs and three very different ideas about how needs motivate, how do we provide a practical answer to managers who just want to know: What leads to effort? Fortunately, the research evidence simplifies things a bit. To start, studies indicate that there are two basic kinds of needs categories.[9] As shown in Exhibit 11.4, *lower-order needs* are concerned with safety and with physiological and existence requirements, whereas *higher-order needs* are concerned with relationships (belongingness, relatedness, and affiliation); challenges and accomplishments (esteem, self-actualization, growth, and achievement); and influence (power). Studies generally show that higher-order needs will not motivate people as long as lower-order needs remain unsatisfied.[10]

So, what leads to effort? In part, needs do. After we discuss rewards in the next section, we'll discuss how managers can use what we know from need–satisfaction theories to motivate workers.

11-1c Extrinsic and Intrinsic Rewards

No discussion of motivation would be complete without considering rewards. Let's add two kinds of rewards, extrinsic and intrinsic, to the model in Exhibit 11.5.[11]

Extrinsic rewards are tangible and visible to others and are given to employees contingent on the performance of specific tasks or behaviors.[12] External agents (e.g., managers) determine and control the distribution, frequency, and amount of extrinsic rewards, such as pay, company stock, benefits, and promotions. Why do companies need extrinsic rewards? To get people to do things they wouldn't otherwise do. Companies use extrinsic rewards to motivate people to perform four basic behaviors: join the organization, regularly attend their jobs, perform their jobs well, and stay with the organization.[13] Would you show up at work every day to do the best possible job that you could just out of

extrinsic reward
a reward that is tangible, visible to others, and given to employees contingent on the performance of specific tasks or behaviors

Exhibit 11.5

Adding Rewards to the Model

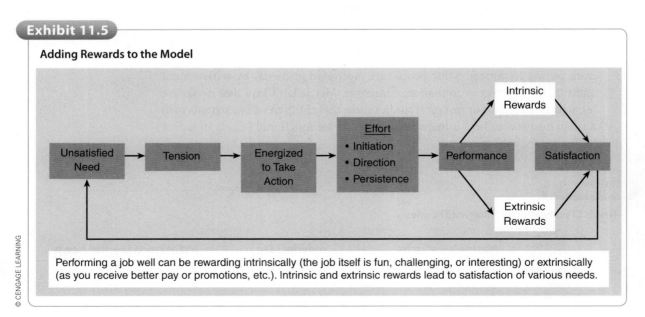

Performing a job well can be rewarding intrinsically (the job itself is fun, challenging, or interesting) or extrinsically (as you receive better pay or promotions, etc.). Intrinsic and extrinsic rewards lead to satisfaction of various needs.

© CENGAGE LEARNING

the goodness of your heart? Very few people would. This is why companies use rewards like cash bonuses or paid vacations.

Intrinsic rewards are the natural rewards associated with performing a task or activity for its own sake. For example, aside from the external rewards management offers for doing something well, employees often find the activities or tasks they perform interesting and enjoyable. Examples of intrinsic rewards include a sense of accomplishment or achievement, a feeling of responsibility, the chance to learn something new or interact with others, or simply the fun that comes from performing an interesting, challenging, and engaging task.

Which types of rewards are most important to workers in general? A number of surveys suggest that both extrinsic and intrinsic rewards are important. One survey found that the most important rewards were good benefits and health insurance, job security, a week or more of vacation (all extrinsic rewards), interesting work, the opportunity to learn new skills, and independent work situations (all intrinsic rewards). And employee preferences for intrinsic and extrinsic rewards appear to be relatively stable. Studies conducted over the last three decades have consistently found that employees are twice as likely to indicate that important and meaningful work matters more to them than what they are paid.[14] Indeed, when asked, "If you were to get enough money to live as comfortably as you would like for the rest of your life, would you continue to work or would you stop working?" Sixty-nine percent of American workers said they would keep working. Clearly, intrinsic rewards matter.[15]

11-1d Motivating with the Basics

So, given the basic model of work motivation in Exhibit 11.5, what practical steps can managers take to motivate employees to increase their effort?

Start by asking people what their needs are. By asking employees what they needed, Aflac has been able to keep its employee turnover rate close to zero. As Dan Amos, the CEO of Aflac says, if you listen, "The survey never lies."[16] So, if you want to meet employees' needs, just ask.

Next, *satisfy lower-order needs first.* Because higher-order needs will not motivate people as long as lower-order needs remain unsatisfied, companies should satisfy lower-order needs first. In practice, this means providing the equipment, training, and knowledge to create a safe workplace free of physical risks, paying employees well enough to provide financial security, and offering a benefits package that will protect employees and their families through good medical coverage and health and disability insurance. Indeed, a survey based on a representative sample of Americans found that when people choose jobs or organizations, three of the four most important factors—starting pay/salary (62%), employee benefits (57%), and job security (47%)—are lower-order needs.[17] Consistent with the idea of satisfying lower-order needs first, a survey of 12,000 employees found that inadequate compensation is the No. 1 reason employees leave organizations.[18]

Third, managers should *expect people's needs to change.* As some needs are satisfied or situations change, what motivated people before may not motivate

intrinsic reward
a natural reward associated with performing a task or activity for its own sake

them now. Likewise, what motivates people to accept a job may not necessarily motivate them once they have the job.

Managers should also expect needs to change as people mature.[19] For older employees, benefits are as important as pay, which is always ranked as more important by younger employees. Older employees also rank job security as more important than personal and family time, which is more important to younger employees.[20]

Finally, *as needs change and lower-order needs are satisfied, create opportunities for employees to satisfy higher-order needs.* Recall that intrinsic rewards such as accomplishment, achievement, learning something new, and interacting with others are the natural rewards associated with performing a task or activity for its own sake. And with the exception of influence (power), intrinsic rewards correspond very closely to higher-order needs that are concerned with relationships (belongingness, relatedness, and affiliation) and challenges and accomplishments (esteem, self-actualization, growth, and achievement). Therefore, one way for managers to meet employees' higher-order needs is to create opportunities for employees to experience intrinsic rewards by providing challenging work, encouraging employees to take greater responsibility for their work, and giving employees the freedom to pursue tasks and projects they find naturally interesting.

REVIEW 11-1

. . . .

Basics of Motivation

Motivation is the set of forces that initiates, directs, and makes people persist in their efforts, over time, to accomplish a goal. Managers often assume motivation to be the only determinant of performance, but job performance is a multiplicative function of motivation times ability times situational constraints. If any one of these components is weak, job performance will suffer. Needs are the physical or psychological requirements that must be met to ensure survival and well-being. When needs are not met, people experience an internal state of tension. But once a particular need is met, it no longer motivates. When this occurs, people become satisfied and are then motivated by other unmet needs.

Different motivational theories, such as Maslow's Hierarchy of Needs (physiological, safety, belongingness, esteem, and self-actualization), Alderfer's ERG Theory (existence, relatedness, and growth), and McClelland's Learned Needs Theory (affiliation, achievement, and power), specify a number of different needs. However, studies show that there are only two general kinds of needs, lower-order needs and higher-order needs, and that higher-order needs will not motivate people as long as lower-order needs remain unsatisfied.

Both extrinsic and intrinsic rewards motivate people. Extrinsic rewards, which include pay, company stock, benefits, and promotions, are used to motivate people to join organizations and attend and perform their jobs. The basic model of motivation suggests that managers can motivate employees by asking them what their needs are, satisfying lower-order needs first, expecting people's needs to change, and satisfying higher-order needs through intrinsic rewards.

11-2 Equity Theory

Perception affects motivation. For example, when employees perceive that they will be unable to perform at a level necessary to obtain rewards, whether extrinsic or intrinsic, they are likely to be *demotivated*.

After reading this section, you should be able to:

11-2 use equity theory to explain how employees' perceptions of fairness affect motivation.

Reward systems at many organizations are geared toward top performers and ignore the mid-level performers. Most banks, for instance, reward the top 10 percent of the sales force; other sales representatives, who don't believe they can generate enough sales to end up in the top category, simply give up. Stephen O'Malley, an independent consultant, says that one way to avoid this scenario is to create an open-ended incentive program that keeps the top-performer programs intact while offering awards for mid-level performers who surpass their annual sales goals by 10 percent. When a large U.S.-based financial services institution implemented such a system, it influenced the perceptions and expectations of its entire sales force—especially its mid-level performers. Because of this change in perception, the company achieved a 47 percent overall increase in sales growth, three times the industry average.[21]

Many would agree that rewarding mid-level performers is only fair. In business, as in life, a person's sense of fairness is a significant factor in his perception, and thus his motivation. In Switzerland, speeding fines are based on the driver's income. A Swiss millionaire driving a red Ferrari Testarossa was caught going 85 mph through a small village, well over the limit, and was fined $290,000 because the court estimated his wealth at $22.7 million.[22]

Is this method of determining speeding fines fair or unfair? Most Americans would argue that their approach is unfair, that fairness requires that fines be proportional to the offense and that everyone who breaks the law to the same degree should pay the same fine. By contrast, most Finns, Swedes, and Swiss believe that fines proportional to income are fair.[23]

Fairness, or what people perceive to be fair, is a critical issue in organizations. **Equity theory** says that people will be motivated at work when they *perceive* that they are being treated fairly. In particular, equity theory stresses the importance of perceptions. So, regardless of the actual level of rewards people receive, they must also perceive that, relative to others, they are being treated fairly. As explained below, equity theory doesn't focus on objective equity (i.e., that CEOs make 344 times more than blue-collar workers). Instead, equity theory says that equity, like beauty, is in the eye of the beholder.

Let's learn more about equity theory by examining **11-2a the components of equity theory, 11-2b how people react to perceived inequities,** and **11-2c how to motivate people using equity theory.**

11-2a Components of Equity Theory

The basic components of equity theory are inputs, outcomes, and referents. **Inputs** are the contributions employees make to the organization. Inputs include

equity theory
a theory that states that people will be motivated when they perceive that they are being treated fairly

inputs
in equity theory, the contributions employees make to the organization

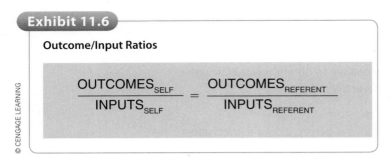

Exhibit 11.6

Outcome/Input Ratios

$$\frac{\text{OUTCOMES}_{\text{SELF}}}{\text{INPUTS}_{\text{SELF}}} = \frac{\text{OUTCOMES}_{\text{REFERENT}}}{\text{INPUTS}_{\text{REFERENT}}}$$

© CENGAGE LEARNING

education and training, intelligence, experience, effort, number of hours worked, and ability. **Outcomes** are what employees receive in exchange for their contributions to the organization. Outcomes include pay, fringe benefits, status symbols, and job titles and assignments. And because perceptions of equity depend on comparisons, **referents** are other people with whom people compare themselves to determine whether they have been treated fairly. Usually, people choose to compare themselves with referents who hold the same or similar jobs or who are otherwise similar in gender, race, age, tenure, or other characteristics.[24]

According to the equity theory process shown in Exhibit 11.6, employees compare their outcomes (the rewards they receive from the organization) with their inputs (their contributions to the organization). This comparison of outcomes with inputs is called the **outcome/input (O/I) ratio**. After an internal comparison in which they compare their outcomes with their inputs, employees then make an external comparison in which they compare their O/I ratio with the O/I ratio of a referent.[25] When people perceive that their O/I ratio is equal to the referent's O/I ratio, they conclude that they are being treated fairly. But when people perceive that their O/I ratio is different from their referent's O/I ratio, they conclude that they have been treated inequitably or unfairly.

Inequity can take two forms, underreward and overreward. **Underreward** occurs when a referent's O/I ratio is better than your O/I ratio. In other words, you are getting fewer outcomes relative to your inputs than the referent you compare yourself with is getting. When people perceive that they have been underrewarded, they tend to experience anger or frustration.

By contrast, **overreward** occurs when a referent's O/I ratio is worse than your O/I ratio. In this case, you are getting more outcomes relative to your inputs than your referent is. In theory, when people perceive that they have been overrewarded, they experience guilt. But, not surprisingly, people have a very high tolerance for overreward. It takes a tremendous amount of overpayment before people decide that their pay or benefits are more than they deserve.

outcomes
in equity theory, the rewards employees receive for their contributions to the organization

referents
in equity theory, others with whom people compare themselves to determine if they have been treated fairly

outcome/input (o/i) ratio
in equity theory, an employee's perception of how the rewards received from an organization compare with the employee's contributions to that organization

underreward
a form of inequity in which you are getting fewer outcomes relative to inputs than your referent is getting

overreward
a form of inequity in which you are getting more outcomes relative to inputs than your referent

11-2b How People React to Perceived Inequity

As a child, do you ever remember calling for a do-over? Even as children, we have a strong desire for fairness, for being treated equitably. When this need isn't met, we are strongly motivated to find a way to restore equity and be fair, hence the do-over. Not surprisingly, equity is just as important at the office as it is on the playground.

So what happens when people perceive that they have been treated inequitably at work? Exhibit 11.7 shows that perceived inequity affects satisfaction. In the case of underreward, this usually translates into frustration or anger; with overreward, the reaction is guilt. These reactions lead to tension and a strong need to take action to restore equity in some way. At first, a slight inequity may not be strong enough to motivate an employee to take immediate action. If the inequity

Exhibit 11.7

Adding Equity Theory to the Model

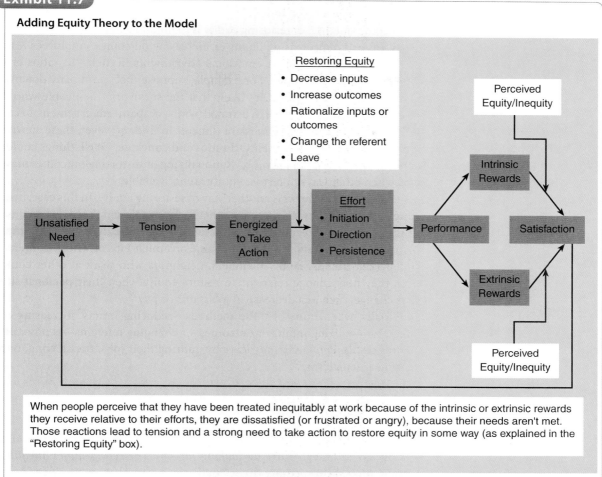

Restoring Equity
- Decrease inputs
- Increase outcomes
- Rationalize inputs or outcomes
- Change the referent
- Leave

Perceived Equity/Inequity

Intrinsic Rewards

Unsatisfied Need → Tension → Energized to Take Action → Effort
- Initiation
- Direction
- Persistence
→ Performance → Satisfaction

Extrinsic Rewards

Perceived Equity/Inequity

When people perceive that they have been treated inequitably at work because of the intrinsic or extrinsic rewards they receive relative to their efforts, they are dissatisfied (or frustrated or angry), because their needs aren't met. Those reactions lead to tension and a strong need to take action to restore equity in some way (as explained in the "Restoring Equity" box).

continues or there are multiple inequities, however, tension may build over time until a point of intolerance is reached, and the person is energized to take action.[26]

When people perceive that they have been treated unfairly, they may try to restore equity by reducing inputs, increasing outcomes, rationalizing inputs or outcomes, changing the referent, or simply leaving. We will discuss these possible responses in terms of the inequity associated with underreward, which is much more common than the inequity associated with overreward.

People who perceive that they have been underrewarded may try to restore equity by *decreasing or withholding their inputs (i.e., effort). Increasing outcomes* is another way people try to restore equity. This might include asking for a raise or pointing out the inequity to the boss and hoping that he or she takes care of it. Sometimes, however, employees may go to external organizations such as labor unions, federal agencies, or the courts for help in increasing outcomes to restore equity. For example, employees of *FAMILY DOLLAR STORES* sued the company, claiming that it had cheated them out of overtime pay by purposefully misclassifying hourly employees (who are eligible for overtime pay) as managers (who are not). The case ultimately went to the U.S. Supreme Court, which upheld a lower court's decision in favor of the workers. Over 1,400 employees will divide $35.6 million.[27]

Another method of restoring equity is to *rationalize or distort inputs or outcomes*. Instead of decreasing inputs or increasing outcomes, employees restore equity by making mental or emotional adjustments in their O/I ratios or the O/I ratios of their referents. For example, suppose that a company downsizes 10 percent of its workforce. It's likely that the survivors (the people who still have jobs) will be angry or frustrated with company management because of the layoffs. If alternative jobs are difficult to find, however, these survivors may rationalize or distort their O/I ratios and conclude, "Well, things could be worse. At least I still have my job." Rationalizing or distorting outcomes may be used when other ways to restore equity aren't available.

Changing the referent is another way of restoring equity. In this case, people compare themselves with someone other than the referent they had been using for previous O/I ratio comparisons. Because people usually choose to compare themselves with others who hold the same or similar jobs or who are otherwise similar (i.e., friends, family members, neighbors who work at other companies), they may change referents to restore equity when their personal situations change, such as a decrease in job status or pay.[28]

Finally, when none of these methods—reducing inputs, increasing outcomes, rationalizing inputs or outcomes, or changing referents—is possible or restores equity, *employees may leave* by quitting their jobs, transferring, or increasing absenteeism.[29]

11-2c Motivating with Equity Theory

What practical steps can managers take to use equity theory to motivate employees? They can *start by looking for and correcting major inequities*. Among other things, equity theory makes us aware that an employee's sense of fairness is based on subjective perceptions. What one employee considers grossly unfair may not affect another employee's perceptions of equity at all. Although these different perceptions make it difficult for managers to create conditions that satisfy all employees, it's critical that they do their best to take care of major inequities that can energize employees to take disruptive, costly, or harmful actions such as decreasing inputs or leaving. So, whenever possible, managers should look for and correct major inequities. At BURGERVILLE, a 39-restaurant fast-food chain in Vancouver, Washington, annual employee turnover was 128 percent per year. The key inequity? Employees making $9 an hour couldn't afford the company's health insurance policy, which cost $42 a month for employees and $105 a month for families, but had a $1,000 deductible and limited benefits. As a result, only 3 percent of employees were enrolled in it. Under Burgerville's revised health plan, employees who work at least 20 hours a week get full health insurance at a cost of just $15 a month for themselves and $90 a month for their families, with no deductible. Although the new plan raised the company' costs to $4.1 million (from $2.1 million), the cost was easily offset by lower employee turnover, which dropped from 128 percent per year to 54 percent per year, and higher sales, which were up 11 percent.[30]

Second, managers can *reduce employees' inputs*. Increasing outcomes is often the first and only strategy that companies use to restore equity, yet reducing employee inputs is just as viable a strategy. In fact, with dual-career couples working 50-hour weeks, more and more employees are looking for ways to reduce stress and restore a balance between work and family. Consequently, it may make sense to ask employees to do less, not more; to have them identify and eliminate the 20 percent of their jobs that doesn't increase productivity or add value for customers; and to eliminate company-imposed requirements that really aren't critical to the performance of managers, employees, or the company (e.g., unnecessary meetings and reports).

Finally, managers should *make sure decision-making processes are fair*. Equity theory focuses on **distributive justice**, the degree to which outcomes and rewards are fairly distributed or allocated. However, **procedural justice**, the fairness of the procedures used to make reward allocation decisions, is just as important.[31] Procedural justice matters because even when employees are unhappy with their outcomes (i.e., low pay), they're much less likely to be unhappy with company management if they believe that the procedures used to allocate outcomes were fair. For example, employees who are laid off tend to be hostile toward their employer when they perceive that the procedures leading to the layoffs were unfair. By contrast, employees who perceive layoff procedures to be fair tend to continue to support and trust their employers.[32] Also, if employees perceive that their outcomes are unfair (i.e., distributive injustice) but that the decisions and procedures leading to those outcomes were fair (i.e., procedural justice), they are much more likely to seek constructive ways of restoring equity, such as discussing these matters with their manager. By contrast, if employees perceive both distributive and procedural injustice, they may resort to more destructive tactics, such as withholding effort, absenteeism, tardiness, or even sabotage and theft.[33]

REVIEW 11-2

. . . .

Equity Theory

The basic components of equity theory are inputs, outcomes, and referents. After an internal comparison in which employees compare their outcomes with their inputs, they then make an external comparison in which they compare their O/I ratio with the O/I ratio of a referent or a person who works in a similar job or is otherwise similar. When their O/I ratio is equal to the referent's O/I ratio, employees perceive that they are being treated fairly. But when their O/I ratio is different from their referent's O/I ratio, they perceive that they have been treated inequitably or unfairly.

There are two kinds of inequity, underreward and overreward. Underreward occurs when a referent's O/I ratio is better than the employee's O/I ratio, and leads to anger or frustration. Overreward occurs when a referent's O/I ratio is worse than the employee's O/I ratio and can lead to guilt, but only when the level of overreward is extreme. When employees perceive that they have been treated inequitably (underrewarded), they may try to restore equity by reducing inputs, increasing outcomes, rationalizing inputs or outcomes, changing the referent, or simply leaving.

Managers can use equity theory to motivate workers by looking for and correcting major inequities, reducing employees' inputs, and emphasizing procedural as well as distributive justice.

distributive justice
the perceived degree to which outcomes and rewards are fairly distributed or allocated

procedural justice
the perceived fairness of the process used to make reward allocation decisions

11-3 Expectancy Theory

How attractive do you find each of the following rewards? A "7 to 7" travel policy stipulating that no one has to leave home for business travel before 7 A.M. on Mondays and that everyone should be home from business travel by 7 P.M. on Fridays. The opportunity to telecommute so that you can feed your kids breakfast, pick them up after school, and tuck them into bed at night.[34]

If you have kids, you might love the chance to telecommute; but if you don't, you may not be interested. If you don't travel much on business, you won't be interested in the "7 to 7" travel policy; but if you do, you'll probably love it.

After reading this section, you should be able to:

11-3 use expectancy theory to describe how workers' expectations about rewards, effort, and the link between rewards and performance influence motivation.

One of the hardest things about motivating people is that not everyone is attracted to the same rewards. **Expectancy theory** says that people will be motivated to the extent to which they believe that their efforts will lead to good performance, that good performance will be rewarded, and that they will be offered attractive rewards.[35]

Let's learn more about expectancy theory by examining **11-3a the components of expectancy theory** and **11-3b how to use expectancy theory as a motivational tool.**

11-3a Components of Expectancy Theory

Expectancy theory holds that people make conscious choices about their motivation. The three factors that affect those choices are valence, expectancy, and instrumentality.

Valence is simply the attractiveness or desirability of various rewards or outcomes. Expectancy theory recognizes that the same reward or outcome—say, a promotion—will be highly attractive to some people, will be highly disliked by others, and will not make much difference one way or the other to still others. Accordingly, when people are deciding how much effort to put forth, expectancy theory says that they will consider the valence of all possible rewards and outcomes that they can receive from their jobs. The greater the sum of those valences, each of which can be positive, negative, or neutral, the more effort people will choose to put forth on the job.

Expectancy is the perceived relationship between effort and performance. When expectancies are strong, employees believe that their hard work and efforts will result in good performance, so they work harder. By contrast, when expectancies are weak, employees figure that no matter what they do or how hard they work, they won't be able to perform their jobs successfully, so they don't work as hard.

Instrumentality is the perceived relationship between performance and rewards. When instrumentality is strong, employees believe that improved

---

expectancy theory
the theory that people will be motivated to the extent to which they believe that their efforts will lead to good performance, that good performance will be rewarded, and that they will be offered attractive rewards

valence
the attractiveness or desirability of a reward or outcome

expectancy
the perceived relationship between effort and performance

instrumentality
the perceived relationship between performance and rewards

performance will lead to better and more rewards, so they choose to work harder. When instrumentality is weak, employees don't believe that better performance will result in more or better rewards, so they choose not to work as hard.

Expectancy theory holds that for people to be highly motivated, all three variables—valence, expectancy, and instrumentality—must be high. Thus, expectancy theory can be represented by the following simple equation:

$$\text{Motivation} = \text{Valence} \times \text{Expectancy} \times \text{Instrumentality}$$

If any one of these variables (valence, expectancy, or instrumentality) declines, overall motivation will decline too.

Exhibit 11.8 incorporates the expectancy theory variables into our motivation model. Valence and instrumentality combine to affect employees' willingness to put forth effort (i.e., the degree to which they are energized to take action), whereas expectancy transforms intended effort ("I'm really going to work hard in this job") into actual effort. If you're offered rewards that you

Exhibit 11.8

Adding Expectancy Theory to the Model

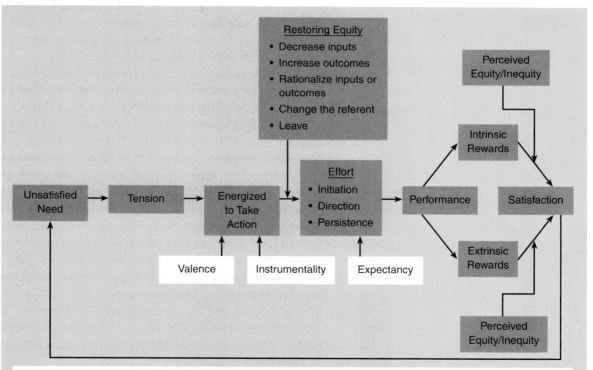

If rewards are attractive (valence) and linked to performance (instrumentality), then people are energized to take action. In other words, good performance gets them rewards that they want. Intended effort (i.e., energized to take action) turns into actual effort when people believe that their hard work and efforts will result in good performance. After all, why work hard if that hard work is wasted?

desire and you believe that you will in fact receive these rewards for good performance, you're highly likely to be energized to take action. However, you're not likely to actually exert effort unless you also believe that you can do the job (i.e., that your efforts will lead to successful performance).

11-3b Motivating with Expectancy Theory

What practical steps can managers take to use expectancy theory to motivate employees? First, they can *systematically gather information to find out what employees want from their jobs.* In addition to individual managers directly asking employees what they want from their jobs (see Section 11-1d, Motivating with the Basics), companies need to survey their employees regularly to determine their wants, needs, and dissatisfactions. Because people consider the valence of all the possible rewards and outcomes that they can receive from their jobs, regular identification of wants, needs, and dissatisfactions gives companies the chance to turn negatively valent rewards and outcomes into positively valent rewards and outcomes, thus raising overall motivation and effort.

Second, managers can *take specific steps to link rewards to individual performance in a way that is clear and understandable to employees.* Unfortunately, most employees are extremely dissatisfied with the link between pay and performance in their organizations. In one study based on a representative sample, 80 percent of the employees surveyed wanted to be paid according to a different kind of pay system! Moreover, only 32 percent of employees were satisfied with how their annual pay raises were determined, and only 22 percent were happy with the way the starting salaries for their jobs were determined.[36]

One way to make sure that employees see the connection between pay and performance (see Chapter 10 for a discussion of compensation strategies) is for managers to publicize the way in which pay decisions are made. This is especially important given that only 41 percent of employees know how their pay increases are determined.[37]

Finally, managers should *empower employees to make decisions if management really wants them to believe that their hard work and effort will lead to good performance.* If valent rewards are linked to good performance, people should be energized to take action. However, this works only if they also believe that their efforts will lead to good performance. One of the ways that managers destroy the expectancy that hard work and effort will lead to good performance is by restricting what employees can do or by ignoring employees' ideas. In Chapter 8, you learned that *empowerment* is a feeling of intrinsic motivation, in which workers perceive their work to have meaning and perceive themselves to be competent, have an impact, and be capable of self-determination.[38] So, if managers want workers to have strong expectancies, they should empower them to make decisions. Doing so will motivate employees to take active rather than passive roles in their work.

REVIEW 11-3
. . . .

Expectancy Theory
Expectancy theory holds that three factors affect the conscious choices people make about their motivation: valence, expectancy, and instrumentality.

Valence is simply the attractiveness or desirability of various rewards or outcomes. Expectancy is the perceived relationship between effort and performance. Instrumentality is the perceived relationship between performance and rewards. Expectancy theory holds that all three factors must be high in order for people to be highly motivated. If any one of these factors declines, overall motivation will decline too. Managers can use expectancy theory to motivate workers by systematically gathering information to find out what employees want from their jobs, by linking rewards to individual performance in a way that is clear and understandable to employees, and by empowering employees to make decisions, which will increase their expectancies that hard work and effort will lead to good performance.

11-4 Reinforcement Theory

When used properly, rewards motivate and energize employees. But when used incorrectly, they can demotivate, baffle, and even anger them. What's the best way to reinforce the behavior you want and minimize or extinguish the behavior you *don't* want?

After reading tthis section, you should be able to:

11-4 explain how reinforcement theory works and how it can be used to motivate.

Reinforcement theory says that behavior is a function of its consequences, that behaviors followed by positive consequences (i.e., reinforced) will occur more frequently, and that behaviors either followed by negative consequences or not followed by positive consequences will occur less frequently.[39] More specifically, **reinforcement** is the process of changing behavior by changing the consequences that follow behavior.[40]

Reinforcement has two parts: reinforcement contingencies and schedules of reinforcement. **Reinforcement contingencies** are the cause-and-effect relationships between the performance of specific behaviors and specific consequences. For example, if you get docked an hour's pay for being late to work, then a reinforcement contingency exists between a behavior (being late to work) and a consequence (losing an hour's pay). A **schedule of reinforcement** is the set of rules regarding reinforcement contingencies such as which behaviors will be reinforced, which consequences will follow those behaviors, and the schedule by which those consequences will be delivered.[41]

Exhibit 11.9 incorporates reinforcement contingencies and reinforcement schedules into our motivation model. First, notice that extrinsic rewards and the schedules of reinforcement used to deliver them are the primary method for creating reinforcement contingencies in organizations. In turn, those reinforcement contingencies directly affect valences (the attractiveness of rewards), instrumentality (the perceived link between rewards and performance), and effort (how hard employees will work).

Let's learn more about reinforcement theory by examining **11-4a the components of reinforcement theory, 11-4b the different schedules for delivering reinforcement,** and **11-4c how to motivate with reinforcement theory.**

reinforcement theory
the theory that behavior is a function of its consequences, that behaviors followed by positive consequences will occur more frequently, and that behaviors followed by negative consequences, or not followed by positive consequences, will occur less frequently

reinforcement
the process of changing behavior by changing the consequences that follow behavior

reinforcement contingencies
cause-and-effect relationships between the performance of specific behaviors and specific consequences

schedule of reinforcement
rules that specify which behaviors will be reinforced, which consequences will follow those behaviors, and the schedule by which those consequences will be delivered

Exhibit 11.9

Adding Reinforcement Theory to the Model

Restoring Equity
- Decrease inputs
- Increase outcomes
- Rationalize inputs or outcomes
- Change the referent
- Leave

Perceived Equity/Inequity

Intrinsic Rewards

Unsatisfied Need → Tension → Energized to Take Action → Effort • Initiation • Direction • Persistence → Performance

Satisfaction

Valence Instrumentality Expectancy

Extrinsic Rewards

Reinforcement Contingencies

Perceived Equity/Inequity

Schedules of Reinforcement

Extrinsic rewards and the schedules of reinforcement used to deliver them are the primary method for creating reinforcement contingencies in organizations. In turn, those reinforcement contingencies directly affect valences (the attractiveness of rewards), instrumentality (the perceived link between rewards and performance), and effort (how hard employees will work).

© CENGAGE LEARNING

11-4a Components of Reinforcement Theory

As just described, *reinforcement contingencies* are the cause-and-effect relationships between the performance of specific behaviors and specific consequences. There are four kinds of reinforcement contingencies: positive reinforcement, negative reinforcement, punishment, and extinction.

Positive reinforcement strengthens behavior (i.e., increases its frequency) by following behaviors with desirable consequences. Pepsi and Waste Management teamed up to create the "dream machine" point system to encourage consumers to recycle. Each bottle or can deposited into a dream machine is rewarded with points that can be used on coupons for shopping, entertainment, dining, travel, and other services.[42] That's instantaneous positive reinforcement.

Negative reinforcement strengthens behavior by withholding an unpleasant consequence when employees perform a specific behavior. Negative reinforcement is also called *avoidance learning*, because workers perform a behavior to *avoid* a negative consequence. Paul English, the cofounder of travel

positive reinforcement
reinforcement that strengthens behavior by following behaviors with desirable consequences

negative reinforcement
reinforcement that strengthens behavior by withholding an unpleasant consequence when employees perform a specific behavior

website, *Kayak.com*, which searches hundreds of travel websites, uses a negative reinforcement strategy to get his 60 software engineers to write better code for Kayak's website—he makes them answer phones and talk to customers—something they'd rather avoid doing. He says, "Anytime anyone contacts us with a question, whether it's by e-mail or telephone, they get a personal reply. The engineers and I handle customer support. People say, 'Why would you pay an engineer $150,000 to answer phones when you could pay someone in Arizona $8 an hour?' If you make the engineers answer e-mails and phone calls from the customers, the second or third time they get the same question, they'll actually stop what they're doing and fix the code. Then we don't have those questions anymore."[43]

By contrast, **punishment** weakens behavior (i.e., decreases its frequency) by following behaviors with undesirable consequences. For example, the standard disciplinary or punishment process in most companies is an oral warning ("Don't ever do that again."), followed by a written warning ("This letter is to discuss the serious problem you're having with . . ."), followed by three days off without pay ("While you're at home not being paid, we want you to think hard about . . ."), followed by being fired ("That was your last chance."). Though punishment can weaken behavior, managers have to be careful to avoid the backlash that sometimes occurs when employees are punished at work.

Extinction is a reinforcement strategy in which a positive consequence is no longer allowed to follow a previously reinforced behavior. By removing the positive consequence, extinction weakens the behavior, making it less likely to occur. Based on the idea of positive reinforcement, most companies give company leaders and managers substantial financial rewards when the company performs well. Based on the idea of extinction, you would then expect that leaders and managers would not be rewarded (i.e., the positive consequence would be removed) when companies perform poorly. If companies really want pay to reinforce the right kinds of behaviors, then rewards have to be removed when company management doesn't produce successful performance. When Toyota saw a decade of low sales, CEO Akio Toyoda and his top managers had their pay cut by 10 percent and did not receive bonuses.[44]

11-4b Schedules for Delivering Reinforcement

As mentioned earlier, a schedule of reinforcement is the set of rules regarding reinforcement contingencies such as which behaviors will be reinforced, which consequences will follow those behaviors, and the schedule by which

punishment
reinforcement that weakens behavior by following behaviors with undesirable consequences

extinction
reinforcement in which a positive consequence is no longer allowed to follow a previously reinforced behavior, thus weakening the behavior

Exhibit 11.10

Intermittent Reinforcement Schedules

	Fixed	Variable
INTERVAL (TIME)	Consequences follow behavior after a fixed time has elapsed.	Consequences follow behavior after different times, some shorter and some longer, that vary around a specific average time.
RATIO (BEHAVIOR)	Consequences follow a specific number of behaviors.	Consequences follow a different number of behaviors, sometimes more and sometimes less, that vary around a specified average number of behaviors.

© CENGAGE LEARNING

continuous reinforcement schedule

a schedule that requires a consequence to be administered following every instance of a behavior

intermittent reinforcement schedule

a schedule in which consequences are delivered after a specified or average time has elapsed or after a specified or average number of behaviors has occurred

fixed interval reinforcement schedule

an intermittent schedule in which consequences follow a behavior only after a fixed time has elapsed

variable interval reinforcement schedules

an intermittent schedule in which the time between a behavior and the following consequences varies around a specified average

fixed ratio reinforcement schedule

an intermittent schedule in which consequences are delivered following a specific number of behaviors

variable ratio reinforcement schedule

an intermittent schedule in which consequences are delivered following a different number of behaviors, sometimes more and sometimes less, that vary around a specified average number of behaviors

those consequences will be delivered. There are two categories of reinforcement schedules: continuous and intermittent.

With **continuous reinforcement schedules**, a consequence follows every instance of a behavior. For example, employees working on a piece-rate pay system earn money (consequence) for every part they manufacture (behavior). The more they produce, the more they earn. By contrast, with **intermittent reinforcement schedules**, consequences are delivered after a specified or average time has elapsed or after a specified or average number of behaviors has occurred. As Exhibit 11.10 shows, there are four types of intermittent reinforcement schedules. Two of these are based on time and are called *interval reinforcement schedules*; the other two, known as *ratio schedules*, are based on behaviors.

With **fixed interval reinforcement schedules**, consequences follow a behavior only after a fixed time has elapsed. For example, most people receive their paychecks on a fixed interval schedule (e.g., once or twice per month). As long as they work (behavior) during a specified pay period (interval), they get a paycheck (consequence). With **variable interval reinforcement schedules**, consequences follow a behavior after different times, some shorter and some longer, that vary around a specified average time. On a 90-day variable interval reinforcement schedule, you might receive a bonus after 80 days or perhaps after 100 days, but the average interval between performing your job well (behavior) and receiving your bonus (consequence) would be 90 days.

With **fixed ratio reinforcement schedules**, consequences are delivered following a specific number of behaviors. For example, a car salesperson might receive a $1,000 bonus after every ten sales. Therefore, a salesperson with only nine sales would not receive the bonus until he or she finally sold a tenth car.

With **variable ratio reinforcement schedules**, consequences are delivered following a different number of behaviors, sometimes more and sometimes less, that vary around a specified average number of behaviors. With a 10-car variable ratio reinforcement schedule, a salesperson might receive the bonus after 7 car sales, or after 12, 11, or 9 sales, but the average number of cars sold before receiving the bonus would be 10 cars.

Which reinforcement schedules work best? In the past, the standard advice was to use continuous reinforcement when employees were learning new behaviors, because reinforcement after each success leads to faster learning.

Likewise, the standard advice was to use intermittent reinforcement schedules to maintain behavior after it is learned, because intermittent rewards are supposed to make behavior much less subject to extinction.[46] Research shows, however, that except for interval-based systems, which usually produce weak results, the effectiveness of continuous reinforcement, fixed ratio, and variable ratio schedules differs very little.[47] In organizational settings, all three consistently produce large increases over noncontingent reward schedules. So managers should choose whichever of these three is easiest to use in their companies.

11-4c Motivating with Reinforcement Theory

What practical steps can managers take to use reinforcement theory to motivate employees? University of Nebraska business professor Fred Luthans, who has been studying the effects of reinforcement theory in organizations for more than a quarter of a century, says that there are five steps to motivating workers with reinforcement theory: *identify, measure, analyze, intervene*, and *evaluate* critical performance-related behaviors.[48]

Identify means singling out critical, observable, performance-related behaviors. These are the behaviors that are most important to successful job performance. In addition, they must also be easily observed so that they can be accurately measured. *Measure* means determining the baseline frequencies of these behaviors. In other words, find out how often workers perform them. *Analyze* means studying the causes and consequences of these behaviors. Analyzing the causes helps managers create the conditions that produce these critical behaviors, and analyzing the consequences helps them determine whether these behaviors produce the results that they want. *Intervene* means changing the organization by using positive and negative reinforcement to increase the frequency of these critical behaviors. *Evaluate* means assessing the extent to which the intervention actually changed workers' behavior. This is done by comparing behavior after the intervention to the original baseline of behavior before the intervention. For more on the effectiveness of reinforcement theory, see the What Really Works feature in this chapter.

In addition to these five steps, managers should remember three other key things when motivating with reinforcement theory. First, *Don't reinforce the wrong behaviors*. Although reinforcement theory sounds simple, it's actually very difficult to put into practice. One of the most common mistakes is accidentally reinforcing the wrong behaviors. Sometimes managers reinforce behaviors that they don't want!

Managers should also *correctly administer punishment at the appropriate time*. Many managers believe that punishment can change workers'

MANAGEMENT FACT

When the Going Gets Tough . . .

It's easy to motivate employees when times are good. A fat bonus check, an extra week of vacation, a remodeled break room with leather sofas, free food, and a high-def TV—all of these things are a drop in the bucket when profits are high. But how do you keep your employees motivated when sales are slow and the economy in all of your major markets is lagging? John Ryan, president of the Center for Creative Leadership, says that three things need to happen if managers are to keep employees happy, motivated, and engaged. First is regular feedback. Managers should not wait for annual reviews, but give regular feedback to let employees know how they are doing and how they can improve. The second is coaching—managers should help employees look at circumstances from a new perspective in order to broaden their thinking and set good goals. Finally, managers must challenge themselves. Instead of just giving advice to others, the effective manager must be willing to receive feedback from others about his or her performance. What is more, managers should identify one or two areas in which they need to improve, so that they always work with the mindset of getting better.[45]

what *really* works

Financial, Nonfinancial, and Social Rewards

Throughout this chapter, we have been making the point that there is more to motivating people than money. But we haven't yet examined how well financial (money or prizes), nonfinancial (performance feedback), and social (recognition and attention) rewards motivate workers by themselves or in combination. However, the results of two meta-analyses, one with 19 studies based on more than 2,800 people (study 1) and another based on 72 studies and 13,301 people (study 2), clearly indicate that rewarding and reinforcing employees greatly improve motivation and performance, especially when combined.

Financial Rewards

On average, there is a 68 percent chance that employees whose behavior is reinforced with financial rewards will outperform employees whose behavior is not reinforced. This increases to 84 percent in manufacturing organizations but drops to 61 percent in service organizations.

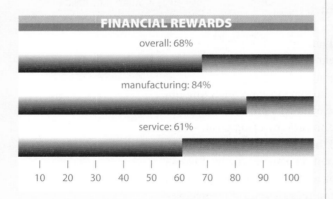

Nonfinancial Rewards

On average, there is a 58 percent chance that employees whose behavior is reinforced with nonfinancial rewards will outperform employees whose behavior is not reinforced. This increases to 87 percent in manufacturing organizations but drops to 54 percent in service organizations.

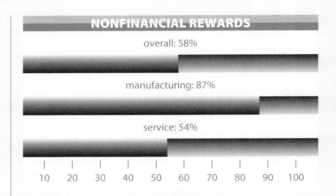

Social Rewards

On average, there is a 63 percent chance that employees whose behavior is reinforced with social rewards will outperform employees whose behavior is not reinforced.

Financial and Nonfinancial Rewards

On average, there is a 62 percent chance that employees whose behavior is reinforced with a combination of financial and nonfinancial rewards will outperform employees whose behavior is not reinforced.

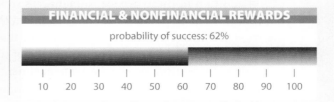

Financial and Social Rewards

On average, there is only a 52 percent chance that employees whose behavior is reinforced with a combination of financial and social rewards will outperform employees whose behavior is not reinforced.

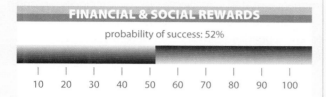

Nonfinancial and Social Rewards

On average, there is a 61 percent chance that employees whose behavior is reinforced with a combination of nonfinancial and social rewards will outperform employees whose behavior is not reinforced.

Financial, Nonfinancial, and Social Rewards

On average, there is a 90 percent chance that employees whose behavior is reinforced with a combination of financial, nonfinancial, and social rewards will outperform employees whose behavior is not reinforced.[52]

behavior and help them improve their job performance. Furthermore, managers believe that fairly punishing workers also lets other workers know what is or isn't acceptable.[49] A danger of using punishment is that it can produce a backlash against managers and companies. But if administered properly, punishment can weaken the frequency of undesirable behaviors without creating a backlash.[50] To be effective, the punishment must be strong enough to stop the undesired behavior and must be administered objectively (same rules applied to everyone), impersonally (without emotion or anger), consistently and contingently (each time improper behavior occurs), and quickly (as soon as possible following the undesirable behavior). In addition, managers should clearly explain what the appropriate behavior is and why the employee is being punished. Employees typically respond well when punishment is administered this way.[51]

Finally, managers should *choose the simplest and most effective schedule of reinforcement*. When choosing a schedule of reinforcement, managers need to balance effectiveness against simplicity. In fact, the more complex the schedule of reinforcement, the more likely it is to be misunderstood and resisted by managers and employees. Since continuous reinforcement, fixed ratio, and variable ratio schedules are about equally effective, continuous reinforcement schedules may be the best choice in many instances by virtue of their simplicity.

REVIEW 11-4
. . . .

Reinforcement Theory
Reinforcement theory says that behavior is a function of its consequences. Reinforcement has two parts: reinforcement contingencies and schedules of reinforcement. The four kinds of reinforcement contingencies are positive

reinforcement and negative reinforcement (which strengthen behavior), and punishment and extinction (which weaken behavior). There are two kinds of reinforcement schedules, continuous and intermittent; intermittent schedules, in turn, can be divided into fixed and variable interval schedules and fixed and variable ratio schedules. Managers can use reinforcement theory to motivate workers by following five steps (identify, measure, analyze, intervene, and evaluate critical performance-related behaviors); not reinforcing the wrong behaviors; correctly administering punishment at the appropriate time; and choosing a reinforcement schedule, such as continuous reinforcement, that balances simplicity and effectiveness.

11-5 Goal-Setting Theory

Leaders who focus blindly on meeting goals at all costs often find that they destroy motivation. A president of a technology company calls his vice president of sales daily and asks, "Did you make your numbers today?" Consultant Richard Hapburg, who works with the vice president who receives these daily calls, says that the VP should be focusing on long-term solutions that increase sales, but "he's under enormous pressure to meet certain sales and profit targets on a daily basis now." The clear danger to using goals in this way, says Hapburg, is "that it's hard to capture employees' hearts, and best efforts, with numbers alone."[53]

After reading this section, you should be able to:

> **11-5** describe the components of goal-setting theory and how managers can use them to motivate workers.

The basic model of motivation with which we began this chapter showed that individuals feel tension after becoming aware of an unfulfilled need. Once they experience tension, they search for and select courses of action that they believe will eliminate this tension. In other words, they direct their behavior toward something. That something is a goal. A **goal** is a target, objective, or result that someone tries to accomplish. For instance, *SINGLE SOURCE SYSTEMS*, a software company in Fishers, Indiana, sets 15 annual goals, such as automating some of the software functions that it uses to write code. But, with 15 goals to accomplish, CEO Tony Petrucciani and his staff divided their efforts and attention in too many directions. Petrucciani said, "Nobody focused on any one thing" and they missed their revenue goal of $8.1 million by 11 percent. Now, Petrucciani sets only a few key goals each year. As a result, with a clearer focus, Single Source Systems met its revenue goal of $10 million last year.[54]

Goal-setting theory says that people will be motivated to the extent to which they accept specific, challenging goals and receive feedback that indicates their progress toward goal achievement.

Let's learn more about goal setting by examining **11-5a the components of goal-setting theory** and **11-5b how to motivate with goal-setting theory.**

11-5a Components of Goal-Setting Theory

The basic components of goal-setting theory are goal specificity, goal difficulty, goal acceptance, and performance feedback.[55] **Goal specificity** is the extent to

---

goal
a target, objective, or result that someone tries to accomplish

goal-setting theory
the theory that people will be motivated to the extent to which they accept specific, challenging goals and receive feedback that indicates their progress toward goal achievement

goal specificity
the extent to which goals are detailed, exact, and unambiguous

which goals are detailed, exact, and unambiguous. Specific goals, such as "I'm going to have a 3.0 average this semester," are more motivating than general goals, such as "I'm going to get better grades this semester."

Goal difficulty is the extent to which a goal is hard or challenging to accomplish. Difficult goals, such as "I'm going to have a 3.5 average and make the Dean's List this semester," are more motivating than easy goals, such as "I'm going to have a 2.0 average this semester."

Goal acceptance, which is similar to the idea of goal commitment discussed in Chapter 4, is the extent to which people consciously understand and agree to goals. Accepted goals, such as "I really want to get a 3.5 average this semester to show my parents how much I've improved," are more motivating than unaccepted goals, such as "My parents really want me to get a 3.5 average this semester, but there's so much more I'd rather do on campus than study!"

Performance feedback is information about the quality or quantity of past performance and indicates whether progress is being made toward the accomplishment of a goal. Performance feedback, such as "My prof said I need a 92 on the final to get an A in that class," is more motivating than no feedback, "I have no idea what my grade is in that class." In short, goal-setting theory says that people will be motivated to the extent to which they accept specific, challenging goals and receive feedback that indicates their progress toward goal achievement.

How does goal setting work? To start, challenging goals focus employees' attention (i.e., direction of effort) on the critical aspects of their jobs and away from unimportant areas. Goals also energize behavior. When faced with unaccomplished goals, employees typically develop plans and strategies to reach those goals. Goals also create tension between the goal, which is the desired future state of affairs, and where the employee or company is now, meaning the current state of affairs. This tension can be satisfied only by achieving or abandoning the goal. Finally, goals influence persistence. Because goals go away only when they are accomplished, employees are more likely to persist in their efforts in the presence of goals. Exhibit 11.11 incorporates goals into the motivation model by showing how goals directly affect tension, effort, and the extent to which employees are energized to take action.

11-5b Motivating with Goal-Setting Theory

What practical steps can managers take to use goal-setting theory to motivate employees? One of the simplest, most effective ways to motivate workers is to give them specific, challenging goals. For example, VALPAK DIRECT MARKETING SYSTEMS is a direct-mailing company that awards regional franchises to people with enough business experience and cash ($43,000 is usually enough for a small region). However, if you work for Valpak and meet the goal of $1.1 million in sales over three years, putting you among the top third of its best salespeople, the company lets you choose your reward: $50,000 toward the purchase of a small regional territory or $10,000 toward getting your MBA. Joe Bourdow, Valpak's president, said, "Sharp people coming out of school have choices, and so

goal difficulty
the extent to which a goal is hard or challenging to accomplish

goal acceptance
the extent to which people consciously understand and agree to goals

performance feedback
information about the quality or quantity of past performance that indicates whether progress is being made toward the accomplishment of a goal

Exhibit 11.11

Adding Goal-Setting Theory to the Model

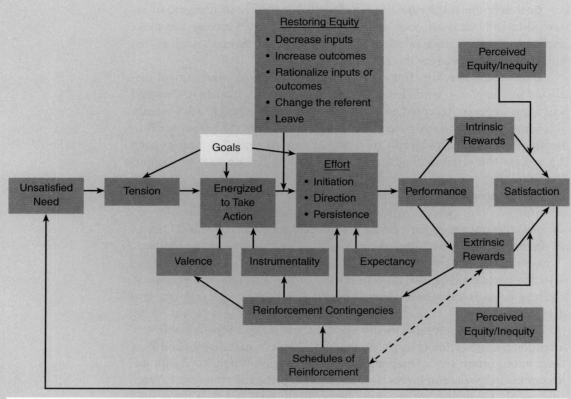

Goals create tension between the goal, which is the desired future state of affairs, and where the employee or company is now, meaning the current state of affairs. This tension can be satisfied only by achieving or abandoning the goal. Goals also energize behavior. When faced with unaccomplished goals, employees typically develop plans and strategies to reach those goals. Finally, goals influence persistence.

we're trying to give them a reason to at least consider us."[56] For more information on assigning specific, challenging goals, see the discussion in Chapter 4 on SMART goals.

Second, managers should *make sure workers truly accept organizational goals*. Specific, challenging goals won't motivate workers unless they really accept, understand, and agree to the organization's goals. For this to occur, people must see the goals as fair and reasonable. Employees must also trust management and believe that managers are using goals to clarify what is expected from them rather than to exploit or threaten them ("If you don't achieve these goals…"). Participative goal setting, in which managers and employees generate goals together, can help increase trust and understanding and thus acceptance of goals. Furthermore, providing workers with training can help increase goal acceptance, particularly when workers don't believe they are capable of reaching the organization's goals.[57]

Finally, managers should *provide frequent, specific, performance-related feedback*. Once employees have accepted specific, challenging goals, they should receive frequent performance-related feedback so that they can track their progress toward goal completion.

Feedback leads to stronger motivation and effort in three ways.[58] Receiving specific feedback about the quality of their performance can encourage employees who don't have specific, challenging goals to set goals to improve their performance. Once people meet goals, performance feedback often encourages them to set higher, more difficult goals. And feedback lets people know whether they need to increase their efforts or change strategies in order to accomplish their goals.

REVIEW 11-5

Goal-Setting Theory

A goal is a target, objective, or result that someone tries to accomplish. Goal-setting theory says that people will be motivated to the extent to which they accept specific, challenging goals and receive feedback that indicates their progress toward goal achievement. The basic components of goal-setting theory are goal specificity, goal difficulty, goal acceptance, and performance feedback. Goal specificity is the extent to which goals are detailed, exact, and unambiguous. Goal difficulty is the extent to which a goal is hard or challenging to accomplish. Goal acceptance is the extent to which people consciously understand and agree to goals. Performance feedback is information about the quality or quantity of past performance and indicates whether progress is being made toward the accomplishment of a goal. Managers can use goal-setting theory to motivate workers by assigning specific, challenging goals, making sure workers truly accept organizational goals, and providing frequent, specific, performance-related feedback.

11-6 Motivating with the Integrated Model

We began this chapter by defining motivation as the set of forces that initiates, directs, and makes people persist in their efforts to accomplish a goal.

After reading this short section, you should be able to:

11-6 discuss how the entire motivation model can be used to motivate workers.

We also asked the basic question that managers ask when they try to figure out how to motivate their workers: What leads to effort? Though the answer to that question is likely to be somewhat different for each employee, Exhibit 11.12 helps you begin to answer it by consolidating the practical advice from the theories reviewed in this chapter in one convenient location. So, if you're having difficulty figuring out why people aren't motivated where you work, Exhibit 11.12 provides a useful, theory-based starting point.

REVIEW 11-6

Motivating with the Integrated Model

Motivating employees can be a difficult process—it can be a challenge even to know where to begin. If you're having difficulty figuring out why people aren't motivated where you work, Exhibit 11.12 provides a useful, theory-based starting point.

Exhibit 11.12

Motivating with the Integrated Model

Motivating With . . .	Managers Should . . .
THE BASICS	Ask people what their needs are.
	Satisfy lower-order needs first.
	Expect people's needs to change.
	As needs change and lower-order needs are satisfied, create opportunities for employees to satisfy higher-order needs.
EQUITY THEORY	Look for and correct major inequities.
	Reduce employees' inputs.
	Make sure decision-making processes are fair.
EXPECTANCY THEORY	Systematically gather information to find out what employees want from their jobs.
	Take specific steps to link rewards to individual performance in a way that is clear and understandable to employees.
	Empower employees to make decisions if management really wants them to believe that their hard work and efforts will lead to good performance.
REINFORCEMENT THEORY	Identify, measure, analyze, intervene, and evaluate critical performance-related behaviors.
	Don't reinforce the wrong behaviors.
	Correctly administer punishment at the appropriate time.
	Choose the simplest and most effective schedule of reinforcement.
GOAL-SETTING THEORY	Assign specific, challenging goals.
	Make sure workers truly accept organizational goals.
	Provide frequent, specific, performance-related feedback.

 # Management Team Decision

Ready for Football?[59]

The CEO of your advertising firm recently put together your team, made up of managers, employees, and even interns, to solve a thorny issue—sports. Almost every Friday and Monday, she has noticed many employees at their desks, looking at their monitors quite intently. At first, she wanted to praise them for working so hard, but on closer inspection, she found that their attention was fixed on fantasy football. These folks, dozens of them all over the office, weren't analyzing company data or working on new sales leads. Instead, they were looking for players to add to their fantasy teams or e-mailing other people in their league about making a trade.

Needless to say, the CEO was quite disheartened to see how preoccupied everyone was with sports. So, she assigned your team the task of putting together an office policy on this issue.

At first glance, the solution seems simple enough—just prohibit employees from playing fantasy sports during work hours. After all, whatever amount of time employees spend on playing or watching games is that much time they spend not working. A study by the outplacement firm Challenger, Gray & Christmas showed that lost productivity costs American companies around $1.5 billion during a football season.

But then again, perhaps the answer is not that simple. Another survey by Challenger, Gray & Christmas shows that fantasy football has little actual impact on productivity. In their survey, 100 human resources officers were asked to rate how big of a distraction fantasy football was on a scale of 1 to 10. The average response—just 3.42. What is more, an office-wide fantasy football league might actually help motivate workers. Letting employees indulge in a fantasy league may actually give them a mental break so that they are even more productive when their attention turns back to work. John Challenger argues that a company that allows employees to participate in fantasy football is likely to see long-term benefits in morale, productivity, and employee retention.

So, the question that your team faces is this: What do we do with fantasy sports?

Should you keep letting employees partake of fantasy leagues during work hours, even though it's often frustrating to see workers do everything else but work? But if you prohibit fantasy sports leagues at work, do you really think that employees will spend their newly found time doing work, or will they just find another distraction? And if you do prohibit, how will you deal with the negative response from employees?

For this Management Team Decision, form a group with three to four other students and consider the questions below.

Questions

1. Do you think that allowing employees to play in fantasy leagues at work is a good motivational tool? Why or why not?

2. What would be an effective method to have employees stop playing fantasy games without destroying their morale or motivation?

 ## Practice Being a Manager

The Makings of Motivation

Motivation is an invisible and powerful force. Strong motivation can drive individuals and organizations to remarkable heights of achievement. A loss of motivation can leave people dispirited and ineffective. One of the fundamental responsibilities of managers is to support healthy worker motivation. This exercise will allow you to practice designing support for worker motivation.

STEP 1 **Divide into groups.** Your professor will organize you in pairs or groups of three.

STEP 2 **Prepare interviews.** Between this class session and the target date set by your professor, you and your partner(s) will each interview two individuals about motivation at work. You should brainstorm about possible types of work, interesting individuals, and so on, and then agree on each partner's list of interviewees/job holders.

Some considerations for brainstorming include jobs or types of work that you consider

particularly interesting, appealing, or mysterious; jobs or types of work that you consider particularly uninteresting, dull, or monotonous (how does a person do that work day after day?); and self-employed or creative work (how do such workers manage their own motivation without a boss or supervisor?)

STEP 3 **Conduct interviews.** Outside of class, students should complete their assigned interviews. Inform the potential interviewee that you are interested in talking about workplace motivation. Set a time that is convenient, and ensure that you arrive on time and are prepared. Make the interview brief, with 15–20 minutes a good target. Go beyond 20 minutes only if the interviewee gives permission and the discussion is lively. Be sure to thank the interviewee for taking the time to visit with you.

Your instructor may give additional instructions for these interviews, and you should carefully follow these guidelines in conducting the interview.

Interview questions might include the following:

1. How would you describe your work? What are some of the things that you particularly like about your work?

2. We are currently studying the topic of motivation in one of my classes. What boosts your motivation at work? If you have ever experienced a period of low motivation, can you identify things that might have contributed to your losing steam in your work?

3. What kinds of rewards or incentives work best to motivate individuals and/or teams who do your type of work? What kinds of rewards or incentives don't work so well?

STEP 4 **Summarize your findings.** Write a one-page paper summarizing your interview findings. Be prepared to compare notes with your partners and to contribute to class discussion.

STEP 5 **Debrief as a class.** Pairs or small groups report their findings and discuss them as a class. What did you learn from your interviews? Did you notice common themes or issues across the interviews you conducted? Did you notice any striking differences across individuals or types of work? What are some possible implications of these interview findings for managers who are responsible for cultivating healthy motivation in a particular work setting?

 ## Self-Assessment

What Do You Need?

What people want out of their jobs is as varied as the jobs themselves.[60] And as you would expect, needs theories show why not everyone wants to be CEO. Take the example of the woman who is extremely organized and efficient in her job as an assistant. She is so effective that she is offered a promotion to management, but she turns it down flatly, saying that she has no interest in moving up the ladder, that she is happy doing what she does. What she needs from work clearly differs from the needs of the person who jumps at every opportunity to move up the corporate hierarchy. Not everyone needs or wants the same things from their jobs.[61] Indicate the extent to which you agree with each of the following statements. Try not to spend too much time on any one item, and be sure to answer all the questions. Use this scale for your responses:

1 **Strongly disagree**
2 **Disagree**
3 **Slightly disagree**
4 **Neutral**
5 **Slightly agree**
6 **Agree**
7 **Strongly agree**

1. I get enough money from my job to live comfortably.

   1   2   3   4   5   6   7

2. Our benefits cover many of the areas they should.

   1   2   3   4   5   6   7

3. My boss encourages people to make suggestions.

   1   2   3   4   5   6   7

4. I can count on my coworkers to give me a hand when I need it.

   1   2   3   4   5   6   7

5. I always get the feeling of learning new things from my work.

   1   2   3   4   5   6   7

6. I often think about how to improve my job performance.

   1   2   3   4   5   6   7

7. My pay is adequate to provide for the basic things in life.

    1   2   3   4   5   6   7

8. The benefit program here gives nearly all the security I want.

    1   2   3   4   5   6   7

9. My boss takes account of my wishes and desires.

    1   2   3   4   5   6   7

10. My coworkers will speak out in my favor if justified.

    1   2   3   4   5   6   7

11. My job requires that a person use a wide range of abilities.

    1   2   3   4   5   6   7

12. I will actively try to improve my job performance in the future.

    1   2   3   4   5   6   7

13. Considering the work required, the pay is what it should be.

    1   2   3   4   5   6   7

14. Compared to other places, our benefits are excellent.

    1   2   3   4   5   6   7

15. My boss keeps me informed about what is happening in the company.

    1   2   3   4   5   6   7

16. I can tell my coworkers how I honestly feel.

    1   2   3   4   5   6   7

17. My job requires making one (or more) important decision(s) every day.

    1   2   3   4   5   6   7

18. I intend to do a lot more at work in the future.

    1   2   3   4   5   6   7

19. Compared to the rates for similar work, here, my pay is good.

    1   2   3   4   5   6   7

20. The benefit program here is adequate.

    1   2   3   4   5   6   7

21. My boss lets me know when I could improve my performance.

    1   2   3   4   5   6   7

22. My coworkers welcome opinions different from their own.

    1   2   3   4   5   6   7

23. I have the opportunity to do challenging things at work.

    1   2   3   4   5   6   7

24. I will probably do my best to perform well on the job in the future.

    1   2   3   4   5   6   7

SCORING

    (A)   Add together your scores for items 1, 2, 7, 8, 13, 14, 19, and 20: _____

    (B)   Add together your scores for items 3, 4, 9, 10, 15, 16, 21, and 22: _____

    (C)   Add together your scores for items 5, 6, 11, 12, 17, 18, 23, and 24: _____

You can find the interpretation for your score at www.cengagebrain.com.

MANAGEMENT WORKPLACE

© CENGAGE LEARNING 2013

LivingSocial Escapes: Motivating Employees

LivingSocial Escapes, which offers a range of outdoor excursions, demands high commitment from employees. When hiring new workers, founder Bram Levy offers only the most basic outline of job responsibilities. "Think about the brand and what we're trying to develop," Levy tells new recruits. "Now take it and formulate what you think will be best and run with it." The employees must then come up with creative ideas and execute them. Though demanding, this approach to motivation has great benefits for employees.

What to Watch For and Ask Yourself

1. Which needs in Maslow's hierarchy are most important to the employees who work for LivingSocial Escapes? How can managers use this information to develop a highly motivated workforce?

2. According to equity theory, how might a LivingSocial Escapes guide react if he or she feels underpaid or unappreciated?

3. What outcomes or rewards possess high valence for managers and guides who work at LivingSocial Escapes?

◢ Endnotes

1   J. Guynn "War Heats up for Top Silicon Valley Talent,"
    Los Angeles Times, November 10, 2010, accessed May 23,
    2011, from http://articles.latimes.com/2010/nov/10/busi-
    ness/la-fi-silicon-pay-war-20101111; D. Chow, "For SAS,
    Asia Presents Risks and Potential," *Wall Street Journal*,
    November 21, 2010, accessed June 4, 2011, from http://
    online.wsj.com/article/SB10001424052748704170404575
    623952475539676.html; M. Hartley, "Business Software's
    'Cadillac'; 'Tough Times are Good Times for Analytics,'
    SAS CEO Jim Goodnight Says," *Financial Post*, July 17,
    2010, 3; D. Kaplan, "The Best Company to Work For,"
    Fortune, February 8, 2010, 56–64; R. Lane, "Pampering the
    Customers, Pampering the Employees," *Forbes*, October
    14, 1996, 74–80; S. Lohr, "SAS Tests Its Business Intel-
    ligence; Top Software Company Confronts New Threat
    from Heavyweight Rivals," *International Herald Tribune*,
    November 23, 2009, 16; and A. Ricadeloa, "IBM vs. SAS:
    The Battle over Data Analysis Software," *Businessweek
    Online*, November 30, 2009), accessed June 4, 2011, from
    www.businessweek.com/technology/content/nov2009/
    tc20091129_192266.htm.

2   J. P. Campbell and R. D. Pritchard, "Motivation Theory in
    Industrial and Organizational Psychology," in *Handbook of
    Industrial and Organizational Psychology*, M. D. Dunnette, ed.
    (Chicago: Rand McNally, 1976).

3   D. Mattioli, "Rewards for Extra Work Come Cheap in Lean
    Times—With Raises and Promotions Scarce, Managers Are
    Generous with Low-Cost Incentives Like Thank-You Notes,
    Gift Cards," *Wall Street Journal*, January 4, 2010, B7.

4   E. A. Locke, "The Nature and Causes of Job Satisfaction," in
    Handbook of Industrial and Organizational Psychology, M. D.
    Dunnette, ed. (Chicago: Rand McNally, 1976).

5   A. H. Maslow, "A Theory of Human Motivation," *Psychological
    Review* 50 (1943): 370–396.

6   C. P. Alderfer, *Existence, Relatedness, and Growth:
    Human Needs in Organizational Settings* (New York: Free
    Press, 1972).

7   D. C. McClelland, "Toward a Theory of Motive Acquisition,"
    American Psychologist 20 (1965): 321–333; and D. C. McClel-
    land and D. H. Burnham, "Power Is the Great Motivator,"
    Harvard Business Review 54, no. 2 (1976): 100–110.

8   J. H. Turner, "Entrepreneurial Environments and the Emer-
    gence of Achievement Motivation in Adolescent Males,"
    Sociometry 33 (1970): 147–165.

9   L. W. Porter, E. E. Lawler III, and J. R. Hackman, *Behavior in
    Organizations* (New York: McGraw-Hill, 1975).

10 C. Ajila, "Maslow's Hierarchy of Needs Theory: Applicability
    to the Nigerian Industrial Setting," *IFE Psychology* (1997):
    162–174.

11 E. E. Lawler III and L. W. Porter, "The Effect of Performance
    on Job Satisfaction," *Industrial Relations* 7 (1967): 20–28.

12 Porter, Lawler, and Hackman, *Behavior in Organizations*.

13 Ibid.

14 C. Caggiano, "What Do Workers Want?" *Inc.*, November
    1992, 101–104; and "National Study of the Changing Work-
    force," Families & Work Institute, accessed May 31, 2005,
    from www.familiesandwork.org/summary/nscw.pdf.

15 A. Brooks, "I LOVE My WORK," *American: A Magazine of
    Ideas* 6 (September–October 2007): 20–28.

16 A. Fisher, "To Keep Employees Loyal, Try Asking What They
    Want," *Fortune*, January 27, 2011, accessed February 15, 2010,
    from http://management.fortune.cnn.com/2011/01/27/to-
    keep-employees-loyal-try-asking-what-they-want/.

17 "America@A Focus on Benefits and Compensation," Aon
    Consulting, accessed June 1, 2011, from www.aon.com/pdf/
    america/awork2.pdf [content no longer available online].

18 H. Dolezalek, "Good Job! Recognition Training," *Training*,
    July 28, 2008.

19 R. Kanfer and P. Ackerman, "Aging, Adult Development, and
    Work Motivation," *Academy of Management Review* (2004):
    440–458.

20 E. White, "The New Recruits: Older Workers," *Wall Street
    Journal*, January 14, 2008, B3.

21 S. J. O'Malley, "Motivate the Middle: How Mid-Level Per-
    formance Can Bring Top Growth to the Bottom Line," *Bank
    Investment Consultant*, February 2007, 39.

22 "Swiss Man Gets Record Fine," BBC News, January 7, 2010,
    accessed June 1, 2011, from http://news.bbc.co.uk/go/pr/fr/-
    /2/hi/europe/8446545.stm.

23 Stecklow, "Fast Finns' Fines Fit Their Finances—Traffic
    Penalties Are Assessed According to Driver Income."

24 C. T. Kulik & M. L. Ambrose, "Personal and Situational
    Determinants of Referent Choice," *Academy of Management
    Review* 17 (1992): 212–237.

25 J. S. Adams, "Toward an Understanding of Inequity," *Journal
    of Abnormal Social Psychology* 67 (1963): 422–436.

26 R. A. Cosier and D. R. Dalton, "Equity Theory and Time: A
    Reformulation," *Academy of Management Review* 8 (1983):
    311–319; and M. R. Carrell and J. E. Dittrich, "Equity Theory:
    The Recent Literature, Methodological Considerations, and
    New Directions," *Academy of Management Review* 3 (1978):
    202–209.

27 N. Maestri, "Supreme Court Lets Stand $36 Million Family
    Dollar Ruling," *Reuters.com*, October 5, 2009, accessed June 1,
    2011, from www.reuters.com/article/domesticNews/
    idUSTRE59447W20091005; and R. Montaigne, "Court
    Rejects Family Dollar Case; Store to Pay Up," *Morning Edition*,
    National Public Radio, October 6, 2009.

28 C. Chen, J. Choi, and S. Chi, "Making Justice Sense of Local-
    Expatriate Compensation Disparity: Mitigation by Local Ref-
    erents, Ideological Explanations, and Interpersonal Sensitivity
    in China-Foreign Joint Ventures," *Academy of Management
    Journal* (2002): 807–817.

29 K. Aquino, R. W. Griffeth, D. G. Allen, and P. W. Hom, "Inte-
    grating Justice Constructs into the Turnover Process: A Test

of a Referent Cognitions Model," *Academy of Management Journal* 40, no. 5 (1997): 1208–1227.

30 S. Needleman, "Burger Chain's Health-Care Recipe—Paying More for Insurance Cuts Turnover, Boosts Sales and Productivity," *Wall Street Journal*, August 31, 2009, B4.

31 R. Folger and M. A. Konovsky, "Effects of Procedural and Distributive Justice on Reactions to Pay Raise Decisions," *Academy of Management Journal* 32 (1989): 115–130; and M. A. Konovsky, "Understanding Procedural Justice and Its Impact on Business Organizations," *Journal of Management* 26 (2000): 489–512.

32 E. Barret-Howard and T. R. Tyler, "Procedural Justice as a Criterion in Allocation Decisions," *Journal of Personality & Social Psychology* 50 (1986): 296–305; and Folger and Konovsky, "Effects of Procedural and Distributive Justice on Reactions to Pay Raise Decisions."

33 R. Folger and J. Greenberg, "Procedural Justice: An Interpretive Analysis of Personnel Systems," in *Research in Personnel and Human Resources Management*, vol. 3, K. Rowland and G. Ferris, eds. (Greenwich, CT: JAI, 1985); R. Folger, D. Rosenfield, J. Grove, and L. Corkran, "Effects of 'Voice' and Peer Opinions on Responses to Inequity," *Journal of Personality & Social Psychology* 37 (1979): 2253–2261; E. A. Lind and T. R. Tyler, *The Social Psychology of Procedural Justice* (New York: Plenum, 1988); and Konovsky, "Understanding Procedural Justice and Its Impact on Business Organizations."

34 K. A. Dolan, "When Money Isn't Enough," *Forbes*, November 18, 1996, 164–170.

35 V. H. Vroom, *Work and Motivation* (New York: John Wiley & Sons, 1964); and L. W. Porter and E. E. Lawler III, *Managerial Attitudes and Performance* (Homewood, IL: Dorsey and Richard D. Irwin, 1968).

36 P. V. LeBlanc and P. W. Mulvey, "How American Workers See the Rewards of Work," *Compensation & Benefits Review* 30 (February 1998): 24–28.

37 A. Fox, "Companies Can Benefit When They Disclose Pay Processes to Employees," *HR Magazine*, July 2002, 25.

38 K. W. Thomas and B. A. Velthouse, "Cognitive Elements of Empowerment," *Academy of Management Review* 15 (1990): 666–681.

39 E. L. Thorndike, *Animal Intelligence* (New York: Macmillan, 1911).

40 B. F. Skinner, *Science and Human Behavior* (New York: Macmillan, 1954); B. F. Skinner, *Beyond Freedom and Dignity* (New York: Bantam, 1971); and B. F. Skinner, *A Matter of Consequences* (New York: New York University Press, 1984).

41 A. M. Dickinson and A. D. Poling, "Schedules of Monetary Reinforcement in Organizational Behavior Management: Latham and Huber Revisited," *Journal of Organizational Behavior Management* 16, no. 1 (1992): 71–91.

42 V. Bauerlein, "PepsiCo Plans Recycling Initiative," *Wall Street Journal*, April 22, 2010, accessed August 23, 2010, from http://online.wsj.com/article/NA_WSJ_PUB:SB100014240527 48703404004575198390481890492.html.

43 L. Welch, "The Way I Work: Paul English of Kayak," *Inc.*, February 1, 2010, accessed June 2, 2011, from www.inc.com/magazine/20100201/the-way-i-work-paul-english-of-kayak.html.

44 H. Tabuchi, "After Tough Year, Pay Cuts and Forfeited Bonuses for Top Toyota Executives," *New York Time,* June 24, 2010, accessed June 2, 2011, from www.nytimes.com/2010/06/25/business/global/25toyota.html?ref=akiotoyod.

45 J. R. Ryan, "Keeping Employees Happy in a Post-Recession World," *Bloomberg Businessweek*, August 31, 2010, accessed October 20, 2010, from www.businessweek.com/managing/content/aug2010/ca20100831_786655.htm.

46 J. B. Miner, *Theories of Organizational Behavior* (Hinsdale, IL: Dryden, 1980).

47 Dickinson and Poling, "Schedules of Monetary Reinforcement in Organizational Behavior Management."

48 F. Luthans and A. D. Stajkovic, "Reinforce for Performance: The Need to Go beyond Pay and Even Rewards," *Academy of Management Executive* 13, no. 2 (1999): 49–57.

49 K. D. Butterfield, L. K. Trevino, and G. A. Ball, "Punishment from the Manager's Perspective: A Grounded Investigation and Inductive Model," *Academy of Management Journal* 39 (1996): 1479–1512.

50 R. D. Arvey and J. M. Ivancevich, "Punishment in Organizations: A Review, Propositions, and Research Suggestions," *Academy of Management Review* 5 (1980): 123–132.

51 R. D. Arvey, G. A. Davis, and S. M. Nelson, "Use of Discipline in an Organization: A Field Study," *Journal of Applied Psychology* 69 (1984): 448–460; and M. E. Schnake, "Vicarious Punishment in a Work Setting," *Journal of Applied Psychology* 71 (1986): 343–345.

52 A. D. Stajkovic and F. Luthans, "A Meta-Analysis of the Effects of Organizational Behavior Modification on Task Performance, 1975–95," *Academy of Management Journal* 40, no. 5 (1997): 1122–1149; and A. D. Stajkovic and F. Luthans, "Behavioral Management and Task Performance in Organizations: Conceptual Background, Meta-Analysis, and Test of Alternative Models," *Personnel Psychology* 56, no. 1 (2003): 155–194.

53 C. Hymowitz, "When Meeting Targets Becomes the Strategy, CEO Is on Wrong Path," *Wall Street Journal*, March 8, 2005, A8.

54 V. Harnish, "Five Ways to Get your Strategy Right," *Fortune*, April 11, 2011, 23.

55 E. A. Locke and G. P. Latham, *Goal Setting: A Motivational Technique That Works* (Englewood Cliffs, NJ: Prentice-Hall, 1984); and E. A. Locke and G. P. Latham, *A Theory of Goal Setting and Task Performance* (Englewood Cliffs, NJ: Prentice-Hall, 1990).

56 "Franchising—In with the New: As More Boomers Retire, Franchisers Set Their Sights on a Much Younger Crowd," *Wall Street Journal*, September 28, 2009, R9.

57 G. P. Latham and E. A. Locke, "Goal Setting—A Motivational Technique That Works," *Organizational Dynamics* 8, no. 2 (1979): 68.

58 Ibid.

59 E. Spitznagel, "Fantasy Football: The New Internet Porn," *Bloomberg Businessweek*, September 9, 2010, accessed February 18, 2010, from www.businessweek.com/magazine/content/10_38/b4195081511463.htm; D. Thompson, "Fantasy Football Is Not Sacking Productivity," *Atlantic*, February 18, 2011, accessed February 18, 2011, from www.theatlantic.com/business/archive/2010/09/study-fantasy-football-is-not-sacking-productivity/63854/; and H. Unger, "New Survey: Fantasy Football Does Not Sack Workplace Productivity," *Atlanta Journal Constitution*, September 30, 2010, accessed February 18, 2010, from http://blogs.ajc.com/business-beat/2010/09/30/new-survey-fantasy-football-not-sacking-workplace-productivity/.

60 C. A. Arnolds and C. Boshoff, "Compensation, Esteem Valence, and Job Performance: An Empirical Assessment of Alderfer's ERG Theory," *International Journal of Human Resource Management* 13, no. 4 (2002): 697–719.

61 Maslow, "A Theory of Human Motivation."

Leadership

OUTLINE

REEL TO REAL

Management Workplace is at Camp Bow Wow.

SELF-ASSESSMENT

What's your leadership orientation? Find out by completing the Least Preferred Coworker Scale in the book or online.

ONLINE QUIZZES

Did you get it? Review the main concepts in the chapter by taking the online quizzes on CourseMate!

VIDEO QUIZZES

Get more out of the videos by taking the multimedia video quizzes online.

What Would You Do?

Apple Headquarters, Cupertino, California[1]

CEO and cofounder Steve Jobs is synonymous with Apple. Fired from Apple in 1985, Jobs founded NeXT Computer, bought the Graphics Group from Lucasfilm, and transformed it into Pixar Studios, and then returned to Apple as CEO in 1995. In his absence, Apple lost billions and its share of the personal computer market dropped from 9 percent to 2 percent. Jobs saved Apple by procuring a $150 million investment from Bill Gates and Microsoft, and launching the iMac, a desktop machine that became one of Apple's leading sellers. Most importantly, though, Jobs directed the development of Apple's new operating system, OS X, an operating system that is speedy, simple to use, incredibly stable, and easy to write software for. OS X, in combination with easy-to-use software for film and picture editing, desktop publishing, presentations, and word processing, stabilized Apple's sales and market share, and put it in a financial position to eventually create the iPod, the iPhone, the iPad, and now iCloud. Today, Apple's 10 percent share of the personal computer market is growing, it has a large market share in smart phones, and a commanding market share in tablets and digital music. Furthermore, its combined stock value is greater than Intel and Microsoft combined.

Jobs was known for his highly demanding and influential leadership at Apple. When Apple's MobileMe service (which synchronized calendar and e-mail and files across Macs, iPhones, and corporate networks) launched to terrible reviews and buggy performance, he berated the MobileMe team, telling them, "You've tarnished Apple's reputation. You should hate each other for having let each other down." He named a replacement manager on the spot. Jobs was also famous for saying "no." A former Apple executive says, "Over and over Steve talks about the power of picking the things you don't do." Jobs once said, "We're always thinking about new markets we could enter. But it's only by saying no . . . that you can concentrate on the things that are really important." Yet, despite his toughness and discipline,

© LUAY BAHOORA/ALAMY

Jobs was able to inspire Apple's managers, software engineers, and designers to create elegant, simple, innovative products. Jeff Robbin, Apple's lead software designer for iTunes and the iPod said, "I remember sitting with Steve and some other people night after night from nine until one, working out the user interface for the first iPod. It evolved by trial and error into something a little simpler every day. We knew we had reached the end when we looked at each other and said, 'Well, of course. Why would we want to do it any other way?'"

Apple's future is bright, but Jobs's health was a long-term concern. In 2004 and 2009, he took medical leaves due to pancreatic cancer, a liver transplant, and an inability to maintain weight. In January 2011, he announced his third medical leave, telling Apple's 50,000 employees, "I love Apple so much and hope to be back as soon as I can. In the meantime, my family and I would deeply appreciate respect for our privacy." In October 2011, Jobs died, one month after handing the CEO job to long-time COO, Tim Cook.

Jobs's charismatic leadership was clearly central to Apple's success. But can Apple succeed without him? What steps should Apple take to increase its chances of continued success without

© DIZZO/ISTOCK PHOTO

Jobs as CEO? Are there ways to substitute for Jobs's leadership at Apple? Next, is Tim Cook the right leader to replace Jobs? Jobs was demanding, creative, and controlling. Cook is not. Should Tim Cook try to emulate Jobs or should he run Apple using a different leadership style? Should Cook focus more on managing or leading Apple? Finally, Jobs was at the center of all of Apple's key decisions over the last decade and a half. Jez Frampton, group CEO of Interbrand says, "Now the worry is the organization has to rewire itself and learn how to make decisions on its own." Should Apple become more participative, involving more managers and employees, or continue to use Jobs's centralized approach to decision making, which was less participative and highly influenced by the founder and former CEO?

If you were in charge at Apple, what would you do?

12-1 Leadership

We begin this chapter by discussing what leadership is, who leaders are (meaning their traits and characteristics), and what leaders do that makes them different from people who aren't leaders. Next we examine four major contingency theories of leadership that specify which leaders are best suited for which situations or how leaders should change their behavior to lead different people in different circumstances. The chapter ends with a review of strategic leadership issues, such as charismatic and transformational leadership, which address how to work with others to meet long-term goals and how to create a viable future for an organization.

How does an ensemble of 100 or more musicians, all playing different parts at different times on different instruments, manage to produce something as beautiful as Beethoven's Fifth Symphony? (Or, if Gustav Mahler's "Symphony of a Thousand" is on the program, a lot more people might be involved!) The conductor, like a CEO, is responsible for managing all of this complexity and ensuring a great performance. But conductors do much more than just keep the beat with a baton. According to Ramona Wis, author of *The Conductor as Leader: Principles of Leadership Applied to Life on the Podium*, conductors must also build connections between people, inspire them with vision, command their trust, and persuade them to participate in the ensemble at their very best.

After reading the next section, you should be able to:

12-1 explain what leadership is.

Whether the end result is a stirring musical performance, innovation of new products, or increased profits, leadership is the process of influencing others to achieve group or organizational goals. If you've ever been in charge, or even just thought about it, chances are you've considered questions like these: Do I have what it takes to lead? What are the most important things leaders do? How can I transform a poorly performing department, division, or company? Do I need to adjust my leadership depending on the situation and the employee? Why doesn't my leadership inspire people? If you feel overwhelmed at the prospect of being a leader, you're not alone—millions of leaders in organizations across the world struggle with these fundamental leadership issues on

leadership
the process of influencing others to achieve group or organizational goals

a daily basis. The knowledge and skills you'll learn in this chapter won't make the task of leadership less daunting, but they will help you navigate it.

In Chapter 1, we defined *management* as getting work done through others. In other words, managers don't do the work themselves. Managers help others do their jobs better. By contrast, *leadership* is the process of influencing others to achieve group or organizational goals. What, then, are the key differences between leaders and managers? Another question that gets at the nature of leadership is this: Is leadership required in every situation? Does leadership always matter? Or are there situations when leadership isn't needed or may even make things worse?

Let's learn more about leadership by exploring **12-1a the differences between leaders and managers**.

12-1a Leaders versus Managers

According to University of Southern California business professor Warren Bennis, the primary difference between leaders and managers, as shown in Exhibit 12.1, is that leaders are concerned with doing the right thing, whereas managers are concerned with doing things right.[2] In other words, leaders begin with the question: What should we be doing? whereas managers start with: How can we do what we're already doing better? Leaders focus on vision, mission, goals, and objectives, whereas managers focus on productivity and efficiency. Managers see themselves as preservers of the status quo, whereas leaders see themselves as promoters of change and challengers of the status quo in that they encourage creativity and risk taking.

Another difference is that managers have a relatively short-term perspective, whereas leaders take a long-term view. Managers are concerned with control and limiting the choices of others, whereas leaders are more concerned with expanding people's choices and options.[3] Managers also solve problems so that others can do their work, whereas leaders inspire and motivate others to find their own solutions.

Finally, managers are also more concerned with *means*, how to get things done, whereas leaders are more concerned with *ends*, what gets done. Although leaders are different from managers, organizations need them both. Managers are critical to getting out the day-to-day work, and

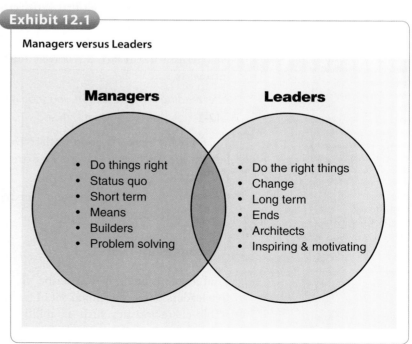

Exhibit 12.1

Managers versus Leaders

Managers	Leaders
• Do things right	• Do the right things
• Status quo	• Change
• Short term	• Long term
• Means	• Ends
• Builders	• Architects
• Problem solving	• Inspiring & motivating

© CENGAGE LEARNING

leaders are critical to inspiring employees and setting the organization's long-term direction. The key issue for any organization is the extent to which it is properly led and properly managed. As Warren Bennis said in summing up the difference between leaders and managers, "American organizations (and probably those in much of the rest of the industrialized world) are under led and overmanaged. They do not pay enough attention to doing the right thing, while they pay too much attention to doing things right."[4]

REVIEW 12-1

· ·

Leadership

Leadership is the process of influencing others to achieve group or organizational goals. Leaders are different from managers. The primary difference is that leaders are concerned with doing the right thing, whereas managers are concerned with doing things right. Furthermore, managers have a short-term focus and are concerned with the status quo, with means rather than ends, and with solving others' problems. By contrast, leaders have a long-term focus and are concerned with change, with ends rather than means, and with inspiring and motivating others to solve their own problems. Organizations need both managers and leaders. But in general, companies are overmanaged and underled.

12-2 Who Leaders Are and What Leaders Do

Indra Nooyi, PepsiCo's CEO, talks straight, has a sharp sense of humor, and sings in the hallways wherever she is. Nooyi is an extrovert. By contrast, JC Penney's former CEO, Mike Ullman, who is soft-spoken and easy to approach, is an introvert.[5] Which one is likely to be successful as a CEO? According to a survey of 1,542 senior managers, it's the extrovert. Forty-seven percent of those 1,542 senior managers felt that extroverts make better CEOs, whereas 65 percent said that being an introvert hurts a CEO's chances of success.[6] So clearly, senior managers believe that extroverted CEOs are better leaders. But are they? Not necessarily. In fact, a relatively high percentage of CEOs, 40 percent, are introverts.

After reading the next section, you should be able to:

12-2 describe who leaders are and what effective leaders do.

So, what makes a good leader? Does leadership success depend on who leaders are, such as introverts or extroverts, or on what leaders do and how they behave?

Let's learn more about who leaders are by investigating **12-2a leadership traits** and **12-2b leadership behaviors**.

12-2a Leadership Traits

Trait theory is one way to describe who leaders are. **Trait theory** says that effective leaders possess a similar set of traits or characteristics. **Traits** are relatively stable characteristics such as abilities, psychological motives, or consistent

trait theory
a leadership theory that holds that effective leaders possess a similar set of traits or characteristics

traits
relatively stable characteristics, such as abilities, psychological motives, or consistent patterns of behavior

patterns of behavior. Trait theory is also known as the "great person" theory because early versions of the theory stated that leaders are born, not made. In other words, you either have the right stuff to be a leader, or you don't. And if you don't, there is no way to get it.

For some time, it was thought that trait theory was wrong and that there are no consistent trait differences between leaders and nonleaders, or between effective and ineffective leaders. However, more recent evidence shows that "successful leaders are not like other people," that successful leaders are indeed different from the rest of us.[7] More specifically, as shown in Exhibit 12.2, leaders are different from nonleaders in the following traits: drive, the desire to lead, honesty/integrity, self-confidence, emotional stability, cognitive ability, and knowledge of the business.[8]

Drive refers to high levels of effort and is characterized by achievement, motivation, initiative, energy, and tenacity. In terms of achievement and ambition, leaders always try to make improvements or achieve success in what they're doing. Because of their initiative, they have strong desires to promote change or solve problems. Leaders typically have more energy—they have to, given the long hours they put in and followers' expectations that they be positive and upbeat. Thus, leaders must have physical, mental, and emotional vitality. Leaders are also more tenacious than nonleaders and are better at overcoming obstacles and problems that would deter most of us.

Successful leaders also have a stronger *desire to lead*. They want to be in charge and think about ways to influence or convince others about what should or shouldn't be done. *Honesty/integrity* is also important to leaders. *Honesty*, being truthful with others, is a cornerstone of leadership. Without it, leaders won't be trusted. When leaders are honest, subordinates are willing to overlook other flaws. For example, one follower said this about the leadership qualities of his manager: "I don't like a lot of the things he does, but he's basically honest. He's a genuine article, and you'll

Exhibit 12.2

Leadership Traits

- Desire to lead
- Honesty and integrity
- Drive
- Self-confidence
- Leadership Traits
- Knowledge of the business
- Emotional stability
- Cognitive ability

© CENGAGE LEARNING

forgive a lot of things because of that. That goes a long way in how much I trust him."[9] *Integrity* is the extent to which leaders do what they say they will do. Leaders may be honest and have good intentions, but if they don't consistently deliver on what they promise, they won't be trusted.

Self-confidence, or believing in one's abilities, also distinguishes leaders from nonleaders. Self-confident leaders are more decisive and assertive and are more likely to gain others' confidence. Moreover, self-confident leaders will admit mistakes because they view them as learning opportunities rather than a refutation of their leadership capabilities. This also means that leaders have *emotional stability*. Even when things go wrong, they remain even-tempered and consistent in their outlook and in the way they treat others. Leaders who can't control their emotions, who anger quickly or attack and blame others for mistakes, are unlikely to be trusted.

Leaders are also smart. Leaders typically have strong *cognitive abilities*. This doesn't mean that leaders are necessarily geniuses—far from it. But it does mean that leaders have the capacity to analyze large amounts of seemingly unrelated, complex information and see patterns, opportunities, or threats where others might not see them. Finally, leaders also know their stuff, which means they have superior technical knowledge about the businesses they run. Leaders who have a good *knowledge of the business* understand the key technological decisions and concerns facing their companies. More often than not, studies indicate that effective leaders have long, extensive experience in their industries.

12-2b Leadership Behaviors

Thus far, you've read about who leaders *are*. But traits alone are not enough to make a successful leader. They are, however, a precondition for success. After all, it's hard to imagine a truly successful leader who lacks most of these qualities. Leaders who have these traits (or many of them) must then take actions that encourage people to achieve group or organizational goals.[10] Accordingly, we now examine what leaders *do*, meaning the behaviors they perform or the actions they take to influence others to achieve group or organizational goals.

Researchers at the University of Michigan, Ohio State University, and the University of Texas examined the specific behaviors that leaders use to improve subordinate satisfaction and performance. Hundreds of studies were conducted and hundreds of leader behaviors were examined. At all three universities, two basic leader behaviors emerged as central to successful leadership: initiating structure (called *job-centered leadership* at the University of Michigan and *concern for production* at the University of Texas) and considerate leader behavior (called *employee-centered leadership* at the University of Michigan and *concern for people* at the University of Texas).[11] These two leader behaviors form the basis for many of the leadership theories discussed in this chapter.

Initiating structure is the degree to which a leader structures the roles of followers by setting goals, giving directions, setting deadlines, and assigning tasks. A leader's ability to initiate structure primarily affects subordinates' job performance.

initiating structure
the degree to which a leader structures the roles of followers by setting goals, giving directions, setting deadlines, and assigning tasks

what *really* works

Leadership Traits That Do Make a Difference

For decades, researchers assumed that leadership traits such as drive, emotional stability, cognitive ability, and charisma were *not* related to effective leadership. More recent evidence, however, shows that there are reliable trait differences between leaders and nonleaders. In fact, 54 studies based on more than 6,000 people clearly indicate that in terms of leadership traits, "successful leaders are not like other people."

Traits and Perceptions of Leadership Effectiveness

Several leadership models argue that in order to be successful, leaders must be viewed as good leaders by their followers. (This is completely different from determining whether leaders actually improve organizational performance.) Consequently, one test of trait theory is whether leaders with particular traits are viewed as more or less effective leaders by their followers.

Intelligence. On average, there is a 75 percent chance that intelligent leaders will be seen as better leaders than less intelligent leaders.

INTELLIGENCE
probability of success: 75%

Dominance. On average, there is only a 57 percent chance that leaders with highly dominant personalities will be seen as better leaders than those with less dominant personalities.

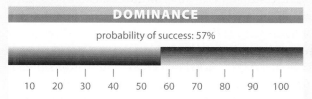

DOMINANCE
probability of success: 57%

Extroversion. On average, there is a 63 percent chance that extroverts will be seen as better leaders than introverts.

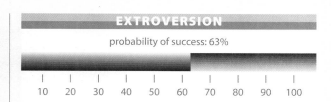

EXTROVERSION
probability of success: 63%

Charisma and Leadership Effectiveness

As discussed at the end of the chapter, *charismatic leadership* is the set of behavioral tendencies and personal characteristics of leaders that creates an exceptionally strong relationship between leaders and their followers. More specifically, charismatic leaders articulate a clear vision for the future that is based on strongly held values or morals; model those values by acting in a way consistent with the company's vision; communicate high performance expectations to followers; and display confidence in followers' abilities to achieve the vision.

Charisma and Performance. On average, there is a 72 percent chance that charismatic leaders will have better-performing followers and organizations than less charismatic leaders.

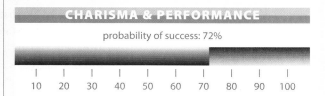

CHARISMA & PERFORMANCE
probability of success: 72%

Charisma and Perceived Leader Effectiveness. On average, there is an 89 percent chance that charismatic leaders will be perceived as more effective leaders than less charismatic leaders.

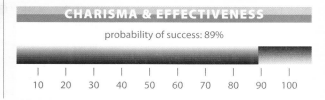

CHARISMA & EFFECTIVENESS
probability of success: 89%

Charisma and Leader Satisfaction. On average, there is a 90 percent chance that the followers of charismatic leaders will be more satisfied with their leaders than the followers of less charismatic leaders.[12]

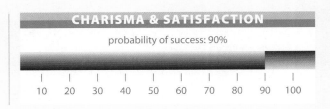

CHARISMA & SATISFACTION

probability of success: 90%

10	20	30	40	50	60	70	80	90	100

© PAUL CHESLEY/STONE/GETTY IMAGES

By briefing hotel staff every day, MGM Grand's CEO demonstrates consideration for the hotel and casino's 10,000 employees.

Consideration is the extent to which a leader is friendly, approachable, and supportive and shows concern for employees. Consideration primarily affects subordinates' job satisfaction. Specific leader consideration behaviors include listening to employees' problems and concerns, consulting with employees before making decisions, and treating employees as equals. When Gamal Azia became president of the *MGM GRAND HOTEL AND CASINO* in Las Vegas, he asked all employees, not just managers, to tell him how the hotel could improve. He was surprised to learn that hotel staff was not told what was happening in the hotel each day. Aziz listened and now the hotel's 10,000 employees start their work shift with a brief meeting, at which they are given a detailed overview of the conventions being held in the hotel, as well as the daily events and specials that the staff could offer to guests. The same approach has long been used in restaurants to let the waitstaff know about daily specials.[13]

Although researchers at all three universities generally agreed that initiating structure and consideration were basic leader behaviors, their interpretation differed on how these two behaviors are related to one another and which are necessary for effective leadership. The University of Michigan studies indicated that initiating structure and consideration were mutually exclusive behaviors on opposite ends of the same continuum. In other words, leaders who wanted to be more considerate would have to do less initiating of structure (and vice versa). The University of Michigan studies also indicated that only considerate leader behaviors (i.e., employee-centered behaviors) were associated with successful leadership. By contrast, researchers at Ohio State University and the University of Texas found that initiating structure and consideration were independent behaviors, meaning that leaders can be considerate and initiate structure at the same time. Additional evidence confirms this finding.[14] The same researchers also concluded that the most effective leaders were strong on both initiating structure and considerate leader behaviors.

consideration
the extent to which a leader is friendly, approachable, and supportive, and shows concern for employees

This "high–high" approach can be seen in the upper right corner of the Blake/Mouton leadership grid, shown in Exhibit 12.3. Blake and Mouton used two leadership behaviors, concern for people (i.e., consideration) and concern for production (i.e., initiating structure), to categorize five different leadership styles. Both behaviors are rated on a 9-point scale, with 1 representing "low" and 9 representing "high." Blake and Mouton suggest that a "high–high," or 9,9, leadership style is the best. They call this style *team management* because leaders who use it display a high concern for people (9) and a high concern for production (9).

By contrast, leaders use a 9,1 *authority–compliance* leadership style when they have a high concern for production and a low concern for people. A 1,9 *country club* style occurs when leaders care about having a friendly, enjoyable work environment but don't really pay much attention to production or performance. The worst leadership style, according to the grid, is the 1,1 *impoverished* leader, who shows little concern for people or production and does the bare minimum needed to keep his or her job. Finally, the 5,5 *middle-of-the-road* style occurs when leaders show a moderate amount of concern for both people and production.

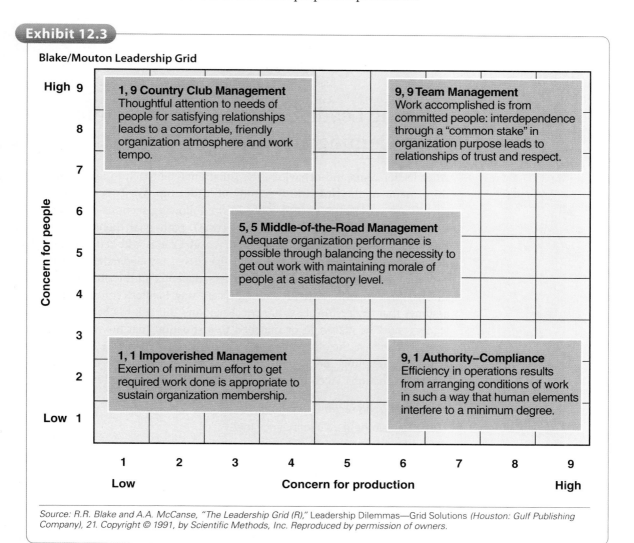

Exhibit 12.3

Blake/Mouton Leadership Grid

1, 9 Country Club Management
Thoughtful attention to needs of people for satisfying relationships leads to a comfortable, friendly organization atmosphere and work tempo.

9, 9 Team Management
Work accomplished is from committed people: interdependence through a "common stake" in organization purpose leads to relationships of trust and respect.

5, 5 Middle-of-the-Road Management
Adequate organization performance is possible through balancing the necessity to get out work with maintaining morale of people at a satisfactory level.

1, 1 Impoverished Management
Exertion of minimum effort to get required work done is appropriate to sustain organization membership.

9, 1 Authority–Compliance
Efficiency in operations results from arranging conditions of work in such a way that human elements interfere to a minimum degree.

Concern for people — High 9, 8, 7, 6, 5, 4, 3, 2, Low 1

Concern for production — Low 1 2 3 4 5 6 7 8 9 High

Source: R.R. Blake and A.A. McCanse, "The Leadership Grid (R)," Leadership Dilemmas—Grid Solutions (Houston: Gulf Publishing Company), 21. Copyright © 1991, by Scientific Methods, Inc. Reproduced by permission of owners.

Is the team management style, with a high concern for production and a high concern for people, the best leadership style? Logically, it would seem so. Why wouldn't you want to show high concern for both people and production? Nonetheless, nearly 50 years of research indicates that there isn't one best leadership style. The best leadership style depends on the situation. In other words, no one leadership behavior by itself and no one combination of leadership behaviors works well across all situations and employees.

REVIEW 12-2
. . . .

Who Leaders Are and What Leaders Do

Trait theory says that effective leaders possess traits or characteristics that differentiate them from nonleaders. Those traits are drive, the desire to lead, honesty/integrity, self-confidence, emotional stability, cognitive ability, and knowledge of the business. Traits alone aren't enough for successful leadership, however; leaders who have these traits (or many of them) must also behave in ways that encourage people to achieve group or organizational goals. Two key leader behaviors are initiating structure, which improves subordinate performance, and consideration, which improves subordinate satisfaction. There is no single best combination of these behaviors. The best leadership style depends on the situation.

12-3 Putting Leaders in the Right Situation: Fiedler's Contingency Theory

After leader traits and behaviors, the situational approach to leadership is the third major method used in the study of leadership. We'll review four major situational approaches to leadership in the following sections—Fiedler's contingency theory (the subject of this section), path–goal theory, Hersey and Blanchard's Situational Leadership theory, and Vroom and Yetton's normative decision model. All assume that the effectiveness of any **leadership style,** the way a leader generally behaves toward followers, depends on the situation.[15] Nonetheless, these theories differ in one significant way. Fiedler's contingency theory assumes that leadership styles are consistent and difficult to change. Therefore, leaders must be placed in or matched to a situation that fits their leadership style. By contrast, the other three situational theories all assume that leaders are capable of adapting and adjusting their leadership styles to fit the demands of different situations. Accordingly, there is no one "best" leadership style.

After reading this section, you should be able to:

12-3 explain Fiedler's contingency theory.

Fiedler's **contingency theory** states that in order to maximize work group performance, leaders must be matched to the right leadership situation.[16]

More specifically, as shown in Exhibit 12.4, the first basic assumption of Fiedler's theory is that leaders are effective when the work groups they lead perform well. So, instead of judging leaders' effectiveness by what they do (i.e., initiating structure and consideration) or who they are (i.e., trait theory),

---

leadership style
the way a leader generally behaves toward followers

contingency theory
a leadership theory that states that in order to maximize work group performance, leaders must be matched to the situation that best fits their leadership style

Fiedler assesses leaders by the conduct and performance of the people they supervise. Second, Fiedler assumes that leaders are generally unable to change their leadership styles and that they will be more effective when their styles are matched to the proper situation. Third, Fiedler assumes that the favorableness of a situation for a leader depends on the degree to which the situation permits the leader to influence the behavior of group members. Fiedler's third assumption is consistent with our definition of leadership as the process of influencing others to achieve group or organizational goals. In other words, in addition to traits, behaviors, and a favorable situation to match, leaders have to be allowed to lead.

Let's learn more about Fiedler's contingency theory by examining **12-3a the least preferred coworker and leadership styles, 12-3b situational favorableness,** and **12-3c how to match leadership styles to situations.**

Exhibit 12.4

Fiedler's Contingency Theory

Situational Favorableness + Leadership Style = Group Performance

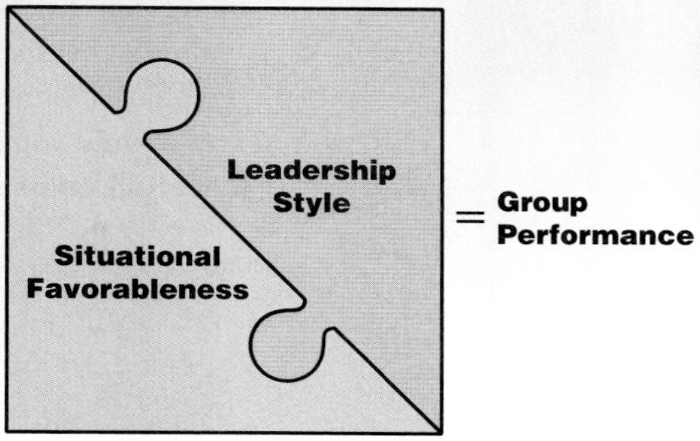

Good fit makes for higher performance levels.

© CENGAGE LEARNING

12-3a Leadership Style: Least Preferred Coworker

When Fiedler refers to *leadership style*, he means the way that leaders generally behave toward their followers. Fiedler also assumes that leadership styles are tied to leaders' underlying needs and personalities. Because personality and needs are relatively stable, he assumes that leaders are generally incapable of changing their leadership styles. In other words, the way that leaders treat people now is probably the way they've always treated others. So, according to Fiedler, if your boss's first instinct is to yell and scream and blame others, chances are he or she has always done that.

Fiedler uses a questionnaire called the Least Preferred Coworker (LPC) scale to measure leadership style; a sample of the scale is shown in Exhibit 12.5.

Exhibit 12.5

Sample from Fiedler's Least Preferred Coworker Scale

Pleasant	8	7	6	5	4	3	2	1	Unpleasant
Friendly	8	7	6	5	4	3	2	1	Unfriendly
Supportive	8	7	6	5	4	3	2	1	Hostile
Boring	1	2	3	4	5	6	7	8	Interesting
Gloomy	1	2	3	4	5	6	7	8	Cheerful
Insincere	1	2	3	4	5	6	7	8	Sincere

Source: F.E. Fiedler and M.M. Chemers, Improving Leadership Effectiveness: The Leader Match Concept, *2nd ed. (New York: John Wiley & Sons, 1984) Available at http://depts.washington.edu/psych/faculty/*cv/fiedler_cv.pdf, 23 March 2002. Reprinted by permission of the authors.*

(See the Self-Assessment at the end of this chapter for the full LPC scale.) When completing the LPC scale, people are instructed to consider all of the people with whom they have ever worked and then to choose the one person with whom they have worked *least* well. Fiedler explains, "This does not have to be the person you liked least well, but should be the one person with whom you have the most trouble getting the job done."[17]

Would you describe your LPC as pleasant, friendly, supportive, interesting, cheerful, and sincere? Or would you describe the person as unpleasant, un-friendly, hostile, boring, gloomy, and insincere? People who describe their LPC in a positive way (scoring 64 and above) have *relationship-oriented* leadership styles. After all, if they can still be positive about their LPC they must be people oriented. By contrast, people who describe their LPC in a negative way (scoring 57 or below) have *task-oriented* leadership styles. Given a choice, they'll focus first on getting the job done and second on making sure everyone gets along. Finally, those with moderate scores (from 58 to 63) have a more flexible leadership style and can be somewhat relationship oriented or somewhat task oriented.

12-3b Situational Favorableness

Fiedler assumes that leaders will be more effective when their leadership styles are matched to the proper situation. More specifically, Fiedler defines **situational favorableness** as the degree to which a particular situation either permits or denies a leader the chance to influence the behavior of group members.[18] In highly favorable situations, leaders find that their actions influence followers. But in highly unfavorable situations, leaders have little or no success influencing the people they are trying to lead.

Three situational factors determine the favorability of a situation: leader–member relations, task structure, and position power. The most important situational factor is **leader–member relations**, which refers to how well followers respect, trust, and like their leaders. When leader–member relations are good, followers trust the leader and there is a friendly work atmosphere. **Task structure** is the degree to which the requirements of a subordinate's tasks are clearly specified. With highly structured tasks, employees have clear job responsibilities, goals, and procedures. **Position power** is the degree to which leaders are able to hire, fire, reward, and punish workers. The more influence leaders have over hiring, firing, rewards, and punishments, the greater their power.

Leader–member relations, task structure, and position power can be combined into eight situations that differ in their favorability to leaders. In general, the most favorable situations for leaders occur when followers like and trust their leaders, when followers know what to do because their tasks are highly structured, and when leaders have the power to hire, fire, reward, and punish workers. In this situation, it's relatively easy for a leader to influence followers. By contrast, the least favorable situations for leaders occur when followers don't like or trust their leaders, when followers are not sure what they're supposed to be doing because their tasks or jobs are highly unstructured, and when leaders don't have the ability to hire, fire, reward, or punish the people who work for them. In short, it's very difficult to influence followers under these conditions.

situational favorableness
the degree to which a particular situation either permits or denies a leader the chance to influence the behavior of group members

leader–member relations
the degree to which followers respect, trust, and like their leaders

task structure
the degree to which the requirements of a subordinate's tasks are clearly specified

position power
the degree to which leaders are able to hire, fire, reward, and punish workers

12-3c Matching Leadership Styles to Situations

After studying thousands of leaders and followers in hundreds of different situations, Fiedler found that the performance of relationship- and task-oriented leaders followed the pattern displayed in Exhibit 12.6.

Relationship-oriented leaders with high LPC scores were better leaders (i.e., their groups performed more effectively) under moderately favorable situations. In moderately favorable situations, the leader may be liked somewhat, tasks may be somewhat structured, and the leader may have some position power. In this situation, a relationship-oriented leader improves leader–member relations, which is the most important of the three situational factors. In turn, morale and performance improve.

By contrast, as Exhibit 12.6 shows, task-oriented leaders with low LPC scores are better leaders in highly favorable and unfavorable situations. Task-oriented leaders do well in favorable situations where leaders are liked, tasks are structured, and the leader has the power to hire, fire, reward, and punish. In these favorable situations, task-oriented leaders effectively step on the gas of a well-tuned car. Their focus on performance sets the goal for the group, which then charges forward to meet it. But task-oriented leaders also do well in unfavorable situations where leaders are disliked, tasks are unstructured, and the leader doesn't have the power to hire, fire, reward, and punish. In these unfavorable situations, the task-oriented leader sets goals, which focus attention on performance and clarify what needs to be done, thus overcoming low task structure. This is enough to jump-start performance even if workers don't like or trust the leader.

Finally, though not shown in Exhibit 12.6, people with moderate LPC scores, who can be somewhat relationship oriented or somewhat task oriented, tend to do fairly well in all situations because they can adapt their behavior. Typically, though, they don't perform quite as well as relationship-oriented or task-oriented leaders whose leadership styles are well matched to the situation.

Recall, however, that Fiedler assumes leaders to be incapable of changing their leadership styles. Accordingly, the key to applying Fiedler's contingency theory in the workplace is to accurately measure and match leaders

Exhibit 12.6

Matching Leadership Styles to Situations

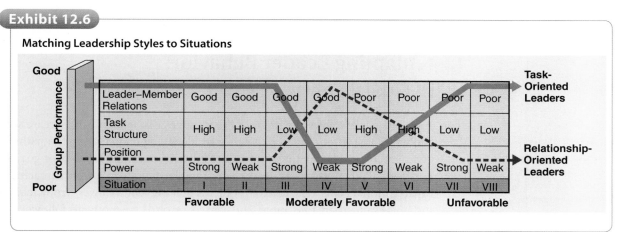

Leader–Member Relations	Good	Good	Good	Good	Poor	Poor	Poor	Poor
Task Structure	High	High	Low	Low	High	High	Low	Low
Position Power	Strong	Weak	Strong	Weak	Strong	Weak	Strong	Weak
Situation	I	II	III	IV	V	VI	VII	VIII

Favorable · Moderately Favorable · Unfavorable

© CENGAGE LEARNING

to situations or to teach leaders how to change situational favorableness by changing leader–member relations, task structure, or position power. Though matching or placing leaders in appropriate situations works particularly well, practicing managers have had little luck reengineering situations to fit their leadership styles. The primary problem, as you've no doubt realized, is the complexity of the theory.

In a study designed to teach leaders how to reengineer their situations to fit their leadership styles, Fiedler found that most of the leaders simply did not understand what they were supposed to do to change their situations. Furthermore, if they didn't like their LPC profile (perhaps they felt they were more relationship oriented than their scores indicated), they arbitrarily changed it to better suit their view of themselves. Of course, the theory won't work as well if leaders are attempting to change situational factors to fit their perceived leadership style rather than their real leadership style.[19]

REVIEW 12-3

....

Putting Leaders in the Right Situation: Fiedler's Contingency Theory
Fiedler's theory assumes that leaders are effective when their work groups perform well, that leaders are unable to change their leadership styles, that leadership styles must be matched to the proper situation, and that favorable situations permit leaders to influence group members. According to the Least Preferred Coworker (LPC) scale, there are two basic leadership styles. People who describe their LPC in a positive way have relationship-oriented leadership styles. People who describe their LPC in a negative way have task-oriented leadership styles. Situational favorableness occurs when leaders can influence followers and is determined by leader–member relations, task structure, and position power. In general, relationship-oriented leaders with high LPC scores are better leaders under moderately favorable situations, whereas task-oriented leaders with low LPC scores are better leaders in highly favorable and unfavorable situations. Because Fiedler assumes that leaders are incapable of changing their leadership styles, the key is to accurately measure and match leaders to situations or to teach leaders how to change situational factors. Although matching or placing leaders in appropriate situations works well, reengineering situations to fit leadership styles doesn't, because the model is complex and difficult for people to understand.

12-4 Adapting Leader Behavior: Path–Goal Theory

path–goal theory
a leadership theory that states that leaders can increase subordinate satisfaction and performance by clarifying and clearing the paths to goals and by increasing the number and kinds of rewards available for goal attainment

Just as its name suggests, **path–goal theory** states that leaders can increase subordinate satisfaction and performance by clarifying and clearing the paths to goals and by increasing the number and kinds of rewards available for goal attainment. Said another way, leaders need to clarify how followers can achieve organizational goals, take care of problems that prevent followers from achieving goals, and then find more and varied rewards to motivate followers to achieve those goals.[20]

After reading this section, you should be able to:

12-4 describe how path–goal theory works.

Leaders must meet two conditions for path clarification, path clearing, and rewards to increase followers' motivation and effort. First, leader behavior must be a source of immediate or future satisfaction for followers. The things you do as a leader must either please your followers today or lead to activities or rewards that will satisfy them in the future. Second, while providing the coaching, guidance, support, and rewards necessary for effective work performance, leader behaviors must complement and not duplicate the characteristics of followers' work environments. Thus, leader behaviors must offer something unique and valuable to followers beyond what they're already experiencing as they do their jobs or what they can already do for themselves. In contrast to Fiedler's contingency theory, path–goal theory assumes that leaders *can* change and adapt their leadership styles. Exhibit 12.7 illustrates this process, showing that leaders change and adapt their leadership styles contingent on their subordinates or the environment in which those subordinates work.

Let's learn more about path–goal theory by examining **12-4a the four kinds of leadership styles that leaders use, 12-4b the subordinate and environmental contingency factors that determine when different leader styles are effective,** and **12-4c the outcomes of path–goal theory in improving employee satisfaction and performance.**

12-4a Leadership Styles

As illustrated in Exhibit 12.7, the four leadership styles in path–goal theory are directive, supportive, participative, and achievement oriented.[21] **Directive leadership** involves letting employees know precisely what is expected of them, giving them specific guidelines for performing tasks, scheduling work, setting standards of performance, and making sure that people follow standard rules and regulations. Frustrated that his Detroit-based executives were focused on North America, *GM* CEO Daniel Akerson told his team, "One of three people on this planet lives in China or India—we need cars for them." When he learned it would take four years to bring model cars to dealer showrooms, he replied, "During World War II, GM

directive leadership
a leadership style in which the leader lets employees know precisely what is expected of them, gives them specific guidelines for performing tasks, schedules work, sets standards of performance, and makes sure that people follow standard rules and regulations

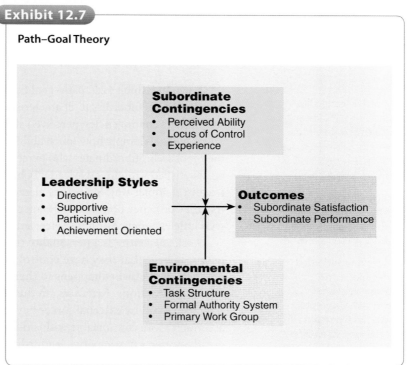

Exhibit 12.7

Path–Goal Theory

Subordinate Contingencies
- Perceived Ability
- Locus of Control
- Experience

Leadership Styles
- Directive
- Supportive
- Participative
- Achievement Oriented

Outcomes
- Subordinate Satisfaction
- Subordinate Performance

Environmental Contingencies
- Task Structure
- Formal Authority System
- Primary Work Group

© CENGAGE LEARNING

produced tanks and equipment within four years. Why should it take four years [with computer-aided design tools] to put a car out?" After reviewing engine plans with top managers, he asked, "Why do we have 18 types of engines? We have only four brands." When told it was GM's tradition to make a variety of engines, Akerson replied, "We have to break out of the old way of thinking around here," and directed his executives to benchmark how many engines Toyota made and then "take out complexity and save money." A year later, GM was producing only a dozen engines.[22]

Supportive leadership involves being approachable and friendly to employees, showing concern for them and their welfare, treating them as equals, and creating a friendly climate. Supportive leadership is very similar to considerate leader behavior. Supportive leadership often results in employee satisfaction with the job and with leaders. This leadership style may also result in improved performance when it increases employee confidence, lowers employee job stress, or improves relations and trust between employees and leaders.[23] **Participative leadership** involves consulting employees for their suggestions and input before making decisions. Participation in decision making should help followers understand which goals are most important and clarify the paths to accomplishing them. Furthermore, when people participate in decisions, they become more committed to making them work.

Achievement-oriented leadership means setting challenging goals, having high expectations of employees, and displaying confidence that employees will assume responsibility and put forth extraordinary effort. Though he's an introvert, *GOOGLE* cofounder and CEO Larry Page is clearly an achievement-oriented leader. A former Google executive says, "When people come to Larry with ideas, he always wants it bigger. His whole point is that only Google has the kind of resources to make big bets. The asset that Larry brings [to the people he leads] is to say, 'Let's go and make big things happen.'"[24]

12-4b Subordinate and Environmental Contingencies

As shown in Exhibit 12.7, path–goal theory specifies that leader behaviors should be adapted to subordinate characteristics. The theory identifies three kinds of subordinate contingencies: perceived ability, experience, and locus of control. *Perceived ability* is simply how much ability subordinates believe they have for doing their jobs well. Subordinates who perceive that they have a great deal of ability will be dissatisfied with directive leader behaviors. Experienced employees are likely to react in a similar way. Since they already know how to do their jobs (or perceive that they do), they don't need or want close supervision. By contrast, subordinates with little experience or little perceived ability will welcome directive leadership.

Locus of control is a personality measure that indicates the extent to which people believe that they have control over what happens to them in life. *Internals* believe that what happens to them, good or bad, is largely a result of their choices and actions. *Externals*, on the other hand, believe that what happens to them is caused by external forces beyond their control. Accordingly, externals are much more comfortable with a directive leadership style, whereas internals greatly prefer a participative leadership style because they like to have a say in what goes on at work.

supportive leadership
a leadership style in which the leader is friendly and approachable to employees, shows concern for employees and their welfare, treats them as equals, and creates a friendly climate

participative leadership
a leadership style in which the leader consults employees for their suggestions and input before making decisions

achievement-oriented leadership
a leadership style in which the leader sets challenging goals, has high expectations of employees, and displays confidence that employees will assume responsibility and put forth extraordinary effort

Path–goal theory specifies that leader behaviors should complement rather than duplicate the characteristics of followers' work environments. There are three kinds of environmental contingencies: task structure, the formal authority system, and the primary work group. As in Fiedler's contingency theory, *task structure* is the degree to which the requirements of a subordinate's tasks are clearly specified. When task structure is low and tasks are unclear, directive leadership should be used because it complements the work environment. When task structure is high and tasks are clear, however, directive leadership is not needed because it duplicates what task structure provides. Alternatively, when tasks are stressful, frustrating, or dissatisfying, leaders should respond with supportive leadership.

The *formal authority system* is an organization's set of procedures, rules, and policies. When the formal authority system is unclear, directive leadership complements the situation by reducing uncertainty and increasing clarity. But when the formal authority system is clear, directive leadership is redundant and should not be used.

Primary work group refers to the amount of work-oriented participation or emotional support that is provided by an employee's immediate work group. Participative leadership should be used when tasks are complex and there is little existing work-oriented participation in the primary work group. When tasks are stressful, frustrating, or repetitive, supportive leadership is called for.

Finally, because keeping track of all of these subordinate and environmental contingencies can get a bit confusing, Exhibit 12.8 provides a summary of when directive, supportive, participative, and achievement-oriented leadership styles should be used.

12-4c Outcomes

Does following path–goal theory improve subordinate satisfaction and performance? Preliminary evidence suggests that it does.[25] In particular, people who

---

Exhibit 12.8

Path–Goal Theory: When to Use Directive, Supportive, Participative, or Achievement-Oriented Leadership

Directive Leadership	Supportive Leadership	Participative Leadership	Achievement-Oriented Leadership
Unstructured tasks	Structured, simple, repetitive tasks	Experienced workers Complex tasks	Unchallenging tasks
Inexperienced workers	Stressful, frustrating tasks	Workers with high perceived ability	
Workers with low perceived ability	When workers lack confidence	Workers with internal locus of control	
Workers with external locus of control	Clear formal authority system	Workers not satisfied with rewards	
Unclear formal authority system			

© CENGAGE LEARNING

work for supportive leaders are much more satisfied with their jobs and their bosses. Likewise, people who work for directive leaders are more satisfied with their jobs and bosses (but not quite as much as when their bosses are supportive) and perform their jobs better too. Does adapting one's leadership style to subordinate and environmental characteristics improve subordinate satisfaction and performance? At this point, because it is difficult to completely test this complex theory, it's too early to tell.[26] However, because the data clearly show that it makes sense for leaders to be both supportive *and* directive, it also makes sense that leaders could improve subordinate satisfaction and performance by adding participative and achievement-oriented leadership styles to their capabilities as leaders.

REVIEW 12-4

Adapting Leader Behavior: Path–Goal Theory

Path–goal theory states that leaders can increase subordinate satisfaction and performance by clarifying and clearing the paths to goals and by increasing the number and kinds of rewards available for goal attainment. For this to work, however, leader behavior must be a source of immediate or future satisfaction for followers and must complement rather than duplicate the characteristics of followers' work environments. In contrast to Fiedler's contingency theory, path–goal theory assumes that leaders can and do change and adapt their leadership styles (directive, supportive, participative, and achievement oriented), depending on their subordinates (experience, perceived ability, internal or external) or the environment in which those subordinates work (task structure, formal authority system, or primary work group).

12-5 Adapting Leader Behavior: Hersey and Blanchard's Situational Leadership® Theory

Have you ever had a new job that you didn't know how to do, and your boss was not around to help you learn it? Conversely, have you ever known exactly how to do your job, but your boss kept treating you as though you didn't?

After reading this section, you should be able to:

12-5 discuss Hersey and Blanchard's Situational Leadership theory.

Hersey and Blanchard's Situational Leadership® theory is based on the idea of follower readiness. Hersey and Blanchard argue that employees have different levels of readiness for handling different jobs, responsibilities, and work assignments. Accordingly, Hersey and Blanchard's **situational theory** states that leaders need to adjust their leadership styles to match followers' readiness.[27]

Let's learn more about Hersey and Blanchard's situational theory by examining **12-5a worker readiness** and **12-5b different leadership styles.**

12-5a Worker Readiness

Worker readiness is the ability and willingness to take responsibility for directing one's behavior at work. Readiness is composed of two components. *Job readiness* consists of the amount of knowledge, skill, ability, and experience people have

situational theory
a leadership theory that states that leaders need to adjust their leadership styles to match their followers' readiness

worker readiness
the ability and willingness to take responsibility for directing one's behavior at work

to perform their jobs. As you would expect, people with greater skill, ability, and experience do a better job of supervising their own work. *Psychological readiness*, on the other hand, is a feeling of self-confidence or self-respect. Confident people are better at guiding their own work than insecure people are. Hersey and Blanchard combine job readiness and psychological readiness to produce four different levels of readiness in their situational leadership theory. The lowest level, R1, represents insecure people who are neither willing nor able to take responsibility for guiding their own work. R2 represents people who are confident and willing, but not able, to take responsibility for guiding their own work. R3 represents people who are insecure and able, but not willing, to take responsibility for guiding their own work. And R4 represents people who are confident, willing, and able to take responsibility for guiding their own work. It's important to note that a follower's readiness is usually task specific. For example, you may be highly confident and capable when it comes to personal computers but know nothing about setting up budgets for planning purposes. You would possess readiness (R4) with respect to computers, but not with respect to budgets.

12-5b Leadership Styles

Similar to Blake and Mouton's managerial grid, situational theory defines leadership styles in terms of task behavior (i.e., concern for production) and relationship behavior (i.e., concern for people). These two behaviors can be combined to form four different leadership styles: telling, selling, participating, and delegating. Leaders choose one of these styles, depending on the readiness a follower has for a specific task.

A *telling* leadership style (high task behavior and low relationship behavior) is based on one-way communication in which followers are told what, how, when, and where to do particular tasks. Telling is used when people are at the R1 stage. For instance, someone using a telling leadership style would identify all the steps in a project and give explicit instructions on exactly how to execute each one.

A *selling* leadership style (high task behavior and high relationship behavior) involves two-way communication and psychological support to encourage followers to own, or buy into, particular ways of doing things. Selling is used most appropriately at the R2 stage.

A *participating* style (low task behavior and high relationship behavior) is based on two-way communication and shared decision making. Participating is used with employees at R3. Because the problem is with motivation rather than ability, someone using a participating leadership style might solicit ideas from a subordinate about a project and let the subordinate get started, but ask to review progress along the way.

A *delegating* style (low task behavior and low relationship behavior) is used when leaders basically let workers run their own show and make their own decisions. Delegating is used for people at R4. For instance, someone using a delegating leadership style might say, "We're going to start a company newsletter. You've got 10 days to do it. Run with it. Let me know when you've got it done. I'll e-mail you a couple of ideas, but other than that, do what you think is best. Thanks."

In general, as people become more ready and thus more willing and able to guide their own behavior, leaders should become less task-oriented and more relationship-oriented. As people become even more ready, leaders should become less task-oriented *and* less relationship-oriented until people eventually manage their own work with little input from their leaders.

How well does Hersey and Blanchard's situational theory work? Despite its intuitive appeal (managers and consultants tend to prefer it over Fiedler's contingency theory because of its underlying logic and simplicity), most studies don't support situational theory.[28] Although managers generally do a good job of judging followers' readiness levels, the theory doesn't seem to work well except at lower levels, where a telling style is recommended for people who are insecure and neither willing nor able to take responsibility for guiding their own work.[29]

REVIEW 12-5
. . . .

Leader Behavior: Hersey and Blanchard's Situational Leadership® Theory
According to situational theory, leaders need to adjust their leadership styles to match their followers' readiness, which is the ability (job readiness) and willingness (psychological readiness) to take responsibility for directing one's work. Job readiness and psychological readiness combine to produce four different levels of readiness (R1–R4). The levels vary based on people's confidence, ability, and willingness to guide their own work. Situational theory combines task and relationship behavior to create four leadership styles—telling (R1), selling (R2), participating (R3), and delegating (R4)—that are used with employees at different readiness levels.

12-6 Adapting Leader Behavior: Normative Decision Theory

For years, your company has insisted on formal business attire for men and women. Now, however, you want to make a change to casual wear. Do you make the decision yourself and announce it, or do you consult your employees before making the decision?

After reading this section, you should be able to:

12-6 explain the normative decision theory.

Many people believe that making tough decisions is at the heart of leadership. Yet experienced leaders will tell you that deciding *how* to make decisions is just as important. The **normative decision theory** (also known as the *Vroom-Yetton-Jago model*) helps leaders decide how much employee participation (from none to letting employees make the entire decision) should be used when making decisions.[30]

Let's learn more about normative decision theory by investigating **12-6a decision styles** and **12-6b decision quality and acceptance.**

12-6a Decision Styles

Unlike nearly all of the other leadership theories discussed in this chapter, which have specified *leadership* styles, that is, the way a leader generally behaves

normative decision theory
a theory that suggests how leaders can determine an appropriate amount of employee participation when making decisions

toward followers, the normative decision theory specifies five different *decision styles*, or ways of making decisions. (See Chapter 4 for a more complete review of decision making in organizations.) As shown in Exhibit 12.9, those styles vary from *autocratic decisions* (AI or AII) on the left, in which leaders make the decisions by themselves, to *consultative decisions* (CI or CII), in which leaders share problems with subordinates but still make the decisions themselves, to *group decisions* (GII) on the right, in which leaders share the problems with subordinates and then have the group make the decisions.

GE AIRCRAFT ENGINES in Durham, North Carolina, uses a similar approach when making decisions. According to *Fast Company* magazine, "At GE/Durham, every decision is either an 'A' decision, a 'B' decision, or a 'C' decision. An 'A' decision is one that the plant manager makes herself, without consulting anyone."[31] " 'B' decisions are also made by the plant manager but with input from the people affected. 'C' decisions, the most common type, are made by consensus, by the people directly involved, with plenty of discussion. With 'C' decisions, the view of the plant manager doesn't necessarily carry more weight than the views of those affected."[32]

12-6b Decision Quality and Acceptance

According to the normative decision theory, using the right degree of employee participation improves the quality of decisions and the extent to which employees accept and are committed to decisions. Exhibit 12.10 lists the decision rules that normative decision theory uses to increase the quality of a decision and the degree to which

Exhibit 12.9

Decision Styles and Levels of Employee Participation

Leader solves the problem or makes the decision

Leader is willing to accept any decision supported by the entire group

AI	AII	CI	CII	GII
Using information available at the time, the leader solves the problem or makes the decision.	The leader obtains necessary information from employees, and then selects a solution to the problem. When asked to share information, employees may or may not be told what the problem is.	The leader shares the problem and gets ideas and suggestions from relevant employees on an individual basis. Individuals are not brought together as a group. Then the leader makes the decision, which may or may not reflect their input.	The leader shares the problem with employees as a group, obtains their ideas and suggestions, and then makes the decision, which may or may not reflect their input.	The leader shares the problem with employees as a group. Together, the leader and employees generate and evaluate alternatives and try to reach an agreement on a solution. The leader acts as a facilitator and does not try to influence the group. The leader is willing to accept and implement any solution that has the support of the entire group.

Source: Adapted from Table 2.1 Decision Methods for Group and Individual Problems and Figure 9.3 Decision-Process Flow Chart for Both Individual and Group Problems, from Leadership and Decision Making, *by Victor H. Vroom and Philip W. Yetton, © 1973. Reprinted by permission of the University of Pittsburg Press.*

Doing the Right Thing

A Leadership Gap

The shift from one leader to another is one of the most crucial times for a company, and very few organizations have planned for the process. A smooth transition to a successor can help a company maintain, and even expand, the company's success. A rough transition, however, can throw the company into chaos as it struggles to find a coherent vision and strategy. This is the reason why 98 percent of global companies recently surveyed believed that a CEO succession plan was critically important to the organization. However, only 35 percent of responding companies actually have a plan set in place. It may sound strange, of course, to think about how you're going to find a new leader when you already have one. But CEOs don't just retire when you're ready for them to; they can resign suddenly, fall ill, or even be fired. So do the right thing, plan for the future, and set up a solid succession plan so that your company's stability isn't jeopardized.[33]

employees accept and commit to it. The quality, leader information, subordinate information, goal congruence, and problem structure rules are used to increase decision quality. For example, the leader information rule states that if a leader doesn't have enough information to make a decision on his or her own, then the leader should not use an autocratic decision style.

The commitment probability, subordinate conflict, and commitment requirement rules shown in Exhibit 12.10 are used to increase employee acceptance and commitment to decisions. For example, the commitment requirement rule says that if decision acceptance and commitment are important, and the subordinates share the organization's goals, then you shouldn't use an autocratic or consultative style. In other words, if followers want to do what's best for the company and you need their acceptance and commitment to make a decision work, then use a group decision style and let them make the decision.

Exhibit 12.10

Normative Theory Decision Rules

Decision Rules to Increase Decision Quality

Quality Rule. If the quality of the decision is important, then don't use an autocratic decision style.

Leader Information Rule. If the quality of the decision is important, and if the leader doesn't have enough information to make the decision on his or her own, then don't use an autocratic decision style.

Subordinate Information Rule. If the quality of the decision is important, and if the subordinates don't have enough information to make the decision themselves, then don't use a group decision style.

Goal Congruence Rule. If the quality of the decision is important, and subordinates' goals are different from the organization's goals, then don't use a group decision style.

Problem Structure Rule. If the quality of the decision is important, the leader doesn't have enough information to make the decision on his or her own, and the problem is unstructured, then don't use an autocratic decision style.

Decision Rules to Increase Decision Acceptance

Commitment Probability Rule. If having subordinates accept and commit to the decision is important, then don't use an autocratic decision style.

Subordinate Conflict Rule. If having subordinates accept the decision is important and critical to successful implementation and subordinates are likely to disagree or end up in conflict over the decision, then don't use an autocratic or consultative decision style.

Commitment Requirement Rule. If having subordinates accept the decision is absolutely required for successful implementation and subordinates share the organization's goals, then don't use an autocratic or consultative style.

Source: V.H. Vroom, "Leadership," in Handbook of Industrial and Organizational Psychology, *ed. M.D. Dunnette (Chicago: Rand McNally, 1976);* V.H. Vroom and A.G. Jago, The New Leadership: Managing Participation in Organizations *(Englewood Cliffs, NJ: Prentice Hall, 1988)*

© ISTOCKPHOTO/LOOPS7

As you can see, these decision rules help leaders improve decision quality and follower acceptance and commitment by eliminating decision styles that don't fit the particular decision or situation they're facing. Normative decision theory then operationalizes these decision rules in the form of yes/no questions, which are shown in the decision tree displayed in Exhibit 12.11. You start at the left side of the model and answer the first question, How important is the technical quality of this decision? by choosing "high" or "low." Then you continue by answering each question as you proceed along the decision tree until you get to a recommended decision style. Let's use the model to make the decision of whether to change from a formal business attire policy to a casual wear policy. The problem sounds simple, but it is actually more complex than you might think. Follow the orange line in Exhibit 12.11 as we work through the decision in the following discussion.

Problem: Change to Casual Wear?

1. *Quality requirement: How important is the technical quality of this decision?* High. This question has to do with whether there are quality differences in the alternatives and whether those quality differences matter. In other words: Is there a lot at stake in this decision? Although most people would assume that quality isn't an issue here, it really is, given the incredibly strong reactions that people have regarding the rules for casual wear at their companies.

2. *Commitment requirement: How important is subordinate commitment to the decision?* High. Changes in culture, like dress codes, require subordinate commitment or they fail.

3. *Leader's information: Do you have sufficient information to make a high-quality decision?* Yes. Let's assume that you've done your homework. Much has been written about casual wear, from how to make the change, to the effects it has in companies (almost all positive).

4. *Commitment probability: If you were to make the decision by yourself, is it reasonably certain that your subordinate(s) would be committed to the decision?* No. Studies of casual wear find that employees' reactions are almost uniformly positive. Nonetheless, employees are likely to be angry if you change something as personal as clothing policies without consulting them.

5. *Goal congruence: Do subordinates share the organizational goals to be attained in solving this problem?* Yes. The goals that usually accompany a change to casual dress policies are a more informal culture, better communication, and less money spent on business attire.

6. *Subordinate information: Do subordinates have sufficient information to make a high-quality decision?* No. Most employees know little about casual wear policies or even what constitutes casual wear in most companies. Consequently, most companies have to educate employees about casual wear practices and policies before making a decision.

7. *CII is the answer:* With a CII, or consultative decision process, the leader shares the problem with employees as a group, obtains their ideas and suggestions, and then makes the decision, which may or may not reflect their input. So, given the answers to these questions (remember, different managers won't necessarily answer these questions the same way), the normative decision theory recommends that leaders consult with their subordinates before deciding whether to change to a casual wear policy.

Exhibit 12.11

Normative Decision Theory Tree for Determining the Level of Participation in Decision Making

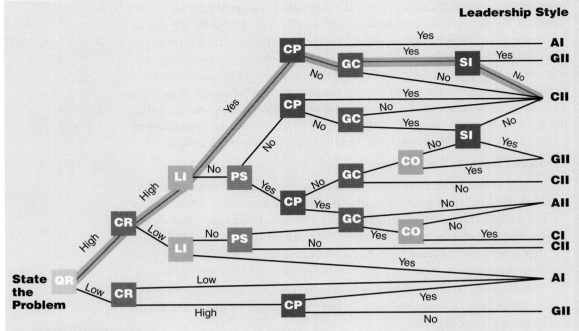

Problem Attributes

QR	Quality requirement:	How important is the technical quality of this decision?
CR	Commitment requirement:	How important is subordinate commitment to the decision?
LI	Leader's information:	Do you have sufficient information to make a high-quality decision?
PS	Problem structure:	Is the problem well structured?
CP	Commitment probability:	If you were to make the decision by yourself, is it reasonably certain that your subordinate(s) would be committed to the decision?
GC	Goal congruence:	Do subordinates share the organizational goals to be attained in solving this problem?
CO	Subordinate conflict:	Is conflict among subordinates over preferred solutions likely?
SI	Subordinate information:	Do subordinates have sufficient information to make a high-quality decision?

Source: Excerpt from Table 2.1 Decision Methods for Group and Individual Problems, and the Normative Decision Theory Tree for Determining the Level of Participation in Decision Making from Figure 9.3 Decision-Process Flow Chart for Both Individual and Group Problems, from Leadership and Decision Making by Victor H. Vroom and Philip W. Yetton, © 1973. Reprinted by permission of the University of Pittsburgh Press.

How well does the normative decision theory work? A prominent leadership scholar has described it as the best supported of all leadership theories.[34] In general, the more managers violate the decision rules in Exhibit 12.10, the less effective their decisions are, especially with respect to subordinate acceptance and commitment.[35]

REVIEW 12-6

. . . .

Adapting Leader Behavior: Normative Decision Theory

The normative decision theory helps leaders decide how much employee participation should be used when making decisions. Using the right degree of employee participation improves the quality of decisions and the extent to which employees accept and are committed to decisions. The theory specifies five different decision styles or ways of making decisions: autocratic decisions (AI or AII), consultative decisions (CI or CII), and group decisions (GII). The theory improves decision quality via the quality, leader information, subordinate information, goal congruence, and unstructured problem decision rules. The theory improves employee commitment and acceptance via the commitment probability, subordinate conflict, and commitment requirement decision rules. These decision rules help leaders improve decision quality and follower acceptance and commitment by eliminating decision styles that don't fit the decision or situation they're facing. Normative decision theory then makes these decision rules more concrete by framing them as yes/no questions, as shown in the decision tree displayed in Exhibit 12.11.

12-7 Strategic Leadership and Visionary Leadership

Thus far, you have read about three major leadership ideas: traits, behaviors, and situational theories. Leader *traits* are relatively stable characteristics such as abilities or psychological motives. Traits capture who effective leaders are. Leader *behaviors* are the actions leaders take to influence others to achieve group or organizational goals. Behaviors capture what effective leaders do (i.e., initiate structure and consideration). And *situational theories* indicate that the effectiveness of a leadership style, the way a leader generally behaves toward followers, depends on the situation. Situational theories capture what leaders need to do or not do in particular situations or circumstances. This final part of the chapter introduces a fourth major leadership idea—strategic leadership—and its components: visionary, charismatic, and transformational leadership.

Strategic leadership is the ability to anticipate, envision, maintain flexibility, think strategically, and work with others to initiate changes that will create a positive future for an organization.[36] HEIDRICK & STRUGGLES (H & S), one of the world's largest executive search firms, helps companies find CEOs, board members, and senior executives. When the economy turned down, CEO Kevin Kelly realized it was time to dramatically change the company's strategy. Currently, 95 percent of its business is executive search. But with online resources like LinkedIn.com making it easier to find and identify talent, and NASDAQ's boardrecruiting.com charging just $350 per candidate to help companies find board members, Kelly wants to shrink search to just 50 percent of the business.

strategic leadership
the ability to anticipate, envision, maintain flexibility, think strategically, and work with others to initiate changes that will create a positive future for an organization

In its place, he wants to grow leadership advisory services, such as executive retention and succession, to 40 percent.[37] Thus, strategic leadership captures how leaders inspire their companies to change and their followers to give extraordinary effort to accomplish organizational goals.

After reading this section, you should be able to:

12-7 explain how visionary leadership (i.e., charismatic and transformational leadership) helps leaders achieve strategic leadership.

In Chapter 4, we defined a purpose statement, which is often referred to as an organizational mission or vision, as a statement of a company's purpose or reason for existing. Similarly, visionary leadership creates a positive image of the future that motivates organizational members and provides direction for future planning and goal setting.[38]

Two kinds of visionary leadership are **12-7a charismatic leadership** and **12-7b transformational leadership**.

12-7a Charismatic Leadership

Charisma is a Greek word meaning "divine gift." The ancient Greeks saw people with charisma as inspired by the gods and capable of incredible accomplishments. German sociologist Max Weber viewed charisma as a special bond between leaders and followers.[39] Weber wrote that the special qualities of charismatic leaders enable them to strongly influence followers.

Indeed, charismatic leaders tend to emerge in times of crisis, and the radical solutions they propose enhance the admiration that followers feel for them. Indeed, charismatic leaders tend to have incredible influence over followers who may be inspired by their leaders and become fanatically devoted to them. From this perspective, charismatic leaders are often seen as larger than life or more special than other employees of the company.

Charismatic leaders have strong, confident, dynamic personalities that attract followers and enable the leaders to create strong bonds with their followers. Followers trust charismatic leaders, are loyal to them, and are inspired to work toward the accomplishment of the leader's vision. Followers who become devoted to charismatic leaders may go to extraordinary lengths to please them. Therefore, we can define charismatic leadership as the behavioral tendencies and personal characteristics of leaders that create an exceptionally strong relationship between them and their followers. Charismatic leaders also

- Articulate a clear vision for the future that is based on strongly held values or morals;
- Model those values by acting in a way consistent with the vision;
- Communicate high performance expectations to followers; and
- Display confidence in followers' abilities to achieve the vision.[40]

Does charismatic leadership work? Studies indicate that it often does. In general, the followers of charismatic leaders are more committed and satisfied, are better performers, are more likely to trust their leaders, and simply work harder.[41] Nonetheless, charismatic leadership also has risks that are at least as large as its

visionary leadership
leadership that creates a positive image of the future that motivates organizational members and provides direction for future planning and goal setting

charismatic leadership
the behavioral tendencies and personal characteristics of leaders that create an exceptionally strong relationship between them and their followers

© FOURMY MARIO/ABACA/NEWSCOM

benefits. The problems are likely to occur with ego-driven charismatic leaders who take advantage of fanatical followers.

In general, there are two kinds of charismatic leaders, ethical charismatics and unethical charismatics.[42] **Ethical charismatics** provide developmental opportunities for followers, are open to positive and negative feedback, recognize others' contributions, share information, and have moral standards that emphasize the larger interests of the group, organization, or society. By contrast, **unethical charismatics** control and manipulate followers, do what is best for themselves instead of their organizations, want to hear only positive feedback, share information that is beneficial only to themselves, and have moral standards that put their interests before everyone else's. Because followers can become just as committed to unethical charismatics as to ethical charismatics, unethical charismatics pose a tremendous risk for companies. According to *Fast Company*, "We're worshipful of top executives who seem charismatic, visionary, and tough. So long as they're lifting profits and stock prices, we're willing to overlook that they can also be callous, cunning, manipulative, deceitful, verbally and psychologically abusive, remorseless, exploitative, self-delusional, irresponsible, and megalomaniacal."[43]

There are stark differences between ethical and unethical charismatics on several leader behaviors: exercising power, creating the vision, communicating with followers, accepting feedback, stimulating followers intellectually, developing followers, and living by moral standards. For example, ethical charismatics account for the concerns and wishes of their followers when creating a vision by having followers participate in the development of the company vision. By contrast, unethical charismatics develop a vision by themselves solely to meet their personal agendas. One unethical charismatic said, "The key thing is that it is my idea; and I am going to win with it at all costs."[44]

What can companies do to reduce the risks associated with unethical charismatics? To start, they need a clearly written code of conduct that is fairly and consistently enforced for all managers. Next, companies should recruit, select, and promote managers with high ethical standards. Also, companies need to train leaders to value, seek, and use diverse points of view. Both leaders and subordinates need training regarding ethical leader behaviors so that abuses can be recognized and corrected. Finally, companies should celebrate and reward people who exhibit ethical behaviors, especially ethical leader behaviors.[45]

12-7b Transformational Leadership

Whereas charismatic leadership involves articulating a clear vision, modeling values consistent with that vision, communicating high performance expectations, and establishing very strong relationships with followers,

Jim McNerney, Boeing's CEO, is an ethical charismatic. He believes that providing development opportunities for followers should be a leader's highest priority because individual growth leads to collective growth.

ethical charismatics
charismatic leaders who provide developmental opportunities for followers, are open to positive and negative feedback, recognize others' contributions, share information, and have moral standards that emphasize the larger interests of the group, organization, or society

unethical charismatics
charismatic leaders who control and manipulate followers, do what is best for themselves instead of their organizations, want to hear only positive feedback, share only information that is beneficial to themselves, and have moral standards that put their interests before everyone else's

Exhibit 12.12

Components of Transformational Leadership

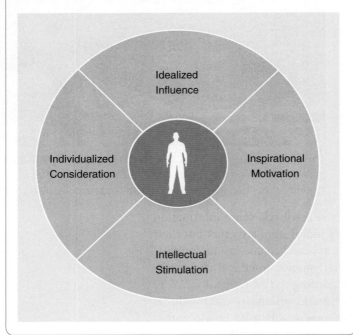

Idealized Influence

Individualized Consideration

Inspirational Motivation

Intellectual Stimulation

© CENGAGE LEARNING

transformational leadership goes further by generating awareness and acceptance of a group's purpose and mission and by getting employees to see beyond their own needs and self-interest, for the good of the group.[46] Like charismatic leaders, transformational leaders are visionary, but they transform their organizations by getting their followers to accomplish more than they intended and even more than they thought possible.

Transformational leaders are able to make their followers feel that they are a vital part of the organization and help them see how their jobs fit with the organization's vision. By linking individual and organizational interests, transformational leaders encourage followers to make sacrifices for the organization because they know that they will prosper when the organization prospers. As Exhibit 12.12 shows, transformational leadership has four components: charismatic leadership or idealized influence, inspirational motivation, intellectual stimulation, and individualized consideration.[47]

Charismatic leadership or idealized influence means that transformational leaders act as role models for their followers. Because transformational leaders put others' needs ahead of their own and share risks with their followers, they are admired, respected, and trusted, and followers want to emulate them. Thus, in contrast to purely charismatic leaders (especially unethical charismatics), transformational leaders can be counted on to do the right thing and maintain high standards for ethical and personal conduct.

Inspirational motivation means that transformational leaders motivate and inspire followers by providing meaning and challenge to their work. By clearly communicating expectations and demonstrating commitment to goals, transformational leaders help followers envision future states, such as the organizational vision or mission. In turn, this leads to greater enthusiasm and optimism about the future.

Intellectual stimulation means that transformational leaders encourage followers to be creative and innovative, question assumptions, and look at problems and situations in new ways, even if their ideas are different from the leaders' ideas.

Individualized consideration means that transformational leaders pay special attention to followers' individual needs by creating learning opportunities, accepting and tolerating individual differences, encouraging two-way communication, and being good listeners.

Finally, a distinction needs to be drawn between transformational leadership and transactional leadership. Whereas transformational leaders use visionary and inspirational appeals to influence followers, **transactional leadership**

transformational leadership
leadership that generates awareness and acceptance of a group's purpose and mission and gets employees to see beyond their own needs and self-interests for the good of the group

transactional leadership
leadership based on an exchange process, in which followers are rewarded for good performance and punished for poor performance

is based on an exchange process in which followers are rewarded for good performance and punished for poor performance. When leaders administer rewards fairly and offer followers the rewards that they want, followers will often reciprocate with effort. A problem, however, is that transactional leaders often rely too heavily on discipline or threats to bring performance up to standards. This may work in the short run, but it's much less effective in the long run. Also, as discussed in Chapters 10 and 11, many leaders and organizations have difficulty successfully linking pay practices to individual performance. As a result, studies consistently show that transformational leadership is much more effective on average than transactional leadership. In the United States, Canada, Japan, and India—and at all organizational levels, from first-level supervisors to upper-level executives—followers view transformational leaders as much better leaders and are much more satisfied when working for them. Furthermore, companies with transformational leaders have significantly better financial performance.[48]

REVIEW 12-7

. . . .

Strategic Leadership

Strategic leadership requires visionary, charismatic, and transformational leadership. Visionary leadership creates a positive image of the future that motivates organizational members and provides direction for future planning and goal setting. Charismatic leaders have strong, confident, dynamic personalities that attract followers, enable the leader to create strong bonds, and inspire followers to accomplish the leader's vision. Followers of ethical charismatic leaders work harder, are more committed and satisfied, are better performers, and are more likely to trust their leaders. Followers can be just as supportive and committed to unethical charismatics, but these leaders can pose a tremendous risk for companies. Unethical charismatics control and manipulate followers and do what is best for themselves instead of their organizations. To reduce the risks associated with unethical charismatics, companies need to enforce a clearly written code of conduct; recruit, select, and promote managers with high ethical standards; train leaders to value, seek, and use diverse points of view; teach everyone in the company to recognize unethical leader behaviors; and celebrate and reward people who exhibit ethical behaviors. Transformational leadership goes beyond charismatic leadership by generating awareness and acceptance of a group's purpose and mission and by getting employees to see beyond their own needs and self-interest for the good of the group. The four components of transformational leadership are charisma, or idealized influence; inspirational motivation; intellectual stimulation; and individualized consideration.

Management Decision

To Cell or Not to Cell[49]

It's a bright Tuesday morning, and you're participating in an important, energizing meeting in which your company's marketing team will present the new fall campaign. It's been an exciting time since you took over as CEO of this small electronics firm, and everyone is anticipating that the new product lineup that the company has been working on will bring new levels of success.

Just as the team is about to start presenting their thoughts on how to market the new products, your phone rings; it's Karen from distribution, asking whether you have five minutes to talk about truck maintenance. "No," you tell her, "I'm in a meeting." As you apologize for the interruption, your phone rings again; it's your assistant, and he wants to know when you can schedule a meeting with the president of a subcontractor. A few minutes after that, Gary from HR calls and asks when the new benefits package will be approved. After that you get calls from the mailroom, the president of the electricians' union, your chief accountant, and your teenage son, asking whether he can drive the car to school. And in between all of those calls, your phone has been buzzing nonstop with e-mails.

With all of these interruptions, a presentation that should have taken 30 minutes took more than two hours, and this isn't the first time something like this has happened either. Day and night, it seems, you're getting bombarded by phone calls and text messages and e-mails, almost to the point that you can't get any real work done. As you trudge back to your office, you remark to your assistant, "Maybe I should just get rid of this phone." And he says, "Maybe you should."

He mentions that he just saw a magazine article about executives who don't use cell phones, even high-powered people like Warren Buffett, Mikhail Prokhorov (owner of the NBA team New Jersey Nets), and Tavis Smiley, a TV and radio host. One manager quoted in the articles says that he got rid of his cell phone to increase his efficiency. With no cell phone, he could focus on one meeting at a time and give exclusive attention to whomever he is talking with. Tavis Smiley says that without a cell phone, employees of his company actually get more conversation time with him than before.

So maybe this is the solution to your problems: Without a cell phone, there would be no more interrupted meetings, no more urgent calls about stuff that isn't really urgent, no more 30-minute appointments that stretch to two hours. When you ask your managers and employees, however, there's a high level of anxiety. Will you be accessible at all? What if there is a real emergency?

Questions

1. Do you believe that the CEO of a company can effectively do his or her job of leading without being always accessible?

2. If you, as the CEO, were to get rid of your phone, how would you ensure that lines of communication remain open?

Practice Being a Manager

Changing Directions

Leadership is a highly prized process and capability. Organizations invest billions of dollars each year in recruiting and developing leadership talent. As more companies compete primarily on the basis of how well they employ their human capabilities, the importance of leadership continues to grow. This exercise will provide you with an opportunity to play coach to a leader entering a challenging situation.

STEP 1 **Get into groups.** Your professor will assign you to pairs or small groups.

Scenario: PepsiCo is a company with a remarkable tradition of product and management innovations, but over the past several years PepsiCo has faced increased competition from its archrival Coca-Cola and struggling to navigate the challenges of an ever-changing marketplace. As the new CEO scans the situation, it is difficult to know how to prioritize. Where to begin?

Assume that the members of your small team are a group of consultants working with Pepsi's new CEO. Your job is behind the scenes—you are simply helping the CEO brainstorm and think carefully about how to lead this company, improve performance, and restore the once-vibrant culture of creativity that made PepsiCo a leader in its industry.

STEP 2 **Outline leadership criteria.** Work as a team to develop a set of leadership recommendations that are well matched to the PepsiCo situation. What do you think employees need most from their new leader? Should the CEO help employees look back and learn from the company's past, or should the CEO encourage employees to move on and focus on the future? What are the trade-offs in each approach? Some key areas of concern include: (1) increased competition; (2) rising cost structures; (3) declining financial and marketing performance; (4) declining brand image (e.g., as a contributor to unhealthy eating habits and childhood obesity). So how would you recommend that the CEO prioritize these issues? Are there creative possibilities for tackling some of these concerns simultaneously?

STEP 3 **Determine a coaching plan.** Prepare to coach the CEO during the process of transforming PepsiCo. How might path–goal thinking help the CEO guide PepsiCo employees through the transition? What should the CEO keep in mind regarding such situational factors as worker readiness, situation favorableness, and environmental contingencies? Assuming the CEO possesses charismatic capabilities, would you recommend relying upon a charismatic leadership style in this situation? Why or why not?

STEP 4 **Debrief as a class.** Share some of the highlights of your recommendations, and discuss what leadership consultants/coaches need to know to effectively advise their clients.

 # Self-Assessment

Leadership Orientation

Think of everyone you have ever worked with in jobs, clubs, volunteer positions, student projects—everything. Now that you have all those situations in mind, try to identify the one person with whom you least liked to work. Who was the most difficult person to work with to get a job done? For whatever reason, you had trouble working with this person. The person can be a peer, boss, or subordinate. Once you have that person in mind, think of how you would describe him or her to another person. The LPC scale uses 18 oppositional adjective pairs to help you build your description.[50] For each pair, choose the number closest to the word that best describes your LPC.

Pleasant	8	7	6	5	4	3	2	1	Unpleasant
Friendly	8	7	6	5	4	3	2	1	Unfriendly
Rejecting	1	2	3	4	5	6	7	8	Accepting
Tense	1	2	3	4	5	6	7	8	Relaxed
Distant	1	2	3	4	5	6	7	8	Close

Cold	1	2	3	4	5	6	7	8	Warm
Supportive	8	7	6	5	4	3	2	1	Hostile
Boring	1	2	3	4	5	6	7	8	Interesting
Quarrelsome	1	2	3	4	5	6	7	8	Harmonious
Gloomy	1	2	3	4	5	6	7	8	Cheerful
Open	8	7	6	5	4	3	2	1	Guarded
Backbiting	1	2	3	4	5	6	7	8	Loyal
Untrustworthy	1	2	3	4	5	6	7	8	Trustworthy
Considerate	8	7	6	5	4	3	2	1	Inconsiderate
Nasty	1	2	3	4	5	6	7	8	Nice
Agreeable	8	7	6	5	4	3	2	1	Disagreeable
Insincere	1	2	3	4	5	6	7	8	Sincere
Kind	8	7	6	5	4	3	2	1	Unkind

TOTAL = _____

SCORING

Determine your leadership style by totaling all the numbers you selected into a single sum. Your score will fall between 18 and 96. You can find the interpretation for your score at www.cengagebrain.com.

MANAGEMENT WORKPLACE

© CENGAGE LEARNING 2013

Camp Bow Wow: Leadership

Although consistency and conformity are critical to the success of any chain, Camp Bow Wow seeks creative input from its franchisees. Founder Heidi Ganahl keeps a door open for anyone who wants to meet and offer feedback. The policy has produced many visible improvements to the company. Because franchise companies attract hundreds of independent business owners into the system, Ganahl has to work with many strong leaders, which requires two-way cooperation and respect. She also has to manage personal relationships and keep every individual focused on business.

What to Watch For and Ask Yourself

1. In what way is Heidi Ganahl's leadership charismatic and visionary? Give examples.
2. Where does Heidi Ganahl's leadership fall on the Blake/Mouton leadership grid? Explain.

Endnotes

1. J. Champy, "Apple's Arrested Development," *Forbes*, April 20, 1998, 132; A. Hesseldahl, "Was Apple 'Adequate but Late' on Jobs?" *Businessweek*, January 6, 2009, 2; Y. Kane, "Jobs, Back at Apple, Focuses on New Tablet," *Wall Street Journal*, August 25, 2009, B1; A. Lashinsky, "Apple: The Genius Behind Steve," *Fortune*, November 24, 2008, 70–80; and A. Lashinsky, "Inside Apple," *Fortune*, May 23, 2011, 125–134; and B. Schlender, "How Big Can Apple Get?" *Fortune*, February 21, 2005, 66–76.

2. W. Bennis, "Why Leaders Can't Lead," *Training & Development Journal* 43, no. 4 (1989).

3. A. Zaleznik, "Managers and Leaders: Are They Different?" *Harvard Business Review* 55 (1977): 76–78; and A. Zaleznik, "The Leadership Gap," *Washington Quarterly* 6 (1983): 32–39.

4. Bennis, "Why Leaders Can't Lead."

5. S. Berfield, "The Best of 2006: Leaders," *Businessweek*, December 18, 2006, 58.

6. D. Jones, "Not All Successful CEOs Are Extroverts," *USA Today*, June 7, 2006, B1.

7. R. J. House and R. M. Aditya, "The Social Scientific Study of Leadership: Quo Vadis?" *Journal of Management* 23 (1997): 409–473; T. Judge, R. Illies, J. Bono, and M. Gerhardt, "Personality and Leadership: A Qualitative and Quantitative Review," *Journal of Applied Psychology* (August 2002): 765–782; and S. A. Kirkpatrick and E. A. Locke, "Leadership: Do Traits Matter?" *Academy of Management Executive* 5, no. 2 (1991): 48–60.

8. House and Aditya, "The Social Scientific Study of Leadership"; and Kirkpatrick and Locke, "Leadership: Do Traits Matter?"

9. J. J. Gabarro, *The Dynamics of Taking Charge* (Boston: Harvard Business School Press, 1987).

10. Kirkpatrick and Locke, "Leadership: Do Traits Matter?"

11. E. A. Fleishman, "The Description of Supervisory Behavior," *Journal of Applied Psychology* 37 (1953): 1–6; and L. R. Katz, *New Patterns of Management* (New York: McGraw-Hill, 1961).

12. B. Fuller, C. E. P. Patterson, K. Hester, and D. Stringer, "A Quantitative Review of Research on Charismatic Leadership," *Psychological Reports* 78 (1996): 271–287; and R. G. Lord, C. L. De Vader, and G. M. Alliger, "A Meta-Analysis of the Relation between Personality Traits and Leadership Perceptions: An Application of Validity Generalization Procedures," *Journal of Applied Psychology* 71, no. 3 (1986): 402–410.

13. N. Byrnes, "The Issue: Maintaining Employee Engagement," *Bloomberg Businessweek*, January 16, 2009, accessed August 20, 2010, from www.businessweek.com/managing/content/jan2009/ca20090116_444132.htm.

14. P. Weissenberg and M. H. Kavanagh, "The Independence of Initiating Structure and Consideration: A Review of the Evidence," *Personnel Psychology* 25 (1972): 119–130.

15. R. J. House and T. R. Mitchell, "Path-Goal Theory of Leadership," *Journal of Contemporary Business* 3 (1974): 81–97;

F. E. Fiedler, "A Contingency Model of Leadership Effectiveness," in L. Berkowitz, (ed.), *Advances in Experimental Social Psychology* (New York: Academic Press, 1964); V. H. Vroom and P. W. Yetton, *Leadership and Decision Making* (Pittsburgh: University of Pittsburgh Press, 1973); P. Hersey and K. H. Blanchard, *The Management of Organizational Behavior*, 4th ed. (Englewood Cliffs, NJ: Prentice Hall, 1984); and Kerr and Jermier, "Substitutes for Leadership."

16. F. E. Fiedler and M. M. Chemers, *Leadership and Effective Management* (Glenview, IL: Scott, Foresman, 1974); and F. E. Fiedler and M. M. Chemers, *Improving Leadership Effectiveness: The Leader Match Concept*, 2nd ed. (New York: Wiley, 1984).

17. Fiedler and Chemers, *Improving Leadership Effectiveness*.

18. F. E. Fiedler, "The Effects of Leadership Training and Experience: A Contingency Model Interpretation," *Administrative Science Quarterly* 17, no. 4 (1972): 455; and F. E. Fiedler, *A Theory of Leadership Effectiveness* (New York: McGraw-Hill, 1967).

19. L. S. Csoka and F. E. Fiedler, "The Effect of Military Leadership Training: A Test of the Contingency Model," *Organizational Behavior & Human Performance* 8 (1972): 395–407.

20. House and Mitchell, "Path-Goal Theory of Leadership."

21. House and Mitchell, "Path-Goal Theory of Leadership."

22. M. Langley and S. Terlep, "'I'm Not a Car Guy': On the Road with the New Man at GM's Wheel," *Wall Street Journal*, January 8, 2011, A1.

23. B. M. Fisher and J. E. Edwards, "Consideration and Initiating Structure and Their Relationships with Leader Effectiveness: A Meta-Analysis," *Proceedings of the Academy of Management*, August 1988, 201–205.

24. F. Manjoo, "Google: The Quest," *Fast Company*, April 2011, 69–120, 9p.

25. J. C. Wofford and L. Z. Liska, "Path-Goal Theories of Leadership: A Meta-Analysis," Journal of Management 19 (1993): 857–876.

26. House and Aditya, "The Social Scientific Study of Leadership."

27. P. Hersey and K. Blanchard, *Management of Organizational Behavior: Leading Human Resources*, 8th ed. (Escondido, CA: Center for Leadership Studies, 2001).

28. W. Blank, J. R. Weitzel, and S. G. Green, "A Test of the Situational Leadership Theory," *Personnel Psychology* 43, no. 3 (1990): 579–597; and W. R. Norris and R. P. Vecchio, "Situational Leadership Theory: A Replication," *Group & Organization Management* 17, no. 3 (1992): 331–342.

29. Ibid.

30. V. H. Vroom and A. G. Jago, *The New Leadership: Managing Participation in Organizations* (Englewood Cliffs, NJ: Prentice Hall, 1988).

31. C. Fishman, "How Teamwork Took Flight: This Team Built a Commercial Engine—and Self-Managing GE Plant—from Scratch," *Fast Company*, October 1, 1999, 188.

32 Ibid.

33 "Korn/Ferry Survey Reveals More Interest than Action in CEO Succession Plan among Companies," Korn/Ferry International. December 21, 2010, accessed June 6, 2011, from http://www.kornferry.com/PressRelease/11916.

34 G. A. Yukl, *Leadership in Organizations,* 3rd ed. (Englewood Cliffs, NJ: Prentice Hall, 1995).

35 B. M. Bass, *Bass & Stogdill's Handbook of Leadership: Theory, Research, and Managerial Applications* (New York: Free Press, 1990).

36 R. D. Ireland and M. A. Hitt, "Achieving and Maintaining Strategic Competitiveness in the 21st Century: The Role of Strategic Leadership," *Academy of Management Executive* 13, no. 1 (1999): 43–57.

37 CEO Insight: Kevin Kelly, "An Executive Recruiter's New Strategy," *Bloomberg Businessweek*, 15 January 2009, accessed June 6, 2011, from www.businessweek.com/managing/content/jan2009/ca20090115_508822.htm.

38 P. Thoms and D. B. Greenberger, "Training Business Leaders to Create Positive Organizational Visions of the Future: Is It Successful?" *Academy of Management Journal* (Best Papers and Proceedings 1995): 212–216.

39 M. Weber, *The Theory of Social and Economic Organizations,* trans. R. A. Henderson and T. Parsons (New York: Free Press, 1947).

40 D. A. Waldman and F. J. Yammarino, "CEO Charismatic Leadership: Levels-of-Management and Levels-of-Analysis Effects," *Academy of Management Review* 24, no. 2 (1999): 266–285.

41 K. B. Lowe, K. G. Kroeck, and N. Sivasubramaniam, "Effectiveness Correlates of Transformational and Transactional Leadership: A Meta-Analytic Review of the MLQ Literature," *Leadership Quarterly* 7 (1996): 385–425.

42 J. M. Howell and B. J. Avolio, "The Ethics of Charismatic Leadership: Submission or Liberation?" Academy of *Management Executive* 6, no. 2 (1992): 43–54.

43 A. Deutschman, "Is Your Boss a Psychopath?" *Fast Company*, July 2005, 44.

44 J. Howell and B. Avolio, "The Ethics of Charismatic Leadership."

45 J. M. Burns, *Leadership* (New York: Harper & Row, 1978); and B. M. Bass, "From Transactional to Transformational Leadership: Learning to Share the Vision," *Organizational Dynamics* 18 (1990): 19–36.

46 Bass, "From Transactional to Transformational Leadership."

47 B. M. Bass, *A New Paradigm of Leadership: An Inquiry into Transformational Leadership* (Alexandria, VA: U.S. Army Research Institute for the Behavioral and Social Sciences, 1996).

48 Bass, "From Transactional to Transformational Leadership."

49 "The Cell-Free Club," *Bloomberg Businessweek*, August 9–15, 2010, 78–79.

50 F. E. Fiedler and M. M. Chemers, *Improving Leadership Effectiveness: The Leader Match Concept* (New York: Wiley, 1984).

Communication

REEL TO REAL

Management Workplace is at Plant Fantasies.

SELF-ASSESSMENT

How do you listen? Are you inquisitive or contemplative? Find out which listening style best describes you by doing the Self-Assessment for this chapter in the book or online.

ONLINE QUIZZES

Did you get it? Review the main concepts in the chapter by taking the online quizzes on CourseMate!

VIDEO QUIZZES

Get more out of the videos by taking the multimedia video quizzes online.

What Would You Do?

Google Headquarters, Mountain View, California[1]

Founded in 1998, Google just had its most dominant year, with its search market share rising from 77 percent to 83 percent and revenues jumping 25 percent. Because most of the revenue came from search, Google is trying to diversify. But it faces intense competition in every market.

In traditional search, Microsoft's Bing search engine and Facebook, which passed Google as the most popular website in the world, pose threats as people desire more personalized and social media-related search information. Searches for local information, such as restaurant reviews or directions, are 20 percent of all Google searches and half of all mobile or smartphone searches. Yet, local-related search advertising is a weakness for Google, but a strength for Groupon, Facebook Places, Living Social, Foursquare, and Bing. Although Google's Android smartphones have more market share than Apple's iPhone, the Android software is open source, so Google makes no money except for built-in Google Ads and services. Likewise, Google trails Apple and Amazon in the number of publishers who use their software, devices (i.e., smartphones, tablets, book readers), and online stores to sell electronic versions of newspapers, magazines, books, music, TV shows, and movies. Finally, Google's Chrome Web browser (13% market share) competes with Microsoft's Internet Explorer (55%), Mozilla's Firefox (22%), and Apple's Safari (7%).

In short, Google is trying to position itself for the day when people won't automatically use a Google search box to find information. Keith Woolcock, founder of 5thColumnIdeas, a technology research firm, doubts Google is up to the task, saying, "The problem for me as an investor is that Google looks a little too [much] like last year's model. It's the chicken in the sandwich— Apple and Facebook are on the opposing sides. Google is in the middle. Really, it looks to me as though it has become the Microsoft of its generation: big, bad and quickly becoming irrelevant."

Unfortunately, you fear that Woolcock might be right, which is why you replaced CEO Eric Schmidt, who now becomes executive chairman. When Google started, you were CEO for three years. But, as an introvert who prefers technology challenges to management issues, you were relieved to hire Schmidt from Sun Microsystems because of his extensive leadership experience. When Schmidt became CEO, Google was much smaller and still in start-up mode, so he focused on management and financial systems, while you and Sergey Brin focused on technology and product development. Google's philosophy was to hire really smart people and then let them do whatever they wanted. It was the norm for Google engineers to have 20 percent of their time to work on whatever they wanted. And it spawned great products like Gmail, which engineer Paul Buchheit designed in a day and then shopped around, to get other Google engineers to join his team. This approach worked well until Google hit 10,000 employees. But at Google's current size, 24,000 employees, with plans to hire another 6,000, it leads to confusion, poor coordination, and a lack of focus.

Today, Google is a much larger, more complicated company. But the biggest problem is that paralyzing bureaucracy has slowed the company. As technology companies grow, this happens. IBM, Apple, Microsoft, and H-P weren't immune, and neither is Google. In fact, the key reason you became CEO again was to streamline decision making and communication, and create clearer lines of responsibility and accountability. But how do you do that in a company of 30,000 people? A related problem is that top management is increasingly isolated from middle- and lower-level managers and employees who are responsible for the research and project management that is key to Google's success. So, what might you do to improve upward communication within the company? Finally, what can Google do to communicate effectively on an organization-wide basis in an organization that has dozens of product lines and hundreds of research projects and that will soon have 30,000 employees?

If you were the new CEO at Google, what would you do?

13-1 Communication and Perception

This chapter begins by examining the role of perception in communication and how perception can make it difficult for managers to communicate effectively. Next, you'll read about the communication process and the various kinds of communication found in most organizations. In the last half of the chapter, the focus is on improving communication in organizations. You'll learn about one-on-one communication and then about how to effectively communicate and listen to others organization-wide.

Communication is the process of transmitting information from one person or place to another. Whereas smart managers understand that effective, straightforward communication between managers and employees is essential for success, some bosses try to make bad news sound good by using phrases like "rightsizing" for layoffs, "merger of equals" for acquisition by another company, "pursuing other interests" for employees who were fired, and "cost efficiencies" for outsourced jobs. Why do managers sugarcoat bad news? Because, says Dartmouth management professor Paul Argenti, they think "they'll get less flak."[2]

After reading this section, you should be able to:

13-1 explain the role that perception plays in communication and communication problems.

It's estimated that managers spend over 80 percent of their day communicating with others.[3] Indeed, much of the basic management process—planning, organizing, leading, and controlling—cannot be performed without effective communication. If this weren't reason enough to study communication, consider that effective oral communication—achieved by listening, following instructions, conversing, and giving feedback—is the most important skill for college graduates who are entering the workforce.[4] Furthermore, across all industries, poor communication skills rank as the single most important reason that people do not advance in their careers.[5]

communication
the process of transmitting information from one person or place to another

One study found that when *employees* were asked whether their supervisor gave recognition for good work, only 13 percent said their supervisor gave a pat on the back, and a mere 14 percent said their supervisor gave sincere and thorough praise. But when the *supervisors* of these employees were asked whether they gave recognition for good work, 82 percent said they gave pats on the back, while 80 percent said that they gave sincere and thorough praise.[6] Given that these managers and employees worked closely together, how could they have had such different perceptions of something as simple as praise?

Let's learn more about perception and communication problems by examining **13-1a the basic perception process, 13-1b perception problems, 13-1c how we perceive others**, and **13-1d how we perceive ourselves**.

We'll also consider how all of these factors make it difficult for managers to communicate effectively.

13-1a Basic Perception Process

As shown in Exhibit 13.1, **perception** is the process by which individuals attend to, organize, interpret, and retain information from their environments. And because communication is the process of transmitting information from one person or place to another, perception is obviously a key part of communication. Yet perception can also be a key obstacle to communication.

As people perform their jobs, they are exposed to a wide variety of informational stimuli such as e-mails, direct conversations with the boss or co-workers, rumors heard over lunch, stories about the company in the press, or a video broadcast of a speech from the CEO to all employees. Just being exposed to an informational stimulus, however, is no guarantee that an individual will pay attention or attend to that stimulus. People experience stimuli through their own **perceptual filters**—the personality-, psychology-, or experience-based differences that influence them to ignore or pay attention to particular stimuli. Because of filtering, people exposed to the same information will often disagree about what they saw or heard.

For example, every major stadium in the National Football League has a huge TV monitor on which fans can watch replays. As the slow-motion video is replayed on the monitor, you can often hear cheers *and* boos, as fans of competing teams perceive the same replay in completely different ways. This happens because the fans' perceptual filters predispose them to attend to stimuli that support their team and not their opponents.[7] The same perceptual filters that affect whether we believe our

perception
the process by which individuals attend to, organize, interpret, and retain information from their environments

perceptual filters
the personality-, psychology-, or experience-based differences that influence people to ignore or pay attention to particular stimuli

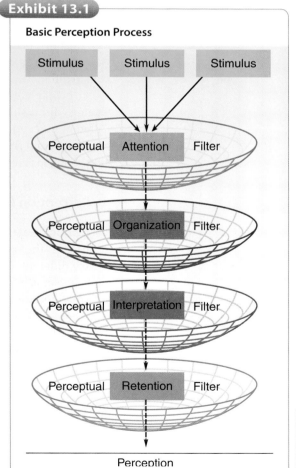

Exhibit 13.1

Basic Perception Process

Stimulus   Stimulus   Stimulus

Perceptual Attention Filter

Perceptual Organization Filter

Perceptual Interpretation Filter

Perceptual Retention Filter

Perception

© CENGAGE LEARNING

favorite team was "robbed" by the referees also affect communication, that is, the transmitting of information from one person or place to another. As shown in Exhibit 13.1, perceptual filters affect each part of the *perception process*: attention, organization, interpretation, and retention.

Attention is the process of noticing, or becoming aware of, particular stimuli. Because of perceptual filters, we attend to some stimuli and not others. For instance, a study at the University of Illinois asked viewers to watch people in black shirts and white shirts toss a basketball back and forth and to count the number of times someone in a black shirt tossed the basketball. Because their perceptual filters had narrowed to track the activities of people in black shirts, half of the viewers did not notice when the experimenters had someone in a gorilla suit walk through the midst of the people tossing the basketball back and forth.[8] *Organization* is the process of incorporating new information (from the stimuli that you notice) into your existing knowledge. Because of perceptual filters, we are more likely to incorporate new knowledge that is consistent with what we already know or believe. *Interpretation* is the process of attaching meaning to new knowledge. Because of perceptual filters, our preferences and beliefs strongly influence the meaning we attach to new information (e.g., "This decision must mean that top management supports our project."). Finally, *retention* is the process of remembering interpreted information. Retention affects what we recall and commit to memory after we have perceived something. Of course, perceptual filters affect retention as much as they do organization and interpretation.

In short, because of perception and perceptual filters, people are likely to pay attention to different things, organize and interpret what they pay attention to differently, and, finally, remember things differently. Consequently, even when people are exposed to the same communications (e.g., organizational memos, discussions with managers or customers), they can end up with very different perceptions and understandings. This is why communication can be so difficult and frustrating for managers. Let's review some of the communication problems created by perception and perceptual filters.

13-1b Perception Problems

Perception creates communication problems for organizations because people exposed to the same communication and information can end up with completely different ideas and understandings. Two of the most common perception problems in organizations are selective perception and closure.

At work, we are constantly bombarded with sensory stimuli: phones ringing, people talking in the background, computers dinging as new e-mail arrives, people calling our names, and so forth. As limited processors of information, we cannot possibly notice, receive, and interpret all of this information. As a result, we attend to and accept some stimuli but screen out and reject others. This isn't a random process.

selective perception
the tendency to notice and accept objects and information consistent with our values, beliefs, and expectations, while ignoring or screening out or not accepting inconsistent information

Selective perception is the tendency to notice and accept objects and information consistent with our values, beliefs, and expectations while ignoring or screening out inconsistent information. A classic case of selective perception occurred when APPLE introduced the iPhone 4 and thousands of customers experienced dropped phone calls and poor reception. With a metal antenna circling its edge, touching the antenna reduced signal reception. But since Apple always cloaks its new phones in covers (so they can't be photographed before product launch), it didn't encounter this problem in testing. Because of selective perception, Apple made matters worse by denying the problem. Then CEO Steve Jobs said, "This has been blown so out of proportion that it's incredible. There is no Antennagate." The iPhone 4, he said, was "perhaps the best product made by Apple."[9] Apple eventually acknowledged the problem and Apple offered each of its iPhone 4 customers a free case that prevented contact with the antenna.

Once we have initial information about a person, event, or process, **closure** is the tendency to fill in the gaps where information is missing, that is, to assume that what we don't know is consistent with what we already do know. If employees are told that budgets must be cut by 10 percent, they may automatically assume that 10 percent of employees will lose their jobs too, even if that isn't the case. Not surprisingly, when closure occurs, people sometimes fill in the gaps with inaccurate information, which can create problems for organizations.

13-1c Perceptions of Others

Attribution theory says that we all have a basic need to understand and explain the causes of other people's behavior.[10] In other words, we need to know why people do what they do. According to attribution theory, we use two general reasons or attributions to explain people's behavior: an *internal attribution*, in which behavior is thought to be voluntary or under the control of the individual; and an *external attribution*, in which behavior is thought to be involuntary and outside of the control of the individual.

Have you ever seen someone changing a flat tire on the side of the road and thought to yourself, "What rotten luck—somebody's having a bad day"? If you did, you perceived the person through an external attribution known as the defensive bias. The **defensive bias** is the tendency for people to perceive themselves as personally and situationally similar to someone who is having difficulty or trouble.[11] When we identify with the person in a situation, we tend to use external attributions (i.e., features related to the situation) to explain the person's behavior. For instance, because flat tires are common, it's easy to perceive ourselves in that same situation and put the blame on external causes such as running over a nail.

Now, let's assume a different situation, this time in the workplace: A utility company worker puts a ladder on a utility pole and then climbs up to do his work. As he's doing his work, he falls from the ladder and seriously injures himself.[12] Answer this question: Who or what caused the accident? If you thought, "It's not the worker's fault. Anybody could fall from a tall ladder," then you interpreted the incident with a defensive bias in which you saw yourself as personally and situationally similar to someone who is having difficulty or trouble. In other words, you made an external attribution by attributing the accident to an external cause, or some feature of the situation.

Most accident investigations, however, initially blame the worker (i.e., an internal attribution) and not the situation (i.e., an external attribution). Typically, 60 percent to 80 percent of workplace accidents each year are blamed on "operator error," that is, the employees themselves. In reality, more complete investigations usually show that workers are responsible for only 30 percent

closure
the tendency to fill in gaps of missing information by assuming that what we don't know is consistent with what we already know

attribution theory
the theory that we all have a basic need to understand and explain the causes of other people's behavior

defensive bias
the tendency for people to perceive themselves as personally and situationally similar to someone who is having difficulty or trouble

to 40 percent of all workplace accidents.[13] Why are accident investigators so quick to blame workers? The reason is that they are committing the **fundamental attribution error**, which is the tendency to ignore external causes of behavior and to attribute other people's actions to internal causes.[14] In other words, when investigators examine the possible causes of an accident, they're much more likely to assume that the accident is a function of the person and not the situation.

Which attribution—the defensive bias or the fundamental attribution error—are workers likely to make when something goes wrong? In general, employees and coworkers are more likely to perceive events and explain behavior from a defensive bias. Because they do the work themselves and see themselves as similar to others who make mistakes, have accidents, or are otherwise held responsible for things that go wrong at work, employees and coworkers are likely to attribute problems to external causes such as failed machinery, poor support, or inadequate training. By contrast, because they are typically observers (who don't do the work themselves) and see themselves as situationally and personally different from workers, managers (i.e., the boss) tend to commit the fundamental attribution error and blame mistakes, accidents, and other things that go wrong on workers (i.e., an internal attribution).

Consequently, workers and managers in most workplaces can be expected to take opposite views when things go wrong. Therefore, the defensive bias, which is typically used by workers, and the fundamental attribution error, which is typically made by managers, together present a significant challenge to effective communication and understanding in organizations.

fundamental attribution error
the tendency to ignore external causes of behavior and to attribute other people's actions to internal causes

self-serving bias
the tendency to overestimate our value by attributing successes to ourselves (internal causes) and attributing failures to others or the environment (external causes)

13-1d Self-Perception

The **self-serving bias** is the tendency to overestimate our value by attributing successes to ourselves (internal causes) and attributing failures to others or the environment (external causes).[15] The self-serving bias can make it especially difficult for managers to talk to employees about performance problems. In general, people have a need to maintain a positive self-image. This need is so strong that when people seek feedback at work, they typically want verification of their worth (rather than information about performance deficiencies) or assurance that mistakes or problems weren't their fault.[16] People can become defensive and emotional when managerial communication threatens their positive self-image. They quit listening, and communication becomes ineffective. In the second half of the chapter, which focuses on improving communication, we'll explain ways in which managers can minimize this self-serving bias and improve effective one-on-one communication with employees.

© ISTOCKPHOTO.COM/PESKYMONKEY

REVIEW 13-1
. . . .
Communication and Perception
Communication is the process of transmitting information from one person or place to another. Perception is the process by which people attend to, organize,

interpret, and retain information from their environments. Perception is not a straightforward process. Because of perceptual filters such as selective perception and closure, people exposed to the same information stimuli often end up with very different perceptions and understandings. Perception-based differences can also lead to differences in the attributions (internal or external) that managers and workers make when explaining workplace behavior. In general, workers are more likely to explain behavior from a defensive bias, in which they attribute problems to external causes (the situation). Managers, on the other hand, tend to commit the fundamental attribution error, attributing problems to internal causes (the worker associated with a mistake or error). Consequently, when things go wrong, it's common for managers to blame workers and for workers to blame the situation or context in which they do their jobs. Finally, this problem is compounded by a self-serving bias that leads people to attribute successes to internal causes and failures to external causes. Some workers may become defensive and emotional and not hear what managers have to say when they receive negative feedback from managers. In short, perceptions and attributions represent a significant challenge to effective communication and understanding in organizations.

13-2 Kinds of Communication

Each year, on the anniversary of your hiring date, you receive a written assessment of your performance from your boss. This year, after receiving your performance appraisal, you gripe about it to your best friend, a coworker in a cubicle down the hall. Despite your griping, however, you appreciate that your boss cut you some slack, allowing you extra days off when you went through a divorce earlier this year. How did your boss know you were having personal problems? He knew something was wrong from your nonverbal communication—your rounded shoulders, the bags under your eyes, and your overall lack of energy.

After reading this section, you should be able to:

13-2 describe the communication process and the various kinds of communication in organizations.

There are many kinds of communication—formal, informal, coaching/counseling, and nonverbal—but they all follow the same fundamental process.

Let's learn more about the different kinds of communication by examining **13-2a the communication process; 13-2b communication channels; 13-2c coaching and counseling, or one-on-one communication**; and **13-2d nonverbal communication**.

13-2a The Communication Process

Earlier in the chapter, we defined *communication* as the process of transmitting information from one person or place to another. Exhibit 13.2 displays a model of the communication process and its major components: the sender (message to be conveyed, encoding the message, transmitting the message); the receiver

Exhibit 13.2

The Interpersonal Communication Process

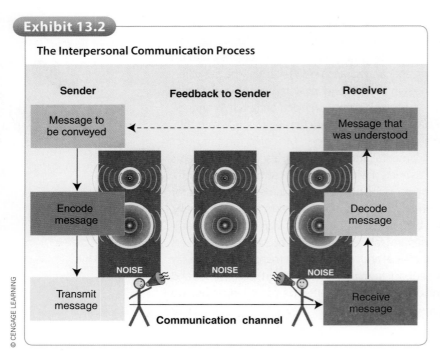

(receiving message, decoding the message, and the message that was understood); and noise, which interferes with the communication process.

The communication process begins when a *sender* thinks of a message he or she wants to convey to another person. On a recent trip to China, WALMART CEO Mike Duke noticed that his Chinese competitors carried domestic and imported bananas. Walmart's Wanda supercenter in Beijing, however, carried only the more expensive, imported bananas. So, Duke wondered why they weren't carrying the cheaper Chinese-grown bananas.

The next step is to encode the message. **Encoding** means putting a message into a verbal (written or spoken) or symbolic form that can be recognized and understood by the receiver. The sender then *transmits the message* via *communication channels*. For example, Duke asked the store manager and the head of Walmart's China division why they sold only the more expensive, imported bananas and not the less expensive bananas from China. With some communication channels such as the telephone and face-to-face communication, the sender receives immediate feedback, whereas with others such as e-mail (or text messages and file attachments), fax, beepers, voice mail, memos, and letters, the sender must wait for the receiver to respond.

After the message is transmitted and received, however, the next step is for the receiver to decode it. **Decoding** is the process by which the receiver translates the written, verbal, or symbolic form of the message into an understood message. In Duke's case, the message was decoded accurately, and the Beijing Wanda store had the cheaper bananas in stock within 24 hours. Within a month, shoppers could find the cheaper Chinese bananas in Walmart's 300 Wanda stores.[17] However, the message as understood by the receiver isn't always the same message that was intended by the sender. Because of different experiences or perceptual filters, receivers may attach a completely different meaning to a message than was intended. The last step of the communication process occurs when the receiver gives the sender feedback. **Feedback to sender** is a return message to the sender that indicates the receiver's understanding of the message (of what the receiver was supposed to know, do, or not do). Feedback makes senders aware of possible miscommunications and enables them to continue communicating until the receiver understands the intended message. Unfortunately, feedback doesn't always occur in the communication process.

encoding
putting a message into a written, verbal, or symbolic form that can be recognized and understood by the receiver

decoding
the process by which the receiver translates the written, verbal, or symbolic form of a message into an understood message

feedback to sender
in the communication process, a return message to the sender that indicates the receiver's understanding of the message

Complacency and overconfidence about the ease and simplicity of communication can lead senders and receivers to simply assume that they share a common understanding of the message and, consequently, not use feedback to improve the effectiveness of their communication. This is a serious mistake, especially because messages and feedback are always transmitted with and against a background of noise. **Noise** is anything that interferes with the transmission of the intended message. Noise can occur in any of the following situations:

- The sender isn't sure what message to communicate.
- The message is not clearly encoded.
- The wrong communication channel is chosen.
- The message is not received or decoded properly.
- The receiver doesn't have the experience or time to understand the message.

When managers wrongly assume that communication is easy, they reduce communication to something called the "conduit metaphor."[18] Strictly speaking, a conduit is a pipe or tube that protects electrical wire. The **conduit metaphor** refers to the mistaken assumption that senders can pipe their intended messages directly into the heads of receivers with perfect clarity and without noise or perceptual filters interfering with the receivers' understanding of the message. However, this just isn't possible. Even if managers could telepathically direct their thoughts straight into receivers' heads, misunderstandings and communication problems would still occur because words and symbols typically have multiple meanings, depending on how they're used. Consider the word "fine." Depending on how you use it, "fine" can mean a penalty; a good job; that something is delicate, small, pure, or flimsy; or that something is okay.

Managers who want to be effective communicators need to carefully choose words and symbols that will help receivers derive the intended meaning of a message. Furthermore, they have to be aware of all steps in the communication process, beginning with the sender (message to be conveyed, encoding the message, transmitting the message) and ending with the receiver (receiving the message, decoding the message, understanding the message, and using feedback to communicate what was understood).

13-2b Communication Channels

Communication channels can be formal or informal. An organization's **formal communication channel** is the system of official channels that carry organizationally approved messages and information. Organizational objectives, rules, policies, procedures, instructions, commands, and requests for information are all transmitted via the formal communication system or channel. There are three formal communication channels: downward communication, upward communication, and horizontal communication.[19]

Downward communication flows from higher to lower levels in an organization. Downward communication is used to issue orders down the organizational hierarchy, to give organizational members job-related information, to give managers and workers performance reviews from upper managers, and to clarify organizational objectives and goals.[20]

noise
anything that interferes with the transmission of the intended message

conduit metaphor
the mistaken assumption that senders can pipe their intended messages directly into the heads of receivers with perfect clarity and without noise or perceptual filters interfering with the receivers' understanding of the message

formal communication channel
the system of official channels that carry organizationally approved messages and information

downward communication
communication that flows from higher to lower levels in an organization

© 2010 COLORBLIND IMAGES/ JUPITERIMAGES

Upward communication flows from lower levels to higher levels in an organization. Upward communication is used to give higher-level managers feedback about operations, issues, and problems; help higher-level managers assess organizational performance and effectiveness; encourage lower-level managers and employees to participate in organizational decision making; and give those at lower levels the chance to share their concerns with higher-level authorities.

Horizontal communication flows among managers and workers who are at the same organizational level, such as when a day shift nurse comes in at 7:30 A.M. for a half-hour discussion with the midnight nurse supervisor who leaves at 8 A.M. Horizontal communication helps facilitate coordination and cooperation between different parts of a company and allows coworkers to share relevant information. It also helps people at the same level resolve conflicts and solve problems without involving high levels of management.

In general, what can managers do to improve formal communication? First, decrease reliance on downward communication. Second, increase chances for upward communication by increasing personal contact with lower-level managers and workers. Third, encourage much better use of horizontal communication. Finally, be aware of the problems associated with downward, upward, and horizontal communication.

An organization's **informal communication channel**, sometimes called the **grapevine**, is the transmission of messages from employee to employee outside of formal communication channels. The grapevine arises out of curiosity, that is, the need to know what is going on in an organization and how it might affect you or others. To satisfy this curiosity, employees need a consistent supply of relevant, accurate, in-depth information about "who is doing what and what changes are occurring within the organization."[21]

Grapevines arise out of informal communication networks such as the gossip or cluster chains shown in Exhibit 13.3. In a *gossip chain*, one highly connected individual shares information with many other managers and workers. By contrast, in a *cluster chain*, numerous people simply tell a few of their friends. The result in both cases is that information flows freely and quickly through the organization. Some believe that grapevines are a waste of employees' time, that they promote gossip and rumors that fuel political speculation, and that they are sources of highly unreliable, inaccurate information. Yet studies clearly show that grapevines are highly accurate sources of information for a number of reasons.[22] First, because grapevines typically carry "juicy" information that is interesting and timely, information spreads rapidly. Second, because information is typically spread by face-to-face conversation, receivers can send feedback to make sure they understand the message that is being communicated.

upward communication
communication that flows from lower to higher levels in an organization

horizontal communication
communication that flows among managers and workers who are at the same organizational level

informal communication channel ("grapevine")
the transmission of messages from employee to employee outside of formal communication channels

This reduces misunderstandings and increases accuracy. Third, because most of the information in a company moves along the grapevine rather than formal communication channels, people can usually verify the accuracy of information by checking it out with others.

What can managers do to manage organizational grapevines? The very worst thing they can do is withhold information or try to punish those who share information with others. The grapevine abhors a vacuum, so rumors and anxiety will flourish in the absence of information from company management. A better strategy is to embrace the grapevine and keep employees informed about possible changes and strategies. Failure to do so will just make things worse.

Finally, in addition to using the grapevine to communicate with others, managers should not overlook the grapevine as a tremendous source of valuable information and feedback. In fact, information flowing through organizational grapevines is estimated to be 75 percent to 95 percent accurate.[23]

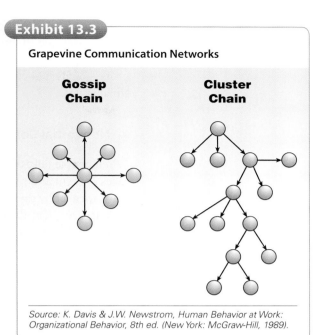

Exhibit 13.3

Grapevine Communication Networks

Source: K. Davis & J.W. Newstrom, Human Behavior at Work: Organizational Behavior, 8th ed. (New York: McGraw-Hill, 1989).

13-2c Coaching and Counseling: One-on-One Communication

Coaching and counseling are two kinds of one-on-one communication. **Coaching** is communicating with someone for the direct purpose of improving the person's on-the-job performance or behavior.[24] George Parsons, chief learning officer for Goldman Sachs says, "As soon as people become good managers, we want them to be good coaches too. You have to be good at getting and giving feedback so you can help individuals fully contribute."[25]

Managers tend to make several mistakes when coaching employees. First, they wait for a problem before coaching. Second, when mistakes *are* made, managers wait much too long before talking to the employee about the problem. Management professor Ray Hilgert says, "A manager must respond as soon as possible after an incident of poor performance. Don't bury your head. . . . When employees are told nothing, they assume everything is okay."[26] In Section 13-3, you'll learn a number of specific steps for effective one-on-one communication and coaching.

By contrast to coaching, **counseling** is communicating with someone about non-job-related issues such as stress, child care, health issues, retirement planning, or legal issues that may be affecting or interfering with the person's performance. But counseling does not mean that managers should try to be clinicians, even though an estimated 20 percent of employees are dealing with personal problems at any one time. Instead, managers should discuss specific performance problems, listen if the employee chooses to share personal issues, and then recommend that the employee call the company's *Employee Assistance*

coaching
communicating with someone for the direct purpose of improving the person's on-the-job performance or behavior

counseling
communicating with someone about non-job-related issues that may be affecting or interfering with the person's performance

Program (EAP). EAPs are typically free when provided as part of a company's benefit package. In emergencies or times of crisis, EAPs can offer immediate counseling and support; they can also provide referrals to organizations and professionals that can help employees and their family members address personal issues.

13-2d Nonverbal Communication

When people talk, they send both verbal and nonverbal messages. Verbal messages are sent and received through the words we speak, as when we congratulate a speaker by saying "That was a great presentation." By contrast, nonverbal messages are sent through body language, facial expressions, or tone of voice. Hearing "*That* was a *great* presentation!" is very different from hearing "Ahem [clearing throat], that was, ahem, ahem, a great presentation."

More generally, **nonverbal communication** is any communication that doesn't involve words. Nonverbal communication almost always accompanies verbal communication and may either support and reinforce the verbal message or contradict it. The importance of nonverbal communication is well established. Researchers have estimated that as much as 93 percent of any message is transmitted nonverbally, with 55 percent coming from body language and facial expressions and 38 percent coming from the tone and pitch of the voice.[27] Because many nonverbal cues are unintentional, receivers often consider nonverbal communication to be a more accurate representation of what senders are thinking and feeling than the words they use. If you have ever asked someone out on a date and been told "yes," but realized that the real answer was "no," then you understand the importance of paying attention to nonverbal communication.

Kinesics and paralanguage are two kinds of nonverbal communication.[28] **Kinesics** (from the Greek word *kinesis*, meaning "movement") are movements of the body and face.[29] These movements include arm and hand gestures, facial expressions, eye contact, folding arms, crossing legs, and leaning toward or away from another person. For example, people tend to avoid eye contact when they are embarrassed or unsure of the message they are sending. Crossed arms or legs usually indicate defensiveness or that the person is not receptive to the message or the sender. Also, people tend to smile frequently when they are seeking someone's approval.

Paralanguage includes the pitch, rate, tone, volume, and speaking pattern (use of silences, pauses, or hesitations) of one's voice. For example, when people are unsure what to say, they tend to decrease their communication effectiveness by speaking softly. When people are nervous, they tend to talk faster and louder. These characteristics have a tremendous influence on whether listeners are receptive to what speakers are saying. In short, because nonverbal communication is so informative, especially when it contradicts verbal communication, managers need to learn how to monitor and control their nonverbal behavior.

REVIEW 13-2
....

Kinds of Communication

Communication within an organization depends on the communication process, formal and informal communication channels, one-on-one

nonverbal communication
any communication that doesn't involve words

kinesics
movements of the body and face

paralanguage
the pitch, rate, tone, volume, and speaking pattern (i.e., use of silences, pauses, or hesitations) of one's voice

Part Four *Leading*

communication, and nonverbal communication. The major components of the communication process are the sender, the receiver, noise, and feedback. The conduit metaphor refers to the mistaken assumption that senders can pipe their intended messages directly into receivers' heads with perfect clarity. With noise, perceptual filters, and little feedback, however, this just isn't possible. Formal communication channels such as downward, upward, and horizontal communication carry organizationally approved messages and information. By contrast, the informal communication channel, called the grapevine, arises out of curiosity and is carried out through gossip or cluster chains. Managers should use the grapevine to keep employees informed and to obtain better, clearer information for themselves. There are two kinds of one-on-one communication. Coaching is used to improve on-the-job performance, whereas counseling is used to communicate about non-job-related issues affecting job performance. Nonverbal communication such as kinesics and paralanguage accounts for as much as 93 percent of a message's content and interpretation. Because nonverbal communication is so informative, managers need to learn how to monitor and control their nonverbal behavior.

13-3 Managing One-on-One Communication

An employee comes in late every day, takes long lunches, and leaves early. His coworkers resent his tardiness and having to do his share of the work. Another employee's job performance has dropped significantly in the last three months. How do you communicate with these employees to begin solving these problems? What sorts of feedback should you give them? What if they are from another country or culture? Turning that around, how can you make yourself accessible so that you can hear what your employees feel and think?

After reading this section, you should be able to:

13-3 explain how managers can manage effective one-on-one communication.

You learned in Chapter 1 that, on average, first-line managers spend 57 percent of their time with people, middle managers spend 63 percent of their time directly with people, and top managers spend as much as 78 percent of their time dealing with people.[30] These numbers make it clear that managers spend a great deal of time in one-on-one communication with others.

Learn more about managing one-on-one communication by reading how to **13-3a choose the right communication medium, 13-3b be a good listener, 13-3c give effective feedback**, and **13-3d improve cross-cultural communication**.

13-3a Choosing the Right Communication Medium

Sometimes messages are poorly communicated simply because they are delivered using the wrong **communication medium**, which is the method used to deliver a message. For example, the wrong communication medium is being used when an employee returns from lunch, picks up the note left on her office chair, and learns she has been fired. The wrong communication medium is also

communication medium
the method used to deliver a message

being used when an employee pops into your office every 10 minutes with a simple request. (An e-mail or IM would be better.)

There are two general kinds of communication media: oral and written communication. *Oral communication* includes face-to-face and group meetings through telephone calls, videoconferencing, or any other means of sending and receiving spoken messages. Studies show that managers generally prefer oral communication over written because it provides the opportunity to ask questions about parts of the message that they don't understand. Oral communication is also a rich communication medium because it allows managers to receive and assess the nonverbal communication that accompanies spoken messages (i.e., body language, facial expressions, and the voice characteristics associated with paralanguage).

Furthermore, you don't need a personal computer and an Internet connection to conduct oral communication. Simply schedule an appointment, track someone down in the hall, or catch someone on the phone. But the oral medium should not be used for *all* communication. In general, when the message is simple, such as a quick request or a presentation of straightforward information, a memo or e-mail is often the better communication medium.

Written communication includes letters, e-mail, and memos. Although most managers still like and use oral communication, e-mail in particular is changing how they communicate with workers, customers, and each other. E-mail is the fastest-growing form of communication in organizations, primarily because of its convenience and speed. For instance, because people read six times faster than they can listen, they usually can read 30 e-mail messages in 10 to 15 minutes.[31] By contrast, dealing with voice messages can take a considerable amount of time.

Written communication such as e-mail is well suited for delivering straightforward messages and information. Furthermore, with e-mail accessible at the office, at home, and on the road (by laptop computer, cell phone, or Web-based e-mail), managers can use e-mail to stay in touch from anywhere at almost any time. And because e-mail and other written communications don't have to be sent and received simultaneously, messages can be sent and stored for reading at any time. Consequently, managers can send and receive many more messages using e-mail than by using oral communication, which requires people to get together in person or by phone or videoconference.

E-mail has its own drawbacks, however. One is that it lacks the formality of paper memos and letters. It is easy to fire off a rushed e-mail that is not well written or fully thought through. Another drawback to e-mail is that it lacks nonverbal cues, making e-mails very easy to misinterpret.

13-3b Listening

Are you a good listener? You probably think so. In fact, most people, including managers, are terrible listeners, retaining only about 25 percent of what they hear.[32] You qualify as a poor listener if you frequently interrupt others, jump to conclusions about what people will say before they've said it, hurry the speaker to finish his or her point, are a passive listener (not actively working at your listening), or simply don't pay attention to what people are saying.[33] On this last point—attentiveness—college students were periodically asked to record their thoughts during a psychology course. On average, 20 percent of the students were paying attention (only 12 percent were actively working at being good listeners), 20 percent were thinking about sex, 20 percent were thinking about things they had done before, and the remaining 40 percent were thinking about other things unrelated to the class (e.g., worries, religion, lunch, daydreaming).[34]

How important is it to be a good listener? In general, about 45 percent of the total time you spend communicating with others is spent listening. Furthermore, listening is important for managerial and business success, even for those at the top of an organization.

So, what can you do to improve your listening ability? First, understand the difference between hearing and listening. According to *Webster's New World Dictionary*, **hearing** is the "act or process of perceiving sounds," whereas **listening** is "making a conscious effort to hear." In other words, we react to sounds, such as bottles breaking or music being played too loud, because hearing is an involuntary physiological process. By contrast, listening is a voluntary behavior. So, if you want to be a good listener, you have to choose to be a good listener. Typically, that means choosing to be an active, empathetic listener.[35]

Active listening means assuming half the responsibility for successful communication by actively giving the speaker nonjudgmental feedback that shows you've accurately heard what he or she said. Active listeners make it clear from their behavior that they are listening carefully to what the speaker has to say. Active listeners put the speaker at ease, maintain eye contact, and show the speaker that they are attentively listening by nodding and making short statements.

Several specific strategies can help you be a better active listener. First, *clarify responses* by asking the speaker to explain confusing or ambiguous statements. Second, when there are natural breaks in the speaker's delivery, use this time to paraphrase or summarize what has been said. *Paraphrasing* is restating what has been said in your own words. *Summarizing* is reviewing the speaker's main points or emotions. Paraphrasing and summarizing give the speaker the chance to correct the message if the active listener has attached the wrong meaning to it. Paraphrasing and summarizing also show the speaker that the active listener is interested in the speaker's message.

Exhibit 13.4 lists specific statements that listeners can use to clarify responses, paraphrase, or summarize what has been said.

Active listeners also avoid evaluating the message or being critical until the message is complete. They recognize that their only responsibility during the transmission of a message is to receive it accurately and derive the intended meaning from it. Evaluation and criticism can take place after the message is accurately received. Finally, active listeners also recognize that a large portion of any message is transmitted nonverbally and thus pay very careful attention to the nonverbal cues transmitted by the speaker.

Empathetic listening means understanding the speaker's perspective and personal frame of reference and giving feedback that conveys that understanding to the speaker. Empathetic listening goes beyond active listening because it depends on our ability to set aside our own attitudes or relationships to be able to see and understand things through someone else's eyes. Empathetic listening is just as important as active listening, especially for managers, because it helps build rapport and trust with others.

hearing
the act or process of perceiving sounds

listening
making a conscious effort to hear

active listening
assuming half the responsibility for successful communication by actively giving the speaker nonjudgmental feedback that shows you've accurately heard what he or she said

empathetic listening
understanding the speaker's perspective and personal frame of reference and giving feedback that conveys that understanding to the speaker

Exhibit 13.4

Clarifying, Paraphrasing, and Summarizing Responses for Active Listeners

Clarifying Responses	Paraphrasing Responses	Summarizing Responses
Could you explain that again?	What you're really saying is . . .	Let me summarize . . .
I don't understand what you mean.	If I understand you correctly . . .	Okay, your main concerns are . . .
I'm not sure how . . .	In other words . . .	To recap what you've said . . .
I'm confused. Would you run through that again?	So your perspective is that . . .	Thus far, you've discussed . . .
		Tell me if I'm wrong, but what you're saying is . . .

Source: E. Atwater, I Hear You, revised ed. (New York: Walker, 1992).

The key to being a more empathetic listener is to show your desire to understand and to reflect people's feelings. You can *show your desire to understand* by listening, that is, asking people to talk about what's most important to them and then by giving them sufficient time to talk before responding or interrupting. Reflecting feelings is also an important part of empathetic listening because it demonstrates that you understand the speaker's emotions. Unlike active listening, in which you restate or summarize the informational content of what has been said, the focus is on the affective part of the message. As an empathetic listener, you can use the following statements to *reflect the speaker's emotions*:

So, right now it sounds like you're feeling. . . .

You seem as if you're. . . .

Do you feel a bit. . . .

I could be wrong, but I'm sensing that you're feeling. . . .

In the end, says management consultant Terry Pearce, empathetic listening can be boiled down to these three steps. First, wait 10 seconds before you respond. It will seem an eternity, but waiting prevents you from interrupting others and rushing your response. Second, to be sure you understand what the speaker wants, ask questions to clarify the speaker's intent. Third, only then should you respond first with feelings and then facts (notice that facts *follow* feelings).[36]

13-3c Giving Feedback

In Chapter 10, you learned that performance appraisal feedback (i.e., judging) should be separated from developmental feedback (i.e., coaching).[37] We can now focus on the steps needed to communicate feedback one-on-one to employees.

To start, managers need to recognize that feedback can be constructive or destructive. **Destructive feedback** is disapproving without any intention of being helpful and almost always causes a negative or defensive reaction in the recipient. By contrast, **constructive feedback** is intended to be helpful, corrective, and/or encouraging. It is aimed at correcting performance deficiencies and motivating employees.

destructive feedback
feedback that disapproves without any intention of being helpful and almost always causes a negative or defensive reaction in the recipient

constructive feedback
feedback intended to be helpful, corrective, and/or encouraging

For feedback to be constructive rather than destructive, it must be immediate, focused on specific behaviors, and problem oriented. *Immediate feedback* is much more effective than delayed feedback because manager and worker can recall the mistake or incident more accurately and discuss it in detail. For example, if a worker is rude to a customer and the customer immediately reports the incident to management, and if the manager, in turn, immediately discusses the incident with the employee, there should be little disagreement over what was said or done. By contrast, it's unlikely that either the manager or the worker will be able to accurately remember the specifics of what occurred if the manager waits several weeks to discuss the incident. When that happens, it's usually too late to have a meaningful conversation.

Specific feedback focuses on particular acts or incidents that are clearly under the control of the employee. For instance, instead of telling an employee that he or she is "always late for work," it's much more constructive to say, "In the last three weeks, you have been 30 minutes late on four occasions and more than an hour late on two others." Furthermore, specific feedback isn't very helpful unless employees have control over the problems that the feedback addresses. Giving negative feedback about behaviors beyond someone's control is likely to be seen as unfair. Similarly, giving positive feedback about behaviors beyond someone's control may be viewed as insincere.

Last, *problem-oriented feedback* focuses on the problems or incidents associated with the poor performance rather than on the worker or the worker's personality. Giving feedback does not give managers the right to personally attack workers. Although managers may be frustrated by a worker's poor performance, the point of problem-oriented feedback is to draw attention to the problem in a nonjudgmental way so that the employee has enough information to correct it.

13-3d Improving Cross-Cultural Communication

As you know by now, effective communication is very difficult to accomplish. **Cross-cultural communication**, which involves transmitting information from a person in one country or culture to a person from another country or culture, is even more difficult.

You can do a number of things to increase your chances for successful cross-cultural communication:

- Familiarize yourself with a culture's general work norms.
- Determine whether a culture is emotionally affective or neutral.
- Develop respect for other cultures.
- Understand how address terms and attitudes toward time differ from culture to culture.

In Chapter 7, you learned that expatriates who receive predeparture language and cross-cultural training make faster adjustments to foreign cultures and perform better on their international assignments.[38] Therefore, the first step for successful cross-cultural communication is *familiarizing yourself with a culture's general work norms*, that is, the shared values, beliefs, and perceptions toward work and how it should be done. (See Chapter 7 for a more complete

cross-cultural communication
transmitting information from a person in one country or culture to a person from another country or culture

discussion of international cultures.) Don't assume that it will be easy; but no matter how difficult, you should work hard to learn different cultures and languages.

Determining whether a culture is emotionally affective or neutral is also important to cross-cultural communication. People in **affective cultures** tend to display their emotions and feelings openly when communicating, whereas people in **neutral cultures** do not.[39] Although Italians are prone to strong bursts of emotion (positive and negative), Chinese don't show strong emotions because doing so is thought to disrupt harmony and lead to conflict. Likewise, a smiling American is displaying happiness, but a smiling Japanese may be trying to hide another emotion or avoid answering a question.[40] The mistake most managers make is misunderstanding the differences between affective and neutral cultures. People from neutral cultures aren't by definition cold and unfeeling. They just don't show their emotions in the same way or with the same intensity as people from affective cultures. The key is to recognize the differences and then make sure your judgments are not based on the lack or presence of emotional reactions. Exhibit 13.5 provides a more detailed explanation of the differences between affective and neutral cultures.

Respecting other cultures is also an important part of improving cross-cultural communication. Because we use our own culture as the standard of comparison, it's very easy to make the common mistake of assuming that *different* means "inferior."[41]

According to Nancy Adler, "Evaluating others' behavior rarely helps in trying to understand, communicate with, or conduct business with people from another culture."[42] The key, she says, is taking a step back and realizing that you don't know or understand everything that is going on and that your assumptions and interpretations of others' behavior and motives may be wrong.

So, instead of judging or evaluating your international business colleagues, observe what they do. Also, delay your judgments until you have more experience with your colleagues and their culture. Last, treat any judgments or

neutral cultures
cultures in which people do not display emotions and feelings when communicating

affective cultures
cultures in which people display emotions and feelings when communicating

---

Exhibit 13.5

Affective and Neutral Cultures

In Affective Cultures, People	In Neutral Cultures, People
1. Reveal thoughts and feelings through verbal and nonverbal communication	1. Don't reveal what they are thinking or feeling
2. Express and show feelings of tension	2. Hide tension and only show it accidentally in face or posture
3. Let their emotions show easily, intensely, and without inhibition	3. Suppress emotions, leading to occasional "explosions"
4. Admire heated, animated, and intense expression of emotion	4. Admire remaining cool, calm, and relaxed
5. Are used to touching, gesturing, and showing strong emotions through facial expressions (all are common)	5. Resist touching, gesturing, and showing strong emotions through facial expressions
6. Make statements with emotion	6. Often make statements in an unexpressive manner

Source: F. Trompenaars, Riding the Waves of Culture: Understanding Diversity in Global Business *(London: Economist Books, 1994).*

---

conclusions you do make as guesses and then double-check those judgments or conclusions with others.[43] The more patient you are in forming opinions and drawing conclusions, the better you'll be at cross-cultural communication.

You can also improve cross-cultural communication by *knowing the address terms* that different cultures use to address each other in the workplace.[44] **Address terms** are the cultural norms that establish whether you address businesspeople by their first names, family names, or titles. An American manager working in one of his company's British subsidiaries introduced himself as "Chuck" to his British employees and coworkers. Nonetheless, even after six months on the job, his British counterparts still referred to him as "Charles." And the more he insisted they call him "Chuck," the more they seemed to dig in their heels and call him "Charles."[45] So, to decrease defensiveness, know your address terms before addressing your international business counterparts.

Understanding different cultural attitudes toward time is another major consideration for effective cross-cultural communication. Cultures tend to be either monochronic or polychronic in their orientation toward time.[46] In **monochronic cultures**, people tend to do one thing at a time and view time as linear, meaning that time is the passage of sequential events. You may have heard the saying, "There are three stages in people's lives: when they believe in Santa Claus, when they don't believe in Santa Claus, and when they are Santa Claus." The progression from childhood, to young adulthood, to parenthood (when they are Santa Claus) reflects a linear view of time. Schedules are important in monochronic cultures because you schedule time to get a particular thing done. By contrast, in **polychronic cultures**, people tend to do more than one thing at a time and view time as circular, meaning that time is a combination of the past, present, and future.

As you can easily imagine, businesspeople from monochronic cultures are driven to distraction by what they perceive as the laxness of polychronic cultures, while people from polychronic cultures chafe under what they perceive as the strict regimentation of monochronic cultures. Exhibit 13.6 provides a more detailed explanation of the differences between monochronic and polychronic cultures.

Differences in monochronic and polychronic time show up in four important temporal concepts that affect cross-cultural communication: appointment time, schedule time, discussion time, and acquaintance time.[47] **Appointment time** refers to how punctual you must be when showing up for scheduled appointments or meetings. In the United States, you are considered late if you arrive more than 5 minutes after the appointed time. By contrast, in Latin countries, people can arrive 20 to 30 minutes after a scheduled appointment and still not be considered late.

Schedule time is the time by which scheduled projects or jobs should actually be completed. In the United States and other Anglo cultures, a premium is placed on completing things on time. By contrast, more relaxed attitudes toward schedule time can be found throughout Asia and Latin America.

Discussion time concerns how much time should be spent in discussion with others. In the United States, we carefully manage discussion time to avoid wasting time on nonbusiness topics. In Brazil, though, because of the emphasis

address terms
cultural norms that establish whether you should address businesspeople by their first names, family names, or titles

monochronic cultures
cultures in which people tend to do one thing at a time and view time as linear

polychronic cultures
cultures in which people tend to do more than one thing at a time and view time as circular

appointment time
a cultural norm for how punctual you must be when showing up for scheduled appointments or meetings

schedule time
a cultural norm for the time by which scheduled projects or jobs should actually be completed

discussion time
a cultural norm for how much time should be spent in discussion with others

Exhibit 13.6

Monochronic versus Polychronic Cultures

People in Monochronic Cultures	People in Polychronic Cultures
• Do one thing at a time	• Do many things at once
• Concentrate on the job	• Are highly distractible and subject to interruptions
• Take time commitments (deadlines, schedules) seriously	• Meet time commitments only if possible without extreme measures
• Are committed to the job	• Are committed to people
• Adhere scrupulously to plans	• Change plans easily and often
• Are concerned about not disturbing others (privacy is to be respected)	• Are more concerned with relationships (family, friends, business associates) than with privacy
• Show respect for private property (rarely lend or borrow things)	• Frequently borrow and lend things
• Emphasize promptness	• Vary their promptness by the relationship
• Are accustomed to short-term relationships	• Tend to build lifetime relationships

Source: E. T. Hall & M. R. Hall, Understanding Cultural Differences (Yarmouth, ME: Intercultural Press, 1990).

on building relationships, as much as two hours of general discussion on non-business topics can take place before moving on to business issues.

Finally, **acquaintance time** is how much time you must spend getting to know someone before the person is prepared to do business with you. Again, in the United States, people quickly get down to business and are willing to strike a deal on the same day if the terms are good and initial impressions are positive. In the Middle East, however, it may take two or three weeks of meetings before reaching this comfort level.

REVIEW 13-3

Managing One-on-One Communication

One-on-one communication can be managed by choosing the right communication medium, being a good listener, giving effective feedback, and understanding cross-cultural communication. Managers generally prefer oral communication because it provides the opportunity to ask questions and assess nonverbal communication. Oral communication is best suited to complex, ambiguous, or emotionally laden topics. Written communication is best suited for delivering straightforward messages and information. Listening is important for managerial success, but most people are terrible listeners. To improve your listening skills, choose to be an active listener (clarify responses, paraphrase, and summarize) and an empathetic listener (show your desire to understand, reflect feelings). Feedback can be constructive or destructive. To be constructive, feedback must be immediate, focused on specific behaviors, and problem oriented. Finally, to increase the chances for successful cross-cultural communication, familiarize yourself with a culture's general work norms, determine whether a culture is emotionally affective or neutral, develop respect for other cultures, and understand how address terms and attitudes toward time

acquaintance time

a cultural norm for how much time you must spend getting to know someone before the person is prepared to do business with you (polychronic vs. monochronic time; appointment, schedule, discussion, and acquaintance time) differ from culture to culture.

13-4 Managing Organization-Wide Communication

Suppose that you supervise a division of 50, 100, or even 1,000 people. How can you communicate effectively with everyone in that division? Although managing one-on-one communication is important, managers must also know how to communicate effectively with a greater number of people throughout an organization. When Bill Zollars became CEO of *Yellow Corporation*, a trucking company, he decided that he needed to communicate directly with all 25,000 of the company's employees. For a year and a half, he traveled across the country conducting small, town hall meetings. Zollars says, "I spent 85 percent of my time on the road talking to people one-on-one or in small groups. I would start off in the morning with the sales force, then talk to drivers, and then the people on the docks. At the end of the day I would have a customer dinner. I would say the same thing to every group and repeat it ad nauseam. The people traveling with me were ready to shoot me. But you have to be relentless in terms of your message."[48]

After reading this section, you should be able to:

13-4 describe how managers can manage effective organization-wide communication.

Effective leaders, however, don't just communicate to others. They also make themselves accessible so they can hear what employees throughout their organizations are thinking and feeling.

Learn more about organization-wide communication by reading the following sections about **13-4a improving transmission by getting the message out** and **13-4b improving reception by finding ways to hear what others feel and think.**

13-4a Improving Transmission: Getting the Message Out

Several methods of electronic communication—e-mail, collaborative discussion sites, televised/videotaped speeches and conferences, and broadcast voice mail—now make it easier for managers to communicate with people throughout the organization and get the message out.

Although we normally think of e-mail, the transmission of messages via computers, as a means of one-on-one communication, it also plays an important role in organization-wide communication. With the click of a button, managers can send e-mail to everyone in the company via distribution lists.

Many CEOs and top executives make their e-mail addresses public and encourage employees to contact them directly. Collaborative websites are another means of electronically promoting organization-wide communication. **Online discussion forums** use Web- or software-based discussion tools to allow

online discussion forums
in-house online newsgroups that use Web- or software-based discussion tools to enable employees throughout the company to ask each other questions and share knowledge

employees across the company to easily ask questions and share knowledge with each other. The point is to share expertise and not duplicate solutions already discovered by others in the company. Furthermore, because collaborative discussion sites remain online, they provide a historical database for people who are dealing with particular problems for the first time. Collaborative discussion sites are typically organized by topic, project, or person and can take the shape of blogs that allow readers to post comments, wikis to allow collaborative discussions, document sharing and editing, or traditional discussion forums (see Chapter 15 on managing information for further explanation).

Televised/videotaped speeches and meetings are a third electronic method of organization-wide communication. **Televised/videotaped speeches and meetings** are simply speeches and meetings originally made to a small audience that are either simultaneously broadcast to other locations in the company or videotaped for subsequent distribution and viewing by a broader audience.

Voice messaging, or voice mail, is a telephone answering system that records audio messages. In one survey, 89 percent of respondents said that voice messaging is critical to business communication, 78 percent said that it improves productivity, and 58 percent said they would rather leave a message on a voice messaging system than with a receptionist.[49] Nonetheless, most people are unfamiliar with the ability to *broadcast voice mail* by sending a recorded message to everyone in the company. Broadcast voice mail gives top managers a quick, convenient way to address their workforces via oral communication, but only if people actually listen to the message, and that turns out to be a challenge with Generation Y workers. Jeff Schwarz, global talent leader at *DELOITTE & TOUCHE*, says, "If you send a message on voicemail or send an e-mail, they are likely to ignore it. It's very frustrating to our leaders, most of whom are boomers [and] some of whom are Gen X'ers. When they broadcast voicemail messages, big swaths of their organization are not hearing it. They're not even listening to it, and they're not even sure it's directed to them because they don't think about being communicated with in that way. CEOs or HR leaders or business leaders think they're sending a direct message, but that is not the most effective way to communicate across the generations." Deloitte's solution—embed the broadcast voice mail in an e-mail.[50]

13-4b Improving Reception: Hearing What Others Feel and Think

When people think of "organization-wide" communication, they think of the CEO and top managers getting their message out to people in the company. But organization-wide communication also means finding ways to hear what people throughout the organization are thinking and feeling. This is important because most employees and managers are reluctant to share their thoughts and feelings with top managers. Surveys indicate that only 29 percent of first-level managers feel that their companies encourage employees to express their opinions openly. Another study of 22 companies found that 70 percent of the people surveyed were afraid to speak up about problems they knew existed at work.

Withholding information about organizational problems or issues is called **organizational silence**. Organizational silence occurs when employees believe

televised/videotaped speeches and meetings speeches and meetings originally made to a smaller audience that are either simultaneously broadcast to other locations in the company or videotaped for subsequent distribution and viewing

organizational silence when employees withhold information about organizational problems or issues

that telling management about problems won't make a difference or that they'll be punished or hurt in some way for sharing such information.[51]

Company hotlines, survey feedback, frequent informal meetings, surprise visits, and blogs are additional ways of overcoming organizational silence. **Company hotlines** are phone numbers that anyone in the company can call anonymously to leave information for upper management. Hotlines are particularly important because 44 percent of employees will not report misconduct. Why not? The reason is twofold: They don't believe anything will be done, *and* they "fear that the report will not be kept confidential."[52] David Childers, CEO of EthicsPoint, which runs hotlines for corporations, says that companies can expect 1 to 1.5 percent of their employees to call their hotlines.[53] Company hotlines are incredibly useful, as 47 percent of the calls placed to them result in an investigation and some form of corrective action within the organization. Anonymity is critical too, because as those investigations proceed, 54 percent of the callers did not want their identities revealed.[54]

Survey feedback is information that is collected by survey from organization members and then compiled, disseminated, and used to develop action plans for improvement. Many organizations make use of survey feedback by surveying their managers and employees several times a year. GUARDIAN NEWS AND MEDIA, the publisher of the British newspaper *The Guardian*, conducts an annual survey of its employees to gauge their satisfaction and confidence in the company.[55]

Frequent *informal meetings* between top managers and lower-level employees are one of the best ways for top managers to hear what others think and feel. Many people assume that top managers are at the center of everything that goes on in organizations, but top managers commonly feel isolated from most of their lower-level managers and employees.[56] Consequently, more and more top managers are scheduling frequent informal meetings with people throughout their companies. Yogesh Gupta, CEO of *FATWIRE* (now owned by Oracle), which makes software to manage business websites, says that managers must not get defensive during informal meetings. Says Gupta, "I've heard so many executives tell employees to be candid and then jump down their throats if they bring up a problem or ask a critical question."[57] Gupta has spent hundreds of hours in informal meetings with his 200 managers and nine executives. He meets with each privately because he believes that it encourages people to be candid. And he asks each these questions:

- What am I doing wrong?
- What would you do differently if you were running the company?
- What's the biggest thing getting in the way of you doing your job well?

As a result of these meetings, Gupta learned that Fatwire was understaffed in marketing and product development.

company hotlines
phone numbers that anyone in the company can call anonymously to leave information for upper management

survey feedback
information that is collected by surveys from organizational members and then compiled, disseminated, and used to develop action plans for improvement

Have you ever been around when a supervisor learns that upper management is going to be paying a visit? First, there's shock. Next, there's anxiety. And then there's panic, as everyone is told to drop what he or she is doing to polish, shine, and spruce up the workplace so that it looks perfect for the visit. Of course, when visits are conducted under these conditions, top managers don't get a realistic look at what's going on in the company. Consequently, one of the ways to get an accurate picture is to pay *surprise visits* to various parts of the organization. These visits should not just be surprise inspections, but should also be used as an opportunity to encourage meaningful upward communication from those who normally don't get a chance to communicate with upper management.

Blogs are another way to hear what people are thinking and saying, both inside and outside the organization. A **blog** is a personal website that provides personal opinions or recommendations, news summaries, and reader comments. At GOOGLE, which owns the blog-hosting service Blogger, hundreds of employees are writing *internal blogs*. One employee even wrote a blog for posting all the notes from the brainstorming sessions used to redesign the search page used by millions each day. Marissa Mayer, former vice president of Google's Search Products & User Experience, said, "Our legal department loves the blogs, because it basically is a written-down, backed-up, permanent, time-stamped version of the scientist's notebook. When you want to file a patent, you can now show in blogs where this idea happened."[58]

External blogs and Twitter sites (micro blogs where entries are limited to 140 characters), written by people outside the company, can be a good way to find out what others are saying or thinking about your organization or its products or actions. But it means that someone in the firm has to actively monitor what is being said on Web, blog, and Twitter sites.

blog
a personal website that provides personal opinions or recommendations, news summaries, and reader comments

REVIEW 13-4
....
Managing Organization-Wide Communication
Managers need methods for managing organization-wide communication and for making themselves accessible so they can hear what employees throughout their organizations are thinking and feeling. E-mail, collaborative discussion sites, televised/videotaped speeches and conferences, and broadcast voice mail make it much easier for managers to improve message transmission and get the message out. By contrast, anonymous company hotlines, survey feedback, frequent informal meetings, and surprise visits help managers avoid organizational silence and improve reception by hearing what others in the organization feel and think. Monitoring internal and external blogs and Twitter sites is another way to find out what people are saying and thinking about your organization.

Management Team Decision

Talking across Time Zones

In the beginning, your company was run out of a small, drab building in the middle of Ohio. With just five employees, your little "factory" produced just a single product—small boat engines. Five years later, against all odds, you somehow landed a lucrative government contract to supply the U.S. Army with small engines for its unmanned vehicles program.

That contract was the turning point that transformed the company from a small local business into a global powerhouse. Gone are the days when the entire company was housed in a small, cramped, converted farmhouse. The entire manufacturing operation was moved to China several years ago. The R&D and engineering division operates out of a sparkling new building in Berlin, Germany. The marketing staff works out of Los Angeles, and the sales and customer service call center is based in Mumbai, India. As for the little farmhouse that you started out in, it's long gone, replaced by a glamorous modern building that's home to executive management.

With facilities located all over the world and an international staff, there have been few challenges that your company has not been able to overcome. It's been able to create low-cost, reliable engines that have been a hit in developing economies. Its alternative fuels research division is among the largest in the world and is poised both to introduce a hydrogen-powered engine and create an infrastructure to give consumers easy access to refueling stations. However, there remains one issue that your company has struggled with for some time. It doesn't have to do with dealing with environmental groups, suppliers, or competitor firms. Instead, it's about communication.

Your company has always emphasized speed—speed in discussing issues, speed in coming to decisions, and speed in executing them. And all this speed requires a great amount of efficient communication within the company. In the early days, of course, this simply meant that Jo in engineering would walk across the hall to talk to Sam in marketing. But now that you have offices all over the world, it's become more difficult to make quick decisions and plans, because it's hard to find a way to get people together to talk. If it's 10 A.M. in Ohio, it's 7 A.M. in Los Angeles, 11 P.M. in Beijing, 8 P.M. in Mumbai, and 4 P.M. in Berlin.

So, how can we talk to each other quickly and efficiently? That's the question that the senior management team has been gathered to try to resolve. Their task is to find, or even create, a communication system that will allow timely, clear, and effective communication throughout the organization without forcing people to wake up at 3 A.M. for a videoconference.

Questions

1. In your opinion, what communication method would be ideal for an organization that has offices in many different countries?

2. Is it necessary to sacrifice speed in communication for the sake of a global presence? That is, can a company have both a global presence and an efficient, timely means of communication?

3. What cross-cultural issues should you keep in mind as you create a new communication system?

Practice Being a Manager

Avoiding Communication Breakdown

When problems occur in organizations, they are frequently attributed to a breakdown in communication. The communication process may get more than its share of the blame for some breakdowns that result from organizational or leadership problems. But there is some truth to the common perception that communication is problematic. In this exercise, you will have the opportunity to consider how you might improve your own communication from two sides of the table—coaching or disciplining an employee and receiving coaching or disciplining from a manager.

STEP 1 **Get into groups and read the scenario.** Your professor will organize you in small groups of three or four students.

Scenario: Chalet is a fine-dining restaurant in a ski resort setting. The restaurant is well known for its gourmet cuisine, fine wine selection, and outstanding service. Dinner for two at Chalet would typically cost $100 or more. A key management responsibility at Chalet is the training and development of waitstaff. Service quality is carefully monitored and standards rigorously maintained. In exchange for meeting these demanding standards, Chalet waitstaff are well compensated and enjoy good benefits. As time permits, you should complete conversations in which you play each of the following roles: Dennis/Denise (new waitstaff member with three months of experience at Chalet); Christy/Chris (service manager); and D.J./R.J. (communication consultant to Chalet).

Here are some basic facts of the situation:

- The service manager has not directly observed any problems with Dennis/Denise interacting with customers of the restaurant.
- Over this past busy weekend, three tables of customers reported problems with the service they received from Dennis/Denise. Only one other table received any negative feedback at all during the weekend, and that concerned the quality of a particular dessert item.
- The reports about Dennis/Denise were rather vague—"server seemed distant, unresponsive" and "acted aloof, like we were a bother."
- Christy/Chris, the service manager, did catch the tail end of what seemed like an argument between Dennis/Denise and one of the cooks on Friday night. When the cook was asked about the incident, she said, "It was nothing... usual cook versus server stuff."
- Dennis/Denise needs this job to pay for college and is taking a full load of classes.

The role-play should involve a brief conversation (5 to 7 minutes) initiated by Christy/Chris on Monday afternoon prior to opening. The focus of this conversation should be to coach and/or discipline regarding the concerns of the previous weekend. Those playing the role of communication consultant should take notes and provide feedback on the communication in this conversation (strengths and areas for improvement). As time allows, rotate roles after completing a conversation and hearing consultant feedback.

STEP 2 **Do the role-play.** Complete a role-play conversation with one person playing the role of the service manager (Christy/Chris) and another person playing the role of the waitstaffer (Dennis/Denise). Communication consultant(s) should listen and take notes in order to provide feedback to the two individuals who are role-playing the coaching/discipline conversation.

STEP 3 **Give feedback.** Communication consultant(s) should give feedback to the role-players at the conclusion of the conversation, considering key aspects of communication discussed in this chapter.

STEP 4 **Switch roles.** Switch roles and repeat the role-play conversation and postconversation feedback as time allows.

STEP 5 **Debrief as a class.** What challenges face the communicators in this scenario? Which role was most difficult for you, and why? Why is it important for managers to coach and discipline effectively? Why might managers avoid (or underutilize) this form of communication?

 Self-Assessment

How Do You Listen?

Have you ever been eager to tell someone a funny story, only to have that person interrupt you repeatedly to ask for details or clarification? And have you ever said in exasperation, "Will you just listen?" Some people prefer an inquisitive listening style, whereas others prefer a contemplative listening style. What listening style best describes you? This listening styles inventory will help you establish a baseline to use as a foundation for developing your listening skills.

The following items relate to listening style.[60] Circle the appropriate responses. Please be candid.

1 Almost always

2 Often

3 Sometimes

4 Seldom

5 Almost never

1. I want to listen to what others have to say when they are talking.
   5   4   3   2   1

2. I do not listen at my capacity when others are talking.
   1   2   3   4   5

3. By listening, I can guess a speaker's intent or purpose without being told.
   5   4   3   2   1

4. I have a purpose for listening when others are talking.
   5   4   3   2   1

5. I keep control of my biases and attitudes when listening to others speak so that these factors won't affect my interpretation of the message.
   5   4   3   2   1

6. I analyze my listening errors so as not to make them again.
   5   4   3   2   1

7. I listen to the complete message before making judgments about what the speaker has said.
   5   4   3   2   1

8. I cannot tell when a speaker's biases or attitudes are affecting his or her message.
   1   2   3   4   5

9. I ask questions when I don't fully understand a speaker's message.
   5   4   3   2   1

10. I am aware of whether or not a speaker's meaning of words and concepts is the same as mine.
    5   4   3   2   1

    TOTAL = _____

SCORING

Determine your listening style by totalling all the numbers you selected into a single sum. You can find the interpretation of your score at www.cengagebrain.com.

MANAGEMENT WORKPLACE

© CENGAGE LEARNING 2013

Plant Fantasies: Managing Communication

In a day when companies use Twitter and Facebook to communicate, Teresa Carleo of Plant Fantasies is a throwback—she doesn't use social media or e-mail. Instead, leaders at Plant Fantasies tailor the communication methods they use to the situation they are in. Not all communication channels are equally suited for each situation. A quick tweet might be a great way to communicate with a landscaper, but a terrible way to reach a new client.

What to Watch For and Ask Yourself

1. Why would Teresa Carleo and Steve Martucci favor face-to-face communication over e-mail when dealing with customers?

2. Why would Carleo and Martucci prefer to use electronic communication methods for certain types of communication within the company?

3. In the video, Carleo says that she worries that at times she communicates too much. What steps could she take to confirm that her messages are being heard and understood by others?

Endnotes

1 "Top Browser Share Trend," NetMarketShare, May 2011, accessed June 19, 2011, from www.netmarketshare.com/browser-market-share.aspx?spider=1&qprid=1; R. Adams and J. Vascellaro, "Google Digital Newsstand Aims to Muscle In on Apple," *Wall Street Journal*, January 3, 2011, B1; L. Edmund and M. Learmonth, "What Larry Page Will Be Up Against at Google," *Advertising Age*, January 24, 2011, 1; A. Efrati, "Google to Test Daily Deals That Challenge Groupon," *Wall Street Journal*, January 22, 2011, B4; A. Efrati and J. Vascellaro, "Power Shifts Atop Google—Internet Giant Says Co-Founder Larry Page Will Replace CEO Eric Schmidt," *Wall Street Journal*, January 21, 2011, A1; M. Farhad, "Google: The Quest," *Fast Company*, April 2011, 68–120, 9p; H. Jenkins Jr., "The Weekend Interview with Eric Schmidt: Google and the Search for the Future," *Wall Street Journal*, August 14, 2010, A9; M. Mangalindan, "Boss Talk: The Grownup at Google; How Eric Schmidt Imposed Better Management Tactics But Didn't Stifle Search Giant," *Wall Street Journal*, March 29, 2004, B1; B. Saporito, "Refreshing Google," *Time*, February 7, 2011, 48–49; and J. Stewart, "WEEKEND INVESTOR—Common Sense: Will Google Survive Facebook?" *Wall Street Journal*, January 29, 2011, B7.

2 J. Sandberg, "Bosses Often Sugarcoat Their Worst News, But Staffers Don't Bite," *Wall Street Journal*, April 21, 2005, http://online.wsj.com/article/SB108249516353388330.html [accessed September 15, 2004].

3 E. E. Lawler III, L. W. Porter, and A. Tannenbaum, "Manager's Attitudes toward Interaction Episodes," *Journal of Applied Psychology* 52 (1968): 423–439; and H. Mintzberg, *The Nature of Managerial Work* (New York: Harper & Row, 1973).

4 J. D. Maes, T. G. Weldy, and M. L. Icenogle, "A Managerial Perspective: Oral Communication Competency Is Most Important for Business Students in the Workplace," *Journal of Business Communication* 34 (1997): 67–80.

5 R. Lepsinger and A. D. Lucia, *The Art and Science of 360 Degree Feedback* (San Francisco: Pfeiffer, 1997).

6 E. E. Jones and K. E. Davis, "From Acts to Dispositions: The Attribution Process in Person Perception," in L. Berkowitz, ed., *Advances in Experimental and Social Psychology*, vol. 2 (New York: Academic Press, 1965), 219–266; and R. G. Lord and J. E. Smith, "Theoretical, Information-Processing, and Situational Factors Affecting Attribution Theory Models of Organizational Behavior," *Academy of Management Review* 8 (1983): 50–60.

7 M. Nicholson and R. Hoye, "Contextual Factors Associated with Poor Sport Spectator Behaviour," *Managing Leisure* 10 (April 2005): 94–105.

8 D. Simons and C. Chabris, "Gorillas in Our Midst: Sustained Inattentional Blindness for Dynamic Events," *Perception* 28 (1999): 1059–1074.

9 G. Fowler and I. Sherr, "A Defiant Steve Jobs Confronts 'Antennagate,'" *Wall Street Journal*, July 17, 2010, B1.

10 H. H. Kelly, *Attribution in Social Interaction* (Morristown, NJ: General Learning Press, 1971).

11 J. M. Burger, "Motivational Biases in the Attribution of Responsibility for an Accident: A Meta-Analysis of the Defensive-Attribution Hypothesis," *Psychological Bulletin* 90 (1981): 496–512.

12 D. A. Hofmann and A. Stetzer, "The Role of Safety Climate and Communication in Accident Interpretation: Implications for Learning from Negative Events," *Academy of Management Journal* 41, no. 6 (1998): 644–657.

13 C. Perrow, *Normal Accidents: Living with High-Risk Technologies* (New York: Basic Books, 1984).

14 A. G. Miller and T. Lawson, "The Effect of an Informational Opinion on the Fundamental Attribution Error," *Journal of Personality & Social Psychology* 47 (1989): 873–896; and J. M. Burger, "Changes in Attribution Errors over Time: The Ephemeral Fundamental Attribution Error," *Social Cognition* 9 (1991): 182–193.

15 F. Heider, *The Psychology of Interpersonal Relations* (New York: Wiley, 1958); and D. T. Miller and M. Ross, "Self-Serving Biases in Attribution of Causality: Fact or Fiction?" *Psychological Bulletin* 82 (1975): 213–225.

16 J. R. Larson Jr., "The Dynamic Interplay between Employees' Feedback-Seeking Strategies and Supervisors' Delivery of Performance Feedback," *Academy of Management Review* 14, no. 3 (1989): 408–422.

17 B. O'Keefe, "Meet the CEO of the Biggest Company on Earth," *Fortune*, September 9, 2010, accessed February 25, 2011, from http://money.cnn.com/2010/09/07/news/companies/mike_duke_walmart_full.fortune/.

18 M. Reddy, "The Conduit Metaphor—A Case of Frame Conflict in Our Language about Our Language," in *Metaphor and Thought*, ed. A. Ortony (Cambridge: Cambridge University Press, 1979), 284–324.

19 G. L. Kreps, *Organizational Communication: Theory and Practice* (New York: Longman, 1990).

20 Ibid.

21 J. Sandberg, "Ruthless Rumors and the Managers Who Enable Them," *Wall Street Journal*, October 29, 2003, B1.

22 W. Davis and J. R. O'Connor, "Serial Transmission of Information: A Study of the Grapevine," *Journal of Applied Communication Research* 5 (1977): 61–72.

23 Davis and O'Connor, "Serial Transmission of Information: A Study of the Grapevine"; and C. Hymowitz, "Managing: Spread the Word, Gossip Is Good," *Wall Street Journal*, October 4, 1988, online, page number not available.

24 D. T. Hall, K. L. Otazo, and G. P. Hollenbeck, "Behind Closed Doors: What Really Happens in Executive Coaching," *Organizational Dynamics* 27, no. 3 (1999): 39–53.

25 P. O'Connell, "Goldman Sachs: Committed to the Next Generation," *Businessweek*, February 17, 2010, 12.

26 R. McGarvey, "Lords of Discipline," *Entrepreneur Magazine*, January 1, 2000, page number not available.

27 A. Mehrabian, "Communication without Words," *Psychology Today* 3 (1968): 53; A. Mehrabian, *Silent Messages* (Belmont,

CA: Wadsworth, 1971); R. Harrison, *Beyond Words: An Introduction to Nonverbal Communication* (Upper Saddle River, NJ: Prentice Hall, 1974); and A. Mehrabian, *Non-Verbal Communication* (Chicago: Aldine, 1972).

28 M. L. Knapp, *Nonverbal Communication in Human Interaction*, 2nd ed. (New York: Holt, Rinehart & Winston, 1978).

29 H. M. Rosenfeld, "Instrumental Affiliative Functions of Facial and Gestural Expressions," *Journal of Personality & Social Psychology* 24 (1966): 65–72; P. Ekman, "Differential Communication of Affect by Head and Body Cues," *Journal of Personality & Social Psychology* 23 (1965): 726–735; and A. Mehrabian, "Significance of Posture and Position in the Communication of Attitude and Status Relationships," *Psychological Bulletin* 71 (1969): 359–372.

30 C. A. Bartlett and S. Ghoshal, "Changing the Role of Top Management beyond Systems to People," *Harvard Business Review,* May–June 1995, 132–142.

31 J. Fry, "When Talk Isn't Cheap: Is E-mailing Colleagues Who Sit Feet Away a Sign of Office Dysfunction, or a Wise Move?" *Wall Street Journal*, November 28, 2005, http://online.wsj.com [content no longer available online].

32 R. G. Nichols, "Do We Know How to Listen? Practical Helps in a Modern Age," in *Communication Concepts and Processes*, ed. J. DeVitor (Englewood Cliffs, NJ: Prentice Hall, 1971); and P. V. Lewis, *Organizational Communication: The Essence of Effective Management* (Columbus, OH: Grid Publishing Company, 1975).

33 E. Atwater, *I Hear You*, rev. ed. (New York: Walker, 1992).

34 R. Adler and N. Towne, *Looking Out/Looking In* (San Francisco: Rinehart Press, 1975).

35 Atwater, *I Hear You.*

36 P. Sellers, A. Diba, and E. Florian, "Get Over Yourself—You're Ego Is out of Control. You're Screwing Up Your Career," *Fortune,* April 30, 2001, 76.

37 H. H. Meyer, "A Solution to the Performance Appraisal Feedback Enigma," *Academy of Management Executive* 5, no. 1 (1991): 68–76.

38 J. S. Black and M. Mendenhall, "Cross-Cultural Training Effectiveness: A Review and Theoretical Framework for Future Research," *Academy of Management Review* 15 (1990): 113–136.

39 F. Trompenaars, Riding the Waves of Culture: Understanding Diversity in Global Business (London: Economist Books, 1994).

40 N. Forster, "Expatriates and the Impact of Cross-Cultural Training," *Human Resource Management* 10 (2000): 63–78.

41 N. Adler, *From Boston to Beijing: Managing with a World View* (Cincinnati, OH: South-Western, 2002), based on A. Laurent, "The Cultural Diversity of Western Conceptions of Management," *International Studies of Management and Organization* 13, no. 1–2 (Spring–Summer 1983): 75–96.

42 Ibid.

43 Ibid.

44 R. Mead, *Cross-Cultural Management* (New York: Wiley, 1990).

45 Ibid.

46 E. T. Hall, *The Dance of Life* (New York: Doubleday, 1983).

47 E. T. Hall and W. F. Whyte, "Intercultural Communication: A Guide to Men of Action," *Human Organization* 19, no. 1 (1961): 5–12.

48 C. Tkaczyk and M. Boyle, "Follow These Leaders," *Fortune*, December 12, 2005, 125.

49 M. Campanelli and N. Friedman, "Welcome to Voice Mail Hell: The New Technology Has Become a Barrier between Salespeople and Customers," *Sales & Marketing Management* 147 (May 1995): 98–101.

50 S. Ali, "Why No One under 30 Answers Your Voicemail," DiversityInc, February 3, 2011, accessed February 22, 2011, from www.diversityinc.com/article/7967/Why-No-One-Under-30-Answers-Your-Voicemail/.

51 E. W. Morrison, "Organizational Silence: A Barrier to Change and Development in a Pluralistic World," *Academy of Management Review* 25 (2000): 706–725.

52 K. Maher, "Global Companies Face Reality of Instituting Ethics Programs," *Wall Street Journal*, November 9, 2004, B8.

53 Ibid.

54 "An Inside Look at Corporate Hotlines," *Security Director's Report*, February 2007, 8.

55 J. Confino, "Guardian Employee Survey Maintains High Scores Despite Radical Restructuring," Guardian.co.uk, January 11, 2010, accessed July 15, 2011, from www.guardian.co.uk/sustainability/corporate-social-responsibility-employee-survey-employee-engagement-sustainability.

56 C. Hymowitz, "Sometimes, Moving Up Makes It Harder to See What Goes on Below," *Wall Street Journal*, October 15, 2007, B1.

57 Ibid.

58 Kirkpatrick and Roth, "Why There's No Escaping the Blog," *Fortune*, January 10, 2005, online, page not available.

59 M. Dollivbre, "Why Companies 'Click' on Twitter," *Adweek*, August 15, 2010, accessed February 13, 2011, from www.adweek.com/aw/content_display/data-center/research/e3i831a0b575c6cd1c617038e29f192cc92.

60 C. G. Pearce, I. W. Johnson, and R. T. Barker, "Assessment of the Listening Styles Inventory: Progress in Establishing Reliability and Validity," Journal of Business and Technical Communication 17, no. 1 (2003): 84–113.

PART FIVE

Controlling

Chapter Fourteen

Control

© KRISTOFFER TRIPPLAAR/ ALAMY

Chapter 14 examines the basic and in-depth methods that companies use to achieve control, as well as those things that companies choose to control (finances, customer retention, and product quality, among others).

Chapter Fifteen

Managing Information

© CHRISTOPHER PARYPA/ SHUTTERSTOCK.COM

Chapter 15 explains why information matters, the value of strategic information to companies, and the cost and characteristics of good information. We investigate how companies capture, process, and protect information, and how information, knowledge, and expertise are shared.

Chapter Sixteen

Managing Service and Manufacturing Operations

© PETER HORREE/ALAMY

Chapter 16 discusses the daily production of goods and services, starting with the basics of productivity and quality. Next, you will read about managing service and manufacturing operations, and the measures, costs, and methods for managing inventory.

© DIZZO/ISTOCK PHOTO

469

Control

REEL TO REAL

Management Workplace is at Barcelona Restaurant Group.

© TETRA IMAGES/CORBIS

SELF-ASSESSMENT

How comfortable are you with receiving feedback? Do the Self-Assessment for this chapter in the book or online to find out.

© ISTOCKPHOTO/ALEXANDER KALINA

ONLINE QUIZZES

Did you get it? Review the main concepts in the chapter by taking the online quizzes on CourseMate!

© ISTOCKPHOTO/PEARLEYE

VIDEO QUIZZES

Get more out of the videos by taking the multimedia video quizzes online.

© ISTOCKPHOTO/DAVID HUGHES

What Would You Do?

Caterpillar Headquarters, Peoria, Illinois[1]

Caterpillar dominates the construction and earth-moving equipment industry, with $50 billion per year in revenues. Komatsu, its next closest competitor, does $25 billion. However, Caterpillar has not been able to master the cyclical nature of its industry. When the heavy machinery industry booms, no one keeps up with demand, and everyone builds new factories and hires thousands of new employees. Indeed, Caterpillar doubled its workforce the last time global demand surged. But when the industry goes bust, factories are closed and tens of thousands of employees are laid off. What kind of dramatic swings does Caterpillar experience? A 43 percent spike in sales in April 2004 and a 52 percent decline in September 2009. Caterpillar's Doug Oberhelman had firsthand experience with an even larger sales swing in Argentina. He says, "We sold 1,200 machines a year in Argentina in the late '70s. In 1981, '82, and '83, while I was there, we sold four total."

© KRISTOFFER TRIPPLAAR/ALAMY

In sudden downturns, Caterpillar learned to switch from selling new equipment to refurbishing used equipment. For customers, the advantages of taking apart, cleaning, repairing, and reassembling the engines, transmissions, and other major parts of heavy machinery are a new factory warranty and a 30 percent to 80 percent lower cost. Globally, the remanufacturing business is worth $100 billion a year, with profit margins as high as 40 percent. So, it has been a good way for Caterpillar to offset the boom-and-bust cycle to some extent.

The second way in which Caterpillar has dealt with sudden swings was to try to predict when they occurred. Company economists told your chief financial officer, "We've got good news and bad news. The good news is we found an indicator that predicts shifts in U.S. GDP with a lead time of six to nine months. The bad news is it's our own sales to users." The problem, though, was that while they could generally predict *when* a shift in sales would occur, they couldn't predict the *severity*. As a result, the last time a severe downturn

occurred, Caterpillar laid off 35,000 managers and workers out of 120,000 worldwide. Furthermore, it cut executive compensation by 50 percent, senior manager pay by up to 35 percent, and manager and support staff pay by 15 percent. To reduce costs further, Caterpillar offered voluntary buyout packages to 25,000 salaried workers.

You've just been named Caterpillar's next CEO, and you've got six months before you take over from the current CEO. You've decided to use this time to pick your 16 top managers and work with them to analyze the company. Caterpillar has entered a lot of businesses in the last two decades and every part, good, bad, and ugly, is on the table for review. The critical issue is how to better manage the cyclical nature of your industry, particularly downturns. While you can see them coming, you can't predict their severity. So, what can the company do to better prepare itself and its customers, suppliers, and dealers for the next severe downturn? Also, what are your goals for company performance for the next

© DIZZO/ISTOCK PHOTO

downswing? Second, severe upswings, though preferable, are disruptive and difficult to manage, particularly when it comes to hiring thousands of workers at one time, restarting mothballed production facilities, procuring the necessary parts from suppliers, and suddenly finding the cash to pay for it all. So, given that there's little warning to when this is coming, what can be done to make sudden increases in production more manageable for you and your suppliers? Finally, sudden upswings and downswings produce opportunities for your competitors to steal customers by undercutting price, delivering products faster, or designing better products. What can Caterpillar and its dealers do to decrease customer losses and defections? What can top management do to make sure it keeps a stronger focus on customers?

If you were the new CEO at Caterpillar, what would you do?

14-1 The Control Process

We begin this chapter by examining the basic control process used in organizations. In the second part of the chapter, we go beyond the basics to an in-depth examination of the different methods that companies use to achieve control. We conclude the chapter by looking at the things that companies choose to control (finances, customer retention, and product quality, among others).

Why is control important? Consider this: A thief robbed the BELLAGIO CASINO in Las Vegas at gunpoint, speeding off with $1.5 million in casino chips that he thought could be cashed in at a later date. But, thanks to the Bellagio's security procedures, the chips that the thief stole were made worthless when the casino's stock of chips was completely replaced. According to Alan Feldman, spokesperson for MGM Resorts International, which owns the Bellagio resort, "The new set was put out probably a half an hour after the robbery took place."[2]

After reading this section, you should be able to:

14-1 describe the basic control process.

Control is a regulatory process of establishing standards to achieve organizational goals, comparing actual performance against the standards, and taking corrective action when necessary to restore performance to those standards. Control is achieved when behavior and work procedures conform to standards and when company goals are accomplished.[3] When the Bellagio Casino engaged its security (control) procedures, the casino was able to achieve its goal of recouping the stolen earnings efficiently and effectively. Control is not just an after-the-fact process, however. Preventive measures are also a form of control.

The basic control process **14-1a begins with the establishment of clear standards of performance; 14-1b involves a comparison of performance to those standards; 14-1c takes corrective action, if needed, to repair performance deficiencies; 14-1d is a dynamic, cybernetic process**; and **14-1e consists of three basic methods: feedback control, concurrent control, and feedforward control.** However, as much as managers would like, **14-1f control isn't always worthwhile or possible.**

control
a regulatory process of establishing standards to achieve organizational goals, comparing actual performance against the standards, and taking corrective action, when necessary

14-1a Standards

The control process begins when managers set goals such as satisfying 90 percent of customers or increasing sales by 5 percent. Companies then specify the performance standards that must be met to accomplish those goals. Standards are a basis of comparison for measuring the extent to which organizational performance is satisfactory or unsatisfactory. For example, many pizzerias use 30–40 minutes as the standard for delivery times. Because anything longer is viewed as unsatisfactory, they'll typically reduce the price if they can't deliver a hot pizza to you within that time period.

So, how do managers set standards? How do they decide which levels of performance are satisfactory and which are unsatisfactory? The first criterion for a good standard is that it must enable goal achievement. If you're meeting the standard but still not achieving company goals, then the standard may have to be changed.

Companies also determine standards by listening to customers' comments, complaints, and suggestions or by observing competitors. Walk into a busy STARBUCKS and you can generally count on a fast-moving line. The focus on speed, however, has also led to customer complaints about "average" quality and inconsistently prepared drinks; for example, a latte tasting differently from barista to barista or store to store. Starbucks is now addressing those concerns. Instead of grinding a day's worth of coffee beans first thing in the morning, beans will be freshly ground for each batch of coffee. Rather than steaming a pitcher of milk to be used in several drinks, baristas will steam just enough fresh milk for the drink they're preparing. Finally, baristas are to prepare only two drinks at a time—and even then, they're only to start the second drink while finishing the first. Starbucks believes these steps will address customers' concerns about quality. However, Starbucks baristas are worried that customers will begin to complain about long lines. If customers complain about long waits, Starbucks may have to reconsider some of these changes and change its standards accordingly.[4]

Standards can also be determined by benchmarking other companies. Benchmarking is the process of determining how well other companies (though not just competitors) perform business functions or tasks. In other words, benchmarking is the process of determining other companies' standards. When setting standards by benchmarking, the first step is to determine what to benchmark. Companies can benchmark anything from cycle time (how fast), to quality (how well), to price (how much).

The next step in establishing standards is to identify the companies against which to benchmark your standards. The last step is to collect data to determine other companies' performance standards.

14-1b Comparison to Standards

The next step in the control process is to compare actual performance to performance standards. Although this sounds straightforward, the quality of the comparison depends largely on the measurement and information systems a

standards
a basis of comparison for measuring the extent to which various kinds of organizational performance are satisfactory or unsatisfactory

benchmarking
the process of identifying outstanding practices, processes, and standards in other companies and adapting them to your company

company uses to keep track of performance. The better the system, the easier it is for companies to track their progress and identify problems that need to be fixed.

14-1c Corrective Action

The next step in the control process is to identify performance deviations, analyze those deviations, and then develop and implement programs to correct them. This is similar to the planning process discussed in Chapter 4. Regular, frequent performance feedback allows workers and managers to track their performance and make adjustments in effort, direction, and strategies.

14-1d Dynamic, Cybernetic Process

As shown in Exhibit 14.1, control is a continuous, dynamic, cybernetic process. Control begins by setting standards, measuring performance, and then comparing performance to the standards. If the performance deviates from the standards, then managers and employees analyze the deviations and develop and implement corrective programs that (they hope) achieve the desired performance by meeting the standards. Managers must repeat the entire process again and again in an endless feedback loop (a continuous process). Thus, control is not a onetime achievement or result. It continues over time (i.e., it is dynamic) and requires daily, weekly, and monthly attention from managers to maintain performance levels at the standard (i.e., it is cybernetic). **Cybernetic** derives from the Greek word *kubernetes*, meaning "steersman," that is, one who steers or keeps on course.[5] The control process shown in Exhibit 14.1 is cybernetic because constant attention to the feedback loop is necessary to keep the company's activity on course.

Keeping control of business expenses is an example of a continuous, dynamic, cybernetic process. A company that doesn't closely monitor expenses usually finds that they quickly get out of control, even for the smallest things. In the first few months of 2011, the price of diesel fuel increased 27 percent. With prices expected to continue rising, managers in all kinds of businesses suddenly needed to deal with this increased expense. PEPSICO addressed this by adding 176 all-electric trucks to its vehicle fleet. Because these trucks don't use diesel fuel, Pepsi will reduce fuel usage by 500,000 gallons per year, resulting in $1.9 million annually in savings.[6] Sure, it's a cliché, but it's just as true in business as in sports: If you take your eye off the ball, you're going to strike out. Control is an ongoing, dynamic, cybernetic process.

cybernetic
the process of steering or keeping on course

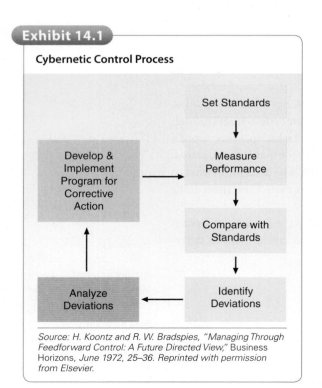

Exhibit 14.1

Cybernetic Control Process

Source: H. Koontz and R. W. Bradspies, "Managing Through Feedforward Control: A Future Directed View," Business Horizons, June 1972, 25–36. Reprinted with permission from Elsevier.

14-1e Feedback, Concurrent, and Feedforward Control

The three basic control methods are feedback control, concurrent control, and feedforward control. **Feedback control** is a mechanism for gathering information about performance deficiencies *after* they occur. This information is then used to correct or prevent performance deficiencies. Study after study has clearly shown that feedback improves both individual and organizational performance. In most instances, any feedback is better than no feedback.

If feedback has a downside, it's that feedback always comes after the fact. That's why **concurrent control** addresses the problems inherent in feedback control by gathering information about performance deficiencies *as* they occur. Thus, it is an improvement over feedback because it attempts to eliminate or shorten the delay between performance and feedback about the performance.

Feedforward control is a mechanism for gathering information about performance deficiencies *before* they occur. In contrast to feedback and concurrent control, which provide feedback on the basis of outcomes and results, feedforward control provides information about performance deficiencies by monitoring inputs rather than outputs. Thus, feedforward control seeks to prevent or minimize performance deficiencies before they happen. Exhibit 14.2 lists guidelines that companies can follow to get the most out of feedforward control.

feedback control
a mechanism for gathering information about performance deficiencies after they occur

concurrent control
a mechanism for gathering information about performance deficiencies as they occur, thereby eliminating or shortening the delay between performance and feedback

feedforward control
a mechanism for monitoring performance inputs rather than outputs to prevent or minimize performance deficiencies before they occur

control loss
the situation in which behavior and work procedures do not conform to standards

14-1f Control Isn't Always Worthwhile or Possible

Control is achieved when behavior and work procedures conform to standards and goals are accomplished. By contrast, **control loss** occurs when behavior and work procedures do not conform to standards.[7] For example, 1,600 people in 17 states became seriously ill from eating eggs contaminated with salmonella bacteria that were processed by *Wright County Egg* and *Hillandale Farms*. Both issued massive recalls covering 500 million eggs sold nationwide. Government inspectors found 4- to 8-foot-high manure piles that pushed open doors, which likely allowed rats, one of the main causes of salmonella, to enter the egg-processing buildings. Furthermore, employees were not required to change protective clothing when moving between henhouses, as required by law. Because of these violations, Wright County Egg was banned from selling eggs for several months and then was allowed to sell eggs only after they had been removed from their shells and treated for potential salmonella infection.[8]

Exhibit 14.2

Guidelines for Using Feedforward Control

1. Thorough planning and analysis are required.
2. Careful discrimination must be applied in selecting input variables.
3. The feedforward system must be kept dynamic.
4. A model of the control system should be developed.
5. Data on input variables must be regularly collected.
6. Data on input variables must be regularly assessed.
7. Feedforward control requires action.

Source: H. Koontz and R. W. Bradspies, "Managing Through Feedforward Control: A Future Directed View," Business Horizons, June 1972, 25–36. Reprinted with permission from Elsevier.

Maintaining control is important because control loss prevents organizations from achieving their goals. When control loss occurs, managers need to find out what, if anything, they could have done to prevent it. Usually, that means identifying deviations from standard performance, analyzing the causes of those deviations, and taking corrective action. Even so, implementing controls isn't always worthwhile or possible. Let's look at regulation costs and cybernetic feasibility to see why this is so.

To determine whether control is worthwhile, managers need to carefully assess **regulation costs**, that is, whether the costs and unintended consequences of control exceed its benefits. If a control process costs more than it benefits, it may not be worthwhile.

An often overlooked factor in determining the cost of control is that *unintended consequences* sometimes accompany increased control. Control systems help companies, managers, and workers accomplish their goals. But although they help solve some problems, they can create others. For example, Six Sigma is a quality control system, originally developed by Motorola, that manufacturers use to achieve the goal of producing only 3.4 defective or nonstandard parts per million parts made. Clearly, manufacturers who reach Six Sigma consistently produce extremely high-quality products. But aligning the constrictive process needed to attain Six Sigma with the need for out-of-the box thinking and innovation can be difficult.

For example, when George Buckley took over as CEO of 3M, he found that the company, long known for innovation, had lost much of its creativity. Under his predecessor, 3M focused on efficiency by streamlining processes, laying off 8,000 employees, and adopting Six Sigma practices. Although this reduced costs, it destroyed creativity in the company's research labs. CEO George Buckley observed, "Invention is by its very nature a disorderly process. You can't put a Six Sigma process into that area and say, well, I'm getting behind on invention, so I'm going to schedule myself for three good ideas on Wednesday and two on Friday. That's not how creativity works."[9] Another factor to consider is **cybernetic feasibility**, the extent to which it is possible to implement each step in the control process: clear standards of performance, comparison of performance against standards, and corrective action. If one or more steps cannot be implemented, then maintaining effective control may be difficult or impossible.

REVIEW 14-1

. . . .

The Control Process

The control process begins by setting standards, measuring performance, and then comparing performance against the standards. The better a company's information and measurement systems, the easier it is to make these comparisons. The control process continues by identifying and analyzing performance deviations and then developing and implementing programs for corrective action. Control is a continuous, dynamic, cybernetic process, not a onetime achievement or result. Control requires frequent managerial attention. The three basic control methods are feedback control (after-the-fact performance information), concurrent control (simultaneous performance information), and feedforward control (preventive performance information). Control has

regulation costs
the costs associated with implementing or maintaining control

cybernetic feasibility
the extent to which it is possible to implement each step in the control process

regulation costs and unanticipated consequences and therefore isn't always worthwhile or possible.

14-2 Control Methods

Auto insurance companies control costs by determining which drivers are higher or lower risks, and then increasing or decreasing auto insurance prices in accordance with that risk. Risk, in turn, is determined in part by your driving record, that is, whether you've had accidents or speeding tickets, and by pooling, that is, looking at the average risk of people similar to yourself. For instance, because male teenagers are much more likely to be in an auto accident, their car insurance costs are generally higher than others. PROGRESSIVE INSURANCE is changing the way it measures and controls driving risk through its Snapshot program, in which customers can have a small monitoring device installed in their cars. The device provides real-time information on driving distance, acceleration, speed, and how hard the brakes are applied. Progressive gets a much more accurate picture of how its customers drive, and thus how much risk it assumes when providing them auto insurance. A. T. Kearney consultant Joe Reifel says, "Snapshot is underwriting based on how people are actually driving. It clearly will make the pricing of insurance more accurate." In turn, Progressive can provide lower costs to its customers, while increasing profits.[10]

After reading this section, you should be able to:

14-2 discuss the various methods that managers can use to maintain control.

Managers can use five different methods to achieve control in their organizations: **14-2a bureaucratic, 14-2b objective, 14-2c normative, 14-2d concertive**, and **14-2e self-control**.

14-2a Bureaucratic Control

When most people think of managerial control, what they have in mind is bureaucratic control. **Bureaucratic control** is top-down control, in which managers try to influence employee behavior by rewarding or punishing employees for compliance or noncompliance with organizational policies, rules, and procedures. Most employees, however, would argue that bureaucratic managers emphasize punishment for noncompliance much more than rewards for compliance.

Bureaucratic management and control were actually created to prevent just this type of managerial behavior. By encouraging managers to apply well-thought-out rules, policies, and procedures in an impartial, consistent manner to everyone in the organization, bureaucratic control is supposed to make companies more efficient, effective, and fair. Ironically, it frequently has just the opposite effect. Managers who use bureaucratic control often emphasize following the rules above all else.

Another characteristic of bureaucratically controlled companies is that, due to their rule- and policy-driven decision making, they are highly resistant to change and slow to respond to customers and competitors. Even Max

bureaucratic control the use of hierarchical authority to influence employee behavior by rewarding or punishing employees for compliance or noncompliance with organizational policies, rules, and procedures

© GOGO IMAGES/JUPITERIMAGES

Weber, the German philosopher who is largely credited with popularizing bureaucratic ideals in the late nineteenth century, referred to bureaucracy as the "iron cage." He said, "Once fully established, bureaucracy is among those social structures which are the hardest to destroy."[11]

14-2b Objective Control

In many companies, bureaucratic control has evolved into **objective control**, which is the use of observable measures of employee behavior or output to assess performance and influence behavior. Whereas bureaucratic control focuses on whether policies and rules are followed, objective control focuses on observing and measuring worker behavior or output. A waitress at *BRIXX PIZZA* in Charlotte, North Carolina, was fired for complaining about some customers on her Facebook page. Two days after the posting, she was called in and fired for violating company policy that restricts employees from criticizing customers and making the restaurant look bad on social networks.[12]

There are two kinds of objective control: behavior control and output control. **Behavior control** is regulating behaviors and actions that workers perform on the job. The basic assumption of behavior control is that if you do the right things (i.e., the right behaviors) every day, then those things should lead to goal achievement. Behavior control is still management based, however, which means that managers are responsible for monitoring and rewarding or punishing workers for exhibiting desired or undesired behaviors.

Instead of measuring what managers and workers do, **output control** measures the results of their efforts. Whereas behavior control regulates, guides, and measures how workers behave on the job, output control gives managers and workers the freedom to behave as they see fit as long as they accomplish prespecified, measurable results. Output control is often coupled with rewards and incentives. Three things must occur for output control to lead to improved business results. First, output control measures must be reliable, fair, and accurate. Second, employees and managers must believe that they can produce the desired results; if they don't, then the output controls won't affect their behavior. Third, the rewards or incentives tied to output control measures must truly be dependent on achieving established standards of performance.

14-2c Normative Control

Rather than monitoring rules, behavior, or output, another way to control what goes on in organizations is to use normative control to shape the beliefs and values of the people who work there. With **normative controls**, a company's widely shared values and beliefs guide workers' behavior and decisions.

---

objective control
the use of observable measures of worker behavior or outputs to assess performance and influence behavior

behavior control
the regulation of the behaviors and actions that workers perform on the job

output control
the regulation of workers' results or outputs through rewards and incentives

normative control
the regulation of workers' behavior and decisions through widely shared organizational values and beliefs

Philip Rosedale, the founder and CEO of *LoveMachine*, an information technology firm, runs his company entirely on one value—transparency. He applies transparency to everything at the company. Every employee, contractor, and freelancer who works for the company has access to everything that others are working on, what others are earning, and what other freelancers are charging and how many hours it took them to complete a project. Even Rosedale's salary and benefits are openly available to everyone. Rosedale believes that this extreme level of transparency is vital for creating an open, collaborative environment in which there is a free exchange of information from one person to another.[13]

Normative controls are created in two ways. First, companies that use normative controls are very careful about whom they hire. Whereas many companies screen potential applicants on the basis of their abilities, normatively controlled companies are just as likely to screen potential applicants based on their attitudes and values. Billionaire Richard Branson, founder of *Virgin*, which has 300 branded companies (Virgin Airways, Virgin Mobile, Virgin Megastore, etc.) employing 50,000 people in 30 countries, hires entrepreneurial people with positive attitudes. He says, "We stumbled on this formula when we were launching our record store business in the late 1960s. We decided to look for employees who were passionate about music, because we thought their enthusiasm and knowledge would be as important a draw as the beanbag chairs, coffee and listening posts we planned to feature in our first stores and that turned out to be correct." Branson says, "This approach helped us to attract and keep great talent.... Virgin has launched 400 businesses in more than 40 years of expansion; our focus on employees is one of the main reasons for our success."[14]

Second, with normative controls, managers and employees learn what they should and should not do by observing experienced employees and listening to the stories they tell about the company. Ed Fuller, the head of international lodging at *Marriott International*, loves to tell stories to illustrate Marriott's commitment to customer service. One of his favorites is when he was a general manager at a Marriott in Boston. A senior executive told him that Bill Marriott, the chairman of the company, was upset about something at his hotel. Fuller was positive that he was going to be fired for being $300,000 behind his catering sales goal. But when Marriott met with him, he wasn't upset about the sales; he was upset that a member of the Marriott family had been served cold clam chowder and that the restaurant manager handled the complaint poorly. Fuller says that the moral of the story is, "If [the family] is treated badly, we assume the customer is treated worse."[15] Nevertheless, this story makes clear the attitude that drives employee performance at Marriott in ways that rules, behavioral guidelines, or output controls could not.

14-2d Concertive Control

Whereas normative controls are based on beliefs that are strongly held and widely shared throughout a company, **concertive controls** are based on beliefs that are shaped and negotiated by work groups.[16] Whereas normative controls are driven by strong organizational cultures, concertive controls usually arise when companies give work groups complete autonomy and responsibility for

concertive control
the regulation of workers' behavior and decisions through work group values and beliefs

task completion. (See Chapter 9, "Managing Teams," for a complete discussion of the role of autonomy in teams and groups.) The most autonomous groups operate without managers and are completely responsible for controlling work group processes, outputs, and behavior. Such groups do their own hiring, firing, worker discipline, work schedules, materials ordering, budget making and meeting, and decision making.

Concertive control is not established overnight. Highly autonomous work groups evolve through two phases as they develop concertive control. In phase one, group members learn to work with each other, supervise each other's work, and develop the values and beliefs that will guide and control their behavior. And because they develop these values and beliefs themselves, work group members feel strongly about following them.

The second phase in the development of concertive control is the emergence and formalization of objective rules to guide and control behavior. The beliefs and values developed in phase one usually develop into more objective rules as new members join teams. The clearer those rules, the easier it becomes for new members to figure out how and how not to behave. Ironically, concertive control may lead to even more stress for workers to conform to expectations than bureaucratic control. Under bureaucratic control, most workers have to worry about pleasing only the boss. But with concertive control, their behavior has to satisfy the rest of their team members. For example, one team member says, "I don't have to sit there and look for the boss to be around; and if the boss is not around, I can sit there and talk to my neighbor or do what I want. Now the whole team is around me and the whole team is observing what I'm doing."[17] Plus, with concertive control, team members have a second, much more stressful role to perform: that of making sure that their team members adhere to team values and rules.

14-2e Self-Control

Self-control, also known as **self-management**, is a control system in which managers and workers control their own behavior.[18] Self-control does not result in anarchy, in which everyone gets to do whatever he or she wants. In self-control or self-management, leaders and managers provide workers with clear boundaries within which they may guide and control their own goals and behaviors.[19] Leaders and managers also contribute to self-control by teaching others the skills they need to maximize and monitor their own work effectiveness. In turn, individuals who manage and lead themselves establish self-control by setting their own goals, monitoring their own progress, rewarding or punishing themselves for achieving or for not achieving their self-set goals, and constructing positive thought patterns that remind them of the importance of their goals and their ability to accomplish them.[20]

For example, let's assume you need to do a better job of praising and recognizing the good work that your staff does for you. You can use goal setting, self-observation, and self-reward to manage this behavior on your own. For self-observation, write "praise/recognition" on a 3-by-5-inch card. Put the card in your pocket. Put a check on the card each time you praise or recognize someone. (Wait until the person has left before you do this.) Keep track for a week. This serves as your baseline or starting point. Simply keeping track will probably

self-control (self-management)
a control system in which managers and workers control their own behavior by setting their own goals, monitoring their own progress, and rewarding themselves for goal achievement

increase how often you do this. After a week, assess your baseline or starting point and then set a specific goal. For instance, if your baseline was twice a day, you might set a specific goal to praise or recognize others' work five times a day. Continue monitoring your performance with your cards. Once you've achieved your goal every day for a week, give yourself a reward (perhaps a CD, a movie, lunch with a friend at a new restaurant) for achieving your goal.[21]

As you can see, the components of self-management, self-set goals, self-observation, and self-reward have their roots in the motivation theories you read about in Chapter 11. The key difference, though, is that the goals, feedback, and rewards originate from employees themselves and not from their managers or organizations.

REVIEW 14-2
. . . .

Control Methods

The five methods of control are bureaucratic, objective, normative, concertive, and self-control (self-management). Bureaucratic and objective controls are top-down, management-based, and measurement-based control methods. Normative and concertive controls represent shared forms of control because they evolve from company-wide or team-based beliefs and values. Self-control, or self-management, is a control system in which managers turn over much, but not all, control to the individuals themselves.

Bureaucratic control is based on organizational policies, rules, and procedures. Objective controls are based on reliable measures of behavior or outputs. Normative control is based on strong corporate beliefs and careful hiring practices. Concertive control is based on the development of values, beliefs, and rules in autonomous work groups. Self-control is based on individuals' setting their own goals, monitoring themselves, and rewarding or punishing themselves with respect to goal achievement.

Each of these control methods may be more or less appropriate depending on the circumstances. Examine Exhibit 14.3 to find out when each of these five control methods should be used.

14-3 What to Control?

In the first section of this chapter, we discussed the basics of the control process and the fact that control isn't always worthwhile or possible. In the second section, we looked at the various ways in which control can be obtained.

After reading this third and final section, you should be able to:

14-3 describe the behaviors, processes, and outcomes that today's managers are choosing to control in their organizations.

Here, we address an equally important issue: What should managers control? Costs? Quality? Customer satisfaction? The way managers answer this question has critical implications for most businesses.

This section explores the question of what to control by explaining **14-3a the balanced scorecard approach to control and how companies can achieve balanced control of company performance by choosing to control; 14-3b**

Exhibit 14.3

When to Use Different Methods of Control

Bureaucratic Control

- When it is necessary to standardize operating procedures
- When it is necessary to establish limits

Behavior Control

- When it is easier to measure what workers do on the job than what they accomplish on the job
- When "cause-effect" relationships are clear, that is, when companies know which behaviors will lead to success and which won't
- When good measures of worker behavior can be created

Output Control

- When it is easier to measure what workers accomplish on the job than what they do on the job
- When good measures of worker output can be created
- When it is possible to set clear goals and standards for worker output
- When "cause-effect" relationships are unclear

Normative Control

- When organizational culture, values, and beliefs are strong
- When it is difficult to create good measures of worker behavior
- When it is difficult to create good measures of worker output

Concertive Control

- When responsibility for task accomplishment is given to autonomous work groups
- When management wants workers to take "ownership" of their behavior and outputs
- When management desires a strong form of worker-based control

Self-Control

- When workers are intrinsically motivated to do their jobs well
- When it is difficult to create good measures of worker behavior
- When it is difficult to create good measures of worker output
- When workers have or are taught self-control and self-leadership skills

Sources: L. J. Kirsch, "The Management of Complex Tasks in Organizations: Controlling the System's Development Process," Organization Science 7 (1996): 1–21; and S. A. Snell, "Control Theory in Strategic Human Resource Management: The Mediating Effect of Administrative Information," Academy of Management Journal 35 (1992): 292–327.

---

budgets, cash flows, and economic value added; **14-3c customer defections; 14-3d quality;** and **14-3e waste and pollution.**

14-3a The Balanced Scorecard

Most companies measure performance using standard financial and accounting measures such as return on capital, return on assets, return on investments, cash flow, net income, and net margins. The **balanced scorecard** encourages managers to look beyond such traditional financial measures to four different perspectives on company performance. How do customers see us (the customer perspective)? At what must we excel (the internal perspective)? Can we continue to improve and create value (the innovation and learning perspective)? How do we look to shareholders (the financial perspective)?[22]

balanced scorecard
measurement of organizational performance in four equally important areas: finances, customers, internal operations, and innovation and learning

The balanced scorecard has several advantages over traditional control processes that rely solely on financial measures. First, it forces managers at each level of the company to set specific goals and measure performance in each of the four areas. For example, Exhibit 14.4 shows that SOUTHWEST AIRLINES uses nine different measures in its balanced scorecard in order to determine whether it is meeting the standards it has set for itself in the control process. Of those, only three—market value, seat revenue, and plane lease costs (at various compounded annual growth rates, or CAGR)—are standard financial measures of performance. In addition, Southwest measures its Federal Aviation Administration (FAA) on-time arrival rating and the cost of its airfares compared with those of competitors (customer perspective); how much time each plane spends on the ground after landing and the percentage of planes that depart on time (internal business perspective); and the percentage of its ground crew workers, such as mechanics and luggage handlers, who own company stock and have received job training (learning perspective).

The second major advantage of the balanced scorecard approach to control is that it minimizes the chances of suboptimization, which occurs when performance improves in one area at the expense of decreased performance in others. Jon Meliones, chief medical director at DUKE CHILDREN'S HOSPITAL, says, "We explained the [balanced scorecard] theory to clinicians and administrators like this: If you sacrifice too much in one quadrant to satisfy another, your organization as a whole is thrown out of balance. We could, for example, cut costs to improve the financial quadrant by firing half the staff, but that would hurt quality of service, and the customer quadrant would fall out of balance. Or

suboptimization
performance improvement in one part of an organization but only at the expense of decreased performance in another part

Exhibit 14.4

Southwest Airlines' Balanced Scorecard

	OBJECTIVES	MEASURES	TARGETS	INITIATIVES
FINANCIAL	Profitability	Market Value	30% CAGR	
	Increased Revenue	Seat Revenue	20% CAGR	
	Lower Costs	Plane Lease Cost	5% CAGR	
CUSTOMER	On-Time Flights	FAA On-Time Arrival Rating	#1	Quality Management, Customer Loyalty Program
	Lowest Prices	Customer Ranking (Market Survey)	#1	
INTERNAL	Fast Ground Turnaround	Time on Ground	30 Minutes	Cycle Time Optimization Program
		On-Time Departure	90%	
LEARNING	Ground Crew Alignment with Company Goals	% Ground Crew Shareholders	Year 1: 70% Year 3: 90% Year 5: 100%	Employee Stock Option Plan Ground Crew Training
		% Ground Crew Trained		

Source: G. Anthes, "ROI Guide: Balanced Scorecard," Computer World, accessed May 5, 2003, from www.computerworld.com/managementtopics/rpo/story/0,10801,78512,00.html.

© CENGAGE LEARNING

we could increase productivity in the internal business quadrant by assigning more patients to a nurse, but doing so would raise the likelihood of errors—an unacceptable trade-off."[23]

Let's examine some of the ways in which companies are controlling the four basic parts of the balanced scorecard: the financial perspective (budgets, cash flows, and economic value added), the customer perspective (customer defections), the internal perspective (total quality management), and the innovation and learning perspective (waste and pollution).

14-3b The Financial Perspective: Controlling Budgets, Cash Flows, and Economic Value Added

The traditional approach to controlling financial performance focuses on accounting tools such as cash flow analysis, balance sheets, income statements, financial ratios, and budgets.

Though no one would dispute their importance for determining the financial health of a business, accounting research also indicates that the complexity and sheer amount of information contained in these accounting tools can shut down the brain and glaze over the eyes of even the most experienced manager.[24] Sometimes there's simply too much information to make sense of. The balanced scorecard simplifies things by focusing on one simple question when it comes to finances: How do we look to shareholders? One way to answer that question is through something called "economic value added."

Conceptually, **economic value added (EVA)** is not the same thing as profits. It is the amount by which profits exceed the cost of capital in a given year. It is based on the simple idea that capital is necessary to run a business and that capital comes at a cost. Although most people think of capital as cash, once it is invested (i.e., spent), capital is more likely to be found in a business in the form of computers, manufacturing plants, employees, raw materials, and so forth. And just like the interest that a homeowner pays on a mortgage or that a college student pays on a student loan, there is a cost to that capital.

The most common costs of capital are the interest paid on long-term bank loans used to buy resources, the interest paid to bondholders (who lend organizations their money), and the dividends (cash payments) and growth in stock value that accrue to shareholders. EVA is positive when company profits (revenues minus expenses minus taxes) exceed the cost of capital in a given year. In other words, if a business is to grow, its revenues must be large enough to cover both short-term costs (annual expenses and taxes) and long-term costs (the cost of borrowing capital from bondholders and shareholders). If you're a bit confused, the late Roberto Goizueta, the former CEO of Coca-Cola, explained it this way: "You borrow

economic value added (EVA)
the amount by which company profits (revenues, minus expenses, minus taxes) exceed the cost of capital in a given year

money at a certain rate and invest it at a higher rate and pocket the difference. It is simple. It is the essence of banking."[25]

Why is EVA so important? First and most importantly, because it includes the cost of capital, it shows whether a business, division, department, profit center, or product is really paying for itself. The key is to make sure that managers and employees can see how their choices and behavior affect the company's EVA. For example, because of EVA training and information systems, factory workers at Herman Miller, a leading office furniture manufacturer, understand that using more efficient materials, such as less expensive wood-dust board instead of real wood sheeting, contributes an extra dollar of EVA from each desk the company makes.[26] Second, because EVA can easily be determined for subsets of a company such as divisions, regional offices, manufacturing plants, and sometimes even departments, it makes managers and workers at all levels pay much closer attention to their segment of the business. In other words, EVA motivates managers and workers to think like small-business owners who must scramble to contain costs and generate enough business to meet their bills each month. And unlike many kinds of financial controls, EVA doesn't specify what should or should not be done to improve performance. Thus, it encourages managers and workers to be creative in looking for ways to improve EVA performance.

EVA is the amount by which profits exceed the cost of capital in a given year. So the more that EVA exceeds the total dollar cost of capital, the better a company has used investors' money that year. For example, APPLE had an EVA of $10.03 billion in 2010, by far the largest EVA in the world. The next closest company was Google, at $5.28 billion. To put Apple's 2010 EVA performance in perspective, note that Apple had an average EVA of $1.7 billion a year from 2005–2009, and that was 2.5 times more than what investors were expecting. Apple's EVA financial performance in 2010 was truly extraordinary.[27]

14-3c The Customer Perspective: Controlling Customer Defections

The second aspect of organizational performance that the balanced scorecard helps managers monitor is customers. It does so by forcing managers to address the question: How do customers see us? Unfortunately, most companies try to answer this question through customer satisfaction surveys, but these are often misleadingly positive. Most customers are reluctant to talk about their problems because they don't know who to complain to or think that complaining will not do any good. Indeed, a study by the federal Office of Consumer Affairs found that 96 percent of unhappy customers never complain to anyone in the company.[28]

One reason that customer satisfaction surveys can be misleading is that sometimes even very satisfied customers will leave to do business with competitors. Another challenge is getting effective feedback when there is a problem. Norm Brodsky founded and ran CITISTORAGE, a document-archive business based in Brooklyn, New York. One day, he found out that one of their biggest customers was leaving when their contract expired. Neither Brodsky or his sales representatives could ever get a response from the company regarding why they left.[29]

Rather than poring over customer satisfaction surveys from current customers, studies indicate that companies may do a better job of answering the question "How do customers see us?" by closely monitoring **customer defections**, that is, by identifying which customers are leaving the company and measuring the rate at which they are leaving. Unlike the results of customer satisfaction surveys, customer defections and retention do have a great effect on profits. For example, very few managers realize that obtaining a new customer costs ten times as much as keeping a current one. In fact, the cost of replacing old customers with new ones is so great that most companies could double their profits by increasing the rate of customer retention by just 5 to 10 percent per year.[30] Retaining customers obviously means having more customers, but how many more?

Consider two companies starting with a customer base of 100,000 customers and an acquisition rate of 20 percent (i.e., yearly each company's customer base grows by 20 percent). Assuming company B has a higher retention rate of just 5 percent (90 percent retention rate for company B versus an 85 percent retention rate for company A), company B will double its customer base around the ninth year, whereas it will take company A slightly more than 15 years to double its customer base. On average, this means company B also profited by a higher percentage.[31] And if a company can keep a customer for life, the benefits are even larger. According to Stew Leonard, owner of the Connecticut-based *STEW LEONARD'S* grocery store chain, "The lifetime value of a customer in a supermarket is about $246,000. Every time a customer comes through our front door I see, stamped on their forehead in big red numbers, '$246,000.' I'm never going to make that person unhappy with me. Or lose her to the competition."[32]

Beyond the clear benefits to the bottom line, the second reason to study customer defections is that customers who have left are much more likely than current customers to tell you what you are doing wrong. Perhaps the best way to tap into this source of good feedback is to have top-level managers from various departments talk directly to customers who have left. It's also worthwhile to have top managers talk to dissatisfied customers who are still with the company. After *CITISTORAGE*'s Norm Brodsky lost the client (above), he said the lesson wasn't that they made mistakes. All firms do. So, Brodsky began renegotiating contracts 18 months before they expire. He says they were surprised to discover they had unhappy customers. For example, one customer wanted a lower price because its storage volume had increased. The customer was right, and they made the change. Another didn't like CitiStorage's inventory system for managing stored documents. So, they changed it. Says Brodsky, "In four months with the new policy, we made four improvements, pleased four customers, and locked up four accounts, and all these benefits came from one failure."[33]

Finally, companies that understand why customers leave should not only take steps to fix ongoing problems, they should also identify which customers are likely to leave and make changes to prevent them from leaving.

14-3d The Internal Perspective: Controlling Quality

The third part of the balanced scorecard, the internal perspective, consists of the processes, decisions, and actions that managers and workers make within the organization. In contrast to the financial perspective of EVA and

customer defections
a performance assessment in which companies identify which customers are leaving and measure the rate at which they are leaving

the outward-looking customer perspective, the internal perspective focuses on internal processes and systems that add value to the organization. For Toyota, it could be reliability—when you turn on your car, it starts, no matter whether the car has 20,000 or 200,000 miles on it. Yet no matter what area a company chooses, the key is to excel in that area. Consequently, the internal perspective of the balanced scorecard usually leads managers to a focus on quality.

Quality is typically defined and measured in three ways: excellence, value, and conformance to expectations.[34] When the company defines its quality goal as *excellence*, managers must try to produce a product or service of unsurpassed performance and features. **Value** is the customer perception that the product quality is excellent for the price offered. At a higher price, for example, customers may perceive the product to be less of a value. When a company emphasizes value as its quality goal, managers must simultaneously control excellence, price, durability, and any other features of a product or service that customers strongly associate with value.

When a company defines its quality goal as conformance to specifications, employees must base decisions and actions on whether services and products measure up to the standard. In contrast to excellence and value-based definitions of quality that can be somewhat ambiguous, measuring whether products and services are "in spec" is relatively easy. Furthermore, whereas conformance to specifications (e.g., precise tolerances for a part's weight or thickness) is usually associated with manufacturing, it can be used equally well to control quality in nonmanufacturing jobs. Exhibit 14.5 shows a checklist that a cook or restaurant owner would use to ensure quality when buying fresh fish.

14-3e The Innovation and Learning Perspective: Controlling Waste and Pollution

The last part of the balanced scorecard, the innovation and learning perspective, addresses the question: Can we continue to improve and create value? Thus, the

value
customer perception that the product quality is excellent for the price offered

---

Exhibit 14.5

Conformance to Specifications Checklist for Buying Fresh Fish

QUALITY CHECKLIST FOR BUYING FRESH FISH		
FRESH WHOLE FISH	**ACCEPTABLE**	**NON ACCEPTABLE**
Gills	bright red; free of slime; clear mucus	brown to grayish; thick, yellow mucus
Eyes	clear, bright, bulging, black pupils	dull, sunken, cloudy, gray pupils
Smell	inoffensive, slight ocean smell	ammonia or putrid smell
Skin	opalescent sheen; scales adhere tightly to skin	dull or faded color; scales missing or easily removed
Flesh	firm and elastic to touch, tight to the bone	soft and flabby, separating from the bone
Belly cavity	no viscera or blood visible; lining intact; no bone protruding	incomplete evisceration; cuts or protruding bones; off odor

Sources:"A Closer Look: Buy It Fresh, Keep It Fresh, ''Consumer Reports Online, accessed June 20, 2005, from www.SeafoodII020101.htm [no longer available]; and National Fisheries Institute, "How to Purchase; Buying Fish," accessed June 20, 2005, from www.aboutseafood.com.

Exhibit 14.6

Advantages and Disadvantages of Different Measures of Quality

QUALITY MEASURE	ADVANTAGES	DISADVANTAGES
Excellence	Promotes clear organizational vision. Being/providing the "best" motivates and inspires managers and employees.	Provides little practical guidance for managers. Excellence is ambiguous. What is it? Who defines it?
Value	Appeals to customers, who "know excellence when they see it." Customers recognize differences in value. Easier to measure and compare whether products/services differ in value.	Difficult to measure and control. Can be difficult to determine what factors influence whether a product/service is seen as having value. Controlling the balance between excellence and cost (i.e., affordable excellence) can be difficult.
Conformance to Specifications	If specifications can be written, conformance to specifications is usually measurable. Should lead to increased efficiency. Promotes consistency in quality.	Many products/services cannot be easily evaluated in terms of conformance to specifications. Promotes standardization, so may hurt performance when adapting to changes is more important. May be less appropriate for services, which are dependent on a high degree of human contact.

Sources: Republished with permission of Academy of Management, PO Box 3020, Briar Cliff Manor, NY, 10510-8020. C. A. Reeves and D. A. Bednar, "Defining Quality: Alternatives and Implications," Academy of Management Review 19 (1994): 419–445. Reproduced by permission of the publisher via Copyright Clearance Center, Inc.

innovation and learning perspective involves continuous improvement in ongoing products and services (discussed in Chapter 16), as well as relearning and redesigning the processes by which products and services are created (discussed in Chapter 6). Because these are discussed in more detail elsewhere in the text, this section reviews an increasingly important topic, waste and pollution minimization. Exhibit 14.7 shows the four levels of waste minimization, ranging from waste disposal, which produces the smallest minimization of waste, to waste prevention and reduction, which produces the greatest minimization.[35]

The goals of the top level, *waste prevention and reduction*, are to prevent waste and pollution before they occur or to reduce them when they do occur. There are three strategies for waste prevention and reduction:

1. *Good housekeeping*—performing regularly scheduled preventive maintenance for offices, plants, and equipment. Examples of good housekeeping include fixing leaky valves quickly to prevent wasted water and making sure machines are running properly so that they don't use more fuel than necessary.

2. *Material/product substitution*—replacing toxic or hazardous materials with less harmful materials.

3. *Process modification*—changing steps or procedures to eliminate or reduce waste.

At the second level of waste minimization, *recycle and reuse*, wastes are reduced by reusing materials as long as possible or by collecting materials for on- or off-site recycling. GENERAL MOTORS uses recycled plastics in the production of its hybrid electric car, the Chevy Volt. The plastic cover for the Volt's radiator fan is made from recycled consumer goods, recycled tires used at GM's test tracks, and the plastic booms that were used to contain the BP oil spill in the Gulf of Mexico. In 2011, GM will use 100,000 pounds of recycled plastics and 100 miles of plastic boom to make radiator fan covers for the Chevy Volt.[36]

A growing trend in recycling is *design for disassembly*, where products are designed from the start for easy disassembly, recycling, and reuse once they are no longer usable. HERMAN MILLER, a manufacturer of office equipment, not only uses recycled material in its award-winning office chairs, it makes it easy to recycle them once they're no longer usable. It clearly labels which parts are recyclable, identifies the type of plastic used in each part, and then minimizes the different types of plastics used. Finally, it designs its chairs so that they are easy to take apart and includes detailed disassembly instructions.[37]

At the third level of waste minimization, waste treatment, companies use biological, chemical, or other processes to turn potentially harmful waste into harmless compounds or useful byproducts. In Africa, animal slaughterhouses often dump untreated animal waste into rivers and lakes. This spreads disease and generates methane and carbon dioxide—greenhouse gases that contribute to global warming. Unlike traditional treatment processes, COWS TO KILOWATTS PARTNERSHIP LIMITED uses an advanced anaerobic reactor to turn animal blood and waste into biogas, which is then processed and compressed into cooking gas or fuel to run household generators. Even the leftover sludge can be reused as environmentally friendly fertilizer.[38]

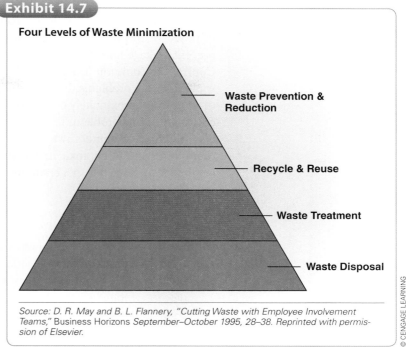

Exhibit 14.7

Four Levels of Waste Minimization

Waste Prevention & Reduction

Recycle & Reuse

Waste Treatment

Waste Disposal

Source: D. R. May and B. L. Flannery, "Cutting Waste with Employee Involvement Teams," Business Horizons *September–October 1995, 28–38. Reprinted with permission of Elsevier.*

© CENGAGE LEARNING

UPS uses GPS and telematic tracking systems to improve the efficiency of its fleet of delivery trucks.

STEPHEN CHERNIN/GETTY IMAGES NEWS/GETTY IMAGES

The fourth and lowest level of waste minimization is *waste disposal.* Wastes that cannot be prevented, reduced, recycled, reused, or treated should be safely disposed of in processing plants or in environmentally secure landfills that prevent leakage and contamination of soil and underground water supplies. Contrary to common belief, all businesses, not just manufacturing firms, have waste disposal problems. For example, with the average computer lasting just three years, approximately 60 million computers come out of service each year, creating disposal problems for offices all over the world. But organizations can't just throw old computers away, because they have lead-containing cathode ray tubes in the monitors, toxic metals in the circuit boards, paint-coated plastic, and metal coatings that can contaminate groundwater.[39]

REVIEW 14-3

What to Control?

Deciding what to control is just as important as deciding whether or how to control. In most companies, performance is measured using financial measures alone. However, the balanced scorecard encourages managers to measure and control company performance from four perspectives: financial, customers, internal operations, and innovation and learning. Traditionally, financial control has been achieved through cash flow analysis, balance sheets, income statements, financial ratios, and budgets. Another way to measure and control financial performance is through economic value added (EVA). Unlike traditional financial measures, EVA helps managers assess whether they are performing well enough to pay the cost of the capital needed to run the business. Instead of using customer satisfaction surveys to measure performance, companies should pay attention to customer defectors, who are more likely to speak up about what the company is doing wrong. Performance of internal operations is often measured in terms of quality, which is defined in three ways: excellence, value, and conformance to expectations. Minimization of waste has become an important part of innovation and learning in companies. The four levels of waste minimization are waste prevention and reduction, recycling and reuse, waste treatment, and waste disposal.

 # Management Decision

Managing or Spying?[40]

Well, it's the last Friday of the month, and that can mean only one thing—time to process the invoices from the freelance workers you hired. A few months ago, your company was overloaded by the amount of data processing that needed to be done. There were a few days when the entire staff, even the janitors, stayed past 11 P.M. to read through, sort, and organize all of your clients' account data. The work wasn't necessarily difficult. But it was time consuming, and you hated it when your employees and managers had to take time off of other important things to get the processing done. You thought you found a perfect solution when you decided to hire some freelancers—part-time outsiders whom you could contract to do all of the processing, freeing up your staff to focus on other things.

What seemed to be a great solution, however, produced a few troubles of its own. It wasn't as if the work wasn't getting done—the freelancers actually did a pretty good job with their assignments. The problem was, though, how much time they seemed to be spending on the work. When you used to do the processing in-house, it usually took one person about 4–5 hours to go through the data for one client. Even employees who didn't have any specialized training could usually get through one client's account in less than 7 hours. Your freelancers, however, have been charging for more hours—a lot more. Six months ago, their time sheet showed that they spent an average of 16 hours per account. Three months ago, their time sheet showed that they spent an average of 19 hours per account. And as you open this month's invoices, you see that they are reporting having spent an average of 21 hours per account.

You think to yourself: This can't be right! You wonder if maybe they are just working extra slowly. Or maybe they are billing you for hours they spend looking up YouTube videos.

As you worry about what the freelancers are doing, one of your managers says he saw a solution on TV the other day. It's a service from a company called oDesk. The company, which helps businesses connect with freelance workers all over the world, also offers a software program that takes pictures of freelancers' computer screens and records their keystrokes and mouse clicks throughout the day. In short, it lets companies like yours know almost every single move that a freelancer makes.

"It's the perfect solution," your manager tells you. No more worries about what the freelancers are doing with their time and your money. You can know every single thing they do during the time they are billing you.

It does seem to be a great solution. But you have some hesitation—isn't this a bit too much like spying? Do I really want to spend my time constantly looking over someone else's shoulder?

Questions

1. Should this company use oDesk's feature to monitor its contractors? Why or why not?

2. In your opinion, do the benefits of using oDesk's surveillance feature outweigh the potential costs?

 ## Practice Being a Manager

In Control or Control Freak?

Control is one of the most controversial aspects of management. Exercising too much control can foster employee resentment and bureaucratic delays. Exercising too little control can raise employee stress and breed organizational chaos. And not only must managers work to achieve a healthy *level* of control, but they must also strive to set controls around the *right targets*. The control process is about more than charts and feedback loops—it is about focusing personal and organizational efforts toward desired outcomes. This exercise will allow you an opportunity to try your hand at developing a control system that is tailored to a particular company and type of work.

STEP 1 **Get into groups.** Your professor will organize your class into teams of three or four students per team. One team will be designated as Company Leadership.

Scenario: Razor's Edge (RE) is a young and growing company that serves the needs of those who engage in extreme sports, adventure/exploration, and guiding services. Some examples of RE's core market include expert/professional mountain climbers, white-water rafting guides, and polar explorers. The founders of RE are the husband and wife team of Dan and Alice Connors, world-famous mountain climbers and explorers. Dan and Alice have both reached the summit of Mount Everest and each is well respected in the rather small and close-knit community of adventurers and explorers. RE is an eclectic company of employees who, like Dan and Alice, share a passion for adventure and extreme sports. The company not only designs and sells its own lines of specialized products such as mountain-climbing shoes and ropes but also develops software designed to support expedition planning, communication and navigation, and simulation and scenario response (i.e., training tools for guides and newer expedition members).

For the first five years of its development, RE did not worry too much about organizational policies or controls. Employees were encouraged to climb, trek, and guide, and attendance issues were addressed on a case-by-case basis. Although officially all employees were given two weeks of paid vacation, many employees were allowed to take up to two months off at half-pay so that they could complete an expedition. Sick days were jokingly referred to as "mountain flu" days, and it was not unusual for the small company to be thinly staffed on Mondays and Fridays. But in the past three years, RE has grown from 25 employees to 85. The company is too big, and the jobs too diverse, for Dan and Alice to deal with each employee request for "expedition time" away from work. And the "mountain flu" has occasionally weakened the company's response to customers. Dan and Alice have also become victims of their own success as they attracted other climbers to join their company—most climbers want time off in the peak climbing seasons. But this also happens to be a peak time for RE orders and service requests.

The company has organized all employees into teams and announced a contest. Each team should come up with an approach for controlling staffing levels to meet or exceed customer expectations for responsiveness, while at the same time preserving RE's tradition as a company of active adventurers and explorers. The company has announced that each member of the employee team that develops the winning solution will receive $2,500 worth of RE gear of their choice.

STEP 2 **Determine staffing levels.** You are a team of workers at RE. Design an approach to controlling daily staffing levels so that RE is able to meet or exceed customer expectations for responsiveness without sacrificing its own identity as a company of adventurers and explorers. Keep in mind that RE is somewhat unusual in that even its accounting staff members (five full-time employees) are experienced adventurers and explorers and are expected to answer customer questions and handle their service needs. You should consider the following elements:

- Paid vacation
- Expedition time
- Sick days and "mountain flu" (Monday/Friday absences)
- Dealing with peak times, and/or most desirable times for vacation or expedition
- Knowing whether customers are pleased with RE's responsiveness to their needs

STEP 3 **Outline a proposal.** Submit a one-page, handwritten outline of your proposal to the Company Leadership team.

STEP 4 **Present the proposal.** Each team will briefly present its proposal to the Company Leadership team, and members of the Company Leadership team may ask questions.

STEP 5 **Vote.** The Company Leadership will confer, vote, and announce the winning proposal.

STEP 6 **Debrief as a class.** What tensions confronted you as you worked to design an approach to staffing control for Razor's Edge? What trade-offs and challenges might you anticipate for the company when it implements the winning proposal? In what ways is control related to employee motivation? In what ways is control related to organizational culture? Do you think that the winning RE proposal would be well suited for use by a major outdoor and casual clothing company such as Lands' End? Why or why not?

Self-Assessment

Too Much Information?

Imagine that your professor handed back term papers, and the only mark on yours was the grade. Would you be content, or would you feel gypped? People have different comfort levels about receiving feedback: Some thrive on it; others are ambivalent. What about you? Would you rather see comments in the margins of your term paper or not? This self-assessment will give you insights into your perceptions of feedback. Understanding your preferences in this area will help you develop the skills you'll need as a manager.[41]

As you complete this feedback inventory, be candid as you circle the appropriate responses. "Extremely Untrue" is 1, and "Extremely True" is 6.

1. It is important for me to obtain useful information about my performance.

    1   2   3   4   5   6

2. If I receive negative feedback, I would have a negative attitude towards myself, so I try to avoid criticism.

    1   2   3   4   5   6

3. I am not really worried about what people will think of me if I ask for feedback about my performance.

    1   2   3   4   5   6

4. I like people to hear about my good performance at work (or at college).

    1   2   3   4   5   6

5. Receiving feedback about my performance helps me to improve my skills.

    1   2   3   4   5   6

6. Negative feedback doesn't really lower my self-worth, so I don't go out of my way to avoid it.

    1   2   3   4   5   6

7. I'm concerned about what people would think of me if I were to ask for feedback.

    1   2   3   4   5   6

8. Seeking feedback from my supervisor (instructor) is one way to show that I want to improve my performance.

    1   2   3   4   5   6

9. I would like to obtain more information to let me know how I am performing.

    1   2   3   4   5   6

10. Receiving negative feedback wouldn't really change the way I feel about myself.

    1   2   3   4   5   6

11. I am worried about the impression I would make if I were to ask for feedback.

    1   2   3   4   5   6

12. I want people to know when I ask for feedback so I can show my responsible nature.

    1   2   3   4   5   6

13. I would like to receive more useful information about my performance.

    1   2   3   4   5   6

14. It's hard to feel good about myself when I receive negative feedback.

    1   2   3   4   5   6

15. I don't really worry about what others would think of me if I asked for feedback.

   1   2   3   4   5   6

16. I don't really care if people hear the good feedback that is given to me.

   1   2   3   4   5   6

17. I'm not really concerned about whether I receive useful information about my performance.

   1   2   3   4   5   6

18. I don't really worry about getting negative feedback because I still feel I am a person of worth.

   1   2   3   4   5   6

19. I don't really care if people know the type of feedback I get.

   1   2   3   4   5   6

20. When I receive praise, I don't really want others to hear it.

   1   2   3   4   5   6

21. Feedback is not really useful to help me improve my performance.

   1   2   3   4   5   6

22. I try to avoid negative feedback because it makes me feel bad about myself.

   1   2   3   4   5   6

23. If I sought feedback about my performance, I wouldn't want other people to know what type of feedback I received.

   1   2   3   4   5   6

24. I don't care either way if people see me asking my supervisor (instructor) for feedback.

   1   2   3   4   5   6

25. Obtaining useful feedback information is not very important to me.

   1   2   3   4   5   6

26. I worry about receiving feedback that is likely to be negative because it hurts to be criticized.

   1   2   3   4   5   6

27. I am usually concerned about other people hearing the content of the individual feedback I receive.

   1   2   3   4   5   6

28. I hope positive feedback about my performance will make a good impression on others.

   1   2   3   4   5   6

29. I don't really require more feedback to let me know how I am performing.

   1   2   3   4   5   6

30. Negative feedback doesn't really worry me because I still have a positive attitude toward myself.

   1   2   3   4   5   6

31. It doesn't worry me if people know how I've performed at something.

   1   2   3   4   5   6

32. I don't really need to impress others by letting them know about the positive feedback I receive regarding my performance.

   1   2   3   4   5   6

SCORING

Determine your average score for each category by entering your response to each survey item below, as follows. In blanks that say *regular score*, simply enter your response for that item. If your response was a 4, place a 4 in the *regular score* blank. In blanks that say *reverse score*, subtract your response from 7 and enter the result. So if your response was a 4, place a 3 (7–4 = 3) in the *reverse score* blank. Total your scores, then compute each average score.

DESIRE FOR USEFUL INFORMATION

1. regular score _____

5. regular score _____

9. regular score _____

13. reverse score _____

17. reverse score _____

21. reverse score _____

25. reverse score _____

29. reverse score _____

TOTAL = _____

DEFENSIVE IMPRESSION MANAGEMENT

3. reverse score _____

7. reverse score _____

11. reverse score _____

15. reverse score _____

19. reverse score _____

23. reverse score _____

27. reverse score _____

31. reverse score _____

TOTAL = _____

EGO DEFENSE

2. regular score _____

6. reverse score _____

10. regular score _____

14. regular score _____

18. reverse score _____

22. reverse score _____

26. regular score _____

30. regular score _____

TOTAL = _____

ASSERTIVE IMPRESSION MANAGEMENT

4. reverse score _____

8. reverse score _____

12. reverse score _____

16. reverse score _____

20. reverse score _____

24. reverse score _____

28. reverse score _____

32. reverse score _____

TOTAL = _____

You can find the interpretation for your score at www.cengagebrain.com.

MANAGEMENT WORKPLACE

© CENGAGE LEARNING 2013

Barcelona Restaurant Group

According to Andy Pforzheimer, food is only 50 percent of the experience at his restaurants. The rest comprises intangibles like ambience and conversation with the staff. To ensure consistent quality across the board, Barcelona uses five "feedback loops" that gauge restaurant performance: a "secret shopper" program, credit card rewards for customers who complete surveys, customer comment cards, e-mails, and surveillance cameras. In addition to these loops, the owners and general managers walk the floor constantly to advise waitstaff and gather feedback from customers.

What to Watch For and Ask Yourself

1. How do managers at Barcelona control the company's financial performance?

2. In what ways does Barcelona use the balanced scorecard approach to control?

3. Describe an instance where Barcelona followed the feedback control model to improve its performance.

Endnotes

1. I. Brat, "Caterpillar Gets Bugs Out of Old Equipment; Growing Remanufacturing Division Is Central to Earnings-Stabilization Plan," *Wall Street Journal*, July 5, 2006, A16; D. Cameron, "Corporate News: Caterpillar Wields Ax on Bonuses—Executive Compensation to Fall as Much as 50%; Other Cutbacks Are Set," *Wall Street Journal*, December 23, 2008, B3; G. Colvin, "Caterpillar Is Absolutely Crushing It," *Fortune*, May 23, 2011, 136–144; S. Oster, "Caterpillar, China Are to Promote Remanufacturing," *Wall Street Journal*, September 15, 2006, A10; and T. Van Hampton, "Down to Earth," *Engineering News-Record*, March 21, 2011, 26–32.

2. S. Mayerowitz, "Casinos Always Win, Even When Robbed," ABC News, January 4, 2011, accessed June 13, 2011, from http://abcnews.go.com/m/story?id=12531632.]

3. R. Leifer and P. K. Mills, "An Information Processing Approach for Deciding upon Control Strategies and Reducing Control Loss in Emerging Organizations," *Journal of Management* 22 (1996): 113–137.

4. J. Jargon, "At Starbucks, Baristas Told No More Than Two Drinks," *Wall Street Journal*, October 13, 2010, accessed April 5, 2011, from http://online.wsj.com/article/SB1000142405274 87041640045755484403514060736.html.

5. N. Wiener, *Cybernetics; Or Control and Communication in the Animal and the Machine* (New York: Wiley, 1948).

6. D. Stanford, "Sustainability Meets the Profit Motive," *Bloomberg Businessweek*, April 4–10, 2011, 25–26.

7. Leifer and Mills, "An Information Processing Approach."

8. A. Mundy, "Flies, Birds, Mice Found at Egg Plant," *Wall Street Journal*, August 31, 2010, accessed April 5, 2011, from http://online.wsj.com/article/SB10001424052748703369704575461881721525848.html; and E. Weise, "Hillandale Farms Can Sell Eggs Again after Salmonella Recall," *USA Today*, October 19, 2010, accessed April 5, 2011, from www.usatoday.com/yourlife/food/safety/2010-10-18-eggs-salmonella_N.htm.

9. M. Gunther, "3M's Innovation Revival," *Fortune*, September 27, 2010, 73–76.

10. E. Holm, "Progressive to Offer Data-Driven Rates," *Wall Street Journal*, March 21, 2011, accessed April 5, 2011, from http://online.wsj.com/article/SB1000142405274870443390457621273123846 4702.html.

11. M. Weber, *The Protestant Ethic and the Spirit of Capitalism* (New York: Scribner's, 1958).

12. E. Frazier, "Facebook Post Costs Waitress Her Job," *Charlotte Observer*, May 17, 2010, accessed April 5, 2011, from www.charlotteobserver.com/2010/05/17/1440447/facebook-post-costs-waitress-her.html.

13. D. Dahl, "Breaking 3 Workplace Taboos," *Inc.*, March 1, 2011, accessed April 5, 2011, from www.inc.com/magazine/20110301/breaking-3-workplace-taboos.html; and D. Dahl, "A Radical Take on the Virtual Company," *Inc.*, March 1, 2011, accessed April 5, 2011, from www.inc.com/magazine/20110301/philip-rosedale-on-freelancing-business-processes.html?nav=related.

14. R. Branson, "Motivated Employees Are Your Greatest Asset," *West Australian*, May 26, 2011, 38.

15. V. Elmer, "How Storytelling Spurs Success," *Fortune*, December 3, 2010, accessed April 5, 2011, from http://management.fortune.cnn.com/2010/12/03/how-storytelling-spurs-success/.

16. J. R. Barker, "Tightening the Iron Cage: Concertive Control in Self-Managing Teams," *Administrative Science Quarterly* 38 (1993): 408–437.

17. Ibid.

18. C. Manz and H. Sims, "Leading Workers to Lead Themselves: The External Leadership of Self-Managed Work Teams," *Administrative Science Quarterly* 32 (1987): 106–128.

19. J. Slocum and H. A. Sims, "Typology for Integrating Technology, Organization and Job Design," *Human Relations* 33 (1980): 193–212.

20. C. C. Manz and H. P. Sims Jr., "Self-Management as a Substitute for Leadership: A Social Learning Perspective," *Academy of Management Review* 5 (1980): 361–367.

21. C. Manz and C. Neck, *Mastering Self-Leadership*, 3rd ed. (Upper Saddle River, NJ: Pearson, Prentice Hall, 2004).

22. R. S. Kaplan and D. P. Norton, "Using the Balanced Scorecard as a Strategic Management System," *Harvard Business Review* (January–February 1996): 75–85; and R. S. Kaplan and D. P. Norton, "The Balanced Scorecard: Measures That Drive Performance," *Harvard Business Review* (January–February 1992): 71–79.

23. J. Meliones, "Saving Money, Saving Lives," *Harvard Business Review* (November–December 2000): 57–65.

24. M. H. Stocks and A. Harrell, "The Impact of an Increase in Accounting Information Level on the Judgment Quality of Individuals and Groups," *Accounting, Organizations & Society* (October–November 1995): 685–700.

25. B. Morris, "Roberto Goizueta and Jack Welch: The Wealth Builders," *Fortune*, December 11, 1995, 80–94.

26. "About Herman Miller: Operational Excellence," Herman Miller, accessed June 20, 2011, from www.hermanmiller.com/About-Us/About-Herman-Miller/Operational-Excellence.

27. "EVA Momentum Ranking for S&P 500," EVA Dimensions, December 15, 2010, accessed June 20, 2011, from http://evadimensions.com/wp-content/rankings/ForbesEVAMomentumRank12142010_website.pdf; and S. Cendrowski, "Buying Apple Stock? Think Twice," CNNMoney, September 28, 2010, accessed June 20, 2011, from http://money.cnn.com/2010/09/09/pf/apple_stock.fortune/index.htm.

28. "Welcome Complaints," Office of Consumer and Business Affairs, Government of South Australia, accessed June 20, 2005, from www.ocba.sa.gov.au/businessadvice/complaints/03_welcome.html.

29 N. Brodsky and B. Burlingham, *The Knack: How Street-Smart Entrepreneurs Learn to Handle Whatever Comes Up* (New York: Portfolio Hardcover, 2008).

30 C. B. Furlong, "12 Rules for Customer Retention," *Bank Marketing* 5 (January 1993): 14.

31 Customer retention graphs, accessed August 1, 2009, from www.voxinc.com/customer-experience-graphs/impact-customer-retention.htm.

32 M. Raphel, "Vanished Customers Are Valuable Customers," *Art Business News*, June 2002, 46.

33 N. Brodsky and B. Burlingham, *The Knack: How Street-Smart Entrepreneurs Learn to Handle Whatever Comes Up*

34 C. A. Reeves and D. A. Bednar, "Defining Quality: Alternatives and Implications," *Academy of Management Review* 19 (1994): 419–445.

35 D. R. May and B. L. Flannery, "Cutting Waste with Employee Involvement Teams," *Business Horizons*, September–October 1995, 28–38.

36 P. Valdes-Dapena, "GM Turning BP Oil Spill Booms into Volt Parts," CNNMoney, December 20, 2010, accessed April 5, 2011, from http://money.cnn.com/2010/12/17/autos/gm_volt_recycling/index.htm.

37 "Herman Miller Earns Design for Recycling Award," *GreenerDesign*, May 12, 2009, accessed July 23, 2010 from www.greenbiz.com/news/2009/05/12/herman-miller-earns-design-recycling-award.

38 J. L. Schenker. "Cows to Kilowatts: A Bounty from Waste," *Businessweek*, December 3, 2008, accessed August 1, 2009, from www.businessweek.com/globalbiz/content/dec2008/gb2008123_181278.htm.

39 "The End of the Road: Schools and Computer Recycling," Intel, accessed September 5, 2008, from www.intel.com/education/recycling_computers/recycling.htm.

40 P. Davidson, "Watching Over Freelancers," *USA Today*, September 13, 2010, accessed March 5, 2011, from www.usatoday.com/printedition/money/20100913/odesk13_st.art.htm.

41 M. Tuckey, N. Brewer, and P. Williamson, "The Influence of Motives and Goal Orientation on Feedback Seeking," *Journal of Occupational and Organizational Psychology* 75, no. 2 (2002): 195.

15

Chapter Fifteen

Managing Information

OUTLINE

REEL TO REAL

Management Workplace is at Numi Organic Tea.

SELF-ASSESSMENT

How comfortable are you with computers and new technology? Do the Self-Assessment for this chapter in the book or online to find out.

ONLINE QUIZZES

Did you get it? Review the main concepts in the chapter by taking the online quizzes on CourseMate!

VIDEO QUIZZES

Get more out of the videos by taking the multimedia video quizzes online.

What Would You Do?

Delta Air Lines Headquarters, Atlanta, Georgia[1]

All airlines and airports lose bags. After all, they must handle thousands of bags per day, sorting through the bags on each plane like a 500-piece puzzle dumped on the table from a just-opened box, and then rush them to the right connecting planes or baggage carousels. The challenging logistics, however, don't make up for the impact of delays on passengers. There's the rabbi flying to Israel, whose lost bag is returned waterlogged, with his belongings covered in black mold. Or the administrative assistant headed to Buffalo, New York, for her cousin's wedding, whose lost luggage contained her bridesmaid dress and her boyfriend's tuxedo. She said, "I was in utter despair. I thought: 'How can I be in this wedding?' You're frustrated, you want to cry, and you're pissed off." Finally, there's the Canadian singer who, on finding his $3,500 guitar damaged, sought and was refused payment by the airline. So he exacted his revenge by making a video and posting it on YouTube, where it has been seen 3.5 million times.

In all, 31 million bags are delivered late worldwide each year, or about 1.4 percent. In the United States, 7 people per 1,000 passengers, or roughly 1 per plane, don't get their luggage on time, and they file 7.5 million mishandled baggage reports a year. Over the last decade, the three largest airlines, American, United, and—yes—Delta Airlines, are the worst offenders. Several key statistics stand out. First, Delta is 30 percent worse compared to the best airlines. Second, 28 percent more bags are delayed today compared to a decade ago. No wonder passengers are frustrated, especially when airlines charge a $25 handling fee for the first checked bag and $35 for the second. Nothing like paying extra to have the airline lose your bags, especially when Delta brings in $952 million a year in bag fees! Third, it costs $15 to transport each bag. Nine dollars is for labor, as ten people touch each bag between check-in and the baggage carousel. U.S. Airways spends $250 million a year on labor for bags alone, or 11 percent of payroll. Four dollars is for sorting systems such as

carousels, conveyors, carts, and tractors. Finally, fuel accounts for the remaining $2. And depending on oil prices, that's sometimes lower, but in the last three to five years, it has generally been higher. Fourth, besides the customer dissatisfaction and ill will created, delayed luggage costs airlines $90 to $100 per bag, or $3 billion to $4 billion a year.

Passengers are beginning to realize that bag fees bring in much more than the cost to deliver bags, so they have every right to expect Delta to do a better job delivering bags. With advances in technology, clearly there have to be ways to use information technology to track bags and sharply decrease the number of delayed bags. If Amazon can send e-mails and texts notifying customers when their orders leave the warehouse, arrive at their local airports, and are delivered to their homes, then why can't Delta do the same thing with luggage that's supposed to never leave the airport, except in passengers' hands? Surely there are ways to do this. What information technology changes would have to be made at the counter; behind the counter as bags are sorted and routed to planes; and then on the tarmac, where bags are sorted one last time as they are put on or taken off planes? Grocery stores and Home Depot have been using self-checkout lanes for several years. What kind of information technology would be required to use self-tagging, where passengers put destination tags on their own bags, and would that help the baggage problem or make it worse? Finally, Delta baggage handlers were caught stealing cameras, laptops, iPods, and jewelry from passengers' bags. If we're going to use technology to get more bags delivered on time, how can we also use technology to deter theft among our own employees?

If you were in charge at Delta Airlines, what would you do?

15-1 Strategic Importance of Information

We begin this chapter by explaining why information matters. In particular, you will learn the value of strategic information to companies, as well as the cost and characteristics of good information. Next, you will investigate how companies capture, process, and protect information. Finally, you'll learn how information is accessed and shared with those both inside and outside the company and how knowledge and expertise (not just information or data) are shared too.

A generation ago, computer hardware and software had little to do with managing business information. Rather than storing information on hard drives, managers stored it in filing cabinets. Instead of uploading daily sales and inventory levels by satellite to corporate headquarters, they mailed hard-copy summaries to headquarters at the end of each month. Today, a generation later, computer hardware and software are an integral part of managing business information. This is due mainly to something called **Moore's law**. Gordon Moore is one of the founders of Intel Corporation, which makes 75 percent of the integrated processors used in personal computers. In 1965, Moore predicted that computer-processing power would double and that its cost would drop by 50 percent every two years.[2]

As Exhibit 15.1 shows, Moore was right. Consequently, the computer sitting in your lap or on your desk is not only smaller but also much cheaper and more powerful than the large mainframe computers used by *Fortune* 500 companies 15 years ago. As computer hardware, software, and networks have become ever more integral to today's hypercompetitive business environment, so too have the vast amounts of information stored on that hardware, processed by that software, and transmitted over those networks. In fact, information has become as important as capital (i.e., money) for business success, whether it's about product inventory, pricing, or costs. It takes money to get businesses started, but businesses can't survive and grow without the right information.

After reading this section, you should be able to:

15-1 explain the strategic importance of information.

Raw data are facts and figures. For example, 11, $452, 32, and 26,100 are some data that I used the day I wrote this section of the chapter. However, facts and figures aren't particularly useful unless they have meaning. For example, you probably can't guess what these four pieces of raw data represent, can you? If you can't, these

Moore's law
the prediction that about every two years, computer processing power would double and its cost would drop by 50 percent

raw data
facts and figures

Exhibit 15.1

Microprocessor Transistor Counts 1971–2011 and Moore's Law

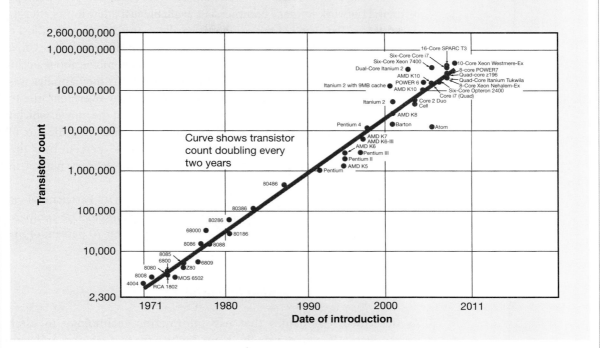

Source: *W. G. Simon, "Microprocessor Transistor Count and Moore's Law—2011," Wikipedia, May 13, 2011, accessed November 24, 2012, from http://en.wikipedia.org/wiki/File:Transistor_Count_and_Moore%27s_Law_-_2011.svg.*

data are useless. That's why researchers make the distinction between raw data and information. Whereas raw data consist of facts and figures, **information** is useful data that can influence someone's choices and behavior. One way to think about the difference between data and information is that information has context.

So, what did those four pieces of data mean to me? Well, 11 stands for Channel 11, the local CBS affiliate on which I watched part of the men's PGA golf tournament; $452 is how much it would cost me to rent a minivan for a week if I go skiing over spring break; 32 is for the 32-gigabyte storage card that I want to add to my digital camera (prices are low, so I'll probably buy it); and 26,100 miles means that it's time to get the oil changed in my car.

While this particular information may not be important to you, information in general has strategic importance for organizations because it can be used to **15-1a obtain first-mover advantage** and **15-1b sustain competitive advantage once it has been created.**

15-1a First-Mover Advantage

First-mover advantage is the strategic advantage that companies earn by being the first in an industry to use new information technology to substantially

information
useful data that can influence people's choices and behavior

first-mover advantage
the strategic advantage that companies earn by being the first in an industry to use new information technology to substantially lower costs or to differentiate a product or service from that of competitors

lower costs or to differentiate a product or service from that of competitors. Texas-based *DG FASTCHANNEL* revolutionized TV marketing when it built its own satellite and Web-based distribution network. Whereas other companies were sending commercials to TV stations on videotapes, DG Fastchannel used its digital network to make commercials available just a few hours after it produced them. The speed of the network also allows the company to adjust commercials based on near-real-time feedback from consumers. When Universal Pictures began advertising *Despicable Me*, an animated movie about a criminal mastermind, DG Fastchannel's research showed that the movie trailer was not polling well among women over the age of 26. Literally overnight, the trailer was remixed to emphasize the heart-warming aspects of the movie, which went on to earn a "female-friendly" reputation and $200 million at the box office. DG Fastchannel has been growing at an average of 43 percent over the last three years and controls almost 65 percent of the ad delivery market in the United States.[3]

First-mover advantages like those established by DG Fastchannel can be sizable. On average, first movers earn a 30 percent market share compared to 19 percent for the companies that follow.[4] Likewise, over 70 percent of market leaders started as first movers.[5]

15-1b Sustaining Competitive Advantage

As described, companies that use information technology to establish first-mover advantage usually have higher market shares and profits. According to the resource-based view of information technology shown in Exhibit 15.2, companies need to address three critical questions in order to sustain a competitive advantage through information technology. First, does the information technology create value for the firm by lowering costs or providing a better product or service? If an information technology doesn't add value, then investing in it would put the firm at a competitive disadvantage to companies that choose information technologies that do add value.

Second, is the information technology the same or different across competing firms? If all the firms have access to the same information technology and use it in the same way, then no firm has an advantage over another (i.e., there is competitive parity). For example, a number of hotels and resorts, such as Marriott, now use social media to improve customer service. Staff members search for any mention of their hotel on Twitter, Facebook, blogs, or websites like TripAdvisor, and other sites. When they find a complaint, they offer an immediate apology and, more often than not, perks like room upgrades and free meals to make up for the problem. When Paul Horan tweeted that his room at the *ORLANDO MARRIOTT WORLD CENTER* was "the crappiest room in the hotel," a member of the hotel's staff saw the tweet, immediately sent an apology note, and upgraded his room. By paying attention to social media, tech-savvy hotels have found a way to get near-instantaneous feedback from customers and quickly resolve problems.[6] But because this technology is available to all companies, it's unlikely that the technology will lead to a sustained competitive advantage.

Exhibit 15.2

Using Information Technology to Sustain a Competitive Advantage

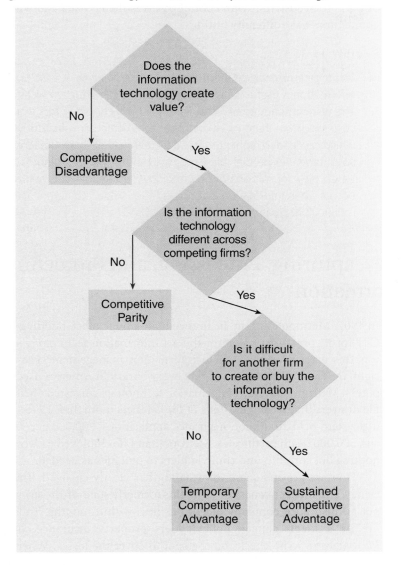

Source: *Adapted from F. J. Mata, W. L. Fuerst, and J. B. Barney, "Information Technology and Sustained Competitive Advantage: A Resource-Based Analysis," MIS Quarterly 19, no. 4, December 1995, 487–505. © 1995, Regents of the University of Minnesota. Reprinted by permission.*

Third, is it difficult for another company to create or buy the information technology used by the firm? If so, then the firm has established a sustainable competitive advantage over competitors through information technology. If not, then the competitive advantage is just temporary, and competitors should eventually be able to duplicate the advantages the leading firm has gained from information technology. For more about sustainable competitive advantage and its sources, see Chapter 5 on organizational strategy.

Companies that achieve first-mover advantage with information technology and then sustain it with continued investment create a moving target that competitors have difficulty hitting.

REVIEW 15-1

Strategic Importance of Information

Information is useful data that can influence someone's choices and behavior. The first company to use new information technology to substantially lower costs or differentiate products or services often gains first-mover advantage, which can lead to higher profits and larger market share. Creating a first-mover advantage can be difficult, expensive, and risky. According to the resource-based view of information technology, sustainable competitive advantage occurs when information technology adds value, is different across firms, and is difficult to create or acquire.

15-2 Capturing, Processing, and Protecting Information

In 1907, Metropolitan Life Insurance built a huge office building in New York City for its brand-new, state-of-the-art information technology system. What was this great breakthrough in information management? Card files. That's right, the same card file system that every library in America used before computers. Metropolitan Life's information technology consisted of 20,000 separate file drawers that sat in hundreds of file cabinets more than 15 feet tall. This filing system held 20 million insurance applications, 700,000 accounting books, and 500,000 death certificates. Metropolitan Life employed 61 workers who did nothing but sort, file, and climb ladders to pull files as needed.[7]

How we get and share information has clearly changed. The cost, inefficiency, and ineffectiveness of using this formerly state-of-the-art system would put an insurance company out of business within months. Today, if storms, fire, or accidents damage policyholders' property, insurance companies like PROGRESSIVE write checks on the spot to cover the losses. When policyholders buy a car, they call their Progressive agent from the dealership to activate their insurance before driving off in their new car. And now, insurance companies are marketing their products and services to customers directly from the Internet—Progressive's fictional spokesperson "Flo" has her own Facebook page with millions of likes. From card files to Internet files, in just under a century, the rate of change in information technology is spectacular.

After reading this section, you should be able to:

15-2 explain the basics of capturing, processing, and protecting information.

Just think about all the information that is processed during a mundane errand. When you go to your local RITE AID pharmacy to pick up a prescription, the pharmacist reviews an electronic file that shows all of the medications you're taking. That same system automatically checks to make sure that your new prescription won't create adverse side effects by interacting with your other medications. When you pay for your prescription, Rite Aid's point-of-sale information system determines whether you've written any bad checks lately (to Rite Aid or other stores), records your payment, and then checks with the computer of the pharmaceutical company that makes your prescription drugs to see whether it's time to reorder. Throughout the process, Rite Aid protects your information to make sure that your data are readily available only to you, your physician, and your pharmacist.

In this section, you will learn about the information technologies that companies like Rite Aid and Progressive use to **15-2a capture, 15-2b process,** and **15-2c protect information**.

15-2a Capturing Information

There are two basic methods of capturing information: manual and electronic. Manual capture of information is a slow, costly, labor-intensive, and often inaccurate process, which entails recording and entering data by hand into a data storage device. For example, when you applied for a driver's license, you probably recorded personal information about yourself by filling out a form. Then, after you passed your driver's test, someone typed your handwritten information into the department of motor vehicles' computer database so that local and state police could access it from their patrol cars in the event they pulled you over for speeding. (Isn't information great?) Consequently, companies are relying more on electronic capture. They use electronic storage devices such as bar codes, radio frequency identification tags, and document scanners to capture and record data electronically.

Bar codes represent numerical data by varying the thickness and pattern of vertical bars. The primary advantage of bar codes is that the data they represent

bar code
a visual pattern that represents numerical data by varying the thickness and pattern of vertical bars

Bar codes have widespread use, from inventory control to paperwork to baggage handling and more.

© VARTANOV ANATOLY/SHUTTERSTOCK.COM

can be read and recorded in an instant with a handheld or pen-type scanner. One pass of the scanner (okay, sometimes several) and "beep!"—the information has been captured. Bar codes cut checkout times in half, reduce data entry errors by 75 percent, and save stores money because stockers don't have to go through the labor-intensive process of putting a price tag on each item in the store.[8] Consumer product companies, like UNILEVER, are now partnering with grocery stores and technology companies to test bar code-based coupons that can be scanned directly from consumers' cell phones.[9]

Radio frequency identification (RFID) tags contain minuscule microchips and antennas that transmit information via radio waves.[10] Unlike bar codes, which require direct line-of-sight scanning, RFID tags are read by turning on an RFID reader that, like a radio, tunes into a specific frequency to determine the number *and* location of products, parts, or anything else to which the RFID tags are attached. Turn on an RFID reader, and every RFID tag within the reader's range (from several hundred to several thousand feet) is accounted for.

Because they are now so inexpensive, RFID tags and readers are being put to thousands of uses in all kinds of businesses. *COCA-COLA* is testing a soft-drink vending machine, the Freestyle, which has 30 different flavor cartridges that can be used to make 100 different Coca-Cola brand drinks. Each cartridge in the Freestyle has an RFID chip attached to it, which allows Coca-Cola to track which drinks are selling, how much they're selling, and when. The RFID tags also indicate when cartridges are running low and must be replaced. Furthermore, RFID can show whether a cartridge has been installed correctly or whether it is a genuine Coca-Cola product. In the case of a product recall, Coca-Cola can even stop particular cartridges from dispensing drinks until they can be pulled from the machines.[11]

Electronic scanners, which convert printed text and pictures into digital images, have become an increasingly popular method of capturing data electronically because they are inexpensive and easy to use. The first requirement for a good scanner is a document feeder that automatically feeds document pages into the scanner or turns the pages (often with a puff of air) when scanning books or bound documents.[12] Text that has been digitized cannot be searched or edited like the regular text in your word-processing software, however, so the second requirement for a good scanner is **optical character recognition** software to scan and convert original or digitized documents into ASCII text (American Standard Code for Information Interchange) or Adobe PDF documents.

15-2b Processing Information

Processing information means transforming raw data into meaningful information that can be applied to business decision making. Evaluating sales data to determine the best- and worst-selling products, examining repair records to determine product reliability, and monitoring the cost of long-distance phone calls are all examples of processing raw data into meaningful information. And with automated, electronic capture of data, increased processing power, and cheaper and more plentiful ways to store data, managers no longer worry about getting data. Instead, they scratch their heads about how to use the

radio frequency identification (RFID) tags
tags containing minuscule microchips that transmit information via radio waves and can be used to track the number and location of the objects into which the tags have been inserted

electronic scanner
an electronic device that converts printed text and pictures into digital images

optical character recognition
the ability of software to convert digitized documents into ASCII text (American Standard Code for Information Interchange) that can be searched, read, and edited by word-processing software as well as other kinds of software

processing information
transforming raw data into meaningful information

overwhelming amount of data that pours into their businesses every day. Furthermore, most managers know little about statistics and have neither the time nor the inclination to learn how to use them to analyze data.

One useful tool to help managers dig out from under the avalanche of data is data mining. **Data mining** is the process of discovering patterns and relationships in large amounts of data.[14] Data mining works by using complex algorithms such as neural networks, rule induction, and decision trees. If you don't know what those are, that's okay. With data mining, you don't have to. Most managers need only to know that data mining looks for patterns that are already in the data but are too complex for them to spot on their own.

Data mining typically splits a data set in half, finds patterns in one half, and then tests the validity of those patterns by trying to find them again in the second half of the data set. The data typically come from a **data warehouse** that stores huge amounts of data that have been prepared for data mining analysis by being cleaned of errors and redundancy. The data in a data warehouse can then be analyzed using two kinds of data mining. **Supervised data mining** usually begins with the user telling the data mining software to look and test for specific patterns and relationships in a data set. Typically, this is done through a series of "what-if" questions or statements. For instance, a grocery store manager might instruct the data mining software to determine whether coupons placed in the Sunday paper increase or decrease sales. By contrast, with **unsupervised data mining**, the user simply tells the data mining software to uncover whatever patterns and relationships it can find in a data set. Unsupervised data mining is particularly good at identifying association or affinity patterns, sequence patterns, and predictive patterns. It can also identify what data mining technicians call data clusters.[15] **Association or affinity patterns** occur when two or more database elements tend to occur together in a significant way. HEAT, short for *HEALTH CARE FRAUD PREVENTION AND ENFORCEMENT ACTION TEAMS*, is a multiagency federal department charged with finding and prosecuting large-scale medical fraud, in which false medical claims are submitted to the U.S. and state governments for Medicare and Medicaid payments. The data mining software helped find factors commonly associated with fraud such as high numbers of out-of-state patients and doctors or one patient buying orthotics for several different body parts. One company raised several red flags, and when sued, pleaded guilty to health care fraud. The owner was sentenced to 54 months in prison.[16]

Sequence patterns occur when two or more database elements occur together in a significant pattern in which one of the elements precedes the other. Most professional baseball teams set the price of tickets for each game at the beginning of the season, varying the price depending on the day of the week

MANAGEMENT TREND

Smart Parking Meters

The city of San Francisco recently introduced "smart" parking meters that are equipped with sensors that can sense when a car is parked in a designated spot, and can communicate with other meters within a certain distance. Other cities have used similar systems to charge different rates at different hours, but San Francisco is the first city to use the real-time information from meters in an effort to reduce traffic congestion and pollution from emissions. Instead of endlessly circling around a block looking for an open parking space, drivers are able to use an application on their smartphones or laptops that shows the precise location of open parking spots. They can even use the application to "feed the meter" digitally.[13]

data mining
the process of discovering unknown patterns and relationships in large amounts of data

data warehouse
stores huge amounts of data that have been prepared for data mining analysis by being cleaned of errors and redundancy

supervised data mining
the process when the user tells the data mining software to look and test for specific patterns and relationships in a data set

unsupervised data mining
the process when the user simply tells the data mining software to uncover whatever patterns and relationships it can find in a data set

association or affinity patterns
when two or more database elements tend to occur together in a significant way

sequence patterns
when two or more database elements occur together in a significant pattern, but one of the elements precedes the other

and the opponent. For example, the SAN FRANCISCO GIANTS use dynamic pricing for all of its single-game tickets. Using data mining, the Giants re-price tickets on a daily basis by calculating the impact of various factors (i.e., database elements) that only become clear a few days before a game, such as the weather, winning streaks, and pitching matchups, all of which influence how many people will want to attend. During the 2009 season, the Giants lowered and raised prices in a small section of seats, using this data, and were able to sell an extra 25,000 tickets, which increased revenue by $500,000. And for the 2010 season, when the Giants switched to dynamic pricing for all single-game seats, ticket revenues were up by 6 percent.[17]

Predictive patterns are just the opposite of association or affinity patterns. Whereas association or affinity patterns look for database elements that seem to go together, **predictive patterns** help identify database elements that are different. Banks and credit card companies use data mining to find predictive patterns that distinguish customers who are good credit risks from those who are poor credit risks and less likely to pay their loans and monthly bills. J. P. Martin, an executive at CANADIAN TIRE, analyzed what customers were buying and identified predictive patterns that accurately forecast whether consumers would pay their debts. For example, he found that people who bought generic motor oil were more likely to miss payments than those who bought more expensive, name-brand oil. People who bought felt furniture pads, which protect wood floors from scratches, were very unlikely to miss payments.[18]

Data clusters are the last kind of pattern found by data mining. **Data clusters** occur when three or more database elements occur together (i.e., cluster) in a significant way.

Traditionally, data mining has been very expensive and very complex. Today, however, data mining services and analysis are much more affordable and within reach of most companies' budgets. And if it follows the path of most technologies, it will become even easier and cheaper to use in the future.

15-2c Protecting Information

Protecting information is the process of ensuring that data are reliably and consistently retrievable in a usable format for authorized users but no one else. For instance, when customers purchase prescription medicine at Drugstore.com, an online drugstore and health-aid retailer, they want to be confident that their medical and credit card information is available only to them, the pharmacists at DRUGSTORE.COM, and their doctors. So Drugstore.com has an extensive privacy policy (click "Privacy Policy" at www.drugstore.com to make sure this is the case).[19]

Companies like Drugstore.com find it necessary to protect information because of the numerous security threats to data and data security. People inside and outside companies can steal or destroy company data in various ways, including denial-of-service Web-server attacks that can bring down some of the busiest and best-run sites on the Internet; viruses and spyware/adware that spread quickly and can result in data loss and business disruption; keystroke monitoring in which every mouse click and keystroke you make is monitored,

predictive patterns
patterns that help identify database elements that are different

data clusters
when three or more database elements occur together (i.e., cluster) in a significant way

protecting information
the process of ensuring that data are reliably and consistently retrievable in a usable format for authorized users, but no one else

stored, and sent to unauthorized users; password-cracking software that steals supposedly secure passwords; and phishing, where fake but real-looking e-mails and websites trick users into sharing personal information (user names, passwords, account numbers), leading to unauthorized account access. There are numerous steps that can be taken to secure data and data networks. Some of the most important are authentication and authorization, firewalls, antivirus software for PCs and e-mail servers, data encryption, and virtual private networks.[20] We will review those steps and then finish this section with a brief review of the dangers of wireless networks.

Two critical steps are required to make sure that data can be accessed by authorized users and no one else. One is authentication, that is, making sure users are who they claim to be.[21] The other is authorization, that is, granting authenticated users approved access to data, software, and systems.[22] When an ATM prompts you to enter your personal identification number (PIN), the bank is authenticating that you are you. Once you've been authenticated, you are authorized to access your funds and no one else's. Of course, as anyone who has lost a PIN or password or had one stolen knows, user authentication systems are not foolproof. In particular, users create security risks by not changing their default account passwords (such as birth dates) or by using weak passwords such as names (e.g., Larry) or complete words (e.g., football) that are quickly guessed by password-cracker software.[23]

This is why many companies are now turning to two-factor authentication, which is based on what users know, such as a password, and what they have, such as a secure ID card.[24] To provide increased security for its users, for example, *Yahoo!* recently introduced two-factor authentication for its Yahoo! Mail service. When logging in, users are first asked for their passwords, as is done with most e-mail accounts. But then they must provide a second authentication factor, such as an answer to a security question or a validation code sent to their mobile phone.[25]

With biometrics, such as fingerprint recognition or iris scanning, users are identified by unique, measurable body features.[26] *24 Hour Fitness USA* has implemented "cardless check-in" by scanning its members' fingerprints. And each time your finger is placed on the scanner, your fingerprint is compared to the identifying number in their system.[27] 24 Hour Fitness emphasizes, however, that it doesn't store images of fingerprints.

Unfortunately, stolen or cracked passwords are not the only way for hackers and electronic thieves to gain access to an organization's computer resources. Unless special safeguards are put in place, every time corporate users are online, there's literally nothing between their personal computers and the Internet (home users with high-speed DSL or cable Internet access face the same risks). Hackers can access files, run programs, and control key parts of computers if precautions aren't taken. To reduce these risks, companies use firewalls, hardware or software devices that sit between the computers in an internal organizational network and outside networks such as the Internet. Firewalls filter and check incoming and outgoing data. They prevent company insiders from accessing unauthorized sites or from sending confidential company information to people outside the company. Firewalls also prevent

authentication
making sure potential users are who they claim to be

authorization
granting authenticated users approved access to data, software, and systems

two-factor authentication
authentication based on what users know, such as a password and what they have in their possession, such as a secure ID card or key

biometrics
identifying users by unique, measurable body features, such as fingerprint recognition or iris scanning

firewall
a protective hardware or software device that sits between the computers in an internal organizational network and outside networks, such as the Internet

outsiders from identifying and gaining access to company computers and data. Indeed, if a firewall is working properly, the computers behind the company firewall literally cannot be seen or accessed by outsiders.

A **virus** is a program or piece of code that, without your knowledge, attaches itself to other programs on your computer and can trigger anything from a harmless flashing message to the reformatting of your hard drive to a systemwide network shutdown. Today's viruses are very sophisticated. In fact, with some viruses, just being connected to a network can infect your computer. *Antivirus software for personal computers* scans e-mail, downloaded files, and computer hard drives, disk drives, and memory to detect and stop computer viruses from doing damage. However, this software is effective only to the extent that users of individual computers have and use up-to-date versions. With new viruses appearing all the time, users should update their antivirus software weekly or, even better, configure their virus software to automatically check for, download, and install updates. By contrast, *corporate antivirus software* automatically scans e-mail attachments such as Microsoft Word documents, graphics, or text files as they come across the company e-mail server. It also monitors and scans all file downloads across company databases and network servers. So, although antivirus software for personal computers prevents individual computers from being infected, corporate antivirus software for e-mail servers, databases, and network servers adds another layer of protection by preventing infected files from multiplying and being sent to others.

Another way of protecting information is to encrypt sensitive data. **Data encryption** transforms data into complex, scrambled digital codes that can be unencrypted only by authorized users who possess unique decryption keys. One method of data encryption is to use products by Pretty Good Privacy (PGP) (www.pgp.com) to encrypt the files stored on personal computers or network servers and databases. This is especially important with laptop computers, which are easily stolen. With people increasingly gaining unauthorized access to e-mail messages—e-mail snooping—it's also important to encrypt sensitive e-mail messages and file attachments. If you want to learn more or want to begin encrypting your own files, download a free copy of Pretty Good Privacy from http://web.mit.edu/pgp.

Although firewalls can protect personal computers and network servers connected to the corporate network, people away from their offices (e.g., salespeople, business travelers, telecommuters) who interact with their company networks via the Internet face a security risk. Because Internet data are not encrypted, packet sniffer software easily allows hackers to read everything sent or received except files that have been encrypted before sending. Previously, the only practical solution was to have employees dial in to secure company phone lines for direct access to the company network. Of course, with international and long-distance phone calls, the costs quickly added up. Now, **virtual private networks (VPNs)** have solved this problem by using software to encrypt all Internet data at both ends of the transmission process. Instead of making long-distance calls, employees connect to the Internet. But unlike typical Internet connections in which data packets are unencrypted, the VPN encrypts the data sent by employees outside the company computer network, decrypts the data when they arrive within the company network, and does the same when data are sent back to the computer outside the network. VPN connections provide secure access to everything on a company's network.

Alternatively, many companies are now adopting Web-based **secure sockets layer (SSL) encryption** to provide secure off-site access to data and programs. If you've ever entered your credit card in a Web browser to make an online purchase, you've used SSL technology to encrypt and protect that information. You can tell whether SSL encryption is being used on a website if you see a padlock icon (gold in Internet Explorer or Firefox; green in Google Chrome, silver in Safari), or if the URL begins with "https." SSL encryption works the same way in the workplace. Managers and employees who aren't at the office simply connect to the Internet, open a Web browser, and then enter a user name and password to gain access to SSL-encrypted data and programs.

Finally, many companies now have wireless networks, which make it possible for anybody with a laptop and a wireless card to access the company network from anywhere in the office. Though wireless networks come equipped with security and encryption capabilities that, in theory, permit only authorized users to access the wireless network, those capabilities are easily bypassed with the right tools. Compounding the problem, many wireless networks are shipped with their security and encryption capabilities turned off for ease of installation.[28] Caution is important even when encryption is turned on because the Wired Equivalent Privacy (WEP) security protocol is easily compromised. If you work at home or are working on the go, extra care is critical because Wi-Fi networks in homes and public places like hotel lobbies are among the most targeted by hackers.[29] See the Wi-Fi Alliance site at www.wi-fi.org for the latest information on wireless security and encryption protocols that provide much stronger protection for your company's wireless network.

REVIEW 15-2

. . . .

Capturing, Processing, and Protecting Information

Electronic data capture (bar codes, radio frequency identification [RFID] tags, scanners, and optical character recognition) is much faster, easier, and cheaper than manual data capture. Processing information means transforming raw data into meaningful information that can be applied to business decision making. Data mining helps managers with this transformation by discovering unknown patterns and relationships in data. Supervised data mining looks for patterns specified by managers; unsupervised data mining looks for four general kinds of data patterns: association/affinity patterns, sequence patterns, predictive patterns, and data clusters. Protecting information ensures that data are reliably and consistently retrievable in a usable format by authorized users but no one else. Authentication and authorization, firewalls, antivirus software for PCs and corporate e-mail and network servers, data encryption, virtual private networks, and Web-based secure sockets layer (SSL) encryption are some of the best ways to protect information. Be careful with wireless networks, which are easily compromised even when security and encryption protocols are in place.

secure sockets layer (SSL) encryption
internet browser-based encryption that provides secure off-site web access to some data and programs

15-3 Accessing and Sharing Information and Knowledge

Today, information technologies are letting companies communicate data, share data, and provide data access to workers, managers, suppliers, and customers in ways that were unthinkable just a few years ago.

After reading this section, you should be able to:

15-3 describe how companies can access and share information and knowledge.

Let's explore how companies use information technology to improve **15-3a internal access and sharing of information, 15-3b external access and sharing of information,** and **15-3c the sharing of knowledge and expertise.**

15-3a Internal Access and Sharing

Executives, managers, and workers inside the company use three kinds of information technology to access and share information: executive information systems, intranets, and portals. An **executive information system (EIS)** uses internal and external sources of data to provide managers and executives the information they need to monitor and analyze organizational performance.[30] The goal of an EIS is to provide accurate, complete, relevant, and timely information to managers.

Managers at *Colgate-Palmolive*, which makes dental (Colgate toothpastes), personal (Irish Spring soap and Speed Stick antiperspirants), and home care (Palmolive dish soaps) products, as well as pet nutrition (Hill's Science Diet), use their EIS, which they call their "dashboard," to see how well the company is running. Ruben Panizza, Colgate's Global IT Director of Business Intelligence, says, "These real-time dashboards are a change for people who are used to seeing a lot of numbers with their data. But they quickly realize they can use the information as it's presented in the dashboards to make faster decisions.... They see the real data as it is in the system much more easily and quickly."[31]

Intranets are private company networks that allow employees to easily access, share, and publish information using Internet software. Intranet websites are just like external websites, but the firewall separating the internal company network from the Internet permits only authorized internal access.[32] Companies typically use intranets to share information (e.g., about benefits) and to replace paper forms with online forms. Many company intranets are built on the Web model as it existed a decade ago. Exhibit 15.3 lists reasons companies use intranets.

Finally, **corporate portals** are a hybrid of executive information systems and intranets. Whereas an EIS provides managers and executives with the information they need to monitor and analyze organizational performance, and

---

executive information system (EIS) a data processing system that uses internal and external data sources to provide the information needed to monitor and analyze organizational performance

intranets private company networks that allow employees to easily access, share, and publish information using internet software

corporate portal a hybrid of executive information systems and intranets that allows managers and employees to use a web browser to gain access to customized company information and to complete specialized transactions

---

Exhibit 15.3

Why Companies Use Intranets

- Intranets are inexpensive.
- Intranets increase efficiencies and reduce costs.
- Intranets are intuitive and easy to use and Web-based.
- Intranets work across all computer systems and platforms (Web-based).
- Intranets can be built on top of an existing computer network.
- Intranets work with software programs that easily convert electronic documents to HTML files for intranet use.
- Much of the software required to set up an intranet is either freeware (no cost) or shareware (try before you buy, usually less expensive than commercial software).

© Cengage Learning 2013

intranets help companies distribute and publish information and forms within the company, corporate portals allow company managers and employees to access customized information *and* complete specialized transactions using a Web browser.

15-3b External Access and Sharing

Historically, companies have been unable or reluctant to let outside groups have access to corporate information. Now, however, a number of information technologies—electronic data interchange, extranets, Web services, and the Internet—are making it easier to share company data with external groups like suppliers and customers. They're also reducing costs, increasing productivity by eliminating manual information processing (70 percent of the data output from one company, like a purchase order, ends up as data input at another company, such as a sales invoice or shipping order), reducing data-entry errors, improving customer service, and speeding communications. As a result, managers are scrambling to adopt these technologies.

With **electronic data interchange** or **EDI** two companies convert purchase and ordering information to a standardized format to enable direct electronic transmission of that information from one company's computer system to the other company's system. For example, when a Walmart checkout clerk drags an Apple iPod across the checkout scanner, Walmart's computerized inventory system automatically reorders another iPod through the direct EDI connection that its computer has with Apple's manufacturing and shipping computer. No one at Walmart or Apple fills out paperwork. No one makes phone calls. There are no delays to wait to find out whether Apple has the iPod in stock. The transaction takes place instantly and automatically because the data from both companies were translated into a standardized, shareable, compatible format.

Web services are another way for companies to directly and automatically transmit purchase and ordering information from one company's computer system to another company's computer system. **Web services** use standardized protocols to describe and transfer data from one company in such a way that those data can automatically be read, understood, transcribed, and processed by different computer systems in another company.[33]

In EDI and Web services, the different purchasing and ordering applications in each company interact automatically without any human input. No one has to lift a finger to click a mouse, enter data, or hit the return key. An **extranet**, by contrast, allows companies to exchange information and conduct transactions by purposely providing outsiders with direct, Web browser-based access to authorized parts of a company's intranet or information system. Typically, user names and passwords are required to access an extranet.[34] PENSKE TRUCK LEASING, which leases truck fleets to companies (just like leasing a car), has created an extranet at MyFleetAtPenske.com for its U.S. customers. Fleet managers use the Penske extranet to track and schedule preventive maintenance, get updates on real-time emergency roadside assistance, generate detailed usage and cost reports, have their drivers participate in online safety-training programs, and manage U.S. Department of Transportation safety compliance requirements (including drug and alcohol testing).[35]

electronic data interchange (EDI)
when two companies convert their purchase and ordering information to a standardized format to enable the direct electronic transmission of that information from one company's computer system to the other company's computer system

web services
using standardized protocols to describe data from one company in such a way that those data can automatically be read, understood, transcribed, and processed by different computer systems in another company

extranets
networks that allow companies to exchange information and conduct transactions with outsiders by providing them direct, web-based access to authorized parts of a company's intranet or information system

Similar to how an extranet digitally manages transactions with suppliers, Chirp's kiosks automate customer transactions for purchases of luxury goods.

Finally, companies are reducing paperwork and manual information processing by using the Internet to electronically automate transactions with customers; this is similar to the way in which extranets are used to handle transactions with suppliers and distributors. For example, Internet purchases, ticketless travel, and automated check-ins have together fully automated the purchase of airline tickets. Use of self-service kiosks is expanding too. Grocery store shoppers in Houston and San Antonio, Texas, can use CHIRP automated kiosks to buy designer handbags from Coach, Michael Kors, or DKNY. Other Chirp machines display high-def scenes from recent movies, while offering shoppers items like jewelry, perfume, or accessories inspired by the films. To buy, customers swipe a credit card, and like a typical vending machine, out comes your purchase. Typically, Chirp's prices are 30 percent to 75 percent below retail because it avoids the cost of retail employees or stores and buys discounted goods in small lots from designers like Gucci, Prada, and others. Returning goods is just as easy. Customers call a toll-free number and Chirp sends them a box with prepaid postage to mail the goods back.[36]

In the long run, the goal is to link customer Internet sites with company intranets (or EDI) and extranets so that everyone—all the employees and managers within a company as well as the suppliers and distributors outside the company—involved in providing a service or making a product for a customer is automatically notified when a purchase is made. Companies that use EDI, Web services, extranets, and the Internet to share data with customers and suppliers achieve increases in productivity 2.7 times larger than those that don't.[37]

15-3c Sharing Knowledge and Expertise

At the beginning of the chapter, we distinguished between raw data, which consist of facts and figures, and information, which consists of useful data that influence someone's choices and behavior. One more important distinction needs to be made, namely, that data and information are not the same as knowledge. **Knowledge** is the understanding that one gains from information. Importantly, knowledge does not reside in information. Knowledge resides in people. That's why companies hire consultants and why family doctors refer patients to specialists. Unfortunately, it can be quite expensive to employ consultants, specialists, and experts. So companies have begun using two information technologies to capture and share the knowledge of consultants, specialists, and experts with other managers and workers: decision support systems and expert systems.

Whereas an executive information system speeds up and simplifies the acquisition of information, a **decision support system (DSS)** helps managers

knowledge
the understanding that one gains from information

decision support system (DSS)
an information system that helps managers understand specific kinds of problems and potential solutions and analyze the impact of different decision options using "what-if" scenarios

understand problems and potential solutions by acquiring and analyzing information with sophisticated models and tools.[38] Furthermore, whereas EIS programs are broad in scope and permit managers to retrieve all kinds of information about a company, DSS programs are usually narrow in scope and targeted toward helping managers solve specific kinds of problems. DSS programs have been developed to help managers pick the shortest and most efficient routes for delivery trucks, select the best combination of stocks for investors, and schedule the flow of inventory through complex manufacturing facilities. It's important to understand that DSS programs don't replace managerial decision making; they *improve* it by furthering managers' and workers' understanding of the problems they face and the solutions that might work.

Expert systems are created by capturing the specialized knowledge and decision rules used by experts and experienced decision makers. They permit nonexpert employees to draw on this expert knowledge base to make decisions. Most expert systems work by using a collection of "if–then" rules to sort through information and recommend a course of action. For example, let's say that you're using your American Express card to help your spouse celebrate a promotion. After dinner and a movie, the two of you stroll by a travel office with a Las Vegas poster in its window. Thirty minutes later, caught up in the moment, you find yourselves at the airport ticket counter trying to purchase last-minute tickets to Vegas. But there's just one problem. American Express didn't approve your purchase. In fact, the ticket counter agent is now on the phone with an American Express customer service agent.

So what put a temporary halt to your weekend escape to Vegas? An expert system that American Express calls "Authorizer's Assistant."[39] The first "if–then" rule that prevented your purchase was the rule "*if* a purchase is much larger than the cardholder's regular spending habits, *then* deny approval of the purchase." This if–then rule, just one of 3,000, is built into American Express's transaction processing system that handles thousands of purchase requests per second. Now that the American Express customer service agent is on the line, he or she is prompted by the Authorizer's Assistant to ask the ticket counter agent to examine your identification. You hand over your driver's license and another credit card to prove you're you. Then the ticket agent asks for your address, phone number, Social Security number, and your mother's maiden name and relays the information to American Express. Finally, your ticket purchase is approved. Why? Because you met the last series of "if–then" rules. *If* the purchaser can provide proof of identity and *if* the purchaser can provide personal information that isn't common knowledge, *then* approve the purchase.

REVIEW 15-3

....

Accessing and Sharing Information and Knowledge

Executive information systems, intranets, and corporate portals facilitate internal sharing and access to company information and transactions. Electronic data interchange, Web services, and the Internet allow external groups like suppliers and customers to easily access company information. All three decrease costs by reducing or eliminating data entry, data errors, and paperwork and by speeding up communication. Organizations use DSS and expert systems to capture and share specialized knowledge with nonexpert employees.

expert system
an information system that contains the specialized knowledge and decision rules used by experts and experienced decision makers so that nonexperts can draw on this knowledge base to make decisions

Management Decision

Switching to the iPad[40]

As part of the antirecession stimulus bill, the federal government allocated $19 billion to subsidize the modernization of medical records. You've been considering making the switch to computer-based records for some time now, and the stimulus funds will certainly make that decision a little easier now. But which system will you buy? You've visited a number of other practices and hospitals to see what they're using, and you've found a dizzying variety—desktops, laptops, PDAs, smartphones, all running different software.

You've heard, though, that Apple's iPad might trump them all. Apple's tablet computer has an elegant design, an easy-to-use operating system, great battery life, and a sharp display. Already, insurance giant Kaiser Permanente, Harvard Medical Schools, and the prestigious Cedars-Sinai Hospital have conducted trial programs to test the iPad's functionality in medical facilities. Best of all, it's relatively cheap compared to other laptop computers, and it has a low learning curve, because most of the doctors in your practice already use the iPhone.

In addition to getting federal funding, then, the iPad can bring several first-mover advantages for your practice. Your medical records will be consolidated and more efficient than competitors, which will make your entire operation run more smoothly. Patients will have to spend less time waiting for you and your staff to retrieve their charts and review their history. And it never hurts to have a reputation for being a practice that uses cutting-edge technology.

But just as you're about to order iPads for everyone in the office, one of your colleagues has some warnings. Do you think that flimsy thing can handle the rigors of a medical setting, he asks? He doesn't think it would last more than a month in a pediatrician's office, much less a hectic emergency room. And what about security? What kind of features does it have that will protect patient confidentiality? And then, he drops this bomb on you: "You know, people who buy first-generation Apple products are suckers." He reminds you that the first iPhone sold for $600 but had a minimal number of applications. Just two months later, the price was cut to $400, and ten months after that, they sold the iPhone 3G, with faster network access and thousands of more apps, for just $300. You could buy the iPad now, he says, but why not wait until Apple releases a cheaper, faster iPad with better features? And then, he reminds you that H-P, Google, Amazon, and Microsoft have competing tablet computers and applications. What if those are even better for medical records and they become the industry standard? Do we want to be left behind?

Questions

1. Considering the various first-mover and second-mover advantages, would you switch to the iPad or wait?

2. How important is it that the medical records system you select for your practice reflects the industry standard?

3. Do the benefits of having a computerized medical records system outweigh the costs involved in setting that system up?

 Practice Being a Manager

Information Pipeline

Information is one of the keys to sustaining a competitive advantage. Growing technological sophistication has also meant growing challenges in maintaining quality and security across far-flung corporate information systems. And managers increasingly feel deluged by the rising flow of e-mail, text messages, and near-instantaneous reports. To thrive in the information-rich environment of modern business, managers must effectively utilize the various tools available. This exercise will give you an opportunity to consider which tools might work best for a given need.

STEP 1 **Get into groups and read the scenario.** Your professor will organize you into pairs or groups of three.

Scenario: Suppose that you and your partner(s) are going into business together. Brainstorm about some new ventures that might interest you. Select one of the ideas, and then talk about how you might build a sustainable competitive advantage for your new business. (*Hint:* You may want to review the first few sections of the chapter.) With this initial sketch of your business plan in mind, discuss how you might use information systems and tools to accomplish the following tasks:

- Researching the likely competition that you will face
- Finding out what steps will be required to get the necessary permits, licenses, and/or

regulatory approvals to open and maintain your business

- Determining what price you should charge for your product(s) or service(s)
- Deciding what computer and communication equipment you will need to buy to support your new venture
- Recruiting and hiring the best people for available jobs in your new company

STEP 2 **Discuss the issues.** Discuss how you might develop the information system that your company needs to successfully launch and grow. Be sure to include security issues/concerns in your discussion.

STEP 3 **Debrief as a class.** What are the major challenges in creating and maintaining a sustainable competitive advantage? What role does information and information technology play in successfully competing with other companies in a given market? Is it possible to secure sensitive information and at the same time share information with employees and/or other key stakeholders (suppliers, customers)?

 ## Self-Assessment

Computer Comfort

Computers are ubiquitous in modern society, but that does not mean that everyone embraces them. As with any innovation, some people are reluctant to adopt computer technology, for whatever reason. How comfortable are you with computer technology?[41] Be candid as you complete the assessment by circling the appropriate responses, from 1, "strongly disagree," to 5, "strongly agree."

1. I hesitate to use a computer for fear of making mistakes that I cannot correct.

   1   2   3   4   5

2. The challenge of learning about computers is exciting.

   1   2   3   4   5

3. I feel apprehensive about using computers.

   1   2   3   4   5

4. I am confident that I can learn computer skills.

   1   2   3   4   5

5. I feel insecure about my ability to interpret a computer printout.

   1   2   3   4   5

6. I look forward to using a computer on my job.

    1   2   3   4   5

7. I have avoided computers because they are unfamiliar and somewhat intimidating to me.

    1   2   3   4   5

8. Learning to operate computers is like learning any new skill—the more you practice, the better you become.

    1   2   3   4   5

9. It scares me to think that I could cause the computer to destroy a large amount of information by hitting the wrong key.

    1   2   3   4   5

10. If given the opportunity, I would like to learn about and use computers.

    1   2   3   4   5

11. I have difficulty in understanding the technical aspects of computers.

    1   2   3   4   5

12. I am sure that with time and practice, I will be as comfortable working with computers as I am working with a typewriter.

    1   2   3   4   5

13. You have to be a genius to understand all the special keys contained on most computer terminals.

    1   2   3   4   5

14. Anyone can learn to use a computer if he or she is patient and motivated.

    1   2   3   4   5

15. I do not think I would be able to learn a computer programming language.

    1   2   3   4   5

16. I feel computers are necessary tools in both educational and work settings.

    1   2   3   4   5

17. I dislike working with machines that are smarter than I am.

    1   2   3   4   5

18. I feel that I will be able to keep up with the advances happening in the computer field.

    1   2   3   4   5

19. I am afraid that if I begin using computers, I will become dependent upon them and lose some of my reasoning skills.

    1   2   3   4   5

TOTAL = _____

SCORING

Reverse scores on even-numbered items. Reverse means, for instance, a 1 becomes a 5; a 4 becomes a 2, and so on. Using the reversed scores and the remaining scores, compute your score for the 19 items by adding up the scores. You can find the interpretation for your score at www.cengagebrain.com.

▶ MANAGEMENT WORKPLACE

© CENGAGE LEARNING 2013

Numi Organic Tea

Brian Durkee is the director of operations at Numi Organic Tea. Right before he joined Numi, the company had just begun to implement an efficient enterprise resource planning (ERP) system with integrated inventory management and accounting to develop an advantage in sustainable supply chain management. In this video, Durkee explains how Numi is dedicated to sustainable supply chain management, eliminating waste, and using recycled materials.

What to Watch For and Ask Yourself

1. What kinds of challenges does Numi face in managing information?
2. Why was it no longer sufficient for Numi to use programs like Excel and QuickBooks to manage its information?
3. What are some of the advantages Durkee mentions that have come with using the ERP system?

Endnotes

1 Research and Innovative Technology Administration, "Baggage Fees by Airline, 2010," Bureau of Transportation Statistics, accessed June 27, 2011, from www.bts.gov/programs/airline_information/baggage_fees/; and F. Levy, "The Airlines' Bag Reflex," *Businessweek Online*, July 31, 2008, 11, accessed June 27, 2011, from www.businessweek.com/lifestyle/content/jul2008/bw20080729_355085.htm; S. McCartney, "Middle Seat Mailbox: Travelers Blast Airlines for Lost Bags; Would Hefty Penalties for Lost Luggage Force Air Carriers to Find a Better Way?" *Wall Street Journal*, January 18, 2007, accessed June 27, 2011, from http://online.wsj.com/article/SB116909017751179834.html; S. McCartney, "Welcome to London: Your Luggage Is Missing; Why British Airways Is Worse Than Even U.S. Airlines at Losing (and Finding) Bags," *Wall Street Journal*, August 21, 2007, D1; S. McCartney, "The Middle Seat: Why Your Bags Aren't Better Off on a Big Airline," *Wall Street Journal*, September 2, 2008, D1; S. McCartney, "The Middle Seat: What It Costs an Airline to Fly Your Luggage," *Wall Street Journal*, November 25, 2008, D1; D. Michaels, "Airlines' Expert on Missing Bags Fights Lost Cause: Mr. Price's Luggage Keeps Getting Mislaid; Buy Insurance, He Says," *Wall Street Journal*, August 13, 2009, A1; and C. Palmeri, "Broken-Guitar Hero," *Businessweek*, August 3, 2009, 17.

2 R. Lenzner, "The Reluctant Entrepreneur," *Forbes*, September 11, 1995, 162–166.

3 R. McGill Murphy, "Rising Stars," *Fortune*, September 6, 2010, 110–116.

4 R. D. Buzzell and B. T. Gale, *The PIMS Principles: Linking Strategy to Performance* (New York: Free Press, 1987); and M. Lambkin, "Order of Entry and Performance in New Markets," *Strategic Management Journal* 9 (1988): 127–140.

5 G. L. Urban, T. Carter, S. Gaskin, and Z. Mucha, "Market Share Rewards to Pioneering Brands: An Empirical Analysis and Strategic Implications," *Management Science* 32 (1986): 645–659.

6 S. Nassauer, "'I Hate My Room' the Traveler Tweeted. Ka-Boom! An Upgrade!" *Wall Street Journal*, June 24, 2010, accessed August 14, 2010, from http: //online.wsj.com/article/NA_WSJ_PUB: SB10001424052748704256304575320730977161348.html.

7 S. Lubar, *Infoculture: The Smithsonian Book of Information Age Inventions* (Boston: Houghton Mifflin, 1993).

8 Ibid.

9 A. Lavallee, "Unilever to Test Mobile Coupons—In Trial at Supermarket, Cellphones Will Be the Medium for Discount Offers," *Wall Street Journal*, 29 May 2009, B8.

10 B. Worthen, "Bar Codes on Steroids," *CIO*, December 15, 2002, 53.

11 C. Swedberg, "RFID to Revolutionize Coca-Cola's Dispensers," *RFID Journal*, June 10, 2009, accessed June 25, 2011, from www.rfidjournal.com/article/view/4967.

12 M. Stone, "Scanning for Business," *PC Magazine*, 10 May 2005, 117.

13 B. Worthen, "New Meters Aim to Cure Parking Headaches," *Wall Street Journal*, January 27, 2011, accessed June 16, 2011, from http://online.wsj.com/article/SB10001424052748703555804576102090737327466.html.

14 N. Rubenking, "Hidden Messages," *PC Magazine*, 22 May 2001, 86.

15 Ibid.

16 M. Schoofs and M. Tamman, "Using a Computer to Fight Medicare Fraud," *Wall Street Journal*, December 22, 2010, accessed June 26, 2011, from http://online.wsj.com/article/SB10001424052748704851204576034332420051722.html.

17 J. Brustein, "Star Pitchers in a Duel? Tickets Will Cost More," *New York Times*, June 27, 2010, accessed June 26, 2011, from www.nytimes.com/2010/06/28/technology/28tickets.html.

18 C. Duhigg, "What Does Your Credit Card Company Know about You?" *New York Times Magazine*, May 12, 2009, accessed June 16, 2010, from www.nytimes.com/2009/05/17/magazine/17credit-t.html?pagewanted=1.

19 "Privacy Policy," accessed June 26, 2011, from http://www.drugstore.com.

20 F. J. Derfler Jr., "Secure Your Network," *PC Magazine*, June 27, 2000, 183–200.

21 "Authentication," Webopedia accessed September 12, 2008, from www.webopedia.com/TERM/a/authentication.html.

22 "Authorization," Webopedia, accessed September 12, 2008, from www.webopedia.com/TERM/a/authorization.html.

23 L. Seltzer, "Password Crackers," *PC Magazine*, February 12, 2002, 68.

24 "Two-Factor Authentication," Information Security Glossary, accessed June 28, 2009, from www.rsa.com.

25 D. Danchev, "Yahoo! Mail Introduces Two-Factor Authentication," ZDNet, December 19, 2011, accessed 3 Apr 2012, http://www.zdnet.com/blog/security/yahoo-mail-introduces-two-factor-authentication/9846

26 B. Grimes, "Biometric Security," *PC Magazine*, April 22, 2003, 74.

27 "Cardless Check-In at 24 Hour Fitness," 24 Hour Fitness, accessed June 26, 2011, from www.24hourfitness.com/health_clubs/cardless_checkin/; and J. Hagerty, "Biometrics Firms Widen Net," *Wall Street Journal*, September 20, 2010, accessed June 26, 2011, from http://online.wsj.com/article/SB10001424052748703376504575492371980339514.html.

28 C. Metz, "Total Security," *PC Magazine*, October 1, 2003, 83.

29 J. DeAvila, "Wi-Fi Users, Beware: Hot Spots Are Weak Spots," *Wall Street Journal,* 16 January 2008, D1.

30 J. van den Hoven, "Executive Support Systems & Decision Making," *Journal of Systems Management* 47, no. 8 (March–April 1996): 48.

31 D. Hannon, "Colgate-Palmolive Empowers Senior Leaders with Executive Dashboards," *InsiderProfiles*, April 1, 2011, accessed June 26, 2011, from http://insiderprofiles.wispubs.com/article.aspx?iArticleId=5720.

32 "Intranet," Webopedia, accessed August 26, 2001, from www.webopedia.com/TERM/i/intranet.html.

33 "Web Services," Webopedia, accessed April 16, 2009, from www.webopedia.com/TERM/W/Web_Services.html.

34 "Extranet," Webopedia, accessed September 12, 2008, from www.webopedia.com/TERM/E/extranet.html.

35 Press Release, "Penske Truck Leasing Launches Improved Customer Extranet," Truckinginfo.com, February 4, 2009, accessed June 26, 2011, from www.truckinginfo.com/news/news-detail.asp?news_id=62365&news_category_id=52; and "Do You Need a Comprehensive Solution? Penske Is an Expert in Fleet Operations," *Penske Truck Leasing*, accessed June 26, 2011, from www.pensketruckleasing.com/leasing/.

36 V. Vaughan, "Smart Little Retail Shops," *Houston Chronicle*, August 17, 2010, accessed March 11, 2011, from www.chron.com/disp/story.mpl/business/7157804.html.

37 S. Hamm, D. Welch, W. Zellner, F. Keenan, and F. Engardio, "Down but Hardly Out: Downturn Be Damned, Companies Are Still Anxious to Expand Online," *Businessweek*, March 26, 2001, 126.

38 K. C. Laudon and J. P. Laudon, *Management Information Systems: Organization and Technology* (Upper Saddle River, NJ: Prentice Hall, 1996).

39 R. Hernandez, "American Express Authorizer's Assistant," *Business Rules Journal*, August 2001, accessed June 26, 2011, from http://bizrules.info/page/art_amexaa.htm.

40 D. Blankenhorn, "Medicine Is the Apple iPad Sweet Spot," ZDNet, January 28, 2010, accessed June 26, 2011, from http://healthcare.zdnet.com/?p=3257; and M. C. White, "An Apple a Day," The Big Money.com, April 7, 2010, accessed June 26, 2011, from www.thebigmoney.com/articles/0s-1s-and-s/2010/04/07/apple-day.

41 R. Heinssen Jr., C. Glass, and L. Knight, "Assessing Computer Anxiety: Development and Validation of the Computer Anxiety Rating Scale," *Computers in Human Behavior* (1987): 49–59.

16

Chapter Sixteen

Managing Service and Manufacturing Operations

OUTLINE

REEL TO REAL

Management Workplace is at Barcelona Restaurant Group.

SELF-ASSESSMENT

What's your approach to handling disgruntled customers? Do the Self-Assessment for this chapter in the book or online to find out.

ONLINE QUIZZES

Did you get it? Review the main concepts in the chapter by taking the online quizzes on CourseMate!

VIDEO QUIZZES

Get more out of the videos by taking the multimedia video quizzes online.

What Would You Do?

Louis Vuitton Headquarters, Paris, France[1]

Louis Vuitton Moët Hennessy (LVMH) is the world's leading luxury goods company. Louis Vuitton, who was employed by wealthy women to pack their clothes, started his company in 1854 and revolutionized travel by offering flat-topped, water-proof trunks that replaced curved, domed-top trunks. Made by hand and with a lifetime guarantee (still so today), Vuitton's expensive trunks were purchased by royalty and well-to-do travelers. Counterfeiters soon produced fakes, forcing the company in 1876 to release a brown and beige striped trunk that was initially difficult to duplicate. By 1888, because of more counterfeiting, Vuitton introduced a patented checkered material that was the forerunner of the distinctive bags it sells today.

LVMH, however, is much more than Louis Vuitton. Among its best known brands, Kenzo, Givenchy, and Celine make up its fashion and leather goods division; Christian Dior, Givenchy, and Guerlain in its perfumes and cosmetics division; Dom Pérignon, Hennessy, Krug, and Moët & Chandon in wine and spirits; TAG Heuer, Chaumet, and Hublot in watches and jewelry; along with Sephora (perfume and cosmetics) and DFS group (duty-free stores).

Over the last decade, the worldwide luxury market has doubled to $220 billion a year, with much of that growth coming from China. Louis Vuitton's CEO, Yves Carcelle, said about China: "There are 1.4 billion people there who suddenly want to treat themselves, and it will continue." That growth has attracted fierce competition, and disagreements about what constitutes luxury.

In practice, LVMH, Coach, and their competitors all walk a tightrope between exclusivity and reaching out to a broader market through diversification. Francesco Trapani, CEO of Bulgari, a luxury Italian jeweler and watchmaker, says, "Diversification is the rule of the game, but you can't do everything. The danger is, you do something badly, and then you don't just lose money but your reputation." Or, you overexpose your product by selling so broadly that it no longer seems like a luxury item.

© PETER HORREE/ALAMY

Louis Vuitton expands production of its most popular products to meet demand, but also produces small numbers or limited editions of a large variety of high-quality luxury items. CEO Yves Carcelle says that "über-luxury" items are a small part of sales, but are growing quickly. He says, "There is demand for things that are incredible and unique. Our paradox is how to grow without diluting our image."

From a production standpoint, this creates a number of challenges. First, don't run out of the most popular products, yet also have the flexibility to produce small batches (i.e., limited editions) of a large number of different luxury goods. But how do you design factories to do both, and increase productivity? Second, because workers complete just one task, such as cutting leather, gluing and sewing, or stitching the lining, it generally takes 30 craftsmen eight days to produce just one Louis Vuitton bag. Production bottlenecks are common as the faster workers are forced to wait on the slower workers. So, how can you restructure production process to add more capacity without building any more factories?

If you were in charge of Louis Vuitton's factories and production system, what would you do?

© DIZZO/ISTOCK PHOTO

16-1 Productivity

As you read in the opening vignette, luxury goods maker Louis Vuitton faces the challenges of adapting its operations, managing inventory, and improving productivity. In this chapter, you will learn about **operations management**—managing the daily production of goods and services. You will begin by learning about the basics of operations management: productivity and quality. Next, you will read about managing operations, beginning with service operations, turning next to manufacturing operations, and finishing with an examination of the types, measures, costs, and methods for managing inventory.

After reading this section, you should be able to:

16-1 discuss the kinds of productivity and their importance in managing operations.

At their core, organizations are production systems. Companies combine inputs such as labor, raw materials, capital, and knowledge to produce outputs in the form of finished products or services. **Productivity** is a measure of performance that indicates how many inputs it takes to produce or create an output.

$$\text{Productivity} = \frac{\text{Outputs}}{\text{Inputs}}$$

The fewer inputs it takes to create an output (or the greater the output from one input), the higher the productivity. For example, a car's gas mileage is a common measure of productivity. A car that gets 35 miles (output) per gallon (input) is more productive and fuel efficient than a car that gets 18 miles per gallon.

To begin a broader discussion on productivity, let's examine **16-1a why productivity matters** and **16-1b the different kinds of productivity**.

16-1a Why Productivity Matters

Why does productivity matter? For companies, higher productivity—that is, doing more with less—results in lower costs for the company, lower prices for consumers, faster service, higher market share, and higher profits. For example, every second saved in the drive-through lane at a fast-food restaurant increases sales by 1 percent. Furthermore, increasing the efficiency of drive-through service by 10 percent adds nearly 10 percent to a fast-food restaurant's sales. And with up to 75 percent of all fast-food restaurant sales coming from the drive-through window, it's no wonder that Wendy's (average drive-through time of 146 seconds per vehicle), Taco Bell (average time of 167 seconds per vehicle), and McDonald's (average time of 184 seconds per vehicle) continue to look for ways to shorten the time it takes to process a drive-through order.[2]

The productivity of businesses within a country matters to that country because it results in a higher standard of living. One way that productivity

operations management
managing the daily production of goods and services

productivity
a measure of performance that indicates how many inputs it takes to produce or create an output

leads to a higher standard of living is through increased wages. When companies can do more with less, they can raise employee wages without increasing prices or sacrificing normal profits. Thanks to long-term increases in business productivity, the average American family today earns 28 percent more than the average family in 1990 and 46 percent more than the average family in 1974—and that's after accounting for inflation.[3] Rising income stemming from increased productivity creates other benefits as well. Productivity increased an average of 2.3 percent between 1995 and 2005, and then slowed to an average of 1.2 percent from 2005 to 2009.[4] And from 1998 to 2008, the U.S. economy created nearly 16.6 million new jobs.[5]

Another benefit of productivity is that it makes products more affordable or better. For example, while inflation has pushed the average cost of a new car to $27,950, increases in manufacturing productivity have actually made cars cheaper. In 1960, the average family needed 26 weeks of income to pay for an average car. Today, the average family needs just 23.2 weeks of income—and today's car is loaded with accessories that weren't available in the 1960s, including air bags, power steering and brakes, CD and DVD players, seat warmers, air conditioning, and satellite navigation. So, in terms of real purchasing power, productivity gains have actually made today's $27,950 car cheaper than the 1960's car that sold for $2,000.[6]

16-1b Kinds of Productivity

Two common measures of productivity are partial productivity and multifactor productivity. **Partial productivity** indicates how much of a particular kind of input it takes to produce an output.

$$\text{Partial Productivity} = \frac{\text{Outputs}}{\text{Single Kind of Input}}$$

Labor is one kind of input that is frequently used when determining partial productivity. *Labor productivity* typically indicates the cost or number of hours of labor it takes to produce an output. In other words, the lower the cost of the labor to produce a unit of output, or the less time it takes to produce a unit of output, the higher the labor productivity. Partial productivity assesses how efficiently companies use only one input, such as labor, when creating outputs. Multifactor productivity is an overall measure of productivity that assesses how efficiently companies use all the inputs it takes to make outputs. More specifically, **multifactor productivity** indicates how much labor, capital, materials, and energy it takes to produce an output.[7]

$$\text{Multifactor Productivity} = \frac{\text{Outputs}}{(\text{Labor} + \text{Capital} + \text{Materials} + \text{Energy})}$$

Exhibit 16.1 shows the trends in multifactor productivity across a number of U.S. industries since 1987. With a 268 percent increase between 2002 (scaled

partial productivity
a measure of performance that indicates how much of a particular kind of input it takes to produce an output

multifactor productivity
an overall measure of performance that indicates how much labor, capital, materials, and energy it takes to produce an output

Exhibit 16.1

Multifactor Productivity Growth across Industries

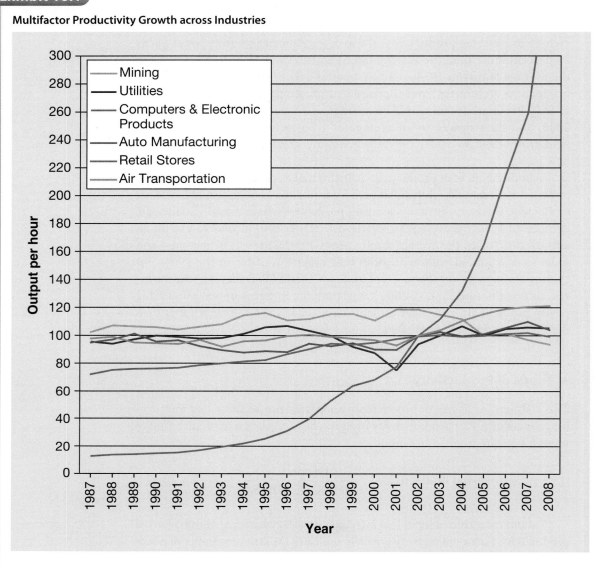

Source: "Industry Productivity Indexes, Detailed 4-Digit NAICS Industries for Multifactor Productivity," Bureau of Labor Statistics, accessed June 27, 2011, from www.bls.gov/mfp/tables.htm.

at 100) and 2008 (when it reached a level of 368), and a thirtyfold increase since 1987, the growth in multifactor productivity in the computer and electronic products industry far exceeded the productivity growth in retail stores, auto manufacturing, mining, utilities, and air transportation, as well as most other industries tracked by the U.S. government.

Should managers use multiple or partial productivity measures? In general, they should use both. Multifactor productivity indicates a company's overall level of productivity relative to its competitors. In the end, that's what counts most. However, multifactor productivity measures don't indicate the specific contributions that labor, capital, materials, or energy make to overall productivity. To analyze the contributions of these individual components, managers need to use partial productivity measures. Doing so can help them determine what factors need to be adjusted or in what areas adjustment can make the greatest difference in overall productivity.

REVIEW 16-1

. . . .

Productivity

At their core, companies are production systems that combine inputs (such as labor), raw materials, capital, and knowledge to produce outputs (such as finished products or services). Productivity is a measure of how many inputs it takes to produce or create an output. The greater the output from one input, or the fewer inputs it takes to create an output, the higher the productivity. Partial productivity measures how much of a single kind of input (such as labor) is needed to produce an output. Multifactor productivity is an overall measure of productivity that indicates how much labor, capital, materials, and energy are needed to produce an output. Increased productivity helps companies lower costs, which can lead to lower prices, higher market share, and higher profits. Increased productivity helps countries by leading to higher wages, lower product prices, and a higher standard of living.

16-2 Quality

With the average car costing $27,950, car buyers want to make sure that they're getting good quality for their money.[8] Fortunately, as indicated by the number of problems per 100 cars (PP100), today's cars are of much higher quality than earlier models. In 1981, Japanese cars averaged 240 PP100. General Motors' cars averaged 670, Ford's averaged 740, and Chrysler's averaged 870 PP100! In other words, as measured by PP100, the quality of American cars was two to three times worse than that of Japanese cars. By 1992, however, U.S. carmakers had made great strides, significantly reducing the number of problems to an average of 155 PP100. Japanese vehicles had improved too, averaging just 125 PP100.

More recently, according to the results of the 2011 J. D. Power and Associates survey of initial car quality, overall quality improved to 107 PP100 in 2011—down from 125 PP100 in 2007, 118 PP100 in 2008, and 108 PP100 in 2010. Lexus, with just 73 PP100, had the best quality, followed by Honda with 86 PP100, Acura with 89 PP100, and Mercedes-Benz with 94 PP100. At the bottom of the list were MINI and Volkswagen tied for 131 PP100, Mitsubishi with 133 PP100, Suzuki with 136 PP100, and Dodge with 137 PP100. In 2011, however, even the worst cars on the J. D. Power and Associates Survey of Initial Car quality beat the scores of the Japanese cars of decades ago. And category leaders like Porsche, Acura, Mercedes-Benz, Lexus, Ford, and Honda came in with scores under 100. That means there's less than one problem per car![9]

After reading this section, you should be able to:

16-2 explain the role that quality plays in managing operations.

The American Society for Quality gives two meanings for **quality**. It can mean a product or service free of deficiencies, such as the number of problems per 100 cars, or it can mean the characteristics of a product or service that satisfy customer needs.[10] Today's cars are of higher quality than those produced 20 years ago in both senses. Not only do they have fewer problems per 100 cars, they also have a number of additional standard features (power brakes and steering, stereo/CD/MP3 player, power windows and locks, air bags, cruise control).

In this part of the chapter, you will learn about **16-2a quality-related characteristics for products and services, 16-2b ISO 9000 and 14000, 16-2c the Baldrige National Quality Award,** and **16-2d total quality management.**

16-2a Quality-Related Characteristics for Products and Services

Quality products usually possess three characteristics: reliability, serviceability, and durability.[11] A breakdown occurs when a product quits working or doesn't do what it was designed to do. The longer it takes for a product to break down or the longer the time between breakdowns, the more reliable the product. Consequently, many companies define *product reliability* in terms of the average time between breakdowns.

Serviceability refers to how easy or difficult it is to fix a product. The easier it is to maintain a working product or fix a broken product, the more serviceable that product is.

A product breakdown assumes that a product can be repaired. However, some products don't break down; they fail. *Product failure* means products can't be repaired. They can only be replaced. *Durability* is defined as the mean time to failure. Typically, for example, when an LCD screen quits working, it "dies" and can't be repaired. Consequently, durability, or the average time before failure, is a key part of LCD quality. Why buy a great-looking LCD if it's going to last only a few years? Indeed, Toshiba is now producing thin-film transistor LCDs with a mean time between failures of 100,000 hours, or 11.4 years.[12]

Whereas high-quality products are characterized by reliability, serviceability, and durability, services are different. There's no point in assessing the durability of a service because services don't last but are consumed the minute they're performed. For example, once a lawn service has mowed your lawn, the job is done until the mowers come back next week to do it again. Services also don't have serviceability. You can't maintain or fix a service. If a service wasn't performed correctly the first time, all you can do is perform it again. Rather than serviceability and durability, the quality of service interactions often depends on how the service provider interacts with the customer. Was the service provider friendly, rude, or helpful?

Five characteristics typically distinguish a quality service: reliability, tangibles, responsiveness, assurance, and empathy.[13] *Service reliability* is the ability to consistently perform a service well. Studies clearly show that reliability matters more to customers than anything else when buying services. When you take your clothes to the dry cleaner, you don't want them returned with cracked

quality
a product or service free of deficiencies, or the characteristics of a product or service that satisfy customer needs

buttons or wrinkles down the front. If your dry cleaner gives you back perfectly clean and pressed clothes every time, it's providing a reliable service.

Also, although services themselves are not tangible (you can't see or touch them), services are provided in tangible places. Thus, *tangibles* refer to the appearance of the offices, equipment, and personnel involved with the delivery of a service. One of the best examples of the effect of tangibles on the perception of quality is the restroom. When you eat at a fancy restaurant, you expect clean, if not upscale, restrooms. How different is your perception of a business, say a gas station, if it has clean rather than filthy restrooms?

Ten years ago, when APPLE launched its retail stores, most experts predicted that they would fail given all of the other locations where consumers could buy computer and electronics equipment. This year, over a quarter billion people will visit Apple's 326 stores, or four times the number of visitors to Walt Disney Companies four largest theme parks. Why? Largely because of the quality characteristics of responsiveness, assurance, and empathy.

Responsiveness is the promptness and willingness with which service providers give good service. Ironically, at Apple stores, this manifests itself in a sales philosophy of not selling. Instead, Apple store employees are trained to help customers solve problems. An Apple training manual says, "Your job is to understand all of your customers' needs—some of which they may not even realize they have." David Ambrose, a former Apple store employee says, "You were never trying to close a sale. It was about finding solutions for a customer and finding their pain points."

Assurance is the confidence that service providers are knowledgeable, courteous, and trustworthy. Apple "geniuses," who staff the "Genius Bars" in each store are trained at Apple headquarters and, according to Apple's website, "can take care of everything from troubleshooting your problems to actual repairs." Geniuses are regularly tested on their knowledge and problem-solving skills to maintain their certification. Other Apple store employees are highly trained too, and are not allowed to help customers until they've spent two to four weeks shadowing experienced store employees.

Empathy is the extent to which service providers give individual attention and care to customers' concerns and problems. The acronym, APPLE, instructs employees how to empathetically engage with customers: "**A**pproach customers with a personalized warm welcome," "**P**robe politely to understand all the customer's needs," "**P**resent a solution for the customer to take home today," "**L**isten for and resolve any issues or concerns," and "**E**nd with a fond farewell and an invitation to return." And when customers are frustrated and become emotional, the advice is to "Listen and limit your responses to simple reassurances that you are doing so. 'Uh-huh,' 'I understand,' etc."

The results from Apple's retail approach speak for themselves, as Apple retail sales average $4,406 per square foot, higher than Tiffany jewelry stores ($3,070), Coach luxury retail ($1,776), or Best Buy ($880), a full-service computer and electronics store.[14]

16-2b ISO 9000 and 14000

ISO, pronounced "eye-so," comes from the Greek word *isos*, meaning "equal, similar, alike, or identical" and is also an acronym for the International Organization for Standardization, which helps set standards for 162 countries. The purpose of this agency is to develop and publish standards that facilitate the international exchange of goods and services.[15] **ISO 9000** is a series of five international standards, from ISO 9000 to ISO 9004, for achieving consistency in quality management and quality assurance in companies throughout the world. **ISO 14000** is a series of international standards for managing, monitoring, and minimizing an organization's harmful effects on the environment.[16] (For more on environmental quality and issues, see Section 3.5 of Chapter 14 on controlling waste and pollution.)

The ISO 9000 and 14000 standards publications, which are available from the American National Standards Institute (see the end of this section), are general and can be used for manufacturing any kind of product or delivering any kind of service. Importantly, the ISO 9000 standards don't describe how to make a better-quality car, computer, or widget. Instead, they describe how companies can extensively document (and thus standardize) the steps they take to create and improve the quality of their products. Studies show that customers clearly prefer to buy from companies that are ISO 9000 certified.[17]

To become ISO certified, a process that can take months, a company must show that it is following its own procedures for improving production, updating design plans and specifications, keeping machinery in top condition, educating and training workers, and satisfactorily dealing with customer complaints.[18] An accredited third party oversees the ISO certification process, just as a certified public accountant verifies that a company's financial accounts are up-to-date and accurate. Once a company has been certified as ISO 9000 compliant, the accredited third party will issue an ISO 9000 certificate that the company can use in its advertising and publications. This is the quality equivalent of the *Good Housekeeping* Seal of Approval. But continued ISO 9000 certification is not guaranteed. Accredited third parties typically conduct periodic audits to make sure the company is still following quality procedures. If it is not, its certification is suspended or canceled.

To get additional information on ISO 9000 guidelines and procedures, see the American National Standards Institute (http://webstore.ansi.org/default.aspx; the ISO 9000 and ISO 14000 standards publications are available here for about $400 and $300, respectively), the American Society for Quality (www.asq.org), and the International Organization for Standardization (www.iso.org).

16-2c Baldrige National Quality Award

The Baldrige National Quality Award, which is administered by the U.S. government's National Institute for Standards and Technology, is given "to recognize U.S. companies for their achievements in quality and business performance and to raise awareness about the importance of quality and performance excellence as a competitive edge."[19] Each year, up to three awards may be given in these categories: manufacturing, education, health care, service, small business, and nonprofit.

The cost of applying for the Baldrige Award includes a $150 eligibility fee, an application fee of $7,500 for manufacturing firms and $4,000 for small businesses, and a site visitation fee of $20,000 to $40,000 for manufacturing firms and $15,000 to $20,000 for small businesses.[20] Why does it cost so much? Because you get a great deal of useful information about your business even if you don't win. At a

ISO 9000
a series of five international standards, from ISO 9000 to ISO 9004, for achieving consistency in quality management and quality assurance in companies throughout the world

ISO 14000
a series of international standards for managing, monitoring, and minimizing an organization's harmful effects on the environment

minimum, each company that applies receives an extensive report based on 300 hours of assessment from at least eight business and quality experts. At $10 an hour for small businesses and about $20 an hour for manufacturing and service businesses, the *Journal for Quality and Participation* called the Baldrige feedback report "the best bargain in consulting in America."[21]

Businesses that apply for the Baldrige Award are judged on a 1,000-point scale based on the seven criteria shown in Exhibit 16.2.[22] The most important category is Results, as it takes up 450 out of 1,000 points. In other words, in addition to the six other criteria, companies must show that they have achieved superior quality when it comes to products and services, customers, financial performance and market share, treatment of employees, work systems and processes, and leadership and social responsibility. This emphasis on results is what differentiates the Baldrige Award from the ISO 9000 standards. The Baldrige Award indicates the extent to which companies have actually achieved world-class quality. The ISO 9000 standards simply indicate whether a company is following the management system it put into place to improve quality. In fact, ISO 9000 certification covers less than 10 percent of the requirements for the Baldrige Award.[23] The companies that have won the Baldrige Award have achieved superior financial returns. Since 1988, an investment in Baldrige Award winners would have outperformed the Standard & Poor's 500 stock index 80 percent of the time.[24] For additional information about the Baldrige Award, see the National Institute of Standards and Technology website at www.nist.gov/baldrige/.

Exhibit 16.2

Criteria for the Baldrige National Quality Award

2012 Categories/Items	Point Values
1 **Leadership**	**120**
Senior Leadership	70
Governance and Societal Responsibilities	50
2 **Strategic Planning**	**85**
Strategy Development	40
Strategy Implementation	45
3 **Customer Focus**	**85**
Voice of the Customer	45
Customer Engagement	40
4 **Measurement, Analysis, and Knowledge Management**	**90**
Measurement, Analysis, and Improvement of Organizational Performance	45
Management of Information, Knowledge, and Information Technology	45
5 **Workforce Focus**	**85**
Workforce Environment	40
Workforce Engagement	45
6 **Operations Focus**	**85**
Work Systems	45
Work Processes	40
7 **Results**	**450**
Product and Process Outcomes	120
Customer-Focused Outcomes	90
Workforce-Focused Outcomes	80
Leadership and Governance Outcomes	80
Financial and Market Outcomes	80
TOTAL POINTS	**1,000**

Source: "2011–2012 Criteria for Performance Excellence," Baldrige Performance Excellence Program, accessed May 23, 2012, from www.nist.gov/baldrige/publications/upload/2011_2012_Business_Nonprofit_Criteria.pdf

16-2d Total Quality Management

Total quality management (TQM) is an integrated, organization-wide strategy for improving product and service quality.[25] TQM is not a specific tool or technique. Rather, TQM is a philosophy or overall approach to management that is characterized by three principles: customer focus and satisfaction, continuous improvement, and teamwork.[26]

Although most economists, accountants, and financiers argue that companies exist to earn profits for shareholders, TQM suggests that customer focus

total quality management (TQM)

an integrated, organization-wide strategy for improving product and service quality and customer satisfaction should be a company's primary goals. **Customer focus** means that the entire organization, from top to bottom, should be focused on meeting customers' needs. The result of that customer focus should be **customer satisfaction**, which occurs when the company's products or services meet or exceed customers' expectations.

Continuous improvement is an ongoing commitment to increase product and service quality by constantly assessing and improving the processes and procedures used to create those products and services. How do companies know whether they're achieving continuous improvement? Besides higher customer satisfaction, continuous improvement is usually associated with a reduction in variation. **Variation** is a deviation in the form, condition, or appearance of a product from the quality standard for that product. The less a product varies from the quality standard, or the more consistently a company's products meet a quality standard, the higher the quality.

The third principle of TQM is teamwork. **Teamwork** means collaboration between managers and nonmanagers, across business functions, and between the company and its customers and suppliers. In short, quality improves when everyone in the company is given the incentive to work together and the responsibility and authority to make improvements and solve problems. Reid Carr, the president of RED DOOR INTERACTIVE, an Internet Presence Management firm, believes that teamwork is critical to his company's success. Therefore, his employees work collaboratively on multiple account teams made up of people from throughout the company.[27]

Customer focus and satisfaction, continuous improvement, and teamwork mutually reinforce each other to improve quality throughout a company. Customer-focused continuous improvement is necessary to increase customer satisfaction. At the same time, continuous improvement depends on teamwork from different functional and hierarchical parts of the company.

REVIEW 16-2
. . . .

Quality

Quality can refer to a product or service free of deficiencies, or the characteristics of a product or service that satisfy customer needs. Quality products usually possess three characteristics: reliability, serviceability, and durability. Quality service involves reliability, tangibles, responsiveness, assurance, and empathy. ISO 9000 is a series of five international standards for achieving consistency in quality management and quality assurance; ISO 14000 is a set of standards for minimizing an organization's harmful effects on the environment. The ISO 9000 standards can be used for any product or service because they ensure that companies carefully document the steps they take to create and improve quality. ISO 9000 certification is awarded following a quality audit from an accredited third party. The Baldrige National Quality Award recognizes U.S. companies for their achievements in quality and business performance. Each year, up to three Baldrige Awards may be given for manufacturing, service, small business, education, and health care. Companies that apply for the Baldrige Award are judged on a 1,000-point scale based on the following: leadership; strategic planning; customer focus; measurement, analysis, and knowledge management; workforce focus; operations focus; and results. Total quality management (TQM) is an integrated, organization-wide

customer focus
an organizational goal to concentrate on meeting customers' needs at all levels of the organization

customer satisfaction
an organizational goal to provide products or services that meet or exceed customers' expectations

continuous improvement
an organization's ongoing commitment to constantly assess and improve the processes and procedures used to create products and services

variation
a deviation in the form, condition, or appearance of a product from the quality standard for that product

teamwork
collaboration between managers and nonmanagers, across business functions, and between companies, customers, and suppliers

strategy for improving product and service quality. TQM is based on three, mutually reinforcing principles: customer focus and satisfaction, continuous improvement, and teamwork.

16-3 Service Operations

At the start of this chapter, you learned that operations management means managing the daily production of goods and services. Then you learned that to manage production, you must oversee the factors that affect productivity and quality. In this half of the chapter, you will learn about managing operations in service and manufacturing businesses. The chapter ends with a discussion of inventory management, a key factor in a company's profitability.

After reading this section, you should be able to:

16-3 explain the essentials of managing a service business.

Imagine that your trusty TiVo digital video recorder (DVR) breaks down as you try to record your favorite TV show. You've got two choices. You can run to Walmart and spend $250 to purchase a new DVR, or you can spend less (you hope) to have it fixed at a repair shop. Either way, you end up with the same thing, a working DVR. However, the first choice, getting a new DVR, involves buying a physical product (a good), whereas the second, dealing with a repair shop, involves buying a service.

Services differ from goods in several ways. First, goods are produced or made, but services are performed. In other words, services are almost always labor-intensive: Someone typically has to perform the service for you. A repair shop could give you the parts needed to repair your old DVR, but you're still going to have a broken DVR. Second, goods are tangible, but services are intangible. You can touch and see that new DVR, but you can't touch or see the service provided by the technician who fixed your old DVR. All you can "see" is that the DVR works. Third, services are perishable and unstorable. If you don't use them when they're available, they're wasted. For example, if your DVR repair shop is backlogged on repair jobs, then you'll just have to wait until next week to get your DVR repaired. You can't store an unused service and use it when you like. By contrast, you can purchase a good, such as motor oil, and store it until you're ready to use it. Finally, services account for 65 percent of gross national product, whereas manufacturing accounts for only 27.7 percent.[28]

Because services are different from goods, managing a service operation is different from managing a manufacturing or production operation.

Let's look at **16-3a the service–profit chain** and **16-3b service recovery and empowerment.**

16-3a The Service–Profit Chain

One of the key assumptions in the service business is that success depends on how well employees—that is, service providers—deliver their services to customers. But success actually begins with how well management treats service employees, as the service–profit chain, depicted in Exhibit 16.3, demonstrates.[29]

Exhibit 16.3

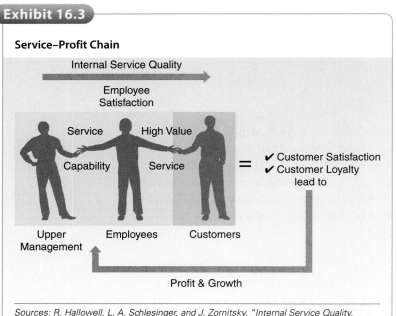

Service–Profit Chain

Internal Service Quality

Employee Satisfaction

Service → High Value
Capability → Service

= ✔ Customer Satisfaction
✔ Customer Loyalty lead to

Upper Management — Employees — Customers

Profit & Growth

Sources: R. Hallowell, L. A. Schlesinger, and J. Zornitsky, "Internal Service Quality, Customer and Job Satisfaction: Linkages and Implications for Management," Human Resource Planning *19 (1996): 20–31;* and J. L. Heskett, T. O. Jones, G. W. Loveman, W. E. Sasser Jr., and L. A. Schlesinger, "Putting the Service–Profit Chain to Work," Harvard Business Review, *March–April 1994, 164–174.*

The key concept behind the service–profit chain is internal service quality, meaning the quality of treatment that employees receive from a company's internal service providers, such as management, payroll and benefits, human resources, and so forth.

As depicted in Exhibit 16.3, good internal service leads to employee satisfaction and service capability. *Employee satisfaction* occurs when companies treat employees in a way that meets or exceeds their expectations. In other words, the better employees are treated, the more satisfied they are, and the more likely they are to give high-value service that satisfies customers. How employers treat employees is important because it affects service capability. *Service capability* is an employee's perception of his or her ability to serve customers well. When an organization serves its employees in ways that help them to do their jobs well, employees, in turn, are more likely to believe that they can and ought to provide high-value service to customers.

Finally, according to the service–profit chain shown in Exhibit 16.3, *high-value service* leads to *customer satisfaction* and *customer loyalty*, which in turn lead to *long-term profits and growth.*[30] What's the link between customer satisfaction and loyalty and profits? To start, the average business keeps only 70 percent to 90 percent of its existing customers each year. No big deal, you say? Just replace leaving customers with new customers. Well, there's one significant problem with that solution. It costs ten times as much to find a new customer as it does to keep an existing customer. Also, new customers typically buy only 20 percent as much as established customers. In fact, keeping existing customers is so cost-effective that most businesses could double their profits by simply keeping 5 percent more customers per year![31] How does this work? Imagine that keeping more of yours customers turns some of those customers into customers for life. How much of a difference would that make to company profits? Consider that just one lifetime customer spends $8,000 on pizza and over $330,000 on luxury cars![32]

16-3b Service Recovery and Empowerment

When mistakes are made, when problems occur, and when customers become dissatisfied with the service they've received, service businesses must switch from the process of service delivery to the process of **service recovery**, or restoring customer satisfaction to strongly dissatisfied customers.[33] Service recovery sometimes requires service employees to not only fix whatever mistake was

service recovery
restoring customer satisfaction to strongly dissatisfied customers

made, but also perform heroic service acts that delight highly dissatisfied customers by far surpassing their expectations of fair treatment. When a SOUTHWEST AIRLINES flight from Fort Lauderdale to Denver was diverted because of storms near the Pueblo, Colorado, airport, the passengers were told they'd have to wait several hours on the plane because the airport terminal had closed at 6 P.M. Expecting a long and unpleasant stay on the ground , the passengers were surprised and pleased when the pilot announced he'd ordered pizza for the entire plane. Chris Mainz, a spokesman for Southwest Airlines, said, "It's not uncommon for our employees to take the extra step to take care of our customers. We do reward and encourage our employees to do something on their own."[34]

Unfortunately, when mistakes occur, service employees often don't have the discretion to resolve customer complaints. Customers who want service employees to correct or make up for poor service are frequently told, "I'm not allowed to do that," "I'm just following company rules," or "I'm sorry, only managers are allowed to make changes of any kind." In other words, company rules prevent them from engaging in acts of service recovery meant to turn dissatisfied customers back into satisfied customers. The result is frustration for customers and service employees, and lost customers for the company.

Now, however, many companies are empowering their service employees.[35] In Chapter 8, you learned that *empowering workers* means permanently passing decision-making authority and responsibility from managers to workers. With respect to service recovery, empowering workers means giving service employees the authority and responsibility to make decisions that immediately solve customer problems.[36] At *DIAPERS.COM*, all customer service agents are empowered to do whatever it takes to take care of the customer, regardless of cost. One customer tried to order a car seat for the weekend, but wouldn't receive it in time because of UPS's delivery schedule. So the customer service rep shipped

Part of what makes Southwest Airlines known for its outstanding customer service is its ability to react quickly to restore satisfaction to dissatisfied customers.

it to her own home (because UPS came to her house in the morning) and then delivered it to the customer's house. Lore says, "We're doing 6,000 orders a day, but that stuff still happens all the time."[37] Empowering service workers does entail some additional costs, but they are usually less than the company's savings from retaining customers.

REVIEW 16-3
....

Service Operations

Services are different from goods. Goods are produced, tangible, and storable. Services are performed, intangible, and perishable. Likewise, managing service operations is different from managing production operations. The service–profit chain indicates that success begins with internal service quality, or how well management treats service employees. Internal service quality leads to employee satisfaction and service capability, which in turn lead to high-value service to customers, customer satisfaction, customer loyalty, and long-term profits and growth. Keeping existing customers is far more cost-effective than finding new ones. Consequently, to prevent disgruntled customers from leaving, some companies are empowering service employees to perform service recovery—restoring customer satisfaction to strongly dissatisfied customers—by giving them the authority and responsibility to immediately solve customer problems. The hope is that empowered service recovery will prevent customer defections.

16-4 Manufacturing Operations

Ford makes cars, and Dell does computers. British Petroleum produces gasoline, whereas Sherwin-Williams makes paint. Boeing makes jet planes, but Budweiser makes beer. Maxtor makes hard drives, and Maytag makes appliances. The *manufacturing operations* of these companies all produce physical goods. But not all manufacturing operations, especially these, are the same.

After reading this section, you should be able to:

16-4 describe the different kinds of manufacturing operations.

Let's learn how various manufacturing operations differ in terms of **16-4a the amount of processing that is done to produce and assemble a product, 16-4b the different types of inventory, 16-4c how to measure inventory levels, 16-4d the costs of maintaining an inventory, and 16-4e the different systems for managing inventory.**

16-4a Amount of Processing in Manufacturing Operations

As Exhibit 16.4 shows, manufacturing operations can be classified according to the amount of processing or assembly that occurs after a customer order is received. The highest degree of processing occurs in **make-to-order operations.** A make-to-order operation does not start processing or assembling products until it receives a customer order. In fact, some make-to-order operations may not even order parts until a customer order is received. Not surprisingly,

make-to-order operation
a manufacturing operation that does not start processing or assembling products until a customer order is received

make-to-order operations produce or assemble highly specialized or customized products for customers.

For example, DELL has one of the most advanced make-to-order operations in the computer business. Because Dell has no finished goods inventory and no component parts inventory, its computers always have the latest, most advanced components, and Dell can pass on price cuts to customers. Plus, Dell can customize all of its orders, big and small. So whether you're ordering 5,000 personal computers for your company or just 1 personal computer for your home, Dell doesn't make the computers until you order them.

A moderate degree of processing occurs in **assemble-to-order operations**. A company using an assemble-to-order operation divides its manufacturing or assembly process into separate parts or modules. The company orders parts and assembles modules ahead of customer orders. Then, based on actual customer orders or on research forecasting what customers will want, those modules are combined to create semicustomized products.

The lowest degree of processing occurs in **make-to-stock operations** (also called "build-to-stock"). Because the products are standardized, meaning each product is exactly the same as the next, a company using a make-to-stock operation starts ordering parts and assembling finished products before receiving customer orders. Customers then purchase these standardized products—such as Rubbermaid storage containers, microwave ovens, and vacuum cleaners—at retail stores or directly from the manufacturer. Because parts are ordered and products are assembled before customers order the products, make-to-stock operations are highly dependent on the accuracy of sales forecasts. If sales forecasts are incorrect, make-to-stock operations may end up building too many or too few products, or they may make products with the wrong features or without the features that customers want.

16-4b Types of Inventory

Inventory is the amount and number of raw materials, parts, and finished products that a company has in its possession. When a devastating earthquake and an accompanying tsunami damaged factories throughout the eastern coast of Japan, inventory shortages, arising from destroyed or damaged Japanese factories, disrupted production around the world.

XIRALLIC is a shiny pigment with coated glass flakes used by nearly all car companies worldwide to paint their cars. It also happens to be made in just one factory, located in Onahama, Japan, which was damaged and without power following the earthquake and tsunami. Consequently, auto manufacturers had

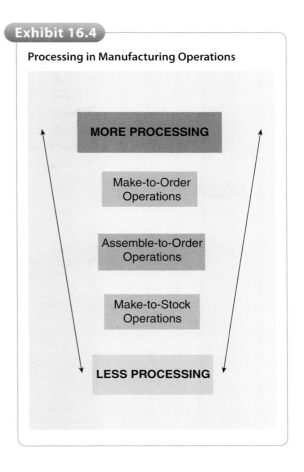

Exhibit 16.4

Processing in Manufacturing Operations

MORE PROCESSING

Make-to-Order Operations

Assemble-to-Order Operations

Make-to-Stock Operations

LESS PROCESSING

assemble-to-order operation
a manufacturing operation that divides manufacturing processes into separate parts or modules that are combined to create semicustomized products

make-to-stock operation
a manufacturing operation that orders parts and assembles standardized products before receiving customer orders

inventory
the amount and number of raw materials, parts, and finished products that a company has in its possession

raw material inventories
the basic inputs in a manufacturing process

component parts inventories
the basic parts used in manufacturing that are fabricated from raw materials

little choice but to ration their pigment inventory. Ford, for example, stopped taking orders for red cars and for "Tuxedo Black" F-150 trucks. Likewise, Chrysler immediately reduced the number of orders it would take for 10 different colors of cars.[38]

Exhibit 16.5 shows the four kinds of inventory a manufacturer stores: raw materials, component parts, work-in-process, and finished goods. The flow of inventory through a manufacturing plant begins when the purchasing department buys raw materials from vendors. **Raw material inventories** are the basic inputs in the manufacturing process. For example, to begin making a car, automobile manufacturers purchase raw materials like steel, iron, aluminum, copper, rubber, and unprocessed plastic.

Next, raw materials are fabricated or processed into **component parts inventories**, meaning the basic parts used in manufacturing a product. For example, in an automobile plant, steel is fabricated or processed into a car's body panels, and steel and iron are melted and shaped into engine parts like pistons or engine blocks. Some component parts are purchased from vendors rather than fabricated in-house.

The component parts are then assembled to make unfinished **work-in-process inventories**, which are also known as "partially finished goods." This process is also called *initial assembly.* For example, steel body panels are welded to each other and to the frame of the car to make a "unibody," which comprises the unpainted interior frame and exterior structure of the car. Likewise, pistons, camshafts, and other engine parts are inserted into the engine block to create a working engine.

Next, all the work-in-process inventories are assembled to create **finished goods inventories**, which are the final outputs of the manufacturing process. This process is also called *final assembly.* For a car, the engine, wheels, brake system, suspension, interior, and electrical system are assembled into a car's painted unibody to make the

Exhibit 16.5

Types of Inventory

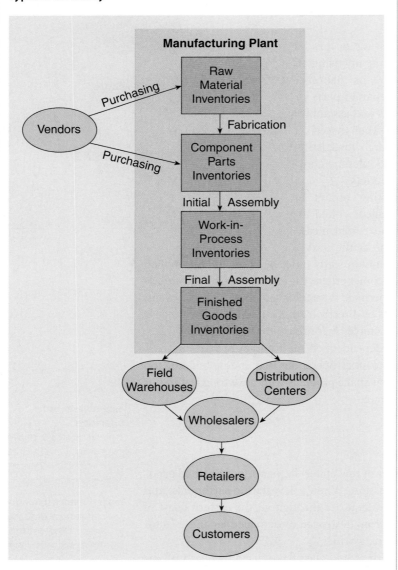

Source: R. E. Markland, S. K. Vickery, and R. A. Davis, Operations Management, 2nd ed. (Mason, OH: South-Western, 1998).

working automobile, which is the factory's finished product. In the last step in the process, the finished goods are sent to field warehouses, distribution centers, or wholesalers, and then to retailers for final sale to customers.

16-4c Measuring Inventory

As you'll learn next, uncontrolled inventory can lead to huge costs for a manufacturing operation. Consequently, managers need good measures of inventory to prevent inventory costs from becoming too large. Three basic measures of inventory are average aggregate inventory, weeks of supply, and inventory turnover.

If you've ever worked in a retail store and had to take inventory, you probably weren't too excited about the process of counting every item in the store and storeroom. It's an extensive task that's a bit easier today because of bar codes that mark items and computers that can count and track them. Nonetheless, inventories still differ from day to day. An inventory count taken at the beginning of the month will likely be different from a count taken at the end of the month. Similarly, an inventory count taken on a Friday will differ from a count taken on a Monday. Because of such differences, companies often measure **average aggregate inventory**, which is the average overall inventory during a particular time period. Average aggregate inventory for a month can be determined by simply averaging the inventory counts at the end of each business day for that month. One way that companies know whether they're carrying too much or too little inventory is to compare their average aggregate inventory with the industry average for aggregate inventory. For example, 72 days of inventory is the average for the automobile industry.

Most industries measure inventory in terms of *weeks of supply*, meaning the number of weeks it would take for a company to run out of its current supply of inventory. In general, there is an acceptable number of weeks of inventory for a particular kind of business. Too few weeks of inventory on hand, and a company risks a **stockout**—running out of inventory. For more than a decade, *LOWE'S* significantly outperformed its key rival Home Depot, but *HOME DEPOT*, however, is catching up because it has done a better job of avoiding stockouts. After a particularly stormy winter across the country, Home Depot's profits rose twice as fast as Lowe's, and its same-store sales rose four times as fast because it had on hand items in high demand like snow blowers, shovels, salt, and other winter-weather items. Lowe's, meanwhile, ran out of these products and lost sales.[40]

Another common inventory measure, **inventory turnover**, is the number of times per year that a company sells, or "turns over," its average inventory. For example, if a company keeps an average of 100 finished widgets in inventory each month, and it sold 1,000 widgets this year, then it turned its inventory 10 times this year.

work-in-process inventories
partially finished goods consisting of assembled component parts

finished goods inventories
the final outputs of manufacturing operations

average aggregate inventory
average overall inventory during a particular time period

stockout
the point when a company runs out of finished product.

inventory turnover
the number of times per year that a company sells, or "turns over," its average inventory

In general, the higher the number of inventory turns, the better. In practice, a high turnover means that a company can continue its daily operations with just a small amount of inventory on hand. For example, let's take two companies, A and B, which have identical inventory levels (520,000 widget parts and raw materials) over the course of a year. If company A turns its inventories 26 times a year, it will completely replenish its inventory every two weeks and have an average inventory of 20,000 widget parts and raw materials. By contrast, if company B turns its inventories only two times a year, it will completely replenish its inventory every 26 weeks and have an average inventory of 260,000 widget parts and raw materials. So, by turning its inventory more often, company A has 92 percent less inventory on hand at any one time than company B.

The average number of inventory turns across all kinds of manufacturing plants is approximately eight per year.[41] The inventory turn rates for some of the best companies in each industry may differ considerably from the average turn rates. Whereas the average auto company turns its entire inventory 13 times per year, some of the best auto companies more than double that rate, turning their inventory 27.8 times per year, or once every two weeks.[42] Turning inventory more frequently than the industry average can cut an auto company's costs by several hundred million dollars per year. Finally, it should be pointed out that even make-to-order companies like Dell turn their inventory. In theory, make-to-order companies have no inventory. In fact, they've got inventory, but you have to measure it in hours. For example, Dell turns the inventory in its facilities 500 times a year, which means that on average it has 17 hours—that's *hours* and not days—of inventory on hand in its factories.[43]

16-4d Costs of Maintaining an Inventory

Maintaining an inventory incurs four kinds of costs: ordering, setup, holding, and stockout. **Ordering cost** is not the cost of the inventory itself but the costs associated with ordering the inventory. It includes the costs of completing paperwork, manually entering data into a computer, making phone calls, getting competing bids, correcting mistakes, and simply determining when and how much new inventory should be reordered.

Setup cost is the cost of changing or adjusting a machine so that it can produce a different kind of inventory.[44] For example, *3M* uses the same production machinery to make several kinds of industrial tape, but it must adjust the machines whenever it switches from one kind of tape to another. There are two kinds of setup costs, downtime and lost efficiency. *Downtime* occurs whenever a machine is not being used to process inventory. If it takes five hours to switch a machine from processing one kind of inventory to another, then five hours of downtime have occurred. Downtime is costly because companies earn an economic return only when machines are actively turning raw materials into parts or parts into finished products. The second setup cost is *lost efficiency*. Recalibrating a machine to its optimal settings after a switchover typically takes some time. It may take several days of fine-tuning before a machine finally produces the number of high-quality parts that it is supposed to. So each time a machine has to be changed to handle a different kind of inventory, setup costs (downtime and lost efficiency) rise.

ordering cost
the costs associated with ordering inventory, including the cost of data entry, phone calls, obtaining bids, correcting mistakes, and determining when and how much inventory to order

setup cost
the costs of downtime and lost efficiency that occur when a machine is changed or adjusted to produce a different kind of inventory

Holding cost, also known as "carrying" or "storage cost," is the cost of keeping inventory until it is used or sold. Holding cost includes the cost of storage facilities, insurance to protect inventory from damage or theft, inventory taxes, the cost of obsolescence (holding inventory that is no longer useful to the company), and the opportunity cost of spending money on inventory that could have been spent elsewhere in the company.

Stockout costs are the costs incurred when a company runs out of a product, as happened to Apple when it failed to have enough iPods during the holiday shopping season. There are two basic kinds of stockout costs. First, the company incurs the transaction costs of overtime work, shipping, and the like, in trying quickly to replace out-of-stock inventories with new inventories. The second and perhaps more damaging cost is the loss of customers' goodwill when a company cannot deliver the products it promised. Stockouts occur more often than you might think. In the United States, the supermarket industry's average out-of-stock rate (the percentage of items that are unavailable at a given time) is 7.9 percent, according to research firm Market6. Most importantly, retailers can increase sales 4 percent if they never run out of stock.[45]

16-4e Managing Inventory

Inventory management has two basic goals. The first is to avoid running out of stock and thus angering and dissatisfying customers. This goal seeks to increase inventory to a safe level that won't risk stockouts. The second is to efficiently reduce inventory levels and costs as much as possible without impairing daily operations. This goal seeks a minimum level of inventory. The following inventory management techniques—economic order quantity (EOQ), just-in-time inventory (JIT), and materials requirement planning (MRP)—are different ways of balancing these competing goals.

Economic order quantity (EOQ) is a system of formulas that helps determine how much and how often inventory should be ordered. EOQ takes into account the overall demand (D) for a product while trying to minimize ordering costs (O) and holding costs (H). The formula for EOQ is:

$$EOQ = \sqrt{\frac{2DO}{H}}$$

For example, if a factory uses 40,000 gallons of paint a year (D), ordering costs (O) are $75 per order, and holding costs (H) are $4 per gallon, then the optimal quantity to order is 1,225 gallons:

$$EOQ = \sqrt{\frac{2(40,000)(75)}{4}} = 1,225 \text{ gallons}$$

With 40,000 gallons of paint being used per year, the factory uses approximately 110 gallons per day:

$$\frac{40,000 \text{ gallons}}{365 \text{ days}} = 110 \text{ gallons/day}$$

© ISTOCKPHOTO.COM/LUIS CARLOS TORRE

Consequently, the factory would order 1,225 new gallons of paint approximately every 11 days:

$$\frac{1{,}225 \text{ gallons}}{110 \text{ gallons per day}} = 11.1 \text{ days}$$

DIAPERS.COM uses EOQ formulas to decide precisely how much inventory to keep on hand. Computational algorithms determine the optimal number of boxes to have in the warehouse and in which sizes. Currently, Diapers.com keeps 23 box sizes on hand, but the company runs the simulation every quarter.[46]

Whereas EOQ formulas try to minimize holding and ordering costs, the JIT approach to inventory management attempts to eliminate holding costs by reducing inventory levels to near zero. With a **just-in-time (JIT) inventory system**, component parts arrive from suppliers just as they are needed at each stage of production. By having parts arrive just in time, the manufacturer has little inventory on hand and thus avoids the costs associated with holding inventory.

To have just the right amount of inventory arrive at just the right time requires a tremendous amount of coordination between manufacturing operations and suppliers. One way to promote tight coordination under JIT is close proximity. A second way to promote close coordination under JIT is to have a shared information system that allows a manufacturer and its suppliers to know the quantity and kinds of parts inventory the other has in stock. Generally, factories and suppliers facilitate information sharing by using the same part numbers and names. Ford's seat supplier accomplishes this by sticking a bar code on each seat, and Ford then uses the sticker to route the seat through its factory.

Manufacturing operations and their parts suppliers can also facilitate close coordination by using the system of kanban. **Kanban**, which is Japanese for "sign," is a simple ticket-based system that indicates when it is time to reorder inventory. Suppliers attach kanban cards to batches of parts. Then, when an assembly-line worker uses the first part out of a batch, the kanban card is removed. The cards are then collected, sorted, and quickly returned to the supplier, who begins resupplying the factory with parts that match the order information on the kanban cards. Because prices and batch sizes are typically agreed to ahead of time, kanban tickets greatly reduce paperwork and ordering costs.[47]

A third method for managing inventory is **materials requirement planning (MRP)**. MRP is a production and inventory system that, from beginning to end, precisely determines the production schedule, production batch sizes, and inventories needed to complete final products. The three key parts of MRP systems are the master production schedule, the bill of materials, and inventory records. The *master production schedule* is a detailed schedule that indicates the quantity of each item to be produced, the planned delivery dates for those items, and the time by which each step of the production process must be completed in order to meet those delivery dates. Based on the quantity and kind of products set forth in the master production schedule, the *bill of materials* identifies all the necessary parts and inventory, the quantity or volume of inventory to be ordered, and the order in which the parts and inventory should be assembled. *Inventory records* indicate the kind, quantity, and location of inventory that is on hand or that has been ordered. When inventory records are

just-in-time (JIT) inventory system
an inventory system in which component parts arrive from suppliers just as they are needed at each stage of production

kanban
a ticket-based JIT system that indicates when to reorder inventory

materials requirement planning (MRP)
a production and inventory system that determines the production schedule, production batch sizes, and inventory needed to complete final products

combined with the bill of materials, the resulting report indicates what to buy, when to buy it, and what it will cost to order. Today, nearly all MRP systems are available in the form of powerful, flexible computer software.[48]

Which inventory management system should you use? Economic order quantity (EOQ) formulas are intended for use with **independent demand systems**, in which the level of one kind of inventory does not depend on another. For example, because inventory levels for automobile tires are unrelated to the inventory levels of women's dresses, Sears could use EOQ formulas to calculate separate optimal order quantities for dresses and tires. By contrast, JIT and MRP are used with **dependent demand systems**, in which the level of inventory depends on the number of finished units to be produced. For example, if Yamaha makes 1,000 motorcycles a day, then it will need 1,000 seats, 1,000 gas tanks, and 2,000 wheels and tires each day. So, when optimal inventory levels depend on the number of products to be produced, use a JIT or MRP management system.

REVIEW 16-4

Manufacturing Operations

Manufacturing operations produce physical goods. Manufacturing operations can be classified according to the amount of processing or assembly that occurs after receiving an order from customers. Make-to-order operations, in which assembly doesn't begin until products are ordered, involve the most processing. The next highest degree of processing occurs in assemble-to-order operations, in which preassembled modules are combined after orders are received to produce semicustomized products. The least processing occurs in make-to-stock operations, in which standard parts are ordered on the basis of sales forecasts and assembled before orders are received.

There are four kinds of inventory: raw materials, component parts, work-in-process, and finished goods. Because companies incur ordering, setup, holding, and sometimes stockout costs when handling inventory, inventory costs can be enormous. To control those costs, companies measure and track inventory in three ways: average aggregate inventory, weeks of supply, and turnover. Companies meet the basic goals of inventory management (avoiding stockouts and reducing inventory without hurting daily operations) through economic order quantity (EOQ) formulas, just-in-time (JIT) inventory systems, and materials requirement planning (MRP).

EOQ formulas minimize holding and ordering costs by determining how much and how often inventory should be ordered. By having parts arrive just when they are needed at each stage of production, JIT systems attempt to minimize inventory levels and holding costs. JIT systems often depend on proximity, shared information, and the system of kanban made popular by Japanese manufacturers. MRP precisely determines the production schedule, production batch sizes, and the ordering of inventories needed to complete final products. The three key parts of MRP systems are the master production schedule, the bill of materials, and inventory records. Use EOQ formulas when inventory levels are independent, and use JIT and MRP when inventory levels are dependent on the number of products to be produced.

independent demand system
an inventory system in which the level of one kind of inventory does not depend on another

dependent demand system
an inventory system in which the level of inventory depends on the number of finished units to be produced

Management Decision

Going Lean at Starbucks [49]

It started off as a day basically like any other. You went into the Starbucks that you manage, helped employees open, and thought about making a dent in the mountain of paperwork left over from the previous week. But then you got an unexpected visit from a team at the corporate office. They started talking about the need to lower labor costs, improve efficiency, and increase productivity. When you asked them how they planned on doing all that, they responded, "Lean production."

They informed you that lean production is a management philosophy derived from Toyota that is focused on reducing waste. Whether it's wasted motion, wasted time, or wasted parts, the goal of lean production is to eliminate waste so that all an organization can do its work efficiently. The executives then show you all the "waste" that's in your stores right now—baristas bending over to scoop coffee from a counter below, others waiting for coffee to fully drain before starting a new pot, one worker carrying trays of pastries from storage to the display case, another spending 10 seconds per drink to read the milk label. They even show you a map showing the winding trail that a barista takes in making a single drink. It looks like a big pile of spaghetti, you think to yourself.

With lean production, the executives tell you, you can reduce the amount of motion that employees spend making drinks and the amount of time they spend reaching for stuff, reading labels, or moving from here to there. This will make your store more efficient and productive so that the same number of employees can serve more customers.

You're intrigued by all of this, as nothing would please your supervisors more than increased revenue and lower costs. But you're also worried about how your employees will react. Many of them came to work at Starbucks because it wasn't like other fast-food chains that focus only on speed, speed, and speed. How will they feel once you tell them that they'll have to change the way they work to become faster? What if they feel like you just want them to be coffee-making robots, leaving them no time to interact with customers or experiment with new drinks? Consider these issues with three or four other students as you discuss the questions below.

Questions

1. How would an increase in efficiency and production benefit your employees?

2. How would you address employees' concerns that they are being transformed into coffee-making robots?

3. What is the best way to ensure that the quality of your products does not decline with increased production speed?

 Practice Being a Manager

Balancing Speed and Accuracy

Success in service and manufacturing operations requires managers to maintain high levels of both productivity and quality. High productivity ensures that the company is cost-competitive with rivals; and high quality helps the company to attract customers and grow revenues and profits. Because productivity and quality are basic drivers of company success, managers must be adept at measuring and improving both. This exercise will give you some practice in developing productivity and quality measures.

STEP 1 Your professor will organize your class into small groups of three or four students.

Scenario: Your group is a management team working to improve productivity and quality in a pharmaceutical company. You have been assigned two units of this company as the focus of your improvement efforts. The first is a pill-packaging unit, and the second is a research and development (R&D) laboratory.

Workers in the packaging unit are responsible for checking to ensure that the pills in the box match the packaging and labeling, placing the appropriate labels and packaging information on each box, and then certifying with a stamp that the box of pills is ready for shipping to wholesale customers, for example, chains like Walgreens and Costco. Mistakes in packaging, if undetected by pharmacists, could have serious, even fatal, outcomes. These manufacturing workers are skilled and highly trained. If they detect a problem, they have the authority to halt production.

Workers in the R&D unit are responsible for developing new drugs and for testing their effectiveness and safety. The company relies for its success upon a steady pipeline of promising new products. At the same time, some basic research (e.g., study of progression of a particular type of cancer) is necessary in order to develop new drugs. These workers are mostly PhDs and highly skilled laboratory technicians.

STEP 2 **Develop metrics.** Working as a team, develop some productivity and quality measures for (a) packaging unit workers and (b) R&D unit workers. Be sure to consider whether productivity and quality should be measured on an individual or unit basis, and why.

STEP 3 **Analyze the metrics.** Critically examine your team's measures for each unit. What unintended consequences might develop as workers in each unit strive to improve on the measures you have designed? Are you more confident of your measures in one unit versus the other? Why or why not?

STEP 4 **Debrief as a class.** What are some of the challenges of measuring productivity and quality? Are these challenges greater for particular types of work? Which level of measurement and accountability—individual or unit—is more likely to generate positive results? Why? What impact do productivity and quality systems of measurement and improvement have on workers? How can firms ensure productivity and quality without overloading workers and/or fostering unhealthy levels of stress?

▶ Self-Assessment

How to Handle Disgruntled Customers

How a company manages its customers is an important indicator of its future success. But managing customers can be as difficult as it is critical. For example, one customer may like to be greeted by an employee and immediately helped upon entering the store. Another might find this approach a bit aggressive. What is your style? If you were responsible for interacting with customers, which approach would you use? The following assessment will evaluate your perspectives on the relationship a company has with its customers. Be candid as you respond to the items, using a scale from 1 to 9, in which 1 means you strongly disagree, 5 means you are neutral, and 9 means you strongly agree (other numbers indicate varying degrees of agreement or disagreement).[50]

1. I try to bring a customer with a problem together with a product/service that helps solve that problem.

   1   2   3   4   5   6   7   8   9

2. I keep alert for weaknesses in a customer's personality so I can use them to put pressure on them to agree with me.

   1   2   3   4   5   6   7   8   9

3. I try to influence a customer by information rather than pressure.

    1   2   3   4   5   6   7   8   9

4. It is necessary to stretch the truth in describing a product to a customer.

    1   2   3   4   5   6   7   8   9

5. I decide what product/service to offer on the basis of what I can convince customers to accept, not on the basis of what will satisfy them in the long run.

    1   2   3   4   5   6   7   8   9

6. I paint too rosy a picture of my product/service to make it sound as good as possible.

    1   2   3   4   5   6   7   8   9

7. I try to find out what kind of products/services will be most helpful to a customer.

    1   2   3   4   5   6   7   8   9

8. I try to sell a customer all I can convince them to buy, even if I think it is more than a wise customer would buy.

    1   2   3   4   5   6   7   8   9

9. I begin talking about the product/service before exploring a customer's need with him or her.

    1   2   3   4   5   6   7   8   9

10. I try to help customers achieve their goals.

    1   2   3   4   5   6   7   8   9

11. I try to figure out what a customer's needs are.

    1   2   3   4   5   6   7   8   9

12. A good employee has to have the customer's best interest in mind.

    1   2   3   4   5   6   7   8   9

13. I try to sell as much as I can rather than to satisfy a customer.

    1   2   3   4   5   6   7   8   9

14. I try to give customers an accurate expectation of what our product/service will do for them.

    1   2   3   4   5   6   7   8   9

15. I imply to a customer that something is beyond my control when it is not.

    1   2   3   4   5   6   7   8   9

16. I try to achieve my goals by satisfying customers.

    1   2   3   4   5   6   7   8   9

17. If I am not sure if our product/service is right for a customer, I will still apply pressure to get him or her to buy.

    1   2   3   4   5   6   7   8   9

18. I answer a customer's question about product/services as correctly as I can.

    1   2   3   4   5   6   7   8   9

19. I offer the product/service that is best suited to the customer's problem.

    1   2   3   4   5   6   7   8   9

20. I treat a customer as a rival.

    1   2   3   4   5   6   7   8   9

21. I spend more time trying to persuade a customer to buy than I do trying to discover his or her needs.

    1   2   3   4   5   6   7   8   9

22. I am willing to disagree with a customer in order to help him or her make a better decision.

     1   2   3   4   5   6   7   8   9

23. I try to get customers to discuss their needs with me.

     1   2   3   4   5   6   7   8   9

24. I pretend to agree with customers to please them.

     1   2   3   4   5   6   7   8   9

SCORING

Enter your response to each survey item below, and then total each column to derive two scores.

CUSTOMER ORIENTATION

1. regular score   _____

3. regular score   _____

7. regular score   _____

10. regular score   _____

11. regular score   _____

12. regular score   _____

14. regular score   _____

16. regular score   _____

18. regular score   _____

19. regular score   _____

22. regular score   _____

23. regular score   _____

    TOTAL =   _____

SELLING ORIENTATION

2. regular score   _____

4. regular score   _____

5. regular score   _____

6. regular score   _____

8. regular score   _____

9. regular score   _____

13. regular score   _____

15. regular score   _____

17. regular score   _____

20. regular score   _____

21. regular score   _____

24. regular score   _____

    TOTAL =   _____

You can find the interpretation for your score at www.cengagebrain.com.

▶ MANAGEMENT WORKPLACE

Barcelona Restaurant Group

At Barcelona Restaurant Group, quality is defined not just by the food, but by the service that the waitstaff delivers. To ensure consistent quality across the board, Barcelona uses five "feedback loops" that gauge restaurant performance: a "secret shopper" program, credit card rewards for customers, customer comment cards, e-mails, and surveillance cameras. In addition, general managers walk the floor constantly to advise waitstaff and gather feedback from customers.

What to Watch For and Ask Yourself

1. How does Barcelona Restaurant Group's approach to customer service fulfill the quality-related characteristics of services?

2. How does Barcelona Restaurant Group's approach to customer service fulfill the three aspects of Total Quality Management?

3. Discuss how Barcelona Restaurant Group implements service recovery and service empowerment.

Endnotes

1. "LVMH Moët Hennessy Louis Vuitton S.A.," International Directory of Company Histories, vol. 113, St. James Press, 2010. Reproduced in Business and Company Resource Center, Farmington Hills, MI: Gale Group, 2011, http://galenet.galegroup.com/servlet/BCRC; P. Gumbel and E. Levenson, "Mass vs. Class," Fortune, September 17, 2007, 82–88; W. Langley, "Louis Vuitton; Not My Bag," Sunday Telegraph (London), August 16, 2009, Features 8; C. Passariello, "At Vuitton, Growth in Small Batches; Luxury-Goods Maker's New French Factory Adds to Capacity but Sticks to Strategy of Tight Rein," Wall Street Journal, June 27, 2011, accessed June 30, 2011, from http://online.wsj.com/article/SB10001424052702303627104576409813842858304.html; and K. Walsh, "He's Got the Whole World in His Handbag," Sunday Times (London), November 21, 2010, Business 7.

2. S. Oches, "QSR Drive-Thru Performance Study," QSR Magazine, October 2011, accessed May 23, 2012, from www.qsrmagazine.com/reports.

3. "Table F-20—Families by Total Money Income, Race, and Hispanic Origin of Householder: 1974 to 2010," U.S. Census Bureau, accessed May 23, 2012, from www.census.gov/hhes/www/income/data/historical/families/.

4. The Conference Board Total Economy Data Base, Summary Statistics 1995–2010 "Table 3: Growth of Labor Productivity, Real GDP and Total Hours Worked by Region for Advanced Countries, 1995–2010," The Conference Board, September 2010, accessed June 27, 2011, from www.conference-board.org/retrievefile.cfm?filename=SummaryTables_Sep20101.pdf&type=subsite.

5. "Employment Projections, Table 1: Civilian Labor Force by Sex, Age, Race, and Hispanic Origin, 1988, 1998, 2008, and projected 2018," in Employment Outlook: 2008–18; Labor Force Projections to 2018: Older Workers Staying More Active, Monthly Labor Review, November 2008, 30–51, accessed June 27, 2011, from www.bls.gov/opub/mlr/2009/11/art3full.pdf.

6. "Are Cars Becoming Less Affordable for the Average American Family?" Cars.com, accessed March 23, 2010, from http://blogs.cars.com/kickingtires/2010/08/are-cars-becoming-less-affordable-for-the-average-american-family.html; and "Auto Affordability Flat in First Quarter of 2011, Comerica Bank Reports," Comerica, May 12, 2011, accessed June 27, 2011, from www.comerica.com/Comerica_Content/Corporate_Communications/Docs/Auto%20Affordability%20Index/Auto_Affordability_Index_Q12011.pdf.

7. "Multifactor Productivity: Frequently Asked Questions," Bureau of Labor Statistics, accessed May 23, 2012 at www.bls.gov/mfp/mprfaq.htm#1.

8. "Study: Auto Makers Initial Quality Improves Considerably," Quality Digest, accessed August 2, 2009, from www.qualitydigest.com/inside/quality-insider-news/study-overall-initial-quality-improves-considerably.html; and "2008 Initial Quality Study Results," accessed August 2, 2009, from www.jdpower.com/autos/articles/2008-Initial-Quality-Study-Results.

9. "2011 Initial Quality Study Results (IQS)," JD Power and Associates, June 23, 2011, accessed June 27, 2011, from www.jdpower.com/autos/articles/2011-Initial-Quality-Study-Results.

10. "Basic Concepts," American Society for Quality, accessed August 2, 2009, from www.asq.org/learn-about-quality/basic-concepts.html.

11. R. E. Markland, S. K. Vickery, and R. A. Davis, "Managing Quality" (Chapter 7) in Operations Management: Concepts in Manufacturing and Services (Cincinnati, OH: South-Western College Publishing, 1998).

12. "New Industrial LCD Panels with 100,000 Hour MTBF LED Backlight Systems from Toshiba America Electronic Components," Your Industry News, August 26, 2009 accessed September 12, 2009, from www.toshiba.com/taec/news/press_releases/2009/lcdb_09_576.jsp.

13. L. L. Berry and A. Parasuraman, Marketing Services (New York: Free Press, 1991).

14. Y, Kane and I. Sherr, "Penney Picks Boss from Apple—Secrets from Genius Bar: Full Loyalty, No Negativity," Wall Street Journal, June 15, 2011, A1.

15. "FAQs—General Information on ISO," International Organization for Standardization, accessed September 12, 2009, from www.iso.org/iso/support/faqs/faqs_general_information_on_iso.htm.

16. "ISO 9000 Essentials," and "ISO 14000 Essentials," International Organization for Standardization, accessed September 12, 2009, from www.iso.org/iso/iso_catalogue/management_standards/iso_9000_iso_14000.htm.

17. J. Briscoe, S. Fawcett, and R. Todd, "The Implementation and Impact of ISO 9000 among Small Manufacturing Enterprises," Journal of Small Business Management 43 (July 1, 2005): 309.

18. R. Henkoff, "The Hot New Seal of Quality (ISO 9000 Standard of Quality Management)," Fortune, June 28, 1993, 116.

19. "Frequently Asked Questions about the Malcolm Baldrige National Quality Award," National Institute of Standards & Technology, accessed September 12, 2009, from www.nist.gov/public_affairs/factsheet/baldfaqs.htm.

20. "2012 Baldrige Award Application Forms," National Institute of Standards & Technology, 3, accessed May 23, 2012, from www.nist.gov/baldrige/publications/upload/Baldrige_Award_Application_Forms.pdf.

21. "Frequently Asked Questions and Answers about the Malcolm Baldrige National Quality Award."

22. "2011–2012 Criteria for Performance Excellence," Baldrige Performance Excellence Program, accessed May 23, 2012, from www.nist.gov/baldrige/publications/upload/2011_2012_Business_Nonprofit_Criteria.pdf.

23. Ibid.

24. "Baldrige Index Beaten by S&P 500 for Second Year," NIST Tech Beat, accessed September 12, 2009, from www.quality.nist.gov/Stock_Studies.htm.

25 J. W. Dean Jr., and J. Evans, *Total Quality: Management, Organization, and Strategy* (St. Paul, MN: West, 1994).

26 J. W. Dean Jr., and D. E. Bowen, "Management Theory and Total Quality: Improving Research and Practice through Theory Development," *Academy of Management Review* 19 (1994): 392–418.

27 R. Carr, "Teamwork at Its Best," *Fast Company*, May 16, 2010, accessed March 23, 2011, from www.fastcompany.com/1648449/teamwork-at-its-best.

28 "Table 669. Gross Domestic Product in Current and Real (2000) Dollars by Type of Product and Sector; 1990 to 2010," *The 2012 Statistical Abstract*, U.S. Census Bureau, accessed May 23, 2012, from www.census.gov/compendia/statab/2012/tables/12s0669.pdf.

29 R. Hallowell, L. A. Schlesinger, and J. Zornitsky, "Internal Service Quality, Customer and Job Satisfaction: Linkages and Implications for Management," *Human Resource Planning* 19 (1996): 20–31; and J. L. Heskett, T. O. Jones, G. W. Loveman, W. E. Sasser Jr., and L. A. Schlesinger, "Putting the Service–Profit Chain to Work," *Harvard Business Review* (March–April 1994): 164–174.

30 J. Paravantis, N. Bouranta, and L. Chitiris, "The Relationship between Internal and External Service Quality," *International Journal of Contemporary Hospital Management* 21 (2009): 275–293.

31 G. Brewer, "The Ultimate Guide to Winning Customers: The Customer Stops Here," *Sales & Marketing Management* 150 (March 1998): 30; and F. F. Reichheld, *The Loyalty Effect: The Hidden Force behind Growth, Profits, and Lasting Value* (Cambridge, MA: Harvard Business School Press, 2001).

32 Heskett et al., "Putting the Service–Profit Chain to Work".

33 L. L. Berry and A. Parasuraman, "Listening to the Customer—The Concept of a Service-Quality Information System," *Sloan Management Review* 38, no. 3 (Spring 1997): 65; and C. W. L. Hart, J. L. Heskett, and W. E. Sasser Jr., "The Profitable Art of Service Recovery," *Harvard Business Review* (July–August 1990): 148–156.

34 D. Stanley, "When Flight Diverted, Crew Ordered Pizza for Passengers," *Denver News*, May 21, 2010, accessed July 7, 2010, from www.thedenverchannel.com/news/23620842/detail.html.

35 D. E. Bowen and E. E. Lawler III, "The Empowerment of Service Workers: What, Why, How, and When," *Sloan Management Review* 33 (Spring 1992): 31–39; and D. E. Bowen and E. E. Lawler III, "Empowering Service Employees," *Sloan Management Review* 36 (Summer 1995): 73–84.

36 Bowen and Lawler, "The Empowerment of Service Workers: What, Why, How, and When."

37 "The Way I Work: Marc Lore of Diapers.com," Inc.com, September 1, 2009, accessed September 2, 2010, from www.inc.com/magazine/20090901/the-way-i-work-marc-lore-of-diaperscom.html.

38 N. E. Boudette and J. Bennett, "Pigment Shortage Hits Auto Makers," *Wall Street Journal*, May 25, 2011, accessed April 9, 2012, http://online.wsj.com/article/SB10001424052748703696704576222990521120106.html.

39 B. Gardiner, "Upcycling Evolves from Recycling," *New York Times*, November 3, 2010, accessed June 27, 2011, from www.nytimes.com/2010/11/04/business/energy-environment/04iht-rbogup.html.

40 M. Bustillo, "For Lowe's, Landscape Begins to Shift," *Wall Street Journal*, February 24, 2011, B3.

41 D. Drickhamer, "Reality Check," *Industry Week*, November 2001, 29.

42 D. Drickhamer, "Zeroing In on World-Class," *Industry Week*, November 2001, 36.

43 J. Zeiler, "The Need for Speed," *Operations & Fulfillment*, April 1, 2004, 38.

44 J. R. Henry, "Minimized Setup Will Make Your Packaging Line S.M.I.L.E.," *Packaging Technology & Engineering*, February 1, 1998, 24.

45 K. Clark, "An Eagle Eye for Inventory," *Chain Store Age*, May 2005, Supplement, 8A.

46 "The Way I Work: Marc Lore of Diapers.com."

47 N. Shirouzu, "Why Toyota Wins Such High Marks on Quality Surveys," *Wall Street Journal*, March 15, 2001, A1.

48 G. Gruman, "Supply on Demand: Manufacturers Need to Know What's Selling before They Can Produce and Deliver Their Wares in the Right Quantities," *Info World*, April 18, 2005, accessed April 15, 2009, from www.infoworld.com/t/data-management/supply-demand-680.

49 J. Jargon, "Latest Starbucks Buzzword: 'Lean' Japanese Techniques," *Wall Street Journal*, August 4, 2009, accessed June 27, 2011, from http://online.wsj.com/article/SB124933474023402611.html.

50 J. A. Perriat, S. LeMay, and S. Chakrabarty, "The Selling Orientation—Customer Orientation (SOCO) Scale: Cross-Validation of the Revised Version," *Journal of Personal Selling & Sales Management* 24, no. 1 (2004): 49–54.

Glossary

360-degree feedback
a performance appraisal process in which feedback is obtained from the boss, subordinates, peers and coworkers, and the employees themselves

A

a-type conflict (affective conflict)
disagreement that focuses on individuals or personal issues

absolute comparisons
a process in which each decision criterion is compared to a standard or ranked on its own merits

accommodative strategy
a social responsiveness strategy in which a company accepts responsibility for a problem and does all that society expects to solve that problem

achievement-oriented leadership
a leadership style in which the leader sets challenging goals, has high expectations of employees, and displays confidence that employees will assume responsibility and put forth extraordinary effort

acquaintance time
a cultural norm for how much time you must spend getting to know someone before the person is prepared to do business with you

acquisition
the purchase of a company by another company

action plan
the specific steps, people, and resources needed to accomplish a goal

active listening
assuming half the responsibility for successful communication by actively giving the speaker nonjudgmental feedback that shows you've accurately heard what he or she said

address terms
cultural norms that establish whether you should address businesspeople by their first names, family names, or titles

adverse impact
unintentional discrimination that occurs when members of a particular race, sex, or ethnic group are unintentionally harmed or disadvantaged because they are hired, promoted, or trained (or any other employment decision) at substantially lower rates than others

advocacy groups
concerned citizens who band together to try to influence the business practices of specific industries, businesses, and professions

affective cultures
cultures in which people display emotions and feelings when communicating

analyzers
companies using an adaptive strategy that seeks to minimize risk and maximize profits by following or imitating the proven successes of prospectors

appointment time
a cultural norm for how punctual you must be when showing up for scheduled appointments or meetings

Asia-Pacific Economic Cooperation (APEC)
a regional trade agreement between Australia, Canada, Chile, the People's Republic of China, Hong Kong, Japan, Mexico, New Zealand, Papua New Guinea, Peru, Russia, South Korea, Taiwan, the United States, and all the members of ASEAN except Cambodia, Laos, and Myanmar

assemble-to-order operation
a manufacturing operation that divides manufacturing processes into separate parts or modules that are combined to create semicustomized products

Association of Southeast Asian Nations (ASEAN)
a regional trade agreement between Brunei Darussalam, Cambodia, Indonesia, Laos, Malaysia, Myanmar, the Philippines, Singapore, Thailand, and Vietnam

association or affinity patterns
when two or more database elements tend to occur together in a significant way

attack
a competitive move designed to reduce a rival's market share or profits

attribution theory
the theory that we all have a basic need to understand and explain the causes of other people's behavior

authentication
making sure potential users are who they claim to be

authority
the right to give commands, take action, and make decisions to achieve organizational objectives

authorization
granting authenticated users approved access to data, software, and systems

autonomy
the degree to which a job gives workers the discretion, freedom, and independence to decide how and when to accomplish the job

average aggregate inventory
average overall inventory during a particular time period

B

background checks
procedures used to verify the truthfulness and accuracy of information that applicants provide about themselves and to uncover negative, job-related background information not provided by applicants

balanced scorecard
measurement of organizational performance in four equally important areas: finances, customers, internal operations, and innovation and learning

bar code
a visual pattern that represents numerical data by varying the thickness and pattern of vertical bars

bargaining power of buyers
measure of the influence that customers have on a firm's prices

bargaining power of suppliers
measure of the influence that suppliers of parts, materials, and services to firms in an industry have on the prices of these inputs

BCG matrix
a portfolio strategy, developed by the Boston Consulting Group, that categorizes a corporation's businesses by growth rate and relative market share, and helps managers decide how to invest corporate funds

behavior control
the regulation of the behaviors and actions that workers perform on the job

behavior observation scale (BOS)
rating scales that indicate the frequency with which workers perform specific behaviors that are representative of the job dimensions critical to successful job performance

behavioral addition
the process of having managers and employees perform new behaviors that are central to and symbolic of the new organizational culture that a company wants to create

behavioral formality
a workplace atmosphere characterized by routine and regimen, specific rules about how to behave, and impersonal detachment

behavioral informality
a workplace atmosphere characterized by spontaneity, casualness, and interpersonal familiarity

behavioral substitution
the process of having managers and employees perform new behaviors central to the "new" organizational culture in place of behaviors that were central to the "old" organizational culture

benchmarking
the process of identifying outstanding practices, processes, and standards in other companies and adapting them to your company

biographical data (biodata)
extensive surveys that ask applicants questions about their personal backgrounds and life experiences

biometrics
identifying users by unique, measurable body features, such as fingerprint recognition or iris scanning

blog
a personal website that provides personal opinions or recommendations, news summaries, and reader comments

bona fide occupational qualification (BFOQ)
an exception in employment law that permits sex, age, religion, and the like to be used when making employment decisions, but only if they are "reasonably necessary to the normal operation of that particular business"; BFOQs are strictly monitored by the Equal Employment Opportunity Commission

bounded rationality
a decision-making process restricted in the real world by limited resources, incomplete and imperfect information, and managers' limited decision-making capabilities

brainstorming
a technique in which group members build on others' ideas for generating a large number of alternative solutions

budgeting
quantitative planning through which managers decide how to allocate available money to best accomplish company goals

bureaucratic control
the use of hierarchical authority to influence employee behavior by rewarding or punishing employees for compliance or noncompliance with organizational policies, rules, and procedures

bureaucratic immunity
the ability to make changes without first getting approval from managers or other parts of an organization

business confidence indices
indices that show managers' level of confidence about future business growth

buyer dependence
the degree to which a supplier relies on a buyer because of the importance of that buyer to the supplier and the difficulty of finding other buyers for its products

C

c-type conflict (cognitive conflict)
disagreement that focuses on problem- and issue-related differences of opinion

cafeteria benefit plans (flexible benefit plans)
plans that allow employees to choose which benefits they receive, up to a certain dollar value

cash cow
a company with a large share of a slow-growing market

Central America Free Trade Agreement (CAFTA-DR)
a regional trade agreement between Costa Rica, the Dominican Republic, El Salvador, Guatemala, Honduras, Nicaragua, and the United States

centralization of authority
the location of most authority at the upper levels of the organization

chain of command
the vertical line of authority that clarifies who reports to whom throughout the organization

change agent
the person formally in charge of guiding a change effort

change forces
forces that produce differences in the form, quality, or condition of an organization over time

change intervention
the process used to get workers and managers to change their behavior and work practices

character of the rivalry
measure of the intensity of competitive behavior between companies in an industry

charismatic leadership
the behavioral tendencies and personal characteristics of leaders that create an exceptionally strong relationship between them and their followers

closure
the tendency to fill in gaps of missing information by assuming that what we don't know is consistent with what we already know

coaching
communicating with someone for the direct purpose of improving the person's on-the-job performance or behavior

coercion
the use of formal power and authority to force others to change

cognitive ability tests
tests that measure the extent to which applicants have abilities in perceptual speed, verbal comprehension, numerical aptitude, general reasoning, and spatial aptitude

cohesiveness
the extent to which team members are attracted to a team and motivated to remain in it

commission
a compensation system in which employees earn a percentage of each sale they make

communication
the process of transmitting information from one person or place to another

communication medium
the method used to deliver a message

company hotlines
phone numbers that anyone in the company can call anonymously to leave information for upper management

company mission
a company's purpose or reason for existing

compensation
the financial and nonfinancial rewards that organizations give employees in exchange for their work

competitive advantage
providing greater value for customers than competitors can

competitive analysis
a process for monitoring the competition that involves identifying competition, anticipating their moves, and determining their strengths and weaknesses

competitive inertia
a reluctance to change strategies or competitive practices that have been successful in the past

competitors
companies in the same industry that sell similar products or services to customers

complex environment
an environment with many environmental factors

complex matrix
a form of matrix departmentalization in which managers in different parts of the matrix report to matrix managers, who help them sort out conflicts and problems

component parts inventories
the basic parts used in manufacturing that are fabricated from raw materials

compression approach to innovation
an approach to innovation that assumes that incremental innovation can be planned using a series of steps and that compressing those steps can speed innovation

concentration of effect
the total harm or benefit that an act produces on the average person

conceptual skills
the ability to see the organization as a whole, understand how the different parts affect each other, and recognize how the company fits into or is affected by its external environment

concertive control
the regulation of workers' behavior and decisions through work group values and beliefs

concurrent control
a mechanism for gathering information about performance deficiencies as they occur, thereby eliminating or shortening the delay between performance and feedback

conduit metaphor
the mistaken assumption that senders can pipe their intended messages directly into the heads of receivers with perfect clarity and without noise or perceptual filters interfering with the receivers' understanding of the message

consideration
the extent to which a leader is friendly, approachable, and supportive and shows concern for employees

consistent organizational culture
a company culture in which the company actively defines and teaches organizational values, beliefs, and attitudes

constructive feedback
feedback intended to be helpful, corrective, and/or encouraging

contingency theory
a leadership theory that states that in order to maximize work group performance, leaders must be matched to the situation that best fits their leadership style

continuous improvement
an organization's ongoing commitment to constantly assess and improve the processes and procedures used to create products and services

continuous reinforcement schedule
a schedule that requires a consequence to be administered following every instance of a behavior

control
a regulatory process of establishing standards to achieve organizational goals, comparing actual performance against the standards, and taking corrective action, when necessary

control loss
the situation in which behavior and work procedures do not conform to standards

controlling
monitoring progress toward goal achievement and taking corrective action when needed

conventional level of moral development
the second level of moral development in which people make decisions that conform to societal expectations

cooperative contract
an agreement in which a foreign business owner pays a company a fee for the right to conduct that business in his or her country

core capabilities
the internal decision-making routines, problem-solving processes, and organizational cultures that determine how efficiently inputs can be turned into outputs

core firms
the central companies in a strategic group

corporate portal
a hybrid of executive information systems and intranets that allows managers and employees to use a Web browser to gain access to customized company information and to complete specialized transactions

corporate-level strategy
the overall organizational strategy that addresses the question: What business or businesses are we in or should we be in?

cost leadership
the positioning strategy of producing a product or service of acceptable quality at consistently lower production costs than competitors can, so that the firm can offer the product or service at the lowest price in the industry

counseling
communicating with someone about non-job-related issues that may be affecting or interfering with the person's performance

creative work environments
workplace cultures in which workers perceive that new ideas are welcomed, valued, and encouraged

creativity
the production of novel and useful ideas

cross-cultural communication
transmitting information from a person in one country or culture to a person from another country or culture

cross-functional team
a team composed of employees from different functional areas of the organization

cross-training
training team members to do all or most of the jobs performed by the other team members

customer defections
a performance assessment in which companies identify which customers are leaving and measure the rate at which they are leaving

customer departmentalization
organizing work and workers into separate units responsible for particular kinds of customers

customer focus
an organizational goal to concentrate on meeting customers' needs at all levels of the organization

customer satisfaction
an organizational goal to provide products or services that meet or exceed customers' expectations

customs classification
a classification assigned to imported products by government officials that affects the size of the tariff and imposition of import quotas

cybernetic
the process of steering or keeping on course

cybernetic feasibility
the extent to which it is possible to implement each step in the control process

D

data clusters
when three or more database elements occur together (ie, cluster) in a significant way

data encryption
the transformation of data into complex, scrambled digital codes that can be unencrypted only by authorized users who possess unique decryption keys

data mining
the process of discovering unknown patterns and relationships in large amounts of data

data warehouse
stores huge amounts of data that have been prepared for data mining analysis by being cleaned of errors and redundancy

de-forming
a reversal of the forming stage, in which team members position themselves to control pieces of the team, avoid each other, and isolate themselves from team leaders

de-norming
a reversal of the norming stage, in which team performance begins to decline as the size, scope, goal, or members of the team change

de-storming
a reversal of the storming phase, in which the team's comfort level decreases, team cohesion weakens, and angry emotions and conflict may flare

decentralization
the location of a significant amount of authority in the lower levels of the organization

decision criteria
the standards used to guide judgments and decisions

decision making
the process of choosing a solution from available alternatives

decision support system (DSS)
an information system that helps managers understand specific kinds of problems and potential solutions and analyze the impact of different decision options using "what-if" scenarios

decoding
the process by which the receiver translates the written, verbal, or symbolic form of a message into an understood message

defenders
companies using an adaptive strategy aimed at defending strategic positions by seeking moderate, steady growth and by offering a limited range of high-quality products and services to a well-defined set of customer

defensive bias
the tendency for people to perceive themselves as personally and situationally similar to someone who is having difficulty or trouble

defensive strategy
a social responsiveness strategy in which a company admits responsibility for a problem but does the least required to meet societal expectations

delegation of authority
the assignment of direct authority and responsibility to a subordinate to complete tasks for which the manager is normally responsible

Delphi technique
a decision-making method in which members of a panel of experts respond to questions and to each other until reaching agreement on an issue

departmentalization
subdividing work and workers into separate organizational units responsible for completing particular tasks

dependent demand system
an inventory system in which the level of inventory depends on the number of finished units to be produced

design competition
competition between old and new technologies to establish a new technological standard or dominant design

design iteration
a cycle of repetition in which a company tests a prototype of a new product or service, improves on that design, and then builds and tests the improved prototype

destructive feedback
feedback that disapproves without any intention of being helpful and almost always causes a negative or defensive reaction in the recipient

devil's advocacy
a decision-making method in which an individual or a subgroup is assigned the role of a critic

dialectical inquiry
a decision-making method in which decision makers state the assumptions of a proposed solution (a thesis) and generate a solution that is the opposite (antithesis) of that solution

differentiation
the positioning strategy of providing a product or service that is sufficiently different from competitors' offerings that customers are willing to pay a premium price for it

direct competition
the rivalry between two companies that offer similar products and services, acknowledge each other as rivals, and act and react to each other's strategic actions

direct foreign investment
a method of investment in which a company builds a new business or buys an existing business in a foreign country

directive leadership
a leadership style in which the leader lets employees know precisely what is expected of them, gives them specific guidelines for performing tasks, schedules work, sets standards of performance, and makes sure that people follow standard rules and regulations

discontinuous change
the phase of a technology cycle characterized by technological substitution and design competition

discretionary responsibilities
the social roles that a company fulfills beyond its economic, legal, and ethical responsibilities

discussion time
a cultural norm for how much time should be spent in discussion with others

disparate treatment
intentional discrimination that occurs when people are purposely not given the same hiring, promotion, or membership opportunities because of their race, color, sex, age, ethnic group, national origin, or religious beliefs

disseminator role
the informational role managers play when they share information with others in their departments or companies

distal goals
long-term or primary goals

distinctive competence
what a company can make, do, or perform better than its competitors

distributive justice
the perceived degree to which outcomes and rewards are fairly distributed or allocated

disturbance handler role
the decisional role managers play when they respond to severe problems that demand immediate action

diversification
a strategy for reducing risk by buying a variety of items (stocks or, in the case of a corporation, types of businesses) so that the failure of one stock or one business does not doom the entire portfolio

dog
a company with a small share of a slow-growing market

dominant design
a new technological design or process that becomes the accepted market standard

downsizing
the planned elimination of jobs in a company

downward communication
communication that flows from higher to lower levels in an organization

dynamic environment
an environment in which the rate of change is fast

dysfunctional turnover
loss of high-performing employees who voluntarily choose to leave a company

E

economic order quantity (EOQ)
a system of formulas that minimizes ordering and holding costs and helps determine how much and how often inventory should be ordered

economic responsibility
a company's social responsibility to make a profit by producing a valued product or service

economic value added (EVA)
the amount by which company profits (revenues, minus expenses, minus taxes) exceed the cost of capital in a given year

effectiveness
accomplishing tasks that help fulfill organizational objectives

efficiency
getting work done with a minimum of effort, expense, or waste

electronic brainstorming
a decision-making method in which group members use computers to build on each others' ideas and generate as many alternative solutions as possible

electronic data interchange (EDI)
when two companies convert their purchase and ordering information to a standardized format to enable the direct electronic transmission of that information from one company's computer system to the other company's computer system

electronic scanner
an electronic device that converts printed text and pictures into digital images

empathetic listening
understanding the speaker's perspective and personal frame of reference and giving feedback that conveys that understanding to the speaker

employee involvement team
team that provides advice or makes suggestions to management concerning specific issues

employee separation
the voluntary or involuntary loss of an employee

employee stock ownership plan (ESOP)
a compensation system that awards employees shares of company stock in addition to their regular compensation

employee turnover
loss of employees who voluntarily choose to leave the company

employment benefits
a method of rewarding employees that includes virtually any kind of compensation other than wages or salaries

employment references
sources such as previous employers or coworkers who can provide job-related information about job candidates

empowering workers
permanently passing decision-making authority and responsibility from managers to workers by giving them the information and resources they need to make and carry out good decisions

empowerment
feelings of intrinsic motivation, in which workers perceive their work to have impact and meaning and perceive themselves to be competent and capable of self-determination

encoding
putting a message into a written, verbal, or symbolic form that can be recognized and understood by the receiver

entrepreneur role
the decisional role managers play when they adapt themselves, their subordinates, and their units to change

environmental change
the rate at which a company's general and specific environments change

environmental complexity
the number and the intensity of external factors in the environment that affect organizations

environmental scanning
searching the environment for important events or issues that might affect an organization

equity theory
a theory that states that people will be motivated when they perceive that they are being treated fairly

ethical behavior
behavior that conforms to a society's accepted principles of right and wrong

ethical charismatics
charismatic leaders who provide developmental opportunities for followers, are open to positive and negative feedback, recognize others' contributions, share information, and have moral standards that emphasize the larger interests of the group, organization, or society

ethical intensity
the degree of concern people have about an ethical issue

ethical responsibility
a company's social responsibility not to violate accepted principles of right and wrong when conducting its business

ethics
the set of moral principles or values that defines right and wrong for a person or group

evaluation apprehension
fear of what others will think of your ideas

executive information system (EIS)
a data processing system that uses internal and external data sources to provide the information needed to monitor and analyze organizational performance

expatriate
someone who lives and works outside his or her native country

expectancy
the perceived relationship between effort and performance

expectancy theory
the theory that people will be motivated to the extent to which they believe that their efforts will lead to good performance, that good performance will be rewarded, and that they will be offered attractive rewards

experiential approach to innovation
an approach to innovation that assumes a highly uncertain environment and uses intuition, flexible options, and hands-on experience to reduce uncertainty and accelerate learning and understanding

expert system
an information system that contains the specialized knowledge and decision rules used by experts and experienced decision makers so that nonexperts can draw on this knowledge base to make decisions

exporting
selling domestically produced products to customers in foreign countries

external environments
all events outside a company that have the potential to influence or affect it

external recruiting
the process of developing a pool of qualified job applicants from outside the company

extinction
reinforcement in which a positive consequence is no longer allowed to follow a previously reinforced behavior, thus weakening the behavior

extranets
networks that allow companies to exchange information and conduct transactions with outsiders by providing them direct, Web-based access to authorized parts of a company's intranet or information system

extrinsic reward
a reward that is tangible, visible to others, and given to employees contingent on the performance of specific tasks or behaviors

F

feedback
the amount of information the job provides to workers about their work performance

feedback control
a mechanism for gathering information about performance deficiencies after they occur

feedback to sender
in the communication process, a return message to the sender that indicates the receiver's understanding of the message

feedforward control
a mechanism for monitoring performance inputs rather than outputs to prevent or minimize performance deficiencies before they occur

figurehead role
the interpersonal role managers play when they perform ceremonial duties

finished goods inventories
the final outputs of manufacturing operations

firewall
a protective hardware or software device that sits between the computers in an internal organizational network and outside networks, such as the Internet

firm-level strategy
a corporate strategy that addresses the question: How should we compete against a particular firm?

first-line managers
managers who train and supervise the performance of nonmanagerial employees who are directly responsible for producing the company's products or services

first-mover advantage
the strategic advantage that companies earn by being the first in an industry to use new information technology to substantially lower costs or to differentiate a product or service from that of competitors

fixed interval reinforcement schedule
an intermittent schedule in which consequences follow a behavior only after a fixed time has elapsed

fixed ratio reinforcement schedule
an intermittent schedule in which consequences are delivered following a specific number of behaviors

flow
a psychological state of effortlessness in which you become completely absorbed in what you're doing and time seems to pass quickly

focus strategy
the positioning strategy of using cost leadership or differentiation to produce a specialized product or service for a limited, specially targeted group of customers in a particular geographic region or market segment

formal communication channel
the system of official channels that carry organizationally approved messages and information

forming
the first stage of team development, in which team members meet each other, form initial impressions, and begin to establish team norms

four-fifths (or 80 percent) rule
a rule of thumb used by the courts and the EEOC to determine whether there is evidence of adverse impact; A violation of this rule occurs when the selection rate for a protected group is less than 80 percent or four-fifths of the selection rate for a nonprotected group

franchise
a collection of networked firms in which the manufacturer or marketer of a product or service, the franchisor, licenses the entire business to another person or organization, the franchisee

functional departmentalization
organizing work and workers into separate units responsible for particular business functions or areas of expertise

functional turnover
loss of poor-performing employees who voluntarily choose to leave a company

fundamental attribution error
the tendency to ignore external causes of behavior and to attribute other people's actions to internal causes

G

gainsharing
a compensation system in which companies share the financial value of performance gains, such as productivity, cost savings, or quality, with their workers

General Agreement on Tariffs and Trade (GATT)
a worldwide trade agreement that reduced and eliminated tariffs, limited government subsidies, and established protections for intellectual property

General Electric workout
a three-day meeting in which managers and employees from different levels and parts of an organization quickly generate and act on solutions to specific business problems

general environment
the economic, technological, sociocultural, and political trends that indirectly affect all organizations

generational change
change based on incremental improvements to a dominant technological design such that the improved technology is fully backward compatible with the older technology

geographic departmentalization
organizing work and workers into separate units responsible for doing business in particular geographic areas

global business
the buying and selling of goods and services by people from different countries

global consistency
when a multinational company has offices, manufacturing plants, and distribution facilities in different countries and runs them all using the same rules, guidelines, policies, and procedures

global new ventures
new companies that are founded with an active global strategy and have sales, employees, and financing in different countries

goal
a target, objective, or result that someone tries to accomplish

goal acceptance
the extent to which people consciously understand and agree to goals

goal commitment
the determination to achieve a goal

goal difficulty
the extent to which a goal is hard or challenging to accomplish

goal specificity
the extent to which goals are detailed, exact, and unambiguous

goal-setting theory
the theory that people will be motivated to the extent to which they accept specific, challenging goals and receive feedback that indicates their progress toward goal achievement

government import standard
a standard ostensibly established to protect the health and safety of citizens but, in reality, often used to restrict imports

grand strategy
a broad corporate-level strategic plan used to achieve strategic goals and guide the strategic alternatives that managers of individual businesses or subunits may use

groupthink
a barrier to good decision making caused by pressure within the group for members to agree with each other

growth strategy
a strategy that focuses on increasing profits, revenues, market share, or the number of places in which the company does business

H

hearing
the act or process of perceiving sounds

holding cost
the cost of keeping inventory until it is used or sold, including storage, insurance, taxes, obsolescence, and opportunity costs

horizontal communication
communication that flows among managers and workers who are at the same organizational level

hostile work environment
a form of sexual harassment in which unwelcome and demeaning sexually related behavior creates an intimidating and offensive work environment

human resource management (HRM)
the process of finding, developing, and keeping the right people to form a qualified workforce

human skills
the ability to work well with others

I

imperfectly imitable resource
a resource that is impossible or extremely costly or difficult for other firms to duplicate

incremental change
the phase of a technology cycle in which companies innovate by lowering costs and improving the functioning and performance of the dominant technological design

independent demand system
an inventory system in which the level of one kind of inventory does not depend on another

individualism–collectivism
the degree to which a person believes that people should be self-sufficient and that loyalty to one's self is more important than loyalty to team or company

industry regulation
regulations and rules that govern the business practices and procedures of specific industries, businesses, and professions

industry-level strategy
corporate strategy that addresses the question: How should we compete in this industry?

informal communication channel ("grapevine")
the transmission of messages from employee to employee outside of formal communication channels

information
useful data that can influence people's choices and behavior

initiating structure
the degree to which a leader structures the roles of followers by setting goals, giving directions, setting deadlines, and assigning tasks

innovation streams
patterns of innovation over time that can create sustainable competitive advantage

inputs
in equity theory, the contributions employees make to the organization

instrumentality
the perceived relationship between performance and rewards

intermittent reinforcement schedule
a schedule in which consequences are delivered after a specified or average time has elapsed or after a specified or average number of behaviors has occurred

internal environment
the events and trends inside an organization that affect management, employees, and organizational culture

internal motivation
motivation that comes from the job itself rather than from outside rewards

internal recruiting
the process of developing a pool of qualified job applicants from people who already work in the company

interorganizational process
a collection of activities that take place among companies to transform inputs into outputs that customers value

interpersonal skills
skills, such as listening, communicating, questioning, and providing feedback, that enable people to have effective working relationships with others

interviews
a selection tool in which company representatives ask job applicants job-related questions to determine whether they are qualified for the job

intranets
private company networks that allow employees to easily access, share, and publish information using internet software

intraorganizational process
the collection of activities that take place within an organization to transform inputs into outputs that customers value

intrinsic reward
a natural reward associated with performing a task or activity for its own sake

inventory
the amount and number of raw materials, parts, and finished products that a company has in its possession

inventory turnover
the number of times per year that a company sells, or "turns over," its average inventory

ISO 14000
a series of international standards for managing, monitoring, and minimizing an organization's harmful effects on the environment

ISO 9000
a series of five international standards, from ISO 9000 to ISO 9004, for achieving consistency in quality management and quality assurance in companies throughout the world

J

job analysis
a "purposeful, systematic process for collecting information on the important work-related aspects of a job"

job characteristics model (JCM)
an approach to job redesign that seeks to formulate jobs in ways that motivate workers and lead to positive work outcomes

job description
a written description of the basic tasks, duties, and responsibilities required of an employee holding a particular job

job design
the number, kind, and variety of tasks that individual workers perform in doing their jobs

job enlargement
increasing the number of different tasks that a worker performs within one particular job

job enrichment
increasing the number of tasks in a particular job and giving workers the authority and control to make meaningful decisions about their work

job evaluation
a process that determines the worth of each job in a company by evaluating the market value of the knowledge, skills, and requirements needed to perform it

job rotation
periodically moving workers from one specialized job to another to give them more variety and the opportunity to use different skills

job specialization
a job composed of a small part of a larger task or process

job specifications
a written summary of the qualifications needed to successfully perform a particular job

joint venture
a strategic alliance in which two existing companies collaborate to form a third, independent company

just-in-time (JIT) inventory system
an inventory system in which component parts arrive from suppliers just as they are needed at each stage of production

K

kanban
a ticket-based JIT system that indicates when to reorder inventory

kinesics
movements of the body and face

knowledge
the understanding that one gains from information

L

leader-member relations
the degree to which followers respect, trust, and like their leaders

leader role
the interpersonal role managers play when they motivate and encourage workers to accomplish organizational objectives

leadership
the process of influencing others to achieve group or organizational goals

leadership style
the way a leader generally behaves toward followers

leading
inspiring and motivating workers to work hard to achieve organizational goals

learning-based planning
learning better ways of achieving goals by continually testing, changing, and improving plans and strategies

legal responsibility
a company's social responsibility to obey society's laws and regulations

liaison role
the interpersonal role managers play when they deal with people outside their units

licensing
an agreement in which a domestic company, the licensor, receives royalty payments for allowing another company, the licensee, to produce the licensor's product, sell its service, or use its brand name in a specified foreign market

line authority
the right to command immediate subordinates in the chain of command

line function
an activity that contributes directly to creating or selling the company's products

listening
making a conscious effort to hear

local adaptation
modifying rules, guidelines, policies, and procedures to adapt to differences in foreign customers, governments, and regulatory agencies

M

Maastricht Treaty of Europe
a regional trade agreement between most European countries

magnitude of consequences
the total harm or benefit derived from an ethical decision

make-to-order operation
a manufacturing operation that does not start processing or assembling products until a customer order is received

make-to-stock operation
a manufacturing operation that orders parts and assembles standardized products before receiving customer orders

management
getting work done through others

management by objectives (MBO)
a four-step process in which managers and employees discuss and select goals, develop tactical plans, and meet regularly to review progress toward goal accomplishment

market commonality
the degree to which two companies have overlapping products, services, or customers in multiple markets

materials requirement planning (MRP)
a production and inventory system that determines the production schedule, production batch sizes, and inventory needed to complete final products

matrix departmentalization
a hybrid organizational structure in which two or more forms of departmentalization, most often product and functional, are used together

maximize
choosing the best alternative

mechanistic organization
an organization characterized by specialized jobs and responsibilities; precisely defined, unchanging roles; and a rigid chain of command based on centralized authority and vertical communication

media advocacy
an advocacy group tactic that involves framing issues as public issues; exposing questionable, exploitative, or unethical practices; and forcing media coverage by buying media time or creating controversy that is likely to receive extensive news coverage

meta-analysis
a study of studies, a statistical approach that provides one of the best scientific estimates of how well management theories and practices work

middle managers
managers responsible for setting objectives consistent with top management's goals and for planning and implementing subunit strategies for achieving these objectives

milestones
formal project review points used to assess progress and performance

modular organization
an organization that outsources noncore business activities to outside companies, suppliers, specialists, or consultants

monitor role
the informational role managers play when they scan their environment for information

monochronic cultures
cultures in which people tend to do one thing at a time and view time as linear

Moore's law
the prediction that about every two years, computer processing power would double and its cost would drop by 50 percent

motivation
the set of forces that initiates, directs, and makes people persist in their efforts to accomplish a goal

motivation to manage
an assessment of how enthusiastic employees are about managing the work of others

multifactor productivity
an overall measure of performance that indicates how much labor, capital, materials, and energy it takes to produce an output

multifunctional teams
work teams composed of people from different departments

multinational corporation
a corporation that owns businesses in two or more countries

N

national culture
the set of shared values and beliefs that affects the perceptions, decisions, and behavior of the people from a particular country

needs
the physical or psychological requirements that must be met to ensure survival and well-being

negative reinforcement
reinforcement that strengthens behavior by withholding an unpleasant consequence when employees perform a specific behavior

negotiator role
the decisional role managers play when they negotiate schedules, projects, goals, outcomes, resources, and employee raises

neutral cultures
cultures in which people do not display emotions and feelings when communicating

noise
anything that interferes with the transmission of the intended message

nominal group technique
a decision-making method that begins and ends by having group members quietly write down and evaluate ideas to be shared with the group

nonsubstitutable resource
a resource that produces value or competitive advantage and has no equivalent substitutes or replacements

nontariff barriers
nontax methods of increasing the cost or reducing the volume of imported goods

nonverbal communication
any communication that doesn't involve words

normative control
the regulation of workers' behavior and decisions through widely shared organizational values and beliefs

normative decision theory
a theory that suggests how leaders can determine an appropriate amount of employee participation when making decisions

norming
the third stage of team development, in which team members begin to settle into their roles, group cohesion grows, and positive team norms develop

norms
informally agreed-on standards that regulate team behavior

North American Free Trade Agreement (NAFTA)
a regional trade agreement between the United States, Canada, and Mexico

 # O

objective control
the use of observable measures of worker behavior or outputs to assess performance and influence behavior

objective performance measures
measures of job performance that are easily and directly counted or quantified

online discussion forums
in-house online newsgroups that use Web- or software-based discussion tools to enable employees throughout the company to ask each other questions and share knowledge

open office systems
offices in which the physical barriers that separate workers have been removed in order to increase communication and interaction

operational plans
day-to-day plans, developed and implemented by lower-level managers, for producing or delivering the organization's products and services over a 30-day to six-month period

operations management
managing the daily production of goods and services

opportunistic behavior
a transaction in which one party in the relationship benefits at the expense of the other

optical character recognition
the ability of software to convert digitized documents into ASCII text (American Standard Code for Information Interchange) that can be searched, read, and edited by word-processing software as well as other kinds of software

options-based planning
maintaining planning flexibility by making small, simultaneous investments in many alternative plans

ordering cost
the costs associated with ordering inventory, including the cost of data entry, phone calls, obtaining bids, correcting mistakes, and determining when and how much inventory to order

organic organization
an organization characterized by broadly defined jobs and responsibility; loosely defined, frequently changing roles; and decentralized authority and horizontal communication based on task knowledge

organizational change
a difference in the form, quality, or condition of an organization over time

organizational culture
the values, beliefs, and attitudes shared by organizational members

organizational development
a philosophy and collection of planned change interventions designed to improve an organization's long-term health and performance

organizational heroes
people celebrated for their qualities and achievements within an organization

organizational innovation
the successful implementation of creative ideas in organizations

organizational process
the collection of activities that transform inputs into outputs that customers value

organizational silence
when employees withhold information about organizational problems or issues

organizational stories
stories told by organizational members to make sense of organizational events and changes and to emphasize culturally consistent assumptions, decisions, and actions

organizational structure
the vertical and horizontal configuration of departments, authority, and jobs within a company

organizing
deciding where decisions will be made, who will do what jobs and tasks, and who will work for whom

outcome/input (O/I) ratio
in equity theory, an employee's perception of how the rewards received from an organization compare with the employee's contributions to that organization

outcomes
in equity theory, the rewards employees receive for their contributions to the organization

outplacement services
employment-counseling services offered to employees who are losing their jobs because of downsizing

output control
the regulation of workers' results or outputs through rewards and incentives

overreward
a form of inequity in which you are getting more outcomes relative to inputs than your referent

overt integrity tests
a written test that estimates job applicants' honesty by directly asking them what they think or feel about theft or about punishment of unethical behaviors

P

paralanguage
the pitch, rate, tone, volume, and speaking pattern (i.e., use of silences, pauses, or hesitations) of one's voice

partial productivity
a measure of performance that indicates how much of a particular kind of input it takes to produce an output

participative leadership
a leadership style in which the leader consults employees for their suggestions and input before making decisions

path–goal theory
a leadership theory that states that leaders can increase subordinate satisfaction and performance by clarifying and clearing the paths to goals and by increasing the number and kinds of rewards available for goal attainment

perception
the process by which individuals attend to, organize, interpret, and retain information from their environments

perceptual filters
the personality-, psychology-, or experience-based differences that influence people to ignore or pay attention to particular stimuli

performance appraisal
the process of assessing how well employees are doing their jobs

performance feedback
information about the quality or quantity of past performance that indicates whether progress is being made toward the accomplishment of a goal

performing
the fourth and final stage of team development, in which performance improves because the team has matured into an effective, fully functioning team

personality tests
tests that measure the extent to which applicants possess different kinds of job-related personality dimensions

personality-based integrity tests
a written test that indirectly estimates job applicants' honesty by measuring psychological traits, such as dependability and conscientiousness

piecework
a compensation system in which employees are paid a set rate for each item they produce

planning
determining organizational goals and a means for achieving them

policies
a standing plan that indicates the general course of action that should be taken in response to a particular event or situation

policy uncertainty
the risk associated with changes in laws and government policies that directly affect the way foreign companies conduct business

political uncertainty
the risk of major changes in political regimes that can result from war, revolution, death of political leaders, social unrest, or other influential events

polychronic cultures
cultures in which people tend to do more than one thing at a time and view time as circular

pooled interdependence
work completed by having each job or department independently contribute to the whole

portfolio strategy
a corporate-level strategy that minimizes risk by diversifying investment among various businesses or product lines

position power
the degree to which leaders are able to hire, fire, reward, and punish workers

positive reinforcement
reinforcement that strengthens behavior by following behaviors with desirable consequences

postconventional level of moral development
the third level of moral development in which people make decisions based on internalized principles

preconventional level of moral development
the first level of moral development in which people make decisions based on selfish reasons

predictive patterns
patterns that help identify database elements that are different

primary stakeholders
any group on which an organization relies for its long-term survival

private spaces
spaces used by and open to just one employee

proactive strategy
a social responsiveness strategy in which a company anticipates responsibility for a problem before it occurs and does more than society expects to address the problem

probability of effect
the chance that something will happen and then harm others

problem
a gap between a desired state and an existing state

procedural justice
the perceived fairness of the process used to make reward allocation decisions

procedures
a standing plan that indicates the specific steps that should be taken in response to a particular event

processing information
transforming raw data into meaningful information

product boycott
an advocacy group tactic that involves protesting a company's actions by persuading consumers not to purchase its product or service

product departmentalization
organizing work and workers into separate units responsible for producing particular products or services

product prototype
a full-scale working model that is being tested for design, function, and reliability

production blocking
a disadvantage of face-to-face brainstorming in which a group member must wait to share an idea because another member is presenting an idea

productivity
a measure of performance that indicates how many inputs it takes to produce or create an output

profit sharing
a compensation system in which a company pays a percentage of its profits to employees in addition to their regular compensation

project team
a team created to complete specific, one-time projects or tasks within a limited time

prospectors
companies using an adaptive strategy that seeks fast growth by searching for new market opportunities, encouraging risk taking, and being the first to bring innovative new products to market

protecting information
the process of ensuring that data are reliably and consistently retrievable in a usable format for authorized users, but no one else

protectionism
a government's use of trade barriers to shield domestic companies and their workers from foreign competition

proximal goals
short-term goals or subgoals

proximity of effect
the social, psychological, cultural, or physical distance between a decision maker and those affected by his or her decisions

public communications
an advocacy group tactic that relies on voluntary participation by the news media and the advertising industry to get the advocacy group's message out

punctuated equilibrium theory
the theory that companies go through long periods of stability (equilibrium) during which incremental changes occur, followed by short, complex periods of dynamic, fundamental change (revolutionary periods), finishing with a return to stability (new equilibrium)

punishment
reinforcement that weakens behavior by following behaviors with undesirable consequences

purchasing power
the relative cost of a standard set of goods and services in different countries

purpose statement
a statement of a company's purpose or reason for existing

Q

quality
a product or service free of deficiencies, or the characteristics of a product or service that satisfy customer needs

question mark
a company with a small share of a fast-growing market

quid pro quo sexual harassment
a form of sexual harassment in which employment outcomes, such as hiring, promotion, or simply keeping one's job, depend on whether an individual submits to sexual harassment

quota
a limit on the number or volume of imported products

R

radio frequency identification (RFID) tags
tags containing minuscule microchips that transmit information via radio waves and can be used to track the number and location of the objects into which the tags have been inserted

rare resource
a resource that is not controlled or possessed by many competing firms

rater training
training performance appraisal raters in how to avoid rating errors and increase rating accuracy

rational decision making
a systematic process of defining problems, evaluating alternatives, and choosing optimal solutions

raw data
facts and figures

raw material inventories
the basic inputs in a manufacturing process

reactive strategy
a social responsiveness strategy in which a company does less than society expects

reactors
companies using an adaptive strategy of not following a consistent strategy, but instead reacting to changes in the external environment after they occur

reciprocal interdependence
work completed by different jobs or groups working together in a back-and-forth manner

recovery
the strategic actions taken after retrenchment to return to a growth strategy

reengineering
fundamental rethinking and radical redesign of business processes to achieve dramatic improvements in critical measures of performance, such as cost, quality, service, and speed

referents
in equity theory, others with whom people compare themselves to determine if they have been treated fairly

refreezing
supporting and reinforcing new changes so that they "stick"

regional trading zones
areas in which tariff and nontariff barriers on trade between countries are reduced or eliminated

regulation costs
the costs associated with implementing or maintaining control

reinforcement
the process of changing behavior by changing the consequences that follow behavior

reinforcement contingencies
cause-and-effect relationships between the performance of specific behaviors and specific consequences

reinforcement theory
the theory that behavior is a function of its consequences, that behaviors followed by positive consequences will occur more frequently, and that behaviors followed by negative consequences, or not followed by positive consequences, will occur less frequently

related diversification
creating or acquiring companies that share similar products, manufacturing, marketing, technology, or cultures

relationship behavior
the establishment of mutually beneficial, long-term exchanges between buyers and suppliers

relative comparisons
a process in which each decision criterion is compared directly with every other criterion

resistance forces
forces that support the existing state of conditions in organizations

resistance to change
opposition to change resulting from self-interest, misunderstanding and distrust, or a general intolerance for change

resource allocator role
the decisional role managers play when they decide who gets what resources

resource scarcity
the abundance or shortage of critical organizational resources in an organization's external environment

resource similarity
the extent to which a competitor has similar amounts and kinds of resources

resources
the assets, capabilities, processes, employee time, information, and knowledge that an organization uses to improve its effectiveness and efficiency, create and sustain competitive advantage, and fulfill a need or solve a problem

response
a competitive countermove, prompted by a rival's attack, to defend or improve a company's market share or profit

results-driven change
change created quickly by focusing on the measurement and improvement of results

retrenchment strategy
a strategy that focuses on turning around very poor company performance by shrinking the size or scope of the business

rules and regulations
standing plans that describe how a particular action should be performed, or what must happen or not happen in response to a particular event

S

S-curve pattern of innovation
a pattern of technological innovation characterized by slow initial progress, then rapid progress, and then slow progress again as a technology matures and reaches its limits

satisficing
choosing a "good enough" alternative

schedule of reinforcement
rules that specify which behaviors will be reinforced, which consequences will follow those behaviors, and the schedule by which those consequences will be delivered

schedule time
a cultural norm for the time by which scheduled projects or jobs should actually be completed

secondary firms
the firms in a strategic group that follow strategies related to but somewhat different from those of the core firms

secondary stakeholders
any group that can influence or be influenced by a company and can affect public perceptions about the company's socially responsible behavior

secure sockets layer (SSL) encryption
Internet browser–based encryption that provides secure off-site Web access to some data and programs

selection
the process of gathering information about job applicants to decide who should be offered a job

selective perception
the tendency to notice and accept objects and information consistent with our values, beliefs, and expectations, while ignoring or screening out or not accepting inconsistent information

self-control (self-management)
a control system in which managers and workers control their own behavior by setting their own goals, monitoring their own progress, and rewarding themselves for goal achievement

self-designing team
a team that has the characteristics of self-managing teams but also controls team design, work tasks, and team membership

self-managing team
a team that manages and controls all of the major tasks of producing a product or service

self-serving bias
the tendency to overestimate our value by attributing successes to ourselves (internal causes) and attributing failures to others or the environment (external causes)

semiautonomous work group
a group that has the authority to make decisions and solve problems related to the major tasks of producing a product or service

sequence patterns
when two or more database elements occur together in a significant pattern, but one of the elements precedes the other

sequential interdependence
work completed in succession, with one group's or job's outputs becoming the inputs for the next group or job

service recovery
restoring customer satisfaction to strongly dissatisfied customers

setup cost
the costs of downtime and lost efficiency that occur when a machine is changed or adjusted to produce a different kind of inventory

sexual harassment
a form of discrimination in which unwelcome sexual advances, requests for sexual favors, or other verbal or physical conduct of a sexual nature occurs while performing one's job

shared spaces
spaces used by and open to all employees

shareholder model
a view of social responsibility that holds that an organization's overriding goal should be profit maximization for the benefit of shareholders

simple environment
an environment with few environmental factors

simple matrix
a form of matrix departmentalization in which managers in different parts of the matrix negotiate conflicts and resources

single-use plans
plans that cover unique, one-time-only events

situational (SWOT) analysis
an assessment of the strengths and weaknesses in an organization's internal environment and the opportunities and threats in its external environment

situational favorableness
the degree to which a particular situation either permits or denies a leader the chance to influence the behavior of group members

situational theory
a leadership theory that states that leaders need to adjust their leadership styles to match their followers' readiness

skill variety
the number of different activities performed in a job

skill-based pay
compensation system that pays employees for learning additional skills or knowledge

slack resources
a cushion of extra resources that can be used with options-based planning to adapt to unanticipated change, problems, or opportunities

SMART goals
goals that are **S**pecific, **M**easurable, **A**ttainable, **R**ealistic, and **T**imely

social consensus
agreement on whether behavior is bad or good

social loafing
behavior in which team members withhold their efforts and fail to perform their share of the work

social responsibility
a business's obligation to pursue policies, make decisions, and take actions that benefit society

social responsiveness
refers to a company's strategy to respond to stakeholders' economic, legal, ethical, or discretionary expectations concerning social responsibility

specific ability tests (aptitude tests)
tests that measure the extent to which an applicant possesses the particular kind of ability needed to do a job well

specific environment
the customers, competitors, suppliers, industry regulations, and advocacy groups that are unique to an industry and directly affect how a company does business

spokesperson role
the informational role managers play when they share information with people outside their departments or companies

stability strategy
a strategy that focuses on improving the way in which the company sells the same products or services to the same customers

stable environment
an environment in which the rate of change is slow

staff authority
the right to advise, but not command, others who are not subordinates in the chain of command

staff function
an activity that does not contribute directly to creating or selling the company's products, but instead supports line activities

stakeholder model
a theory of corporate responsibility that holds that management's most important responsibility, long-term survival, is achieved by satisfying the interests of multiple corporate stakeholders

stakeholders
persons or groups with a "stake" or legitimate interest in a company's actions

standardization
solving problems by consistently applying the same rules, procedures, and processes

standards
a basis of comparison for measuring the extent to which various kinds of organizational performance are satisfactory or unsatisfactory

standing plans
plans used repeatedly to handle frequently recurring events

star
a company with a large share of a fast-growing market

stepladder technique
a decision-making method in which group members are added to a group discussion one at a time (like a stepladder); The existing group members listen to each new member's thoughts, ideas, and recommendations; then the group shares the ideas and suggestions that it had already considered, discusses the new and old ideas, and makes a decision.

stock options
a compensation system that gives employees the right to purchase shares of stock at a set price, even if the value of the stock increases above that price

stockout
the point when a company runs out of finished product

stockout costs
the costs incurred when a company runs out of a product, including transaction costs to replace inventory and the loss of customers' goodwill

storming
the second stage of development, characterized by conflict and disagreement, in which team members disagree over what the team should do and how it should do it

strategic alliance
an agreement in which companies combine key resources, costs, risk, technology, and people

strategic dissonance
a discrepancy between a company's intended strategy and the strategic actions managers take when implementing that strategy

strategic group
a group of companies within an industry against which top managers compare, evaluate, and benchmark strategic threats and opportunities

strategic leadership
the ability to anticipate, envision, maintain flexibility, think strategically, and work with others to initiate changes that will create a positive future for an organization

strategic objective
a more specific goal that unifies company-wide efforts, stretches and challenges the organization, and possesses a finish line and a time frame

strategic plans
overall company plans that clarify how the company will serve customers and position itself against competitors over the next two to five years

strategic reference points
the strategic targets managers use to measure whether a firm has developed the core competencies it needs to achieve a sustainable competitive advantage

structural accommodation
the ability to change organizational structures, policies, and practices in order to meet stretch goals

structured interviews
interviews in which all applicants are asked the same set of standardized questions, usually including situational, behavioral, background, and job-knowledge questions

subjective performance measures
measures of job performance that require someone to judge or assess a worker's performance

suboptimization
performance improvement in one part of an organization but only at the expense of decreased performance in another part

subsidies
government loans, grants, and tax deferments given to domestic companies to protect them from foreign competition

supervised data mining
the process when the user tells the data mining software to look and test for specific patterns and relationships in a data set

supplier dependence
the degree to which a company relies on a supplier because of the importance of the supplier's product to the company and the difficulty of finding other sources of that product

suppliers
companies that provide material, human, financial, and informational resources to other companies

supportive leadership
a leadership style in which the leader is friendly and approachable to employees, shows concern for employees and their welfare, treats them as equals, and creates a friendly climate

survey feedback
information that is collected by surveys from organizational members and then compiled, disseminated, and used to develop action plans for improvement

sustainable competitive advantage
a competitive advantage that other companies have tried unsuccessfully to duplicate and have, for the moment, stopped trying to duplicate

T

tactical plans
plans created and implemented by middle managers that specify how the company will use resources, budgets, and people over the next six months to two years to accomplish specific goals within its mission

tariff
a direct tax on imported goods

task identity
the degree to which a job, from beginning to end, requires the completion of a whole and identifiable piece of work

task interdependence
the extent to which collective action is required to complete an entire piece of work

task significance
the degree to which a job is perceived to have a substantial impact on others inside or outside the organization

task structure
the degree to which the requirements of a subordinate's tasks are clearly specified

team diversity
the variances or differences in ability, experience, personality, or any other factor on a team

team leaders
managers responsible for facilitating team activities toward goal accomplishment

team level
the average level of ability, experience, personality, or any other factor on a team

teamwork
collaboration between managers and nonmanagers, across business functions, and between companies, customers, and suppliers

technical skills
the ability to apply the specialized procedures, techniques, and knowledge required to get the job done

technological discontinuity
the phase of an innovation stream in which a scientific advance or unique combination of existing technologies creates a significant breakthrough in performance or function

technological lockout
the inability of a company to competitively sell its products because it relied on old technology or a nondominant design

technological substitution
the purchase of new technologies to replace older ones

technology
the knowledge, tools, and techniques used to transform input into output

technology cycle
a cycle that begins with the "birth" of a new technology and ends when that technology reaches its limits and is replaced by a newer, substantially better technology

televised/videotaped speeches and meetings
speeches and meetings originally made to a smaller audience that are either simultaneously broadcast to other locations in the company or videotaped for subsequent distribution and viewing

temporal immediacy
the time between an act and the consequences the act produces

testing
the systematic comparison of different product designs or design iterations

threat of new entrants
measure of the degree to which barriers to entry make it easy or difficult for new companies to get started in an industry

threat of substitute products or services
measure of the ease with which customers can find substitutes for an industry's products or services

top managers
executives responsible for the overall direction of the organization

total quality management (TQM)
an integrated, organization-wide strategy for improving product and service quality

trade barriers
government-imposed regulations that increase the cost and restrict the number of imported goods

traditional work group
a group composed of two or more people who work together to achieve a shared goal

training
developing the skills, experience, and knowledge employees need to perform their jobs or improve their performance

trait theory
a leadership theory that holds that effective leaders possess a similar set of traits or characteristics

traits
relatively stable characteristics, such as abilities, psychological motives, or consistent patterns of behavior

transactional leadership
leadership based on an exchange process, in which followers are rewarded for good performance and punished for poor performance

transformational leadership
leadership that generates awareness and acceptance of a group's purpose and mission and gets employees to see beyond their own needs and self-interests for the good of the group

transition management team (TMT)
a group of 8 to 12 people whose full-time job is to manage and coordinate a company's change process

two-factor authentication
authentication based on what users know, such as a password and what they have in their possession, such as a secure ID card or key

U

uncertainty
the extent to which managers can understand or predict which environmental changes and trends will affect their businesses

underreward
a form of inequity in which you are getting fewer outcomes relative to inputs than your referent is getting

unethical charismatics
charismatic leaders who control and manipulate followers, do what is best for themselves instead of their organizations, want to hear only positive feedback, share only information that is beneficial to themselves, and have moral standards that put their interests before everyone else's

unfreezing
getting the people affected by change to believe that change is needed

Union of South American Nations (UNASUR)
a regional trade agreement between the former Mercosur nations, the Andean Community, and Guyana, Suriname, and Chile

unity of command
a management principle that workers should report to just one boss

unrelated diversification
creating or acquiring companies in completely unrelated businesses

unstructured interviews
interviews in which interviewers are free to ask the applicants anything they want

unsupervised data mining
the process when the user simply tells the data mining software to uncover whatever patterns and relationships it can find in a data set

upward communication
communication that flows from lower to higher levels in an organization

V

valence
the attractiveness or desirability of a reward or outcome

validation
the process of determining how well a selection test or procedure predicts future job performance; the better or more accurate the prediction of future job performance, the more valid a test is said to be

valuable resources
resources that allow companies to improve their efficiency and effectiveness

value
customer perception that the product quality is excellent for the price offered

variable interval reinforcement schedules
an intermittent schedule in which the time between a behavior and the following consequences varies around a specified average

variable ratio reinforcement schedule
an intermittent schedule in which consequences are delivered following a different number of behaviors, sometimes more and sometimes less, that vary around a specified average number of behaviors

variation
a deviation in the form, condition, or appearance of a product from the quality standard for that product

virtual organization
an organization that is part of a network in which many companies share skills, costs, capabilities, markets, and customers to collectively solve customer problems or provide specific products or services

virtual private network (VPN)
software that securely encrypts data sent by employees outside the company network, decrypts the data when they arrive within the company computer network, and does the same when data are sent back to employees outside the network

virtual team
a team composed of geographically and/or organizationally dispersed coworkers who use telecommunication and information technologies to accomplish an organizational task

virus
a program or piece of code that, without your knowledge, attaches itself to other programs on your computer and can trigger anything from a harmless flashing message to the reformatting of your hard drive to a systemwide network shutdown

visible artifacts
visible signs of an organization's culture, such as the office design and layout, company dress code, and company benefits and perks, like stock options, personal parking spaces, or the private company dining room

visionary leadership
leadership that creates a positive image of the future that motivates organizational members and provides direction for future planning and goal setting

voluntary export restraints

voluntarily imposed limits on the number or volume of products exported to a particular country

W

web services

using standardized protocols to describe data from one company in such a way that those data can automatically be read, understood, transcribed, and processed by different computer systems in another company

whistleblowing

reporting others' ethics violations to management or legal authorities

wholly owned affiliates

foreign offices, facilities, and manufacturing plants that are 100 percent owned by the parent company

work sample tests

tests that require applicants to perform tasks that are actually done on the job

work team

a small number of people with complementary skills who hold themselves mutually accountable for pursuing a common purpose, achieving performance goals, and improving interdependent work processes

work-in-process inventories

partially finished goods consisting of assembled component parts

worker readiness

the ability and willingness to take responsibility for directing one's behavior at work

World Trade Organization (WTO)

the successor to GATT; the only international organization dealing with the global rules of trade between nations; Its main function is to ensure that trade flows as smoothly, predictably, and freely as possible

wrongful discharge

a legal doctrine that requires employers to have a job-related reason to terminate employees

Name Index

ExlService Holdings, 349
Exxon, 205

F

Facebook, 4, 46, 87, 213, 291, 356, 478, 504
Family and Medical Leave Act (FMLA), 43, 327, 329
Family Dollar Stores, 377
Family Feud, 224
Fandray, Dayton, 80
Farnsworth, Philo T., 190
Fast Company, 423, 429
Fatwire, 461
Faxon, Roger, 17, 18
Fayol, Henri, 5, 10
Federal Aviation Administration (FAA), 483
Federal Reserve, 41
Feldman, Alan, 472
Fiedler, 412–416, 419, 422
FiOS, 51
Fitlogic, 121
Folley, Greg, 12
Foo Fighters, 250
Food and Drug Administration, 47–48
Ford, 45, 202, 529, 538, 540
Ford Fusion, 167
Ford, Henry, 183
Ford Motor Company, 8
Fortune 500, 69, 83, 91, 367, 502
Fortune magazine, 26, 127, 325
Fosamax, 249
Fowler, Geoffrey, 231
Fox News, 45, 230
Framestore, 277
Frampton, Jez, 404
Fremantle Media, 224
Friedman, Milton, 83–84
Friedman, Thomas, 215
Frito-Lay, 90
Fuller, Ed, 479
Funtleyder, Les, 249

G

G-Star, 209
Galleon Group, 69–70
Ganahl, Heidi, 62, 435
Garden Sensation, 170
Garmin, 226
Garner, Don, 67
Gates, Bill, 52

Gawande, Atul, 301
GE Aircraft Engines, 423
Genentech, 163
General Aviation Revitalization Act, 289
General Electric (GE), 86, 91, 181, 193, 201–202, 205, 291
General Motors (GM), 10, 107, 136, 166, 205, 280–281, 417–418, 489, 529
Givenchy, 525
Goizueta, Roberto, 485
The Golden Compass, 277
Goldman Sachs, 308, 449
GolinHarris Change, 82–83
Good Housekeeping Seal of Approval, 532
Google, 4, 88, 148, 149, 150, 195, 213, 296, 368, 418, 439–440, 462, 485, 513, 518
Google Music, 150
Great Depression, 86
Greenfield, Jerry, 91
Groupon, 213–214
Guardian News and Media, 461
Gupta, Yogesh, 461
Gutenberg, 183

H

H&M, 223
Hamilton Sundstrand, 255
Hammer, Michael, 197, 272–273, 272–274
Handy Andy, 155
Hapburg, Richard, 390
Harrah's casinos, 45
Harris Interactive, 11
Harry Potter, 277
Harry Potter and the Deathly Hallows, 277
Harvard Medical School, 518
Hasbro, 152
Hastings, Reed, 3
Hatch, Jeff, 266
Hay Group, 349
Hazard Analysis and Critical Control Points, 47–48
HBO, 3
HCL Technologies, 5
HEAT (Health Care Fraud Prevention and Enforcement Action Teams), 509
Heidrick & Struggles (H & S), 427
Herman Miller, 489
Herman Miller Aeron, 276
Hersey, 412, 420–422
Hershey Co., 215–216
Hewlett-Packard (HP), 4, 14, 126, 342
Hilgert, Ray, 449

Hill, Allen, 17
Hill, Linda, 22–24
Hillandale Farms, 475
Hitachi Automotive Systems, 166
Hoffman, Michael, 79
Hofstede, Geert, 231, 232
Holden Outerwear, 209, 243, 317
Hollenbeck, John, 310
Home Depot, 57, 154, 155, 156, 158, 501, 541
Honda, 84, 91, 153, 201, 202, 205
Honda Civic, 167
Honda FCX Clarity, 205
Hooters, 324
Hoover, 45
Horan, Paul, 504
Hormel Foods, 162
Hostmann, Bill, 367
HRIS (Human Resource Information System), 352
HSBC, 83
Hsieh, Tony, 54
The Human Equation: Building Profits by Putting People First, 24
Hyland-Savage, Gail, 330
Hyundai, 201–202

I

IBM, 46, 52, 74, 75, 367
IBM Credit, 273
iCloud, 150, 403
iComp, 183–185
iComp Index, 183–184
IdeaMax, 191
iMac, 403
Immelt, Jeffrey, 91
Imperial Sugar, 116
InBev, 163
Inception, 277
Independent Carton Group (ICG), 279
Infoseek, 147
Infosys, 215
Intel, 17, 183–185, 502
International Organization for Standardization (ISO), 531–532
International Space Station, 115
International Telecommunication Union (ITU), 188
Internet Explorer, 513
Internet Phone, 46
iPad, 122, 148, 150
iPad 2, 36, 278, 403, 518

iPhone, 36, 106, 149, 150, 182, 183, 195, 227, 298
iPhone 3G, 518
iPhone 4, 51, 52, 89, 403, 442–443, 518
iPod, 17, 36, 52, 149, 403, 502, 515, 543
iPod Touch, 51, 149
ISO, 531–532
iTunes, 148, 150

J

J. D. Power and Associates, 201–202, 529
J. J. Keller & Associates, Inc., 335
Jack Resnick & Sons, 141
JCPenney, 55, 296, 406
Jeopardy!, 250
Jernhusen AB, 182
Jobs, Steve, 51, 89, 147, 403–404, 443
John Jay College, 141
Johns Hopkins University, 21
Johnson & Johnson (J&J), 12, 86
Johnson, Doug, 294
Jones Apparel, 121
Journal for Quality and Participation, 532–533
Journal of Applied Psychology, 7

K

Kahn, Robert, 190
Kaiser Permanente, 518
Kayak.com, 385
Kelleher, Herb, 56
Kelly, Kevin, 427
Kempa, Kevin, 12
Kennedy, John F., 115
Kentucky Fried Chicken (KFC), 226
Kenzo, 525
Kerr, Steve, 308
Kessler, Eric, 3
Kew Gardens Principles, 78
Kia, 45
Kilburg, Richard, 21
Kimberly-Clark, 113
Kindermusik International, 116
Kindler, Jeffrey, 8
King, Jan, 118
Kmart, 155
Knox, David, 330
Kohlberg, Lawrence, 76, 77
Komatsu, 471
Kors, Michael, 516
Kotter, John, 199–201

Mount Everest, 491

Mountain Safety Research, 163

Mouton, 421

Movie Gallery, 187

Muhlhauser, Craig, 199–201

Mulally, Alan, 8–9

MySpace, 87

N

Nalco, 38–39

Napier, Sharon, 56

NASA, 115

National Business Ethics Survey, 2009, 79–80

National Center for Employee Ownership, 350

National Football League (NFL), 441

National Institute of Standards and Technology (NIST), 532, 533

National Labor Relations Board (NLRB), 326, 329

National Transportation Safety Board (NTSB), 310

Nayar, Vineet, 5

NBC, 45

Nestlé, 163

Netflix, 3–4, 148, 187

New York Times, 167, 215

Nextel, 169

Nick's Pizza & Pub, 323–324

Nilekani, Nandan, 215

Nintendo's Wii game, 172

Nissan, 109

Nissan Leaf, 205

Nobel Prize, 83

Nokia-Siemens Networks, 215

Nook Simple Touch, 42, 171

Nooyi, Indra, 84, 406

Nordstrom, 121

Nortel, 78

Novo Nordisk, 54

Numi Organic Tea, 521

O

Obama, Michelle, 173

Oberhelman, Doug, 471

Occupational Safety and Health Act (OSHA), 326, 329

Ocean Spray Cranberries, Inc., 113

Office of Consumer Affairs, 485

Okabe, Toru, 46

Olofsson, Lars, 151

O'Malley, Stephen, 375

1-800-Got-Junk, 127

100 Best Companies to Work for in America, 26

Oreck, 45

Orlando Marriott World Center, 504

OS X, 403

Otis, 255

P

Page, Larry, 418

Panizza, Ruben, 514

Pantene, 259

Parsons, George, 449

Partners + Napier, 56

Patagonia, 9

Paycycle, 12

PayPal, 6

PC Connection, 126

PC Magazine, 153

Pearce, Terry, 454

Pelton, Jack, 15

Penske Automotive Group, 349

Penske, Roger, 349

Penske Truck Leasing, 515

Pentagon, 38

Pentium, II, III, 4, 183, 185

Pep Boys, 349

Pepsi, 45, 173, 237, 384

PepsiCo, 406, 433, 474

People for the Ethical Treatment of Animals (PETA), 49

Peto, Richard, 7

Petrucciani, Tony, 390

Pfeffer, Jeffrey, 24

Pfizer, 8, 163, 249

Pforzheimer, Andy, 496

PGA golf tournament, 503

Pink, 250

Pioneer Fund, 93

Pixar Studios, 147

Pizza Hut, 226

Plant Fantasies, 141, 466

Plants vs. Zombies, 196

PlayStation 2 (PS2), 194

PlayStation, 250

PlayStation 3 (PS3), 36, 169, 172, 194

Pordon, Tony, 349

Porsche, 202, 529

Porter, Michael, 165, 167, 169

Post-it notes, 162, 181

Pratt & Whitney, 255–256

Pregnancy Discrimination Act, 327, 329

Pretty Good Privacy (PGP), 512

The Price Is Right, 224

Prime View International, 42

Princess Leia, 183

Prius, 107

Procter & Gamble, 259, 260, 291

Progressive Insurance, 477, 506

Prokhorov, Mikhail, 432

Prozac, 249

Prudential Relocation Management, 235

PSA Peugeot-Citroen, 166

Publishers Weekly, 167

Puckett, John, 306

Puflea, Susan, 83

Q

Qualcomm, 42

QVC, 121

QWERTY keyboard, 188

R

Raju, Ramalinga, 69

Razor's Edge (RE), 491

Red Door Interactive, 534

Red Lobster, 169

Reengineering the Corporation, 272

REI Adventures, 163

Reifel, Joe, 477

Reinboth, Gary, 52

Research in Motion (RIM), 195, 230

Reuters, 16

Reynolds, Beverly, 293

Riccitiello, John, 5

Ricks, David, 234

Ringlemann, Maximilian, 293

Rite Aid, 506–507

Robbin, Jeff, 403

Robert Bosch GmbH, 166

Roche, 163

Rosedale, Philip, 479

Royal Dutch Shell, 205

Royal, Mark, 349

Ryan, Sue, 31

Ryder Cup, 309

Ryla Teleservices, 198

S

SAIC-GM-Wuling, 281

SAIC Motor Corporation, 280

Sam's Club, 9

Samsung, 36, 160, 278

San Francisco Giants, 510

Sandbox, The, 198

Santa Claus, 457

Santos, Ltd., 330

Sarbanes-Oxley Act of 2002, 80

SAS (Statistical Analysis System), 367–368

Satyam Computer, 69

Savills, 295

S.C. Johnson, 370

Scharffen Berger Chocolate Maker, 262

Schlage Lock Company, 115

Schmidt, Eric, 439

Scholastic Aptitude Test (SAT), 82, 336

Schultz, Howard, 121, 213

Schwarz, Jeff, 460

Scotchgard, 162

Scott, Lee, 53

Scoutmob, 213

Scudamore, Brian, 127

Search Products & User Experience, 462

Sears Roebuck, 86

Seinfeld, 250

Serena Software, 16

Shakira, 250

Shanghai General Motors, 281

Shapiro, Paul, 49

Shell Oil, 367

Sherer, Paul, 67

Sherwin-Williams, 538

Shetty, Ajit, 12

Siemens AG, 166

Sierra Club, 36

Sigma-Aladrich, 276

Sikorsky, 255–256

Single Source Systems, 390

Singulair, 249

Six Sigma, 181, 476

Skype, 6

Slocum, Tyson, 49

Small Business Research Board, 41–42

Smiley, Tavis, 432

Social Security, 118

V

V-J Day, 236
VAIO Business Group, 250, 261
Valpak Direct Marketing Systems, 391
Van Houten, 215
van Musschenbroek, Pieter, 190
Van Natta, Owen, 87
Vaynerchuk, Gary, 17
Verizon, 46, 51, 169
Virgin, 479
Vizio, 36
VoIP (Voice over Internet Protocol), 46, 50–51
Volkswagen, 529
Volvo Penta, 226
Vonage, 46
Vuitton, Louis, 525, 526

W

Waffenschmidt, John, 35
Walgreens, 547
Walkman, 36, 250
Wall Street Journal, 7, 16, 28, 38, 231
Walmart, 9, 35, 52, 53, 83–84, 85, 209, 213, 214, 446, 515, 535
Walt Disney Company, 115, 147–148
Walton, Sam, 52, 53
Warner Bros. Pictures, 188, 277
Waste Management, 35–36, 384
Watson, Thomas J., Sr., 52
Web Phone, 46
Weber, Max, 428, 477–478
Webster's New World Dictionary, 453
Wells Fargo, 83
Wendy's, 10, 170, 526
Weyco, 67
Wheatley, Marie, 49
Wheeler, Brian, 43
Whinney, Joe, 98, 176
Whitehead, Jay, 67

W (continued)

Whittle, Sir Frank, 190
Whole Foods, 292
Wi-Fi, 513
Wii, 172
William J. Clinton Foundation, 173
Wilson, Mark, 198
Windows 7, 251
Windows 8 phones, 183
Winnie-the-Pooh, 147
Wintek, 278
Wired Equivalent Privacy (WEP) security protocol, 513
Wis, Ramona, 404
Wolfgang, Mel, 333
Wong, Mary, 276
Woolcock, Keith, 439
World Heart Federation, 173
World of Warcraft (WOW), 44–45
World Trade Center, 38
World Trade Organization (WTO), 217, 218, 219
Worn Again, 541
Wright County Egg, 475
Wyeth, 8, 163

X

Xbox, 199
Xbox 360, 36, 37, 52, 169, 172
XEL Communications, 306
Xirallic, 539

Y

Yahoo!, 345, 511
Yamaha, 545
Yellow Corporation, 459
YouTube, 491, 501

Z

Zaffino, Ian, 168
Zappos.com, 53, 54
Zollars, Bill, 459

Subject Index

A

A-type conflict, 129, 304
Absenteeism, 270
Absolute comparisons, 122
Accommodative strategy, 90
Achievement-oriented leadership, 418
Acquaintance time, 458
Acquisition, 159
   portfolio strategy, 159
Action plan, 110
Active listening, 453
Adaptability, 53
Adaptability screening, 235
Adaptive strategies, 167–168
   analyzers, 168
   defenders, 167–168
   prospectors, 168
   reactors, 168
Address terms, 457
Adverse impact, 328
Advocacy groups, 48
   media advocacy, 49
   product boycott, 49
   public communications, 49
   specific environment component, 48–49
Affective conflict, 304
Affective culture, 456
Albemarle Paper Co. v. Moody, 332
Alderfer's ERG Theory, 371, 374
Ambiguity, 59–61
Analyzers, 168
APEC. *See* Asia-Pacific Economic Cooperation (APEC)
Application forms, 334–335
Appointment time, 457
Aptitude tests, 336
Arrivers, 20–21
ASEAN. *See* Association of Southeast Asian Nations (ASEAN)
Asia-Pacific Economic Cooperation (APEC), 218, 220–221, 222
Assemble-to-order operations, 539

Association of Southeast Asian Nations (ASEAN), 218, 220–221, 222
Association or affinity patterns, 509–510
Attack, in direct competition, 171–172
Attribution theory, 443
Authentication of information, 511
Authority, 261
   centralization, 263–264
   chain of command, 261
   decentralization, 25, 263–264
   delegation of, 262–263
   line authority, 262
   staff authority, 262
   standardization, 264
   unity of command, 261
Authorization of information, 511
Autonomy, 268
   of teams, 296–298
Average aggregate inventory, 541
Avoidance learning, 384
Avoidance strategy, 230

B

Background checks, 335–336
Balanced scorecard, 482–484
Baldrige National Quality Award, 532–533, 534
Bar code, 507–508
Bargaining power
   of buyers, 166
   of suppliers, 166
Base fine, 71–72
BCG matrix, 160–162
Behavior control, 478, 482
Behavior observation scale (BOS), 346
Behavioral addition, 55
Behavioral informality, 275–277
   behavioral formality, 275
   open office systems, 275
   private spaces, 275
   shared spaces, 275

objective control, 478, 481

output control, 478, 482

self-control, 480–481, 482

political risks, 230

process, 472–477

benchmarking, 473

concurrent control, 475

control loss, 475

corrective action, 474

cybernetic feasibility, 476

dynamic, cybernetic process, 474

feedback, 475

feedforward control, 475

regulation costs, 476

standards, 473

standards comparison, 473–474

Conventional level of moral development, 76

Cooperation, political risks of, 230

Cooperative contracts, 224–225

franchise, 225–226

licensing agreement, 225

Core capabilities, 153

Core change coalition, 199

Core firms, 154

Corporate-level strategies, 158–164

grand strategy, 162–164

portfolio strategy, 158–164

acquisitions, 159

BCG matrix, 160–162

cash cows, 160–162

diversification, 159

dogs, 160–162

question marks, 160–162

related diversification, 162

stars, 160–162

unrelated diversification, 160

Corporate portals, 514

Cost leadership, 167

Counseling, 449–450

Counterproductive behaviors, integrity tests, 81

Creative work environments, 190–191

Cross-cultural communication, 455

acquaintance time, 458

address terms, 457

affective cultures, 456

appointment time, 457

discussion time, 457–458

monochronic cultures, 457

neutral cultures, 456

polychronic cultures, 457

schedule time, 457

Cross-functional teams, 298

Cross-training, 292

Culpability score, 71

Culture

affective cultures, 456

awareness of differences, 231–233

cross-cultural training, 233–234, 236–237

cultural simulations, 234

global business concerns, 231–233

individualism, 232

making a new culture, 57

masculinity and femininity, 232

monochronic cultures, 457

national culture, 231

neutral cultures, 456

organization's culture, 201

orientation, 232

polychronic cultures, 457

power distance, 231

uncertainty avoidance, 232

Customers

customer focus, 533–534

customer satisfaction, 534

defections, 485–486

departmentalization, 256, 257

handling disgruntled customers, 547–549

proactive monitoring, 45

reactive monitoring, 44

specific environment component, 44–45

trade barriers and trade agreements and, 221–222

work teams and customer satisfaction, 291

Customs classification, 217

Cybernetic feasibility, 476

Cybernetic process, 474

D

Data clusters, 510

Data encryption, 512

Data mining, 509

Data warehouse, 509

De-forming stage of team development, 306–307

De-norming stage of team development, 306

De-storming stage of team development, 306

Decentralization

of authority, 263–264

management practices, 25

E

E-mail, 452

Economics

    economic order quantity, 543–544

    economic responsibility, 87

    economic value added, 484

    general environment, 42

    social responsibility and economic performance, 90–92

EDI. *See* Electronic data interchange (EDI)

Effectiveness, 5

Efficiency, 5

EIS. *See* Executive information system (EIS)

Electronic data interchange (EDI), 515–516

Electronic scanner, 508

Emotional stability of leaders, 407, 408

Empathetic listening, 453–454

Employee stock ownership plan (ESOP), 350

Employees. *See also* Human resources

    benefits, 351

    decision-making involvement, 53

    Employee Assistance Program, 449–450

    employee involvement teams, 296–297

    empowerment, 537–538

    selection of, 333–338, 340–341

        application forms and résumés, 334–335

        background checks, 335–336

        interviews, 338, 340

        references, 335–336

        tests, 336–338, 339–340

        validation, 334

    separations, 352–355

        downsizing, 354

        outplacement services, 354

        terminations, 353

        turnover, 355

        wrongful discharge, 353

Employment benefits, 351–352

Employment references, 335–336

Employment security, management practices, 25

Empowerment, 274

    empowering workers, 274, 537–538

Encoding, 446

Enterprise resource planning (ERP), 521

Entrepreneur role of managers, 16

Environment

    complexity, 38

    creative work environments, 190–191

    environmental change, 37–38

    environmental contingencies, 418–419

    environmental scanning, 50, 154

    external. *See* External environments

    general. *See* General environment

    hostile work environment, 328

    internal. *See* Internal environment

    pollution minimization, 489–490

    resource scarcity, 38–39

    specific environment, 41, 44–50

        advocacy groups, 48–50

        competitors, 45–46

        customers, 44–45

        industry regulation, 47–48

        suppliers, 46–47

    uncertainty, 39

    work environment

        changing, 204

        creative, 190–191

        hostile work environment, 328

Equity theory, 375–379

    distributive justice, 379

    inputs, 375–376

    integrated model, 394

    motivating with, 378–379

    outcome/input (O/I) ratio, 376

    outcomes, 376

    overreward, 376

    procedural justice, 379

    reaction to perceived inequity, 376–378

    referents, 376

    underreward, 376

ERG Theory, 371, 374

ERP. *See* Enterprise resource planning (ERP)

ESOP. *See* Employee stock ownership plan (ESOP)

Ethics, 68. *See also* Social responsibility

    baseline, 94–97

    decision-making

        code of ethics, 78

        concentration of effect, 75

        ethical climate, 79–80

        ethical intensity, 74–76

        ethics training, 78–79

        influences on, 74–77

        magnitude of consequences, 75

        moral development, 76–77

        practical steps, 77–80

        probability of effect, 75

        proximity of effect, 75

Ethics (*Continued*)

    social consensus, 75

    temporal immediacy, 75

  ethical behavior, 69

  ethical charismatics, 429

  ethical responsibility, 88

  integrity tests, 81

  management jobs and, 68–70

  office scavenging, 276

  responding to tragedy, 92

  unethical behavior, discerning, 93–94

  unethical charismatics, 429

  U.S. Sentencing Commission Guidelines for Organizations, 70–74

    base fine, 71–72

    culpability score, 71

    level of offense, 71

    offenses covered, 71

    overview, 70–73

    punishment, 71–73

  whistleblowing, 80

Evaluation apprehension, 134

Executive information system (EIS), 514

Expatriate, 233

  cross-cultural training, 233–234, 236–237

  language training, 233–234

  spouse, family, and dual-career issues, 235

Expectancy theory, 380–383

  expectancy, 380

  instrumentality, 380–381

  integrated model, 394

  motivating with, 382

  valence, 380

Expenses

  cost leadership, 167

  inventory maintenance, 542–543

    holding cost, 543

    ordering cost, 542

    setup cost, 542

    stockout cost, 543

  regulation costs, 476

Experiential approach of innovation management, 192–193

Expert system, 517

Exporting, 224

External environments, 36

  advocacy groups, 48–49

  changing environments, 36–40

    dynamic environments, 37

    environmental complexity, 38, 39–40

    punctuated equilibrium theory, 37–38

    resource scarcity, 38–39, 40

    stable environments, 37

    uncertainty, 39

  competitors, 45–46

  customers, 44–45

  environmental scanning, 50

  general environment, 40–44

    economy, 41–42

    political/legal component, 43–44

    sociocultural component, 42–43

    specific environment, 41

    technology, 42

  industry regulation, 47–48

  interpreting environmental factors, 50–51

  opportunities, acting on, 51

  suppliers, 46–47

  threats, acting on, 51

Extinction, 385

Extranet, 515

Extrinsic rewards, 372–373

Extroversion of leaders, 409

F

Fakelaki, 48

Feedback, 268

  360-degree feedback, 347–348

  constructive, 454

  control, 475

  destructive, 454

  feedback to sender, 446

  immediate, 455

  job performance, 346–348

  performance feedback, 391

  problem-oriented, 455

  specific, 455

  survey feedback, 461

Feedforward control, 475

Fiedler's contingency theory, 412–416

  Least Preferred Coworker (LPC) scale, 413–414

  matching leadership styles to situations, 415–416

  situational favorableness, 414

Field simulation training, 234

Figurehead role of managers, 15

Financial control perspective

  budgets, 484–485

  cash flows, 484–485

  economic value added, 484–485

Finished goods inventory, 540–541

Firewall, 511

Firm-level strategies, 169–172
    direct competition, 169–173
    direct competition strategic moves, 169, 171–172
        attack, 171–172
        market commonality, 169–170
        resource similarity, 169–170
        response, 171–172
First-line managers, 12
    jobs and responsibilities summary, 11, 12–13
    responsibilities, 12–13
First-mover advantage, 503–504
Flexible benefit plans, 351–352
Flow, 191
Focus strategy, 167
Formal communication channel, 447
Forming stage of team development, 305
Four-fifths (80 percent) rule, 328
Franchise, 225
Freedom in the work environment, 191
Functional departmentalization, 254
Functional turnover, 355
Fundamental attribution error, 443–444

G

Gainsharing, 312
GATT. *See* General Agreement on Tariffs and Trade (GATT)
General Agreement on Tariffs and Trade (GATT), 218
General Electric workout, 201–202
General environment, 40–44
    economy, 41–42
    political/legal component, 43–44
    sociocultural component, 42–43
    specific environment, 41
    technology, 42
General mental ability test, 8
Generational change, 194
Geographic departmentalization, 256–258
Global business, 214
    cooperative contracts, 224–226
    direct foreign investment, 215
    exporting, 224
    global new ventures, 227
    impact of, 215–216
    multinational corporations, 215
    new ventures, 227
    strategic alliances, 226–227
    trade agreements, 218–221
    trade barriers, 216–217, 221–222

    wholly owned affiliates, 227
Global management
    best business climate, 228–231
        growing markets, 228–229
        office/manufacturing location, 229
        political risk, 230
        purchasing power, 228
    global business forms, 223–228
        cooperative contracts, 224–226
        exporting, 224
        global new ventures, 227
        strategic alliances, 226–227
        wholly owned affiliates, 227
    global consistency, 222–223
    how to go global, 222–227
    where to go global, 228
        best business climate, 228–231
        cross-cultural training, 233–234, 236–237
        cultural differences, 231–233
        global business forms, 223–228
        global consistency, 222–223
        international assignments, 233–235
        language, 233–234
        local adaptation, 223
        spouse, family, and dual-career issues, 235
Goals, 390
    distal goals, 111–112
    goal commitment, 109–110
    goal-setting theory, 390–393
        goal acceptance, 391
        goal difficulty, 391
        goal specificity, 390–391
        integrated model, 394
        motivating with, 391–393
        performance feedback, 391
    proximal goals, 111–112
    setting goals, 108–109
    SMART, 109, 308, 392
    stretch goals, 308
    for team effectiveness, 307–309
Gossip chain, 448–449
Government import standards, 217
Grand strategy, 162–164
    growth strategy, 163
    recovery, 164
    retrenchment strategy, 164
    stability strategy, 164
Grapevine, 448–449

"Green" products, 90

Greenwashing, 83

Griggs v. Duke Power Co., 332

Groupthink, 127, 293–294

Growth strategy, 164

H

Hearing, 453

Hersey and Blanchard's situational leadership® theory, 420–422

Hierarchy of Needs, 371

Hiring, selective, management practices, 25

Honesty of leaders, 407

Horizontal communication, 448

Hostile work environment, 328

Human resources. *See also* Employees

    compensation, 349–352

        decisions, 349–351

        employment benefits, 351–352

    employee separations, 352–355

        downsizing, 354

        outplacement services, 354

        terminations, 353

        turnover, 355

        wrongful discharge, 353

    employment legislation, 324–330

        adverse impact, 328

        background, 324–325

        bona fide occupational qualification, 326

        disparate treatment, 328

        federal employment laws, 326–327

        four-fifths (80 percent) rule, 328

        hostile work environment, 328

        quid pro quo sexual harassment, 328

        sexual harassment, 328–329

    human resource management, 324

    performance appraisal, 344–349

    recruiting, 330

        external recruiting, 332

        internal recruiting, 332

        job analysis, 330–332

        job description, 331

        job specifications, 331

    selection of employees, 333–338, 340–341

        application forms and résumés, 334–335

        background checks, 335–336

        interviews, 338, 340

        references, 335–336

        tests, 336–338, 339–340

        validation, 334

        training, 341–344

Human skills for managers, 19

I

Idealized influence, 430

Imperfectly imitable resources, 150

Incremental change, 188

Independent demand systems, 545

Individualism-collectivism, 309

Individualized consideration, 430

Industry-level strategies, 165–169

    adaptive strategies, 167–168

    five industry forces, 165–166

        bargaining power of buyers, 166

        bargaining power of suppliers, 166

        character of the rivalry, 165

        threat of new entrants, 165–166

        threat of substitute products or services, 166

    positioning strategies, 167

Industry regulation, 47

    specific environment component, 47–48

Informal communication channel (grapevine), 448–449

Information, 503

    capturing, 507–508

        bar codes, 507–508

        electronic scanners, 507–508

        optical character recognition, 508

        radio frequency identification tags, 508

    competitive advantage, sustaining, 504–506

    external access and sharing, 515–516

        electronic data interchange, 515

        extranet, 515

        Web services, 515

    first-move advantage, 503–504

    information pipeline, 518–519

    informational roles of managers, 15–16

        disseminator, 16

        monitor, 16

        spokesperson, 16

    internal access and sharing, 514–515

        corporate portals, 514

        executive information system, 514

        intranets, 514

Moore's law, 502

    processing information, 508–510

        association or affinity patterns, 509–510

        data clusters, 510

        data mining, 509

Leading, 8–9

Learned Needs Theory, 371

Learning-based planning, 112–113

Least Preferred Coworker (LPC) scale, 413–414

Legal component, general environment, 43–44

Legal responsibility, 87–88

Legislation, employment, 324–330

    adverse impact, 328

    bona fide occupational qualification, 326

    disparate treatment, 328

    federal employment laws, 326–327

    four-fifths (80 percent) rule, 328

    hostile work environment, 328

    quid pro quo sexual harassment, 328

    sexual harassment, 328–329

Liaison role of managers, 15

Licensing agreement, 225

Line authority, 262

Line function, 262

Listening, 452–454

    active listening, 453

    empathetic listening, 453–454

    hearing, 453

Local adaptation, 223

M

Maastricht Treaty, 218, 222

Magnitude of consequences, from ethical decisions, 75

Make-to-order operations, 538–539

Make-to-stock operations, 539

Management, 5

    competitive advantage through people, 24–27

    first-year transition, 22–24

    functions, 5–10

        controlling, 9

        leading, 8–9

        organizing, 8

        planning, 6

    importance of, 24–26

    meta-analysis, 7–8

    responsibilities, 5

    self-management, 137

Management by objectives (MBO), 116, 117

Managers

    arrivers, 20–21

    derailers, 20–21

    ethics, 68–70

    first-line managers, 12

    jobs and responsibilities summary, 11, 12–13

        responsibilities, 12–13

    leaders vs., 405–406

    middle managers, 12

        jobs and responsibilities summary, 11, 12

        responsibilities, 12

    requirements for, 18–20

        first-year transition, 22–24

        mistakes managers make, 20–22

        skills needed, 18–20

    roles, decisional, 16–18

        disturbance handler, 17

        entrepreneur, 16

        example, 27

        negotiator, 18

        resource allocator, 17

    roles, informational, 15–16

        disseminator, 16

        monitor, 16

        spokesperson, 16

    roles, interpersonal, 15

        figurehead, 15

        leader, 15

        liaison, 15

    skills needed, 18–20

        conceptual, 19–20

        human, 19

        motivation to manage, 19

        technical, 19

    team leaders, 13

        jobs and responsibilities summary, 11, 13–14

        responsibilities, 13–14

    top managers, 10–11

        jobs and responsibilities summary, 11

        responsibilities, 10–11

Manufacturing operations, 538–545

    assemble-to-order operations, 539

    inventory, 539–545

    location, choosing of, 229

    make-to-order operations, 538–539

    make-to-stock operations, 539

Market commonality, 169–170

Market, growing markets, 228–229

Maslow's Hierarchy of Needs, 371

Materials requirement planning, 544–545

Matrix departmentalization, 259–260

    complex matrix, 260

    simple matrix, 260

Maximize decisions, 126

MBO. *See* Management by objectives (MBO)

McClelland's Learned Needs Theory, 371

Mechanistic organization, 271

Media advocacy, 49

Meta-analysis, 8

    purpose of, 7

    uses for, 7–8

Middle managers, 12

    jobs and responsibilities summary, 12

    responsibilities, 12

Milestones, 192–193

Modular organization, 277–278

Monitor role of managers, 16

Monochronic culture, 457

Moore's law, 502

Moral development, 76–77

    conventional level, 76

    postconventional level, 76

    preconventional level, 76

Motivation, 368

    direction of effort, 368

    effort and performance, 369–370

    equity theory, 375–379

        distributive justice, 379

        inputs, 375–376

        integrated model, 394

        motivating with, 378–379

        outcome/input (O/I) ratio, 376

        outcomes, 376

        overreward, 376

        procedural justice, 379

        reaction to perceived inequity, 376–378

        referents, 376

        underreward, 376

    expectancy theory, 380–383

        expectancy, 380

        instrumentality, 380–381

        integrated model, 394

        motivating with, 382

        valence, 380

    extrinsic rewards, 372–373

    goal-setting theory, 390–393

        goal acceptance, 391

        goal, 392. *See also* Goals

        goal difficulty, 391

        goal specificity, 391

        integrated model, 394

        motivating with, 391–393

        performance feedback, 391

    initiation of effort, 368

    inspirational, 430

    integrated model, 393–394

    internal motivation, 267

    intrinsic rewards, 373

    management for managers, 19

    need satisfaction, 370–372

    persistence of effort, 368

    reinforcement theory, 383–387, 389–390

        extinction, 385

        integrated model, 394

        motivating with, 387, 389

        negative reinforcement, 384–385

        positive reinforcement, 384

        punishment, 385

        reinforcement contingencies, 383

        rewards, 388–389

        schedule of reinforcement, 383

        schedules for delivering reinforcement, 385–387

    with the basics, 373–374

Multifactor productivity, 527–529

Multifunctional teams, 193

Multinational corporation, 215

N

NAFTA. *See* North American Free Trade Agreement (NAFTA)

National culture, 231

Needs, 370

    Alderfer's ERG Theory, 371, 374

    Maslow's Hierarchy of Needs, 371

    McClelland's Learned Needs Theory, 371

    need satisfaction, 370–372

Negative consequences, 132–133

Negative reinforcement, 384–385

Negotiator role of managers, 18

Neutral culture, 456

Noise, 447

Nominal group technique, 130

Nonsubstitutable resources, 150

Nontariff barrier, 217

Nonverbal communication, 450

Normative control, 478–479, 482

Normative decision theory, 422–427

    decision quality and acceptance, 423–427

    decision styles, 422–423

    decision tree, 426

Norming stage of team development, 306

Norms of teams, 300

North American Free Trade Agreement (NAFTA), 218, 219, 222

O

Objective control, 478, 482

Objective performance measures, 346

Office location, choosing of, 229

One-on-one communication, 451–459
    communication mediums, 451–452
    cross-cultural communication, 455–458
    feedback, 454–455
    listening, 452–454

Online discussion forums, 459–460

Open office systems, 275

Operational plans, 116

Operations management, 526
    balancing speed and accuracy, 546–547
    disgruntled customers, 547
    manufacturing operations, 538–545
        assemble-to-order operations, 539
        inventory, 539–545
        make-to-order operations, 538–539
        make-to-stock operations, 539
    operations management, 526
    productivity, 526–529
        importance of, 526–527
        labor productivity, 527
        multifactor productivity, 527–529
        partial productivity, 527
    quality, 529–535
        assurance, 531
        Baldrige National Quality Award, 532–533, 534
        durability, 530
        empathy, 531
        ISO 9000 and 14000, 531–532
        product failure, 530
        product reliability, 530
        responsiveness, 531
        service reliability, 530–531
        serviceability, 530
        tangibles, 531
        total quality management, 533–534
    service operations, 535–538
        empowering workers, 537–538
        service-profit chain, 535–536
        service recovery, 536–537

Opportunistic behavior, 47

Optical character recognition, 508

Options-based planning, 112

Organic organization, 271

Organisation for Economic Cooperation and Development (OECD), 230

Organizational change, 182
    change tools and techniques, 201–203
    leading change, 199–201
    managing resistance to change, 196–203
        change forces, 196
        change intervention, 197
        coercion, 198
        overview, 195–198
        refreezing, 197
        resistance forces, 196
        unfreezing, 197
    people, changing, 204
    work setting change, 204

Organizational culture, internal environments, 52
    changing, 54–56
        behavioral addition, 55
        behavioral substitution, 55
        visible artifacts, 55
    creation and maintenance of
        organizational heroes, 53
        organizational stories, 52
    successful organizational cultures, 53–54
        company mission, 54
        consistent organizational culture, 54

Organizational development, 202, 203

Organizational innovation, 182
    creativity, 182
    innovation streams, 186–189
        design competition, 187
        discontinuous change, 187
        dominant design, 187–188
        incremental change, 188
        technological discontinuity, 186
        technological lockout, 188
        technological substitution, 187
    managing innovation, 189–195
        compression approach, incremental change, 193–195
        creative work environments, 190–191
        experiential approach, discontinuous change, 192–193
        flow psychological state, 191
        sources of innovation, 190–191
    S-curve pattern of innovation, 183–185
    technology cycle, 183

TQM. *See* Total quality management (TQM)

Trade agreements, 218–221

Trade barriers, 216–217

Traditional work group, 296

Training, 341

    competitive advantage through people, 25

    conflict resolution skills, 311

    cross-cultural, 233–234, 236–237

    cross-training, 292

    decision-making skills, 311

    documentary, 234

    e-learning, 343–344

    ethics, 78–79

    evaluations, 344

    field simulation, 234

    human resources, 341–344

    interpersonal skills, 311

    language, 233–234

    methods, 342–344

    objectives and methods, 343

    problem-solving skills, 311

    rater training, 346

    work teams, 311

Trait theory, 406

Traits of leaders, 406–408, 409–410

Transactional leadership, 430–431

Transformational leadership, 429–431

Transition management team (TMT), 202

Twitter, 462

Two-factor authentication, 511

U

UNASUR. *See* Union of South American Nations
    (UNASUR)

Uncertainty, 39

Underreward, 376

Unethical charismatics, 429

Unfreezing, 197

Union of South American Nations (UNASUR), 218, 220

Unity of command, 261

Unrelated diversification, 160

Unsupervised data mining, 509

Upward communication, 448

U.S. Sentencing Commission Guidelines for Organizations,
    70–74

    base fine, 71–72

    culpability score, 71

    level of offense, 71

    offenses covered, 71

    overview, 70

    punishment, 71–73, 81

USAN, 222

V

Valence, 380

Validation of job applicant information, 334

Value, 487

    economic value added, 484–485

    valuable resources, 149

Variation, 534

Virtual organization, 278–280

Virtual private network (VPN), 512

Virtual teams, 298–299

Virus, 512

Visible artifacts, 55

Vision, 200

Visionary leadership, 427–431

    charismatic leadership, 409–410, 428–429

    transactional leadership, 430–431

    transformational leadership, 429–431

Voluntary export restraints, 217

VPN. *See* Virtual private network (VPN)

W

Wages. *See* Compensation

Waste minimization, 489–490

Web services, 515

WEP. *See* Wired Equivalent Privacy (WEP)

Whistleblowing, 80

Wholly owned affiliates, 227

Wired Equivalent Privacy (WEP), 513

Work environment

    changing, 204

    creative, 190–191

    hostile work environment, 328

Work-in-process inventory, 540

Work sample tests, 337–338

Work teams, 290. *See also* Teams

    cohesiveness, 301–303

    conflict, 303–304

    effectiveness, enhancing of, 307–313

        bureaucratic immunity, 308–309

        compensation and recognition, 312–313

        individualism-collectivism, 309

        selecting people, 309–311

        setting goals and priorities, 307–309

        structural accommodation, 308

        team diversity, 310